Date Due

# THE DRAMA
## OF THE
# MEDIEVAL CHURCH

FIRST PUBLISHED 1933

REPRINTED LITHOGRAPHICALLY IN GREAT BRITAIN
AT THE UNIVERSITY PRESS, OXFORD
FROM CORRECTED SHEETS OF THE FIRST EDITION
1962, 1967

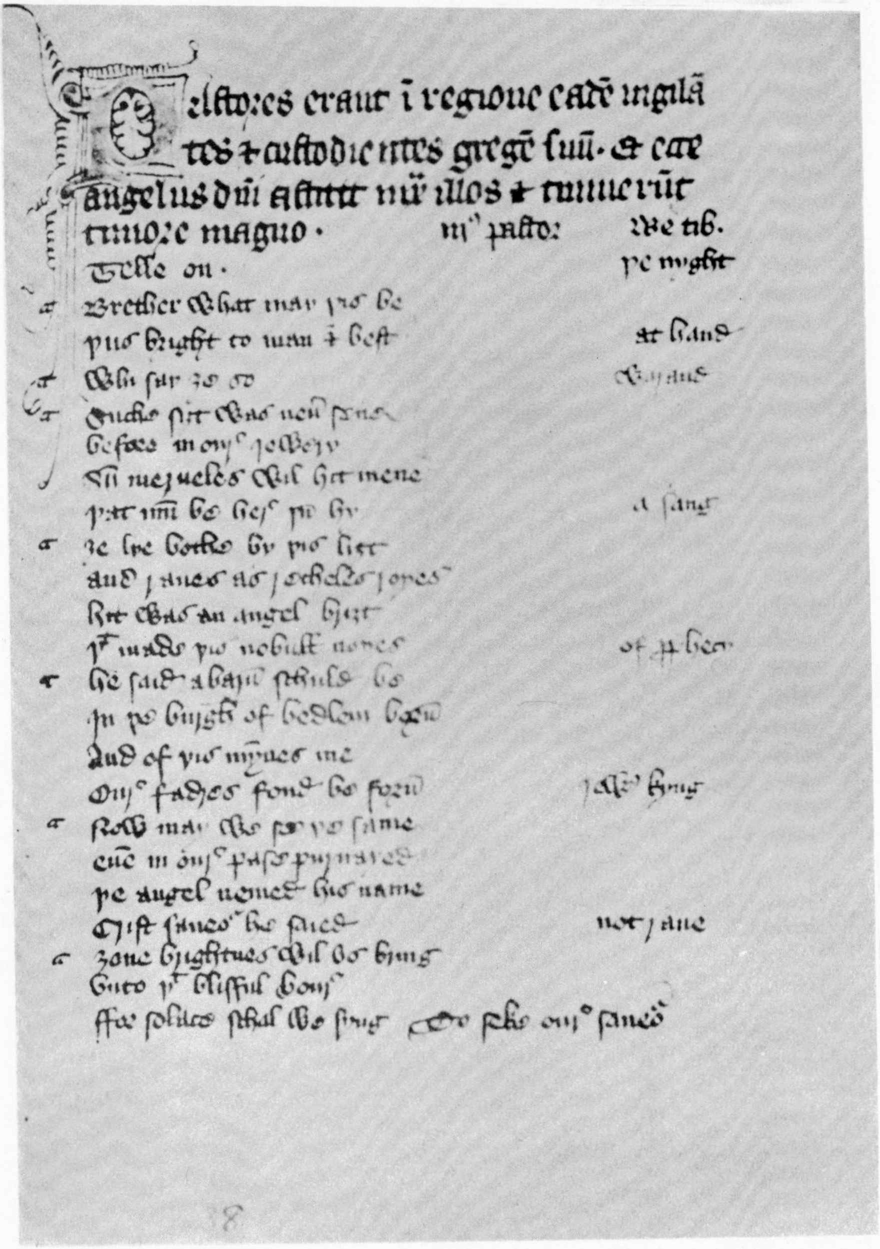

XIII. Play of the Shepherds, from the 'Shrewsbury Fragments', in the Library of Shrewsbury School, MS VI (Mus. iii. 42), fol. 38r

# THE DRAMA
## OF THE
# MEDIEVAL CHURCH

BY

KARL YOUNG

*Professor of English in Yale University*

VOLUME II

OXFORD

AT THE CLARENDON PRESS

*Oxford University Press, Ely House, London W. 1*
GLASGOW NEW YORK TORONTO MELBOURNE WELLINGTON
CAPE TOWN SALISBURY IBADAN NAIROBI LUSAKA ADDIS ABABA
BOMBAY CALCUTTA MADRAS KARACHI LAHORE DACCA
KUALA LUMPUR HONG KONG TOKYO

# CONTENTS

## *VOLUME II*

### PLAYS ASSOCIATED WITH THE NATIVITY



### PLAYS UPON OTHER SUBJECTS FROM THE BIBLE AND FROM LEGENDS

# LIST OF ILLUSTRATIONS

## *VOLUME II*

# ABBREVIATIONS

Brev. = Breviarium
Grad. = Graduale
Lib. resp. = Liber responsalis
Miss. = Missale
Ordin. = Ordinarium
Process. = Processionale
sæc. = sæculum
Trop. = Troparium

# PLAYS ASSOCIATED WITH THE NATIVITY

## CHAPTER XVII

# THE SHEPHERDS AT THE HOLY MANGER

THE survey of the plays of Easter Day, which has occupied the greater part of the first volume, may be regarded, fairly enough, as an introduction to the dramatic pieces presenting the Nativity, for, in their simpler forms, the latter are imitations of the former. In the dramatizing of occurrences immediately associated with the birth of Jesus the pattern used was the *Visitatio Sepulchri*.[1]

## I

The natural centre of a dramatic performance on Christmas Day was, of course, the *præsepe* at Bethlehem, and the action inevitably chosen was the visit of the shepherds, the description of which forms the most conspicuous part of the only circumstantial account of Christ's birth given in the Gospels, that in the second chapter of St Luke:[2]

7. Et peperit filium suum primogenitum, et pannis eum involvit, et reclinavit eum in præsepio, quia non erat eis locus in diversorio.

8. Et pastores erant in regione eadem vigilantes, et custodientes vigilias noctis super gregem suum.

9. Et ecce angelus Domini stetit juxta illos, et claritas Dei circumfulsit illos, et timuerunt timore magno.

10. Et dixit illis angelus: Nolite timere, ecce enim evangelizo vobis gaudium magnum, quod erit omni populo,

11. Quia natus est vobis hodie Salvator, qui est Christus Dominus in civitate David.

12. Et hoc vobis signum: Invenietis infantem pannis involutum, et positum in præsepio.

13. Et subito facta est cum angelo multitudo militiæ cœlestis laudantium Deum, et dicentium:

14. Gloria in altissimis Deo, et in terra pax hominibus bonæ voluntatis.

15. Et factum est ut discesserunt ab eis angeli in cœlum, pastores loquebantur ad invicem: Transeamus usque Bethlehem, et videamus hoc verbum quod factum est, quod Dominus ostendit nobis.

16. Et venerunt festinantes, et invenerunt Mariam et Joseph et infantem positum in præsepio.

[1] For bibliography bearing upon the plays of Christmas see Notes, p. 427.

[2] Luke ii, 7–20.

17. Videntes autem cognoverunt de verbo, quod dictum erat illis de puero hoc.
18. Et omnes qui audierunt mirati sunt, et de his quæ dicta erant a pastoribus ad ipsos.
19. Maria autem conservabat omnia verba hæc, conferens in corde suo.
20 Et reversi sunt pastores glorificantes et laudantes Deum in omnibus quæ audierant et viderant, sicut dictum est ad illos.

In all its serene beauty and angelic joyfulness, however, this narrative fails to provide all the details desired by a playwright. From it, indeed, one might fancy that the scene at the manger was a silent one, in which the shepherds were completely awed by what they saw before them. The required dialogue, therefore, had to be devised.[1] For this, the model employed was the Easter introit trope *Quem quæritis*,[2] and the result may be illustrated by the following text of the eleventh century from Limoges:[3]

AD DOMINICAM MISSAM

*Quem queritis in presepe, pastores, dicite?*

*Saluatorem Christum Dominum, infantem pannis inuolutum, secundum sermonem angelicum.*[4]

*Adest hic paruulus cum Maria matre sua, de qua dudum uaticinando Isaias dixerat propheta: Ecce uirgo concipiet et pariet filium;*[5] *et nunc euntes dicite quia natus est.*

*Alleluia, alleluia! Iam uere scimus Christum natum in terris, de quo canite omnes cum propheta, dicentes:*

Psalmus: *Puer natus est.*

Just as the Easter trope is assumed to be a dialogue between the Marys and the angel at the sepulchre, so the short composition before us consists in a similar exchange of utterances between the shepherds and certain persons stationed at the manger. The Christmas piece, moreover, resembles the Easter trope not only in its arrangement as a dialogue and in its attachment to the

[1] Schiffmann (*Drama*, p. 9) seems to imply that the element of dialogue is already supplied by the Gospel.

[2] For the relevant texts of the Easter tropes see above, chapter vii.

[3] Paris, Bibl. Nat., MS lat. 887, Trop. Lemovicense sæc. xi, fol. 9$^v$, previously edited by Young, *Officium Pastorum*, pp. 300–1. The MS provides music. For references to other texts of this form of trope see Notes, p. 427.

[4] It is entirely possible that the rhyming of *Dominum*, *inuolutum*, and *angelicum* is intentional.

[5] See Isaiah vii, 14: *Propter hoc dabit Dominus ipse vobis signum. Ecce virgo concipiet, et pariet filium, et vocabitur nomen ejus Emmanuel.*

introit of the Mass,[1] but also in such turns of phrase as appear in the following parallels:[2]

Quem quæritis in sepulchro, o Christicolæ?
Quem quæritis in præsepe, pastores, dicite?[3]

Jesum Nazarenum crucifixum.
Salvatorem Christum Dominum.

Non est hic.
Adest hic.

Ite, nuntiate quia surrexit.
Nunc euntes dicite quia natus est.

. . . illud quod olim ipse per prophetam dixerat ad Patrem taliter inquiens.

. . . de quo canite omnes cum propheta dicentes.

That the indebtedness is upon the part of the Christmas trope is indicated sufficiently by the fact that the earliest extant texts of it, from the eleventh century, are decidedly later than the earliest texts of the Easter trope.[4]

In one respect the Christmas trope is distinctly unlike its model: it does not tell us with whom the shepherds are assumed to be conversing. From later texts, however, we learn that the other interlocutors are midwives, or *obstetrices*.[5] These personages appear first in the apocryphal *Protevangelium Jacobi* of the second century, in which they bear testimony to the Immaculate Conception.[6] This Greek version circulated widely in the East. The dissemination of the story in Western Europe seems to have been due to a Latin version, of the fourth century or earlier, in the *Pseudo-evangelium Matthæi*.[7] Here the midwives are two in number, and from the sixth century onwards they are represented in art as serving Mary in her childbearing. These are the personages who are assumed to be addressing the shepherds in the Christmas dialogue now before us.[8]

[1] The last three words of the printed text are the beginning of the introit of the third Mass of Christmas Day, the full text of which is as follows: *Puer natus est nobis, et filius datus est nobis; cujus imperium super humerum ejus, et vocabitur nomen ejus, magni consilii angelus.* Psalmus: *Cantate Domino canticum novum, quia mirabilia fecit.* Concerning the three Masses of Christmas see above, i, 547.

[2] These resemblances are effectively indicated by Böhme, pp. 33–6. On the imitating of the Easter trope see also Brinkmann, pp. 108–9, 130–3.

[3] This sentence appears to show the influence also of the responsory *Quem vidistis, pastores, dicite* (see above, i, 57), or of the antiphon beginning with the same words, concerning which see below, pp. 20 sqq.

[4] See the texts from St Gall and Limoges above, i, 201, 210.

[5] See, for example, the version of the *Officium Pastorum* from Padua below, p. 9.

[6] See Tischendorff, *Evangelia*, pp. 35 sqq.

[7] See *id.*, pp. 76 sqq.

[8] On the tradition of the *obstetrices* see Anz, pp. 19 sqq. In his zealous demonstration of

Among the extant examples of the Christmas trope the variety in content is not very great. A slight addition to the text appears in the following of the eleventh century from Ivrea:[1]

TRO*pus*

*Quem queritis in presepe, pastores, dicite?*

Versus: *Saluatorem Christum Dominum, infantem pannis inuolutum, secundum sermonem angelicum.*

Versus: *Adest hic paruulus cum Maria matre sua, de quo dudum uaticinando Ysayas dixerat propheta:*

Versus: *Ecce uirgo concipiet et pariet filium; et nunc euntes dicite quia natus est.*

Versus: *Alleluia, alleluia! Iam uere scimus Christum natum in terris, de quo canite omnes cum propheta dicentes:*

*Puer natus est nobis, ⟨et filius datus est nobis; cujus imperium super humerum ejus; et vocabitur nomen ejus, magni consilii angelus.⟩*

Versus: *⟨H⟩ora est, psallite; jube, Domne, canere*[2] *eia!*[3]

*⟨Cantate Domino canticum novum, quia mirabilia fecit.⟩*

In so far as we can judge from the rubrics, the choral distribution of the sentences here is made without any precise dramatic intention. If the word *Versus* indicates an alternation between two groups of singers, then those who speak for the shepherds sing, inappropriately, the sentence *Ecce virgo*, and leave to the mid-wives, also inappropriately, the sentence *Iam vere scimus*. The text of the trope itself is extended by the passage beginning *Hora est, psallite*, inserted, probably, between the antiphon and verse of the introit.[4] This textual addition is, no doubt, borrowed from the Easter tropes.[5]

Another addition to the text of the trope appears in the following version from Bobbio:[6]

*Quem queritis | in presepe, pastores, dicite?*

Versus: *Saluatorem Christum Dominum.*

Versus: *Infantem pannis inuolutum, secundum sermonem angelicum.*

Versus: *Adest hic paruulus cum Maria matre sua, de qua dudum uaticinando*

the dependence of the Christmas play upon that of Easter, Böhme (pp. 37–9) holds that the personages who address the shepherds were originally conceived not as midwives, but as mere attendants imitated from the *angeli* of the *Visitatio Sepulchri*.

[1] Ivrea, Bibl. Capit., MS 60, Trop. Eporediense sæc. xi, fol. 10$^v$, previously edited by Young, *op. cit.*, p. 302–3. The MS provides music. For a similar trope from Limoges see Notes, p. 427.

[2] canere] canetet (MS).

[3] Followed by another separate trope of the introit, beginning thus: Tropus *Gaudeamus hodie quia Deus descendit*.

[4] Concerning the structure of the introit see above, i, 21.

[5] See, for example, above, i, 210, 211.

[6] Turin, Bibl. Reg., MS F. IV. 18, Trop. Bobbiense sæc. xii, fol. 9$^v$–10$^r$, now first printed. The MS provides music. For a similar text, without the rubric *Versus*, found *ibid.*, MS G. V. 20, Trop. Bobbiense sæc. xi, fol. 20$^v$, see Young, *op. cit.*, p. 305.

*Ysaias dixerat propheta: Ecce uirgo concipiet et pariet filium, et nunc*[1] *euntes dicite quia natus est.*

*Alleluia, alleluia! Iam uere scimus Christum natum in terris, de quo canite omnes cum propheta dicentes:*

*Puer natus* ⟨*est nobis, et filius datus est nobis; cujus imperium super humerum ejus; et vocabitur nomen ejus, magni consilii angelus*⟩.

*Gloria tibi, Christe, gloria tibi, sancte, gloria tibi, Domine, quia uenisti omne genus liberare. Omnes gaudentes dicite:*

*Puer* ⟨*natus est*⟩.[2]

The part added to the trope here is of a liturgical, rather than a dramatic, nature. After it the introit was probably sung through without interruption.

In the following version from Mantua are more precise indications as to the distribution of parts:[3]

ITE*m* ALIA.[4]

*Quem queritis in presepe, pastores, dicite?*

R*espondet* scol*a*:

*Saluatorem Christum Dominum.*

R*espondent* cant*ores*:

*Infantem pannis inuolutum, secundum sermonem angelicum.*

R*espondet* scol*a*:

*Adest hic paruulus cum Maria matre sua, de qua dudum uaticinando*[5] *Esaias dixerat propheta:*

R*espondent* cant*ores*:

*Ecce uirgo concipiet et pariet filium; et nunc euntes dicite quia natus est.*

R*espondet* scol*a*:

*Alleluia, alleluia!* | *Iam uere s*⟨*c*⟩*imus Christum natum in terra, de quo*[6] *canite omnes cum propheta dicentes:*

*Puer natus est.*

Although the division of the dialogue here between the chorus and selected members of it[7] contributed, no doubt, a certain animation to the singing, it represents nothing definitely dramatic. A far more explicit advance toward drama is shown in a text from Novalesa:[8]

1 nunc] nunc et (MS).

2 Followed by another separate trope of the introit, beginning thus: Tropi. *Quem nasci mundo docuere.*

3 Verona, Bibl. Capit., MS 107, Trop. Mantuanum sæc. xi, fol. 5v–6r, previously edited by Young, *op. cit.*, pp. 305–6. The text is incompletely indicated in *A.H.*, xlix, 8–9. The MS provides music.

4 This rubric indicates that the trope printed here is only one of a series of tropes of the introit *Puer natus est*.

5 uaticinando] uaticinandum (MS).

6 quo] co (MS).

7 The response to the chorus may be sung by a *single* cantor—the rubric is ambiguous. Concerning the term *schola* for the chorus see above, i, 210.

8 Oxford, Bibl. Bodl., MS Douce 222, Trop. Novaliciense sæc. xi, fol. 6r–6v, previously

In Natiuitate Domini ad Missam sint parati duo diaconi induti dalmaticis retro altare dicentes:

*Quem queritis in presepe, pastores, dicite?*

Respondeant duo cantores in choro | versum:

*Saluatorem Christum Dominum, infantem pannis inuolutum, secundum sermonem angelicum.*

It*em* diaconi versum:

*Adest hic paruulus cum Maria matre sua, de qua dudum uaticinando Ysaias dixerat propheta: Ecce uirgo concipiet et pariet filium; et nunc euntes dicite quia natus est.*

Tunc cantor dicat excelsa uoce:

*Alleluia, alleluia! Iam uere scimus Christum natum in terris, cui canite omnes cum propheta dicentes:*

*Puer natus est nobis.*

The rubrics before us here, though far too brief, indicate something that may be called *mise en scène*. Deacons standing behind the altar address as *pastores* two cantors standing in front of it, in the choir. The stage-setting, then, if one may use so ambitious a term, is the altar itself. In trying to account for this arrangement we may, if we wish, assume that it is merely one more example of imitation of the Easter trope, versions of which were not infrequently sung across the altar.[1] Possibly, however, one may seek an explanation also in symbolism. Just as the altar could provide a setting for the Easter dialogue through symbolizing the *sepulchrum*, so, perhaps, it could symbolize also the *præsepe*. In the *Theoria* of Germanus I, Patriarch of Constantinople (†733), for example, we read, *Altare est et dicitur præsepe, et sepulchrum Domini*;[2] and the Cistercian abbot, Guerricus (†circa 1157), writes in a Christmas sermon, *Fratres, et vos invenietis hodie infantem pannis involutum, et positum in præsepio altaris.*[3] If this association of ideas between altar and *præsepe* had any general currency during the Middle Ages, it might well be that the manner of singing the Christmas dialogue prescribed in the text before us was due neither to imitation nor to accident. In addressing the cantors as *pastores*, the deacons behind the altar may have regarded themselves as representing, though not impersonating, the *obstetrices* at the manger.

edited by Young, *op. cit.*, pp. 306–7. Anz (p. 38), following Gautier (*Tropes*, pp. 136, 218), erroneously assigns this troper to St Gall. This text is incompletely indicated in *A.H.*, xlix, 8–9.

[1] See above, i, 214 sqq.

[2] *Maxima Bibliotheca Veterum Patrum*, xiii, Lyons, 1677, p. 51. See above, i, 220.

[3] Migne, *P.L.*, clxxxv, 46.

## II

Even assuming that the altar over which the Christmas dialogue was sometimes sung was actually felt to represent the Holy Manger at Bethlehem, we cannot regard any of the versions of *Quem quæritis in præsepe* reviewed hitherto as being true drama. The fact is that this dramatic trope of Christmas, like that of Easter, failed to achieve impersonation while it remained attached to the introit of the Magna Missa, and became a genuine play only after it had been transported to a place at the end of the office of Matins.[1] The dramatic performance which developed in this position is conveniently called *Officium Pastorum*.[2] The choosing of Matins as the place for the Christmas play may have been determined by the custom of Easter, already established in the tenth century. The appropriateness of this arrangement, in any case, is established by the fact that the visit of the shepherds to Bethlehem as recounted by St Luke must have occurred during the night or early morning.

At Matins the *Officium Pastorum*, like the *Visitatio Sepulchri* of Easter, was usually performed at the conclusion of the normal liturgical service. But the Christmas play sometimes preceded Matins, as is shown by the following *ordo* of the thirteenth century from the cathedral of Padua:[3]

Ad Matutinum, pulsatis duabus campanis, canonici uadunt pro episcopo tali modo. Duo scolares precedunt archipresbyterum cum duobus cereis, et canonici secuntur[4] archipresbyterum; et omnes oscu- | lantur manum episcopi, et sic conducunt ipsum in ecclesiam. Et pulsatis campanis, episcopus in medio choro incip*it* Matutinum. Et ibi aliquantulum inferius ab altari preparata est quedam ancona, cum Beata Uirgine Maria et Filio, nitido pallio cooperta, per quam Presepium Domini presentatur. Et post dictam anconam sunt duo canonici cum duobus pluuialibus, qui uocantur Obstetrices; ante uero dictam anconam aliquantulum inferius in medio choro stant magister scolarum et cantor cum duobus pluuialibus, qui dicuntur Pastores. Et tunc Obstetrices cantant:

*Quem queritis in presepe, ⟨pastores, dicite?⟩*

[1] See above, i, 231 sqq.

[2] For the use of this term see the text from Rouen below, p. 14.

[3] Padua, Bibl. Capit., MS S, Ordin. Patavinense sæc. xiii, fol. 40v–41v. This text is described, and published in part, by Dondi Orologio, p. 42. It is described again, and published completely, by Bartholomaeis, pp. 147–8, 525–6. For observations on the MS see above, i, 552.

[4] secuntur] Partly rubbed away, but the reading is fairly certain.

R*espond*ent Pastores:

*Saluatorem Christum Dominum, ⟨infantem pannis involutum, secundum sermonem angelicum.⟩*

R*espond*ent Obstetrices discooperiendo anconam, flexis genibus:

*Adest hic paruulus ⟨cum Maria matre sua, de qua dudum vaticinando Isaias dixerat propheta: Ecce virgo concipiet et pariet filium; et nunc euntes dicite quia natus est⟩.*

Et dum Obstetrices cantant hoc, Pastores etiam stant flexis genibus. Finito cantu Obstetricum, Pastores surgunt et uertunt se uersus populum, et incipiunt vitatorium, scilicet *Christus natus est nobis*. *Venite*; et uertunt se ad supradictam anconam, et flexis genibus dicunt *Adoremus*. Et tunc chorus incipit vitatorium, scilicet *Christus natus est*. | Et tunc Obstetrices simul cum Pastoribus descendunt iuxta pergamum, et Obstetrices primo cantant *Venite, exultemus Domino*. Pastores uero secundo loco secundum uersum cantant, et sic prosecuntur uicissim totum *Venite*. In fine Obstetrices simul cum Pastoribus iterum cantant vitatorium, et tunc Obstetrices deponunt pluuialia. Pastores uero stant et regunt chorum et officium conferendo antiphonas et uersus et cetera, que dicuntur ordinatim per ordinem, ut dictum est supra ubi tractatur de ordine officii[1] in Matutino sollempnitatum.[2]

At Padua the play is introduced immediately after the arrival of the bishop and the recital of the opening formulæ of the service, and before the singing of the invitatory.[3] The *præsepe*, or *ancona*, is placed in the middle of the choir, a short distance in front of the altar, and in it, or upon it, are figures of the Virgin and Child.[4] Behind the *præsepe* stand two canons vested in copes, who are called *obstetrices*; and in front appear the two cantors in similar vestments, representing the *pastores*. At the conclusion of the dialogue, the latter very appropriately begin the invitatory *Christus natus est*, genuflecting toward the *præsepe* at the word *adoremus*; and the midwives join in the further singing of the invitatory psalm.[5] Throughout Matins the two shepherds direct the ceremonial and begin the choral pieces. In this way the extra-liturgical dramatic ceremony is made an organic part of the regular liturgical service.

As to the element of impersonation here the text leaves us in some uncertainty. The setting provided by the *præsepe* is explicit

[1] officii] offitii (MS).

[2] Followed immediately by the rubric *Prima lectio*.

[3] The formulæ at the opening of Matins are explained above, i, 49–50.

[4] These may be living figures. In any case they have no part in the action. In the play from Rouen the figure in the *præsepe* is called *Ymago Sancte Marie*. See below, p. 14.

[5] The form of the invitatory is explained above, i, 50–1.

and complete; but the costuming and gestures of the actors appear to be primarily liturgical. Since these persons are named *pastores* and *obstetrices*, however, we inevitably infer some sort of physical imitation sufficient for characterizing the performance as a play. More generous indications of impersonation will appear in other versions considered below.

Unlike the play from Padua, the other extant versions of the *Officium Pastorum* are found not at the beginning of Matins, but at the end, outside the normal liturgical frame-work of the service. The play could not, like the *Visitatio Sepulchri* of Easter, be conveniently performed between the last responsory and the *Te Deum*, for this position was occupied by the recital of the Genealogy of Christ, taken from the Gospel of Matthew.[1] The dramatic text, therefore, was placed *after* the *Te Deum*; and in this location it was treated not as a conclusion to Matins, but as an introduction to the first Mass of Christmas, which immediately followed.[2] This arrangement is seen in the following text from the cathedral of Clermont-Ferrand:[3]

Quo dicto,[4] duo pueri iuxta altare hunc prosellum cantent.

Versus: *Quem queritis in presepe, pastores, dicite?*

Versus: *Saluatorem Christum Dominum, infantem pannis inuolutum, secundum sermonem angelicum.*

Versus: *Adest hic paruulus cum Maria matre sua, de qua dudum uaticinando Ysaias dixerat propheta: Ecce uirgo concipiet et pariet filium; et nunc euntes dicite quia natus est.*

Versus: *Alleluya, alleluya!*

Versus: *Iam uere scimus Christum natum in terris, de quo canite omnes cum propheta dicente⟨s⟩.*

Quo finito, immediate incipiant ad Missam officium *Dominus dixit ad me*.[5]

The word *prosellus* in the introductory rubric indicates that the text before us is regarded as a mere embellishment of the official liturgy, and the closing words assure us that the dramatic trope is directly attached to the introit of the first Christmas Mass, the opening words of which are *Dominus dixit ad me*. The manner in

[1] This medieval liturgical custom is illustrated by Young, *Officium Pastorum*, pp. 313, 375, 385–6.

[2] In regard to the three Masses of Christmas see above, i, 547.

[3] Clermont-Ferrand, Bibl. de la Ville, MS 67, Brev. Claromontense sæc. xv, fol. 28v, previously edited incompletely by R. Twigge, in *Dublin Review*, cxxi (1897), 362, and re-edited from the MS by Young, *op. cit.*, p. 321.

[4] The reference is to the *Te Deum*.

[5] These are the opening words of the introit of the first Mass of Christmas. In France *officium* is the usual term for introit.

which the sentences are sung is shown more explicitly in another example from the same church:[1]

Quo dicto, duo pueri cantent iuxta altare versum:

*Quem queritis in presepe, pastores, dicite?*

Pastores versum:

*Saluatorem ⟨Christum⟩ Dominum, infantem pannis inuolutum, secundum sermonem angelicum.*

Pueri versum:

*Adest hic paruulus cum Maria matre sua, de qua dudum vaticinando Ysaias dixerat propheta: Ecce uirgo concipiet et pariet filium; et nunc euntes dicite quia natus est.*

Pastores:

*Alleluia, alleluia! Iam uere scimus Christum natum in terris, ⟨de quo⟩ canite omnes cum propheta dicentes.*

Quo finito, chori prouisores incipiant ad Missam in Gallicantu.

From this text it appears that the speeches are appropriately assigned to two boys standing beside the altar, who represent the *obstetrices*, and to another group of singers called *pastores*. Whether the stage-setting is furnished merely by the altar or by a special *præsepe* we cannot tell. The shepherds and midwives may, or may not, be explicitly impersonated.

Virtually all such uncertainties as to theatrical detail are absent from the more highly developed versions of the *Officium Pastorum* belonging to the liturgical traditions of Rouen. The simpler form of Christmas play from this ecclesiastical province is as follows:[2]

In Natiuitate Domini, finito *Te Deum laudamus*, pueri[3] in uno loco ecclesie baculis se sustentantes in similitudine Pastorum consistant; vnus autem puer in excelso, amictu et alba indutus, in similitudine Angeli natiuitatem Domini annuntiantis, hunc versum dicens:

*Nolite timere, ecce enim euangelizo uobis gaudium magnum, quod erit omni populo, quia natus est uobis hodie Saluator mundi in ciuitate Dauid, et hoc uobis signum: Inuenietis infantem pannis inuolutum et positum in presepio.*[4]

[1] Paris, Bibl. Nat., MS lat. 1274, Brev. Claromontense sæc. xiv, fol. 40v, previously edited by Young, *op. cit.*, pp. 322. The complete text of Matins and Lauds, including the dramatic trope, is published *ibid.*, pp. 369–78. In the MS the text now before us is immediately preceded by the *Te Deum*.

[2] Montpellier, Bibl. de la Faculté de Médecine, MS H. 304, Miscellanea ecclesiastica sæc. xii, fol. 41r–41v, published by Young, *op. cit.*, pp. 323–4; Young, *Rouen*, pp. 207–8. For observations on the MS see Notes, p. 428.

[3] pueri] Between this word and the preceding is what I take to be a mark indicating an omission. Probably the corrector had in mind the omission of the numeral vii. See below, p. 13, note 6.

[4] For this speech, and the two succeeding ones, see Luke ii, 10–2, 14–5.

Sint item plures pueri dextra et sinistra parte similiter induti, qui, finita prefata antiphona, incipiant cantando:

*Gloria in excelsis Deo, et in terra pax hominibus bone uoluntatis, alleluia, alleluia.*

Hoc it*eru*m finito, Pastores subsequentem antiphonam cantantes, ad locum in quo paratum fuit[1] Presepe accedant:

*Transeamus usque Bethleem, et uideamus hoc uerbum quod factum est, quod fecit Dominus et ostendit nobis.*

Quem dum intrauerint, duo clerici qui | ad Presepe fuerint incipiant cantare:

*Quem queritis in presepe, pastores, dicite?*

Pastores respondebunt:

*Saluatorem Christum Dominum, infantem pannis inuolutum, secundum sermonem angelicum.*

Ad Presepe stantes it*eru*m dicant:

*Adest hic paruulus cum Maria matre sua, de quo dudum uaticinando Ysaias dixerat propheta: Ecce uirgo concipiet et pariet filium, et nomen eius Emmanuel dicetur.*

Pastores:

*Natus est nobis hodie Saluator qui est Christus Dominus in ciuitate Dauid. Te Deum laudamus.*

Quo finito, idem Pastores incipiant introitum *Dominus dixit ad me*, et regant chorum ad omnem Missam.[2] Finita Missa, incipiat presul uersum *Benedictus qui uenit in nomine Domini*. Deinde[3] *Deus in adiutorium*, cum *Gloria Patri*, et *Alleluia*. Postea incipiat cantor antiphonam *Quem uidistis*, usque, *Quis apparuit*, et Pastores dicant *Natum uidimus*, usque in finem. Postea incipiant Pastores *Dominus regnauit*, et ad finem regendo chorum ipsi Matutinas[4] perducant. Finita collecta Matutinarum, cantetur antiphona *Ecce completa sunt omnia*, cum subsequenti collecta *Deus qui salutis eterne*.[5]

During the singing of the *Te Deum* which immediately precedes this play seven youths costume themselves with amices, albs, tunics, and staffs, to represent shepherds.[6] As they take their places in the church at the beginning of the action, a choir-boy stationed aloft, costumed as an angel, announces the Nativity to them (*Nolite timere*), and is supported by other angels who sing

[1] fuit] The reading may be *fuet*, and the author may have intended *fuerat*.

[2] The first Mass.

[3] Here begins Lauds.

[4] This is Lauds (*Matutinæ Laudes*).

[5] Followed by the rubric *Officivm Stelle ita celebretvr*. For the text of this *Officium Stellæ* see below, p. 68.

[6] This we know from the following passage in an earlier part of the treatise to which the play is attached (Montpellier MS H. 304, fol. 32$^{r}$): *Te Deum laudamus* alta uoce incipiat. Interim preparentur vij iuuenes amictis et albis et tunicis induti, baculos in manibus ferentes in similitudine Pastorum, qui finito Presepis Officio, in prima Missa usque ad finem Matutinorum regent chorum. See Young, *Rouen*, p. 207, note 2.

*Gloria in excelsis.* The shepherds then proceed to the *præsepe*—situated, presumably, behind the main altar[1]—singing the appropriate processional *Transeamus usque Bethlehem.* Here occurs the usual dialogue, only slightly modified, between the shepherds and two clerics whom we may assume to be costumed for representing the midwives. In the Mass which follows,[2] the shepherds begin the introit and rule the choir. They assume a similar responsibility also in Lauds.[3]

A considerably more elaborate version of the *Officium Pastorum* as it was performed in the cathedral of Rouen itself is described as follows in an ordinary of the fourteenth century:[4]

Finito *Te Deum laudamus*, peragatur Officium Pastorum hoc modo secundum Rothomagensem usum. Presepe sit paratum retro altare, et Ymago Sancte Marie sit in eo posita. In primis quidam puer ante chorum in excelso in similitudinem Angeli natiuitatem Domini annuncians ad quinque canonicos quindecim marcharum et librarum, vel ad eorum uicarios de secunda sede,[5] Pastores intrantes per magnum hostium chori per medium chorum transeuntes, tunicis et amictis indutos, hunc versum ita dicens:

*Nolite timere, ecce enim,*

usque *in presepio.*[6] Sint plures[7] pueri in uoltis ecclesie quasi Angeli, qui alta uoce incipiant:

*Gloria in excelsis Deo,*

et cantent usque *uoluntatis.* Hoc audientes Pastores ad locum in quo paratum est Presepe accedant cantantes hunc versum:

*Pax in terris,*|

totum. Quod dum intrauerint, duo presbyteri dalmaticati de maiori sede, quasi Obstetrices qui ad Presepe fuerint, dicant:

*Quem queritis,*

usque *dicite.* Pastores respondeant:

*Saluatorem Christum,*

usque *angelicum.* Item Obstetrices cortinam aperientes Puerum demonstrent, dicentes:

[1] This, at any rate, is the arrangement in the cathedral of Rouen. See the play from Rouen MS 384, below.

[2] The repetition of the *Te Deum* in the text at this point is probably an error.

[3] The dramatic activities of the *pastores* in Lauds are further explained below, pp. 20 sqq.

[4] Rouen, Bibl. de la Ville, MS 384 (*olim* Y. 110), Ordin. ad usum cathedralis Rothomagensis sæc. xiv, 22r–23r, previously edited by Gasté, pp. 25–32; Young, *Officium Pastorum*, pp. 330–3. Gasté's text is reprinted by Adams, pp. 25–7. Concerning others see Notes, p. 428.

[5] In regard to these terms bearing upon the ranking and endowment of canons at Rouen see Gasté, pp. 25–6.

[6] The speeches are given completely in the text from Paris MS lat. 904 printed below, p. 16.

[7] From Paris MS lat. 904 we learn that the number of *pueri* was seven.

*Adest hic paruulus*,

usque *Ysaias dixerat propheta*. Hic ostendant Matrem Pueri dicentes:

*Ecce uirgo*,

vsque *quia natus est*. Tunc, eo uiso, inclinatis ceruicibus adorent Puerum et salutent dicentes:

*Salue, uirgo singularis*,

usque *frui natus uisione*. Deinde uertant se ad chorum redeuntes et dicentes:

*Alleluia, alleluia! Iam uere scimus*,

vsque *cum propheta dicentes*. Hoc finito, incipiatur Missa, et Pastores regant chorum. Dominus archiepiscopus, si presens fuerit, cantet Missam. Officium *Dominus dixit ad me*. *Kyrie* festiue.[1] *Gloria in excelsis*. Pastores cant*ent* prosam *Quem ciues celici*. Oratio *Deus qui hanc sacratissimam*. De Beata Maria oratio *Deus qui salutis eterne*. Quidam de Pastoribus cantet *Populus gentium*. Sine interuallo subdiaconus legat epistolam *Apparuit gratia Dei saluatoris*. Duo Pastores de secunda sede responsum *Tecum principium*. Versus *Dixit Dominus*. Reiteretur responsum *Tecum principium*. Duo de maiori sede *Alleluia*. Versus *Dominus dixit ad me*. Sequentia *Nato canunt omnia*. Euuangelium *Exiit edictum*. *Credo in unum*. Offertorium *Letentur celi*. Offerant omnes qui uoluerint, et recipiatur a Pastoribus et distribuatur inter eos. Secreta *Accepta tibi sit, Domine*. Alia secreta *Muneribus nostris*. Prefatio *Quia per incarnati*. Hec prefatio suprascripta dicatur omnibus festiuis diebus usque ad Purificationem, excepto die Epyphanie Domini cum eius octaua. *Communicantes et noctem sacratissimam* dicatur. *Sanctus* et *Agnus Dei* festiue. Communio *In splendoribus*. Postcommunio *Da nobis, quesumus, Domine, Deus noster*. Alia Communio *Hec nos communio Deo*. *Ite missa est*.

Finita Missa, archiepiscopus uel alius ad altare dicat versum *Benedictus qui | uenit in nomine Domini*. *Deus Dominus*. *Deus in adiutorium*. *Gloria Patri*. *Sicut erat*, et cetera. *Alleluia*. Archiepiscopus uel alius sacerdos uersus ad Pastores dicat:

*Quem uidistis, pastores, dicite? Annunciate nobis in terris quis apparuit?*

Pastores respond*eant:*

*Natum uidimus*,

et cetera, et totam antiphonam finiant. Dehinc incipi*at* quidam Pastorum a dextera parte psalmum *Dominus regnauit*. Antiphona *Quem uidistis*. Pastores alias antiphonas incipiant, unusquisque suam secundum ordinem, et omnes cum neumis finiantur, et Pastores regant chorum. Antiphona *Genuit puerpera*. Psalmus *Iubilate*. Antiphona *Angelus ad pastores*. Psalmus *Deus, Deus*. Antiphona *Facta est cum angelo*. Psalmus *Benedicite*. Antiphona *Paruulus filius*. Psalmus *Laudate*. Capitulum *Populus gentium*. Ymnus *A solis ortus cardine*. Versus *Viderunt omnes fines terre*. Antiphona sicut in Vesperis repetatur *Gloria in excelsis*. Psalmus

[1] festiue] Partly erased (MS).

*Benedictus.* Oratio *Concede, quesumus, omnipotens Deus. Benedicamus* cantetur a Pastoribus, *Verbum Patris hodie.* Quo finito, Pastores cantent hanc antiphonam totam in pulpito: *Ecce completa sunt.* Archiepiscopus vel sacerdos dicat versum *Post partum uirgo.* Oratio *Deus, qui salutis eterne. Benedicamus* tres de prima sede.[1]

Although this text provides invaluable rubrics, it presents the speeches and liturgical pieces very incompletely. It is fortunate, therefore, that the Rouen play is preserved also in the following form in a gradual of the thirteenth century:[2]

In sancta nocte Natiuitatis Domini post *Te Deum*, Angelus assistet, annunciet Christum natum esse, et hoc dicet:

*Nolite timere, ecce enim euangelizo uobis gaudium magnum, quod*[3] *erit omni populo, quia natus est uobis hodie Saluator mundi in ciuitate Dauid, et hoc uobis signum: Inuenietis infantem pannis inuolutum | et positum in presepio.*

Hoc audientes vii pueri stantes in alto loco dicant:

*Gloria in excelsis Deo, et in terra pax hominibus bone uoluntatis.*

Audientes Pastores eant uersus Presepe cantantes hoc r*esponsorium*:[4]

*Pax in terris nunciatur,*
*in excelsis gloria.*
*Terra ⟨cælo⟩ federatur,*
*mediante gratia.*

*Mediator, homo, Deus*
*descendit in propria,*
*ut ascendat homo reus*
*ad admissa gaudia. Eya! Eya!*

*Transeamus, uideamus*
*uerbum hoc quod factum est;*
*transeamus ut sciamus*
*quod ⟨an⟩nuntiatum est.*

Versus:

*In Iudea puer uagit,*
*puer salus populi,*
*quo bellandum se presagit*
*uetus hospes seculi.*

[1] Followed by the rubric *Sequatur Missa de luce.*

[2] Paris, Bibl. Nat., MS lat. 904, Grad. Rothomagense sæc. xiii, fol. 11$^{v}$–14$^{r}$, previously edited by Young, *op. cit.*, pp. 325–9. The *Officium Pastorum* itself, without the liturgical sequel, has been published by Coussemaker, pp. 235–41 (with the music), and by Mme Chasles, pp. 177–9, with facsimiles, pp. 174–6. The entire MS is reproduced in photographic facsimile by Loriquet, *Graduel*, vol. ii, with comment on the *Officium Pastorum* in i, 13–8. See also plate xiv in the present treatise.

[3] quod] Preceded by *quia*, expunged (MS).

[4] See Chevalier, *R.H.*, no. 14777.

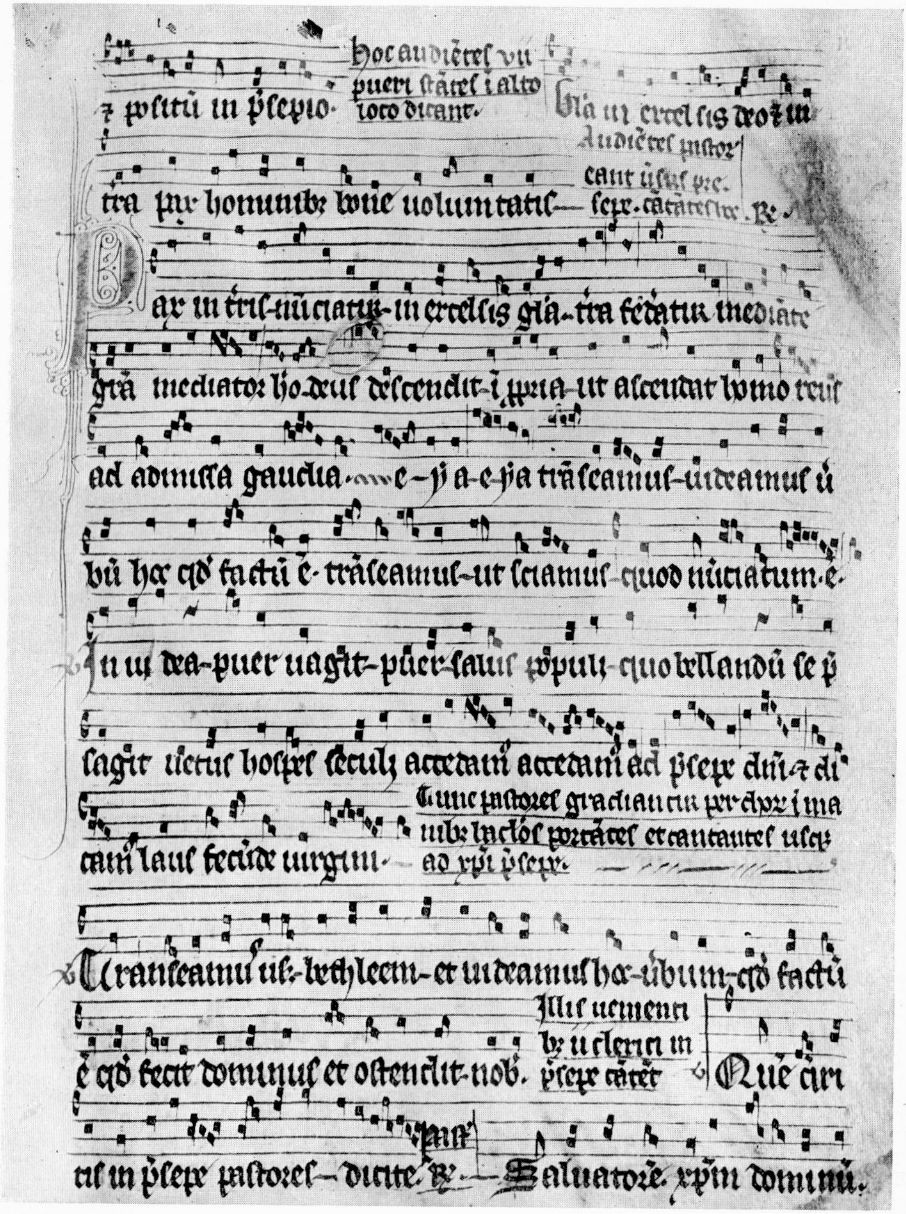

XIV. Play of the Shepherds from Rouen, in Paris, Bibliothèque Nationale, MS lat. 904, fol. 12ʳ

*Accedamus, accedamus*
*ad presepe Domini,*
*et dicamus, ⟨et dicamus:⟩*
*Laus fecunde uirgini.*

Tunc Pastores gradiantur per chorum, in manibus baculos portantes, et cantantes usque ad Christi Presepe versum:

*Transeamus usque Bethleem, et uideamus hoc uerbum quod factum est, quod fecit Dominus et ostendit nobis.*

Illis uenientibus ii clerici in Presepe cantent versum:

*Quem queritis in presepe, pastores, dicite?*

Pastores r*espondeant:*

*Saluatorem Christum Dominum,* | *infantem pannis inuolutum, secundum sermonem angelicum.*

It*em* Obstetrices cortinam aperientes, Puerum demonstrent dicentes versum:

*Adest hic paruulus cum Maria matre sua, de quo dudum uaticinando Ysayas dixerat propheta:*

Ostendant Matrem Pueri dicentes:

*Ecce uirgo concipiet et pariet filium; et euntes dicite quia natus est.*

Tunc salutent Pastores Uirginem ita dicentes:[1]

*Salue, uirgo singularis,*
*uirgo manens Deum paris*
*ante secla generatum*
*corde Patris.*
*Adoremus nunc creatum*
*carne matris.*

Versus:

*Nos, Maria, tua prece*
*a peccati purga fece*
*nostri cursum incolatus;*
*sic dispone*
*ut det sua frui natus*
*uisione.*

Tunc, uiso Puero, Pastores adorent eum. Deinde uertant se ad chorum dicentes:

*Alleluia, alleluia! Iam uere scimus Christum natum in terris, de quo canite omnes cum propheta*[2] *dicentes.*

Postea statim incipiatur Missa, et Pastores regant chorum et cantent *Gloria in excelsis Deo*, et epistolam, et tropa. Et unus[3] Pastorum legat lectionem *Populus gencium.* Subdiaconus tunica inductus legat epistolam, nullo gradale intercerto. Duo Pastores cantent in pulpito gradale *Tecum*

[1] See Chevalier, *R.H.*, no. 18306.

[2] propheta] Corrected from *prophetis* (MS).

[3] unus] After this is written, and expunged, the following: *cus legat epistolam.*

*principium.* Duo de maiori sede cantent in pulpito *Alleluia. Dixit Dominus.*[1] Finita Missa, sacerdos qui Missam cantauerit uertat se uersus Pastores et dicat hanc antiphonam[2] usque ad *Natum.* Officium incipit. Officium *Dominus dixit ad me: Filius meus es tu; ego hodie genui te.* Psalmus *Quare fremuerunt. Gloria, seculorum, amen.* Oratio *Deus qui hanc sacratissimam.* Memoria Beate Marie *Deus qui salutis.* Lectio prima *Populus gentium.* Epistola *Apparuit gratia.* Responsum *Tecum* | *principium in die uirtutis tue, in splendoribus san⟨c⟩torum, ex utero ante luciferum genui te.* Versus *Dixit Dominus Domino meo: Sede a dextris meis, donec ponam inimicos tuos scabellum pedum tuorum. Alleluia.* Versus *Dominus dixit ad me: Filius meus es tu; ego hodie genui te.*

Sequentia[3]

*Nato canunt omnia   Domino pie agmina*
*Sillabatim pneumata   perstringendo organica.*
*Hec dies sacrata,   in qua noua sunt gaudia   mundo plene dedita;*
*Hac nocte precelsa   intonuit et gloria   in uoce angelica.*
*Fulserunt et immania*[4] *nocte media   pastoribus lumina;*
*Dum* | *fouent sua pecora,   subito diua   percipiunt monita.*
*Natus alma   uirgine, qui extat   ante secula,*
*Est immensa   in celo gloria,   pax et in terra.*
*Hic ergo celi caterua   altissime iubilat,*
*Et tanto canore tremat   alta poli machina.*
*Sonet et per omnia   hac in die gloria*[5] *uoce clara reddita.*
*Humana concrepent cuncta   Deum natum in terra;*
*Confracta sunt imperia   hostis crudelissima;*
*Pax in terra reddita. Nunc letantur omnia   nati per exordia.*
*Solus qui tuetur omnia,   solus qui condidit omnia,*
*Ipse sua   pietate soluat omnia   peccata nostra.*

Euangelium *Exiit editum a Cesare.*[6] Offertorium *Letentur celi et exultet terra ante faciem Domini, quoniam uenit.* Communio *In splendoribus sanctorum ex utero ante luciferum genui te.* Finita Missa, sacerdos uel episcopus qui Missam cantauerit uertat se ad Pastores et dicat hanc antiphonam usque ad *Natum*:[7]

*Quem uidistis, pastores, dicite? Annunciate nobis in terris quid apparuit?*

⟨Pastores respondeant:⟩

*Natum uidimus et choros angelorum collaudantes Dominum, alleluia, alleluia.*

Chorus dexter incip*iat Dominus regnauit*, et cetera. Finitis Laudibus, Pastores loco *Benedicamus* dicant: |

[1] Dominus] dix̄ (MS).

[2] This antiphon is omitted, and the text is confused.

[3] For this sequence see Chevalier, *R.H.*, no. 11890, printed in *A.H.*, liii, 41–2.

[4] Fulserunt et immania] Pulserunt et innania (MS).

[5] gloria] gioria (MS).

[6] Euangelium . . . Cesare] Written in the margin (MS).

[7] Finita . . . Natum] Written in the margin (MS).

*Uerbum Patris hodie*[1]
*processit ex uirgine;*
*uenit nos redimere,*
*et celesti patrie*
*uoluit nos reddere.*
*Uirtutes angelice*
*cum canore iubilo*
*benedicant Domino.*

R*esponsio*:

*Refulgens pastoribus*
*nunciauit angelus*
*pacem, pacis nuncius.*
*Tu, Pastor ecclesie,*
*pacem tum et dirige,*
*filios et instrue*
*Redemptori debitas*
*iubilando gracias.*

Post *Benedicamus* omnes Pastores cantent in pulpito hanc antiphonam: *Ecce completa sunt omnia que dicta sunt per angelum de Uirgine Maria.* Oratio *Deus qui salutis.*[2]

From these two texts together we have ample information concerning the Rouen play, and concerning the participation of the *pastores* in the normal liturgy of the day. The *præsepe*, it appears, was behind the main altar, and contained artificial figures of the Virgin Mary and the Child, behind a curtain. As the five shepherds, suitably costumed, enter the west door of the choir, a boy up under the vaulting, representing an angel, announces the Nativity. After seven other angels have sung *Gloria in excelsis*, the shepherds begin their march to the *præsepe*, singing, as they traverse the choir, first a responsorial poem *Pax in terris*, and then, as they round the altar, the verse *Transeamus*. At the manger they find two priests in dalmatics, who represent midwives, and with whom they carry on the familiar dialogue. At the words *Adest hic parvulus*, the *obstetrices* draw aside the curtain, and point first to the Child, and then, at the words *Ecce virgo*, to the Mother. The shepherds kneel before the figure of the Virgin, singing the verses *Salve, virgo singularis*, and after obeisance to the Child, they turn to the chorus, singing the usual sentence *Iam vere scimus*.[3] This leads directly into the Mass,

[1] For a somewhat similar version of the trope *Verbum Patris hodie* see Chevalier, *R.H.*, no. 21374, printed in *A.H.*, xx, 226.

[2] Followed by the rubric *Missa in diluculo*.

[3] For speculative suggestions as to the parts of the church in which different parts of the action were performed see Böhme, pp. 25–7, 39–40.

during which the *pastores* rule the choir, and read or sing considerable parts of the liturgical text. In Lauds they take part in a dramatic rendering of the first antiphon,[1] and at the end sing a trope of the *Benedicamus*, and a special antiphon.

After reviewing the few versions of the *Officium Pastorum* which have come to light, one cannot avoid a feeling of surprise over the smallness of their number and the restriction of their content.[2] The Rouen play, which appears to represent the highest stage of development achieved by this dramatic type, has the charm naturally inherent in the subject, as well as a certain amount of literary finish and dramatic effectiveness. In comparison with the Easter plays, however, the dramatizations of the Nativity seem to have inspired strangely little literary effort. This failure may have resulted from two causes: the relative meagreness and uneventfulness of the Gospel narratives, and the superior dramatic opportunities offered for an Epiphany play of the Magi, which, as we shall see,[3] seems to have overshadowed, and to some extent to have absorbed, the Christmas play of the shepherds.

## III

In one of its dramatic aspects, however, the *Officium Pastorum* was singularly effectual. The impersonated characters of no other play so freely extend their activities outside the strict limits of the representation itself, and take a ceremonial, and sometimes a dramatic, part in the official liturgy. Though Christmas Day is not impressively adorned by highly developed dramatic pieces, its liturgy is uniquely enlivened by incidental dramatic movement. Of this a very good example is the treatment of the following antiphon of Christmas:[4]

Quem vidistis, pastores, dicite? Annuntiate nobis in terris quis apparuit? Natum vidimus in choro angelorum Salvatorem Dominum, alleluia, alleluia.

In the liturgy of Rouen this, the first antiphon of Lauds, was sung dramatically between the archbishop or priest and the *pastores*, the former singing the question, and the latter, the answer.[5]

[1] This dramatic manifestation in Lauds is considered in the next section of this chapter.

[2] For a record of an *Officium Pastorum* at Lichfield in the twelfth century, or later, see appendix B below, p. 522; and for the Shrewsbury fragment, of the fifteenth century, see appendix B below, p. 514.

[3] See chapters xviii and xix.

[4] Hartker, p. 50. On the dramatic aspects of this antiphon see Böhme, pp. 30–2, 44.

[5] See above, pp. 15, 18. For further observations on *Quem vidistis, pastores*, see Notes, p. 429.

In certain other communities a somewhat more conspicuous dramatic use was made of another antiphon of Lauds:[1]

Pastores, dicite, quidnam vidistis, et annuntiate Christi nativitatem. Infantem vidimus pannis inuolutum, et choros angelorum laudantes Salvatorem.

This text was sometimes recited as a dialogue immediately before the introit of the first Mass of Christmas.[2] More commonly, perhaps, it was sung at the close of this Mass, as follows:[3]

Non dicitur *Ite, missa est.* Si Missa celebratur cum cantu, ne populus licenciatum se credens, non audito Matutino, discedat, dicitur a diachono:

*Pastores, dicite, quidnam uidistis, et annunciate Christi natiuitatem,*

et cetera. Chorus respondeat:

*Infantem uidi|mus pannis inuolutum, et choros angelorum laudantes Saluatorem,*

ut habetur in breviariis. Dicitur *Te Deum laudamus.*

The most striking use of this dialogue is in connexion with the psalmody of Lauds, where it may be found, sung singly or in several repetitions, in any one of at least three positions: before the fifth antiphon, or in the midst of the singing of the first psalm or of the fifth. In one instance it is repeated three times during the singing of the first psalm, and in another, four times during the singing of the fifth psalm.[4] These festal practices may be illustrated by the following simple text from Senlis:[5]

Finita communione prime Misse, cantantur Matutine Laudes, in quibus non d*icatu*r capitulum nec hymnus, sed incipitur sequens antiphona: *Quem uidistis, pastores, dicite? Annunciate nobis in terris quis apparuit. Natum uidimus in choro angelorum Saluatorem Dominum, alleluia, alleluia.* |

Psalmus: *Dominus regnauit.*

Antiphona: *Genuit puerpera regem, cui nomen eternum et gaudium matris habens cum uirginitatis honore; nec primam similem uisa est, nec habere sequentem, alleluia.*

Psalmus: *Iubilate.*

Antiphona: *Angelus ad pastores ait: Annuncio uobis gaudium magnum, quia natus est nobis hodie Saluator mundi, alleluia.*

[1] Hartker, p. 51. See Young, *Officium Pastorum*, pp. 351–62.

[2] See Notes, p. 429.

[3] Paris, Bibl. Mazarine, MS 420 (*olim* 216), Miss. Pictaviense sæc. xiv, fol. 18ʳ–18ᵛ, previously printed by Young, *op. cit.*, p. 352, along with other examples of the same practice.

[4] Full texts showing all of these practices are printed by Young, *op. cit.*, pp. 353–61. The normal structure of Lauds is explained above, i, 64 sqq.

[5] Paris, Bibl. Nat., MS lat. 1268, Brev. Silvanectense sæc. xiv, fol. 175ᵛ–176ᵛ, previously edited by Young, *op. cit.*, pp. 355–6. See also Grenier, p. 390.

Psalmus: *Deus, Deus.*

Antiphona: *Facta est cum angelo multitudo celestis exercitus*[1] *laudantium et dicentium: Gloria in excelsis Deo, et in terra pax hominibus bonae uoluntatis, alleluia.*

Psalmus: *Benedicite.*

Dum cantatur psalmus *Benedicite*, uadunt pueri retro altare, et finita antiphona illius psalmi, illi qui chorum seruant uenientes ante altare dicant antiphonam:

*Pastores, dicite, quidnam uidistis, et annunciate Christi natiuitatem.*

Et pueri stantes retro altare dicant:

*Infantem uidimus pannis inuolutum, et choros angelorum laudantes Saluatorem.*

Antiphona: *Paruulus filius hodie natus est nobis, et uocabitur Deus fortis, alleluia.*

Psalmus: *Laudate.*

Quo finito et antiphona eius cantata, ille qui Missam cantat stans ad altare incipit antiphonam super *Benedictus*, et totam cantat, quam ei defert unus custodum chori. Ad *Benedictus* antiphona *Gloria in excelsis Deo, et in terra pax hominibus bone uoluntatis, alleluia.* Psalmus *Benedictus.* | Oratio *Da nobis, quesumus, Domine, Deus noster, ut qui natiuitatem Domini nostri Ihesu Christi nos frequentare gaudemus, dignis conuersationibus ad eius mereamur pertingere consorcium. Per eundem.*[2]

In this case the special dialogue is merely inserted before the fifth antiphon, the normal liturgical arrangement being otherwise undisturbed. The interrogation is spoken by cantors standing in the choir, and the reply, by choirboys stationed behind the altar. There appears to be no intention of impersonation or *mise en scène*, unless we wish to regard the altar itself as symbolizing the *præsepe*.[3] The dialogue, as a matter of fact, is really adapted for recital not at the manger, but at some place on the journey away from Bethlehem; for it must be assumed that the question is asked by persons inquiring concerning the occurrences there. It is for this reason that these sentences were incorporated in several plays dealing with the Magi and Herod, in which the shepherds, returning from Bethlehem, are interrogated by the Magi or others.[4]

As a final example of the dramatic enlivening of the liturgy of Christmas we may cite the famous trope *Hodie cantandus est*, which, as we have seen, was well known as an introduction to the

[1] exercitus] excercitus (MS).

[2] Followed by the rubric *Per horas antiphone de Laudibus.*

[3] See above, p. 8.

[4] See, for example, below, pp. 61, 65–6, 71, 79.

introit of the third Mass of the day.[1] A representative text, with rubrics, is the following from Mantua:[2]

In Natiuitate Domini ad Missam sint omnes ornati in choro stantes, et pronunciet scola hunc versum:

*Hodie cantandus est nobis puer, quem ⟨g⟩ignebat ineffabiliter ante tempora Pater, et eundem*[3] *sub tempore generauit inclita mater.*

R*espondeant* cant*ores*:

*Quis est iste puer, que⟨m⟩ tam magnis preconiis dignum uociferatis? Dicite nobis, ut conlaudatores esse possimus.*

R*espondeat* scola:

*Hic enim est que⟨m⟩ presagus et electus simixta Dei ad terram uenturum preuidens longe ante prenotauit, sicque predixit:*

*Puer natus est.*[4]

The rubrics here show that the dialogue is sung between the whole chorus (*scola*) and a selected group of special cantors.[5] The following text, from Arras, appears to be regarded merely as a processional for use before Mass:[6]

In die Natalis Domini ad Processionem Tr*opus*.

*Hodie cantandus est nobis puer, quem gignebat ineffabiliter ante tempora Pater, et eundem sub tempore generauit inclita mater.*

Chorus:

*Quis est iste puer quem tam magnis preconiis dignum uociferatis? Dicite nobis, ut collaudatores esse possimus.*

Processio:

*Hic enim est quem presagus et electus symmista Dei ad terras uenturum praeuidens longe ante praenotauit, sicque praedixit:*

Antiphona: *Puer natus ⟨est nobis⟩*.[7]

A slightly more detailed indication of the manner in which the trope was sung is given by the following rubric from the liturgical tradition of Rouen:[8]

Post Terciam uero fiet processio. Qua finita, duo clerici circa altare stabunt, qui uersus, scilicet *Hodie cantandus est*, cantabunt. Quibus secundum uersum regentes chorum respondebunt. Primi tertium dicent. Et hoc finito, cantores officium[9] incipient, et celebre perfinient.

[1] See above, i, 195.

[2] Verona, Bibl. Capit., MS 107, Trop. Sancti Benedicti Mantuani sæc. xi, fol. 4$^{v}$, previously edited by Young, *op. cit.*, pp. 366–7.

[3] eundem] euntem (MS).

[4] Followed by a fresh introit trope beginning *Ecce adest de quo*⟨MS *co*⟩ *prophete*.

[5] For conjectures as to a more specific distribution of the parts of such a text see Chasles, pp. 68–9.

[6] Cambrai, Bibl. de la Ville, MS 75, Grad. Sancti Vedasti Atrebatensis sæc. xi, fol. 7$^{v}$, previously edited by Young, *op. cit.*, p. 366.

[7] Followed by a fresh introit trope beginning *Ecce adest de quo prophetae*.

[8] Montpellier, Bibl. de la Faculté de Médecine, MS H. 304, fol. 32$^{r}$.

[9] In French MSS *officium* is often used as meaning *introitus*.

According to this *ordo* the first and third sentences are sung by two clerics standing at the altar, and the question is asked by the cantors who have charge of the choir. One would be glad to infer that the altar is regarded as symbolizing the *præsepe*, and that the groups of speakers are assumed to be the midwives and shepherds respectively; but such an inference is insufficiently supported by the available facts. So far as we know, the trope *Hodie cantandus est* had no place in the genuine drama of the Christmas season.[1]

## IV

One dramatic, or more precisely, *theatrical*, aspect of the ceremonies of Christmas still remains to be explained: the prevalence during the later Middle Ages and into modern times of plastic representations of the Holy Manger. In view of the meagreness of the dramatic texts, one is called upon to account for the astonishing popularity of what might seem to be the related dramatic *mise en scène*.[2]

The history of the *præsepe* begins in the very grotto traditionally venerated as the birth-place of Christ. As early as the third century, according to Origen, this veneration was well established, and a specific manger was the centre of pious devotion.[3] Over this spot the empress, Helena, erected a basilica, visited during the fourth century and after by numerous pilgrims, of whose spiritual edification through seeing the holy place St Jerome speaks expressly.[4] The grotto was richly decorated, and the manger itself was adorned with gold and silver.[5] It has, indeed, been asserted that not only ornaments, but also figures of the Holy Family were placed in the manger at Bethlehem as early as the year 400; but this is unproved.[6]

Whatever may have been the reaches of the early cult of the *præsepe* in the East, the widest development of this form of devo-

[1] This is the view of Creizenach (i, 52) and Chambers (ii, 9). The contrary opinion has been expressed numerous times. Gautier (*Tropes*, p. 218) speaks of this trope as 'le premier germe d'un futur théâtre'; and after quoting Gautier, W. H. Grattan Flood (*The Month*, cxxxviii [1921], 545) calls it 'the bed-rock of mediaeval drama', and, along with *Quem quæritis in præsepe*, 'the foundation of liturgical drama'. This latter view is expressed also by G. Vale (*Rassegna Gregoriana*, v [1906], 532), C. Blume (*A.H.*, xlix, 7) and Sepet (*Origines*, pp. 15–6).

[2] For bibliography relating to the *præsepe*, or *præsepium*, see Notes, p. 429.

[3] See Origen, *Contra Celsum*, i, 51, in Migne *P.G.*, xi, 756.

[4] See Usener, pp. 283–4. The archaeology of the church at Bethlehem is treated by E. Weigand, *Die Geburtskirche von Bethlehem*, Leipzig, 1911.

[5] See Wetzer and Welte, vii, 1195–6; Usener, pp. 284–5.

[6] The assertion is made by Usener, p. 287. See Young, *op. cit.*, p. 335.

tion occurred during the later Middle Ages in the West. In 354, at Rome, Pope Liberius first established the Nativity as a special feast to be celebrated on December 25th, distinct from the feast of Epiphany, of which it had previously been a part on January 6th. As a church dedicated especially to the observance of the Nativity he erected the Basilica Liberii, which during the fifth century became known as Basilica Sanctæ Mariæ, and after the ninth century, as Sancta Maria Major. Meanwhile, in the time of Pope Theodore (642–9), relics of the true *præsepe* were brought from Bethlehem and deposited in this building, which was henceforth known also by the name, Sancta Maria ad Præsepe. As a shelter for these relics a chapel was built in the right aisle, to the decoration of which Pope Gregory III (731–41) contributed gold figures of Mary and her Child. When Pope Sixtus V (1585–90) built the new chapel in the right transept, the old chapel of the *præsepe*, already once restored in the thirteenth century, was moved to a position beneath the main altar.[1]

As to the use of the relics themselves in the church of St Mary we have only meagre information. It appears that the venerated boards of wood originally deposited in the side-chapel were not encased in a reliquary, as are the modern fragments, but were joined together in the form of an actual manger.[2] This, moreover, was the veritable altar upon which the pope laid the consecrated *Corpus Christi* when he celebrated his annual Mass in this church on the vigil of Christmas. Thus the altar became in every sense the *præsepe Christi*, and in numerous examples of medieval plastic art the Child Himself may be seen lying upon the altar-table.[3]

We may infer that the manger of Sancta Maria ad Præsepe was imitated in other Roman churches. We know, indeed, that Pope Gregory IV (827–44) placed a similar one in the church of Sancta Maria trans Tiberim;[4] but from the first ten Christian centuries we have virtually no further relevant information. Whether or not the representations of the manger in these two churches held figures of the Holy Family we cannot tell. That

[1] For the facts supporting the statements in this paragraph see Usener, pp. 275–7, 280, 281, 282, 291.

[2] See Usener, pp. 282–3.

[3] See Mâle, *XIII^e Siècle*, p. 224. For representations of the Nativity in art in general see F. Noack, *Die Geburt Christi in der bildenden Kunst bis zur Renaissance*, Darmstadt, 1894; Rohault de Fleury, *Vierge*, i, 109–36; Rietschel, *Weihnachten*, pp. 1–99.

[4] See *Le Liber Pontificalis*, ed. L. Duchesne, ii, Paris, 1892, p. 78; Usener, pp. 280–1; Cabrol and Leclercq, iii, 3025–7.

the *chapel* in each case was supplied with such images there can be no doubt;[1] but that the ancient cribs themselves closely resembled the elaborate contrivances of the later Middle Ages we have no indication.[2]

Passing from the tradition of the actual *præsepe* of Bethlehem and Rome to a consideration of the structure used as *mise en scène* for dramatic performances, we find much less information than we could desire. Certain external evidences are supplied by Gerhoh of Reichersberg and the chronicler, Galvano Flamma (1283–1344). The former, writing about 1160, speaks of plays of the Nativity thus: *Exhibent præterea imaginaliter et Salvatoris infantiæ cunabula, parvuli vagitum, puerperæ Virginis matronalem habitum.*[3] The latter, in his account of an Epiphany play at Milan in 1336, mentions the *præsepe* as follows: *Tres reges . . . pervenerunt ad ecclesiam Sancti Eustorgii. Ubi in latere altaris majoris erat præsepium cum bove et asino, et in præsepio erat Christus parvulus in brachiis Virginis matris.*[4] From such passages we may infer that during the period from the twelfth century to the fourteenth a structural crib was familiar in dramatic performances, and that it was sometimes provided with appropriate plastic figures.

The actual dramatic texts in which the *præsepe* is mentioned give us relatively little information as to details. From the *Officium Pastorum* at Rouen we learn that it was erected behind the main altar, and if we may interpret the rubrics literally, it was sufficiently large for the two midwives to stand in it.[5] It was provided with figures representing Mary and the Child, which were hidden, until the appropriate moment, by a curtain.[6] In the *Officium Stellæ* from the same church, as we shall see in the next chapter, the statuette of the Mother and Child probably stood upon the altar itself.[7] We know also that the crib used for the Christmas play of Benediktbeuern contained a figure of the infant Christ.[8]

As a source for such dramatic furnishings it is scarcely necessary to search beyond the natural inventiveness of those who produced the plays. Although the cult of the relics of the true

[1] See Usener, p. 291.

[2] Concerning the preservation of the relics in Sancta Maria ad Præsepe in modern times see Vigouroux, ii, 1107–8; Cabrol and Leclercq, iii, 3022–5.

[3] Scheibelberger, i, 27. See Appendix C, p. 525.

[4] L. A. Muratori, *Rerum Italicarum Scriptores*, xii, Milan, 1728, col. 1017–8. See D'Ancona, i, 97–8.

[5] See above, pp. 14, 17.

[6] See above, p. 17.

[7] See below, p. 44.

[8] See below, p. 188.

*præsepe* at Rome must have been known all over Europe, one would not be justified in attempting to derive directly from this the dramatic use now under consideration. If the clerics concerned with the plays had required a model, they could have found it most effectually in the representations of the Mother and Child in independent plastic art.

Roman tradition, dramatic custom, and early ecclesiastical art, however, all fail to account for the astonishing European popularity of the Christmas crib in both public and private devotion during the later Middle Ages and in modern times. Of this widespread and still flourishing cult the chief origin seems to be an ecstatic episode in the life of St Francis of Assisi. The description of this occurrence by St Bonaventura (1221–74) may be summarized as follows:[1]

In the year 1223, in order to stir the people to a more devout observance of the Nativity, Francis obtained papal permission to erect at Greccio a *præsepium*, at which he stationed a live ox and ass, with a supply of provender. Crowds gathered, and the Holy Night was made festal with clustered lights and glad sounds. Before the manger, which served as the altar, stood Francis, his eyes suffused with tears of joy. At Mass, celebrated *super præsepium*, he himself sang the gospel, and preached a sermon on the Nativity. A certain John of Greccio reported that he had seen sleeping in the manger a beautiful child, whom Francis roused from sleep and embraced. The hay from the *præsepium* was preserved as a miraculous panacea for diseases of animals.

Thomas of Celano, in an account written about the middle of the thirteenth century, emphasizes somewhat the miraculous aspect of the occasion.[2] He reports that a child lying lifeless in the manger was resuscitated by the holy Francis, that the hay became a panacea for diseases of both men and animals, and that a church was built on the spot, with an altar over the *præsepium*.

Although we do not know what specifically inspired St Francis to erect his Christmas crib, we may infer that he was

[1] *Acta Sanctorum*, Oct., ii, Paris and Rome, 1866, p. 770. For the text see Notes, p. 430. See also P. Sabatier, *Vie de S. François d'Assise*, Paris, 1894, pp. lxxxi–lxxxviii, 328–9; Wetzer and Welte, vii, 1196–7; Gougaud, pp. 26–7; N. Tamassia, *S. Francesco d'Assisi e la sua Leggenda*, Padua and Verona, 1906, pp. 83–7; H. Dausend, *Die Weihnachtsfeier des hl. Franziskus von Assisi in Deutschland und Greccio*, in *Franziskanische Studien*, xiii (1926), 294–304. See also the fresco by Giotto in the Upper Church at Assisi, reproduced, for example, by H. Thode, *Franz von Assisi und die Anfänge der Kunst der Renaissance in Italien*, Berlin, 1904, plate 32.

[2] For the text, from *Acta Sanctorum*, Oct., ii, p. 706, see Notes, p. 430. See Sabatier, *op. cit.*, pp. li–lvi; Gougaud, p. 26.

influenced by traditions from both Bethlehem and Rome. During the period 1219–20 he had journeyed in the East, and the ceremony at Greccio may have been 'the crystallization of haunting memories carried away from the real Bethlehem'.[1] The influence of the tradition of the church of Sancta Maria ad Præsepe at Rome is to be seen, perhaps, in the use of the manger as the altar for the Mass. Whether St Francis knew of the use of the *præsepe* in Church plays of the Christmas season we cannot tell. His own legend, however, may have transmitted to later writers a dramatic inspiration which we are unable to trace.[2]

After the thirteenth century, as a matter of fact, the *præsepe* was much less important as a dramatic *mise en scène* than as a centre of public and private devotion. Through the enthusiasm of Franciscans and others, Christmas cribs were used throughout Western Europe. Churches, dwellings and public squares were brightened annually by silent representations of the scene at Bethlehem. The dumb figures from the hands of artisans were the centre not of dramatic action, but of prayers and Christmas carols. Finally, through the addition of scores of human and animal effigies, through scenic elaboration, and through lavish adornments of jewels and fabrics, the *præsepe* became increasingly, at the end of the Middle Ages and in modern times, a mere curiosity of plastic ingenuity.[3]

[1] See Evelyn M. Cesaresco, in *Contemporary Review*, lxxvii (1900), 117.

[2] Thode (p. 451) and Hager (p. 12) erroneously assume that the celebration at Greccio was itself a play. For the correct view see D'Ancona, i, 117.

[3] Concerning the *præsepe* during the Renaissance and in modern times see, for example, Hager, pp. 18–145, and the published parts of the treatise by Berliner. Modern examples may be seen conveniently in the Musée de Cluny in Paris, the Museo Civico in Naples, and the Bayerisches Nationalmuseum in Munich.

## CHAPTER XVIII

# THE COMING OF THE MAGI

THE dramatic ceremonies of Christmas Day, as we have seen, are unexpectedly meagre. The number of churches which can be shown to have cultivated them is small, and the extant examples are of relatively slight scope. Decidedly more impressive are the plays of the Magi for Epiphany, January 6th. Of these we have an ample number, exhibiting an unusual variety in their content, a considerable breadth of action, and, in several instances, a rather remarkable literary sophistication. The more highly developed of them, indeed, actually contribute somewhat toward enlarging the range of the pieces performed on Christmas Day; for several versions of the Magi play, or *Officium Stellæ*, represent, in brief episodes, the experiences of the Christmas shepherds after their visit to Bethlehem, and thus amplify the action of the *Officium Pastorum* itself.[1]

## I

The central theme of the feast of Epiphany and of the dramatic *Officium Stellæ* is the coming of the Magi to Jerusalem and Bethlehem, recounted in the following passages in the second chapter of the Gospel of Matthew:[2]

1. Cum ergo natus esset Jesus in Bethlehem Juda in diebus Herodis regis, ecce Magi ab oriente venerunt Ierosolymam,

2. Dicentes: Ubi est qui natus est rex Judæorum? Vidimus enim stellam ejus in oriente, et venimus adorare eum.

3. Audiens autem Herodes rex, turbatus est, et omnis Ierosolyma cum illo.

4. Et congregans omnes principes sacerdotum, et scribas populi, sciscitabatur ab eis ubi Christus nasceretur.

5. At illi dixerunt ei: In Bethlehem Judæ; sic enim scriptum est per prophetam:

6. Et tu Bethlehem terra Juda, nequaquam minima es in principibus Juda; ex te enim exiet dux qui regat populum meum Israel.

7. Tunc Herodes clam vocatis Magis, diligenter didicit ab eis tempus stellæ quæ apparuit eis;

8. Et mittens illos in Bethlehem dixit: Ite, et interrogate diligenter de

[1] For bibliography relating to the *Officium Stellæ* see Notes, p. 432.

[2] Matt. ii, 1–12, 16.

puero; et cum inveneritis, renuntiate mihi, ut et ego veniens adorem eum.

9. Qui cum audissent regem, abierunt. Et ecce stella, quam viderant in oriente, antecedebat eos usque dum veniens staret supra ubi erat puer.

10. Videntes autem stellam gavisi sunt gaudio magno valde.

11. Et intrantes domum invenerunt puerum cum Maria matre ejus, et procidentes adoraverunt eum; et apertis thesauris suis, obtulerunt ei munera: aurum, thus, et myrrham.

12. Et responso accepto in somnis ne redirent ad Herodem, per aliam viam reversi sunt in regionem suam. . . .

16. Tunc Herodes videns quoniam illusus esset a Magis, iratus est valde, et mittens occidit omnes pueros qui erant in Bethlehem et in omnibus finibus ejus, a bimatu et infra, secundum tempus quod exquisierat a Magis.

About this narrative accumulated, during the Middle Ages, a very considerable body of patristic and apocryphal tradition, some of which is essential to our present purpose.[1] The term *magus* (μάγος), for example, was interpreted variously. Commentators and homilists often explained it in its least favourable sense as indicating a magician or sorcerer, and emphasized the notion that magic was discredited at the advent of Christ. The Gospel itself, however, contains no hint of reprobation, and seems to use the word not with reference to a special sacerdotal or professional class, but as indicating merely heathen sages from the East who were apt in astronomy and, perhaps, in the interpretation of dreams. Christian writers associated them variously with Persia, Arabia, or Chaldæa.[2] During the sixth century, if not before, the tradition arose that the Magi were kings, and this belief prevailed throughout the Middle Ages.[3] Hence the feast of Epiphany received the name *Festum Trium Regum*. Although the Gospel and the apocrypha give no support to this identification, it found ample justification in numerous prophetic passages, of which the following is, perhaps, the most conspicuous:[4]

Reges Tharsis et insulæ munera offerent; reges Arabum et Saba dona adducent.

This psalm-verse acquired especial prominence through its use as the offertory of the Mass of Epiphany.[5]

[1] For a general survey of this tradition in its bearings upon the drama see Sturdevant, pp. 8–34.

[2] See Kehrer, *Legende*, pp. 5–11, 30–1; P. V. M. Benecke, in Hastings, *Bible*, iii, 204.

[3] Kehrer, *Legende*, pp. 11–6; Kehrer, *Literatur*, i, 36, 52; Benecke, in Hastings, *Bible*, iii, 206; Hirn, p. 376.

[4] Ps. lxxi, 10. See also, for example, Isaiah xlix, 7, 23; lx, 3, 10.

[5] See Migne, *P.L.*, lxxviii, 649, and below, p. 33.

We do not know the exact nature of the sidereal appearance which moved the Magi to make their journey, and from which they inferred the birth of the Messiah of the Jews.[1] They probably based this inference not primarily upon a gentile tradition, such as that established by Balaam's prophecy,[2] but upon some Rabbinical teaching which associated the appearance of a star with the coming of the Messiah.[3] The ancient belief that a special guiding star rises at the birth of important persons is reflected in the patristic tradition that the star of Bethlehem was a special creation of a particular nature, such as an unusual form of angel.[4]

Since the Gospel and the apocrypha are silent in regard to the number of the Magi, ancient authorities differ on this point. In the East the traditional number was twelve or thirteen, and some evidence exists for the numbers two and four.[5] For the West, however, from the fifth century on, Church writers established three as the correct number, this number being chosen, probably, because the Gospel mentions the gifts of the Magi as being three.[6]

The names assigned to the three Magi at different periods were numerous.[7] From among the various triads there arose, apparently during the course of the twelfth century, the familiar Melchior, Caspar (Gaspar, Jasper), and Balthasar, of whom the *Collectanea et Flores* of Pseudo-Beda provides the following description:[8]

Magi sunt qui munera Domino dederunt: primus fuisse dicitur Melchior, senex et canus, barba prolixa et capillis, tunica hyacinthina, sagoque mileno, et calceamentis hyacinthino et albo mixto opere, pro mitrario variæ compositionis indutus; aurum obtulit regi Domino. Secundus, nomine Caspar, juvenis imberbis, rubicundus, mylenica tunica, sago rubeo, calceamentis hyacinthinis vestitus; thure quasi Deo oblatione digna, Deum honorabat. Tertius, fuscus, integre barbatus, Balthasar nomine, habens tunicam rubeam, albo vario, calceamentis

[1] For references to astronomical discussions of the *stella* mentioned in the Gospel see Kehrer, *Legende*, pp. 18–9.

[2] Numbers xxiv, 17: *Orietur stella ex Jacob, et consurget virga de Israel; et percutiet duces Moab, vastabitque omnes filios Seth.*

[3] See Benecke, in Hastings, *Bible*, iii, 204–5.

[4] See Kehrer, *Legende*, pp. 18–21.

[5] See Vigouroux, iv, 546–7; Benecke, in Hastings, *Bible*, iii, 204–6.

[6] See Kehrer, *Legende*, pp. 22–3.

[7] See Hartmann, *Dreikönigsspiel*, pp. 51–79; Kehrer, *Legende*, pp. 25–30; Kehrer, *Literatur*, i, 64–75.

[8] Migne, *P.L.*, xciv, 541. The *Collectanea et Flores* is usually assigned to the twelfth century. See Kehrer, *Legende*, pp. 25–6; Kehrer, *Literatur*, i, 66–8. For the unusual names Zoroaster and Fadizarda see below, pp. 78, 444.

milenicis amictus, per myrrham filium hominis moriturum professus est. Omnia autem vestimenta eorum Syriaca sunt.

The conventional individualizations recorded here were, no doubt, frequently presented in the plays of Epiphany, though the dramatic texts themselves seldom record the fact.[1]

The symbolistic interpreting of the three gifts of the Magi began to flourish, apparently, in the second century, at which time Irenæus, bishop of Lyons, wrote of them as follows:[2]

Myrrham quidem, quod ipse erat, qui pro mortali humano genere moreretur et sepeliretur; aurum vero, quoniam Rex, cujus regni finis non est; thus vero, quoniam Deus, qui et notus in Judæa factus est, et manifestus eis qui non quærebant eum.

That this interpretation was adopted early into the liturgy is manifest from the following antiphon of Epiphany:[3]

Ab oriente venerunt Magi ut in Bethlehem adorarent Dominum; et apertis thesauris suis, pretiosa munera obtulerunt: aurum sicut regi magno, thus sicut Deo vero, myrram sepulturæ ejus, alleluia.

This liturgical piece contains what may be called the normal symbolizing of the gifts throughout the Middle Ages.

## II

The plays which embody the legends of the Magi are by no means uniform either in their content or in the nature of their attachment to the liturgy. The most elementary of them are associated with the Mass, though not as appendages to the liturgical text, after the manner of the introit tropes of Easter and Christmas, but rather as vivid amplifications of essential parts of the usual ceremonial. Since, for example, the Magi brought with them gifts and presented them to the new-born king, it was altogether appropriate that a dramatic representation of this action should sometimes attach itself to the oblation, particularly in view of the fact that during the Middle Ages this part of the Mass was a far more elaborate and vivid ceremony than would be inferred from modern custom. In the early period there were two offerings: one by the people, *oblatio populi*, and one by the clergy, *oblatio sacerdotalis*. From about the fifth century to the eleventh or twelfth, the *oblatio populi* was more or less obliga-

[1] See below, pp. 41, 73.

[2] Migne, *P.G.*, vii, 870–1.

[3] Hartker, p. 77. On the symbolizing of the gifts in general see Kehrer, *Legende*, pp. 31–5.

tory. The offerings of the general congregation were of two sorts, treated separately in the liturgy. There were, in the first place, miscellaneous objects—intended for the support of the clergy, of the church fabric, and of the poor—such as food, wax, oil, clothing, ornaments or money. These offerings (*munera*), for which there were no established liturgical forms, were made before the Mass began, or, at least, before the singing of the gospel. The other gifts of the people (*oblata*), consisting of bread and wine destined for use in the Eucharistic sacrifice, were made at the time of the liturgical oblation by the persons who expected to take part in the subsequent communion. Because of the inconvenience entailed by the participation of the congregation in this ceremony, the offering was delegated, during the later Middle Ages, to particular members of the clergy, and thus became an *oblatio sacerdotalis*.[1]

The offering of bread and wine for actual use in the Mass of the day was often, if not always, accompanied by a somewhat elaborate ceremonial and by the choral singing of the offertory. Since the presenting and receiving of the *offerenda* occupied considerable time, particularly if many of the congregation took part, the liturgical chant had to be correspondingly prolonged. During the earlier Christian centuries, therefore, the *offertorium* consisted of a whole psalm, or a large part of it, the verses of which were sung in alternation by two halves of the chorus. By the time of Gregory the Great (590–604), however, the custom had arisen of assigning the psalm-verses to a cantor, the whole chorus singing a special verse, or antiphon, at the beginning and end of the psalm, or even after each verse of it. With the gradual reduction of the number of the persons offering, the *offertorium* was shortened until, during the later Middle Ages, it survived, in its present form, as a mere antiphon without verses.[2] What we may regard as an intermediate form between the prolonged chant of the early Middle Ages and the residual antiphon of modern times is the offertory of Epiphany found in certain service-books of the tenth century:[3]

Reges Tharsis et insulæ munera offerent, reges Arabum et Saba dona adducent; et adorabunt eum omnes reges terræ, omnes gentes servient ei.

[1] See Corblet, i, 215–25; Thalhofer, ii, 120–3.

[2] See Wagner, pp. 112–6; Thalhofer, ii, 106. The modern form of the *offertorium* is explained above, i, 29–30.

[3] *Paléographie musicale*, i, 18–9; Migne, *P.L.*, lxxviii, 649–50.

Versus: Deus, judicium tuum Regi da, et justitiam tuam Filio Regis; judicare populum tuum cum justitia, et pauperes tuos in judicio.

Versus: Orietur in diebus ejus justitia, et abundantia pacis, donec extollatur luna; et dominabitur a mari usque ad mare.

Versus: Suscipiant montes pacem populo tuo, et colles justitiam.

The text in the modern Roman missal consists merely of the opening sentence, without the verses. The longer form before us was probably intended to accompany a somewhat elaborate form of oblation, the nature of which we cannot determine. For the moment, however, we are concerned not so much with speculation as to the authorized liturgical ceremonial which may have prevailed in one medieval community or another, as with the text itself, recounting the bringing of gifts by the kings of the East.[1] Such a passage would seem to convey a direct invitation to the clergy to transform their oblation into a scene representing the kings bringing their gifts to the manger at Bethlehem. That this dramatic opportunity was not lost is shown by the following text, of uncertain date, from the use of Limoges:[2]

Cantato offertorio, antequam eant ad offerendam, tres chorarii induti vestibus sericis, habentes singuli coronam auream in capite suo, et cyphum deauratum,[3] seu aliud jocale pretiosum in manibus suis, ad instar trium Regum qui venerunt adorare Dominum, ingrediuntur per portam majorem chori, incedentes cum gravitate, cantantes sequentem prosulam:[4]

*O quam dignis celebranda dies ista laudibus,*
*In qua Christi genitura propalatur gentibus.*
*Pax terrenis nunciatur, gloria cælestibus:*
*Novi partus signum fulget orientis patria.*
*Currunt Reges orientis stella sibi prævia;*
*Currunt Reges, et adorant Deum ad præsepia.*
*Tres adorant Reges unum, triplex est oblatio.*

Primus dicit elevando cyphum:

*Aurum primo.*

Deinde secundus dicit:

*Thus secundo.*

[1] For further observations on ceremonies at the offertory see Notes, p. 432.

[2] Martene, iii, 44, from an 'ordinarium ecclesiæ Lemovicensis', of which the editor (i, p. xxi) does not give the date. This text has been reprinted by Du Méril, pp. 151–3; Daniel, *Codex*, i, 128–9; Anz, pp. 140–1; Böhme, pp. 48–9. Meyer (p. 38) observes that the dissyllabic rhymes of the opening *prosula* indicate a date later than 1100. The play is discussed by Anz, pp. 42–4; Böhme, pp. 47–55.

[3] deauratum] doauratum (Print).

[4] See Chevalier, *R.H.*, no. 13496.

Item tertius:

*Myrrham dante tertio.*

Ordine prædicto primus dicit:

*Aurum Regem.*

Secundus:

*Thus cælestem.*

Tertius:

*Mori notat unctio.*

Deinde existentes circa medium chori, unus eorum elevat manum ostendentem Stellam pendentem in filo, quæ antecedit eos, cantando altiori voce:

*Hoc signum magni Regis.*[1]

Tunc tres simul pergunt versus majus altare cantantes:

*Eamus, inquiramus eum, et offeramus ei munera: aurum, thus, et myrrham.*

Et vadunt ad offerendam, relinquentes ibi sua jocalia. Post hæc unus puer psallit retro majus altare, ad instar Angeli; alloquendo Reges cantat:

*Nuncium vobis fero de supernis:*
*Natus est Christus, Dominator orbis,*
*in Bethleem Judæ, sic enim propheta*
*dixerat ante.*[2]

Qua visione attoniti Reges et admirantes redeunt per portam quæ ducit ad sacristiam cantando antiphonam:

*In Bethleem natus est Rex cælorum.*

From this brief text it appears that after the singing of the offertory,[3] and before the actual oblation, three cantors, dressed to represent the three kings, enter the choir through the main door, proceeding with measured tread and singing the prose *O quam dignis*. Announcing their gifts, they proceed to the middle of the choir, where one of them points to a star hanging from a cord, and sings the words *Hoc signum magni regis*. Guided by the star, which precedes them, the three kings, singing *Eamus, inquiramus*, approach the high altar, where they deposit their gifts. Then a boy behind the altar, in the likeness of an angel, sings to the kings the hymn *Nuntium vobis fero de supernis*. Astonished at what they see and hear, the kings withdraw from the choir by the door leading into the sacristy, singing *In Bethlehem natus est rex cælorum*.

[1] This speech, and the next, are taken from the following antiphon in Lauds of Epiphany: *Magi videntes stellam dixerunt ad invicem: Hoc signum magni Regis est; eamus et inquiramus eum, et offeramus ei munera: aurum, thus, et myrrham*. See Hartker, p. 76.

[2] For the hymn *Nuncium vobis fero de supernis* see Chevalier, *R.H.*, no. 12625, printed in *A.H.*, l, 283. For the complete text see Notes, p. 433.

[3] The text is, no doubt, *Reges Tharsis*; but whether there are also verses we do not know.

This play, then, merely dramatizes the traditional oblation, the clergy, or members of the congregation, being represented by the three *Reges*. In depositing their vessels or reliquaries upon the altar the kings seem to be following one of the established traditions of the *oblatio populi*, for Belethus, in this *Rationale Divinorum Officiorum*, of the twelfth century, refers to such gifts thus:[1]

In quibusdam ecclesiis in magnis solemnitatibus pretiosa offeruntur ecclesiæ utensilia, et in altari ponuntur vel in locis competentibus.

For the utterances of his personages the composer of this dramatic piece resorts not to the Gospel and the apocrypha, but to the liturgy itself. The opening processional of the Magi, *O quam dignis*, consists of three stanzas from a relatively rare *prosula*, which, it will be observed, includes the symbolical interpretation of the gifts mentioned above. The stational chant *Hoc signum* and the processional *Eamus, inquiramus* are skilfully selected from a well-known antiphon in Lauds of Epiphany. The song of the angel, *Nuntium vobis*, is the first stanza of a traditional hymn. The antiphon *In Bethlehem*, sung by the Magi as they withdraw from the choir, appears not to be easily identified.[2] The result of this liberal use of liturgical pieces is the presence of at least one slight dramatic impropriety, in that the three kings, in their opening processional, are made to speak of themselves in the third person.

For so simple a performance the stage arrangements are quite ample. The kings, with their silk garments, crowns and vessels are clearly impersonated. The *Stella pendens in filo* locates the scene in Bethlehem. The crib is represented only by the altar itself, which may, to be sure, have been decorated in some appropriate manner, or may have been felt to represent the crib symbolically according to patristic tradition.[3]

The slight dramatic action confines itself to the visit of the kings to the manger in Bethlehem, and thus omits the part of the Biblical narrative which would have submitted most readily to a rendering in dialogue—the meeting of the kings with Herod in Jerusalem. It is possible that the first station, in the middle of the choir, was intended to represent the arrival of the visitors

[1] Migne, *P.L.*, ccii, 50.

[2] See Du Méril, p. 153. Böhme (p. 54) infers, very reasonably, that this announcement of the Nativity reveals the influence of the plays, or ceremonies, of Christmas Day.

[3] See above, p. 8. I find no support for the inference of Böhme (p. 54) that there is an actual *præsepe* behind the altar.

in the Holy City, and the procession onward to the altar, the journey thence to Bethlehem. Of such intention, however, there is no specific indication.

## III

Although the play from Limoges is the only extant Magi play which is directly attached to the offertory, it is highly probable that in this part of the liturgy dramatic ceremonies were developed often. Limoges, in any case, is not the only community from which we have actual evidence of mimetic observances within the Mass of Epiphany, for in the metropolitan churches of Besançon a representation of the Three Kings was customary in association with the reciting of the gospel.

As we have already observed, in an earlier chapter, the reading, or singing, of the gospel in the liturgy has always been accompanied by a certain amount of impressive ceremonial.[1] The mere procession of the deacon with the gospel-book to the left side of the choir, and the censing before the reading, give special prominence to this moment in the early part of the Mass. On certain feasts extra-liturgical pieces, or tropes, were sometimes sung here.[2] In the Mass of Epiphany, as observed in the cathedral of Bayeux in the thirteenth century and earlier, the intoning of the gospel was introduced by this appropriate antiphon:[3]

Ab Oriente venerunt Magi ut in Bethlehem adorarent Dominum, et apertis thesauris suis, pretiosa munera obtulerunt: aurum sicut regi magno; thus sicut Deo vero: myrrham sepulture ejus, alleluia.

Such a liturgical piece suggests at once the appropriateness of including in the ceremonial at the gospel actual impersonations of the Magi; and at Besançon these personages actually appeared in the procession, and took part in the reading itself. These dramatic activities are described in the following passages from service-books of the churches of St Stephen and St John:[4]

In Missa, ante euangelium, fit processio Trium Regum, qui induuntur

[1] See above, i, 27–8; *Catholic Encyclopedia*, vi, 660–2.

[2] See Gautier, *Tropes*, pp. 159–60.

[3] Chevalier, *Bayeux*, p. 79. See Hartker, p. 77.

[4] H. Crombach, *Primitiæ Gentium, seu Historia SS. Trium Regum Magorum*, Cologne, 1654, pp. 732–4, reprinted by Anz, pp. 142–5, and by Young, *Trois Rois*, pp. 76–9. The dates of the MSS upon which Crombach draws cannot be determined. As is indicated in the foot-notes, the opening and closing passages in the text now reprinted are from a service-book of the church of St Stephen at Besançon; the main body of the text is from the use of the church of St John. It appears that dramatic ceremony was virtually the same in the two churches. For discussion of the ceremony see Anz, pp. 44–7; Böhme, pp. 55–6. For additional information see Notes, p. 433.

amictis, albis, paratis, stolis, et tunicis colore differentibus. Apponuntur etiam humeris cappæ, dantur capelli cum coronis, et vnicuique famuli, qui deferant phialas. Finita prosa, egrediuntur e vestiario, præcedentibus cereis, et thuribulo, et duobus choristis quorum iunior cum suo baculo præcedit, senior vero sequitur Reges.[1] Reges eant vsque ante altare Beatæ Mariæ cantando:

*Nouæ geniture*
*cedit ius naturæ;*
*contra carnis iura*
*parit virgo pura;*
*nouo quodam iure*
*premitur natura,*
*nato Christo.*

*Audit non auditum;*
*seruat non attritum*
*virgineum florem*
*mater præter morem;*
*irritansque ritum*
*retinet pudorem,*
*nato Christo.*

*Totum reseratur,*
*quidquid tegebatur*
*clausum sub figura;*
*prodeunt obscura,*
*iamque iudicatur*
*literæ litura,*
*nato Christo.*

*Ortus veri Dei,*
*quem respirant rei,*
*miserans eduxit,*
*gratiam reduxit,*
*dies nostræ spei*
*dies et illuxit,*
*nato Christo.*[2]

Cum autem venerint ante altare B. Mariæ, vertendo ante chorum Tres Reges simul dicant:[3]

[1] To this point, the text of Crombach is derived 'ex codice rituum Ecclesiæ Metropolitanæ S. Stephani Bisonticensis'.

[2] These four stanzas are from a *cantio* listed by Chevalier, *R.H.*, no. 12329, and printed in *A.H.*, xx, 63. For a fifth stanza, omitted here, see Notes, p. 435.

[3] The four stanzas sung by the *Reges* here are found in a piece listed by Chevalier, *R.H.*, no. 12241, and printed by Mone, *Hymni*, i, 80. A slightly different version, which does not contain the fourth stanza of the text before us, is printed in *A.H.*, i, 160.

*Nos respectu gratiæ*
*gentium primitiæ*
*spem totius veniæ*
*vobis damus hodie.*

Cum venerint in medium simul dicant:

*Cuius stellam vidimus,*
*verum lumen credimus;*
*quem Deum cognoscimus*
*adorare venimus.*

Cum autem processerint paulo ultra, dicant simul:

*Dona damus talia,*
*per quæ Regis gloria*
*patet, et potentia,*
*qui gubernat omnia.*

In introitu chori dicant simul:

*Ius in auro regium,*
*thure sacerdotium,*
*myrrha munus tertium*
*mortis est indicium.*

Cum autem adscenderint supra ad pulpitum, legant euangelium vnusquisque versum suum in hunc modum:

Reges simul: *Dominus vobiscum.*
Cantores: *Et cum spiritu tuo.*
Reges: *Sequentia S. Euangelij secundum Matthæum.*
Cantores: *Gloria tibi, Domine.*
1. Rex: *Cum natus esset Iesus in Bethlehem Iudæ, in diebus Herodis regis, ecce Magi ab oriente venerunt Ierosolymam, dicentes.*
2. Rex: *Vbi est, qui natus est Rex Iudæorum?*
3. Rex: *Vidimus enim stellam eius in oriente.*
Cantores: *Et venimus adorare eum.*
1. Rex: *Audiens autem Herodes rex turbatus est, et omnis Ierosolyma cum illo.*
2. Rex: *Et congregans omnes principes sacerdotum, et scribas populi sciscitabatur ab eis, vbi Christus nasceretur.*
3. Rex: *At illi dixerunt ei.*
Cantores: *In Bethlehem Iudæ.*
1. Rex: *Sic enim scriptum est per prophetam.*
2. Rex: *Et tu, Bethlehem, terra Iuda, nequaquam minima es in principibus Iuda.*
3. Rex: *Ex te exiet dux.*
Cantores: *Qui regat populum meum Israel.*
1. Rex: *Tunc Herodes, clam vocatis Magis, diligenter ab eis didicit tempus stellæ quæ apparuit eis.*
2. Rex: *Et mittens illos in Bethlehem, dixit.*

3. Rex: *Ite et interrogate diligenter de puero; et cum inueneritis, renunciate mihi.*

Cantores: *Vt et ego veniens adorem eum.*

1. Rex: *Qui cum audissent regem, abierunt.*

2. Rex: *Et ecce stella, quam viderant in oriente, antecedebat eos, vsque dum veniens staret supra vbi erat puer.*

3. Rex: *Videntes autem stellam.*

Cantores: *Gauisi sunt gaudio magno valde.*

1. Rex: *Et intrantes domum inuenerunt puerum cum Maria matre eius.*

2. Rex: *Et procidentes adorauerunt eum.*

3. Rex: *Et apertis thesauris suis.*

Cantores: *Obtulerunt ei munera.*

1. Rex: *Aurum.*

2. Rex: *Thus.*

3. Rex: *Et myrrham.*

1. Rex: *Et responso accepto in somnis.*

2. Rex: *Ne redirent ad Herodem.*

3. Rex: *Per aliam viam reuersi sunt in regionem suam.*

In eodem loco dicat 1. Rex, ostendens stellam alijs: *Ecce stella!*

2. Rex: *Ecce stella!*

3. Rex: *Ecce stella!*

Omnes simul: *In oriente præuisa, iterum præcedet nos lucida.*

Postea descendunt. Cum descenderint vsque in introitum chori, dicant pariter:

*Cuius stellam vidimus,*
*verum lumen credimus;*
*quem Deum cognouimus*
*adorare venimus.*

Cum venerint iuxta candelabrum, dicant simul:

*Dona damus talia,*
*per quæ Regis gloria*
*patet, et potentia,*
*qui gubernat omnia.*

Cum autem venerint ante altare maius, offerant super altare, scilicet:

1. Rex cum auro et dicat: *Ius in auro regium.*

2. Rex offerat similiter dicens: *Thure sacerdotium.*

3. Rex pariter offerens dicat: *Myrrha munus tertium*
*mortis est indicium.*

[1]Postea pergunt ante maius altare; ibique flexis genibus offerunt sua munera cum coronis, inde recedentes vnus per ianuam S. Agapiti, alius per magnam ianuam, et tertius per portam Beatæ Mariæ in vestiarium reuertuntur.

[1] From this point the text of Crombach is found 'in libro S. Stephani'.

According to the information available from Besançon it appears that before the singing of the gospel three of the clergy costume themselves with crowns and differently coloured regal garments.[1] They are accompanied by attendants carrying gifts in gold vases, and by other clerics bearing silver staffs, lighted candles, and thuribles. The attendants are dressed as Persians, and one of them is blacked to represent a Moor.[2] Singing four stanzas of the chant *Novæ genituræ* the kings advance to the altar of the Blessed Virgin, and in their procession thence to the pulpit—presumably in the nave—they sing *Nos respectu gratiæ*. After the gospel has been announced in the usual liturgical forms,[3] the kings take part in the reading in a special manner. After each of the kings in turn has read a short passage, the cantors read a few words in unison. The words *aurum*, *thus*, *et myrrham*, are distributed among the three kings. At the conclusion of the gospel they exclaim *Ecce stella*, pointing to the star, and advance from the pulpit through the door of the choir up to the main altar, where each in turn deposits his gift and crown. In their procession they sing two stanzas of *Nos respectu gratiæ*, and in making his offering each sings an appropriate part of a third stanza from the same composition.

This dramatic office, then, may be said to consist of two parts: (1) a procession of the three kings to the pulpit and a reading of the liturgical gospel, and (2) a procession of the kings to the main altar, and their offering there. The first procession may have been regarded as a representation of the journey to Jerusalem. The second procession, under the guidance of the star, clearly represents the journey to Bethlehem, completed by the offering of gifts. We may assume that the second procession is not meant to supplant the usual liturgical oblation, and that after the withdrawal of the kings the chorus proceeds with the creed and offertory in the normal manner.[4]

The spoken text of these ceremonials is supplied almost completely by two independent choral compositions and by the liturgical gospel. The passage beginning *Ecce stella in oriente* may be considered an adaptation of the Biblical sentence *Et ecce stella, quam viderant in oriente, antecedebat eos*.[5] As in the ceremony

[1] In my description I draw, in part, upon texts printed below, pp. 433 sqq.

[2] See the French text below, p. 434.

[3] See above, i, 27–8.

[4] In regard to the order of the Mass at this point see above, i, 28–30.

[5] Matt. ii, 9. See Anz, p. 46. From this Biblical passage was formed a liturgical responsory beginning *Stella quam viderant Magi in oriente antecedebat eos*. See Hartker, p. 73.

from Limoges, the gifts are interpreted symbolically, in the present case through the use of the stanza,

> Ius in auro regium,
> thure sacerdotium,
> myrrha munus tertium
> mortis est indicium.

The word *sacerdotium* attached to the second gift here, in place of the *cœlestem* of the Limoges text, may show the influence of the responsory beginning *Tria sunt munera pretiosa quæ obtulerunt Magi Domino in die ista; et habent in se divina mysteria: in auro ut ostendatur regis potentia, in thure sacerdotem magnum considera, et in myrrha Dominicam sepulturam.*[1]

The striking device of partitioning the liturgical gospel among the three kings and the cantors has a parallel in the Mass of the Annunciation as celebrated at Cividale, Padua, and elsewhere;[2] and it may have been due to the same tendency which resulted, during the late Middle Ages, in the distribution of the text of the *Passiones* of Holy Week among three singers.[3] In the case before us the result is not completely satisfying, since both the cantors and the kings are forced to utter passages quite alien to their roles. The cantors, for example, usurp from the kings the words *Et venimus adorare eum*, and the third king recites a speech of Herod beginning *Ite et interrogate*.

The dramatic ceremony as a whole is a true play in that the kings are genuinely impersonated, and the stage-setting is adequate. A *stella*—presumably drawn on a string—guides the kings to the manger at Bethlehem, which is represented, or at least symbolized, by the main altar itself.[4] The three separate doors through which the three kings respectively withdraw may, possibly, be understood to represent the three countries to which these personages belong.

## IV

The dramatic ceremonies of Limoges and Besançon are the only available ones which occupy a position in the interior of the Mass of Epiphany; and although similar performances must have occurred in other communities, especially at the offertory, it is unlikely that they exceeded very much in scope the two examples that we have just considered. It is obvious that an elaborated

[1] Hartker, p. 74; Migne, *P.L.*, lxxviii, 742. See Anz, p. 46.
[2] See below, chapter xxiv.
[3] See above, i, 100–1.
[4] See above, p. 8.

play in this liturgical position would probably have been, not an aid to devotion, but rather, an effectual distraction. For the more highly developed versions of the *Officium Stellæ*, then, we must look elsewhere than within the Mass. In so doing we may give our attention first to a play which might be said to represent an intermediate stage between the dramatic ceremonials within the confines of the Eucharistic service and those which are dissociated from the Mass altogether. Although the *Officium Stellæ* of Rouen, to which I am referring, is performed before the opening of the Mass of Epiphany, it has a kind of epilogue which recalls the dramatization of the offertory at Limoges. Of the several texts of the Rouen play, the most illuminating is the following, from a service-book of the fourteenth century:[1]

### Officium Regum Trium secundum Usum Rothomagensem

Die Epyphanie, Tercia cantata, tres de maiori sede more Regum induti—et debent esse scripti in tabula—ex tribus partibus ante altare conueniant cum suis famulis portantibus Regum oblaciones, induti tunicis et amictis—et debent esse de secunda sede scripti in tabula ad placitum scriptoris. Ex tribus Regibus medius ab oriente ueniens, Stellam cum baculo ostendens, dicat alte:

*Stella fulgore nimio ⟨rutilat⟩.*

Secundus Rex a dextra parte respondeat:

*Que regem regum ⟨natum demonstrat⟩.*

Tercius Rex a sinistra parte dicat:

*Quem venturum olim ⟨prophetiæ signauerant⟩.*

Tunc Magi ante altare sese osculentur, et simul cantent:

*Eamus ergo et inquiramus ⟨eum, offerentes ei munera: aurum, thus, et mirram⟩.*

Hoc finito, cantor incipiat responsorium:[2]

*Magi ueniunt ⟨ab oriente, Ierosolymam quærentes, et dicentes: Ubi est qui natus est, cujus stellam vidimus, et venimus adorare Dominum⟩.*

Et moueat processio. Versus:

*Cum natus ⟨esset Jesus in Bethlehem Judæ in diebus Herodis regis, ecce Magi ab oriente venerunt Ierosolymam dicentes. Ubi est⟩.*

Sequatur aliud responsorium, si necesse fuerit:

*Interrogabat Magos ⟨Herodes: Quod signum vidistis super natum Regem? Stellam magnam fulgentem, cujus splendor illuminat mundum; et nos cognovimus*

[1] Rouen, Bibl. de la Ville, MS 384 (*olim* Y. 110), Ordin. Rothomagense sæc. xiv, fol. $38^{v}$–$39^{v}$, previously edited by Gasté, pp. 49–52, and reprinted from him by Böhme, pp. 58–60; Adams, pp. 28–31. In my text I complete the speeches and liturgical forms from the *Officium Stellæ* in the Rouen gradual of the thirteenth century (Paris, Bibl. Nat., MS lat. 904). For the text of the latter, and for other information concerning the Rouen play, see Notes, p. 435.

[2] For this responsory, with a different verse, see Hartker, p. 74; Migne, *P.L.*, lxxviii, 742.

*et venimus adorare Dominum.* Versus: *Magi veniunt ab oriente inquirentes faciem Domini, et dicentes. Et nos*⟩.[1]

Processio in naui ecclesie consti|tuta stationem faciat. Dum autem processio nauem ecclesie intrare ceperit, corona ante crucem pendens in modum Stelle accendatur, et Magi, Stellam ostendentes, ad Ymaginem Sancte Marie super Altare Crucis prius positam cantantes pergant:

*Ecce stella in oriente ⟨prævisa iterum præcedit nos lucida. Hæc, inquam, stella natum demonstrat de quo Balaam cecinerat dicens.* Versus: *Oritur stella ex Jacob, et exsurget homo de Israel, et confringet omnes duces alienigenarum, et erit omnis terra possessio ejus*⟩.

Hoc finito, duo de maiori sede cum dalmaticis, ex utraque altaris parte stantes, suauiter respondeant:

*Qui sunt hij qui, stella ⟨duce, nos adeuntes inaudita ferunt⟩?*

Magi respondeant:

*Nos sumus, quos cernitis, ⟨reges Tharsis et Arabum et Saba dona ferentes Christo, Regi, nato Domino, quem, stella deducente, adorare venimus.⟩*

Tunc duo dalmaticati aperientes cortinam dicant:

*Ecce puer adest ⟨quem quæritis; iam properate adorare, quia ipse est redemptio mundi*⟩.

Tunc procidentes Reges ad terram simul salutent Puerum, ita dicentes:

*Salue, Princeps seculorum.*

Tunc vnus a suo famulo aurum accipiat et dicat:

*Suscipe, Rex, aurum,*

et offerat. Secundus ita dicat et offerat:

*Tolle thus, tu uere ⟨Deus⟩.*

Tercius ita dicat et offerat:

*Mirram, signum sepulture.*

Interim fiant oblaciones a clero et populo, et diuidatur oblacio predictis duobus canonicis. Tunc Magis orantibus et quasi sompno sopitis, quidam puer, alba indutus quasi Angelus, illis ante altare dicat:

*Impleta sunt omnia que prophetice, ⟨dicta sunt. Ite, viam remeantes aliam, ne delatores tanti regis puniendi eritis,⟩*

et cetera. Hoc finito, cantor incipiat ad introitum chori responsorium:

*Tria sunt munera ⟨pretiosa quæ obtulerunt Magi Domino in die ista, et habent in se divina mysteria: in auro ut ostendatur regis potentia; in thure sacerdotem magnum considera; et in myrrha dominicam sepulturam*⟩. Versus: *Salutis nostre auctorem ⟨Magi venerati sunt in cunabulis, et de thesauris suis mysticas ei munerum species obtulerunt. In auro*⟩.[2]

Ad Missam tres Reges chorum regant, qui *Kyrie fons bonitatis*, *Alleluia*, *Sanctus*, et *Agnus* festiue cantent. Officium *Ecce aduenit.* Psalmus *Deus iudicium tuum. Kyrieleyson* et *Gloria* festiue. Oratio *Deus qui hodierna die.* Si archiepiscopus cantauerit, memorie pro Domino Papa et pro Rege

[1] For this responsory see Hartker, p. 73; Migne, *P.L.*, lxxviii, 742.

[2] For this responsory, with a different verse, see Hartker, p. 74.

tantum. Sin autem, nulla memoria fiat. Epistola *Surge, illuminare.* Predicti famuli cantent responsum *Omnes de Sabba.* Versus *Surge, illuminare. Alleluia.* Versus *Vidimus stellam.* Sequencia *Epyphaniam Domino.* Euangelium *Cum natus esset Ihesus. Credo in unum Deum.* Offertorium *Reges Tharsis.* Deinde offerent Reges et omnes qui voluerint, et diuidatur oblacio inter famulos predictos. | Secreta *Ecclesie tue, quesumus, Domine.* Prefacio *Quia cum vnigenitus. Communicantes, et diem.* Communio *Vidimus stellam eius.* Postcommunio *Presta, quesumus, omnipotens Deus.* Prefacio et *Communicantes* dicantur per octauam eciam ad[1] Missam Beate Marie.[2]

At the opening of the Rouen play, immediately after Terce, three of the superior clergy, dressed in copes and crowns to represent kings,[3] come from separate directions and meet before the main altar. Each king is accompanied by his servant, from the lower stalls, dressed in tunic and amice, who carries his gift. The king who comes from the East, pointing with his staff to a star, sings *Stella fulgore nimio rutilat*, to which the other two appropriately respond. After exchanging kisses, the three sing in unison *Eamus ergo*, and, guided by the star, move westward in procession, while the chorus sings one or two responsories. As they pass from the choir into the nave, they observe a star-shaped cluster of lights over the altar of the Holy Cross. At this altar, upon which are figures of the mother and child behind a curtain, the kings halt. Two clerics in dalmatics, one at each end of the altar, interrogate the visitors, and having heard of their errand, draw aside the curtain and disclose the child. The kings prostrate themselves in adoration, and present their gifts. Then both clergy and congregation bring additional offerings to the same altar. The kings now kneel in prayer, and presently fall asleep. Then a choir-boy, dressed in an alb to represent an angel, rouses them and warns them to return home by another route, lest they give information which shall imperil the new-born child. Accordingly, while the chorus sings the responsory *Tria sunt munera*, the kings leave the altar of the Holy Cross, and proceeding down the left aisle re-enter the choir by the side door.[4]

At the Mass, which follows immediately, the kings direct the ceremonial, and sing the troped *Kyrie*, the *Alleluia*, the *Sanctus*, and the *Agnus Dei*. Their attendants sing the gradual. At the

[1] ad] Illegible in MS.

[2] Followed immediately by the rubric *Ad vi ymnus.*

[3] For details see the text from Paris MS 904 below, p. 436.

[4] See the texts from Paris MS 1213 and Rouen MS 382 below, p. 437.

regular offertory of the Mass, the kings, and all others who so desire, bring gifts to the altar, and divide them among the attendants.

The Rouen play, then, falls into three divisions: the gathering of the three kings before the main altar, their dialogue and oblation at the *Altare Crucis*, and their second oblation at the offertory of the Mass. Of these three parts the first two, constituting virtually the whole of the dramatic action proper, precede the Mass, and are united to it only through the fact that the Magi rule the choir during Mass, and take part in the oblation at the offertory. For the dramatic action the position before the Mass is by no means inappropriate. Since it appears that this place in the liturgy was traditionally occupied by an oblation from the congregation, a ceremony centring in an offering by the Magi could be accommodated here very fittingly. On important feast days, moreover, the Mass was commonly preceded by a liturgical procession, for which a representation of the journey of the Magi could be considered a fair substitute.

Since the greater part of the speeches in the play come before us here for the first time, we are called upon to consider their sources with some care. The first three utterances, spoken by the Magi in turn, seem to have been fashioned, with some originality, from a well-known antiphon of Lauds, the first half of which runs thus: *Stella ista sicut flamma coruscat, et regem regum Deum demonstrat.*[1] The passage spoken by the Magi in unison (*Eamus ergo*) is virtually identical with a speech in the ceremony of Limoges, the origin of which has already been considered;[2] and the piece which they sing as they approach the altar of the Holy Cross (*Ecce stella*) appears to have been drawn from a verse in the narrative of Matthew,[3] with some use of the following responsory:[4]

> Orietur stella ex Jacob, et consurget homo de Israel, et confringet omnes duces alienigenarum, et erit omnis terra possessio ejus. Versus: Et adorabunt eum omnes reges, omnes gentes servient ei. Et erit.

The most striking innovation is, of course, the scene at the altar of the Holy Cross, which appears to be modelled, in large measure, upon dramatic traditions of Christmas day. This influence appears, for example, in matters connected with the

[1] See Migne, *P.L.*, lxxviii, 743; Hartker, p. 77.

[2] See above, p. 35.

[3] Matt. ii, 9. See above, p. 30; and Anz, p. 46.

[4] Hartker, p. 34. The responsory arises from Numbers xxiv, 17. See Meyer, p. 43.

*præsepe*. In the dramatic ceremonies of Limoges and Besançon the altar seems to have represented the manger, if at all, only in a symbolic sense. At Rouen, on the other hand, the *mise en scène* is made realistic through the presence upon the altar of plastic figures representing Mary and Jesus; and this arrangement raises a query as to the age of the child at the time of the visit of the Magi, and as to the circumstances under which the adoration took place.[1] From the account in the Gospel of Matthew one would infer that the visitors arrived at Bethlehem a considerable time after the Nativity—two years according to some patristic writers[2]—and that the adoration occurred in a house or inn.[3] The majority of medieval commentators, however, held that the Magi had been summoned by the star some two years before the Nativity itself, and hence reached Bethlehem only some thirteen days after this event. It is generally agreed, likewise, that they found the child at the manger, and not in a house or inn.[4] There is less agreement on the question as to whether the child was, on this occasion, lying recumbent in the *præsepe*, or was sitting in Mary's lap; but since there is substantial ecclesiastical tradition in support of each of these situations, and since the dramatic text before us is non-committal, the matter need not be pursued here.

That the two interlocutors of the Magi at the *præsepe* are, in the play before us, the apocryphal midwives seems to be sufficiently established by their being designated *obstetrices* in other versions of the *Officium Stellæ*.[5] Their presence in the shepherd play of Christmas has, as we have seen, every justification; but this cannot be said of their use in the Magi play. Whether the visitors reached Bethlehem two years or thirteen days after the birth of Jesus, the presence of midwives would scarcely be expected. It seems clear, then, that the appearance of *obstetrices* in the *Officium Stellæ* of Rouen, unsupported by Scriptural or patristic tradition, arises from demands of stagecraft. Speakers being needed for a conversation with the Magi at the manger, the writer adopted for this role the midwives from the tradition of Christmas.[6]

In the text of the dialogue itself, for which the Bible offers nothing, we readily discern the influence of the Christmas trope

[1] These matters are ably discussed by Anz, pp. 15–21.

[2] See Matt. ii, 16, especially the words, *a bimatu et infra, secundum tempus quod exquisierat a Magis*; Anz, p. 16.

[3] See Matt. ii, 11, containing the words *Et intrantes domum*.

[4] See Anz, pp. 16–7.

[5] See below, pp. 61, 66, 71.

[6] See Anz, pp. 19–21.

*Quem quæritis in præsepe*, both in general design and in some verbal details.[1] The words *Quem quæritis* and *Adest hic parvulus* of the trope, for example, seem to be reflected in the second speech of the midwives, *Ecce puer adest quem quæritis*, as does also the sentence *Nunc euntes dicite*, in the passage beginning *Iam properate*.[2]

The representation of the offering by the Magi employs the usual symbolism of the three gifts. The words with which the angel wakes and dismisses the visitors are written without very close adherence to the Biblical passage that inspired them. The second sentence of the angel's speech arises obviously from the verse *Et responso accepto in somnis ne redirent ad Herodem, per aliam viam reversi sunt in regionem suam*.[3] Since Herod does not appear in the play, the Biblical reference to him is omitted; and to the sentence under consideration is prefixed a formula of a somewhat conventional nature, beginning *Impleta sunt omnia*.[4]

From certain evidences in the text before us one might infer that, short though it be, the Rouen play is not a completely simple composition, but, rather, a combination of dramatic ceremonies originally independent of each other. One such evidence is the presence of two separate *stellæ*, one hovering over an action which occurs in front of the main altar, in the choir, and the other suspended over the *Altare Crucis* in the nave, to accompany a separate action there.[5] Still more striking is the performing of two oblations by the kings: one in the presence of the *puer*, at the altar of the Cross, and the other at the main altar during the singing of the normal liturgical offertory. In seeking an explanation of these features one critic has found significance in the fact that the *Officium Stellæ* at Rouen did not at all periods occupy the same liturgical position.[6] All the manuscripts which contain the play place it immediately before the Mass; but Jean d'Avranches, writing concerning the uses of Rouen in the eleventh century, speaks of it as being performed immediately before the *Te Deum* at the end of Matins.[7] The placing of the

[1] See Anz, p. 41–2; Böhme, pp. 65–8. For texts of the Christmas trope see above, pp. 4 sqq.

[2] It may be that the passage beginning *Iam properate* is under the influence of *Ite, nuntiate* in the Easter introit trope *Quem quæritis in sepulchro*. Concerning the latter, and its relations to the Christmas *Quem quæritis*, see above, i, 201 sqq.; ii, 4 sqq.

[3] Matt. ii, 12.

[4] This formula resembles, in a general way, the sentence *En ecce completum* of the Easter introit trope, printed above, i, 209, 212, and the following antiphon: *Ecce completa sunt omnia quæ dicta sunt per angelum de Virgine Maria* (Hartker, p. 81). See Anz, p. 41.

[5] The use of the two separate stars is discussed by Anz, pp. 21–3; Böhme, pp. 61–2.

[6] See Anz, pp. 23–4, 32–4.

[7] See Migne, *P.L.*, cxlvii, 43.

play at this point in the liturgy may have been due to the example of Easter,[1] or possibly of Christmas; or the dramatic ceremony may have been felt to be a fitting sequel to the reading of the Genealogy of Christ, from Saint Luke, which occurred normally immediately before the *Te Deum*.[2] Whatever the reason for the location of the performance at one place or another in the liturgy, the fact that it changed its position has been thought to account for the somewhat exceptional features of the extant version from Rouen. Anz surmises that the Rouen play began merely as an *Oblatio Magorum* in connexion with the offertory of the Mass; that this simple dramatic ceremony was transferred to the end of Matins, and was there enlarged by the addition of the dialogue between the kings and the midwives; and that this longer play was later transferred to a position just before the Mass, where it became associated with, or supplanted, the usual liturgical procession.[3]

Anz's explanation does, no doubt, account for the facts, but there is no proof for it, nor any great need of it. We may, if we wish, draw the simpler inference that the Rouen performance, having begun as a mere *Oblatio Magorum* within the Mass, was transferred to a position before the Mass and there enlarged. Exactly how the *Officium Stellæ* referred to by Jean d'Avranches was constituted we do not know. It may have differed very greatly from the play now under discussion, after the manner of the version from Normandy to be considered below.[4] The use of two different *stellæ* in separate parts of the present play may have been dictated by convenience, or by a desire to use the full theatrical resources of the church.[5]

Whatever the process through which the Rouen version of the *Officium Stellæ* arose, in its extant form it is an orderly and successful play. The journey of the Magi to Jerusalem is represented by the entry of these personages and by their halt before the main altar; and their visit to Bethlehem is accomplished through the procession from choir to nave, and by the dialogue at the altar of the Cross, arranged as a *præsepe*. The completion of this action before the Mass would seem to render unnecessary the participation of the Magi in the oblation at the regular liturgical *offertorium* later; but this additional activity of personages from the

[1] See above, i, 231 sqq.
[2] See Migne, *P.L.*, cxlvii, 43.
[3] See Anz, pp. 32–4.
[4] See pp. 68 sqq.
[5] For patristic explanation of the peculiar sidereal phenomenon recorded in the Gospel see Kehrer, *Legende*, pp. 17–9.

play proper in no way mars the dramatic office, and it has the merit of further enlivening the occasion. Although the rubrics are none too generous in detail, we may safely infer that impersonation of Magi, servants, midwives, and angel is adequate. In a literary way the play shows a notable advance in freedom of expression. The writer makes considerable use of authorized liturgical pieces, and obviously imitates the dramatic dialogues of Christmas; but he exhibits flexibility in revising his sources and his model.

## V

Although the Rouen play shows a marked advance in the development of the role of the Magi, it leaves still unused the most conspicuous element in the Biblical narrative: the encounter between the visitors and King Herod.[1] This episode, to be sure, is referred to in the Rouen play in the processional responsory *Interrogabat Magos Herodes*; and the danger of a meeting with Herod is implied in the angel's warning to the Magi at the end of the scene at the *præsepe*: *Ite, viam remeantes aliam, ne delatores tanti regis puniendi eritis.* The king himself, however, does not appear in person. For an actual representation of him upon the stage we may turn to the following relatively simple form of the play from the cathedral of Nevers:[2]

Finitis lectionibus, lubeat Domnus Presul preparare tres clericos in trium transfiguratione Magorum, quos preparatos terque a presule uocatos ita: *Venite*; pergant ante altare hunc uersum dicentes:

*Stella fulgore nimio rutilat,*
*que regem regum natum monstrat,*
*quem uenturum olim prophetie signauerant.*

Quo finito, uerso eorum uultu ad populum pergent usque ad Regem. Dicant hunc uersum:

*Eamus ergo et inquiramus eum, offerentes ei munera: aurum, thus, et myrram.*

Quibus respondens Rex dicat:

*Regem quem queritis, natum esse quo signo didicistis? Si illum regnare creditis, dicite nobis.*

Adcontra ipsi:

*Illum natum esse didicimus in oriente stella monstr⟨an⟩te.*

[1] Matt. ii, 3–8.

[2] Paris, Bibl. Mazarine, MS 1708, Lib. resp. Nivernensis sæc. xi, fol. 81$^v$, previously edited by Young, *Some Texts*, pp. 296–7. The MS provides music. The dramatic text is immediately preceded, at the very bottom of fol. 81$^r$, by the ninth responsory of Epiphany, *Rex magnus natus est*. For related texts of the play see Notes, p. 439.

Quo audito, dicat iterum Rex:

*Ite et de puero diligenter inuestigate,*
*Et inuentum redeuntes michi renuntiate.*

Accepta licentia, pergant:

*Ecce stella in oriente preuisa iterum preueniet. Vidimus stellam eius in oriente, et agnouimus regem regum natum esse.*

Quibus respondeant Custodes ita:

*Qui sunt hi qui, stella duce, nos adeuntes*[1] *inaudita ferentes?*

Atcontra ipsi:

*Nos sumus, quos cernitis, reges Tarsis et Arabum et Saba dona ferentes Christo, Regi, nato Domino, quem,*[2] *stella deducente, uenimus adorare.*

Ostendentibus illis Imaginem dicant:

*Ecce puer adest quem queritis; iam properate, adorate, quia ipse est redemptio uestra.*

Quorum Magorum unus offerens aurum dicat:

*Salue, Rex seculorum, suscipe nunc*[3] *aurum.*

Et secundus offerens thus dicat:

*Tolle thus, tu uerus Deus.*

Necnon tercius ⟨offerens⟩ mirram dicat:

*Mirram, signum sepulture.*

His itaque gestis, dicat puer stans in excelso loco:

*Impleta sunt omnia que prophetice dicta sunt. Ite, uiam remeantes aliam, ne delatores tanti regis puniendi eritis.*

Omnibus peractis, dicat presul *Te Deum laudamus.*[4]

The play of Nevers is performed immediately after the ninth responsory of Matins. The bishop arranges that three clerics shall be costumed in the likeness of Magi, whom he summons by thrice pronouncing the word *Venite.* The Magi respond by appearing before the main altar, singing, apparently in unison, the passage beginning *Stella fulgore nimio.* Facing the congregation, and singing *Eamus ergo*, they advance, without introduction, directly to King Herod, who appears to be fully informed as to their errand, and abruptly inquires concerning the source of their information about the new-born king. When the Magi reply that they have learned of his birth through the appearance of a star in the East, Herod promptly bids them seek the child, and bring back their report. The visitors obediently proceed, singing *Ecce stella in oriente.* When they arrive at the *præsepe*, they take part in an action similar to that seen in the play of Rouen, consisting of a dialogue with the midwives, an oblation, and a

[1] adeuntes] adientes (MS).
[2] quem] qui (MS).
[3] nunc] First *n* erased (MS).
[4] Followed by *In Matutinis Laudibus.*

dismissal by an angel. The bishop brings the performance to a conclusion by intoning the opening words of the *Te Deum*.

In large part, then, the play before us resembles that of Rouen,[1] the one substantial addition being the dialogue between the Magi and Herod. For this innovation there are obvious textual sources in the Vulgate itself,[2] in the responsory *Interrogabat Magos Herodes*,[3] used in the Rouen play, and in the antiphon *Vidimus stellam ejus in oriente*.[4] The sentence *Si illum regnare creditis, dicite nobis* may, apparently, be conceded to the originality of the dramatic writer.[5] As a general model for the new dialogue he may have used either the trope *Quem quæritis in præsepe* of the Christmas introit,[6] or, possibly, the dialogue between the Magi and the midwives (*Qui sunt hi*), if this latter was already in existence.[7]

The resulting scene, in any case, brings Herod before us in the briefest and simplest form possible. Unprovided with attendants, he deals with the Magi with the utmost directness, and after delivering his two speeches, disappears from view. The abruptness of his opening question to the Magi in the play before us is somewhat mitigated in another version of the Nevers play, in which, after the processional *Eamus ergo*, is inserted the sentence *Vidimus stellam ejus in oriente, et agnovimus regem regum esse natum*.[8] This provides at least a more acceptable transition to Herod's first words. To the latter part of his first speech, however, the play offers no reply; and that this omission was regarded as a defect appears from the fact that in the more highly developed versions of the *Officium Stellæ* some effort was made, as we shall see, to supply a suitable answer.[9]

As to *mise en scène* our text is decidedly uninforming. Since the Magi are appropriately costumed, we may infer the same for Herod, the midwives (*custodes*), and the angel. The three divisions

[1] The processional *Ecce stella in oriente* differs somewhat from the parallel passage in the Rouen play, possibly through the use of the Epiphany antiphon *Vidimus stellam ejus in oriente, et venimus cum muneribus adorare Dominum* (Migne, *P.L.*, lxxviii, 743), or of Matt. ii, 2.

[2] Matt. ii, 2, 7–8.

[3] For the aprocryphal sources of this responsory, with which we are not directly concerned, see Anz, p. 53.

[4] See note 1 above.

[5] Anz (p. 56) refers to the use of *dicite* and *dicite nobis* in various liturgical and extra-liturgical forms, such as the Christmas introit trope *Quem quæritis in præsepe, pastores, dicite*.

[6] See above, pp. 4 sqq.

[7] There appears to be no support for Madame Chasles' opinion (pp. 258–9) that the dialogue between the Magi and Herod arose from an independent trope.

[8] See the text from Paris MS lat. 9449 below, p. 439.

[9] See below, for example, pp. 54, 65. See also Anz, pp. 54, 57, 149.

of the action occurred, no doubt, in separate parts of the church: the meeting of the Magi, in front of the main altar; the dialogue with Herod, at a special *sedes*, perhaps near the choir-screen; and the scene at the manger, probably in the nave or transept. We may safely assume the use of some sort of *præsepe*, and the heading *Versus ad Stellam faciendam*, over one of the Nevers texts,[1] points to the presence of a star, drawn, presumably, on a string as a guide to the Magi in their journey. In locating the performance at the end of Matins the clerics of Nevers may be following either the tradition of the Easter plays, or simple convenience.[2]

## VI

In the play from Nevers Herod enters upon the medieval stage in a distinctly sedate and inoffensive manner. His appearance here may, or may not, be the earliest in the history of the drama; it is, in any case, the quietest. Both the narrative of St Matthew and ecclesiastical tradition assign to him a much more turbulent and a much less solitary role. In the Gospel we are told that when the Magi arrived at Jerusalem, he was 'troubled', and summoned the chief priests and scribes; and that after the escape of the visitors he was 'exceeding wroth'.[3] The impression conveyed by the Bible and by the patristic commentators is that of an irascible potentate surrounded by attendants and advisers.[4] We are prepared to observe, therefore, that in all versions of the *Officium Stellæ* in which Herod appears, except that from Nevers, he is provided with a theatrical *entourage* justified by Scripture and designed to amplify his role, enhance his pomp, or increase the comic aspect of his behaviour. Among the persons who attend him the most significant are the learned men, or *scribæ*. The part played by them, and by certain other servitors, in the more adequately developed forms of the play is illustrated in the following version of the eleventh century from Compiègne:[5]

Primvs:

*Stella fulgore nimio rutilat.*

[1] See below, p. 439.

[2] See above, pp. 48–9.

[3] For the narrative of the Vulgate see above, pp. 29–30.

[4] In regard to the patristic tradition see Anz, pp. 51–2.

[5] Paris, Bibl. Nat., MS lat. 16819, Lectionarium Compendiense sæc. xi, fol. 49r–49v, previously edited by Hartmann, *Dreikönigsspiel*, pp. 43–6. The dramatic text, with its neums, is entered, by a separate hand, immediately after a sermon on Epiphany, but with no indication of its position in the liturgy of the day. With the present text may be associated certain fragments printed, or referred to, in Notes, p. 443.

Secundvs veniens a meridie:

*Que regem regum natum monstrat.*

Tertivs ab avstrali parte:

*Quem uenturum olim prophetia signauerat.*

Postea dant oscvla inuicem; deinceps dicunt:

*Eamus ergo et inquiramus eum, offerentes ei munera: aurum, tus, et mirram; quia scriptum didicimus: Adorabunt eum omnes reges, omnes gentes seruient ei.*

Legati Regis ad Magos:

*Principis edictu, reges, prescire uenimus*
*Quo sit directus hic uester et unde profectus.*

Magi:[1]

*Regem quesitum duce stella significatum,*
*Munere prouiso properamus eum uenerando.*

Nuntius:[2]

*En magi ueniunt,*
*Et regem regum natum, stella duce, requirunt.*

Iussvs Regis:

*Ante uenire iube, ut possim singula scire*
*Qui sint, cur ueniant, quo nos rumore requirant.*

Iterum Legati ad Magos:

*Reges eximii, prestante decore uerendi,*
*Rex petit ad sese, placeant mandata, uenite.*

Venivnt ante Regem. Oscvlatvs est eos.

*Regem quem queritis, natum esse quo signo didicistis?*

Magi:

*Illum natum esse didicimus in oriente stella monstrante.*

Rex:

*Si illum regnare creditis, dicite michi.*

Magi:

*Hunc regnare fatentes, cum misticis muneribus de terra longinqua adorare uenimus, trinum Deum uenerantes tribus in muneribus.*

Primvs:

*Auro regem.*

Secvndus:

*Ture sacerdotem.*

Tertivs:

*Mirra mortalem.*

Rex:

*Huc, simiste mei, disertos pagina scribas prophetica ad me uocate.*

Nvncii ad Scribas:

*Vos, legis periti, a rege uocati cum prophetarum libris properando uenite.*

Rex:

*O uos scribe, interrogati dicite si quid de hoc puero scriptum uideretis in libro.*

[1] Magi] Inserted above the line (MS). [2] Nuntius] Inserted above the line (MS).

Scribe:

*Vidimus, Domine, in prophetarum lineis quod manifeste scriptum est: Bethleem,*[1] *non es minima in principibus Iuda, ex te enim exiet dux qui regat populum meum Israel; ipse enim saluum faciet populum suum a peccatis eorum.*

Rex:

*Ite et de puero diligenter inuestigate,*
*Et inuento, redeuntes michi renuntiate.*

Ter:

*Ecce stella,*
*Et ecce stella in oriente preuisa*
*Iterum precedit nos lucida,*
*Quam Balaam ex Iudaica*
*Orituram dixerat prosapia;*
*Que nostrorum oculos fulgoranti lumine perstrinxit pauidos lucida.*
*Ipsam simul congrediendo sectantes non relinquamus ultra,*
*Donec nos perducat ad cunabula.*

Mulieres:

*Qui sunt hi qui, stella duce, nos adeuntes inaudita ferunt?*

Magi:

*Nos sumus, quos cernitis, reges Tharsis et Arabum et Saba, dona ferentes Christo, Regi, nato Domino, quem, stella deducente, adorare uenimus.*

Mulieres:

*Ecce puer adest quem queritis; iam properantes adorate, quia ipse est redemptio mundi.*

Magi:

*Ave, Rex seculorum.*

Primus:

*Suscipe, Rex, aurum.*

Secundus:

*Tolle tus, tu uerus Deus.*

Tertius:

*Mirram, signum sepulture.*

Angelus:

*Impleta sunt omnia ⟨quæ prophetice dicta sunt. Ite, viam remeantes aliam, ne delatores tanti regis puniendi eritis⟩.*

Nuncius ad Regem:

*Delusus es, Domine; magi uiam redierunt aliam.*

Armiger:

*Decerne, domine, uindicari iram tuam, et stricto mucrone querere iube puerum; forte inter occisos | occidetur et puer.*

Rex:

*Indolis eximie, pueros fac ense perire.*

[1] Bethleem] Belleem (MS).

Angelus:

*Sinite paruulos uenire ad me, talium est enim regnum celorum.*[1]

In the Compiègne play the first conspicuous addition to what we have seen in other versions is the colloquy in hexameters between Herod's courtiers and the Magi, in which the latter declare the purpose of their coming. After this has been reported to Herod, he commands that the visitors be brought before him, and the courtiers carry out the summons, their last two speeches also taking the form of hexameters. The Magi appear before the king, are greeted with a kiss, and are questioned in sentences which we have already seen in the play from Nevers. In the present case, however, the inquiry *Si illum regnare creditis* receives an appropriate answer. Turning aside from the Magi for the moment, Herod sends a messenger to summon the scribes, and by the latter is assured that from Bethlehem shall arise the ruler of Israel. Herod now bids the Magi seek out the new-born child, and return to him with their report. They obey, and at Bethlehem carry out a dialogue with the midwives, and are warned by the angel, in a form with which we are already familiar. After the Magi have withdrawn from the stage occurs a scene at the court of Herod which we now encounter for the first time. A messenger reports that the Magi have escaped, a military attendant advises the slaughter of the children, and Herod assents. An angel, however, brings the performance to a peaceful conclusion by singing the antiphon *Sinite parvulos*.

When we inquire more closely into the sources of the innovations in this play we observe that the writer has not only followed courageously the suggestions found in the Gospel, but has also drawn upon other parts of the Vulgate, upon the liturgy and ecclesiastical poetry, and upon his own invention. The processional *Eamus ergo*, for example, has been enlarged beyond the forms of it examined previously, through the use of verse 11 of Psalm lxxi; the dialogue between Herod and the Magi has been extended through a redistribution of sentences seen in the Nevers play, and the invention of a new speech for the Magi (*Hunc regnare*); and at the close of the performance is sung an antiphon from Innocents' Day found in no other version of the play. Particularly noticeable also is the amplification of the

[1] Followed by the rubric *In die sancto Epyphanie lectio prima Isaie prophete*. For the antiphon *Sinite parvulos* see Hartker, p. 68; Migne, *P.L.*, lxxviii, 740.

processional *Ecce stella in oriente* beyond its form in the Rouen play, the alteration arising through the use of passages from the sequence *Quem non prævalent.*[1]

These verbal enlargements, however, are of relatively slight importance in comparison with the addition to the play of new roles, such as that of the messengers, or emissaries, of Herod. Although these personages are implied in the narrative of St Matthew, they are not explicitly referred to, and their invention must be attributed to one of the writers who developed the *Officium Stellæ*—possibly, in this instance, under the influence, direct or indirect, of the apocryphal *Protevangelium Jacobi*, in which such emissaries are at least mentioned.[2] Since the playwright is following his own fancy, he not unnaturally gives rein to his literary talent and composes original hexameters.[3]

A recession from this ambitious versifying is apparent in the scene between Herod and the scribes, which rests in large measure upon the Scriptural narrative. Even the messengers who summon the scribes, and whose words have no source in the Vulgate, abjure their earlier formality.[4] On the other hand, the part of the scene which draws most closely upon the Biblical account, does not do so slavishly. The speech of the scribes follows literally neither the relevant passage in the Vulgate nor the liturgical antiphon based upon it.[5]

The boldest of all the additions to the play is the brief scene between Herod and his military attendant. For this latter personage there is no Biblical or apocryphal antecedent; and although Herod's action here is indicated in the Gospel, his words are invented.[6] Hence we hear an appropriate formal prose speech from the *armiger*, and a hortatory hexameter from Herod.

As to the position of the play in the liturgy, and as to *mise en*

[1] For the passage in the Rouen play see above, p. 44; and concerning *Quem non prævalent* and related compositions see Notes, p. 446.

[2] See Anz, p. 63; Sondheimer, p. 39; Sturdevant, p. 9. Anz (pp. 63–8, 89–90) and Sondheimer (pp. 39–52) attempt to isolate as a 'Botenspiel' a particular stage in the development of the *Officium Stellæ* in which the messengers of Herod are prominent.

[3] The speech of *Nuntius* beginning *En Magi veniunt* may possibly be influenced by the responsory *Magi veniunt*, which we have already observed in the Rouen play above, p. 43.

[4] Herod addresses the messengers as *symmistæ*. The writers do not always discriminate rigidly among such words as *legatus*, *nuntius*, *symmista*, and *discipulus*. See Böhme, p. 78; Wilmart, p. 8.

[5] See Matt. ii, 5–6, and the antiphon *Tu, Bethlehem, terra Juda, non eris minima inter principes Juda, ex te enim exiet qui regat populum meum Israel* (Migne, *P.L.*, lxxviii, 732). A briefer form of this antiphon is found in Hartker, p. 37. See also Micah v, 2.

[6] See Anz, p. 69.

*scène*, the text is silent. No costume or stage-property is mentioned, not even the *stella*. We must, however, assume the usual intention of impersonation, and the usual *sedes* for Herod and the *præsepe*.

In arranging his dramatic events the writer has shown independence in departing from the Gospel sequence. According to St Matthew, Herod consults the chief priests and scribes before his actual interview with the Magi, whereas in the play before us he summons the scribes between the two parts of his talk with his visitors, and in so far as we can determine, in their very presence.[1] One critic finds in this arrangement a dramatic difficulty, in that the Magi appear to overhear a conversation between Herod and the scribes which was not intended for their ears.[2] It does not appear certain, however, that the *Herodes iratus* who appears at the end of the play would have felt embarrassment over the presence of three harmless Magi; and if he did wish them to be dramatically absent, they might have humoured him by withdrawing up stage while the scribes were being consulted. From the dramatic point of view the sequence of events in the play seems neither better nor worse than that in the Gospel.

Looked at broadly, the play from Compiègne shows a marked advance in dramatic vivacity, in literary form, and in characterization. The movement of messengers from station to station and the ceremonious entry of Magi and scribes contribute liveliness to the scene and add a characteristic formality to Herod's court. This formality is to some extent reflected in the use of verse. The desire for hexameters and rhyme appears not only in scenes which are freely invented, but also in speeches for which the Vulgate provides the full substance.[3] The play is no longer a compilation of liturgical and Biblical passages, but an independent literary composition. Through this freedom and inventiveness, moreover, is achieved a highly acceptable gain in characterization. Herod himself begins to disclose those traits of pomposity, impetuousness and violence which promise well both for dramatic conflict and for comedy.

[1] Anz (p. 63) conjectures that in this arrangement the writer of the play is influenced by the *Protevangelium Jacobi*.

[2] See Sondheimer, pp. 18, 65.

[3] See Herod's speech beginning *Ite et de puero*, from Matt. ii, 8.

## CHAPTER XIX

# THE COMING OF THE MAGI (*continued*)

IN the several plays reviewed in the preceding chapter we have had ample occasion to observe the adaptation to the uses of Epiphany of dramatic and legendary themes from the tradition of Christmas. This borrowing, or imitation, has appeared especially in the presence in the *Officium Stellæ* of the *præsepe* and of the dialogue there between the midwives and the Magi. This scene we found to be very obviously modelled upon the dialogue of the midwives and shepherds which constitutes the essential part of the *Officium Pastorum*. We are now to observe that the more highly developed forms of the Epiphany play have a contact with Christmas of a still more appealing kind, in that they bring upon the stage the *pastores* themselves. Since the shepherds had preceded the Magi in visiting Bethlehem, nothing could be more appropriate dramatically than that, in returning from their visit, the former should meet the strangers on the road from Jerusalem, and should speak of their experience at the *præsepe*. For this meeting there is no hint in the Gospels and no warrant in early medieval tradition; hence we can scarcely withhold from the clerical playwrights themselves the credit for a charming invention.[1]

## I

The simplest extant version of the *Officium Stellæ* in which the shepherds appear is the following, which seems to represent the Norman-French liturgical custom current in the kingdom of Sicily in the twelfth century:[2]

### VERSUS AD HERODEM FACIENDUM

⟨Primus dicat:⟩

*Stella fulgore nimio rutilat.*[3]

[1] Though he can cite no non-dramatic mention of this meeting earlier than the year 1514, Anz (pp. 90–1) infers that the tradition is much older, and insists that it is 'kein Originalgedanke des Bearbeiters unsres Spieltextes'. Meyer (p. 39) and Böhme (p. 99), however, appear to regard the scene as a fortunate dramatic invention.

[2] Madrid, Biblioteca Nacional, MS 289 (*olim* C. 153), Trop. ad usum ecclesiæ Siculorum sæc. xii, fol. $107^v$–$110^r$, previously edited by Young, *Some Texts*, pp. 325–9, and reprinted therefrom by Bartholomaeis, pp. 528–30, and Beeson, pp. 202–4. The MS provides music. The text before us is immediately preceded in the MS by the *Te Deum* at the end of Matins of Epiphany.

[3] rutilat] rudilat (MS).

Alivs dicat:

*Que regem regum natum monstrat.*

Ter⟨t⟩ivs:

*Quem uenturum olim prophecie signauerant.*

Primus: |

*Venite.*

Alivs:

*Venite.*

Tercivs:

*Venite, adoremus eum, quia ipse est Dominus Deus noster.*[1]

Tunc iungant se simvl et dicant:

*Eamus ergo et inquiramus eum, offerentes ei munera: aurum, thus, et mirram, quia scriptum didicimus: Adorabunt eum omnes reges, omnes gentes seruient ei.*

Nvncivs ad Herodem:

*Salue, Rex Iudeorum.*
*En Magi ueniunt,*
*Et regem regum natum, stella duce,*[2] *requirunt.*

Herodes ad Nuncivm:

*Ante uenire iube, quo possim singula scire*
*Qui sint, cur ueniant, quo nos rumore requirunt.*

Nvncivs ad Magos:

*Regia uos mandata uocant; non segniter ite.*

Magi ad Herodem:

*Israhelitarum rex fortis uiuat in euum.* |

Herodes ad Magos:

*Quem queritis, aduene?*

Magi:

*Regem Iudeorum natum querimus.*

Herodes:

*Regem quem queritis, natum esse quo signo didicistis?*

Magi:

*Illum natum esse didicimus in oriente stella monstrante.*

Herodes:

*Si illum regnare creditis, dicite nobis.*

Magi:

*Hunc regnare fatentes, cum misticis muneribus de terra longinqua adorare uenimus, trinum Deum uenerantes tribus in muneribus.*

Vnvs dicat:

*Auro regem.*

Alivs:

*Thure sacerdotem.*

[1] For this antiphon of Epiphany see Hartker, p. 74.

[2] natum, stella duce] stella duce natum (MS).

Tercivs:

*Mirra mortalem.*

Herodes ad Nvncios:

*Huc, simiste mei, dissertos pagina scribas prophetica ad me uocate.*

Nuncius ad Scribas:

*Vos, legis periti,* | *a rege uocati cum prophetarum libris properando uenite.*

Scribe ad Herodem:

*Salue, Rex Iudeorum.*

Herodes:

*O, uos scribe, interrogati dicite si quid de hoc puero scriptum uideritis in libris.*

Scribe ad Herodem:

*Vidimus, Domine, in prophetarum lineis nasci Christum in Bethleem, ciuitate Dauid, Ysaia sic uaticinante: Bethleem, non eris minima in principibus Iuda, ex te enim exiet dux qui regat populum meum Israhel; ipse enim saluum faciet populum suum a peccatis eorum.*

Herodes ad Magos:

*Ite et de puero diligenter inuestigate,*
*Et inuentum redeuntes michi renunciate,*
*Ut et ego ueniens adorem eum.*

Magi ad Pastores: |

*Pastores, dicite quidnam uidistis, et annunciate Christi natiuitatem.*

Pastores ad Magos:

*Infantem uidimus pannis inuolutum, et choros angelorum laudantes Saluatorem.*

Magi:

*Ecce stella in oriente preuisa*
*Iterum precedit nos lucida,*
*Quam Balaam ex Iudaica*
*Orituram dixerat prosapia;*
*Que nostrorum oculos*
*Fulguranti lumine perstri⟨n⟩xit pauidos.*[1]

Obstetrices:

*Qui sunt hi qui, stella duce, nos adeuntes inaudita ferunt?*

Magi:

*Nos sumus, quos cernitis, reges Tharsis et Arabum et Saba dona ferentes Christo, Regi, nato Domino, quem, stella deducente, adorare uenimus.*

Obstetrices:

*Ecce puer adest quem queritis; iam properate et adorate, quia ipse est redemp|tio nostra.*

Primvs dicat:

*Salue, Deus Deorum.*

[1] See the sequence *Quem non prævalent* below, p. 446.

Secundus:

*Salue, Princeps seculorum.*

Tercius:

*Salue, uita mortuorum.*

Primus:

*Suscipe, Rex, aurum.*

Secundus:

*Tolle thus, tu uere Deus.*

Tercius:

*Mirram, signum sepulture.*

Angelus:

*Impleta sunt omnia que prophetice dicta sunt. Ite, uia remeantes alia, ne delatores tanti regis puniendi sitis.*[1]

*Nuncium uobis fero de supernis:*
*Natus est Christus, dominator orbis*
*in Bethleem Iude, sic enim propheta*
*dixerat ante.*[2]
*Te Deum laudamus.*[3]

The dialogue between the Magi and the shepherds is introduced here in the appropriate place, immediately after the former have been dismissed by Herod and are, presumably, on their way to Bethlehem. The absence of a processional piece at this point in the action, however, gives to the new scene an effect of abruptness. The dialogue itself appears to be taken over bodily from the liturgy of Christmas, where we have already observed it both before and after the first Mass, and among the psalms of Lauds.[4]

The other novelties of the play are, obviously, less important. The sentence *Venite adoremus*, sung by the Magi after their entrance, is an antiphon from Matins of Epiphany. The action preceding their interview with Herod shows a notable increase in formality. First, the king is ceremoniously informed that the Magi have arrived. Then, at his command, they are formally summoned, in a hexameter verse which we now see for the first time (*Regia vos mandata*). Likewise new are the first three speeches of the interview itself, the first being a hexameter (*Israelitarum rex*) designed to express the humility of the Magi, and enhance the impressiveness of the royal presence. The *Quem quæritis* of

[1] Here follows a blank space in the MS, apparently for an unwritten rubric.

[2] Concerning the hymn *Nuncium vobis fero de supernis* see below, p. 433.

[3] Followed by a farced epistle for Epiphany beginning *Deus ante tempora genitus*.

[4] See above, pp. 21–2.

Herod may be an echo of the dramatic trope of Christmas or of Easter.

The formality of the court is further indicated by the words *Salve, Rex Judæorum*, sung by the scribes at their entrance. Their pronouncement to Herod (*Vidimus, Domine*) takes a somewhat longer form than in the play from Compiègne. This form we shall find prevailing in the plays to be considered below, except for the word *Ysaia*, which is elsewhere supplanted by the general term *propheta*. Since the scriptural passage cited by the Magi is not found in the Book of Isaiah, the mention of this prophet here must be regarded as an aberration.[1] During Herod's consultation with the scribes, as in the similar scene in the play from Compiègne, the Magi appear to remain beside, or near, the throne.

The scene at the *præsepe* is noteworthy only for the thrice-repeated *Salve* of the adoring Magi, and for the enlargement of the angel's speech of dismissal through the inclusion of a stanza of the hymn *Nuntium vobis fero*, already brought to our notice in the play from Limoges.[2]

As to the staging of the play the meagre rubrics provide us, once more, only a basis for conjecture. The words *Magi, Herodes, Obstetrices* and the like are a sufficient assurance of impersonation, although details are lacking. From the closing *Te Deum* we may infer that the performance occurred at Matins, and from the general arrangement of the text we may assume that *sedes* for Herod and the *præsepe* were constructed in appropriate parts of the church.

Although the presence of the shepherds lends a pleasant variety to the play, it does not alter the centre of dramatic interest. That centre, as we observe, becomes less and less the visit of the Magi to the manger at Bethlehem, and more and more the occurrences at the court of Herod. In the play before us the extension of the dialogue in which he is concerned, and the increased formality of his surroundings, are appropriately reflected in the heading of the text in the manuscript: *Versus ad Herodem faciendum*.

[1] The prophetic passage most closely resembling that cited in the Gospel (Matt. ii, 6) and in the play is found in Micah v, 2.

[2] See above, p. 35.

## II

Similar to the Sicilian play in general content, but somewhat more highly wrought in its details, is the following version of about the year 1200 from Strassburg:[1]

Magus unus *cantet:*
*Stella fulgore nimio rutilat.*

Alter:
*Que regem regum natum monstrat.*

Tercius:
*Quem uenturum olim profecia signauerat.*

Internuncius:
*Assunt nobis, Domine Rex, uiri ignoti ab oriente uenientes, nouiter natum quendam regem | queritantes.*[2]

Rex:
*Ad nos uocentur, ut eorum a nobis sermones audiantur.*

Internuncius ad Magos:
*Rex uos uocat, ut, quem queratis regem, et ipse agnoscat.*

Nequaquam dicunt Magi.[3] Armiger ad Regem:
*Uiue, Rex, in eternum.*

Rex:
*Quid rumoris habes?*

Armiger:
*En magi ueniunt,*
*Et regem regum natum, stella duce, requirunt.*

Rex:
*Ante uenire iube, quo possim singula scire*
*Qui sint, cur ueniant, quo nos rumore requirant.*

Armiger ad Magos:
*Regia uos mandata uocant; non segniter ite.*

Cum steterint ante Regem, dicat Rex:
*Que sit cau|sa uie, qui uos, uel unde uenitis?*
*Dicite nobis.*

Magi:
*Rex est causa uie; reges sumus ex Arabitis*
*Huc uenientes.*

Rex ad Sim⟨m⟩istas:
*Huc, simmiste mei, disertos pagine scribas prophetice ad me uocate.*

[1] London, Brit. Mus., Additional MS 23922, Lib. resp. Argentoratensis sæc. xii–xiii, fol. $8^{v}$–$11^{r}$, previously edited by W. de G. Birch, in *Transactions of the Royal Society of Literature*, 2d series, x (1874), 413–6; C. Lange, in *Z.f.d.A.*, xxxii (1888), 413–5; Wilmart, pp. 8–10. The MS provides music. See plate xv. Concerning the position of this play in the liturgy see Notes, p. 446.

[2] In this speech, and in the two succeeding ones, the effort toward metre and rhyme is clear, but still tentative.

[3] Nequaquam dicunt Magi] This passage has no musical notation, but it is written in the black script used for the spoken text throughout.

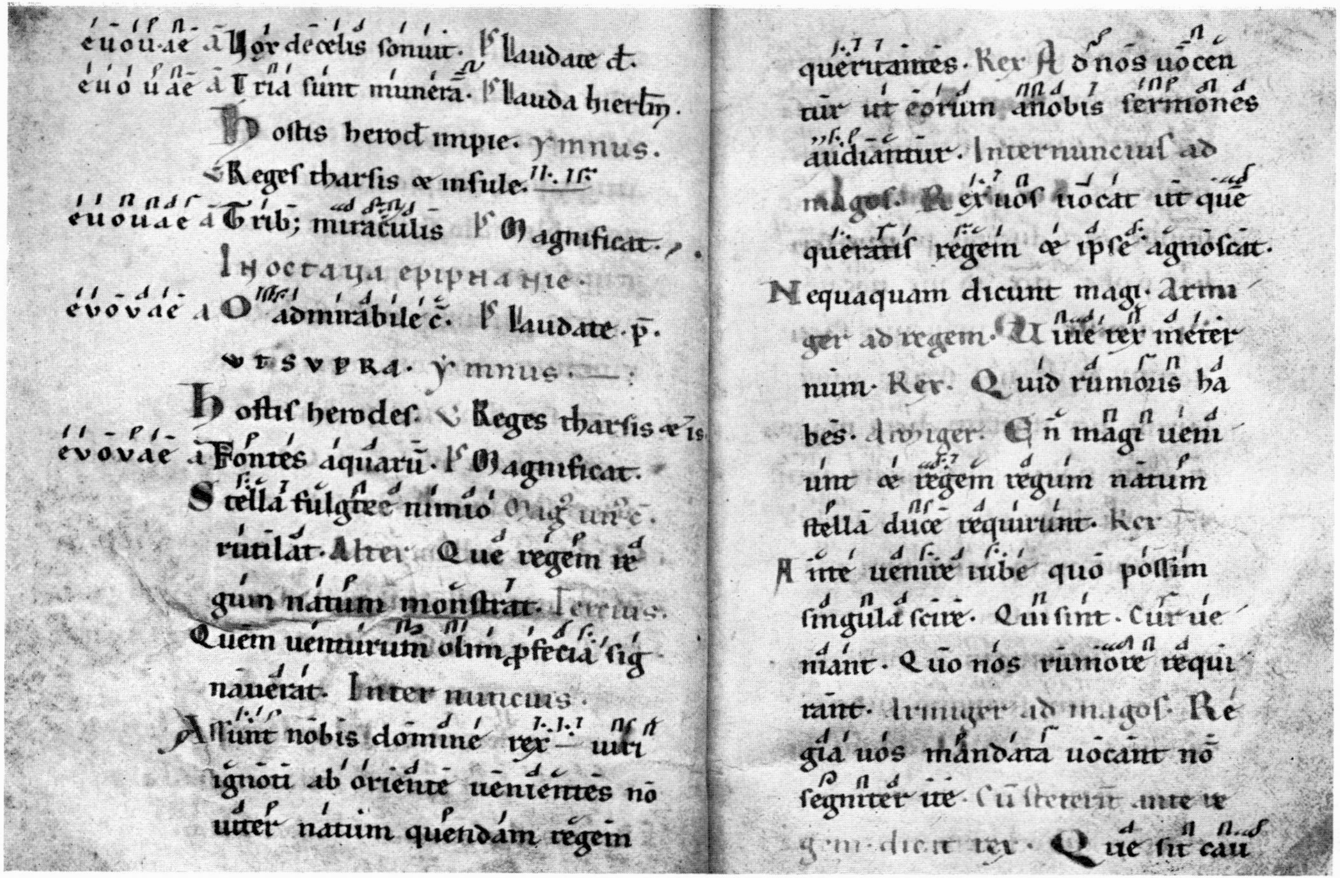

xv. Play of the Magi from Strassburg, in London, British Museum, MS Add. 23922, fol. $8^v$–$9^r$.

Symmiste:

*O principes sacerdotum, et o uos scribe populorum,*
*pertractate dicta magorum,*
*et dicite nobis tanti pueri ortum.*
*Si scripta illum probauerint, solus regnabit,*
*nostraque lex coram illo silebit.*

Rex ad Scribas:

*O uos scribe, interrogati dicite si quid de hoc puero scriptum uideretis in libris.*

Scribe:

*Uidimus, Domine, in prophetarum lineis nasci Christum in Bethleem, ciuitate Da|uid, propheta sic uaticinante.*

Chorus antiphonam:

*Bethleem, non es minima ⟨in principibus Juda, ex te enim exiet dux qui regat populum meum Israel; ipse enim salvum faciet populum suum a peccatis eorum⟩.*

Rex ad Magos:

*Regem quem queritis, natum esse quo signo didicistis?*

Magi:

*Illum natum esse didicimus in oriente stella monstrante.*

Rex:

*Si illum regnare creditis, dicite nobis.*[1]

Magi:

*Hunc regnare fatentes, cum mysticis muneribus de terra longinqua adorare uenimus, trinum Deum uenerantes tribus in muneribus.*

Primus:

*Auro regem.*

Secundus:

*Thure sacerdotem.*

Tertius:[2]

*Mirra mortalem.*

Rex ad Magos:

*Ite et de puero diligenter inuestigate,*
*Et inuento, redeuntes michi renunciate,*
*Vt et ego ueniens adorem | eum.*

Magi in eundo cantant:

*Eamus ergo et inquiramus eum, offerentes ei munera: aurum, thus, et mirram.*

Item Magi:

*Ecce stella in oriente preuisa*
*Iterum precedet nos lucida.*

Pastores:

*Pastores loquebantur ad inuicem.*

Magi ad Pastores:

*Pastores, dicite quidnam uidistis?*

[1] dicite nobis] Not supplied with music (MS).

[2] The rubrics *Primus, Secundus, Tertius* appear in the MS as mere numerals: i., ii., iii.

Responsio Pastorum:

*Infantem uidimus ⟨pannis involutum, et choros angelorum laudantes Salvatorem⟩.*

Obstetrices:

*Qui sunt hi, quos stella ducit, nos adeuntes, inaudita ferentes?*

Magi:

*Nos sumus, quos cernitis, reges Tharsis et Arabum et Saba dona offerentes Christo, Regi, nato Domino, quem, stella deducente, adorare uenimus.*

Obstetrices:

*Ecce puer | adest quem queritis; iam properate, adorate, quia ipse est redemptio mundi.*

Tunc cantet unus Magorum:

*Salue, Princeps seculorum. Suscipe, Rex, aurum.*

Secundus:

*Tolle thus, tu uere Deus.*

Tertius:[1]

*Myrram, signum sepulture.*

Angelus:

*Impleta sunt omnia que prophetice dicta sunt. Ite, uiam remeantes aliam.*

Armiger:

*Delusus es, Domine; magi uiam redierunt aliam.*

Rex:

*Incendium meum ruina extinguam.*[2]

The notable activities of the messengers and attendants of Herod in the Sicilian play are here strikingly amplified. Herod is first notified of the arrival of the Magi by *Internuntius*, whom he promptly commands to bring them forward. After the speech of the messenger summoning the visitors, occurs the rubric *Nequaquam dicunt Magi*, which may mean either that they ignore the summons, or that they silently advance part way toward Herod's throne. In any case, a second attendant, *Armiger*, informs Herod again of the advent and errand of the Magi, and again Herod commands that they be brought to him. To the pointed words *non segniter ite* of the second summons they respond, it appears, with alacrity. From the words *Nequaquam dicunt Magi* we may, if we wish, infer that the Magi at first resist the summons of the ordinary messenger, and comply with the king's desire only after they have been addressed in more vigorous phrase by an armed attendant.

The scene before the throne of Herod is striking, in the first

[1] Tertius] .iii. (MS).

[2] Followed immediately by the rubric *De Sancto Hilario*.

place, in that the first two speeches, containing each a hexameter, have appeared in none of the plays examined above. Herod's opening utterance is composed, apparently, under the influence of the Virgilian passage,

> State viri; quæ causa viæ? quive estis in armis?
> Quove tenetis iter?[1]

The skilful metrical imitation of Herod's phrases in the reply of the Magi may undertake to convey either their quiet confidence, or it may be a mere display of the writer's literary facility. The scene is noteworthy also in that Herod's interview with the scribes occurs not at the end of his questioning of the Magi, but in the midst of it.[2] It is not apparent that the one speech which he has heard from the Magi need move him to consult the interpreters of the prophets; nor have the previous utterances been such as to prompt the somewhat headlong appeal of the *symmistæ* to the chief priests and scribes. It must be observed, however, that this rather precipitate procedure seems fairly to conform to the narrative of St Matthew.[3] The concessions in the latter part of the speech of the *symmistæ* may have been motivated, in the stage-action, by frightened whisperings between Herod and his attendants.[4] One must fairly say, in any case, that the speech of the attendants rather overshadows the utterance of Herod which follows (*O vos scribæ*). One other noticeable feature of the present scene is the assigning of the prophecy *Bethlehem, non es minima* to the chorus. This arrangement is usual in the versions of the play to be considered below.

For their departure from Jerusalem the Magi are provided with two processional utterances: *Eamus ergo* and *Ecce stella*. The fluency of the play might have been improved by placing the second of these after the dialogue of the Magi and the shepherds. This dialogue is introduced by the words *Pastores loquebantur ad invicem*, spoken, if the text is to be trusted, by the shepherds. The dramatic inappropriateness of their speaking of themselves in the third person would be avoided by assigning this utterance

[1] *Æneid* ix, 376–7. There is no obvious use of *Æneid* i, 369–70,

> Sed vos qui tandem, quibus aut venistis ab oris,
> Quove tenetis iter?

Herod's speech may, or may not, be influenced by *Æneid* viii, 112–4,

> 'Juvenes, quæ causa subegit
> Ignotas temptare vias? quo tenditis?' inquit.
> 'Qui genus? unde domo? pacemne huc fertis, an arma?'

[2] See above, p. 58.

[3] See Matt. ii, 3–4, quoted above, p. 29.

[4] Anz (p. 62) regards the latter part of this speech as 'sinnlos'.

to the chorus—which we may surmise to have been the writer's intention.

Passing over the scene at the *præsepe*, which is in all respects conventional, we note, finally, the rudimentary nature of the scene at Herod's court with which the play ends. In replying to the abrupt disclosure of his military attendant the king bombastically replies with a passage from Sallust,[1] thus further enriching the tradition of *Herodes iratus*.

From the classical flavour of Herod's closing utterance, the echoes from Virgil in an earlier scene, and the general absence of liturgical formulæ, one might be tempted to infer that this play was designed for performance outside the scheme of public worship, or even outside the church. The text, however, is entered in an official service-book, and we are still at liberty to surmise that it was performed in the usual liturgical position—at the end of Matins of Epiphany.[2]

## III

Further notable advances in dramatic expression are to be seen in the following play, which, though in some way related to the traditions of Rouen, differs substantially from the *Officium Trium Regum* of that cathedral described in the preceding chapter:[3]

Officivm Stelle ita celebretvr. Vbi Stella apparebit, dicat Rex stans post altare maivs:

*Stella fulgore nimio rutilat.*

Alter, aliunde ueniens ex dextera parte, dicat:

*Que regem regum natum monstrat.*

Tercius a sinistra ueniens dicat:

*Quem uenturum olim prophetia signauerat.*

Regi a dextera uenienti dicat Rex medius:

*Pax tibi, frater.*

Cui respondeat idem cum alio a sinistra ueniente:

*Pax quoque tibi,*

[1] Sallust, *De Conjuratione Catilinæ*, cap. xxxi, ed. A. W. Ahlberg, Leipzig, 1919, p. 25: Tum ille furibundus, 'Quoniam quidem circumventus,' inquit, 'ab inimicis præceps agor, incendium meum ruina restinguam.'

[2] For the data in the MS see below, p. 446.

[3] Montpellier, Bibl. de la Faculté de Médecine, MS H. 304, Miscellanea ecclesiastica sæc. xii, fol. 41$^{v}$–42$^{v}$, described, with extracts, by Gasté, pp. 53–7, and edited by Young, *Rouen*, pp. 208–11. Concerning the place of the play among the several pieces in the MS see below, p. 428. The text now before us is immediately preceded by the *Officium Pastorum* printed above, pp. 12–3.

sese osculando. Quo finito, chorus cantet antiphonam:[1]

*Hec primum orientales fines collustrans illarum colonis partium magne rei prebuit signum; hec illos tres magos insignes prudentie capaces ad adorandum regem natum perduxit dicentes.*

Et interim Reges, alter alteri ostendendo Stellam, baculis innuentes erectis, dicat medius:

*Ecce stella!*

Alter in dextera dicat:

*Et ecce stella!*

Tercius in sinistra dicat:

*Et ecce uere[2] stella!*

Quo finito, dicant Reges:

*Eamus ergo et inquiramus eum, offerentes ei munera: aurum, thus, et myrram.*

Herodi in throno svo residenti dicat Internvntivs:

*Salue, Rex Iudeorum.*

Huic Rex econtra:

*Salue⟨t⟩ te gratia mea.*

Item Internuntius:

*Assunt nobis, Domine Rex, uiri ignoti ab oriente uenientes, nouiter natum quendam regem queritantes.*

Rex econtra:

*Ante uenire iube, quo possim singula scire*
*Qui sint, cur ueniant, quo nos rumore requirant.*

Item Internuntius:

*Quod mandas, citius, Rex inclite, perficietur.*

Quo peracto, Internuntius rediens ad Magos dicat:

*Que sit causa uie, qui uos, uel unde uenitis?*
*Dicite.*

Cui Magi: |

*Rex est causa uie; reges sumus ex Arabitis*
*Huc uenientes.*
*Querimus hic regem regnantibus imperitantem,*
*Quem natum mundo lactat Iudaica uirgo.*

Internuntius Herodi:

*Reges sunt, ut dicunt, ex Arabitis, regem regum regnantibus imperitantem queritantes.*

Rex Internuntio:

*Ad nos uocentur, ut eorum a nobis sermones audiantur.*

Internuntius Magis:

*Regia uos mandata uocant; non segniter ite.*

Internuntius precedens Reges Herodi nuntiat, baculo innuendo:

*En magi ueniunt,*

[1] This antiphon—if it be such—I have not found elsewhere.

[2] uere] uerae (?MS).

*Et regem regum natum stella duce requirunt.*
*Portant insonti*[1] *sua munera cuncta regenti.*

Quo finito, medius Rex Herodi dicat:

*Salue, rex populi fortis, dominator et orbis.*
*Quid uis edissere nobis?*

Quem osculetur Herodes, faciendo eum sedere in dextera parte sui. Alter in dextera Herodi dicat:

*Ase ai ase elo allo abadac crazai nubera satai loamedech amos ebraisim loasetiedet inbedo addoro otiso bedoranso i et o iomo bello o illa et cum marmoysen aharon et cum cizarene rauidete qui adonay moy.*

Hunc osculando iubeat Herodes sedere iuxta priorem. Tercius in sinistra Herodi dicat:

*O some tholica lama ha osome tholica lama ma chenapi ha thomena.*

De quo Herodes faciat ut de prioribus, quibus Herodes dicat:

*Regem quem queritis, natum esse quo signo didicistis?*

Magi econtra:

*Illum natum esse didicimus in oriente stella monstrante.*

Hic ostendant Magi Stellam baculis, quibus Rex:

*Si illum regnare creditis, dicite nobis.*

Item Magi:

*Illum regnare fatentes, cum misticis muneribus de terra longinqua adorare uenimus, trinum Deum uenerantes tribus cum muneribus.*

Primus Rex erigens se a sede genuflexo ante Herodem dicat:

*Auro regem.*

Secundus similiter dicat:

*Thure sacerdotem.*

Tercius similiter dicat:

*Myrra mortalem.*

Herodes Episcopis:

*Huc, simiste mei, disertos pagina scribas prophetica ad me uocate.*

Quo finito, Episcopi uenientes ad Scribas dicant:

*Vos, legis periti, a rege uocati cum prophetarum libris properando uenite.*

Scribe cum Episcopis uenientes dicant Herodi:

*Dissere, Rex, quid uis, assumus ecce tibi.*

Quibus Rex:

*O uos scribe, interrogati dicite si quid de hoc puero scriptum uideretis in libro.*

Huic Scribe:

*Vidimus, Domine, in prophetarum lineis nasci Christum in Bethleem, ciuitate Dauid, propheta sic uaticinante.*

Quo finito, chorus dicat:

*Betleem, non es minima,*

[1] insonti] Unquestionably the reading of the MS; but see *infanti* of the play from Bilsen below, p. 77.

vsque in finem. Quo audito, Herodes prospiciens in libro prophetie iratus proiciat. Deinde dicat Magis:

*Ite et de puero diligenter inuestigate,*
*Et inuento, redeuntes mihi renunciate,*
*Ut et ego | ueniens adorem eum.*

Qui redeuntes ab Herode, insinuando sibi inter se preuisam Stellam, dicant:

*Ecce stella in oriente preuisa*
*Iterum precedit nos lucida.*

Qui gradientes uersus Presepe interrogent Pastores obuiam factos:

*Pastores, dicite quidnam uidistis, et annunciate Christi natiuitatem.*

Quibus Pastores respondeant:

*Infantem uidimus pannis inuolutum, et choros angelorum laudantes Saluatorem.*

Quo audito, Magi inde transeuntes cantent:

*Quem non preualent propria magnitudine*
*Celi, terre atque maria anphisepere,*
*De uirgineo natus utero    ponitur in presepio,*
*Sermo cecinit quem uatidicus    stant simul bos et asinus.*
*Sed oritur stella lucida,    prebitura Domino obsequia.*
*Quem Balaam ex Iudaica    oriturum dixerat prosapia.*
*Hec nostrorum oculos    fulguranti lumine perstrinxit prouidos,*
*Atque ipsos preuia    ducens ad cunabula perduxit uilia.*[1]

His peruenientibus ad Presepe dicant Obstetrices:

*Qui sunt hii qui, stella duce, nos adeuntes inaudita ferunt?*

Magi econtra:

*Nos sumus, quos cernitis, reges Tharsis et Arabum et Saba dona ferentes Christo, Regi, nato Domino, quem, stella deducente, adorare uenimus.*

Item Obstetrices aperiendo Presepe dicant:

*Ecce puer adest quem queritis; iam properate, adorate, quia ipse est redemptio mundi.*

Quo uiso, primus Magus aurum offerendo in terram prostratus dicat:

*Salue, Rex seculorum, cuius ad imperium uniuersa pauescunt, suscipe nunc aurum, regis signum.*

Secundus thus offerendo subinfera⟨t⟩:

*Domine, Rex eterne glorie, suscipere dignare thus, sicut Deus uerus.*

Tercius mirram offerendo dicat:

*Puer iacens in presepe,*
*tamen imperans ubique,*
*suscipe mirram signum sepulture.*

His adorantibus puer quasi Angelus desuper stans cantet:

*Impleta sunt omnia que prophetice dicta sunt. Ite, uiam remeantes aliam, nec delatores tanti regis*[2] *puniendi eritis.*

[1] For the sequence *Quem non prævalent* see below, p. 446.
[2] regis] reges (MS).

Quo expleto, Magi aliunde redeuntes cantent:

*O magnum misterium,*[1]

usque in finem. Illis redeuntibus Internuntius dicat Herodi:

*Delusus es, Domine; magi uiam redierunt aliam.*

Qua peracta, Filius Herodis ad patrem:

*Salue, pater inclite,*
*salue, Rex egregie,*
*qui ubique imperans,*
*sceptra tenens regia.*

Cui Herodes:

*Fili amantissime,*
*digne laudis munere,*
*laudis pompam regie*
*tuo gerens nomine,*
*rex est natus fortior*
*nobis et potentior.*
*Uereor ne nos exturbet*
*nostri*[2] *regni solio.*

Item Filius patri:

*Contra natum puerum,*
*contra illum regulum,*
*iube, Pater, maximum*
*imminere premium.*

Hac peracta, Duces tenentes nudatos gladios dicant Herodi:

*Decerne, Domine, uindicari iram tuam; iube occidi pueros; forte inter occisos occidetur et puer.*

Herodes acceptum gladium librans hac et illac reddat a[3] quo sumpsit.[4]

Although this play may be said to resemble that from Strassburg in its general structure, it exhibits dramatic amplification in virtually every scene. The representation of the meeting of the Magi, and of their journey toward Jerusalem, for example, is enlarged by passages which we have not seen hitherto. After they have exchanged the kiss of peace at the main altar, with the words *Pax tibi, frater*, and while they are proceeding, presumably, through the choir, the chorus sings the passage *Hæc primum orientales*, explaining the occasion of the journey. This so-called antiphon appears not to be found in the medieval service-books.

[1] The Magi sing part, or all, of the following Christmas responsory (Hartker, p. 47; Migne, *P.L.*, lxxviii, 734): *O magnum mysterium, et admirabile sacramentum, ut animalia viderent Dominum natum jacentem in præsepio! Beata Virgo, cujus viscera meruerunt portare Christum Dominum.* Versus: *Domine, audivi auditum tuum et timui; consideravi opera tua, et expavi, in medio duorum animalium.*

[2] nostri] nostris (MS).

[3] a] Corrected from *hac* (MS).

[4] Here end fol. $42^v$ and the fragment. The text on fol. $43^r$ is irrelevant.

The role of the messenger who conducts the Magi to Herod's court shows an unusually high stage of development. This appears both in the exchange of ceremonious salutations at the entrance of *Internuntius*, and in the responsibilities which he assumes. Part of the questioning of the Magi undertaken by the king in the Strassburg play (*Quæ sit causa viæ?*) is here committed to the messenger; and the reply of the Magi (*Rex est causa*) is enlarged by two new hexameters. Another fresh hexameter (*Portant insonti*) appears at the end of the processional piece sung by the messenger as he finally brings the visitors before the throne. The most striking of all the innovations in the play appears in the first speeches of the Magi to Herod. Without awaiting any prompting from the *dominator orbis*, the first Magus elegantly inquires concerning his purpose in the interview. The next two speakers utter unintelligible gibberish, designed, apparently, to convey a realistic impression of their foreign nationality. At the end of each of these first three speeches Herod kisses the speaker and assigns to him a seat beside the throne. In this position the Magi appear to remain throughout the conversation, and throughout the consultation with the scribes. The unintelligible jargon used by two of the oriental strangers represents the boldest effort toward realistic impersonation which we have encountered thus far; and in view of the writer's ingenious originality, we may overlook the possible inconsistency arising from the use of acceptable Latin by these two foreigners in other parts of the play. The purpose of the gibberish here appears to be the serious differentiation of personalities, rather than comic diversion.[1]

After leaving the court of Herod, the Magi meet the shepherds, and question them in the usual way. As they proceed toward Bethlehem they sing a more substantial part of the sequence *Quem non prævalent* than is found in any of the plays reviewed above. The scene at the *præsepe* is exceptional in respect to the unique utterances used by the Magi in making their offerings, and to the processional responsory *O magnum mysterium*, sung by them, appropriately enough, as they flee from Bethlehem.[2]

The final scene, at the court of Herod, introduces a new personage into the play.[3] After the king has been informed of the escape of the Magi, his son, Archelaus, enters with verses of

[1] Anz (pp. 110–1, 117) and Jacobsen (p. 86) regard this jargon as comic. Concerning the comic uses of such language in later religious plays see Gasté, pp. 54–5.

[2] For the text of the responsory see above p. 72.

[3] See Anz, p. 86.

pompous greeting. To this salutation the father replies in kind, but with an added confession of apprehension concerning the power of the new-born king. The prince urges aggressive action against the *regulus*, and this policy is vehemently supported by the military officers, who enter with drawn swords. Herod promptly accepts their advice, and at our last glimpse of him he is precariously brandishing a weapon.

In surveying the play as a whole one is impressed by its dramatic merits. The general structure is good, and the transitions from scene to scene are, in general, amply provided for. Literary skill appears in the increasing proportion of the verse. Differentiation of personality is attempted through such means as the jargon of two of the Magi, and the special form of verse with which the young Archelaus enters into the closing scene. Comedy lurks in the violence and apprehensiveness of Herod.

Particularly illuminating in the text before us are the rubrics in regard to impersonation, stage-action, and stage-setting. We learn that the Magi enter the playing-space from different directions, as from different countries, that they exchange the kiss of peace, that they point to the guiding star with their staffs, that they take seats beside Herod, and that, in presenting his gift at the *præsepe*, the first of them prostrates himself upon the ground. Herod, we are told, greets each of the Magi with a kiss, inspects and angrily throws down the book of prophecies used by the scribes, and in the closing scene threateningly brandishes a sword. The *stella*—from which the play is here explicitly named *Officium Stellæ*—is mentioned at least three times. It appears to have been drawn on a string in such a way as to be always above the heads of the Magi in their journeying. Herod is specifically provided with a throne (*Herodi in throno suo residenti*), but as to where it was placed we are not informed. Likewise unknown is the position of the *præsepe*, although we are told that it had a curtain which could be drawn for disclosing the figure of the *puer* within it.

In the absence of evidence, we can only surmise that the play was performed at the end of Matins. This is the position to which the *Officium Stellæ* was assigned by Jean d'Avranches, archbishop of Rouen, in the eleventh century;[1] and since our twelfth-century text is in some way connected with the traditions of that ecclesiastical province, it probably follows that early arrangement.

[1] See Migne, *P.L.*, cxlvii, 43.

## IV

The tendency toward adding passages in verse, and toward enlivening the role of Herod, which we have observed in the Norman play, is still more strikingly present in a version of the twelfth century from the monastery of Bilsen, in Belgium:[1]

ORDO ⟨STELLE⟩[2]

Post *Benedicamus* puerorum splendide cetus
Ad regem pariter debent protendere gressu,
Preclara uoce necnon istud[3] resonare:
*Eia dicamus! Regias hic fert dies annua laudes;*
*Hoc lux ista dedit quod mens sperare nequiuit:*
*At⟨t⟩ulit et uere uotorum gaudia mille,*
*Et regnum regi, pacem quoque reddidit orbi,*
*Nobis diuicias, decus, odas, fæsta, choreas.*
*Eia dicamus!*
*Hunc regnare decet et regni sceptra tenere:*
*Regis nomen amat, nomen quia moribus ornat.*

Chorvs, ascendente Rege:

*Super solium David, ⟨et super regnum ejus sedebit in æternum, alleluia.⟩*[4]

Angelus, ab altis, Pastoribus ista predicit:

*Pastores, an⟨n⟩untio uobis ⟨gaudium magnum, quia natus est nobis hodie Salvator mundi, alleluia⟩.*[5]

Multitudo Angelorum:

*Gloria in excelsis*[6] *⟨Deo, et in terra pax hominibus bonæ voluntatis, alleluia, alleluia⟩.*[7]

Bethleem[8] Pastores tunc pergant[9] h*ec* resonantes:

[1] Brussels, Bibl. des Bollandistes, MS 299, Evangeliarium Belisiense sæc. xii, fol. 179v–180v, previously edited by C. Cahier and A. Martin, *Mélanges d'Archéologie, d'Histoire et de Littérature*, i, Paris, 1847–9, pp. 258–60; Clément, pp. 115–8; Cohen and Young, pp. 359–68; and by Gessler, pp. 19–30. The MS provides music. In the present text, illegible passages, and those lost through tearing, are indicated by two devices: (1) dots, representing passages for which no restorations are offered; and (2) pointed brackets, enclosing passages that may be restored with certainty or reasonable probability. When pointed brackets are used also to indicate the editorial completing of *incipits*, the fact is noted. For further observations on the MS see Notes, p. 446.

[2] After the word *Ordo* occurs an erasure, probably of a single word. *Stelle* satisfies the sense, and fits the space; and possibly the first letter may still be read.

[3] istud] istut (?MS).

[4] Antiphon for the second Sunday of Advent. See Hartker, p. 24; Migne, *P.L.*, lxxviii, 728. The bracketed passage is the editor's addition.

[5] See the following antiphon of Christmas (Hartker, p. 50; Migne, *P.L.*, lxxviii, 735): *Angelus ad pastores ait: Annuntio vobis gaudium magnum, quia natus est nobis hodie Salvator mundi, alleluia.* The bracketed passage is the editor's addition.

[6] excelsis] hecelsis (MS).

[7] Antiphon of Christmas. See Hartker, p. 51; Migne, *P.L.*, lxxviii, 735. The bracketed passage is the editor's addition.

[8] Bethleem] Behtleem (MS).

[9] pergant] The reading may be *pergunt* (MS).

*Transeamus Bethleem et ⟨videamus hoc verbum quod Dominus ostendit nobis, alleluia⟩.*[1]

Magus[2] primus, qui stat tunc in medio, cantet:

*Stella fulgore nimio rutilat.*

Secundus, qui stat ad dexteram:

*Que regem*[3] *regvm natvm monstrat.*

Tercivs, qui stat ad sinistram:

*Quem*[4] *uenturvm olim prophetia signauerat.*

Insimvl hi pergent ac oscula dulcia figent.

Tunc p*ergun*t pariter hoc[5] verbvm uociferantes:

*Hac ducente, pergamus ubi eius sit natiuitatis locvs.*

Conpellat taliter uox Internuncii Magos:

*Regia uos mandata uocant; non segniter ite.*

Magi:

*Qui rex sic per te uult nos reuocando uenire?*

Magos[6] tunc ense iugulari Preco minatur.

Internuncius:

*Rex est qui totum regnando possidet orbem.*

⟨Magi:⟩

*Et nos cernemus quis regvm sic sit herilis.*

Illos dimittit[7] rege . . .: |

*Viuas eternus Rex, semper uiuere dignvs!*

Rex econtra:

*Quid maioris opvs? mea sit tibi*[8] *gracia munus.*

*Quid rumoris affers?*

Non moram faciens respondet Nuncius[9] ista:

*Nuncia dura satis refero, presagia uatis.*

Rex:

*Que sunt presagia uatis?*

Internuncivs:

*Adsunt nobis, Domine, tres uiri ignoti ab oriente nouiter natum quendam regem queritantes.*

Occurrens alter, cui tunc hec sunt patefacta:

*Rex, Rex, Rex!*

*Rex, regem natvm constat per carmina uatvm.*

*Constat per lumen natvm de uirgine natvm.*

Tercivs accedat, hos qui monstrat uenientes:

*En magi veniunt,*[10]

[1] See the following antiphon of Christmas (Hartker, p. 54): *Pastores loquebantur ad invicem: Transeamus Bethleem et videamus hoc verbum quod Dominus ostendit nobis, alleluia.* The bracketed passage is the editor's addition.

[2] Magus] Ineffectually erased. Above the erasure a later hand has written *Rex*.

[3] regem] cegem (MS).

[4] Quem] Quēn (MS).

[5] hoc] hunc (MS).

[6] Magos] Erased, and above the erasure, *Reges*, by a later hand.

[7] dimittit] dimitit (MS).

[8] tibi] Written above the line (MS).

[9] nuncius] noncius (?MS).

[10] veniunt] venient (MS).

*Et regem regvm natvm, stella dvce, requirvnt;*
*Portant infanti sva munera, cuncta regenti.*
Talibus auditis, Rex illi talia profert:
*Ante venire iube, quo possim singvla scire*
*Qui sint, cur ueniant, quo nos rumore requirant.*
Armiger ad ⟨Magos⟩[1] sic inplet iussa potentis:
*Regia ⟨vos mandata vocant; non segniter ite⟩.*[2]
Ad Regem ueniunt; pariter sic ore salutant;
*Salue, Princeps Iudeorum.*
Rex:
*Que sit causa uie, qui vos, uel unde uenitis?*
*Dicite nobis.*
Magi:
*Rex est causa uie; reges sumus ex Arabitis,*
*Huc venientes,*[3] *regem regvm querentes.*
Rex:
*Regem quem queritis, natvm esse quo signo didicistis?*
Cantant Magi:
*Illum natvm esse didicimus*[4] *in oriente,*
Monstrant[5] stellam fvste leuato:
*Stella monstrante.*
Ira tumens gladios sternens ⟨Rex⟩ ista ⟨red⟩undat:
*Si illum regnare creditis, dicite nobis.*
De Christo rege[6] noli mendacia loqui:[7]
*Hunc regnare fatentes, cvm misticis muneribus de terra longinqua adorare venimus.*
Tunc monstrant[8] dona que portant Omnipotenti.
Primus:
*Auro regem.*
Secundus:
*Tvre sacerdotem.*
Tercius:
*Mirra mortalem.*
Rex, his auditis, iubet hos in carcere trvdi.
Aduocat D⟨isci⟩pulos[9] ac illis talia pandit:
*Hvc, simiste mei, disertos*[10] *pagina scribas prophetica ad me vocate.*
Discipvli ad Scribas:
*Vos, legis periti, a rege uocati cum prophetarvm lineis properando venite.*

[1] Magos] Completely erased, and above the erasure, *reges*, by a later hand.
[2] The bracketed passage is the editor's addition.
[3] venientes] veniente (MS).
[4] didicimus] The third and fourth letters are supplied by a marginal entry in the same hand.
[5] monstrant] monstrat (MS).
[6] rege] regi (MS).
[7] De Christo . . . loqui] Clearly written as a rubric, without music and explicable as an 'aside' of the Magi, who certainly speak what follows.
[8] monstrant] monstrat (MS).
[9] D⟨isci⟩pulos] Partly erased. Above the erasure a later hand has written *alumnos*.
[10] disertos] desertos (MS).

Scribe ad Regem:

*Salue.*

Talia cantando Scribas[1] baculo quoque cedri:

*O, uos scribe, interrogati dicite si quid de hoc pvero scriptvm*[2] *videretis in libris.*

Scribe:

*Vidimus, Domine, in proph⟨etarum⟩ lineis nasci Christum in Betleem, ciuitate Dauid, propheta sic vaticinando.*

⟨Chorus:⟩

*Bet⟨leem, non es minima in principibus Juda, ex te enim exiet dux qui regat populum meum Israel; ipse enim salvum faciet populum suum a peccatis eorum⟩.*[3]

Inspiciat libros ac illos reddat amare;

Precones mittit; Reges iubet ante venire;

⟨Primo⟩ Regi[4] cantet rex fuste minando:

*Tv michi responde*[5] *stans primus in or⟨dine, fare⟩:*
*Tv, ergo, vnde es?*

Magus:

*Tarsensis regio me rege nitet Zoroastro.*

⟨Rex:⟩

*Tv alter, vnde es?*

Magus:

*Me metvunt Arabes, mihi parent vsque fideles.*

⟨Rex:

*Tu tercius, unde es?*⟩[6]

Magus:

*Inpero Caldeis dominans rex omnibus illis.*

Advocat Armiger⟨um⟩ . . .:

*Vestris consiliis,*[7] *uestris uolo uiribus vti;*
*Consilium nobis date quod sit et it . . .*

⟨. . . . Armiger:⟩

*Audi que facias, Rex, audi pauca set apta.*
*Eois des do⟨na Magis⟩ | nec mitte morari,*
*Vt nouiter nato, quem*[8] *querunt regem, reperto,*
*Rex, per te redeant, ut et ipse scias quod adorent.*

Tunc tribus ⟨Rex⟩ dona remittit . . .:

*Ite et de puero diligenter inuestigate,*
*Et inuento, redeuntes mihi renuntiate.*

1 Scribas] Written above an erasure; reading uncertain.

2 scriptvm] scritvm (MS).

3 Through laceration of the leaf, only the first three letters of *Betleem* remain. The MS never contained more than an *incipit* of one or two words.

4 regi] Written above an illegible word crossed out.

5 responde] respondes (MS).

6 In this suggested restoration I follow, in part, the proposal of Gessler, prompted by the text from Freising. See below, p. 95.

7 consiliis] consilii (MS).

8 quem] Apparently *quom* (MS).

Magi descendentes de sede:

*Eamus ergo et inquiramus evm; offeramus ei mvnera: aurvm, thvs, et mirra⟨m⟩.*

Videntes Stellam cantant celesti uoce.[1]

⟨Primus:⟩

*Ecce stella!*

Secundus:

*Ecce stella!*

Tercius:

*Ecce stella!*

Insimul:

*In oriente previsa,*
*Qvam[2] Balaan ex Iudaica[3]*
*Orituram predixerat prosapia,*
*Iterum precedet nos lucida.*
*Non relinquamus vltra,*
*Donec nos perdvcat ad cunabula.*

M⟨agi⟩ ad Pastores:

*Pastores, dicite ⟨quidnam vidistis, et annuntiate Christi nativitatem⟩.*[4]

Pastores:

*Infantem ⟨vidimus pannis involutum, et choros angelorum laudantes Salvatorem⟩.*

⟨Magi:⟩[5]

*Ecce patere domus nobis pia claustra rogamus*
*Hoc quibus est votis regem donis uenerari*
*Qvem prefert regnis astrum quod prenitet astris.*

⟨Obstetrices:⟩

*Qui sunt hi, quos stella ducit, nos adeuntes, inaudita ferentes?*

Magi:

*Nos svmus, quos cernitis, reges Tharsis et Arabum[6] et Saba dona ferentes Christo, Regi, nato Domino, quem, stella deducente, adorare venimus.*

Obstet⟨rices⟩:

*Ecce pver adest quem[7] queritis; iam properate, adorate, quia ipse est redemptio mundi.*

Magi:

*Salue, Princeps secvlorum.*

⟨Primus:⟩

*Svscipe, Rex, aurvm.*

Secundus:

*Tolle thvs, tv uere Deus.*

[1] celesti uoce] *celesti* written *celetsti* (MS); *uoce* very doubtfully legible.

[2] Qvam] qvem (MS).

[3] Iudaica] iudaico (MS).

[4] This bracketed passage and the one in the next speech are the editor's additions.

[5] This illegible rubric probably contained several words.

[6] Arabum] arabunt (MS).

[7] quem] que (MS).

⟨Tercius:⟩

*Mirram, signvm sepvlture.*

Angelus:

*Inpleta sunt omnia que prophetice dicta sunt. Ite,*[1] *uiam remeantes aliam, ne delatores tanti regis*[2] *pvniendi eritis.*

⟨Chorus:⟩

*Deo gracias.*

Magi reuertentes . . .:

*O Regem celi ⟨cui talia famulantur obsequia! Stabulo ponitur qui continet mundum; jacet in præsepio, et in nubibus tonat⟩.*[3]

⟨Chorus:⟩

*Hostis Herodes.*[4]

Armiger . . .:

*Delusvs es,*[5] *Domine; magi viam redierunt aliam.*[6]

In view of the fact that this play contains innovations of a somewhat subtle character, and is preserved in a very defective text, it is desirable that the action be sketched in some detail.

The play opens with the singing by the chorus of a succession of hexameters introduced, and once interrupted, by the exclamation *Eia dicamus!* Then, as Herod ascends his throne, the chorus sings the antiphon *Super solium David.* The action proper begins with a scene in which the shepherds receive the announcement of the Nativity from an angel on high, listen to the *Gloria in excelsis* of the angelic throng, and set out toward Bethlehem singing the processional *Transeamus.* The Magi now appear, sing their well-known sentences, exchange the kiss of peace, and proceed upon their journey singing *Hac ducente, pergamus.* On their way they are promptly challenged by a messenger, who commands them to hasten to court. For inquiring who the king should be, they are at first threatened with violence, but are presently told that they are summoned by the king of the whole world. Not unnaturally they express their desire to make the acquaintance of so mighty a monarch. The messenger now appears ceremoniously before Herod, and to the king's request for news, refers to menacing prophecies of a certain sage, and

[1] ite] corrected from *ita* (?MS).

[2] regis] regi (MS).

[3] For this Christmas antiphon see Hartker, p. 54. The bracketed passage is the editor's addition. The piece sung by the Magi may have been the following responsory from Matins of Christmas (Hartker, p. 45; Migne, *P.L.*, lxxviii, 735: *O Regem cœli cui talia famulantur obsequia! Stabulo ponitur qui continet mundum; jacet in præsepio et in cœlis regnat.* Versus: *Domine, audivi auditum tuum, et timui; consideravi opera tua, et expavi, in medio duorum animalium.*

[4] For the hymn *Hostis Herodes impie* see Notes, p. 447.

[5] es] Corrected from *est* (MS).

[6] The remaining two or three lines on the page are blank.

then discloses the fact that three strangers from the East have arrived, seeking a new-born king. A second messenger now rushes into Herod's presence with the excited report that both the utterances of sages and the light of the skies indicate that a king has been born of a virgin. A third messenger now brings the Magi before Herod's presence, and they approach the throne with respectful greeting. When he has elicited from the Magi the information that they come, under the guidance of a star, to seek the King of kings, Herod, swelling with anger and throwing swords to the ground, asks for an explicit statement of their belief in the new monarch. Having made their confession, and having displayed to Herod the gifts that they bear for the child, the Magi are, by Herod's command, promptly haled to prison. The king now sends for the scribes, and learns from them the familiar prophecy, which prompts him to examine the prophetic books, and to return them bitterly. Summoning the Magi from prison, he threateningly interrogates each in turn as to the land from which he comes. Having received explicit answers, Herod, on the advice of his squire, speeds the Magi on their way to Bethlehem.

After encountering the shepherds, in a scene familiar to us, the Magi arrive at Bethlehem, and ask that they be admitted to the dwelling in which Jesus is sheltered. Upon this request follow the usual dialogue with the midwives, the oblation, and the dismissal by the angel. The visitors depart singing the antiphon *O Regem cœli*. Of the scene in the presence of Herod which follows we have only the first speech, and the hymn *Hostis Herodes*, which serves to introduce it.

When we examine these scenes in detail we observe a considerable amount of originality, and, perhaps, some caprice. The introductory hexameters are found also at the close of the Epiphany play from Freising, and, apparently, nowhere else.[1] In the text now before us these verses may be regarded as a trope of the *Benedicamus* found, during the Middle Ages, at, or near, the close of all the canonical *horæ* except Matins.[2] The words *Post Benedicamus* of the rubric seem to show that the performance occurred at the end of one of these liturgical offices. One critic infers that the *rex* who mounts the throne during the singing of

[1] See below, p. 97.

[2] See Gautier, *Tropes*, pp. 171–3; Cabrol and Leclercq, ii, 659–60. According to the Roman tradition the *Benedicamus* occurs at the end of Matins only very rarely. See Thalhofer, ii, 571, 587; and above, i, 67. In regard to the appropriateness of the verses *Eia dicamus* see the opinions expressed below, p. 98.

the antiphon *Super solium David* was almost certainly a *rex fatuorum*.[1] To the present writer he appears clearly to be merely the Herod of the play itself.

The shepherds assume here an unexpected prominence, appearing not only in the usual fictitious encounter with the Magi, but also in a preliminary scene in the fields, according to the Gospel of Luke.[2] The utterances of the shepherds and angels appear to be established liturgical pieces.

In the scene in which the Magi enter upon the stage the only novelty is the passage beginning *Hac ducente, pergamus*, which they sing as they proceed toward Jerusalem. This bit of original composition supersedes the processional *Eamus ergo*, which is usually found in this position, and which now superfluously occupies a place later in the play. The dialogue in which the visitors are commanded to appear before Herod is composed chiefly of new sentences designed to express the personalities of the speakers. By their two speeches the Magi exhibit a self-possession, or defiance, which is an agreeable enrichment of their role.[3]

The dialogue between Herod and his messengers shows a formality of utterance and a facility in the construction of hexameters which exceeds anything that we have seen in the parallel parts of other plays. A touch of unusual animation, and possibly of humour, appears in the excited *Rex*, *Rex*, *Rex!* of the second messenger. The reference implied in the *præsagia vatis*, concerning which the king so eagerly inquires, is not made entirely clear. Certainly the messenger who immediately replies to him does not elucidate it, and the second messenger increases one's curiosity by his mention of *carmina vatum*. The writer may have in mind merely the prophets, whose writings are to be consulted in a later scene; or he may, in his obviously classical manner, be referring to famous lines in the Fourth Eclogue of Virgil.[4]

The spoken text of the first scene between Herod and the Magi, and of the dialogue between him and the scribes, contains no notable innovations. The next two stages in the action, however, have no parallel in the plays reviewed above. Moved by the

[1] See Chambers, ii, 56; and above, i, 104 sqq.

[2] Luke, ii, 10–5, quoted above, p. 3.

[3] Anz (p. 104) regards their second speech as an expression of timidity.

[4] Ultima Cumæi venit iam carminis ætas;
Magnus ab integro sæclorum nascitur ordo.
Iam redit et Virgo, redeunt Saturnia regna;
Iam nova progenies cælo demittitur alto.
*Ecl.* iv, 4–7.

disclosures of the scribes, Herod summons the Magi from prison,[1] and threateningly interrogates them as to the regions from which they come. Although the hexameter speeches are obviously original, the scene may have been suggested by the Virgilian passage,

> 'Qui genus? unde domo?' . . .
> 'Troiugenas ac tela vides inimica Latinis.'[2]

The assigning of the name, Zoroaster, to the first Magus appears to be a personal fancy of the writer of this play.[3] It has been urged that in its position in the play this scene is inept, in that, after the pronouncement of the scribes, such a dialogue is unintelligible, or superfluous.[4] This opinion I do not share. Although the addition is, perhaps, somewhat too obviously designed to enlarge the role of Herod, it may be said to represent his natural desire to learn more about the visitors who bring news so alarming; and this desire is further indulged in his consultation with his military attendant which immediately follows. This latter dialogue, in original hexameters, motivates Herod's dismissal of the Magi.

The final innovation in the spoken text which forces itself upon our attention is the passage in hexameters sung by the Magi as they approach the *præsepe* (*Ecce patere domus*). Although these lines supply a needed transition between the brief scene with the shepherds and the dialogue with the midwives, they are unhappily verbose and obscure.[5]

The most striking literary feature of the play, however, is not the content or form of the dialogue, but the versifying of the rubrics. The writer who undertakes to present his stage-directions in hexameters would seem to have abandoned the purpose of moving an audience, and to have occupied himself in a mere literary exercise with the intent of impressing the reader. It may be, then, that the text before us was not designed for use upon the stage. This possibility is suggested also by the general absence from the rubrics of indications of costume or stage-furnishings. The gestures of Herod, on the other hand, are described with a care that points towards an actual performance.

Whether or not this version of the *Officium Stellæ* was intended

[1] Sondheimer (p. 18), misled by defective printed texts, errs in saying that the playwright makes no provision for the return of the Magi from imprisonment.

[2] *Æneid* viii, 114, 117. See above, p. 67.

[3] For the names traditionally assigned to the Magi see above, p. 31.

[4] See Anz, pp. 95–6.

[5] Anz (p. 105) unsparingly characterizes these lines as 'eine monströse Neuschöpfung'.

primarily for an audience, it is a substantial contribution to the history of comedy. Herod's impetuosity and gestures of anger, his lofty language, his prevailing bewilderment, and the precipitate actions of his attendants all aid in advancing this personage substantially nearer to the comic type which was to persist throughout the course of later medieval drama.

## V

Similar to the play from Bilsen in general structure, but still more highly developed in some of its scenes, is the version of the Epiphany play from the monastery of St-Benoît-sur-Loire, at Fleury:[1]

⟨I⟩NCIP*it*[2] ORDO AD REPRESENTANDUM HERODEM

Parato Herode et ceteris personis, tunc quidam Angelus cum multitudine in excelsis ap⟨p⟩areat. Quo uiso, Pastores perterriti; salutem[3] annunciet eis de ceteris adhuc tacencibus:

*Nolite timere uos, ecce*[4] *enim euuangelizo uobis gaudium magnum, quod erit omni populo, quia natus est nobis ⟨h⟩odie Saluator mundi in ciuitate Dauid, et hoc uobis signum: Inuenietis infantem pannis inuolutum et positum in presepio in medio duum animalium.*

Et subito omnis multitudo cum Angelo dicat:

*Gloria in excelsis Deo, et in terra pax hominibus bone uoluntatis, alleluia, alleluia!*

Tunc demum surgentes cantent intra se *Transeamus*, et cetera; et sic procedant usque ad Presepe, quod ad ianuas monasterii paratum erit:

*Transeamus usque Bethleem, et uideamus | hoc uerbum quod factum est, quod fecit Dominus et ostendit nobis.*

Tunc due Mulieres custodientes Presepe interrogent Pastores, dicentes:

*Quem queritis, pastores, dicite?*

Respondeant Pastores:

*Saluatorem Christum Dominum, infantem pannis inuolutum, secundum sermonem angelicum.*

Mulieres:

*Adest paruulus cum Maria matre eius, de quo dudum uaticinando Ysaias propheta dixerat: Ecce uirgo concipiet et pariet filium.*

[1] Orleans, Bibl. de la Ville, MS 201 (*olim* 178), Miscellanea Floriacensia sæc. xiii, pp. 205–14, previously edited by Monmerqué, in *Mélanges*, vii, 133–44; Wright, pp. 23–8; Du Méril, pp. 162–71; Coussemaker, pp. 143–65. The music is included only by Coussemaker. Wright's text is reprinted by Davidson, pp. 51–65, and Coussemaker's, by Adams, pp. 32–40. The text has been translated into modern French by Piolin, *Théâtre*, pp. 21–32. This translation appears to have been mistaken by Chambers (ii, 49) for an independent play 'from Mans,' and Anz (p. 10) repeats the error.

[2] Preceding this opening rubric is the rubricated word *Tunc*, very faintly preserved, and probably erased intentionally.

[3] salutem] salus (MS).

[4] ecce] Inserted above the line by a second hand (MS).

Tunc Pastores procidentes adorent Infantem dicentes:

*Salue, Rex seculorum.*

Postea surgentes inuitent populum circumstantem adorandum Infantem, dicentes tribus vicibus:

*Venite, uenite, uenite, adoremus Deum, quia ipse est Saluator noster.*

Interim Magi prodeuntes, quisquam de angulo suo quasi de regione sua, conueniant ante altare uel ad ortum Stelle, et dum appropinquant, primus dicat:

*Stella fulgore nimio rutilat.* |

Secundus:

*Quem uenturum olim propheta signauerat.*

Tunc stantes collaterales, dicat dexter ad medium: *Pax tibi, frater.*[1] Et ille respon*deat*: *Pax quoque tibi.* Et osculentur sese; sic medius ad sinistrum, sic sinister ad dextrum. Salutacio cuiusque:

*Pax tibi, frater.*

Responsio[2] cuiusque:

*Pax quoque tibi.*

Tunc ostendant sibi mutuo:[3]

*Ecce stella, ecce stella, ecce stella!*

Procedente autem Stella, sequentur et ipsi precedentem Stellam, dicentes:

*Eamus ergo et inquiramus eum, offerentes ei munera: aurum, thus, et mirram; quia scriptum didicimus: Adorabunt eum omnes reges, omnes gentes seruient et.*

Uenientes ad hostium chori interrogent astantes:

*Dicite nobis, O Ierosolimitani ciues, ubi est expectacio gencium; ubi est qui natus est rex Iudeorum, quem signis celestibus agnitum uenimus adorare?*

Quibus uisis, Herodes mit⟨t⟩at ad eos Armigerum dicentem:[4]

*Que rerum* | *nouitas, aut que causa subegit uos*
*Ignotas temptare uias? Quo tenditis ergo?*
*Quod genus? Vnde domo? Pacemne huc fertis an arma?*[5]

Responsio Magorum:

*Caldei sumus;*
*pacem ferimus;*
*regem regum querimus,*
*quem natum esse stella indicat,*
*que fulgore ceteris clarior rutilat.*

Armiger reuersus salutat Regem; flexo genu dicat:

*Viuat Rex in eternum.*

Herodes:

*Saluet te gratia mea.*

[1] For the two short speeches within this rubric the music is provided only when they are repeated, immediately below.

[2] Responsio] Respond̄ (MS).

[3] mutuo] Corrected from something like *mutia* (MS).

[4] dicentem] dicens (MS).

[5] For the Virgilian parallels see above, p. 67.

Armiger ad Regem:

*Adsunt nobis, Domine, tres uiri ignoti ab oriente uenientes, nouiter natum quendam regem queritantes.*

Tunc mittat Herodes Oratores uel Interpretes suos ad Magos dicens:[1]

*Leti inquisitores, qui sunt inquirite reges,*
*Affore quos nostris iam fama reuoluit in oris.*[2]

Interpretes ad Magos:

*Principis edictu, reges, | prescire uenimus*
*Quo sit profectus*[3] *hic*[4] *uester et unde perfectus.*

Magi:

*Regem quesitum duce stella significatum,*
*Munere prouiso properamus eum uenerando.*

Oratores reuersi ad ⟨H⟩erodem:

*Reges sunt Arabum; cum trino munere natum*
*Querunt infantem, quem monstrant sidera regem.*

Herodes mittens Armigerum pro Magis:

*Ante uenire iube, quo possim singula scire*
*Qui sunt, cur ueniant, quo nos rumore requirant.*

Armiger:

*Quod mandas, cicius, Rex inclite, perficietur.*

Armiger ad Magos:

*Regia uos mandata uocant; non segniter*[5] *ite.*

Armiger adducens Magos ad Herodem:

*En Magi ueniunt,*
*Et regem natum, stella duce, requirunt.*

Herodes ad Magos:

*Que sit causa uie; qui uos, uel unde uenitis?*
*Dicite.*

Magi:

*Rex est causa uie; reges sumus ex Arabitis*
*Huc ueni|entes.*
*Querimus en regem regnantibus imperitantem,*
*Quem natum mundo lactat Iudaica uirgo.*

Herodes ad Magos:

*Regem quem queritis, natum esse quo signo didicistis?*

Magi:

*Illum natum esse didicimus in oriente stella monstrante.*

Herodes:

*Si illum regnare creditis, dicite nobis.*

[1] dicens] dicentes (MS).
[2] oris] Corrected from something like *choris* (MS).
[3] profectus] perfectus (MS).
[4] hic] Inserted above the line (MS).
[5] segniter] signiter (MS).

Magi:

*Illum regnare fatentes, cum misticis muneribus de terra longinqua adorare uenimus, trinum Deum uenerantes tribus cum muneribus.*

Et ostendant munera. Primus dicat:

*Auro regem.*

Secundus:

*Thure Deum.*

Tercius:

*Mirra mortalem.*

Tunc Herodes imperet Symmistis[1] qui cum eo sedent in habitu iuuenili, ut adducant Scribas qui in diuersorio parati sunt barbati:

*Vos, mei simiste, legis peritos ascite ut discant in prophetis quid senciant ex his.*

Simiste ad Scribas, et adducant eos cum libris prophetarum:

*Vos, legis periti, ad regem uocati, cum prophetarum libris properando uenite.*

Postea Herodes interroget Scribas dicens:|

*O uos scribe, interrogati dicite si quid de hoc puero scriptum uideritis in libro.*

Tunc Scribe diu reuoluant librum, et tandem, inuenta quasi prophetia, dicant *Vidimus, Domine*, et osten⟨den⟩tes cum digito, Regi incredulo tradant librum:

*Vidimus, Domine, in prophetarum lineis nasci Christum in Bethleem[2] Iude, ciuitate Dauid, propheta sic uaticinante.*

Chorus:

*Bethleem, non es minima ⟨in principibus Juda, ex te enim exiet dux qui regat populum meum Israel; ipse enim salvum faciet populum suum a peccatis eorum⟩.*

Tunc Herodes, uisa prophetia, furore accessus, proiciat librum; at Filius eius, audito tumultu, procedat pacificaturus patrem, et stans salutet eum:

*Salue, pater inclite;*
*salue, Rex egregie,*
*qui ubique imperas,*
*⟨s⟩ceptra tenens regia.*

Herodes:

*Fili amantissime,*
*digne laudis munere,*
*laudis pompam regie*
*tuo gerens nomine,*
*rex est natus forcior*
*nobis et potencior.*
*Uereor ne solio*
*nos extrahet[3] regio.*

Tunc Filius despectiue loquens[4] de Christo offerat[4] se ad uindictam dicens:

[1] symmistis] sinistris (MS).
[2] Bethleem] belleem (MS).
[3] extrahet] extrabet (MS).
[4] The latter part of *loquens* and *offerat* is effaced; hence the readings given here are not certain.

*Contra illum regulum,*
*contra natum paruulum*
*iube, pater, filium*
*hoc inire prelium.*

Tunc demum dimittat Herodes Magos, ut inquirant de Puero, et coram eis spondeat Regi nato, dicens:|

*Ite, et de puero diligenter inuestigate,*
*Et inuento, redeuntes michi renunciate,*
*Ut et ego ueniens adorem eum.*

Magis egredientibus, precedat Stella eos, que nondum in conspectu Herodis ap⟨p⟩aruit. Quam ipsi sibi mutuo ostendentes, procedant. Qua uisa, Herodes et Filius minentur cum gladiis. ⟨Magi:⟩

*Ecce stella in oriente preuisa*
*Iterum precedit nos lucida.*

Interim Pastores redeuntes a Presepe ueniant gaudentes et cantantes in eundo:

*O Regem celi ⟨cui talia famulantur obsequia! Stabulo ponitur qui continet mundum; jacet in præsepio, et in nubibus tonat.⟩*[1]

Ad quos Magi:

*Quem uidistis?*

Pastores:

*Secundum quod dictum est nobis ab*[2] *angelo de puero isto, inuenimus infantem pannis inuolutum et positum in presepio in medio duum animalium.*

Postea Pastoribus abeuntibus, Magi procedant post Stellam usque ad Presepe cantantes:[3]

*Que⟨m⟩ non preualent propria magnitudine*
*Celum, terra atque maria lata capere,*
*De uirgineo natus utero    ponitur in presepio.*
*Sermo cecinit quem uatidicus,    sta⟨n⟩t simul bos et asinus.*|
*Sed oritur stella lucida,    prebitura*[4] *Domino obsequia.*
*Quem Balaam ex Iudaica    nasciturum dixerat prosapia.*
*Hec nostrorum oculos    fulguranti lumine prest⟨r⟩inxit lucida,*
*Et nos ipsos prouide    ducens ad cunabula resplendens fulgida.*

Tunc Obstetrices uidentes Magos alloquantur:

*Qui sunt hii qui, stella duce, nos adeuntes inaudita ferunt?*

Magi:

*Nos sumus, quos cernitis, reges Tharsis et Arabum et Saba dona ferentes Christo nato, Regi, Domino, quem, stella ducente, adorare uenimus.*

Obstetrices ostendentes Puerum:

*Ecce puer adest quem queritis; iam properate et adorate, quia ipse est redempcio mundi.*

[1] Concerning this antiphon and a related responsory see above, p. 80.

[2] ab] ad (MS).

[3] For a text of the sequence *Quem non prævalent* see below, p. 446.

[4] prebitura] prehitum (MS).

Magi:

*Salue, Rex seculorum.*
*Salue, Deus deorum.*
*Salue, salus | mortuorum.*

Tunc procidentes Magi adorent Puerum et offerent. Primus dicat:

*Suscipe, Rex, aurum, regis signum.*

Secundus:

*Suscipe mirram, signum sepulture.*

Tercius:

*Suscipe thus, tu*[1] *uere Deus.*

Istis factis, Magi incipiant dormire ibi ante Presepe, donec Angelus desuper ap⟨p⟩arens moneat in sompnis ut redeant in regionem suam per aliam[2] uiam. Angelus dicat:

*Impleta sunt omnia que prophetice scripta sunt. Ite, uiam remeantes aliam, nec delatores tanti regis puniendi eritis.*

Magi euigilantes:

*Deo gracias. Surgamus ergo uisione moniti angelica, et calle mutato lateant Herodem que uidimus de puero.*

Tunc Magi abeuntes cantent per aliam uiam, non uidente Herode:

*O admirabile commercium! Creator generis ⟨humani animatum corpus sumens, de virgine nasci dignatus est. Et procedens homo sine semine, largitus est nobis suam deitatem⟩.*[3]

Tunc uenientes in[4] choro dicentes:

*Gaudete, fratres,*
*Christus nobis natus est,*
*Deus homo factus est.*

Tunc cantor incipit *Te Deum*. Sic finit.[5]

The play from Fleury opens with a complete version of a scene which, in its independent forms, we have called *Officium Pastorum*.[6] The *præsepe*, as we are told explicitly, is placed at one of the doors of the church (*ad januas monasterii*), possibly the door at the west or south.[7] To this place, after the angelic announcement, the shepherds proceed, and here occurs the usual dialogue with the midwives. The conclusion of this scene is unique in that after adoring the Child themselves, the shepherds invite the congregation to do likewise. For this invitation they use a slightly modified form of an antiphon which has already appeared in one other version of the Epiphany play.[8]

[1] tu] Inserted above the line by a later hand (MS).

[2] per aliam] Written twice (MS).

[3] For this antiphon of the Christmas season see Hartker, p. 70; Migne, *P.L.*, lxxviii, 741.

[4] in] Almost completely hidden by the rubrication.

[5] Followed by the rubric beginning ⟨*A*⟩*d interfectionem puerorum*. See below, p. 110.

[6] See above, chapter xvii.

[7] See below, pp. 91, 117.

[8] See above, p. 60.

Meanwhile the Magi, coming from separate directions, meet before the main altar with their usual mutual salutations, and guided by the star, proceed toward the door between the choir and the nave. At this point they address to the bystanders a passage beginning *Dicite nobis, o Ierosolimitani cives*, which is an original and rhythmical rendering of two verses from the Gospel.[1] In this utterance we are explicitly assured, for the first time in the Epiphany plays, that the passage of Magi from the altar through the choir is meant to represent their journey from the East to Jerusalem. This passage, moreover, removes the abruptness of the messenger's first approach to the visitors.

The part of the play in which the emissaries of Herod treat with the Magi is highly amplified and, in some details, unique. The introductory rubric is significant in showing that, as in the Biblical narrative, the king himself takes the initiative in arranging that the Magi be questioned. The opening address to them by Herod's attendant achieves literary elevation through imitating the following Virgilian lines:[2]

> 'iuvenes, quæ causa subegit
> Ignotas temptare vias? quo tenditis?' inquit.
> 'Qui genus? unde domo? pacemne huc fertis, an arma?'

The rhymed lines in which the Magi reply to *Armiger* follow his questions closely, and resemble somewhat their own first speeches in the play. The remaining utterances in this part of the action, except for two pairs of hexameters (*Læti inquisitores* and *Reges sunt*), have appeared in plays examined above, particularly in the play from Compiègne.

Over the scenes in which Herod converses with the Magi and consults the scribes we need not pause here. The appearing of Archelaus, in a dialogue already seen in the Norman play,[3] has, however, a bearing upon the structure of the play which we may consider below.

The text of the dialogue between the Magi and the shepherds is somewhat carefully brought into conformity with the *Officium Pastorum* which constitutes the opening part of the play. In place of their usual reply to the Magi, the shepherds refer to the earlier announcement of the angel to themselves, and repeat some of his words.

The processional which the Magi sing on their way to the

[1] See Matt. ii, 1–2. In this passage in the play Anz (p. 97) detects conscious rhyming.

[2] *Æneid* viii, 112–4. See above, p. 67.

[3] See above, p. 72.

*præsepe*, and the scene there, are already sufficiently familiar. After they have been warned by the angel, however, they are given several utterances which we have not seen before. The speech beginning *Deo gracias* expresses their readiness to outwit Herod, and the antiphon *O admirabile commercium* serves appropriately as a recessional. The return of the Magi to the choir with the announcement *Gaudete, fratres* provides the performance with a fitting conclusion. The absence of a final scene in which Herod orders the slaughter of the Innocents may be due to the fact that at Fleury this subject is treated in a separate play.[1]

From the generous rubrics in this text we can infer at least the general arrangement of the stations at which the several scenes were acted. The *præsepe* was placed at one of the doors of the church,[2] and somewhere in the nave between this and the door of the choir was the throne of Herod. The *stella* appears to have been drawn on a string from its original position, over the main altar, to the door of the choir, thence to Herod's throne and, eventually, to the *præsepe*. The meeting of the Magi and the shepherds occurred, no doubt, in the nave, between the *præsepe* and the throne. In escaping from Herod, at the end of the play, the Magi probably passed behind the throne down one of the aisles.

Concerning impersonation we are given a number of informing details. Herod, for example, rages appropriately at the disclosures of the scribes, and joins Archelaus in threatening gestures toward the departing Magi. The scribes are dignified with beards, and they turn the pages of the prophetic writings with becoming diligence (*Scribæ diu revolvant librum*). The *symmistæ* who serve as Herod's messengers are costumed as young men (*in habitu juvenili*). The shepherds show their fright when they first see the angel, and as they return from Bethlehem, they outwardly express their rejoicing.

The play as a whole is successfully constructed. The *Officium Pastorum* provides an agreeable introduction, and prepares dramatically for the later meeting of the shepherds and the Magi. The presence of this introductory action here points forward to

[1] See below, p. 110.

[2] The rubric runs, *ad praesepe, quod ad ianuas monasterii paratum erit*. The word *monasterium* probably denotes here not 'the cloister' or 'the conventual buildings,' but 'the church'. I formerly believed that the door mentioned was that leading through the south wall of the nave into the cloister, and I still regard this identification as one among several possibilities. The archaeological and architectural facts are surveyed by Young, *Ordo Rachelis*, pp. 37–9. See below, p. 117.

the amalgamation of the several plays of the Christmas season in a large composition such as that from Benediktbeuern.[1] The play before us, however, is sufficiently centred in the personality of Herod, and is faithful to the words of the opening rubric: *Ordo ad representandum Herodem.* The entrance of this royal personage is provided for at the very outset, the greater part of the action occurs about his throne, and at the very end of the performance the dominating effect of his presence is revealed in the words *non vidente Herode.* The placing of the scene of Herod and his son before the dismissal of the Magi from the court is, perhaps, less successful than the use of the same passage at the end of the longer Norman play.[2] After the contemptuous and threatening words of Archelaus, and the obvious anger of Herod, one is scarcely prepared for the king's words to the Magi in regard to the possibility of his joining in worshipping the new-born child. It may be, on the other hand, that the writer means to represent Herod as consciously deceiving the Magi; and if this interpretation is correct, the psychological interest of the latter part of the play is palpably increased.[3]

In spite of its several novelties in characterization, in passages of verse, and in general construction, the Fleury play maintains the dignified tone which may be considered characteristic of a Church play.[4] In some measure, no doubt, this effect arises from the considerable proportion of prose in the composition, and from the presence of several pieces from the authorized liturgy. The closing *Te Deum* may be assumed to indicate that the performance occurred at the end of Matins of Epiphany.

## VI

The increasing violence of *Herodes iratus*, which we have observed as the dominant characteristic of the more extended versions of the *Officium Stellæ*, reaches its culmination in a play of the eleventh century from the cathedral of Freising:[5]

[1] See below, chapter xxii.

[2] See above, p. 72.

[3] See Sondheimer, pp. 158–9.

[4] See Anz, pp. 106–8.

[5] Munich, Staatsbibl., MS lat. 6264$^{a}$, Miscellanea Frisingensia, fol. 1$^{r}$. This page, with its musical notation, was written in the eleventh century. Fol. 1$^{v}$ begins with the rubric *In vigilia Sancti Andree*, introducing a *lectio* irrelevant to the matter now before us. The text of the *Officium Stellæ*, which is very defectively preserved, has been previously edited by Du Méril, pp. 156–62; Wilken, pp. 6–9; Weinhold, pp. 56–61; Anz, pp. 154–8. Davidson (pp. 50–64) prints a text based upon Du Méril and Weinhold. Meyer (p. 41) speaks slightingly of the texts of Du Méril and Weinhold; and it must be confessed that Anz, for example, omits at least one whole speech and several other words.

*Ascendat rex et sedeat in solio;*
*audiat senten⟨tia⟩m;*
*ex se ipso querat consilium.*
*Exeat edictum,*
*vt pereant continuo*
*qui detrahunt eius imperio.*[1]

Angelus inprimis:
*Pastores, annuntio vobis gaudivm magnum.*

P⟨ast⟩ores:
*Transeamus Bethlehem et videamvs hoc verbum.*

Ch⟨oru⟩s:
*Gloria in excelsis Deo, et in terra pax h⟨ominibus⟩ b⟨one⟩ v⟨oluntatis⟩.*[2]

Magi proced*ant*. Primus:
*Stella fulgore nimio rutilat.*

⟨Secundus:⟩
*Que regem regum natum monstrat.*

Te⟨rti⟩us:
*Quem uenturum olim prophetie signauerant.*

⟨Ma⟩gi ⟨simu⟩l:
*Eamus ergo et inquiramus eum, offerentes ei munera: avrum, thvs, et mirram.*

⟨Ad c⟩iues H⟨iero⟩solim⟨itanos⟩:
*Dicite nobis, o Hierosolimitani cives, vbi est expectatio gentium; nouiter natus rex Ivdeorum, quem signis celestibus agnitum venimus adorare?*

Inter⟨nuntius⟩ cvrrens:
*Salue, Rex Iudeorum!*

Rex:
*Quid rumoris affers?*

In⟨ternu⟩ntius:
*Assvnt nobis, Domine, tres viri ignoti ab oriente venientes, nouiter natum regem quendam queritantes.*

Rex . . .:
*Que sit causa uie iamiam citus, impero, quere.*

Intern⟨untius ad M⟩agos:
*Que rerum nouitas, aut que uos causa subegit*
*Ignotas temptare vias?*
*Qui genvs? Vnde domo? Pa⟨cemne⟩ huc fertis an arma?*

From so defective a MS, however, a flawless text is beyond the range of possibility. In the present text illegible passages are indicated by two devices: (1) dots, representing passages for which no restorations are offered; and (2) pointed brackets, enclosing passages that may be restored with certainty or reasonable probability. When pointed brackets are used also to indicate the editorial completing of *incipits*, the fact is noted. With the version before us may be associated the fragment from Einsiedeln MS 366 printed in Notes, p. 447.

[1] Since these opening lines have musical notation, they cannot be regarded as a rubric.

[2] The bracketed passages are the editor's additions.

Magi resp*ondent*:
*Chaldei sumvs;*
*pacem ferimvs;*
*regem regum querimvs,*
*quem natum esse stella indicat,*
*que fulgore ceteris clarior rvtilat.*

⟨Ar⟩m⟨i⟩ge⟨r⟩ ad Regem:
*Viue, Rex, in eternum.*

R⟨ex⟩ . . .:
*Quid ⟨rumo⟩ris habes, que fers, . . . nuntia, uiues.*

Internuntius:
*Rex, miranda fero: tres reges ecce . . .*

R⟨ex⟩ . . .:
*Ad nos uocemus, ut eorum sermones audiamus.*

⟨Inter⟩nunti⟨us⟩:
*Regia uos mandata vocant; ⟨non⟩ segniter ite!*

⟨Internuntius preced⟩ens:
*En magi uenivnt,*
*⟨Et⟩ regem regum natum stella duce requirunt.*

R⟨ex⟩ . . .:
*Ante venir⟨e iub⟩e, quo possim singula scire*
*Qui sint, cur veniant, quo nos ru⟨more⟩ requirant.*

Magi ad Regem:
*⟨Sa⟩l⟨ue, Princ⟩eps Iudeorum!*

Rex . . .:
*⟨Que sit causa uie, qui⟩ vos, aut unde venitis?*
*Dicite.*

Mag⟨i⟩:
*Rex ⟨est causa uie; reg⟩es sumus ex ⟨Arabitis⟩*
*Hvc ⟨uenientes⟩.*

Rex:
*Regem quem queritis, natum esse quo signo didicistis?*

Magi resp*ondent*:
*Illum natum esse didicimus in oriente stella monstrante.*

Rex econtra:
*Si illum regnare creditis, dicite nobis.*

Magi resp*ondent*:
*Hvnc regnare fatentes, cum mysticis muneribus de terra longinqva adorare venimus.*

Primus:
*Avro regem.*

ii.
*Thvre sacerdotem.*

iii:

*Mirra mortalem.*

Rex ad Milites:

*H⟨uc⟩, symmiste*[1] *mei, disertos pagina scribas prophetica ⟨uo⟩cate.*

Milites ad Scribas:

*Vos, legis periti, a rege vocati cum prophetarum libris properando venite.*

Rex ad Scribas:

*O, vos scribe, interrogati dicite si quid de hoc puero scriptum habetis in libris.*

Resp*ondent* Scribe:

*Vidimus, Domine, in prophetarum libris nasci Christum in Bethlehem, civitate David, propheta s⟨ic⟩ vaticinante.*

Antiphona:

*Bethlehem, ⟨non es minima in principibus Juda, ex te enim exiet dux qui regat populum meum Israel; ipse enim salvum faciet populum suum a peccatis eorum.⟩*[2]

Rex ad Scribas:

*H . . . nem spectat prudentia rerum.*
*Vadite cum vestris qui digni vatibvs estis.*

Et proiciat librum. Rex ad . . .:

*Consilium nobis, proceres, date laudis, honoris.*

Armiger ad R⟨egem⟩:

*Audi que facias, Rex, audi pauca sed apta.*
*Eois des dona magis, nec mitte morari,*
*Vt nouiter nato quem querunt rege reperto,*
*Rex, per te redeant, vt et ipse scias quid adores.*

Rex ad Armigerum:

*Addvc externos citivs, uassalle, tyrannos.*

Armiger ad Magos:

*Regia uos mandata ⟨uocan⟩t.*

Rex ad Magos. Ad i:

*Tv mihi responde, stans primus in ordine, fare.*

Resp*ondet* i:

*Impero Chaldeis dominans rex omnibus illis.*

Ad secundum:

*Tv ai, vnde es?*

Resp*ondet* ii:

*Tharsensis regio me rege nitet Zoroastro.*

Ad tercivm:

*Tv tertius, vnde es?*

Resp*ondet* iii:

*Me metuunt Arabes, mihi parent vsque fideles.*

[1] symmiste] symniste (MS).

[2] The bracketed passage is the editor's addition.

Rex consilio habito dic*it*:

*Ite, et de puero diligenter inuestigate,*
*Et inuento, redeuntes mihi renvnciate,*
*Ut et ego ⟨veniens⟩ adorem eum.*

Magi aspicientes stellam cantent:

*Ecce stella in oriente previsa*
*Iterum precedet nos lucida.*

Magi ad Pastores:

*Pastores, dicite, quidnam ⟨uidistis⟩?*[1]

Pastores:

*Infantem vidimus pannis inuolutum.*

Angelus a lon⟨gin⟩quo:[2]

*Qui sunt h⟨i⟩ quos stella ducit, nos adeuntes, inaudita ferentes?*

Magi resp*ondent;*

*Nos sumvs, quos cernitis, reges Tharsis et Arabum et Saba dona ferentes Christo, ⟨Reg⟩i, nato Domino, quem, stella duce, adorare venimus.*

Obstetrices:

*Ecce puer adest quem queritis; iam properate et orate, quia ipse est redemptio mundi.*

Intrantes Magi:

*Salue, Princeps seculorum!*

Primus:

*Svscipe, Rex, aurum.*

Secundus:

*Tolle thus, tu uere Devs.*

Tercius:

*Mirram, signum sepulture.*

Angelus ad prostratos Magos:

*Impleta sunt omnia que prophetice dicta sunt. Ite, viam remeantes aliam, ne delatores tanti regis puniendi sitis.*

Magi red*euntes* antiphonam:

*O Regem celi ⟨cui talia famulantur obsequia! Stabulo ponitur qui continet mundum; jacet in præsepio, et in nubibus tonat⟩.*[3]

Internuntius:

*Delusvs es, Domine; magi viam redierunt aliam.*

. . . probant. Rex prosiliens:

*Incendium meum ruina extinguam.*[4]

. . . Armiger econtra:

*Decerne, Domine, vindicare iram tuam, et estricto mucrone querere ivbe pueros; forte inter occisos occidetur et puer.*

[1] The bracketed word is the editor's addition.

[2] That *angelus* should speak here is surprising. As to the reading of the MS there is no doubt.

[3] Concerning this antiphon and a related responsory see above, p. 80.

[4] See above, p. 68.

Rex gladivm versans Armigero reddit[1] dicens:

*Armiger o prime, pueros fac ense perire.*

Vel:

*Mas omnis ⟨infans occidat,*
*scrutare nutricum sinus,*
*fraus ne qua furtim subtrahat*
*prolem virilis indolis⟩.*[2]

Hos versvs cantent pueri in processione Regis:

*Eia dicamus! regias ⟨hic⟩ fert dies annua laudes;*
*Hoc lux ista dedit, quod mens sperare nequiuit:*
*⟨Attulit et⟩ uere uotorum gaudia mille,*
*Hoc regnum regi, pacem quoque reddidit orbi,*
*N⟨obis diui⟩cias, decus, odas, festa, choreas.*
*Hunc regna⟨re decet⟩ et reg⟨ni⟩ sceptra tenere;*
*Regis ⟨nomen⟩ amat, nomen quia moribus or⟨nat⟩.*[3]

Expleto officio, pueri cantent . . .:

*Letabundus exultat fidelis chorus angelorum.*
*Angelus cons⟨ilii⟩ natus est de uirgine sol de ste⟨l⟩la.*
*Sicut sidus ⟨ra⟩dium profert uirgo ⟨fi⟩lium ⟨pari forma⟩.*[4]

The play from Freising opens with what may be called a processional for the entrance of Herod, sung presumably by the chorus. These unique sentences announce, somewhat vaguely, the main drift of the scenes in which he is to be the dominating figure.[5] The action itself begins with a brief scene between the shepherds and angels, followed by the usual forgathering of the Magi. As these latter proceed on their journey, they pause, as in the play from Fleury, to address the citizens of Jerusalem.

Our attention is now shifted to the court of Herod, and to the passing to and fro of the messengers who, at the king's command, summon the Magi into his presence. The activities and utterances of *Internuntius* and *Armiger* here exceed somewhat in elaborateness even what we have observed in the plays from Bilsen and Fleury. A similar prominence is given to Herod's *entourage* in the subsequent scenes in which he interviews the Magi and the scribes. His demand for comment upon the disclosures of the scribes, for example, elicits from one of his courtiers four

[1] reddit] redit (? MS).

[2] The bracketed passage is the editor's addition. For the hymn, *Salvete, flores martyrum*, of which this is the fifth stanza, see Notes, p. 449.

[3] These verses are found also at the beginning of the play from Bilsen. See above, p. 75.

[4] For the text of the sequence *Lætabundus exultet fidelis*, see Notes, p. 450.

[5] I cannot see that this introductory passage needs to be accompanied by the pantomimic action that Anz (pp. 94, 100) suggests.

hexameters (*Audi quæ facias*) which we have already observed in the highly literary text of Bilsen. In a general way these scenes follow the course familiar to us in plays already examined, but Herod's consultation with his attendants is preëminent at least in producing the delightfully insolent line,

Adduc externos citius, vasalle, tyrannos.

The humour of the word *tyrannus* from the lips of this monarch requires no emphasizing.

Passing over the several succeeding scenes, which have close parallels in other plays, we need pause only over the conclusion of the text before us. After a messenger has informed Herod of the escape of the Magi, and the king has uttered his Sallustian threat (*Incendium meum*), his armed attendant explicitly proposes the slaughter of the male children. For giving his assent to this proposal, Herod is provided with alternative utterances: either the hexameter *Armiger o prime, pueros fac ense perire*, or a stanza, *Mas omnis infans occidat*, from the hymn *Salvete, flores martyrum*. Either of these is sufficiently appropriate to the situation; the latter is found in no other play.[1] The verses beginning *Eia dicamus*, which are difficult enough to understand in their position at the opening of the play from Bilsen,[2] are still more perplexing in the present instance. If they are intended as a processional for the withdrawal of Herod from the stage, they are totally incongruous; and if they are sung in honour of the new-born king, they clash abruptly with the tone of the scene immediately preceding. The latter seems more likely to have been the intention of the writer, in view of the singing of the sequence *Lætabundus exultet fidelis* by the *pueri* immediately after.[3]

Viewed as a whole, the play is orderly in structure and smooth in its transitions. If, in the opening scene of the shepherds, the *Gloria in excelsis* is sung by the chorus, the effect is liturgical rather than dramatic.[4] As to stage-action, impersonation, and scenery the fragmentary rubrics provide almost no information. The spoken text clearly requires that during Herod's interview with the scribes the Magi be conducted out of the scene, until

[1] The corresponding hexameter in the play from Compiègne has the more acceptable metrical form, *Indolis eximie, pueros fac ense perire*. See above, p. 55.

[2] See above, p. 75.

[3] Anz (p. 93) regards the use of the verses *Eia dicamus* here as scarcely intelligible, and as more acceptable in their place in the play from Bilsen. Böhme (p. 102) views the matter conversely.

[4] My reading, *Ch⟨oru⟩s*, is not certain. Anz (p. 154) finds the rubric totally illegible and conjectures ⟨*Multitudo angelorum*⟩.

Herod commands their return (*Adduc externos . . . tyrannos*).[1] One would like to infer that the stage was furnished with a *carcer*, such as that in the play from Bilsen. Aside from the indispensable *stella*, there must have been also a *præsepe* and a throne for Herod. Of the violence of this personage we are left in no doubt. He dashes the book of prophecies to the ground, makes impulsive gestures, and, no doubt, brandishes his sword. These movements are abundantly supported by his utterances, which are, as we have seen, superlatively angry and arrogant.

## VII

The angry Herod, as a matter of fact, did more than merely dominate the dramatic performance in which he had an inevitable role; he also invaded parts of the liturgy where his violence was an unseemly intrusion only to be tolerated under the general spirit of misrule prevailing during the Christmas season.[2] Of this particular form of dramatic licence a striking example is the following bit of ceremonial from the cathedral of Padua:[3]

### Representatio Herodis in Nocte Epyphanie

Finita octaua lectione, exit Herodes de secrestia superiori cum capellano suo; et sunt induti uilissimis strictis et infulis. Et cum hasta lignea in manu, et cum maximo furore prohic*it* eam uersus chorum, et cum tanto furore ascendit pergamum, et duo scolares defer*unt* cereos ante eum, et cum tanto furore incip*it* nonam lectionem. Et interim ministri eius cum magno furore circuunt chorum percutiendo episcopum, canonicos et scolares uesica | inflata, et etiam uiros et mulieres in ecclesia existentes; et q*uando*q*ue* deportant dictam hastam Herodi, qui prohicit eam per ecclesiam. Finita lectione, descendit Herodes cum ministris suis, et cum supradicto furore iterum circuunt chorum percuciendo ut supra. Finito responsorio, quidam diaconus indutus dalmatica ascendit pergamum cum dicto Herode et capellano suo, et capellanus defert turribulum, precedentibus duobus scolaribus cum cereis. Et interim episcopus incip*it* antiphonam *In Bethleem Iude*. Et postea diaconus dic*it* euangelium, scilicet: *Genealogia Domini*. Quo finito, episcopus incipit *Te Deum laudamus*. Et Herodes defert librum euangeliorum, et capellanus cum turribulo incensat episcopum et

[1] See Sondheimer, p. 18.

[2] See above, i, 104. Concerning abuses associated with such representations see the observations of Herrad of Landsberg quoted below, pp. 412 sqq.

[3] Padua, Bibl. Capit., MS S Ordin. Patavinense sæc. xiii, fol. 58ʳ–58ᵛ, described by Dondi Orologio, pp. 43–4, and by Bartholomaeis, pp. 151–2, and published by the latter, pp. 530–1. Concerning the manuscript see above, i, 552.

can*onicos*, qui osculantur librum euangeliorum, quem defert eis supradictus Herodes; et postea incensantur scolares sine libro. Et chorarii prosecuntur antiphonam Laudum *Caput*,[1] ut supra. Et tunc quidam scolaris superius ad altare Sancti Michaelis cantat primum uersum ymni, scilicet: *Nuntium uobis*.[2] Quo finito, ostendit candelam accensam ad similitudinem Stelle, quam prohic*it* uersus chorum, et chorus prosequitur ymnum.[3]

At Padua, it appears, in the absence of a decorous play of the Magi, Herod takes a lawless part in the concluding parts of Matins itself. After the eighth lesson he and his chaplain come from the sacristy, clad in untidy tunics, and carrying wooden spears. Before he mounts the platform, Herod angrily hurls his spear towards the chorus, and then proceeds, *cum tanto furore*, to read the ninth lesson. Meanwhile his attendants dash about the choir belabouring bishop, canons and choristers with an inflated bladder. At the conclusion of his reading, Herod joins in these antics *cum supradicto furore*—presumably while the chorus is attempting to sing the last responsory. Then Herod, preceded by acolytes and thuribles, again ascends the platform, where he remains, possibly quiescent, while the deacon reads the Genealogy. At the conclusion of this somewhat extended recital Herod carries the gospel-book to the bishop and cantors to be kissed by them. The chorus now proceeds with Lauds, and the liturgy is no further disturbed, except that at the beginning of the hymn a chorister, standing in an elevated position at the altar of St Michael, tosses towards the chorus a lighted candle, in the likeness of a star.

Thus our survey of the plays of Epiphany, having begun with the reverent participation of the Magi in the oblation of the Mass, ends with the boisterous antics which, it appears, were ever lurking on the outskirts of the liturgy of the twelve days of the Christmas season.[4]

The order in which the dramatic texts have been presented in the last two chapters has, it is hoped, at least the virtue of making clear their increasing complexity. Although this arrangement does not undertake to demonstrate the exact textual

[1] Hartker (p. 80) gives the following as one of the antiphons of Lauds on the octave of Epiphany: *Caput draconis Salvator conteruit in Jordane flumine, ab ejus potestate omnes eripiens.*

[2] Concerning the hymn *Nuntium vobis fero de supernis* see above, p. 35.

[3] The text proceeds as follows: Versus *Adorate Dominum*. Ad *Benedictus* antiphona *Hodie celesti sponso*. In the *ordo* for Epiphany there are no further details of dramatic interest.

[4] See Chambers, ii, 56. For further references to dramatic texts and records connected with Epiphany see Notes, p. 451.

development historically, it probably represents fairly enough the general course of actual dramatic growth. The original date of the dramatic ceremonies of Limoges and Besançon, in which the impersonated Magi make offerings at the altar during Mass, cannot be determined.[1] Such ceremonies may, or may not, have antedated and inspired the more regular dramatic performances at the *præsepe* and at the throne of Herod.[2] Whether or not a simple play such as that from Rouen had antecedents such as the performances at Limoges and Besançon, the general development from the Rouen type of play to that found at Fleury and Freising is not difficult to trace in its broad outlines. To the play consisting essentially in the visit of the Magi to the *præsepe* was added a scene in which they appear before Herod. This was enlarged by a scene in which Herod confers with the scribes. To these two additional scenes—through a process that cannot be successfully unravelled in all its details—were added secondary actions in which the emissaries of Herod treat, more or less elaborately, with the Magi or the scribes, or with both. Finally the *Officium Stellæ* included within its scope one or more scenes presenting the shepherds.[3]

From the plain fact that the simplest and oldest forms of the play are found only in France, one draws the obvious conclusion that it originated there.[4] From the additional fact that French communities furnish most of the texts of the play in all its stages, one infers that it throve chiefly on French soil. As to the epoch during which the *Officium Stellæ* arose there can be no substantial doubt. Both the records and the texts point to the eleventh century.[5]

[1] See above, pp. 34, 37.

[2] Böhme (pp. 47–69) undertakes to convey the impression that something like the Limoges ceremony may have existed in the tenth century, and that it was the basis upon which simple plays like that of Rouen (see above, p. 43) may have been developed in the eleventh century.

[3] The development roughly outlined in this paragraph conforms to the general views of Anz, as slightly modified by Schiffmann, *Review*, pp. 13–7. Many of Anz's theoretical reconstructions, represented in part by his 'Uebersichtstabelle' (p. 129), are no more convincing to me than they are to Böhme (pp. 83–6).

[4] See Anz, pp. 124–7; Schiffmann, *Review*, p. 12. Concerning Meyer's view (pp. 42–4), that the play arose in Germany, see Notes, p. 452.

[5] See Anz, pp. 122–4.

# CHAPTER XX

# THE SLAUGHTER OF THE INNOCENTS

THE treatment here of the few extant dramatizations of the slaughter of the Innocents is to be regarded as a direct continuation of the discussion of the Magi plays in the two preceding chapters.[1] Both through its position in the Gospel narrative and through its liturgical history the theme of the Innocents is closely associated with that of the visit of the wise men from the East. In the account of St Matthew we are told that after he heard of the escape of the Magi, Herod promptly indulged his anger by ordering the slaughter of all the male children in the region of Bethlehem of the age of two years or less; and that thus was fulfilled the prophecy of Jeremiah concerning Rachel's mourning for her children. The brief record in the Vulgate runs as follows:[2]

Tunc Herodes videns quoniam illusus esset a Magis, iratus est valde, et mittens occidit omnes pueros qui erant in Bethlehem et in omnibus finibus ejus a bimatu et infra, secundum tempus quod exquisierat a Magis.

Tunc adimpletum est quod dictum est per Jeremiam prophetam dicentem:

Vox in Rama audita est, ploratus et ululatus multus: Rachel plorans filios suos, et noluit consolari, quia non sunt.

The association of the two events was maintained for a time in the Roman liturgical calendar, for during the early Christian centuries they were commemorated in a single feast, the separate celebration of the Slaughter of the Innocents on December 28th being unknown before the fourth or fifth century.[3] It was entirely natural, therefore, that the close relationship between the two themes should sometimes continue when they were dramatized, the representation of the fate of the Innocents serving as a kind of epilogue to the play of the Magi.

## I

This dramatic sequence has, indeed, already been indicated in several of the versions of the *Officium Stellæ* considered in the foregoing chapters. At the close of the version from Freising, for

[1] For bibliography bearing on the play of the Innocents see Notes, p. 452.

[2] Matt. ii, 16–8.

[3] See Rietschel, *Lehrbuch*, i, 189; Anz, p. 70.

example, one of Herod's soldiers explicitly urges him to order the slaughter of the male children, the king accedes with vehemence, and the *pueri* actually appear upon the stage, as if to show that the execution of Herod's design is imminent.[1] In the play from Compiègne Herod issues the same command, and the children appear to have been rescued from destruction only through the sudden ending of the play with the angel's merciful utterance *Sinite parvulos venire ad me*.[2] The Norman play ends with a scene in which Herod is incited to the slaughter both by his soldiers and by his son, Archelaus, and brandishes his sword angrily in acquiescence. Since the scene ends fragmentarily, the outcome cannot be determined.[3]

To these versions of the *Officium Stellæ* which end with only a tentative, or fragmentary, approach to a dramatization of our theme we may now add at least one example of a Magi play which presents the subject completely. This is found in a service-book of the cathedral of Laon:[4]

ORDO STELLE

Stella apparente, tres Reges e diuersis partibus ueniunt, et primus dicit:

*Stella fulgore nimio rutilat.*

Secundus dicit:

*Que | regem regum natum monstrat.*

Tertius dicit:

*Quem uenturum olim prophetia signauerat.*

Tres simul:

*Eamus ergo et inquiramus eum, offerentes ei munera: aurum, thus, et mirram; quia scriptum didicimus: Adorabunt eum omnes reges, omnes gentes seruient ei.*

Nuntius ad Magos:

*Qui uos? quid queritis? uel quo iam tendere uultis?*

Magi:

*Ex oriente sumus, Iherosolimam tendentes; natum regem querimus.*

Nuntius ad Regem:

*Viuat Rex in eternum!*

Item Nuntius ad Regem:

*En magi ueniunt,*
*Et regem regum natum, stella duce, requirunt.*

[1] See above, p. 97.

[2] See above, pp. 55–6.

[3] See above, p. 72. See also p. 66, and Young, *Ordo Rachelis*, pp. 5–13.

[4] Laon, Bibl. de la Ville, MS 263, Troparium-Hymnarium Laudunense sæc. xiii, fol. 149r–151r, previously edited by Chevalier, *Laon*, pp. 389–94; and by Young, *Ordo Rachelis*, pp. 13–7. The text before us is immediately preceded in the MS by the ending of the *Ordo Prophetarum* printed below, pp. 145 sqq.

Rex ad Nuntium:

*Ante uenire iube, quod possim singula scire*
*Qui sint, cur ueniant, quo nos rumore requirant.*

Nuntius ad Magos:

*Regia uos mandata uocant; non segniter*[1] *ite.*

Magi Regem salutant:

*Aue, Rex Iudeorum!*

Rex ad Magos:

*Regem quem queritis, natum esse quo signo didicistis?*

Magi:

*Illum natum esse didicimus in oriente stella monstrante.*

Rex ad Magos:

*Si illum regnare creditis, dicite michi.*

Magi:

*Hunc regnare fatentes, cum misticis muneribus de terra longinqua adorare uenimus, trinum Deum uenerantes tribus in muneribus.*

Primus:

*Auro regem.*

Secundus:

*Thure sacerdotem.*

Tertius:

*Mirra mortalem.*

Rex ad Symmistas:

*Huc simmiste*[2] *mei, disertos pagina scribas prophetica ad me uocate.*|

Simmiste ad Scribas:

*Vos, legis periti, a rege uocati cum prophetarum libris properando uenite.*

Rex ad Scribas:

*O uos scribe, interrogati dicite si quid de hoc puero scriptum uideritis in libro.*

Respondent Scribe:

*Vidimus, Domine, in prophetarum libris: Bethleem, non es minima in principibus Iuda, ex te enim exiet dux qui regat populum meum Israel; ipse enim saluum faciet populum suum a peccatis eorum.*

Rex ad Magos:

*Ite et de puero diligenter inuestigate,*
*Et inuento, redeuntes mihi renuntiate.*

Magi inclinantes discedunt, et iterum uidentes Stellam dicunt:

*Ecce stella, ecce stella, et ecce stella in oriente preuisa*
*Iterum reducit nos lucida, lucida, lucida,*
*Quam Balaam ex Iudaica orituram*[3] *dixerat prosapia;*
*Que nostrorum oculos*[4] *fulguranti lumine perstrinxit*[5] *pauidos lucida, lucida, lucida.*

[1] segniter] senniter (MS).
[2] simmiste] simite (MS).
[3] orituram] oriturum (MS).
[4] oculos] oculis (MS).
[5] perstrinxit] perstrinexit (MS).

*Ipsam simul, ipsam simul, ipsam simul congrediendo sectantes non relinquamus ultra,*

*Donec nos perducat ad cunabula.*

Obstetrices ad Magos, antequam intrent:

*Qui sunt hi qui, stella duce, nos adeuntes inaudita*[1] *ferunt?*

Magi:

*Nos sumus, quos cernitis, reges Tharsis et Arabum et Sabba dona ferentes Christo, Regi,*[2] *nato Domino, quem, stella deducente, adorare uenimus.*

Obstetrices introducentes Magos, ostendunt Puerum et dicunt:

*Ecce puer adest quem queritis; | introeuntes adorate, quia ipse est redemptio mundi.*

Accedunt Magi et genuflexo primus dicit:

*Suscipe, Rex, aurum.*

Secundus:

*Tolle thus, tu uere Deus.*

Tertius:

*Mirram, signum sepulture.*

Ioseph ad Magos:

*Multi reges et prophete*
*uoluerunt hec uidere;*
*que auditis et uidetis*
*nec concessum fuit illis.*

Angelus:

*Impleta sunt omnia que prophetice dicta sunt. Ite, uiam redeuntes aliam, ne delatores tanti regis puniendi eritis.*

Magi redeuntes cantant:

*Secundum quod dictum est nobis ab angelo de puero isto, inuenimus infantem pannis inuolutum et positum in presepio in medio duum animalium.*

Nuntius ad Regem:

*Delusus es, Domine; Magi uiam redierunt aliam.*

Archelaus ad Regem:

*Decerne, Domine, uindicari iram tuam, et stricto mucrone querere iube pueros; forte inter occisos occidetur et puer.*

Rex gladium reddens Archelao dicit:

*Indolis eximie, pueros fac ense perire.*

Interim Pueri, agnum portantes, intrant cantantes:

*Ecce Agnus Dei, ecce qui tollit peccata mundi, alleluia.*

Iterum et tertio ueniunt Armati. Clamant Pueri dum occiduntur:

*Quare non defendis sanguinem nostrum?*

Angelus:

*Adhuc sustinete modicum tempus, donec impleatur numerus fratrum uestrorum.*

[1]. inaudita] mandata (MS). [2] Regi] rege (MS).

Venit Rachel, et exclamans cum fletu dicit:

*O dulces innocentum acies!*
*O pia lactantum pro Christo certamina!*
*Paruorum truci|dantur milia;*
*membris ex teneris manant lactis flumina.*

Consolatrix:

*Noli, uirgo Rachel,   noli, dulcissima mater,*
*Pro nece paruorum   fletus reticere dolorum.*

Rachel:

*Gaudia non possunt,*[1]   *nam dulcia pignora non sunt,*
*Iudee florem,   patrie lacrimando decorem.*

Consolatrix:

*Tu, que tristaris,   exulta, que lacrimaris,*
*Namque tui nati   uiuunt super astra beati.*

Rachel:

*Heu! Heu!*
*Quomodo gaudebo   dum mortua membra uidebo?*
*Dum sic commota   fuero per uiscera tota*
*Me facient uere   pueri sine fine dolere.*

Consolatrix:

*Supplico ne plores,   que tanto sanguine flores*
*Ast oculos flentes,   lacrimas quoque terge fluentes.*

Rachel:

*In dolorem est conuersum   quod habebam gaudium.*

Consolatrix:

*Quam beata sunt innocentum ab Herode cesa corpuscula!*
*Quam felices existunt matres, fuderunt que talia pignora!*

Rachel:

*Planctus matrum et Rachelis   equa sunt suspiria*
*Nulla quidem consolatur   magna pre tristitia.*
*Ey dolor est! Nolo consolari, quia non sunt.*[2]

This is, in large part, a normal version of the play of the Magi, so generally similar to versions of the *Officium Stellæ* already examined that a detailed analysis may be omitted. In the scene of the adoration of the Magi, however, at least one matter requires a word of comment: namely, the participation of Joseph. Although he is not specifically mentioned in St Matthew's narrative, he appears in the apocryphal Pseudo-Matthew,[3] and his presence must, in any case, be assumed. One wonders, indeed, why this appealing figure is not brought forward prominently in other versions of the *Officium Stellæ*. In the absence of any

[1] possunt] possum (MS).
[2] Followed by the rubric *Ordo Ioseph*, introducing the play printed below, pp. 267 sqq.
[3] See Tischendorf, *Evangelia*, p. 83.

traditional utterance for Joseph on this occasion, the writer at Laon rather skilfully adopts and versifies the following utterance of Christ from the Gospel of Luke: *Dico enim vobis quod multi prophetæ et reges voluerunt videre quæ vos videtis, et non viderunt; et audire quæ auditis, et non audierunt.*[1]

In the role of the Magi we need observe only one other detail: the passage which they sing as they withdraw from the stage (*Secundum quod dictum*). This utterance—appropriate only to the shepherds, and here assigned to the Magi somewhat ineptly—may possibly be a remnant of a scene of the *pastores*, incompletely eliminated at Laon.[2]

Proceeding, then, to the scene of the massacre of the Innocents, which follows immediately and naturally after Herod's command, we observe that it opens with a processional entry of the boys, carrying a lamb and singing *Ecce Agnus Dei*. As the soldiers rush in and begin the slaughter, the *pueri* utter their despairing cry *Quare non defendis?* and receive the angelic assurance *Adhuc sustinete*. Rachel now enters, and a succession of laments from her, accompanied by the comforting utterances of *Consolatrix*, constitute the greater part of the scene, and conclude the play.

The literary elements of the new scene of the Innocents are in part traditional and liturgical, and in part original. The presence of the lamb carried by the boys at their entrance upon the stage is amply explained by the liturgical epistle of the day, in which we read the following:[3]

> Et vidi, et ecce Agnus stabat supra montem Sion, et cum eo centum quadraginta quattuor millia . . . Hi sunt qui cum mulieribus non sunt coinquinati; virgines enim sunt. Hi sequuntur Agnum quocumque ierit.

The passage which the *pueri* actually sing appears to be taken directly from the Gospel of John (i, 29)—*Ecce Agnus Dei, ecce qui tollit peccatum mundi*—rather than from the adaptations of this text in the liturgy.[4]

The killing of the children is dramatized very briefly. The soldiers who perform the deed say nothing, but the boys and the

[1] Luke x, 24. See Anz, p. 86.

[2] See Anz, p. 87. For the use of this speech by the *pastores* in the *Officium Stellæ* from Fleury see above, p. 88.

[3] Rev. xiv, 1, 4.

[4] I refer especially to the *Agnus Dei* of the Mass, and to the Christmas responsory *Ecce Agnus Dei* (see Hartker, p. 49). In regard to these liturgical pieces see Young, *op. cit.*, p. 19, and above, i, 39. As to the frequent use of the theme of the procession of the lamb in liturgical poetry see Anz, p. 71.

angel exchange utterances drawn from the following responsory of Matins of Innocents Day:[1]

Sub altare Dei audivi voces occisorum: Quare non defendis sanguinem nostrum? Et acceperunt divinum responsum: Adhuc sustinete modicum, donec impleatur numerus fratrum vestrorum. Versus: Vidi sub altare Dei animas sanctorum, propter verbum Domini quod habebant, et clara voce dicebant. Quare non.

The rest of the scene consists of the laments of Rachel, the representative Jewish mother, and the responses of *Consolatrix*. These two figures arise ultimately from the prophecy of Jeremiah: *Vox in excelso audita est lamentationis, luctus, et fletus Rachel plorantis filios suos, et nolentis consolari super eis, quia non sunt.*[2] This passage re-appears, slightly modified, in the Gospel narrative upon which the present scene is based,[3] and thus finds a prominent place in the liturgy of Innocents Day both in the liturgical gospel and in the *communio* of the Mass.[4] In all these places Rachel is explicitly named, and the presence of her comforter is clearly implied in the words *noluit consolari.* Their utterances, however, remained to be supplied by the imaginations of liturgical poets, among whose independent productions are found several passages of the scene before us. Rachel's first speech (*O dulces . . . lactis flumina*) and the last speech of her consoler (*Quam beata . . . talia pignora*) are supplied by passages in the sequence *Celsa pueri concrepent melodia.*[5] From another sequence *Misit Herodes innocentum*[6] are derived the first two lines of Rachel's last speech (*Planctus matrum . . . præ tristitia*), the third line of which seems to rest upon a passage in the Vulgate.[7] For the remaining speeches of the two women no sources can be cited. It will be observed that some dozen lines of this part of the dialogue (*Noli, virgo . . . terge fluentes*) are leonine hexameters.[8]

Concerning the staging of the play before us the text is almost silent. For the earlier part of the action, in which the Magi are concerned, are provided a star and a manger; but for the scene of the slaughter no special arrangements are mentioned. In the

[1] Migne, *P.L.*, lxxviii, 739–40. A slightly different form is given by Hartker, p. 65. See Young, *op. cit.*, p. 19.

[2] Jeremiah, xxxi, 15.

[3] See Matt. ii, 17–8, quoted above, p. 102.

[4] See Migne, *P.L.*, lxxviii, 648.

[5] Chevalier, *R.H.*, no. 2747, For the complete text see Notes, p. 452.

[6] Chevalier, *R.H.*, no. 11620. For the complete text see Notes, p. 453.

[7] See Matt. ii, 18, quoted above, p. 102.

[8] Meyer (pp. 45–6) and Anz (pp. 74–7) discern verbal relationships between certain of these lines and passages in the versions from Freising and Limoges to be considered below. These relationships are treated as largely indecisive by Young, *op. cit.*, pp. 22, 53–62.

representation of the killing of the children there was, presumably, no industrious attempt at realism. At what point in the liturgy the play was performed we do not know. Probably it could have been given most conveniently at the close of Matins of Epiphany.

## II

Only in the *Officium Stellæ* of Laon is a fully developed scene of the Innocents found directly attached to an Epiphany play. The three other extant dramatic treatments of this subject are independent pieces. Of these the simplest and briefest is the following, of the eleventh or twelfth century, from the monastery of St Martial at Limoges:[1]

⟨Responsorium:⟩ *Svb altare Dei audiui uoces occisorum dicentivm.* Versus:[2] *Quare non defendis sanguinem nostrum? Et acceperunt diuinum responsum: Adhuc sustinete modicum tempus, donec impleatur numerus fratrum uestrorum.* ⟨Versus:⟩ *Vidi* ⟨*sub altare Dei animas sanctorum, propter verbum Domini quod habebant, et clara voce dicebant. Quare non*⟩.

Lamentatio Rachel*is*:

*O dvlces filii, quos nunc progenui,*|
*Olim dicta mater, quod nomen tenui?*
*Olim per pignora uocor puerpera,*
*Modo sum misera, natorum uidua.*
*Heu! michi misere! cum possim uiuere,*
*Cum natos coram me uideo perdere,*
*Atque lacerare parum detruncare.*
*Herodes impius, furore repletus,*
*Nimium superbus perdit meos*[3] *partus.*

Angelus:

*Noli, Rachel, deflere pignora.*
*Cvr*[4] *tristaris, et tundis pectora?*
*Noli flere, sed gaude potius,*
*cui nati uiuunt felicius.*
*Ergo gaude!*
*Svmmi patris eterni*[5] *filius,*
*hic est ille quem querit perdere,*
*qvi uos facit eterne uiuere.*
*Ergo gaude!*[6]

[1] Paris, Bibl. Nat., MS lat. 1139, Trop. Martialense sæc. xi-xii, fol. $32^v$–$33^r$, previously edited by Magnin, *Review*, p. 93; Coussemaker, *Histoire*, p. 128; Gautier, *Tropes*, p. 168; Chasles, p. 407; Young, *op. cit.*, pp. 24–5. Gautier's text is reprinted by Anz, pp. 72–3; and a fragmentary text is provided by Du Méril, p. 46. For observations on the MS see Notes, p. 453.

[2] Versus] Apparently misplaced by the scribe.

[3] meos] mons (MS).

[4] Cvr] Cor (?MS).

[5] eterni] eterun (MS).

[6] Thus ends fol. $33^r$. At the top of fol. $33^v$

From its form and associations the text before us may be described as a dramatic trope of the liturgical responsory *Sub altare Dei*.[1] The dramatic nature of the responsory itself we have already noted in our examination of the scene of the Innocents in the Epiphany play from Laon. There the dialogue embedded in the responsory is extracted and made part of the dramatic action, whereas in the Limoges text the responsory remains intact as a purely liturgical element, and the dramatic dialogue consists merely of two affecting utterances: a lament of Rachel and a comforting response from the angel. Rachel's lament takes the form of a stanza of twelve-syllable lines, with prevailing internal rhyme, and the angel replies in a succession of seven ten-syllable lines broken by the effectual use of the refrain *Ergo gaude*. The composition appears to be the original production of the Limoges poet,[2] and the part of it assigned to the sorrowing mother has true emotional power. As to the manner in which the dialogue was rendered there is no evidence. In the absence of assurance that the speeches were delivered by impersonated characters, we may regard the composition more safely as a dramatic poem than as a miniature play.

## III

For genuine and independent dramatizations of our theme, then, we must proceed to more ambitious compositions of a type which, in at least one manuscript, has been fittingly designated *Ordo Rachelis*.[3] Such is the following piece from the Fleury playbook:[4]

⟨A⟩d interfectionem Puerorum induantur Innocentes stolis albis, et gaudentes per monasterium, orent Deum dicentes:[5]

*⟨O⟩ quam gloriosum est regnum ⟨in quo cum Christo gaudent omnes sancti amicti stolis albis; sequuntur agnum quocumque ierit⟩.*[6]

begins a fresh trope (probably of the *Benedicamus*): *In hoc festo breuiter iubilemus pariter*.

[1] Gautier (*Tropes*, p. 168) adopts this interpretation, but with misgivings in which I do not share.

[2] The remote possibility of certain liturgical influences is suggested by Young, *op. cit.*, p. 26.

[3] See the version from Freising below, p. 117.

[4] Orleans, Bibl. de la Ville, MS 201 (*olim* 178), Miscellanea Floriacensia sæc. xiii, pp. 214–20, previously edited by Monmerqué, in *Mélanges*, vii, 147–54 (M); Wright, pp. 29–31 (W); Du Méril, pp. 175–9 (D); Coussemaker, pp. 166–77 (C); Young, *op. cit.*, pp. 27–31. Only Coussemaker includes the music. Concerning the MS see above, i, 665.

[5] In the MS the word *dicentes* is followed by a small blank space, after which the text proceeds as follows: Tunc Agnus ex inprouiso ueniens portans crucem antecedat eos huc et illuc, et illi sequentes cantent | ⟨*O*⟩ *quam gloriosum* ⟨MS *glosiosum*⟩ *est regnum. Emitte agnum, domine*. Interim armiger.

[6] Antiphon of Vespers for the Vigil of All Saints. See Hartker, p. 331.

Tunc Agnus ex inprouiso ueniens, portans crucem, antecedat eos huc et illuc, et illi sequentes cantent:

*Emitte agnum, Domine,* ⟨*dominatorem terræ, de petra deserti, ad montem filiæ Sion.*⟩[1]

Interim Armiger quidam offerat Herodi sedenti sceptrum suum dicens:

*Super solium Dauid,* ⟨ *et super regnum ejus sedebit in æternum, alleluia.*⟩[2]

Interea Angelus super Presepe apparens moneat Ioseph fugere in Egiptum cum Maria. Angelus dicat tribus vicibus *Ioseph*:

*Ioseph, Ioseph, Ioseph, fili Dauid!*

Postea dicat hec:

*Tolle puerum et matrem eius, et uade in Egiptum, et esto ibi usque dum dicam tibi. Futurum est enim ut Herodes querat puerum ad perdendum eum.*

Ioseph abiens, non uidente Herode, cum Maria portante Puerum, dicens:

*Egipte, noli flere,* ⟨*quia dominator tuus veniet tibi, ante cujus conspectum movebuntur abyssi, liberare populum suum de manu potentium.* Versus: *Ecce dominator Dominus cum virtute veniet.*⟩[3]

Interim Armiger, nuncians Magos per aliam uiam redisse salutat prius Regem; postea dicat:

*Rex, in eternum uiue! Delusus es, Domine; magi uiam redierunt aliam.*

Tunc Herodes, quasi corruptus, arrepto gladio, paret seipsum occidere; sed prohibeatur tandem a suis et pacificetur, dicens:

*Incendium meum ruina restinguam.*

Interea Innocentes, adhuc gradientes post Agnum, decantent:

*Agno sacrato pro nobis mortificato,|*
*Splendorem patris splendorem uirginitatis*
*Offerimus Christo sub signo luminis isto.*
*Multis ira modis ut quos inquirit Herodis*
*Agno saluemur, cum Christo conmoriemur.*

Armiger suggerat Herodi dicens:[4]

*Discerne, Domine, uindicare iram tuam, et stricto mucrone iube occidi pueros; forte inter occisos*[5] *occidetur et Christus.*

Herodes tradens ei gladium dicens:

*Armiger eximie, pueros fac ense perire.*

Interim, occisoribus uenientibus, subtrahatur agnus clam, quem abeuntem[6] salutant Innocentes:

*Salue, Agnus Dei! Salue, qui tollis*[7] *peccata mundi, alleluia!*

Tunc Matres occidentes orent occisos:

*Oremus, tenere natorum parcite uite.*

[1] Antiphon of Lauds in Advent. See Hartker, p. 37; Migne, *P.L.*, lxxviii, 731.

[2] Antiphon of Lauds of the second Sunday before Christmas. See Hartker, p. 24.

[3] Responsory of Matins of the third Sunday before Christmas. See Hartker, p. 28.

[4] Herodi dicens] Herodes dicentes (MS).

[5] occisos] oculos (MS).

[6] quem abeuntem] qui abeuntes (MS).

[7] tollis] tollit (MS).

Postea, iacentibus Infantibus, Angelus ab excelso admoneat[1] eos, dicens:

*Vos qui in puluere estis, expergiscimini et clamate.*

Infantes iacentes:

*Quare non defendis | sanguinem nostrum, Deus noster?*

Angelus:

*Adhuc sustinete modicum tempus, donec impleatur numerus fratrum uestrorum.*

Tunc inducatur Rachel, et due Consolatrices; et stans super Pueros plangat, cadens aliquando, dicens:

*Heu! teneri partus, laceros quos cernimus artus!*
*Heu! dulces nati, sola rabie iugulati!*
*Heu! quem nec pietas nec uestra coercuit etas!*
*Heu! matres misere, que cogimur ista uidere!*
*Heu! quid nunc agimus cur non hec facta subimus!*
*Heu! quia memores*[2] *nostrosque leuare dolores*
*Gaudia non possunt, nam dulcia pignora desunt!*

Consolatrices excipientes eam cadentem dicentes:

*Noli, uirgo Rachel, noli dulcissima mater,*
*Pro nece paruorum fletus retinere dolorum.*
*Si que tristaris, exulta que lacrimaris.* |
*Namque tui nati uiuunt super astra beati.*

Item Rachel dolens:

*Heu! Heu! Heu!*
*Quomodo gaudebo, dum mortua membra uidebo;*
*Dum sic commota fuero per uiscera tota?*
*Me facient uere pueri sine fine dolere.*
*O dolor! O patrum mutataque gaudia matrum*
*Ad lugubres luctus; lacrimarum fundite fletus,*
*Iudee florem patrie lacrimando dolorem.*

Item Consolatrices:

*Quid tu, uirgo,*
*mater Rachel, ploras*[3] *formosa,*
*cuius uultus*[4] *Iacob delectat?*
*Ceu sororis annicule*
*lippitudo*[5] *eum iuuat!*
*Terge, mater, flentes oculos.*
*Quam te decent genarum*[6] *riuuli?*

Item Rachel:

*Heu, heu, heu! Quid*[7] | *me incusastis fletus incassum fudisse,*
*Cum sim orbata nato, paupertatem meam ⟨qui solus⟩ curaret,*

[1] admoneat] ut moneant (MS).

[2] quia memores] quid memores (M. D). For *memores* D and C suggest *moerores* (*merores*). Anz (p. 76) emends the first half-line to *Heu!* (*luctus*) *memores*.

[3] ploras] plorans (MS).

[4] uultus] uultum (MS).

[5] Ceu . . . lippitudo] seu sororis agnicule limpitudo (MS).

[6] genarum] genatum (MS).

[7] Quid] Written twice (MS).

*Qui non hostibus cederet angustos terminos, quos michi Iacob adquisiuit,*

*Quique stolidis fratribus, quo⟨s⟩ multos, pro⟨h⟩ dolor, extuli,*[1] *esset profuturus?*

Tunc Consolatrices, esupinantes Infantes, dicentes:

*Numquid flendus est iste, qui regnum possidet celeste,*

*Quique prece frequenti*[2] *miseris fratribus apud Deum auxilietur?*

Item Rachel cadens super Pueros:

*Anxiatus est in me spiritus meus; in me turbatum est cor meum.*[3]

Tunc Consolatrices abducant Rachel, et Angelus interim de supernis dicat antiphonam que sequitur:

*Sinite paruulos ⟨venire ad me, talium est enim regnum cœlorum⟩.*[4]

Ad uocem Angeli surgentes Pueri intrent chorum dicentes:

*O Christe, quantum patri exercitum iuuenis, doctus ad bella maxima; populis predicans, colligis, umbras suggens cum tantum miseris.*

Dum hec fiunt, tollatur Herodes et substituatur in loco eius Filius eius, Archelaus, et exaltetur in regem. Interim Angelus ammoneat Ioseph in Egiptum, quo prius secessit, dicens:

*Ioseph, Ioseph, Ioseph, fili Dauid! Reuertere | in terram Iudam, defuncti sunt enim qui querebant animam pueri.*

Tunc Ioseph reuertatur cum Maria et Puero, secedens in parte⟨s⟩ Galilee dicens:

*Gaude, gaude, gaude, Maria uirgo; cunctas hereses,*

et cetera.[5] Cantor incipit *Te Deum laudamus*. Sic finit.

The play opens with a procession of the boys through the church[6] singing the antiphon *O quam gloriosum*. Then a lamb, with a cross attached to it, takes its place at the head of the procession, and the boys follow, singing the antiphon *Emitte agnum*. Meanwhile Herod mounts his throne, and ceremoniously receives his sword from his armour-bearer, who sings the antiphon *Super solium David*.

The action proper begins with a scene in which the angel appears above the *præsepe*, commanding Joseph to flee with Mary and Jesus into Egypt. As the Holy Family depart, Joseph sings the responsory *Ægypte, noli flere*.

The next scene recalls a situation which we have observed at the end of several versions of the *Officium Stellæ*. Informed of the

[1] extuli] extulit (MS).

[2] frequenti] frequenta (MS).

[3] Antiphon of Lauds of Good Friday. See Hartker, p. 220.

[4] Antiphon of Lauds of Innocents Day. See Hartker, p. 68.

[5] Among the antiphons for the Assumption is the following: *Gaude, Maria virgo, cunctas hæreses sola intemeristi in universo mundo*. See Migne, *P.L.*, lxxviii, 799; Hartker, p. 117. For a responsory with the same *incipit* see Hartker, p. 118.

[6] The meaning of the phrase *per monasterium* and the location of the play in the church are considered below, p. 117.

escape of the Magi, Herod is enraged to the point of attempting suicide. He is, however, restrained from this, and contents himself with ordering the destruction of the male children, who have meanwhile appeared singing the verses *Agno sacrato*.

Now is represented the slaughter of the Innocents. As the slayers approach, the lamb is removed, and the destruction of the boys promptly begins, the mothers uttering a vain prayer for mercy. The prostrate children address their appeal to the angel, and receive in reply the familiar admonition *Adhuc sustinete*.

With the entrance of Rachel, accompanied by two *Consolatrices*, begins the most ambitious part of the composition, which might be called the *Lamentatio Rachelis*.[1] Over the bodies of the dead boys Rachel sings a succession of four laments, interrupted by comforting assurances from her companions, and supported by them in her moments of fainting.

After the consolers have conducted Rachel from the scene, the angel sings the antiphon *Sinite parvulos*, in response to which the slaughtered Innocents rise and enter the choir. Meanwhile, in dumb show, Herod is removed from the throne in favour of his son Archelaus. The action ends with a scene representing the return of the Holy Family from Egypt and their departure into Galilee.

The Fleury play shows a notable advance over the versions already examined, both in the enlargement of familiar elements and in the addition of new roles. The procession of the lamb, the killing of the children, and the lament of Rachel are all somewhat amplified beyond what we have found in the pieces from Laon and Limoges; and the scope of the play is greatly increased through the presence of Herod and the Holy Family.[2] The result of these modifications is a highly successful composition, both in its arrangement and in its completeness. The Innocents, for example, enter processionally at the outset, subsequently pass before Herod, perish at the hands of Herod's soldiers, and at the end of the play are resuscitated. The *lamentatio* is enlarged both through an extension of the utterances of Rachel and her consolers, and through the presence and unavailing appeal of the group of Jewish mothers. With similar care are

[1] Böhme (p. 110) conjectures—not very plausibly—that the presence of *two* comforters here may reflect the use of *two* midwives in the shepherd plays.

[2] In connexion with the dramatization of the flight of the Holy Family should be noticed the representation of this event in dumb-show as part of the revels on Innocents' Day in the cathedral of Padua. See above, i, 107–8.

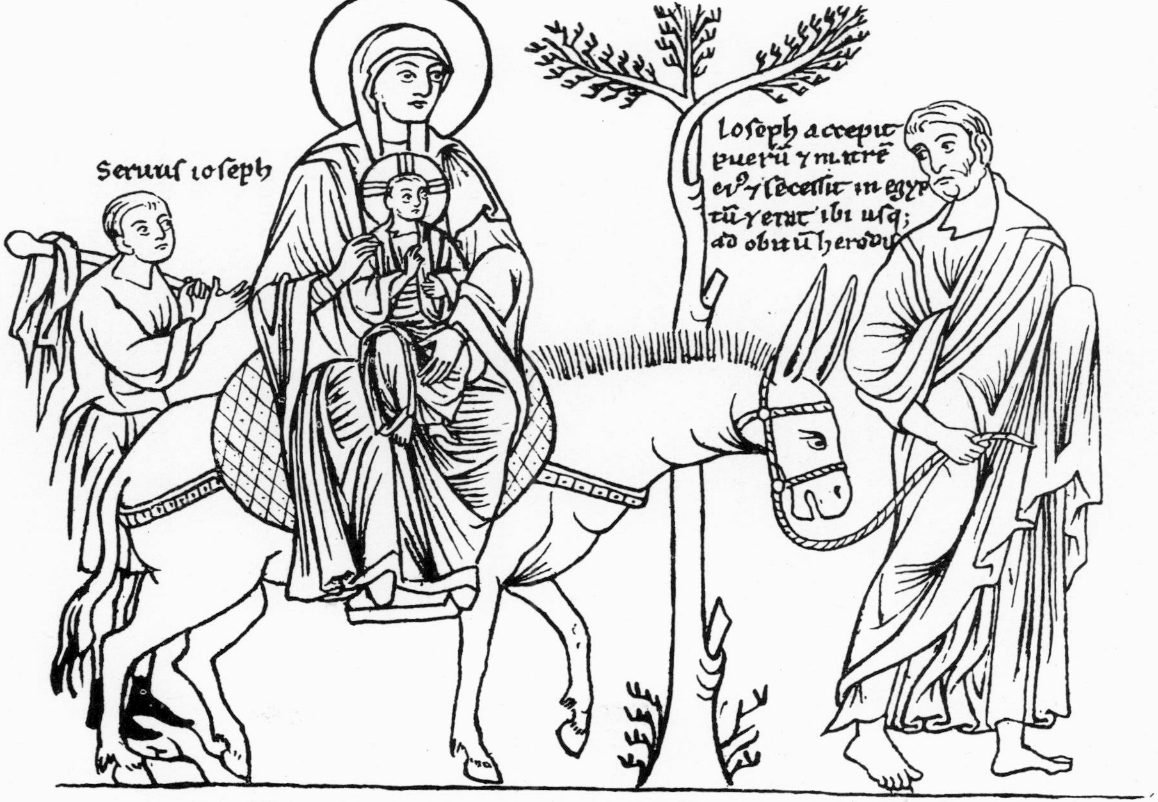


XVI. The Flight to Egypt, from the *Hortus Deliciarum* of Herrad of Landsberg

developed the roles of Herod and the Holy Family. Herod enters ceremoniously at the opening of the play, and after the flight of the family of Joseph, appears in a scene in which he orders the general slaughter. Finally his death and the accession of Archelaus appropriately precede the return of the refugees from Egypt.

For his text, the author has drawn, to a striking extent, upon the liturgy and the Vulgate. The three processional pieces at the beginning are well-known antiphons.[1] The scenes in which the Holy Family appear arise ultimately, of course, from the following narrative in the second chapter of St Matthew:[2]

13. Qui cum recessissent, ecce angelus Domini apparuit in somnis Joseph, dicens: Surge, et accipe puerum et matrem ejus, et fuge in Ægyptum, et esto ibi usque dum dicam tibi. Futurum est enim ut Herodes quærat puerum ad perdendum eum.

14. Qui consurgens accepit puerum et matrem ejus nocte, et secessit in Ægyptum.

15. Et erat ibi usque ad obitum Herodis, ut adimpleretur quod dictum est a Domino per prophetam dicentem: Ex Ægypto vocavi filium meum....

19. Defuncto autem Herode, ecce angelus Domini apparuit in somnis Joseph in Ægypto,

20. Dicens: Surge, et accipe puerum et matrem ejus, et vade in terram Israel, defuncti sunt enim qui quærebant animam pueri.

21. Qui consurgens accepit puerum et matrem ejus, et venit in terram Israel.

22. Audiens autem quod Archelaus regnaret in Judæa pro Herode patre suo, timuit illo ire; et admonitus in somnis, secessit in partes Galilææ.

23. Et veniens habitavit in civitate quæ vocatur Nazareth, ut adimpleretur quod dictum est per prophetas: Quoniam Nazaræus vocabitur.

From this account, it appears, the speeches of the angel to Joseph, at the beginning of the action, are adapted directly. Joseph's reply, however, is a liturgical antiphon. With the exception of five leonine hexameters, not found elsewhere, the scene in which Herod takes counsel against the Innocents (*Rex, in æternum . . . ense perire*) is generally similar to the closing part of certain versions of the *Officium Stellæ*.[3] The scene of the killing of the children (*Salve, Agnus . . . fratrum vestrorum*) is formed from a variety of sources, the liturgical *Agnus Dei* and the responsory *Sub altare* supplying three of the speeches.[4] The appeal of the

[1] These, and the other liturgical pieces contained in the play, are referred to in the notes to the text itself.

[2] Matt. ii, 13–5, 19–23.

[3] See, for example, above, pp. 55–6, 96.

[4] See above, pp. 108, 109.

mothers (*Oremus . . . vite*) appears to be an original hexameter, and the succeeding speech of the angel to the prostrate victims probably derives from a passage of Isaiah: *Expergiscimini et laudate, qui habitatis in pulvere.*[1]

The lament of Rachel consists of a part in verse, and another in prose. Among the verses (*Heu! teneri . . . lacrimando dolorem*), for which no sources can be cited, are a number of lines found also in the plays from Laon and Freising.[2] Of the part in prose, the first three speeches (*Quid tu . . . Deum auxilietur*) represent the complete text of a well-known Notkerian sequence, which, as we shall see, forms also a substantial part of the play from Freising.[3] Rachel's final speech is an antiphon from Lauds of Good Friday.

Of the four remaining speeches of the play, the first and the last are traditional antiphons. The utterance of the resuscitated children is a passage from the sequence *Festa Christi*,[4] and the address of the angel to Joseph is adapted either from the narrative of St Matthew quoted above,[5] or from some liturgical piece.[6]

In summary, then, the text of the Fleury play might be characterized as a mosaic of passages from the service-books and the Vulgate, in the midst of which appear certain passages of original verse. Considering the wide range from which the liturgical passages are selected, one must remark that they are chosen with skill and appropriateness. The sequence of events is smooth and orderly, and the utterances of the chief personages are not wanting in force and vividness. Particularly fortunate is the dramatic adaptation of the Notkerian composition *Quid tu, virgo*, supplying Rachel's consolers with touching appeals such as *Quam te decent genarum rivuli?*

Concerning the staging of the play the rubrics give us considerable information. The closing *Te Deum* points to a performance at the end of Matins, probably, but not necessarily, on the feast of the Innocents.[7] Numerous details of impersonation have been mentioned in the summary of the action given above. As to the location of the action in the church, however, we are left in some doubt. Since towards the close of the play the resuscitated children are said to enter the choir (*surgentes Pueri*

[1] Isaiah xxvi, 19.

[2] See pp. 106, 120.

[3] For passage in the Freising play, see below, p. 120. For the text of the sequence *Quid tu, virgo, mater* (Chevalier, *R.H.*, no. 16675) see Notes, p. 454.

[4] Chevalier, *R.H.*, no. 6111. For the complete text see Notes, p. 454.

[5] See Matt. ii, 19–20.

[6] As to the liturgical possibilities see Notes, p. 455.

[7] For observations upon this matter see Notes, p. 455.

*intrent chorum*), we may infer that the play was performed in some other part of the building, probably in the space in front of the choir-screen, between the nave and the choir. At the opening of the performance the boys pass in procession *per monasterium*, and from the *Officium Stellæ* of Fleury we know that the *præsepe*, which is used in the present play, was stationed *ad januas monasterii*.[1] Hence one might infer that at least part of the action occurred at the door in the south side of the nave leading from the cloister into the church.[2] But in the texts under consideration the word *monasterium* probably denotes not the monastic buildings, such as the cloister and its conventual surroundings, but merely the church itself, or more particularly the nave.[3] It would appear, therefore, that the phrase *per monasterium* means merely that the boys approached the playing-space 'through the church', and that a crib placed *ad januas monasterii* might be near any door of the church building. In any case, the space for the performance had to be sufficiently large to provide places for Jerusalem, the manger at Bethlehem, Egypt, and the locality in which the Innocents were slaughtered. We may, then, conjecture that in addition to the space in front of the choir-screen the players used also parts of the nave and aisles.

## IV

In marked contrast to the *Ordo Rachelis* of Fleury, both in literary texture and in general organization, is the following dramatization of this theme from the cathedral of Freising:[4]

### Ordo Rachelis

Angelus:

*Ortum pastoris, Pastores, nuncio uobis,*
*Qui redimet proprias, pastor et agnus, oues.*
*Pannis obductus, decus orbis, gloria regum,*
*In feno situs est qui cibat omne quod est.*
*In Bethleem uite panem queratis eundem.*[5]

[1] See above, pp. 84, 89.

[2] The architectural arrangement of the monastic church at Fleury is discussed in some detail by Young, *op. cit.*, pp. 37–41. In that place the present writer—with what now seems to him undue assurance—inferred that the word *monasterium* denoted the monastic buildings, such as the cloister, apart from the church.

[3] For a clear example of this use of *monasterium* see above, i, 295.

[4] Munich, Staatsbibl., MS lat. 6264, Lectionarium Frisingense sæc. xi–xii, fol. 27$^{v}$, previously edited by Du Méril, pp. 171–5; Weinhold, pp. 62–5; Young, *op. cit.*, pp. 42–5. Weinhold's text is reprinted by Froning, pp. 871–4. The MS provides musical notation.

[5] Du Méril reasonably conjectures that after this line the second line of a distich has been lost.

Angeli:

*Gloria in excelsis Deo!*

Pastores:

*Quis audiuit his similia,*
*ab eterno mirabilia?*
*O mirandum puerperium,*
*tantum habens ministerium!*
*Transeamus ergo Bethleem*
*explorare rei seriem.*

Venientes ad Presepe dicant:

*O regem celi, cui celicole famulantur!*
*Clauditur in stabulo concludens cuncta pugillo,*
*Despectissimus in terris habitus, et summus in astris.*

Chorus dicat:

*Pastores, dicite quidnam uidistis?*

Respondeant Pastores:

*Infantem uidimus pannis inuolutvm.*

Angelus ad Ioseph cantet:

*Ioseph, Ioseph surge!*
*Ioseph, in Egyptum cum matre feras cito Christum,*
*Ne cum mactandis pueris rex mactet et ipsum.*
*Admonitus redeas ubi nex, fraus, rexque quiescunt.*

Ioseph surgens de stratu dicat ad Mariam:

*Quod prophetica dudum uox insonuit,*
*angelica tuba nunc admonuit.*
*Intrat Egyptum lux mundi, Dominus,*
*leui carnis nube superpositus.*
*Ydolis Egipti corruentibus,*
*adest salus expectata gentibus.*

Iterum Ioseph dicat ad Mariam:

*Angelus a patria   nos precipit ire, Maria;*
*Rex fugiendus erit   puerum qui perdere querit.*

Maria dicat ad Ioseph:

*Omnia dura pati   uitando pericula nati*
*Mater sum presto;   iam uadam; tu comes esto.*

Ioseph pergens in Egiptum cantet:

*Egipte, noli flere,* ⟨*quia dominator tuus veniet tibi, ante cujus conspectum movebuntur abyssi, liberare populum suum de manu potentium.* Versus: *Ecce dominator Dominus cum virtute veniet.*⟩[1]

Internuncius properans ad Regem d*icat*:

*Felix et uiuus   sit Rex per secula diuus.*

Rex Internuncio respo*ndeat*:

*Quid rumoris habes?   Est pax an bellica clades?*

[1] Responsory of Matins of the third Sunday before Christmas. See Hartker, p. 28.

Internuncius respond*eat*:

*Reges illi quos misisti*
*explorare cunas Christi,*
*iusso calle permutato,*
*redierunt, te frustrato.*
*Quid facturus sis exquire;*
*constat eos non redire.*

Rex Internuncio resp*o*nd*eat*:

*Rex nouus ut pereat, regisque furor requiescat,*
*Omnimodis, ui, fraude, dolis, mecum satagatis.*

Internuncius dicat:

*In Bethleem natum probat istum pagina uatum.*[1]
*In qua mactetur mas lactens quisquis habetur,*
*Nullus ut euadat; sic puer ipse cadat.*

Rex de solio prosiliens can*tet*:

*Sic, sic quando quidem delusus sencio fraudem,*
*Incendium meum ruina extinguam.*

Armiger Regi respondens et cantet:[2]

*Ecce*[3] *miles ego regius;*
*ecce uindex regis gladius,*
*paratus ad omne facinus*
*quod iubebit noster Dominus,*
*qui placabit iram principis*
*multa strage turbe simplicis.*

Rex ad Armigerum:

*Etatis bime pueros fac ense perire.*

Armiger interficiens Pueros dicat:

*Disce mori, puer.*

Angelus e longinquo can*tet*:

*Christus sospes abiit, strages quem tanta requrit;*
*Illius in populum trux furit in uacuum.*

Chorus cantet:

*Hostis Herodes impie,*
*Christum uenire qui times.*[4]

Rachel plorans super Pueros d*icat*:

*O dolor! O patrum mutataque gaudia matrum*
*Ad lugubres luctus; lacrimarum fundite fluctus!*
*Ah!*[5] *teneri partus, laceros quos cernimus artus!*
*Heu! dulces nati, sola rabie iugulati!*
*Quid commisistis, quod talia facta subistis?*

[1] Du Méril reasonably conjectures that after this line the second line of a distich has been lost.

[2] cantet] Reading doubtful.

[3] Ecce] Preceded by an erasure of the words *Miles ego*, and of others.

[4] For the text of the hymn *Hostis Herodes impie* see below, p. 447.

[5] Ah] Ach, with the *c* expunged (MS).

*Cur uitam uobis liuor subtraxit Herodis,*
*Quam nondum uere uos cognouistis habere?*
*Heu! quem nec pietas nec uestra coercuit etas!*
*Ach! matres misere, que cogimur ista uidere!*
*Cur autem natis patimur superesse necatis?*
*Saltim morte pari nobis licet hos comitari.*

Consolatrix acced*at*:

*Quid tu, uirgo,*
*mater, ploras, Rachel formosa,*
*cuius uultum Iacob electat?*
*Ceu sororis annicule*
*lippitudo eum*[1] *iuuat!*

Terg*at* hic Consolatrix oculos Rachelis:

*Terge, terge, mater, fluentes oculos.*
*Quam te decent genarum rimule?*

Iterum Rachel d*icat*:

*Heu, heu, heu! Quid tu me incusas fletus incassum fudisse,*
*Cum sim orbata nato, paupertatem meam qui solus curaret,*
*Qui non hostibus cederet angustos terminos, quos michi Iacob acquisiuit?*[2]

Consolatrix accedens d*icat*:

*Numquid flendus est iste,*[3] *qui regnum possedit celeste,*
*Quique preces frequentans miseris fratribus apud Deum auxiliatur?*
*Te Deum laudamus.*[4]

The Freising play begins, somewhat abruptly, with a scene representing the visit of the shepherds to the *præsepe* at Bethlehem. Without transition, this is followed by a representation of the flight of the Holy Family. Commanded by the angel to depart into Egypt, Joseph rises from the ground, explains to Mary the angelic message, and receives her willing consent to the undertaking. On their journey Joseph sings the liturgical piece *Ægypte, noli flere*.

The action now shifts to the court of Herod, to whom a messenger reports the flight of the Magi and urges that their escape be prevented. Ignoring the precise counsel of the messenger, Herod immediately commands the death of the new-born king, and the messenger proposes that the slaughter include all the male children in Bethlehem, a proposal which Herod ardently adopts. A soldier offers to carry out the massacre, and receives Herod's final commission (*Ætatis bimæ . . . perire*).

[1] eum] An unintelligible correction appears to have been attempted (MS).

[2] Followed by an erasure covering two or three words.

[3] Numquid . . . iste] Written twice (MS).

[4] The remaining five lines on the page are largely blank. The few passages of text are irrelevant or mostly illegible. One illegible passage appears to begin *Iterum Rachel*.

From the text one infers that the actual slaughter of the children is effected by a single soldier, who, as he dispatches each boy, utters his brief *Disce mori, puer*, without response from his victims or protest from their mothers. From afar an angel rejoices in the safety of Jesus, and the chorus comments by singing some part of the hymn *Hostis Herodes*.

The play concludes with the *Lamentatio Rachelis*, containing two utterances from Rachel and two from her consoler. Rachel's first speech, in leonine hexameters, contains some six lines which we have already seen in the play from Fleury.[1] The three succeeding speeches, in prose, are drawn from the sequence *Quid tu, virgo*, which we have found similarly employed in the Fleury piece.[2]

Since the author at Freising has accomplished a rather thoroughgoing versifying of the text, the sources that he may have used are generally transformed and concealed.[3] The opening shepherd scene, for example, differs considerably from what we have found in the extant versions of the *Officium Pastorum*,[4] but resembles, in part, the brief scenes of the *Pastores* in some texts of the *Officium Stellæ*.[5] The scene representing the flight of the Holy Family has in common with the parallel part of the Fleury play only the responsory *Ægypte, noli flere*.[6] The scene of which Herod is the centre discloses certain inevitable resemblances to passages in several versions of the *Officium Stellæ*; but the tenuousness of these likenesses only emphasizes the independence of the Freising author.[7] In the text accompanying the actual slaughter of the children he is original, except in using the hymn *Hostis Herodes*, which appears also in the Epiphany play from Bilsen.[8] Only in the lament of Rachel does our author resort copiously, as we have seen, to a liturgical source, and only in one speech of Rachel does he employ a noticeable number of verses found elsewhere.

Although, then, a large part of the Freising play shows striking originality in literary composition, in comparison with the Fleury version it reveals palpable defects in dramatic scope, sequence, and motivation.[9] The scene of the shepherds, for example, not only is irrelevant to the rest of the Freising play in

[1] See above, pp. 112–3.

[2] See above, p. 112. For the text of the sequence see below, p. 454.

[3] This aspect of the play is discussed by Meyer, p. 48, Anz, p. 78, and Young, *op. cit.*, pp. 47–50.

[4] See above, pp. 11 sqq.

[5] See above, for example, pp. 71, 96.

[6] See above, p. 111.

[7] See Young, *op. cit.*, pp. 49–50.

[8] See above, p. 80.

[9] These matters are discussed by Meyer, pp. 45–8; Chambers, ii, 50; Anz, p. 78.

content, but also lacks a transitional connexion with the scene of the flight to Egypt which follows. As motivation for this second scene is required at least a reference to the escape of the Magi and to the threatening anger of Herod. The flight of the Holy Family is somewhat more fully developed than the parallel part of the Fleury play, in that it contains a dialogue between Joseph and Mary;[1] but the absence of provision for the return from Egypt conveys an impression of incompleteness. A similar impression arises from the silence of the play as to the ultimate fate of Herod. A defect in the sequence of the action connected with Herod appears in the fact, already noticed, that when he is informed of the secret departure of the Magi, and is advised to capture them, he immediately issues, not the expected order for preventing this escape, but a command for the death of the new king. This defect in dramatic sequence—present, to be sure, in the Gospel narrative—is skilfully repaired in the Fleury play, where Herod, before ordering the slaughter, is not only informed of the escape of the Magi, but is also explicitly advised to insure the death of the new-born child. Particularly paltry in the Freising play is the role of the Innocents. Whereas in the Fleury version they enter processionally at the outset, appear during Herod's colloquy with his armour-bearer, suffer martyrdom, and subsequently come to life again, in the play before us they merely appear silently in the brief scene of the slaughter. Finally one observes the abruptness with which the piece ends. In view of these numerous faults in composition one would like to regard the *Ordo Rachelis* of Freising as avowedly a mere tentative dramatic sketch. In the manuscript, however, it is presented as a completed effort, with an introductory rubric, and with the *Te Deum* as the conventional liturgical ending.[2]

Although the rubrics are scanty, they at least point towards adequate *mise en scène*. The playing-space is equipped with some sort of structural *præsepe*, with a throne for Herod, and probably with other stage-properties.[3] At least a few details of stage-action are provided for Joseph, Herod, and Rachel. The *Te Deum* at the end of the play seems to imply a performance at Matins, possibly on Innocents Day.[4]

[1] Joseph's reference to the falling of the Egyptian idols, and Mary's speech, have parallels in a dramatic text from Benediktbeuern. See below, pp. 465–6.

[2] For further observations on the defects of the play see Chambers, ii, 50.

[3] For conjectures as to staging see Böhme, p. 114.

[4] As to the liturgical position of such a play see above, p. 116.

## V

In the light of the facts now before us we are at liberty to consider briefly, in conclusion, two general matters relating to the extant versions of the *Ordo Rachelis*: namely, their textual interrelations, and the question as to whether the Innocents play arose as a mere extension of the *Officium Stellæ* or as an independant dramatic invention.[1]

From the textual similarities of the several versions Meyer has inferred that the original form of the *Ordo Rachelis*—upon which the Freising play, for example, rests—arose in Germany; that a version similar to the Freising play is the basis, or inspiration, of the Laon version; and that the Fleury play is indebted both to the Freising play (or its original) and to the Innocents scene from Laon.[2] From the fact that the simple Limoges text consists merely in a dialogue of lament and consolation appended to the responsory *Sub altare*, and that likewise in the plays from Fleury and Laon a dialogue of lament and consolation is associated with at least part of the same responsory, Meyer further infers that a dialogue between Rachel and her comforter is the kernel of the plays which we call collectively *Ordo Rachelis*. Thus from a lost original in South Germany, he thinks, developed, on the one hand, the Freising play, and by another tradition, a lost French intermediary which is the source of the compositions of Limoges, Laon, and Fleury.

Through a still more elaborate and tenuous investigation of textual relationships Anz concludes that the piece from Limoges is an early and independent production; that this composition, or a related one, is the source of a substantial part of the Rachel scene in the Laon play; and that the Fleury play is indebted to both the Laon and the Freising plays, or to their originals. According to this view, then, the original of the extant plays is a version similar to the Limoges text; and from this original developed the two traditions which produced respectively the plays of Laon and Freising, and which are in some fashion united in the version from Fleury.[3]

My scepticism as to the details of these attempted demonstrations I have expressed elsewhere, along with my own conclusion that we can be sure only of a French tradition which includes

[1] These matters are treated more amply by Young, *op. cit.*, pp. 52–65.

[2] See Meyer, pp. 44–8.

[3] See Anz, pp. 73–8.

the compositions from Limoges and Laon, of a German tradition represented by the play from Freising, and of a union of the two traditions, in some manner, in the play from Fleury.[1]

As to whether the *Ordo Rachelis* originated as a mere extension of the *Officium Stellæ* or as an independent creation, we cannot, I think, be certain. Evidence for an independent origin appears in the fact that the characteristic and central element of this type of play—the lament of Rachel—is found in the version from Limoges, in an early manuscript, as a separate dramatic composition attached to the responsory *Sub altare*. In two plays, moreover—those of Laon and Fleury—the association of the lament with at least part of the responsory persists. Still further, the Innocents scene in such a play as that from Laon contains almost nothing else than the lament and the sentences from the responsory. From these facts alone one might reasonably infer that the lament originated as a trope of the responsory, as at Limoges, and was then appended to the *Officium Stellæ* as the chief element in a scene of the Innocents. On the other hand, however, we have observed that several versions of the *Officium Stellæ* end with an explicit promise of an Innocents scene, and that the Innocents plays of Fleury and Freising contain passages which seem to be borrowed from the Magi plays.

The probability, therefore, seems to be as follows. Under the general influences that inspired the great body of liturgical poetry, arose a trope, or tropes, of the responsory *Sub altare*, which are adequately represented by the text from Limoges. Certain ecclesiastical writers, wishing to carry out dramatically the implications of Herod's threats at the end of various versions of the *Officium Stellæ*, used such a trope as the essential part of a scene representing the slaughter of the Innocents. The *Ordo Rachelis* thus created sometimes served as the conclusion of an *Officium Stellæ*, as at Laon; sometimes, as at Fleury and Freising, it formed a separate play. The relative simplicity of the Innocents scene at Laon points toward the probability that the use of the trope in a concluding scene of the Magi play preceded its use in an independent dramatic composition.

[1] See Young, *op. cit.*, pp. 56–63.

CHAPTER XXI

# THE PROCESSION OF PROPHETS

AMONG the several separate groups of dramatic performances designed for the Christmas season there remains for consideration a small body of pieces, presented on Christmas Day or a week later, containing utterances of the prophets concerning the coming of Christ. A convenient medieval designation for this kind of play is *Ordo Prophetarum*.[1]

## I

The play of the prophets differs from all the other dramatic compositions of Christmas in its origin, for it arises not from tropes, antiphons, responsories, or lyric poems, but from a sermon. This substantial homiletic piece, found among the spurious works attributed to St Augustine, is entitled *Contra Judæos, Paganos, et Arianos Sermo de Symbolo*.[2] Although the Augustinian authorship is now discredited, the attribution to the great bishop persisted throughout the Middle Ages. The sermon appears to have been written during the fifth or sixth century.[3] Of the twenty-two chapters, or sections, into which the discourse is divided in the modern edition, we are concerned only with the eight (xi–xviii) which are addressed specifically to the Jews, and which undertake to convict them of error through utterances of their own prophets and of certain pagans. The preacher summons the selected witnesses singly by name, and announces their successive testimonies.[4]

The fame of this part of the sermon is established through the fact that almost the whole of it is frequently found during the Middle Ages as a separate liturgical *lectio* for use in Matins of Christmas or of some other day of the Christmas season. The use of it as the sixth *lectio* of Matins is seen, for example, in the following text found in a lectionary of the twelfth century from Arles:[5]

[1] This designation is attached to the play from Laon printed below, pp. 145 sqq. For bibliography see Notes, p. 456.

[2] Printed in *Sancti Aurelii Augustini . . . Opera*, viii, Paris, 1688, Appendix, col. 11–20; Migne, *P.L.*, xlii, 1117 sqq.

[3] For further discussion of this point see Young, *Ordo Prophetarum*, pp. 2–3. For some discussion of the real, and alleged, relations of this sermon and its dramatic derivatives to Greek sermons see La Piana, pp. 283–302, 308–9, and Young, pp. 15, 36–7.

[4] A translation of this part of the sermon is given by Stone, *Pseudo-Augustinian Sermon*, pp. 200–8.

[5] Paris, Bibl. Nat., MS lat. 1018, Lectio-

SERMO BEATI AUGUSTINI EPISCOPI DE NATALE DOMINI

Lectio Sexta.

Vos, inquam, conuenio, o Iudei, qui usque in hodiernum diem negatis Filium Dei. Nonne uox uestra est illa, quando eum uidebatis miracula facientem atque temptantes dicebatis: Quousque animas nostras suspendis? Si tu es Christus, dic nobis palam. Ille autem uos ad considerationem mittebat miraculorum, dicens: Opera que ego facio ipsa testimonium perhibent de me; vt Christo testimonium dicerent non uerba, sed facta. Vos autem non agnoscentes Saluatorem qui operabatur salutem in medio uestre terre, adicientes in malo aistis: Tu de te ipso testimonium dicis; testimonium tuum non est uerum. Sed ad hec ille quid uobis responderit, aduertere noluistis. Nonne scriptum est in lege uestra quod duorum hominum testimonium uerum sit? Preuaricatores legis, intendite legem. Testimonium queritis de Christo: in lege uestra scriptum est quod duorum hominum testimonium uerum sit. Procedant ex lege non tantum duo, sed eciam plures testes Christi, et conuincant auditores legis, non factores.

Dic, Ysaya,[1] testimonium Christo. *Ecce*, inquit, *uirgo in utero concipiet et pariet filium, et uocabitur nomen eius Hemanuhel*, quod est interpretatum: Nobiscum Deus.[2]

Accedat et alius testis. Dic et tu, Iheremia,[3] testimonium Christo. *Hic est*, inquit, *Deus noster, et non | estimabitur alius absque illo qui inuenit omnem uiam scientie et dedit eam Iacop puero suo et*[4] *Israel dilecto suo. Post hec in terris uisus est, et cum hominibus conuersatus est.*[5] Ecce duo testes idonei ex lege uestra ad quorum testimonia non sunt compuncta corda uestra. Sed alij atque alij ex lege testes Christi introducantur, ut frontes durissime inimicorum conterantur.

Veniat et ille Danihel[6] sanctus, iuuenis quidem etate, senior uero scientia ac mansuetudine, et conuincat omnes falsos testes et sicut conuicit seniores impudicos, ita suo testimonio Christi conterat inimicos. Dic, sancte Danihel, dic de Christo quod nosti. *Cum uenerit*, inquit, *Sanctus*

narium Arelatense sæc. xii–xiii, fol. 129$^r$–132$^v$ (A). This is the text printed by Sepet, pp. 3–8, and re-edited from the MS by Young, *op. cit.*, pp. 5–10. This *lectio* is found in numerous MSS. A text of the eleventh century is found in Paris, Bibl. Nat., MS lat. 16819, Lectionarium Compendiense, fol. 12$^v$–14$^r$. See Young, p. 4. In the foot-notes I indicate the marginal entries and unusual rubrications found in Rome, Bibl. Vatic., MS Vat. Regin. 125, Lectionarium Forcalqueriense sæc. xiii, fol. 74$^r$–76$^v$ (B), and Oxford, Bibl. Bodl., MS Canon. Liturg. 391, Lectionarium sæc. xii, fol. 11$^v$–14$^r$ (C).

[1] Ysaya] In the right margin, opposite the line in which the name occurs, is written the rubric *Ysayas* (A. C). All the marginal entries in C appear to be of the fifteenth century. In the left margin, a later hand has written *i^a prophetia* (B).

[2] Ecce inquit . . . Nobiscum Deus] Encircled by red lines, with marginal numeral *i* (B).

[3] Iheremia] Opposite this name in the margin *Iheremias* (A); *Ieremias* (C).

[4] dedit . . . suo et] Written in the margin by a later hand (A).

[5] Hic est inquit . . . conuersatus est] encircled by red lines, with marginal numeral *ii* (B).

[6] Danihel] Opposite this name in the margin *Daniel* (C).

*Sanctorum, cessabit unctio.*[1] Quare, illo presente, cui insultantes dicebatis: Tu de te testimonium dicis, testimonium tuum non est uerum; cessauit unctio uestra? Nisi quia ipse est qui uenerat Sanctus Sanctorum. Si enim, sicut uos dicitis, non dum uenit, sed expectatur ut ueniat Sanctus Sanctorum, demonstrate unctionem; si autem, quod uerum est, cessauit uestra unctio, agnoscite uenisse Sanctum Sanctorum. Ipse est enim et lapis ille abscisus de monte sine manibus concidentium, id est Christus natus de uirgine sine manibus complectentium, qui tantum creuit ut mons magnus fieret, et impleret uniuersam faciem terre. De quo monte dicit propheta: Venite, ascendamus in montem Domini; et de quo Dauid dicit: Mons Dei, mons uber, ut quid suspicamini montes incaseatos, montem in quo placuit Deo habitare in ipso. Cum enim ipse Dominus Christus discipulos suos interrogaret quem dicerent esse homines Filium hominis, responderunt: Alij Helyam, alij Iheremiam, aut unum ex prophetis; et ille, vt quid suspicamini montes incaseatos, montem in quo placuit Deo habitare in eo, hunc cognouit Petrus dicens: Tu es Christus, Filius Dei. Agnouit montem et ascendit in montem; testimonium dix*it* ueritati, et dilectus est a ueritate. Super petram fundatus est Petrus, ut montem susciperet illum amando quem ter negauerat timendo.

Dic et Moyses,[2] legislator, dux populi Israel, testimonium Christo. *Prophetam*, inquit, *uobis suscitabit Deus de fratribus uestris; omnis anima que non audierit prophetam illum*, *exterminabitur de populo suo.*[3] Prophetam autem dictum Christum ipsum audi in Euangelio dicentem: Non est, inquit, propheta sine honore, nisi in patria sua.[4]

Accedat autem Dauid[5] sanctus, testis fidelis, ex cuius semine processit ipse | cui lex et prophete testimonium dicunt, dicat et ipse de Christo. *Adorabunt*, inquit, *eum omnes reges terre, omnes gentes seruient illi.*[6] Cui seruient? dic, cui seruient? Vis audire cui? *Dixit Dominus Domino meo: Sede ad dexteram meam, donec ponam inimicos tuos scabellum pedum tuorum.*[7] Et expressius atque nominatim: Quare, inquit, tumultuate sunt gentes, et populi meditati sunt inania? Astiterunt reges terre, et principes conuenerunt in unum aduersus Dominum et aduersus Christum eius.

Accedat et alius testis. Dic et tu, Abacuch[8] propheta, testimonium de Christo. *Domine*, inquit, *audiui auditum tuum et timui; consideraui opera tua et expaui.*[9] Que opera Dei iste miratus expauit? Numquid fabricam mundi

[1] Cum uenerit . . . cessabit unctio] Encircled by red lines, with marginal numeral *iii* (B).

[2] Moyses] Opposite this name in the margin *Moyses* (C).

[3] Prophetam inquit . . . de populo suo] Encircled by red lines, with illegible marginal numeral (B).

[4] Non est . . . patria sua] Encircled by red lines, without marginal numeral (B).

[5] Dauid] Opposite this name in the margin *Dauid* (C).

[6] Adorabunt . . . seruient illi] Encircled by red lines, with marginal numeral *v* (B).

[7] Dixit Dominus . . . pedum tuorum] Encircled by red lines, without marginal numeral (B).

[8] Abacuch] Opposite this name in the margin *Abacuc* (C).

[9] Domine . . . et expaui] Encircled by red lines, with marginal numeral *vi*[a] (B).

iste miratus expauit? Absit. Sed, audi, aliquid expauit. *In medio*, inquit, *duum animalium cognosceris. Opera tua*, *Deus*, *Uerbum caro factum est.* In medio duum animalium cognosceris. Qui quousque descendisti, expauescere me fecisti; Uerbum, per quod facta sunt omnia, in presepe iacuisti. Agnouit bos possessorem suum, et asinus presepe Domini sui. In medio duum animalium cognosceris. Quid est in medio duum animalium cognosceris, nisi aut in medio duorum testamentorum, aut in medio duorum latronum, aut in medio Moysi[1] et Helye cum eo in monte sermocinantium? Ambulauit, inquit, Uerbum et exiuit in campis. Verbum caro factum est et habitauit in nobis. Hoc et Iheremias ait: *Post hec in terris uisus est*, *et cum hominibus conuersatus est.*[2] Ecce quemadmodum sibi conueniunt testes ueritatis, ecce quemadmodum conuincunt filios falsitatis. Sufficiunt uobis ista, o Iudei, an adhuc ad uestram confusionem ex lege et ex gente uestra alios introducemus testes, ut illi testimonium perhibeant cui perdita mente insultantes dicebatis: Tu de te ipso testimonium dicis, testimonium[3] tuum non est verum? Quod si uelim ex lege et ex prophetis omnia que de Christo dicta sunt colligere, facilius me tempus quam copia deseret.

Verumptamen senem[4] illum ex gente uestra natum, sed in errore uestro non relictum, Symeonem sanctum in medio introducam, qui meruit teneri decrepitus in hac luce quousque uideret lucem. Quem quidem iam etas compellebat ire, sed expectabat suscipĕre quem sciebat uenire; cum iste senex admonitus esset a Spiritu sancto quod non ante moreretur quam uideret Christum Dei natum, quem cognoscens perrex*it* ad templum. | Vbi uero eum portari matris manibus uidit et diuinam infantiam pia senectus agnouit, tulit infantem in manibus suis. Ille quidem Christum ⟨infantem⟩[5] ferebat, sed Christus senem regebat. Regebat qui portabatur ne ille ante promissum a corpore solueretur. Quid tamen dixerit, quem tamen confessus fuerit aduertite inimici, non Christi sed uestri. Benedicens Dominum exclamauit senex ille et dixit: *Nunc dimittis*, *Domine*, *seruum tuum in pace*, *quia uiderunt oculi mei salutare tuum.*[6]

Illi eciam parentes Iohannis, Zacharias et Elisabeth,[7] iuuenes steriles, in senecta fecundi, dicant eciam ipsi testimonium Christo; dicant de Christo quid sentiant et testem idoneum Christo nutriant. Aiunt enim suo paruulo nato: *Tu puer propheta Altissimi uocaberis*, *preibis enim ante faciem Domini parare uiam eius.*[8] Ipsique matri et uirgini, Helisabeth ait:

[1] Moysi] The last letter of this word is blurred in the MS.

[2] Post hec . . . conuersatus est] Encircled by red lines, with marginal numeral *vii* (B).

[3] dicis testimonium] Supplied in the right margin by a later hand (A).

[4] senem] Opposite this word in the margin *Symeon* (C).

[5] Following Sepet, I supply the word *infantem* from the Benedictine edition of the entire sermon *Contra Judæos*, mentioned above. The word is absent from A, B, and C.

[6] Nunc dimittis . . . salutare tuum] Encircled by red lines, with marginal numeral *viii*, written twice (B).

[7] Zacharias et Elisabeth] Opposite these names in the margin *Zacharias*, *Helisabeth* (C).

[8] Tu puer . . . uiam eius] Encircled by red lines, with marginal numeral *ix* (B).

*Vnde mihi hoc ut ueniat Mater Domini mei ad me? Ecce enim ut facta est uox salutationis tue in auribus meis, exultauit in gaudio infans in utero meo.*[1] Intelligens enim Iohannes[2] matrem Domini sui uenisse ad suam matrem inter ipsas angustias uteri adhuc positus, motu salutauit quem uoce non poterat. Qui postea ipse Iohannes precursor et amicus, humillimus et fidelissimus seruus, testis fidelis idoneus effectus, tanto maior inter natos mulierum quanto existimabatur esse quod non erat. Christum enim eum esse Iudei credebant, sed ille non se esse clamabat dicens: *Quem me suspicamini esse, non sum ego. Sed ecce uenit post me cuius pedum non sum dignus soluere corrigiam calciamenti.*[3] O fidelis testis et amice ueri sponsi, quanto te humiliauisses si ad corrigiam calciamenti eius soluendam dignum te esse dixisses! Sed dum ad hoc non te dignum dicis, Iudeis falsis testibus contradicis. Et hec a te dicta sunt antequam Christum videres, qui cum ad te ipse uenit excelsus humilis, implende dispensationis sue gratia, ut a te baptizaretur qui nullum habebat omnino peccatum, quid responderis, quem cognoueris, quod testimonium protuleris audiant inimici qui audire nolunt. *Ecce*, inquit, *agnus Dei*, *ecce qui tollit peccata mundi.* Et adiecit: *Tu ad me uenis baptizari. Ego a te debeo baptizari.*[4] Agnouit seruus dominum, agnouit uinculis | originalis peccati obligatus ab omni nexu peccati liberum. Agnouit preco iudicem, agnouit creatura creatorem, agnouit paranimphus sponsum. Nam et hec uox Iohannis est: Qui habet sponsam sponsus est; amicus autem sponsi qui stat et audit eum gaudio gaudet propter uocem sponsi.

Sufficiunt uobis ista, O Iudei, sufficiunt uobis tanti testes, tot testimonia ex lege uestra et ex gente uestra? An adhuc inpudentia nimia audebitis dicere quod alterius gentis uel nationis homines Christo deberent testimonium perhibere? Sed si hoc dicitis, respondet quidem ille uobis: Non sum missus nisi ad oues que perierunt domus Israel. Sed, sicut uos in Actibus Apostolorum increpat Paulus, uobis primum oportuerat annuntiare Uerbum Dei, sed quia repulistis illud nec uos dignos uite eterne iudicastis: Ecce, inquit, conuertimus nos ad gentes. Demonstremus eciam nos ex gentibus testimonium Christo fuisse prolatum, quoniam ueritas non tacuit clamando eciam per linguas inimicorum suorum. Nonne quando ille poeta[5] facundissimus inter sua carmina:

*Iam noua progenies*[6] *celo demittitur alto*,[7]

dicebat, Christo testimonium perhibebat? In dubium hoc ueniat nisi alios ex gentibus idoneos testes pluraque dicentes in medio introducam.

[1] Vnde mihi . . . in utero meo] Encircled by red lines, with marginal numeral *x* (B).

[2] Iohannes] Opposite this name in the margin *Iohannes* (C).

[3] Quem me suspicamini . . . corrigiam calciamenti] Encircled by red lines, with marginal numeral *xi* (B).

[4] Ecce inquit agnus . . . debeo baptizari] Encircled by red lines, without marginal numeral (B).

[5] poeta] Opposite this word in the margin *Virgilius* (C).

[6] progenies] proienies (A).

[7] Iam noua . . . demittitur alto] Encircled by red lines, without marginal numeral (B).

Illum, illum[1] regem qui uestram superbiam captiuando perdomuit, Nabuchodonosor, regem scilicet Babilonis, non pretermittam. Dic, Nabuchodonosor, quid in fornace uidisti quando tres uiros iustos iniuste illuc miseras, dic, dic quid tibi fuerit reuelatum. *Nonne,* inquit, *tres uiros misimus in fornace ligatos?* Et aiunt ei: *Vere, rex. Ecce,* inquit, *ego uideo quatuor uiros solutos deambulantes in medio ignis, et corruptio nulla est in eis, et aspectus quarti similis est Filio Dei.*[2] Alienigena, unde tibi hoc? Quis tibi annunciauit Filium Dei? Que lex? Quis propheta tibi annuntiauit Filium Dei? Nondum quidem mundo nascitur et similitudo nascentis a te cognoscitur? Vnde tibi hoc? Quis tibi istud annuntiauit nisi quia sic te diuinus ignis intus illuminauit ut cum illic apud te captiui tenerentur inimici Iudei, sic diceres testimonium Filio Dei? Sed quia in ore duorum uel trium testium stat omne uerbum, sicut ipse Dominus uestram contumaciam confutans: | In lege, inquit, uestra scriptum est quod duorum hominum testimonium uerum sit; etiam ex gentibus tercius testis introducatur ut testimonium ueritatis ex omni parte roboretur.

Quid Sibilla[3] uaticinando etiam de Christo clamauerit in medium proferamus, ut ex uno lapide utrorumque frontes percuciantur, Iudeorum scilicet atque paganorum, atque suo gladio, sicut Golias, Christi omnes percuciantur inimici. Audite quid dixerit:

*Ivdicij*[4] *signum: Tellus sudore madescet;*
*E celo rex adueniet per secla futurus,*
*⟨S⟩cilicet in carne presens ut iudicet orbem,*
*Vnde Deum cernent incredulus atque fidelis*
*Celsum*[5] *cum sanctis, eui iam termino in ipso.*
*Sic anime cum carne aderunt quas iudicat ipse.*
*Cum iacet incultus densis in uepribus orbis,*
*Reicient simulacra uiri, cunctam quoque gazam.*
*Exuret terras ignis, pontumque polumque;* |
*Inquirens tetri portas effringet Auerni;*
*Sanctorum sed enim cuncte lux libera carni,*
*Tradetur;*[6] *sontes eterna flamma cremabit.*
*Occultos actus retegens, tunc quisque loquetur*
*Secreta, atque Deus reserabit pectora luci.*[7]
*Tunc erit et luctus, stridebunt dentibus omnes.*
*Eripitur solis iubar, et chorus interit astris;*
*Soluetur celum, lunaris splendor obibit;*
*Deiciet colles, ualles extollet ab imo.*

[1] illum] Opposite this word in the margin *Nabuchodonosor* (C).

[2] Ecce inquit ego . . . Filio Dei] Encircled by red lines, with marginal numeral *xii* (B).

[3] Sibilla] Opposite this word in the margin *Sibilla* (C).

[4] The verses of the Sibyl (*Judicij signum* . . . *sulphuris amnis*) are furnished with musical notation in A, and the first two verses are thus furnished in B.

[5] Celsum] Selsum (A).

[6] Tradetur] Tradentur (A).

[7] luci] lucis (A).

*Non erit in rebus hominum sublime uel altum.*
*Tum equantur campis montes, et cerula ponti.*|
*Omnia cessabunt, tellus confracta peribit.*
*Sic pariter fontes torrentur, fluminaque igni.*
*Et tuba tunc sonitum tristem demittet ab alto*
*Orbe, gemens facinus miserum, uariosque labores,*
*Tarthareumque chaos monstrabit terra de⟨h⟩i⟨s⟩cens;*
*Et coram hic Domino reges sistentur ad unum;*
*Decidet e celo ignisque et sulphuris amnis.*

Hec de Christi Natiuitate, Passione, et Resurrectione atque secundo eius Aduentu ita dicta sunt ut, si quis in greco capita horum uersuum discernere uoluerit, inueniet *Ihesus Christus, Yos Theu, Soter*; quod in latino ita interpretatur: *Ihesus Christus, Filius Dei, Saluator*; quod et in latinum translatis eisdem uersibus apparet, preter hoc quod grecarum litterarum proprietas non adeo potuit obseruari. Credo iam uos, o inimici Iudei, tantis testibus ita obrutos confutatosque esse ipsa ueritate ut nichil ultra repugnare, nichil querere debeatis.[1]

In some churches this *lectio* was substantially abbreviated. Thus in a French breviary of the thirteenth century, where it appears as the sixth *lectio* of Christmas Matins, it is reduced in length by almost one-half, retaining only the introduction, the prophecies of Isaiah, Jeremiah, and Daniel, and the concluding prophecy of the Sibyl.[2] In a still shorter form, used as the sixth *lectio* on Christmas at Saintes in the fourteenth century, it includes only the usual introduction and the prophecies of Isaiah and Jeremiah.[3] The sermon shows variations also in liturgical position, being found as the fifth, sixth, eighth, or ninth *lectio* in Christmas Matins; as the fourth *lectio*, or as the fourth, fifth, and sixth *lectiones*, on the fourth Sunday of Advent; as the fourth *lectio* on the day before Christmas; as all three *lectiones* in ferial Matins on any day of the week preceding Christmas; and as the sixth *lectio* on the feast of the Circumcision (January 1).[4] Its use appears to be confined to the season of Christmas.

Returning to the relevant part of the sermon itself, in the

[1] Followed immediately by the rubric *Lectio Sancti Euangeli secundum Lucam* (A).

[2] Paris, Bibl. Nat., MS lat. 1255, Brev. Gallicanum sæc. xiii, fol. $84^r$–$85^v$. See Young, *op. cit.*, p. 11. From a MS of the ninth century (Karlsruhe, Landesbibl., Cod. Augiensis xviii), K. Künstle (*Forschungen zur christlichen Litteratur- und Dogmengeschichte*, ed. A. Ehrhard and J. P. Kirsch, i, 4, Mainz, 1900, pp. 163–7) publishes the relevant part of the sermon in a form considerably briefer than that printed above. The prophecies are the same, but the homiletic exposition is much reduced. As to its liturgical use there is no evidence.

[3] See Paris, Bibl. Nat., MS lat. 16309, Brev. Santonense sæc. xiv, fol. $31^r$, published by Young, *op. cit.*, pp. 11–2.

[4] Evidences for all these uses are given by Young, *op. cit.*, pp. 12–5.

complete and normal form printed above from the lectionary of Arles, we observe that it opens with a direct arraignment of the Jews for their perverse disbelief in the Messiahship of Christ. Since the Jews stubbornly demand evidence, the preacher grimly proposes to bring testimony from their own law. He first summons Isaiah, bidding him testify concerning Christ. As if receiving a response directly from Isaiah in person, the preacher reports the prophet's utterance. Similarly are summoned the prophets Jeremiah, Daniel, Moses, David, and Habbakuk. After each summons, the preacher reports the prophet's utterance, and adds a few words of elucidation. With the taunt that he might readily extend this succession of witnesses from the Old Testament, the preacher passes on to the premonitions regarding Christ in the New Testament, quoting utterances from Simeon, Zacharias, Elisabeth, and John. With a tart reminder to the Jews that the testimony already adduced should be ample, the preacher adds utterances from the Gentiles, Virgil[1] and Nebuchadnezzar, and finally a prophetic passage in hexameters from the Erythræan Sibyl.[2] After elucidating the Christian acrostic of the Sibylline verses, the speaker darts at the hostile Jews a concluding shaft of scorn.

Viewed as a literary production the *lectio* is particularly noteworthy for its energetic dramatic style. The direct denunciations of the Jews are presented in effective, though artificial, antitheses; and the verbal playfulness of some passages, though strained, contributes at least a certain vivacity. The monotony inherent in the formula of repeated summonses and responses is somewhat mitigated through variety in the expository narratives. The circumstance that the prophets are not summoned in chronological order does not seriously impair the structure of the composition.

[1] For information concerning the famous lines from Virgil see J. B. Mayor, W. W. Fowler, and R. S. Conway, *Virgil's Messianic Ecologue*, London, 1907.

[2] These prophetic verses are quoted and interpreted by St Augustine in his *De Civitate Dei* (lib. xviii, cap. 23, Migne, *P.L.*, xli, 579–81). Their appearance throughout the Middle Ages is frequent. See F. Neri, *Le Tradizioni italiene della Sibilla*, in *Studi Medievali*, ed. Novati and Renier, iv (1912–3), 220–1; F. Kampers, *Die Sibylle von Tibur und Vergil*, in *Historisches Jahrbuch*, xxix (1908), 3, 244; Chevalier, *R.H.*, no. 9876; La Piana, pp. 308–9. It will be observed that, in the text printed above, the last seven witnesses (Simeon, Zacharias, Elisabeth, John, Virgil, Nebuchadnezzar, and Sibyl) are not summoned after the formula (*Dic, Ysaia; Dic et tu, Iheremia; Dic, sancte Danihel*, &c.) employed for the six preceding. The actual presence of Simeon, Zacharias, and Elisabeth, John, Nebuchadnezzar, and the Sibyl, however, might be understood as suggested in various utterances of the preacher, such as the following: *Symeonem . . . introducam; Illi etiam parentes Iohannis, Zacharias et Elisabeth . . . dicant; O fidelis testis; In dubium hoc ueniat nisi alios ex*

## II

In the form presented above, the *lectio* seems clearly not to be designed for delivery as a dialogue by separate persons. The use of the word *inquit* in the responses seems to prove conclusively that the utterances of the prophets summoned are delivered not by separate speakers, but by the single person who recites the expository part of the sermon.[1] The most that we can infer is the lector's altering of his voice in such a way as to distinguish between summons and response. That there were other versions of the *lectio*, however, in the reciting of which the several prophecies were probably spoken by separate persons is shown by the following text from the cathedral of Salerno:[2]

In Nativitatis Nocte post Primam Missam legitur Sermo Sancti Augustini Episcopi, More Salernitano

*Vos (inquam) conuenio, O Iudæi, qui vsque in hodiernum diem negatis Filium Dei. Nonne vox vestra est illa, quando eum videbatis miracula facientem, atque tentantes dicebatis: Quousque animas nostras suspendis? Si tu es Christus, dic nobis palam. Ille autem vos ad considerationem miraculorum mittebat, dicens: Opera que ego facio, ipsa testimonium perhibent de me; vt Christo testimonium dicerent, non verba, sed facta. Vos autem, non cognoscentes Saluatorem, adijcientes in malo dixistis: Tu de te testimonium dicis; testimonium tuum non est verum. Sed ad hæc ille quid vobis responderit, aduertere noluistis. Nonne scriptum est (inquit) in lege vestra quod duorum hominum testimonium verum sit? Præuaricatores legis intendite legem. Testimonium quæritis de Christo; in lege vestra scriptum est quod duorum hominum ⟨testimonium⟩ verum sit. Procedant de lege non tantum duo sed etiam plures testes Christi, et conuincant auditores legis, nec factores. Dic et tu, Isaias propheta, testimonium Christo.*

Isaias:

*Ecce virgo concipiet et pariet filium, et vocabitur nomen eius Emanuel, quod est interpretatum: Nobiscum Deus.*

Lector:

*Accedat et alius testis. Dic et tu, Hieremia, testimonium Christo.*

Ieremias:

*gentibus idoneos testes pluraque dicentes in medio introducam.* I find in the text nothing that could possibly imply the actual presence of Virgil.

[1] At one moment Sepet (*Prophètes*, p. 9) seems to affirm the presence of dialogue in the *lectio*; but he subsequently corrects himself (*id.*, p. 23). Madame Chasles (p. 123) sees clearly that the use of *inquit* precludes dialogue.

[2] *Officia propria Festorum Salernitanæ Ecclesiæ*, Naples, 1594, pp. 75–9, previously reprinted from the copy in the British Museum by Young, *op. cit.*, pp. 18–22. Sepet knew of no such version, but, upon somewhat erroneous grounds, he courageously conjectured the existence of it (pp. 10–3, 42, 96–7). His conjectures are considered by Young, *op. cit.*, pp. 17–8.

*Hic est Deus noster, et non æstimabitur alius absque eo qui inuenit omnem viam scientiæ, et dedit eam Iacob puero suo et Israel dilecto suo. Post hæc in terris visus est, et cum hominibus conuersatus est.*

Lector:

*Ecce duo testes idonei ex lege vestra, ex quorum testimonio non sunt compuncta corda vestra. Sed alij atque alij ex lege Christi testes introducantur vt frontes durissimi inimicorum conterantur. Veniat et Daniel sanctus, iuuenis quidem ætate, senior vero scientia ac mansuetudine, conuincat omnes falsos testes, et sicut conuicit seniores impudicos, ita suo testimonio Christi conterat inimicos. Dic, sancte Daniel, dic de Christo quod nosti.*

Daniel:

*Cum venerit Sanctus Sanctorum, cessabit vnctio vestra.*

Lector:

*Quare, illo præsente ⟨cui⟩ insultantes dicebatis: Tu de te ipso testimonium dicis, testimonium tuum non est verum, cessauit vnctio vestra nisi quia ipse est qui venerat Sanctus Sanctorum? Sed si, ut*[1] *vos dicitis, nondum venit, sed expectatur, vt veniat Sanctus Sanctorum, demonstrate vnctionem. Si autem, quod verum est, cessauit vnctio vestra, cognoscite venisse Sanctum Sanctorum. Accedat et alius testis. Dic et tu, Moyses, legislator, dux populi Israel, testimonium Christo.*

Moyses:

*Prophetam vobis excitabit Deus de fratribus vestris; omnis anima quæ non audierit prophetam illum, exterminabitur de populo suo.*

Lector:

*Prophetam dictum Christum, ipsum Christum audi in Euangelio dicentem: Non est propheta sine honore, nisi in patria sua. Accedat enim Dauid sanctus testis fidelis, ex cuius semine processit ipse cui lex et prophete testimonium dicunt; dicat et ipse de Christo. Dic et tu, Dauid, propheta, testimonium Christo.*

Dauid:

*Adorabunt eum omnes reges terræ, omnes gentes seruient ei.*

Lector:

*Cui seruient? Dic, cui seruient?*

Dauid:

*Vis audire cui?*

Lector:

*Volo.*

Dauid:

*Dixit Dominus Domino meo: Sede ad dexteram meam, donec ponam inimicos tuos scabellum pedum tuorum.*

Lector:

*Et espressius atque nominatim: Quare (Quare, inquit) tumultuatæ sunt gentes, et populi meditati sunt inania? Astiterunt reges terræ, et principes conue-*

[1] si, ut] sicut (Print).

*nerunt in vnum aduersus Dominum et aduersus Christum eius. Accedat et alius testis. Dic et tu Abachuc, propheta, testimonium Christo.*

Abachuc:

*Domine, audiui auditum tuum et timui, consideraui opera tua et expaui. In medio duorum animalium cognosceris. Opera tua, Deus, et verbum caro factvm est.*

Lector:

*Ecce quemadmodum conueniunt testes veritatis; ecce quemadmodum conueniunt testes falsitatis. Sufficiunt vobis ista, O Iudei?*[1] *An adhuc ad vestram confusionem et ex lege et ex gente vestra alios introducemus testes, et illi testimonium præbeant cui perdita mente insultantes dicebatis: Tu de te ipso testimonium perhibes; testimonium tuum non est verum? Accedat et alius testis. Benedicens Dominum Simeon, exclamauit senex ille et dixit. Dic et tu, Simeon, propheta, testimonium Christo.*

Simeon:

*Nunc dimittis,*[2] *Domine,*[3] *seruum tuum secundum verbum tuum in pace, quia viderunt oculi mei salutare tuum.*

Lector:

*Illi etiam parentes Ioannis, Zaccharias et Elizabeth, iuuenes steriles et in senectute fecundi, dicant etiam ipsi testimonium Christo; dicant de Christo quod sentiunt et testem idoneum Christo nutriant. Aiunt enim suo paruulo nato. Dic et tu, Zacharias, propheta, testimonium Christo.*

Zaccharias:

*Tu puer, propheta Altissimi vocaberis, præibis enim ante faciem Domini parare vias eius.*

Lector:

*Ipsique matri et virgini Elizabeth ait. Dic et tu, Elizabeth, testimonium Christo.*

Elizabet:

*Vnde hoc mihi, vt veniat Mater Domini mei ad me? Ecce enim vt facta est vox salutationis in auribus meis, exultauit in gaudio infans in vtero meo.*

Lector:

*Intelligens enim Ioannes Matrem Domini sui venisse ad suam matrem, inter ipsas angustias vteri adhuc positus motu salutauit, quem voce non poterat. Dic et tu, Ioannes, testimonium Christo.*

Ioannes:

*Ecce Agnus Dei; ecce qui tollit peccata mundi.*

Lector:

*Et adiecit: Tu ad me venis baptizari; ego a te debeo baptizari. Agnouit seruus Dominum, cognouit vinculis originalis peccati obligatus omni nexu peccati liberum. Agnouit peccator iudicem, agnouit creatura creatorem, cognouit paranymphus sponsum. Nam et hæc vox Ioannis est: Qui habet sponsam, sponsus est. Nonne quando ille facundissimus poeta inter sua carmina dicit? Dic et tu, Virgiii, testimonium Christo.*

[1] O Iudei?] Within marks of parenthesis (Print). [2] dimittis] dimictis (Print). [3] Domine] Within marks of parenthesis (Print).

Virgilius:

*Iam noua progenies cœlo demittitur alto.*

Lector:

*Dicebat Christo testimonium propheta? In dubium hoc veniat nisi alios ex gentibus idoneos testes pluraque dicentes in medium introducat. Illum regem qui vestram superbiam captiuando perdomuit, Nabuchdonosor, regem scilicet Babylonis, non prætermittam. Dic et tu, Nabuchdonosor, testimonium Christo.*

Nabuchdonosor:

*Nonne tres viros misimus in fornacem ligatos?*

Lector:

*Et aiunt ei.*

Famulus Regis:

*Vere, Rex.*

Nabuchdonosor:

*Ecce video quatuor viros solutos deambulantes in medio ignis, et corruptio nulla est in eis, et aspectus quarti similis est Filio Dei.*

Lector:

*O alienigena, vnde tibi hoc? Quis tibi annunciauit Filium Dei? Nondum quidem mundo nascitur, et similitudo nascentis a te cognoscitur. Quid Sibilla vaticinando etiam de Christo clamauerit, in medium proferamus, vt ex vno latere vtrorumque frontes percutiantur, Iudæorum, scilicet atque paganorum, atque suo gladio, sicut Golias, Christi omnes percutiantur inimici. Audite quid dixerit. Dic et tu, Sybilla, testimonium Christo.*

Sibilla Erythræa:

*Ivdicii signum: Tellus sudore madescet;*
*E cœlo Rex adueniet, per sæcla futurus,*
*Scilicet in carne*[1] *presens vt iudicet orbem.*
*Vnde Deum cernent incredulus atque fidelis*
*Celsum cum sanctis, æui iam termino in ipso.*
*Sic animæ cum carne aderunt, quas iudicet ipse.*
*Cum iacet incultus densis in vepribus orbis,*
*Deiicient simulachra viri, cunctam quoque gazam.*
*Exuret terras ignis, pontumque polumque;*
*Inquirens tetri portas effringet Auerni;*
*Sanctorum sed enim cunctæ lux libera carni*
*Tradetur; sontes æterna flamma cremabit.*
*Occultos actus retegens, tunc quisque loquetur*
*Secreta, atque Deus reserabit pectora luci.*
*Tunc erit et luctus, stridebunt dentibus omnes.*
*Eripitur solis iubar, et chorus interit astris;*
*Soluetur cœlum, lunaris splendor obibit;*
*Deiiciet colles, valles extollet ab imo.*

[1] Carne] carnem (Print).

*Non erit in rebus hominum sublime vel altum.*
*Iam æquantur campis montes, et cærula ponti.*
*Omnia cessabunt, tellus confracta peribit.*
*Sic pariter fontes torrentur, fluminaque igni.*
*Et tuba tunc sonitum tristem demittet ab alto*
*Orbe, gemens facinus miserum, variosque labores,*
*Tartareumque chaos monstrabit terra dehiscens;*
*Et coram hic Domino reges sistentur ad vnum;*
*Decidet e cœlo ignis et sulphuris amnis.*

Lector:

*Hæc de Christi Natiuitate, Passione, et Resurrectione, atque secundo eius Aduentu ita dicta sunt vt, si quis in græco capita eorum discere voluerit, inueniet* IESVS,[1] CHRISTOS YOS THEV, SOTIR; *quod est in latino* IESVS CHRISTVS, FILIVS DEI, SALVATOR; *quod et in latinum translatis eisdem versibus apparet præter quod græcarum literarum proprietas non adeo potuit obseruari. Tu* ⟨*autem, Domine, misere nobis*⟩.[2]

The unusual liturgical position of the *lectio* before us is indicated by the introductory rubric *In Natiuitatis Nocte post primam Missam.* The recitation occurs, then, at the conclusion of the first of the three Christmas Masses, which is sung immediately after the *Te Deum* at the close of Matins.[3] The sermon is no longer used as a lesson in Matins, but has become liturgically independent. The manner of the recital is obvious. The lector reads the introductory passage addressed to the Jews, and then summons, in turn, the thirteen witnesses. Each testimony is recited, presumably, by a separate person; but there is no evidence of impersonation.

The change in the manner of recitation is accompanied by several alterations in the text of the sermon. The utterances of the lector, for example, are substantially reduced in length, and the summonses are given a new uniformity.[4] The parts spoken by David and Nabuchadnezzar are somewhat amplified. In the dialogue of the latter we encounter, for the first time, the *famulus Regis.*

It cannot be asserted positively that the version now before us represents a chronological stage between the use of the sermon as a mere lesson in Matins and the use of it as unmistakable drama. Since the *lectio* of Salerno is known to us only in a printed text of the late sixteenth century, one might infer that it repre-

[1] IESVS] IISVS (Print).

[2] Followed immediately by the rubric *De officio Beati Matthæi in Feria quinta.*

[3] See above, i, 547.

[4] See, for example, *Dic et tu, Simeon,* and *Dic et tu, Ioannes.*

sents not a pre-dramatic stage of development, but a later stage in which the influence of the fully dramatized *Ordo Prophetarum* merely survives. The presence of the dialogued *lectio* in a service-book of 1594, however, does not argue against its having had a long tradition; and while awaiting further information concerning the medieval customs of the church of Salerno, we are free to regard the text before us as representing a transition rather than a survival.

## III

The dramatic text from Salerno still retains the essential outline and language of the Augustinian *lectio*. The prophecies are still merely incidental to an expository address—an address which has, to be sure, been considerably reduced, but which still serves as the backbone of the piece. We pass, then, to the following version from the monastery of St Martial at Limoges, in which the prophecies are virtually free from enclosing exposition, are given an original literary form, and are set to music:[1]

⟨Cantor:⟩[2]

*Omnes gentes,*
*congaudentes,*
*dent cantum leticie.*
*Deus homo*
*fit de domo*
*Dauid,*[3] *natus hodie.* |

*O Iudei,*
*Uerbum Dei*
*qui negatis hominem,*
*vestre legis*
*teste⟨s⟩ regis*
*audite per ordinem.*

[1] Paris, Bibl. Nat., MS lat. 1139, Trop. Martialense sæc. xi–xii, fol. $55^{v}$–$58^{r}$, published by Monmerqué and Michel, pp. 6–9, Magnin, *Review*, pp. 88–93, Du Méril, pp. 179–87, Coussemaker, pp. 11–20, and Young, *op. cit.*, pp. 25–31. Wright (pp. 60–2) uses the text of Monmerqué and Michel (see Wright, p. xiv); and the second text of Coussemaker (*Histoire*, pp. 134 sqq.) is dependent upon the readings of Magnin and Du Méril. The text of Monmerqué and Michel is reprinted and translated into English by Stone, *Pseudo-Augustinian Sermon*, pp. 209–13. For additional remarks on the MS see Notes, p. 456.

[2] I enter the conjectural *cantor* at appropriate places throughout the text merely for general intelligibility. Since the text is sung, the word seems acceptable; and its indefiniteness accords with our ignorance of the precise facts. *Cantores* or *chorus* might serve equally well. Du Méril's *Præcentor* and Magnin's *Dicat Sacerdos* seem to imply undue editorial certainty.

[3] Dauid] Dauit (MS).

*Et uos gentes*
*non credentes*
*peperisse uirginem,*
*vestre gentis*
*documentis*
*pellite caliginem.*

ISRael

⟨Cantor:⟩

*Israel, uir lenis, inque*
*de Christo ⟨quæ⟩ nosti firme.*

R*esponsum*:

*Dux de Iuda non tolletur*[1]
*donec adsit qui mit⟨t⟩etur;*
*salutare Dei uerbum*
*expectabunt gentes mecum.*

MOYSES

⟨Cantor:⟩

*Legislator,*[2] *huc propinqua,*
*et de Christo prome digna.*

R*esponsum*:

*Dabit Deus uobis uatem;*
*huic ut mihi aurem date;*
*qui non audit hunc audientem*[3]
*expellitur sua gente.*

ISAIAS

⟨Cantor:⟩

*Isayas, uerum qui scis,*
*ueritatem cur | non dicis?*

R*esponsum*:

*Est necesse*
*uirga⟨m⟩ Iesse*
*de radice proue⟨h⟩i;*
*flos deinde*
*surget inde,*
*qui est spiritus Dei.*

IEREMIAS

⟨Cantor:⟩

*Hvc accede, Ieremias;*
*dic de Christo prophetias.*

[1] tolletur] tollitur (MS).
[2] Legislator] Legislatvr (MS).
[3] audientem] Magnin plausibly emends to *dicentem*.

R*esponsum*:

*Sic est,*
*hic est*
*Deus noster,*
*sine quo non erit alter.*

DANIEL

⟨Cantor:⟩

*Daniel, indica*
*uoce prophetica*
*facta dominica.*

R*esponsum*:[1]

*Sanctus Sanctorum ueniet,*
*et unctio deficiet.*

⟨ABACUC

Cantor:⟩

*Abacuc, regis celestis*
*nunc ostende quod sis testis.*

R*esponsum*:

*Et expectaui,*
*mox expaui*
*metu mirabilium,*
*opus tuum*
*inter duum*
*corpus animalium.*

DAVID

⟨Cantor:⟩

*Dic tu, Dauid,*[2] *de nepote*
*causas que sunt tibi note.*

R*esponsum*:

*Vniuersus*
*grex conuersus*
*adorabit*[3] *Dominum,*
*cui futurum*
*seruiturum*
*omne genus ho|minum.*
*Dixit Dominus Domino meo:*
*Sede a*[4] *dextris meis.*

[1] Responsum] Preceded by a superfluous scribal capital *S* (MS).
[2] Dauid] Dauit (MS).
[3] adorabit] adorabat (MS).
[4] a] ad (MS).

### Simeon

⟨Cantor:⟩

*Nvnc Symeon adueniat,*
*qui responsum acceperat,*
*qui non ⟨h⟩aberet terminum*
*donec uideret Dominum.*

R*esponsum*:

*Nunc me dimittas, Domine,*
*finire uitam in pace;*
*quia mei modo cernunt oculi*
*quem misisti*
*hunc mundum pro salute populi.*[1]

### Elisabet

⟨Cantor:⟩

*Illud, Helisabet, in medium*
*de Domino profer*[2] *eloquium.*

R*esponsum*:

*Quid est rei*
*quod me mei*
*mater ⟨h⟩eri uisitat?*
*Nam ex eo*
*uentre meo*
*letus infans palpitat.*[3]

### ⟨Johannes Baptista

Cantor:⟩

*Dic,*[4] *Babtista,*
*uentris cista*
*clausus*
*qua*[5] *dedisti*
*causa Christo |*
*plausus?*
*Cui dedisti gaudium*
*profer*[6] *et testimonium.*

R*esponsum*:

*Venit talis*
*sotularis*
*cuius non sum etiam*
*tam benignus*

[1] For the entire part of Simeon (*Nvnc Symeon . . . salute populi*) the musical notation is omitted.
[2] profer] profert (MS).
[3] Here follows a blank space, left, no doubt, for a rubric.
[4] Dic] De (MS).
[5] qua] Quod (MS).
[6] profer] Profert (MS).

*ut sim ausus*
*soluere corrigiam.*

VIRGILIUS

⟨Cantor:⟩

*Vates, Maro,*[1] *gentilium,*
*da*[2] *Christo testimonium.*

R*esponsum*:

*Ecce polo demissa solo noua progenies est.*

NABUCODO⟨NO⟩SOR

⟨Cantor:⟩

*Age, fare, os laguene,*
*que de Christo nosti uere.*[3]
*Nabucodonosor, propheti⟨z⟩a,*
*auctorem omnium auctoriza.*

R*esponsum*:

*Cum reuisi*
*tres quo⟨s⟩ misi*
*uiros in incendium,*
*vidi iustis*
*inconbustis*
*mixtum Dei filium;*
*viros tres in ignem misi,*
*quartum cerno*[4] *prolem Dei.*

SIBILLA |

⟨Cantor:⟩

*Vera pande iam, Sibilla,*
*que de Christo pre⟨s⟩cis signa.*

R*esponsum*:

*Ivditii signum: Tellus sudore madescet;*
*E celo rex adueniet per secla futurus,*
*Scilicet in carne presens, ut iudicet orbem.*

⟨Cantor:⟩

*Ivdea incredula,*
*cur manes*[5] *adhuc inuerecunda?*

⟨H⟩ic incoant *Benedicamus*.[6]

A mere glance at this dramatic text suggests its derivation from the pseudo-Augustinian *lectio*. The prophetic witnesses in

[1] Maro] Moro (MS).
[2] da] dea (MS).
[3] uere] uere Responsum (MS).
[4] cerno] cerna (MS).
[5] manes] manens (MS).
[6] In regard to what immediately follows in the MS see below, p. 456.

the two may be listed as follows, in the order in which they occur in the texts themselves:

| *Lectio* | *Ordo of Limoges* |
| --- | --- |
| Isaiah | Israel |
| Jeremiah | Moses |
| Daniel | Isaiah |
| Moses | Jeremiah |
| David | Daniel |
| Habakkuk | Habakkuk |
| Simeon | David |
| Zacharias | Simeon |
| Elizabeth | Elisabeth |
| John the Baptist | John the Baptist |
| Virgil | Virgil |
| Nebuchadnezzar | Nebuchadnezzar |
| Sibyl | Sibyl |

It will be observed that at Limoges Israel has been added, and Zacharias has been omitted. These changes are minimized, however, by the fact that in the *lectio* Israel is at least mentioned,[1] and Zacharias is represented by his wife, Elisabeth. Although neither list is completely chronological, the Limoges writer appears to have attempted an improvement in this respect. The first six names are arranged in virtually the correct order. Then appears David, appropriately enough, before the contemporaries of Christ. The pagan witnesses are left in their original positions.

The prophecies themselves in the Limoges text are, in general, free and pleasing versifications of the parallel utterances in the *lectio*.[2] A divergence appears, however, between the testimonies of Isaiah in the two texts:

*Lectio*

Ecce virgo in utero concipiet et pariet filium, et vocabitur nomen ejus Hemanuhel, quod est interpretatum: Nobiscum Deus.[3]

*Ordo of Limoges*

Est necesse
virga⟨m⟩ Iesse
de radice prove⟨h⟩i;
flos deinde
surget inde,
qui est spiritus Dei.

[1] See the prophecy of Jeremiah above, p. 126.

[2] These parallels are listed *in extenso* by Young, *op. cit.*, pp. 33–6.

[3] See Isaiah vii, 14: *Ecce virgo concipiet, et pariet filium, et vocabitur nomen ejus Emmanuel.*

The stanza here is formed not from the text of the *lectio*, but from the following unrelated passage in the book of Isaiah:[1]

Et egredietur virga de radice Jesse, et flos de radice ejus ascendet. Et requiescet super eum spiritus Domini.

As to the arrangement for singing the dramatic text the meagre rubrics provide extremely little information. One may reasonably suppose that the introductory stanzas and the summonses were sung by a choral group, as in the plays from Laon and Rouen to be considered below. We may infer also that at each summons one of the prophets appeared in person and responded with his testimony. Of actual impersonation, however, we cannot be sure.[2] As to the part of the church in which the performance occurred, and as to stage-setting we know nothing at all.[3]

We are left in uncertainty also as to the day on which the ceremony was performed, and as to its position in the liturgy. The words *natus hodie*, of the opening stanza, point directly to Christmas Day; but the same words are found also in the Rouen play, which was undeniably presented on the feast of the Circumcision (January 1).[4] Concerning the attachment of the performance to the liturgy our only possible shred of evidence is the rubric at the end: *Hic incoant Benedicamus*. This may mean that the representation was brought to a close with the singing of the *Benedicamus*; and since this liturgical piece was sung at the end of each of the canonical *horæ*, even of Matins,[5] this interpretation might seem to place the dramatic performance at one of these services.[6] The rubric, on the other hand, may have been entered to indicate merely that at this point in the manuscript the *Benedicamuses* begin.[7] It is followed, as a matter of fact, by a series of metrical pieces evidently composed as tropes of the *Benedicamus*. Between the two interpretations it is difficult to choose.

However uncertain we may be as to external matters of per-

[1] Isaiah xi, 1–2. See Isa. xi, 10; Rom. xv, 12–3; Num. xvii, 5–6.

[2] Sepet (*Prophètes*, p. 25) considers impersonation not improbable.

[3] For Magnin's conjectural description see Notes, p. 456.

[4] See below, pp. 156, 168. Du Méril (p. 180) chooses to assign the performance to the day before Christmas; Sepet (pp. 14–5) is unconditionally for Christmas Day.

[5] See above, i, 67; ii, 81.

[6] Sepet (*Prophètes*, pp. 25–6, 84) not only considers the rubric and the subsequent lines as organically related to the preceding dramatic text, but he also regards the dramatic text itself as a sort of trope of the *Benedicamus*. Petit de Julleville (i, 36) appears to accept Sepet's view. For what immediately follows the rubric in the MS see Notes, p. 456.

[7] This appears to be the interpretation of Magnin (*Review*, p. 92) and Monmerqué and Michel (pp. 3, 9).

formance and liturgical relationship, we readily recognize in the Limoges text a significant advance in the literary treatment of the theme which we are considering. Particularly noteworthy are the force and aptness of the opening stanzas, the elimination of the narrative and expository element of the *lectio*, and the graceful versifying of both summonses and responses.

## IV

In spite of its success as a literary composition, the *Ordo Prophetarum* of Limoges, as we have seen, cannot be characterized with certainty as a genuine drama, because of the absence of rubrics indicating impersonation. This deficiency is abundantly supplied by the following version of the thirteenth century from the cathedral of Laon:[1]

### Ordo Prophetarum

Ysaias: barbatus, dalmatica indutus, stola rubea per medium uerticis ante et retro dependens.[2]

Iheremias: similiter, absque stola.

Daniel: adolescens, ueste splendida indutus.

Moyses: cum dalmatica, barbatus, tabulas legis ferens.

Dauid: regio habitu.

Abacuc: barbatus, curuus, gibosus.

Elisabeth: femineo habitu, pregnans.

Iohannes Baptista: pilosa ueste et longis capillis, barbatus, palmam tenens.

Virgilius: cum cornu et calamo, edera coronatus, scriptorium tenens.

Nabugodonosor: regio habitu, superbo incessu.

Sibilla: ueste feminea, decapillata, edera coronata, insanienti simillima.

Symeon: barbatus, capa serica in|dutus, palmam tenens.

Balaam: super asinam, curuus, barbatus, palmam tenens, calcaribus urgens.

*Gloriosi*
*et famosi*
*regis festum*
*celebrantes*
*gaudeamus.*

[1] Laon, Bibl. de la Ville, MS 263, Troparium-Hymnarium Laudunense sæc. xiii, fol. $147^v$–$149^r$, previously edited by Chevalier, *Laon*, pp. 385–9, and by Young, *op. cit.*, pp. 40–5. Chevalier's text is reprinted by Chasles, pp. 129–34, and by Adams, pp. 41–8. The opening rubric *Ordo Prophetarum* is immediately preceded by the following irrelevant *incipit*: *De Sancto Nicholao, Congaudentes.* For the *Ordo Prophetarum* the MS provides no music.

[2] dependens] Emendation *dependente* permissible (Chevalier).

*Cuius ortum,*
*uite portum,*
*nobis datum,*
*predicantes*
*habeamus.*

*Ecce regem*
*nouam legem*
*dantem orbis*
*circuitu*
*predicamus.*

Duo cantores:

*Omnes gentes,*
*congaudentes,*
*dent cantus letitie.*
*Deus homo*
*fit de domo*
*Dauid, natus hodie.*

Ad Iudeos:

*O Iudei,*
*Uerbum Dei*
*qui negastis hominem,*
*vestre legis*
*testes regis*
*audite per ordinem.*

Ad Paganos:

*Et uos gentes*
*non credentes*
*peperisse uirginem,*
*vestre legis*
*documentis*
*pellite caliginem.*

Appellatores:

*Isaias, uerum qui scis,*
*ueritatem cur non dicis?*

Isaias:

*Est necesse*
*uirgam Iesse*
*de radice prouehi;*
*flos deinde*
*surget inde,*
*qui est filius Dei.*

Appellatores:

*Iste cetus*
*psallat letus;*
*error uetus*
*condempnetur.*

Omnis chorus:

*Quod Iudea*
*perit rea,*
*hec chorea*
*gratulatur.*

Appellatores:

*Huc accede, Iheremias;*
*dic de Christo prophetias.*

Hieremias:

*Sic est,*
*hic est*
*Deus noster.*

Duo:

*Iste cetus.*

Item chorus:

*Quod Iudea.*

Duo:

*Daniel, indica*
*uoce prophetica*
*facta dominica.*

Daniel:

*Sanctus Sanctorum ueniet,*
*et unctio deficiet.*[1]

Duo:

*Iste cetus.*

Chorus:

*Quod Iudea.*

Ap⟨p⟩ellatores:

*Dic tu, Moyses, legislator,*
*quis sit Christus | et Saluator.*

Moises:

*Prophetam accipietis*
*tamquam me hunc audietis.*

Duo:

*Iste cetus.*

Chorus:

*Quod Iudea.*

[1] deficiet] defitiet (MS).

Ap⟨p⟩ellatores:

*Dic tu, Dauid, de nepote*
*causas que sunt tibi note.*

Dauid:

*Vniuersus*
*rex conuersus*
*adorabit Dominum,*
*cui futurum*
*seruiturum*
*omne genus hominum.*

Duo:

*Iste cetus.*

Chorus:

*Quod Iudea.*

Appellatores:

*Abacuc, regis celestis*
*nunc ostende quod sis testis.*

Abacuc:

*Opus tuum*
*inter duum*
*latus animalium*
*ut cognoui,*
*mox expaui*
*metu mirabilium.*

Duo:

*Iste cetus.*

Chorus:

*Quod Iudea.*

Ap⟨p⟩ellatores:

*Illud, Elisabeth, in medium*
*de Domino profer eloquium.*

Elisabeth:

*Quid est rei*
*quod me mei*
*mater regis uisitat?*
*nam ex eo*
*uentre meo*
*letus infans palpitat.*

Duo:

*Iste cetus.*

Chorus:

*Quod Iudea.*

Item duo:

*Da, Baptista,*
*uentris cista*
*clausus,*
*quos dedisti*
*causa Christi*
*plausus?*
*Cui dedisti gaudium,*
*profer et testimonium.*

Iohannes:

*Venit talis*
*sotularis*
*cuius non sum etiam*
*tam benignus*
*ut sim dignus*
*soluere corrigiam.*

Duo:

*Iste cetus.*

Chorus:

*Quod Iudea.*

Duo:

*Maro, uates gentilium,*
*da Christo testimonium.*

Maro:

*Ecce polo dimissa sola noua progenies est.*

Duo:

*Iste cetus.*

Chorus:

*Quod Iudea.*

Appellatores reducunt Danielem, et dic*un*t ad Regem:

*Puerum cum pueris,*
*Nabugodonosor,*
*cum in igne uideris,*
*quid dixisti?*

Nabugodonosor:

*Tres in igne positi pueri*
*quarto gau|dent comite liberi.*

Duo:

*Iste cetus.*

Chorus:

*Quod Iudea.*

Ap⟨p⟩ellatores:

*Tu, Sibilla,*
*uates illa,*
*dic aduentum iudicis,*
*dic signum iudicij.*

Sibilla:

*Iudicij signum: Tellus sudore madescet;*
*E celo rex adueniet per secla futurus,*
*Scilicet in carne presens, ut iudicet orbem.*
*Vnde Deum cernent incredulus atque fidelis*
*Celsum cum sanctis, eui iam termino in ipso.*

Duo:

*Iste cetus.*

Chorus:

*Quod Iudea.*

Appellatores:

*Symeon, inter prophetas*
*pande nobis quid expectas.*

Symeon:

*Vite non spero terminum*
*donec uideam Dominum.*

Duo:

*Iste cetus.*

Chorus:

*Quod Iudea.*

Symeon accipiens Puerum dicit:

*Tuum sub pacis tegmine*
*seruum dimittis, Domine.*

Ap⟨p⟩ellatores:

*Dic, Balaam, ex Iudaica*
*oriturum Dominum prosapia.*

Balaam:

*Exibit de Iacob rutilans noua stella*
*et confringet ducum agmina*
*regionis Moab maxima potentia.*

Hic ueniat Angelus cum gladio. Balaam tangit Asinam, et illa non procedente, dicit iratus:

*Quid moraris, asina,*
*obstinata bestia?*
*Iam scindent calcaria*
*costas et precordia.*

Puer sub Asina respondet:

*Angelus cum gladio,*
*quem adstare uideo,*
*prohibet ne transeam;*
*timeo ne peream.*[1]

In its careful provision for details of impersonation this text is

[1] Followed immediately by the rubric *Ordo Stelle*, introducing the version of the Epiphany play printed above, pp. 103 sqq.

exceptionally impressive. Daniel's youthful appearance, Moses' tables of the law, Elisabeth's pregnancy, John the Baptist's hairy shirt and palm-branch, Virgil's writing materials and crown of ivy, the Sibyl's expression of mad inspiration, Balaam's ass—all these are prescribed specifically.

The performance opens with the stanzas *Gloriosi et famosi*, sung, presumably, by the chorus as the *prophetæ* enter. Two cantors then deliver three stanzas, the second and third of which are addressed to the Jews and Gentiles respectively, bidding them prepare for enlightenment. Two special summoners (*appellatores*) call forth the prophets, one by one, and after each prophecy deliver the stanza *Iste cœtus*, to which the chorus responds with its own stanza *Quod Judæa*.

The close kinship of the Laon play to the Limoges version and to the original *lectio* is obvious. Each of these three compositions presents thirteen witnesses, and twelve of these are common to all three: namely, Isaiah, Jeremiah, Daniel, Moses, David, Habakkuk, Elisabeth, John the Baptist, Virgil, Nebuchadnezzar, Sibyl, and Simeon. Balaam is peculiar to the Laon version, as Israel and Zacharias are to the Limoges version and the *lectio* respectively. The similarity of the three versions is further apparent in the textual content of the prophecies. In eight of these[1] the Limoges and Laon versions agree in presenting metrical versions of the utterances provided by the *lectio*. In the utterance of Isaiah, the Limoges and Laon versions agree as against the *lectio*. In the prophecies of Moses and Nebuchadnezzar the two dramatic versions differ from each other in expression, but both derive from the *lectio*. The utterance of Simeon in the Laon play is developed somewhat beyond what is found either in the Limoges text or in the *lectio*.

In general arrangement the Laon play differs considerably from the two preceding versions. The non-chronological order in which the first six prophets appear reproduces what we have observed in the original sermon. The presence of Simeon and Balaam at the end, after Sibyl, suggests that those two prophets were attached to the series in a relatively mechanical way. Probably the copy from which the present text was made was in disorder. This impression is indeed strengthened by the inconclusiveness with which the play ends.[2]

[1] Jeremiah, Daniel, David, Habakkuk, Elisabeth, John the Baptist, Virgil, and the Sibyl.

[2] See Chambers, ii, 54, 56–7; Chasles, p. 127, note 2.

From the point of view of dramatic delivery the most arresting of the prophecies are those of Nebuchadnezzar, Simeon, and Balaam. The first of these may be dismissed briefly, for although the rubric *Appellatores reducunt Danielem* suggests a special action of some sort, the nature of it is not specified. The theatrical movements accompanying the role of Simeon can be visualized somewhat more clearly. It appears that *Simeon barbatus* is represented as standing in the temple in the presence of Joseph, Mary, and Jesus, and that after his first utterance has been heralded by the cantors and chorus, he takes the child in his arms and speaks the versified *Nunc dimittis*.[1]

Most animated of all is the scene in which Balaam appears, digging his spurs into the sides of his ass—*calcaribus urgens*. After he has uttered his prophecy, an angel appears and obstructs his progress. When Balaam impatiently urges the ass forward, the boy concealed underneath explains the cause of his halting; and thus the play abruptly ends. The action of this little episode is, of course, derived from the Biblical narrative; but the dialogue shows no dependence upon the text of the Vulgate.[2] The speech of the *appellatores* seems clearly to be adapted from the following passage in a well-known sequence of Epiphany: *Quam Balaam ex Judaica orituram dixerat prosapia*;[3] and the response of Balaam is from another Epiphany sequence *Epiphaniam Domino canamus*.[4] The second speech of Balaam and the reply of *Puer sub asina* seem to have been invented for the present scene.[5]

It is clear that the episodes in which Simeon and Balaam figure stand apart from the rest of the performance as small dramatic units. Possibly they were composed separately, before being added at the end of the text before us. The modern reader who is tempted to infer that Balaam's ass is introduced here with a comic intention may appropriately be reminded of the medieval attribution of noble virtues to this patient and sober beast, who had borne an important prophet, the Virgin Mary and Christ, and had been present benevolently at the manger in Bethlehem.[6]

[1] Craig (p. 475, note 4) refers to this scene as 'probably the most primitive form known of the play of the Presentation in the Temple'. See the dramatic ceremonies of the Purification treated below, pp. 250 sqq.

[2] See Numbers xxii, 21–31.

[3] See the sequence *Quem non prævalent*, considered below, p. 446. See Meyer, p. 52.

[4] Chevalier, *R.H.*, no. 5497; see Meyer, p. 52. For the complete text from *A.H.*, liii, 47–8, see Notes, p. 457.

[5] For remarks on the progress in dramatic development represented by the Balaam scene of the Laon play see Sepet, p. 35, and Chasles, p. 127, summarized by Young, *op. cit.*, p. 47, note 15.

[6] Concerning the reverent medieval symbolizing of the ass see Clément, pp. 172 sqq.;

Since the text of the Laon play, like that from Limoges, does not indicate its position in the liturgy, we may, perhaps, derive indirect evidence upon this point from other sources. From Tours, for example, we have the following rubrics for the feast of the Circumcision:[1]

Ad Matutinas cantent duo et duo versus invitatorii et antiphonas similiter, et hymnos sicut ad Vesperas. . . . Post nonam lectionem ducunt Prophetas de capitulo ad portam thesaurarii cantilenas cantando, et post in chorum, ubi dicunt cantori prophetias, et duo clericuli in pulpito cantando eos appellant. Post dicitur nonum responsorium in pulpito. . . . Post prandium debent choros ducere in claustro in supelliciis donec ecclesia aperiatur, et totum luminare accendatur. Quo facto, incipiunt Nonam et Vesperas; faciunt totum sicut ad primas ⟨Vesperas⟩, et dictis psalmis et antiphonis, ducunt ad portam thesaurarii Prophetas sicut ad Matutinum, et reducunt in chorum similiter, et habent clerici virgas plenas candelis ardentibus. Vocant eos clerici duo sicut ad Vesperas.

At Tours the *Ordo Prophetarum* was performed in Matins of January 1st, after the reading of the ninth lesson and before the singing of the ninth responsory. The prophets entered the choir during the singing of certain *cantilenæ*. The summonses to the individual *prophetæ* were delivered by *duo clericuli in pulpito*, and the several prophecies seem to have been addressed to a sort of presiding *cantor*. The repetition of the *ordo* at Vespers is mentioned, but not described in detail. Although the actual utterances of the participants are not known, the nature of the performance must have been similar to that of the Laon play. We may safely infer that the prophets were specifically impersonated, and that they spoke in the formal sequence already familiar to us. It may be that certain of the preceding *lectiones* in Matins were supplied by the pseudo-Augustinian sermon, and that the prophets were introduced after the final *lectio* by way of didactic illustration. If we may assume that the performance at Tours resembles that at Laon in its general procedure, we may reasonably conjecture a similarity in liturgical position. It may well be, then, that the Laon *Ordo*—and the Limoges version also—is to be associated with the liturgy of the Circumcision. This conjecture, indeed, receives further support from the circumstances surrounding the dramatic piece which we are to consider next.

Cabrol and Leclercq, i, 2047–68. Meyer (pp. 52–3), however, unhesitatingly infers that in the *Ordo Prophetarum* the ass is comic.

[1] Martene, iii, 41–2.

## V

In the number and names of the prophets presented the two versions of the *Ordo Prophetarum* which have now been examined adhere closely to the original pseudo-Augustinian *lectio*. To the speakers summoned in the sermon the Limoges text adds only Israel, and the Laon version, only Balaam. The full possibilities in the way of addition are realized only in such a play as the so-called *Festum Asinorum*, from the cathedral of Rouen:[1]

ORDO PROCESSIONIS ASINORUM SECUNDUM ROTHOMAGENSEM VSUM[2]

Tercia cantata, paratis Prophetis iuxta suum ordinem, fornace in medio nauis ecclesie lintheo et stupis constituta, processio moueat de claustro, et duo clerici de secunda sede in cappis processionem regant, hos versus canentes;[3]

*Gloriosi*
*et famosi*
*⟨regis festum*
*celebrantes*
*gaudeamus⟩.*

Chorus:

*Gloriosi*
*⟨et famosi*
*regis festum*
*celebrantes*
*gaudeamus⟩.*

Versus:

*Cuius ortum*
*⟨vitæ portum*
*nobis datum*
*prædicantes*
*habeamus⟩.*

[1] Rouen, Bibl. de la Ville, MS 384 (*olim* Y. 110), Ordin. Rothomagense sæc. xiv, fol. 33ʳ–35ʳ (A), with variants (except for a few meaningless divergences in spelling) from Rouen, *ibid.*, MS 382 (*olim* Y. 108), Ordin. Rothomagense sæc. xv, fol. 31ᵛ–33ʳ (B). A modern hand, probably of the seventeenth century, has copied the text, apparently from MS 384, into MS lat. 1232, of the Bibl. Nat., Paris, fol. 26ʳ–27ʳ. None of the MSS contains musical notation. The text has been edited by Du Cange, iii, 460–1, from an unidentified 'Ordinarius MS' of Rouen; by Gasté, pp. 4–20, from MS 384 with some of the variants from MS 382; and by Young, *Ordo Prophetarum*, pp. 50–63, from all three MSS. For further observations on MSS and editions see Young, *op. cit.*, pp. 49–50, and Young, *Rouen*, pp. 224–7. The text before us is immediately preceded in the MSS by the rubric *Nota, Cantor: Si Festum Asinorum fiat, processio ⟨processio et (B)⟩ ordinetur post Terciam; si non fiat Festum, tunc fiat processio ut prenotatur.* See plate xvii.

[2] Processionis Asinorum secundum Rothomagensem Vsum] processio asinorum secundum Vsum Rothomagensem (B).

[3] hos versus canentes] cantantes hos versus (B).

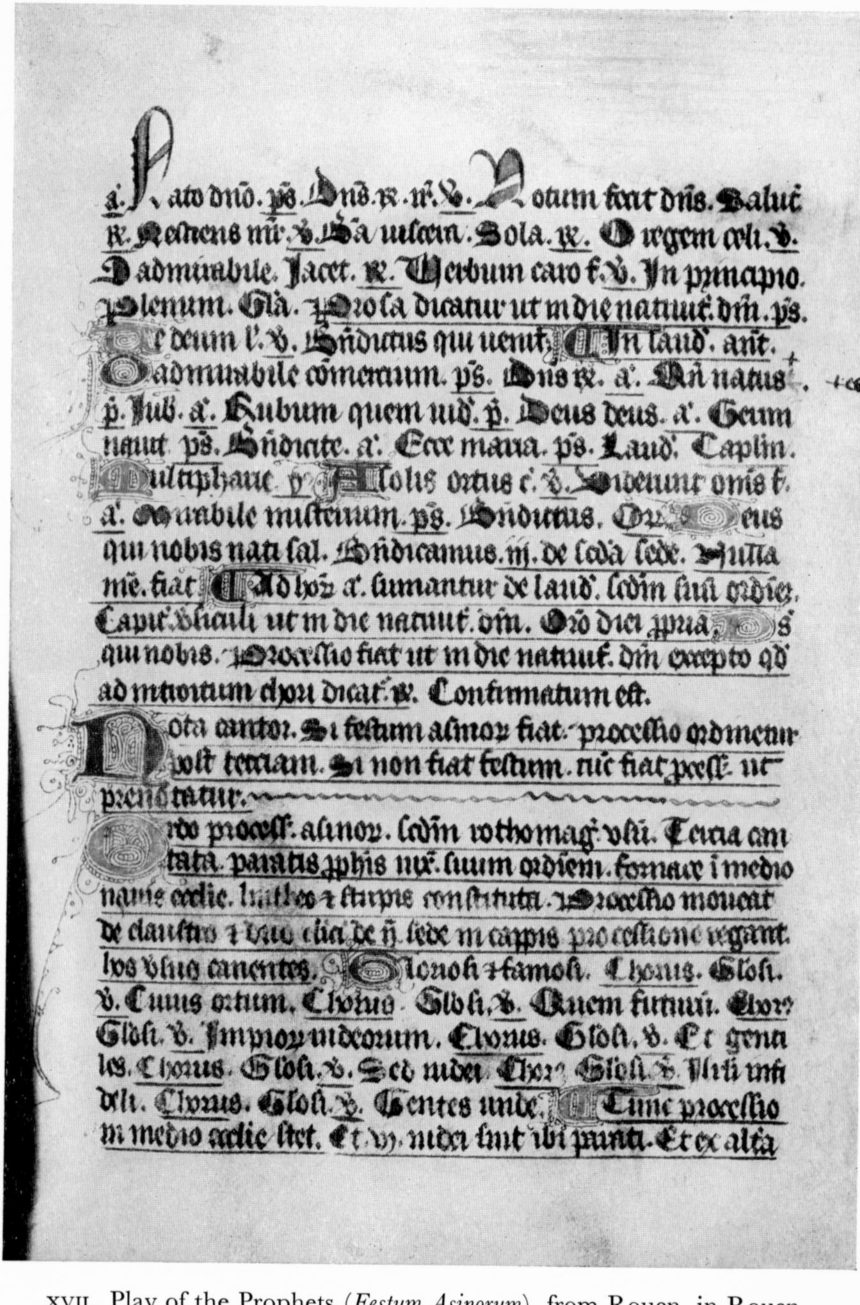

XVII. Play of the Prophets (*Festum Asinorum*), from Rouen, in Rouen, Bibliothèque de la Ville, MS 384 (Y. 110), fol. 33r

Chorus:

*Gloriosi.*

Versus:

*Quem futurum*
*⟨regnaturum*
*prophetico*
*admonitu*
*nuntiamus⟩.*

Chorus:

*Gloriosi.*

Versus:

*Impiorum*
*Iudeorum*
*⟨corda negant*
*regnaturo*
*sua lege⟩.*

Chorus:

*Gloriosi.*

Versus:

*Et gentiles*
*⟨prius viles*
*convertuntur*
*majestate*
*ætherea⟩.*

Chorus:

*Gloriosi.*

Versus:

*Sed Iudei*
*⟨facti rei*
*condemnantes*
*sacrum regem*
*damnabuntur⟩.*

Chorus:

*Gloriosi.*

Versus:

*Israeli*
*infideli*[1]
*⟨jam Maria*
*natus scitur*
*hic adesse⟩.*

Chorus:

*Gloriosi.*

[1] infideli] infideles (B).

Versus:

*Gentes unde.*

Tunc processio in medio ecclesie stet. Et sex Iudei sint ibi parati, et ex altera | parte sex Gentiles, et omnes Gentes uocent ita Uocatores:

*Omnes gentes,*
*⟨congaudentes,*
*dent cantus lætitiæ⟩.*
*Deus homo*
*Fit*[1] *⟨de domo*
*David, natus hodie⟩.*

Hic uertant se Uocatores ad Iudeos dicentes:

*O Iudei,*
*Uerbum Dei*
*⟨qui negastis hominem⟩.*

Versus:

*Vestre legis*
*testes ⟨regis*
*audite per ordinem⟩.*

Iudei respondeant:

*Nos mandatum uobis.*

Vocatores ad Gentiles dicant:

*Et uos gentes*
*non credentes*
*⟨peperisse virginem.*

Versus:

*Vestræ legis*
*documentis*
*pellite caliginem⟩.*

Gentiles respondeant:

*Deum uerum*
*Regem rerum.*[2]

Vocatores prius Moysen,[3] ita dicentes:

*Tu, Moyses,*
*legislator,*
*⟨huc propinqua,*
*et de Christo*
*prome digna.⟩*

Tunc Moyses, tenens tabulas legis apertas, indutus alba et cappa, et cornuta facie, barbatus, tenens uirgam in manu, dicat:

*Vir post me veniet exortus.*

[1] Deus homo fit] Dominus homo sit (A. B).

[2] Deum uerum regem rerum] Deum regem verum (B).

[3] Moysen] Omitted (B).

Hoc dicto, Vocatores eum ducant ultra fornacem dicentes:

*Iste cetus*
*psallat letus;*
*⟨error vetus*
*condemnetur.⟩*

Chorus:

*Quod Iudea*
*⟨perit rea,*
*hæc chorea*
*gratulatur⟩.*

Vocatores dicant ad Amos:

*Amos mentis.*

Tunc Amos, senex barbatus, spicam tenens, dicat:

*Ecce dies uenient.*[1]

Vocatores:

*⟨Iste cetus.⟩*

Chorus:

*Quod Iudea.*

Vocatores dicant Ysaye:

*Ysaias, verbum qui scis,*[2]
*⟨veritatem cur non dicis?⟩*

Ysaias, barbatus, alba indutus, per mediam[3] frontem rubea stola discrinitus, dicat:

*Est necesse*
*uirga⟨m⟩ Yesse*
*⟨de radice provehi;*
*flos deinde*
*surget inde,*
*qui est Filius Dei⟩.*

Vocatores:

*Iste cetus.*

Chorus:

*Quod Iudea.*

Vocatores ad Aaron:

*Aaron, doce populum.*

Aaron, ornatus pontificalibus indumentis et mitra, barbatus, tenens florem dicat:

*Virga Iesse florida.*[4]

[1] uenient] ueniunt (B). See Amos viii, 11: *Ecce dies veniunt, dicit Dominus, et mittam famem in terram; non famem panis, neque sitim aquæ, sed audiendi verbum Domini.*

[2] scis] scit (A.B).

[3] mediam] medium (B).

[4] See Num. xvii, 5–8: *Quem ex his elegero, germinabit virga ejus . . . fueruntque virgæ duodecim absque virga Aaron . . . Sequenti die regressus invenit germinasse virgam Aaron in domo Levi; et turgentibus gemmis eruperant flores, qui, foliis dilatatis, in amygdalas deformati sunt.*

Vocatores:

*Iste cetus.*

Chorus:

*Quod Iudea.*

Vocacio Iheremie:

*Qui vocaris, Iheremias.*[1]

Iheremias sacerdotali habitu ornatus et barbatus[2] tenens rotulum dicat:

*Sic est,*
*hic est*
*Deus noster,*
*⟨sine quo non erit alter.⟩*

Vocatores:

*Iste cetus.*

Chorus:

*Quod Iudea.*

Vocacio Danielis:

*Daniel, indica*
*uoce prophetica*
*⟨facta dominica⟩.*

Daniel, indutus uiridi tunica, iuuenilem uultum habens, tenens spicam, dicat:

*Sanctus Sanctorum ueniet,*
*⟨et unctio deficiet.⟩*

Vocatores:

*Iste cetus.*

Chorus:

*Quod Iudea.*

Vocacio Abacuc:

*Abacuc, regis celestis*
*⟨nunc ostende quod sis testis⟩.*

Abacuc, senex claudus, dalmatica indutus,[3] habens in peram radices, et longas palmas habens unde gentes per|cuciat, comedens, dicat:

*Opus tuum*
*inter duum*[4]
*⟨latus animalium*
*ut cognovi,*
*mox expavi*
*metu mirabilium⟩.*

Vocatores:

*Iste cetus.*

Chorus:

*Quod Iudea.*

[1] Iheremias] Omitted (B).

[2] ornatus et barbatus] indutus et ornatus barbatus (B).

[3] indutus] Omitted (B).

[4] inter duum] in triduum (B).

Duo missi a rege Balac dicant:

*Balaam, veni et fac.*

Tunc Balaam, ornatus, sedens super Asinam, habens calcaria retineat lora et calcaribus percuciat Asinam. Et quidam iuuenis habens alas, tenens gladium, obstet Asine. Quidam sub Asina dicat:

*Cur me cum calcaribus miseram sic leditis?*

Hoc dicto, Angelus ei dicat:

*Desine regis Balac preceptum perficere.*

Vocacio Balaam:

*Balaam, esto uaticinans.*

Tunc Balaam respondeat;

*Exibit ex Iacob rutilans ⟨nova stella,*
*et confringet ducum agmina*
*regionis Moab maxima potentia⟩.*

Vocatores:[1]

*Iste cetus.*

Chorus:

*Quod Iudea.*

Vocacio Samuelis:

*Accede, Samuel.*

Samuel, religiose indutus, dicat:[2]

*In Israel faciet rex verbum.*[3]

Vocatores:[4]

*Iste cetus.*

Chorus:

*Quod Iudea.*

Vocacio Dauid:

*Dic tu, Dauid, de nepote*
*causas ⟨ quæ sunt tibi notæ⟩.*

Dauid, ornatus regalibus ornamentis, dicat:

*Vniuersus*
*grex conuersus*
*adorabit Dominum,*
*⟨cui futurum*
*servitrum*
*omne genus hominum.⟩*

Vocatores:

*Iste cetus.*

Chorus:

*Quod Iudea.*

[1] Vocatores] Vocant (B).

[2] dicat] doceat (B).

[3] See 1 Samuel iii, 11: *Et dixit Dominus ad Samuelem: Ecce ego facio verbum in Israel, quod quicumque audierit, tinnient ambæ aures ejus.*

[4] Vocatores] Vocant (B).

Vocacio Osee:

*Auffer, Osee,*
*plebi Hebree*
*cecitatem.*

Osee, barbatus, dicat:

*Deus nunciauit de filio Dauid in presenti.*[1]

Vocatores:[2]

*Iste cetus.*

Chorus:

*Quod Iudea.*

Vocacio Iohelis:

*Iohel, leua uocem cum ceteris.*

Iohel, diuersum habens cultum, et barbatus dicat:

*Effundam de spiritu meo, dicit Dominus.*[3]

Vocatores:[4]

*Iste cetus.*

Chorus:

*Quod Iudea.*

Vocacio Abdie:

*Fac, Abdia, preconia uenturi Saluatoris.*

Abdias, diuersum habens cultum, barbatus, dicat:

*Et in monte Syon saluacio erit.*[5]

Vocatores:[6]

*Iste cetus.*

Chorus:

*Quod Iudea.*

Vocacio Ione:

*De persona*
*Christi, Iona,*[7]
*que sunt in te mistica?*

Ionas, caluus, alba indutus, dicat:

*O Iudei,*
*huius rei*
*signum, genus fatuum.*[8]

[1] See Hosea iii, 5: *Et post hæc revertentur filii Israel, et quærent Dominum Deum suum, et David regem suum; et pavebunt ad Dominum, et ad bonum ejus, in novissimo dierum.*

[2] Vocatores] Vocant (B).

[3] See Joel ii, 28: *Et erit post hæc: Effundam spiritum meum super omnem carnem; et prophetabunt filii vestri et filiæ vestræ; senes vestri somnia somniabunt, et juvenes vestri visiones videbunt.*

[4] Vocatores] Vocant (B).

[5] See Obadiah, 17: *Et in monte Sion erit salvatio, et erit sanctus; et possidebit domus Jacob eos qui se possederant.*

[6] Vocatores] Vocant (B).

[7] Iona] Omitted (B).

[8] See Matt. xii, 39–40: *Qui respondens ait illis: Generatio mala et adultera signum quærit, et signum non dabitur ei, nisi signum Jonæ prophetæ. Sicut enim fuit Jonas in ventre ceti tribus diebus et tribus noctibus, sic erit Filius hominis in corde terræ tribus diebus et tribus noctibus.*

Vocatores:

*Iste cetus.*

Chorus:

*Quod Iudea.*

Vocacio Michee:

*Effice, Michea, quod credat plebs.*

Micheas, diuersum cultum habens, barbatus, dicat:

*Descendet Dominus*
*cui non est terminus.*[1]

Vocatores:

*Iste cetus.*

Chorus:

*Quod Iudea.*

Vocacio Naum:

*Naum,*[2] *plebi Iudaice dic.*

Naum[3] | senex respond*eat*:

*Super montes euuangelizantis.*[4]

Vocatores:

*Iste cetus.*

Chorus:

*Quod Iudea.*

Vocacio Sophonie:

*Esto nobis, Sophonia.*

Sophonias, barbatus, dicat:

*In medio tui Syon rex regnabit.*[5]

Vocatores:

*Iste cetus.*

Chorus:

*Quod Iudea.*

Vocacio Aggei:

*Audiamus os Aggei ut expon*at.

Aggeus, senilem uultum gerens, dicat:

*Veniet cunctis gentibus rex desideratissimus.*[6]

Vocatores:

*Iste cetus.*

[1] See Micah i, 3: *Quia ecce Dominus egredietur de loco suo; et descendet, et calcabit super excelsa terræ;* Mich. v, 2: *Et tu, Bethlehem Ephrata, parvulus es in millibus Juda; ex te mihi egredietur qui sit dominator in Israel, et egressus ejus ab initio, a diebus æternitatis;* Mich. v, 4: *Et convertentur, quia nunc magnificabitur usque ad terminos terræ.*

[2] Naum: Naum] Nain (B).

[3] Naum] Nain (B).

[4] See Nahum i, 15: *Ecce super montes pedes evangelizantis, et annuntiantis pacem.*

[5] See Zephaniah iii, 14: *Lauda, filia Sion; jubila, Israel; lætare, et exulta in omni corde, filia Jerusalem.*

[6] See Haggai ii, 8: *Et movebo omnes gentes, et veniet desideratus cunctis gentibus; et implebo domum istam gloria, dicit Dominus exercituum.*

Chorus:

*Quod Iudea.*

Vocacio Zacharie:

*Veni, Zacharia, fili Barachie.*

Zacharias, barbatus, dicat:

*En rex tuus uenit tibi iustus, filia Syon.*[1]

Vocatores:

*Iste cetus.*

Chorus:

*Quod Iudea.*

Vocacio Ezechielis:

*Profer nobis, Ezechiel, aduentum.*

Responsio eiusdem:

*Per clausam ianuam rex intrabit solus.*[2]

Vocatores:

*Iste cetus.*

Chorus:

*Quod Iudea.*

Vocacio Malachie:

*Palam nobis refer, Malachia.*[3]

Responsio eiusdem:

*Scimus hec dicentem Deum.*[4]

Vocatores:

*Iste cetus.*

Chorus:

*Quod Iudea.*

Vocacio Zacharie patris Sancti Iohannis:

*Zacharia, os aperi.*

Ipse, ornatus quasi Iudeus, dicat:

*Per uiscera dulciflue*
*Dei misericordie.*[5]

Vocatores:

*Iste cetus.*

[1] See Zechariah ix, 9: *Exulta satis, filia Sion; jubila, filia Jerusalem; ecce rex tuus veniet tibi justus, et salvator; ipse pauper, et ascendens super asinam et super pullum filium asinæ.*

[2] See Ezekiel xliv, 1–3: *Et convertit me ad viam portæ sanctuarii exterioris, quæ respiciebat ad orientem; et erat clausa. Et dixit Dominus ad me: Porta hæc clausa erit; non aperietur, et vir non transibit per eam, quoniam Dominus, Deus Israel, ingressus est per eam; eritque clausa principi.*

[3] nobis refer Malachia] refer nobis Mathia (B).

[4] See Malach. iii, i: *Ecce ego mitto angelum meum, et præparabit viam ante faciem meam; et statim veniet ad templum suum Dominator quem vos quæritis, et angelus testamenti quem vos vultis. Ecce venit, dicit Dominus exercituum.*

[5] See Luke i, 78: *Per viscera misericordiæ Dei nostri, in quibus visitavit nos, oriens ex alto.* It will be observed that the prophecy assigned to Zacharias in the Rouen version is not the same as that (Luke i, 76) assigned to him in the pseudo-Augustinian *lectio*. See above, p. 128.

Chorus:

*Quod Iudea.*

Vocacio Elyzabeth:

*Illud, Elyzabeth, in medium*
*⟨de Domino profer eloquium⟩.*

In persona alba, quasi pregnans, dicat:

*Quid est rei*
*quod me*[1] *mei*
*⟨mater heri visitat?*
*nam ex eo*
*ventre meo*
*lætus infans palpitat⟩.*

Vocatores:

*Iste cetus.*

Chorus:

*Quod Iudea.*

Vocacio Sancti Iohannis Baptiste:

*Da, Baptista,*
*uentris*[2] *cista*
*clausus,*
*⟨quos dedisti*
*causa Christi*
*plausus?*
*Cui dedisti gaudium,*
*profer et testimonium.⟩*

Ipse, nudus pedes, tenens textum, dicat:

*Venit talis*
*sotularis*
*cuius non sum ⟨etiam*
*tam benignus*
*ut sim dignus*
*solvere corrigiam⟩.*

Vocatores:

*Iste cetus.*

Chorus:

*Quod Iudea.*

Vocacio Symeonis:

*Quid dixisti, Symeon, cum in tua?*

Symeon, senex, respondeat:

*Dei nostri, Saluatoris, conspexerunt*[3] *oculi.*

Vocatores:

*Iste cetus.*

[1] me] Omitted (B).
[2] uentris] Ventrix (B).
[3] conspexerunt] cum surrexerunt (B).

Chorus:

*Quod Iudea.*

Vocacio Uirgilii:

*Maro, Maro,*[1] *uates gentilium,*
*da Christo* ⟨*testimonium*⟩.

Virgilius, in iuuenili habitu bene ornatus, respond*eat*:

*Ecce polo demissa solo* ⟨*nova progenies est.*⟩

Vocatores:

*Iste cetus.*

Chorus:

*Quod Iudea.*

Interim Nabugodonosor, quasi rex paratus, | ostendens ymaginem, duobus Armatis dicat:

*Huc venite, uos armati.*

Tunc Armati ostendant ymaginem prius[2] dicentes:

*Regi gratum*
*famulatum.*

Interim ostendant[3] ymaginem tribus Pueris dicentes:

*Huic sacro*
*simulacro.*

Tunc Pueri ymaginem respuentes dicant:

*Deo soli*
*digno coli.*

Hoc audito, Armati Pueros Regi ducant, dicentes:

*Quia ritum*
*stabilitum*
*non timetis.*

Tunc ostendant[4] Regi Pueros, dicentes:

[5]*Rex, tua saluentur.*

Tunc Rex iratus dicat:

*Ergo tales assumantur.*

Tunc Armati ducentes Pueros ad fornacem dicentes:[5]

*Reos digne*[6]
*iam in igne.*

Tunc mittantur Pueri in fornace⟨m⟩, et accendatur. At illi, facti liberi, dicant:

*Benedictus es, Domine Deus,*

et cetera. Rex, hoc audiens, admirans dicat:

*En quid cantant*[7] *illi tres?*

[1] Maro Maro] Mars Mars (B).

[2] prius] pueris (A.B). The reading *prius* (adopted from MS 1232) results in avoiding a repetition of the summons to the *Pueri*—a repetition which may, or may not, be objectionable. See Gasté, p. 17, note.

[3] ostendant] ostendat (B).

[4] ostendant] respondeant (B).

[5–5] Omitted (B).

[6] Reos digne] Digne reos (B).

[7] cantant] cantent (B).

Armati dicant:

*Deum laudant.*[1]

Tunc Uocatores dicant Regi:

*Puerum cum pueris,*
*Nabugodonosor,*
*⟨cum in igne videris,*
*quid dixisti?⟩*

Rex fornacem ostendens[2] dicat:

*Tres in igne positi pueri*
*⟨quarto gaudent comite liberi⟩.*

Vocatores:[3]

*Iste cetus.*[4]

Chorus:

*Quod Iudea.*

Vocacio Sibille:

*Tu, Sibilla,*[5]
*uates illa,*
*⟨dic adventum judicis,*
*dic signum judicii.⟩*

Sibilla, coronata et muliebri habitu ornata, dicat:

*Iudicii signum: Tellus sudore ⟨madescet⟩.*

Vocatores:[6]

*Iste cetus.*

Chorus:

*Quod Iudea.*

Quo finito, omnes Prophete et Ministri in pulpito cantent[7] hos versus:

*Ortum predestinacio*
*paruo sabbati spacio.*[8]

Hoc finito, cantor incipiat ad introitum chori responsorium *Confirmatum est cor uirginis.*[9] Prophete et Ministri regentes chorum secundum suum ordinem incipiant ad Missam officium *Puer natus.*[10]

The representation at Rouen clearly begins immediately after Terce. During the singing of the stanzas *Gloriosi et famosi* by two clerics, with responses from the chorus, the procession of prophets

[1] laudant] laudent (B).

[2] fornacem ostendens] ostendens fornacem (B).

[3] Vocatores] Vocant (B).

[4] cetus] Omitted (B).

[5] Vocacio Sibille Tu Sibilla] Vocatis Sibila En Sibila (B).

[6] Vocatores] Vocant (B).

[7] cantent] cantant (B).

[8] For the complete text of *Hortum prædestinatio* see above, i, 615, 616.

[9] cor uirginis] Omitted (B). For the following Christmas responsory see Hartker, p. 49: *Confirmatum est cor virginis, in quo divina mysteria angelo narrante concepit te, formam præ filiis hominum castis concepit visceribus; et benedicta in æternum Deum nobis protulit et hominem.* Versus: *Domus pudici pectoris templum repente fit Dei, intacta nesciens virum verbo concepit filium.*

[10] *Puer natus est nobis* is the *incipit* of the introit both for the feast of the Circumcision (Jan. 1) and for the third Mass of Christmas. As to the three masses of Christmas see above, i, 547.

leaves the cloister and advances toward the nave. In the middle of the church a halt is made between a row of six Jews on one side and a row of six Gentiles on the other. After exhorting both groups to rejoice in Christ's birth, the summoners address in turn the recalcitrant Jews and the unbelieving Gentiles, receiving a response from each. The *vocatores* now call upon Moses to testify concerning Christ, and after he has delivered his testimony, they conduct him to a position beyond the furnace that has been constructed in the middle of the nave. Next in order Amos is appropriately summoned, utters his prophecy, and is conducted to a position beside Moses. Similarly are treated Isaiah, Aaron, Jeremiah, Daniel, Habakkuk, Balaam, Samuel, David, Hosea, Joel, Obadiah, Jonah, Micah, Nahum, Zephaniah, Haggai, Zechariah, Ezekiel, Malachi, Zacharias, Elisabeth, Saint John the Baptist, Simeon, Virgil, Nebuchadnezzar, and the Sibyl. After the Sibyl has been escorted to her place among the prophets, the whole company of prophets and attendants unite in singing from a pulpit[1] the prose *Hortum prædestinatio*. The procession now advances into the choir for Mass, the prophets and ministers beginning the introit (*officium*) and ruling the choir.

In its general arrangements for impersonation this play resembles that from Laon. Each of the two texts mentions details of costume which are lacking in the other, but there are no noteworthy discrepancies. In its content, likewise, the Rouen play shows certain marked similarities to other versions. Like the Laon play it opens with the processional stanzas *Gloriosi et famosi*, adding a considerable number of lines which we have not seen hitherto. The appropriateness of this composition to the general theme of the *Ordo Prophetarum* is so complete as to suggest that it was invented specifically for use in this dramatic procession. A like appropriateness cannot be claimed, however, for the closing chant *Hortum prædestinatio*, which we now find in the play of the prophets for the first time. In its content this poem is related, not to the theme under present consideration, but to the story of the Resurrection, in certain dramatizations of which we have already observed it.[2]

The most obvious difference between the Rouen play and the versions previously considered is, of course, the notable increase in the number of the prophets. Against the thirteen personages

[1] The phrase *in pulpito* may apply to the rood-loft over the choir-screen. See Gasté, pp. 19–20.

[2] See above, i, 575, 615, and below, p. 460.

summoned in the *lectio*, and in the Limoges and Laon versions, the Rouen text provides twenty-eight, in non-chronological order, including all of the major and minor prophets of the Bible. Excepting Israel, these twenty-eight include all the prophets found in the shorter dramatic texts, and fourteen others.[1] This expansion of the dramatic text was accomplished easily, since the names and utterances of the added personages lay ready to hand in the Vulgate, and the sermonizer of the pseudo-Augustinian *lectio* had himself suggested the process: *Quod si velim ex lege et ex prophetis omnia quæ de Christo dicta sunt colligere, facilius me tempus quam copia deseret.*[2]

Of the fourteen prophets that the Rouen version has in common with the shorter versions, some nine[3] use utterances that we have already seen in both the Limoges and the Laon texts. The other five present special cases. Balaam, found only at Laon and Rouen, uses the same prophecies in the two versions. The Moses and Simeon of Rouen—if we may judge from their brief *initia*—deliver speeches unlike those of Limoges and Laon in text, but like them in ultimate derivation from the *lectio*. Zacharias appears only in the *lectio* and in the Rouen play, and in the two versions his utterances are not the same. The Rouen Nebuchadnezzar utters the prophecy that we have already seen in the Laon version.

The peculiar interest of the Rouen play lies, however, not in textual details, but in two amplified scenes, centring respectively in Balaam and Nebuchadnezzar.

The dramatization of the story of Balaam is brief, but more comprehensive than what we have seen in the Laon play. In the spoken text of the Rouen play, to be sure, less attention is given to the *asina*; but, on the other hand, specific notice is taken of the relation of Balaam to King Balak. It is, indeed, two emissaries of this king, rather than the usual *vocatores*, who first summon Balaam forth, and bid him come to Balak's court. Balaam now rides forth upon his ass, vigorously plying his spurs, until the person concealed under the animal cries out in protest. Meanwhile a youth costumed as an angel, with wings and sword, stands in the path and commands Balaam to cease serving Balak.

[1] Amos, Aaron, Samuel, Hosea, Joel, Obadiah, Jonah, Micah, Nahum, Zephaniah, Haggai, Zechariah, Ezekiel, and Malachi.

[2] See above, p. 128. Concerning this tendency to assimilate additional prophets, or *loi d'assimilation*, see Sepet, pp. 27–38.

[3] Isaiah, Jeremiah, Daniel, Habakkuk, David, Elisabeth, John the Baptist, Virgil, and the Sibyl.

The official *vocatores* now call upon Balaam for his prophecy, and he delivers the utterance that we have already observed in the Laon play.[1]

For enlivening the prophecy of Nebuchadnezzar a still more elaborate action is devised. As a stage-setting are provided a furnace made of cloth and oakum, and some sort of figure to serve as the golden idol of the Biblical account. Pointing to this image, the king begins the action abruptly by ordering two of his soldiers to command the youths, Shadrach, Meshach, and Abednego, to fall down in worship. When they respond by spurning the idol, the three young men are haled into the presence of Nebuchadnezzar. Hearing of their contumacy, the king angrily orders that they be cast into the furnace. After this order has been executed, and the furnace lighted, the *pueri* sing *Benedictus es, Domine Deus*. Aroused by the sound of their voices, Nebuchadnezzar asks his attendants what the youths are singing, and is told that they are praising God. The *vocatores* now interrupt the action, asking the king what he said at this juncture. Nebuchadnezzar brings the episode to a close by delivering the testimony already known to us from the Laon version.[2]

In contrast to the brief and formal treatment accorded to the other prophets, the elaboration of the roles of Balaam and Nebuchadnezzar yields two small episodes which, in their completeness, may almost be considered independent dramatic units. To the further question as to whether such scenes eventually severed their connexion with the defile of prophets and became separate plays, we must recur in a moment.

As to the day on which the Rouen play was performed the commentators have not agreed, some assigning it to Christmas Day,[3] others to the preceding day,[4] and still others to the feast of the Circumcision (January 1).[5] This last date is unquestionably correct, for in our best manuscript the dramatic text is found in the very midst of the *ordo* for the services of January

[1] For the source of the whole action see Numbers xxii, 1–35. It will be observed that the dramatic writer does not use the phraseology of the Vulgate.

[2] For the source of this whole episode see Daniel iii, 13 sqq.

[3] See Du Cange, iii, 460; Sepet, p. 42; Chambers, ii, 55; Bartholomaeis, p. 212. Chambers assigns the performance to Christmas, rather than to the preceding day, because 'the *Introit* with which the text concludes is *Puer natus est*, which belongs to the *Magna missa* of the feast-day, and not to the eve.' *Puer natus est*, as a matter of fact, is the introit also of the Mass of the feast of the Circumcision. As Villetard has observed (*Corbeil*, p. 47), the entire liturgy of the Circumcision is essentially a compilation from other feasts, chiefly Christmas. See Chasles, p. 126.

[4] See Gasté, p. 4.

[5] See Du Méril, p. 181; Chasles, p. 126.

1st, and directly introduces the Mass for that day.[1] From the rubric introducing the dramatic text we learn that the performance might or might not be performed in any particular year, an option to which we need attach no special significance.[2]

The attachment of this dramatic performance to the liturgy of the feast of the Circumcision, the name *Festum Asinorum* given to it in the manuscript, and the presence of the *asina* in the action —all these circumstances combine to raise the question of the relation of the play before us to the famous liturgical revels of the Christmas season known collectively as the Feast of Fools.[3] Of the four special celebrations composing these revels the most pertinent to our immediate inquiry is that which occurred, most commonly, on the day of the Circumcision. In churches in which such 'misrule' was permitted, the subdeacons assumed control of the liturgy, and, as we have seen, conducted services which were abnormal in various particulars. At Beauvais in the thirteenth century, for example, the normal *form* of the Mass and Canonical Office is retained, but the official *text* was extended by interpolations, or tropes, and the ceremonial included a considerable amount of boisterous buffoonery. At Sens, during the same century, the ceremony, although it is revealingly referred to as *asinaria festa*, appears to have been decorously 'reformed' so as to exclude burlesque and irreverence. Both at Sens and at Beauvais the introductory chants to the *cursus* include the famous Prose of the Ass, *Orientis partibus*, during the singing of which at Beauvais the animal appears to have been brought into the church.[4]

What, then, is the relation between the *asinaria festa* of the Feast of Fools and the so-called *Festum Asinorum* of Rouen, along with any other dramatic representation of the prophets which may include the perturbing figure of Balaam's ass? In answering this question we may assume, in the first place, that the Augustinian sermon and the dramatic *Ordo Prophetarum* which developed from it antedate such ecclesiastical revels as the Feast of Fools of Beauvais and Sens. It is not to be inferred, however, that the

[1] In Rouen MS 384 the complete *ordo* for the Circumcision occupies fol. $32^{v}$–$35^{r}$, the play of the prophets occurring on fol. $33^{r}$–$35^{r}$. Further details are given by Young, *op. cit.*, p. 67.

[2] This option is discussed by Young, *op. cit.*, pp. 67–8. There appears to be no basis for Sepet's conjecture (pp. 38–40) that the presenting of the play may have been contingent upon the decorous conduct of the spectators during the performance of the previous year.

[3] Concerning the Feast of Fools see above, i, 104 sqq.

[4] See Chambers, i, 286, 331; Villetard, *Corbeil*, pp. 49, 232. For the text of the Prose of the Ass see above, i, 551.

riotous *asinaria festa* of the Feast of Fools were derived from the play of the prophets, as at least one critic has held.[1] On the contrary, in so far as Balaam and his ass are concerned, the borrowing was, no doubt, in the other direction. In the sermon and the dramatic version from Limoges Balaam does not appear; and in the play at Laon his role seems to have been a concluding addition to the text. It would appear, then, that in the course of time the figure of the ass was introduced from the Feast of Fools into the play of the prophets, and that sometimes, as at Rouen, the *asina* forced upon the pious dramatic performance the name *Festum Asinorum*.[2] The Rouen play on the feast of the Circumcision, of which our earliest text is of the fourteenth century, may actually supersede an earlier Feast of Fools on the same day. Whether the ass brought with him into the *Ordo Prophetarum* the comic associations of the liturgical revels we cannot say with final assurance. From the Laon and Rouen texts themselves we may reasonably infer that the performances were intended to be serious throughout, and that the conduct of the ass itself was altogether decorous.[3]

## VI

The most obvious effect of such episodes as those of Balaam and Nebuchadnezzar is to animate and vary the otherwise rather dull uniformity of the fundamental dramatic scheme of the *Ordo Prophetarum*. However carefully the personages may be differentiated through costume and other details of impersonation, an unrelieved succession of summonings and respondings cannot escape monotony; and in the Rouen play the placing of the respective scenes of Balaam and of Nebuchadnezzar relatively early and late in the performance may have been designed to secure with limited resources a maximum of diversity. But in these two scenes at least one critic has discerned a somewhat wider significance. Sepet conjectures, in the first place, a form of the dramatic procession in which still further speakers are summoned to testify, and in which other prophets beside Balaam and Nabuchadnezzar were centres of dramatic expansion—

[1] See Gasté, pp. 20–1. His position is challenged by Chambers (ii, 56–7), with whose views I am in accord in the present paragraph.

[2] Of a Feast of Fools in the cathedral of Rouen itself we have no information. Chambers (i, 303–4) traces its presence at Laon from about 1280 to the sixteenth century.

[3] Sepet (p. 28) makes this inference with complete confidence. For other texts and fragments related, directly or indirectly, to the *Ordo Prophetarum* see Notes, pp. 458 sqq.

Abraham, for example, and Joseph, Moses, or David.[1] He infers, moreover, that certain of these special episodes may have been amplified considerably beyond anything that we have seen in the plays from Laon and Rouen. He then reasons that certain of these more highly developed episodes may have detached themselves from the *Ordo Prophetarum*, and have maintained themselves as independent dramatic pieces. Finally Sepet arrives at the conclusion that after existing for a time as independent units, these isolated plays re-united in the form of cycles collectively dramatizing large portions of the narrative of the Old Testament—cycles such as are found in several of the vernaculars of Western Europe.[2]

Conjectures so comprehensive as these reach far beyond the limits of the present study, and cannot be examined in detail here. Scholars have not failed to challenge one step or another in Sepet's argument, and it is obvious to all students of the subject that his proposals cannot be accepted in their entirety.[3] Within the present treatise, however, are found evidences sufficient for establishing the soundness of some of his less ambitious conjectures. Clearly a few scenes within the *Ordo Prophetarum* itself were expanded into episodes of independent dramatic interest, and texts of the *Ordo* now lost must have contained other similar, or even more extensive, amplifications. Among the plays of the Church, moreover, are independent pieces which centre in personages found in the versions of the *Ordo Prophetarum* reviewed above, and which, as we shall see, bear evidences of having been, at some stage, attached to the more comprehensive dramatic performance.[4] To this extent, at least, the brilliant inferences of Sepet are firmly substantiated.

[1] For a conjecture concerning a scene, or play, of Moses, at Lincoln, see Chambers, ii, 377–8.

[2] See Sepet, *passim*—especially pp. 48–147, 165–79.

[3] See Meyer, pp. 53–6; W. Creizenach, in *Literaturblatt für germanische und romanische Philologie*, xxiii (1902), 203; Craig, pp. 473–87; Jenney, pp. 59–64.

[4] See below, pp. 304 sqq.

## CHAPTER XXII

# THE CHRISTMAS PLAY FROM BENEDIKTBEUERN

THE chapters immediately preceding have brought before us the several kinds of play which arose on separate days during the Christmas season, dramatizing the visit of the shepherds to the manger at Bethlehem (*Officium Pastorum*), the coming of the Magi (*Officium Stellæ*), the slaughter of the Innocents (*Ordo Rachelis*), and the testimonies of the prophets (*Ordo Prophetarum*). Although each of these four dramatic types is to be regarded as an independent development, some of them, as we have observed, show a tendency to combine among themselves into somewhat larger units. Thus some versions of the *Officium Stellæ*, particularly those from Bilsen, Fleury, and Freising, contain scenes in which the shepherds appear, as does also the *Ordo Rachelis* from Freising;[1] and the *Officium Stellæ* from Laon ends with a representation of the slaughter of the Innocents.[2] Among the Christmas plays in general, however, combinations such as these may be regarded as tentative and exceptional. For a truly comprehensive play, uniting all the dramatic themes of Christmas, we turn to the celebrated composition found among the *Carmina Burana*:[3]

Primo ponatur sedes Augustino in fronte ecclesie, et Augustinus habeat a dextera parte Ysaiam et Danielem et alios Prophetas, a sinistra autem Archisynagogum et suos Iudeos. Postea surgat Ysaias cum prophetia sua sic:

*Ecce uirgo pariet*
*sine uiri semine,*
*per quod mundum abluet*
*a peccati crimine.*
*De uenturo gaudeat*
*Iudea numine,*
*et nunc ceca fugiat*
*ab erroris limine!*[4]

[1] See above, pp. 79, 84, 96, 117–8.

[2] See above, p. 105.

[3] Munich, Staatsbibl., MS lat. 4660, Carmina Burana sæc. xiii, fol. $99^r$–$104^v$, previously edited by Schmeller, pp. 80–91 (S); Du Méril, pp. 187–206 (D); Froning, pp. 877–96 (F). The text of Hilka and Schumann will be no. 227. For observations upon the MS see above, i, 686. Unpublished textual notes from the pen of the late Professor Wilhelm Meyer have reached me through the generosity of Professor Hilka. With the exceptions indicated in the foot-notes below, the spoken text is provided with musical notation. For references to commentary upon the present play see Notes, p. 463. See also plate xviii.

[4] limine] lumine (S.F).

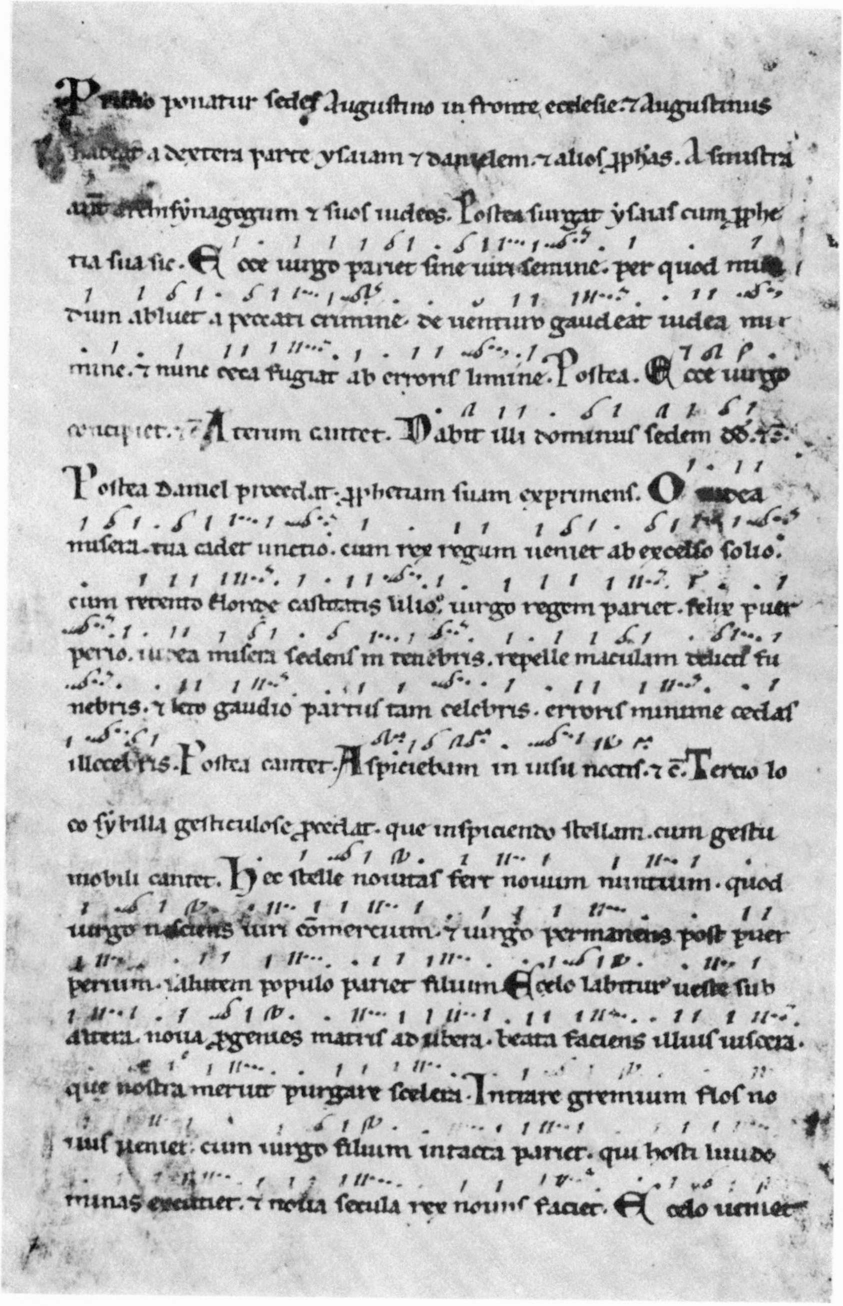

Primitus ponatur sedes Augustino in fronte ecclesie, et Augustinus habeat a dextera parte Ysaiam et Danielem et alios prophetas, a sinistra autem Archisynagogum et suos Iudeos. Postea surgat Ysaias cum prophetia sua sic: Ecce virgo pariet sine viri semine, per quod mundum abluet a peccati crimine. De venturo gaudeat Iudea numine, et nunc ceca fugiat ab erroris limine. Postea: Ecce virgo concipiet, et cetera. Iterum cantet: Dabit illi dominus sedem, et cetera. Postea Daniel procedat prophetiam suam exprimens: O Iudea misera, tua cadet unctio, cum rex regum veniet ab excelso solio, cum decenti flore castitatis lilio virgo regem pariet felix puerperio. Iudea misera, sedens in tenebris, repelle maculam delicti funebris, et leto gaudio partus tam celebris erroris minime cedas illecebris. Postea cantet: Aspiciebam in visu noctis, et cetera. Tertio loco Sybilla gesticulose procedat, que inspiciendo stellam cum gestu mobili cantet: Hec stelle novitas fert novum nuntium, quod virgo nasciens viri commercium et virgo permanens post puerperium salutem populo pariet filium. E celo labitur veste sub altera nova progenies matris ad ubera, beata faciens illius viscera, que nostra meruit purgare scelera. Intrare gremium flos novus veniet, cum virgo filium intacta pariet, qui hosti livido minas excutiet et nova secula rex novus faciet. E celo veniet

XVIII. Christmas Play, from *Carmina Burana*, in Munich, Staatsbibliothek, MS lat. 4660, fol. 99[r]

Postea:

*Ecce uirgo concipiet,*

et cetera.[1] Iterum cantet:

*Dabit illi Dominus sedem David,*

et cetera.[2] Postea Daniel procedat prophetiam suam exprimens:

*O Iudea misera!*
*Tua cadet unctio,*
*cum rex regum ueniet*
*ab excelso solio,*
*cum retento floridę*
*castitatis lilio*
*uirgo regem pariet*
*felix puerperio!*

*Iudea misera,*
*sedens in tenebris,*
*repelle maculam*
*delicti funebris,*
*et leto gaudio*
*partus tam celebris*
*erroris minime*
*cedas illecebris!*

Postea cantet:

*Aspiciebam in uisu noctis,*

et cetera.[3] Tercio loco Sybilla gesticulose procedat, que inspiciendo Stellam cum gestu mobili cantet:

*Hec stelle nouitas*
*fert nouum nuntium,*
*quod uirgo nesciens*
*uiri commercium,*
*et uirgo permanens*
*post puerperium,*
*salutem populo*
*pariet filium!*

*E celo labitur*
*ueste sub altera*
*noua progenies*
*matris ad ubera,*

[1] The following responsory is found in Hartker, p. 17: *Ecce virgo concipiet et pariet filium, dicit Dominus, et vocabitur nomen ejus admirabilis, Deus fortis.* Versus: *Tollite portas, principes, vestras, et elevamini portæ æternales, et introibit Deus.* In the text above, the word *concipiet* has no music.

[2] The following antiphon is found in Hartker, p. 38: *Dabit ei Dominus sedem David, patris sui, et regnabit in æternum.*

[3] The following responsory is found in Hartker, p. 16: *Aspiciebam in visu noctis, et ecce in nubibus cœli filius hominis venit, et datum est ei regnum et honor, et omnes populi, tribus et linguæ servient ei.* Versus: *Ecce dominator Dominus cum virtute veniet.*

*beata faciens*
*illius uiscera,*
*quę nostra meruit*
*purgare scelera!*

*Intrare gremium*
*flos nouus ueniet,*
*cum uirgo filium*
*intacta pariet,*
*qui hosti liuido*
*minas excutiet,*
*et noua secula*
*rex nouus faciet.*

*E celo ueniet* |
*rex magni nominis,*
*coniungens federa*
*Dei et hominis,*
*et sugens ubera*
*intacte uirginis,*[1]
*reatum diluens*
*mundani criminis!*

Item cantet hos uersus:

*Iudicii signum: Tellus,*

et cetera.[2] Deinde procedat Aaron, quartus propheta, portans uirgam, que sumpta super altare inter xii uirgas aridas sola floruit. Illam personam conducat chorus cum hoc responsorio:

*Salue, nobilis uirga.*[3]

Et dicat hanc prophetiam:

*Ecce nouo more frondes dat amigdala nostra*
*Virgula: nux Christus, sed uirgula uirgo beata!*

Et dicat:

*Vt hec* ⟨*uirga*⟩ *floruit*
*omni carens nutrimento,*
*sic et uirgo pariet*
*sine carnis detrimento.*

*Vt hic ramus uiruit*
*non nature copia,*
*uerum ut in uirgine*
*figuret misteria.*

[1] intacte uirginis] dei et hominis (MS)—emended by S.

[2] For these verses see above, p. 130.

[3] The following responsory is found in Hartker, p. 304; *Salve, nobilis virga Jesse; salve, flos campi, Maria, unde ortum est lilium convallium.* Versus: *Odor tuus super cuncta, pretiosa unguenta favus distillans, labia tua mel et lac sub lingua tua.*

*Clausa erunt uirginis*
*sic pudoris ostia,*
*quando uirgo pariet*
*spiritali gratia!*

Quinto loco procedat Balaam sedens in Asina et cantans:

*Vadam, uadam, ut maledicam populo huic!*

Cui occurrat Angelus euaginato gladio dicens:

*Caue, caue, ne quicquam aliud quam tibi dixero loquaris!*

Et Asinus, cui insidet Balaam, perterritus retrocedat. Postea recedat Angelus, et Balaam cantet hoc responsorium:

*Orietur stella ex Iacob,*

et cetera.[1] Archisynagogus cum suis Iudeis ualde obstrepet auditis prophetiis, et dicat trudendo socium suum, mouendo caput suum et totum corpus et percuciendo terram pede, baculo etiam imitando gestus Iudei in omnibus, et sociis suis indignando dicat:

*Dic michi, quid predicat*
*dealbatus paries!*
*Dic | michi, quid asserat*
*ueritatis caries!*
*Dic michi, quid fuerit,*
*quod audiui pluries!*
*Vellem esset cognita*
*rerum michi series!*

*Illos, reor, audio*
*in hec uerba fluere,*
*quod sine conmercio*
*uirgo debet parere!*
*O quanta simplicitas*
*cogit hos desipere,*
*qui de boue predicant*
*camelum descendere!*

Auditis tumultu et errore Iudeorum, dicat Episcopus Puerorum:[2]

*Horum sermo uacuus*
*sensus peregrini,*
*quos et furor agitat*
*et libertas uini!*
*Sed restat consulere*
*mentem Augustini,*
*per quem disputatio*
*concedatur fini!*

[1] For this responsory see Hartker, p. 34, and above, p. 46.

[2] For the speech that follows there is no music.

Statim Prophete uadant ante Augustinum et dicant:

*Multum nobis obuiat*
*lingua Iudeorum,*
*quibus adhuc adiacet*
*uetus fex errorum.*
*Cum de Christo loquimur,*
*rident et suorum*
*argumenta proferunt*
*nobis animorum!*

R*espondeat* Augustinus:

*Ad nos illa prodeat*[1]
*tenebris abscondita*
*et se nobis offerat*
*gens errori dedita,*
*vt et error claudicet*
*re*[2] *ipsis exposita,*
*et scripture pateat*
*ipsis clausa semita!*

Veniat Archisynagogus cum magno murmure sui et suorum, quibus dicat Augustinus:

*Nunc aures aperi,*
*Iudea misera!*
*Rex regum ueniet*
*ueste sub altera,*
*qui matris uirginis*
*dum sugit ubera,*
*Dei et hominis*
*coniunget federa!*

R*espondeat* Archisynagogus cum nimio cachinno:

*O Augustine,*
*de profundo maxime*
*portans hec ingenio,*[3]
*dum futurum predicas,*
*id quod negat ratio!*
*Nam si 'uirgo pariet'*
*et sine commercio,*
*id nature rubor est,*[4]
*et rerum confusio!*

[1] prodeat] Over the last two letters a later hand has placed a bar, as if to indicate *prodeant*.

[2] re] res, with *s* expunged (MS).

[3] O Augustine . . . ingenio] De profundo, maxime, portas hæc ingenio (emendation suggested D).

[4] id . . . est] nature robur est (MS. S. F); naturæ robur esset (emend. suggested D). From Hilka I adopt the emendation of Meyer.

*Tu quid contra resonas,*
*labe tactus ueteri,*
*qui non illud respicis,*
*quod est iustum fieri?*
*Nam si 'uirgo pa|riet,'*
*quod prophetant pueri,*
*natura de proprio*
*iure potest conqueri!*

*Quando 'uirgo pariet,'*
*Xante, retro propera!*
*Lupus agnum fugiet,*
*plana fient aspera!*
*Si moderna colligis*
*et attendis uetera,*
*in adiecto ponitur*
*'est uirgo puerpera,'*

*Vt propheta garrulus*
*incessanter asserit;*
*uel si 'uirgo pariet,'*
*uel iam forte peperit,*
*que non carnis copulam*
*ante partum*[1] *senserit,*
*quod fantasma fuerit,*
*lex docet et aperit!*

*Quod de clausa uirgine*
*sic procedat paruulus,*
*est erroris credere,*
*non doctrine cumulus!*
*Uel ergo respondeat*
*ad obiectum emulus,*
*uel erroris fugiat*
*et ruboris baiolus!*

Voce sobria et discreta respondeat Augustinus:

*In euentu prospero*
*talis casus unici*
*argumenta claudicent*[2]
*moresque sophistici;*
*docet enim ratio,*
*naturam non reici,*
*si quid preter solitum*
*semel uides obici!*

[1] carnis . . . partum] ante partum carnis copulam (MS. F).
[2] claudicent] claudicant (S.D).

⟨Archisynagogus:⟩

*Dicat 'homo mortuus';*[1]
*in adiecto ponitur,*
*quod in Aristotile*
*pueris exprimitur;*
*sed hec uestra regula*
*tunc repulsam patitur,*
*cum de 'matre uirgine'*
*sermo nobis oritur!*

Augustinus dicat:

*Ne fantasma dixeris*
*quod uirgo concipiet,*
*quod pudoris ostio*
*non aperto pariet:*
*De Iudea multiplex*
*testis nobis ueniet,*
*qui uobis contrarius*
*et nobiscum faciet!*

*Vt specular solidum*
*solis intrat radius,*
*et sincere transitus*
*seruit ei peruius,*
*sic in aulam uirginis*
*summi Patris Filius*
*lapsum quidem faciet,*
*et tamen innoxius!*

Postea incipiat Augustinus cantare:

*Letabundus* ⟨*exultet fidelis chorus,*
*Alleluia!*⟩,

primum uersum; et secundum, Prophete:

*Regem regum intacte profudit thorus,*
*Res mi|randa,*[2]

et cetera.[3] Dicat Archysinagogus cum suis:

*Res neganda!*

Iterum Augustinus cum suis:

*Res miranda!*[4]

[1] Archisynagogus: Dicat 'homo mortuus'] *Dicat* begins with a capital, and has musical notation, as if it were part of the spoken text—though it is followed by a point. D prints *Archisynagogus* as if it were in the MS, regards *dicat* as part of the rubric, and suggests inserting *movens* in the spoken text to restore the metre. S and F merely supply *Archisynagogus*, and use *dicat* along with it as part of the rubric.

[2] In the lower margin of fol. 100$^{v}$ another hand has written the poem *Furibundi cum aceto* (Hilka and Schumann, no. 5*; Schmeller, no. CC).

[3] For the complete text of the sequence *Lætabundus exultet fidelis* see below, p. 450.

[4] For this utterance no music is provided.

Iterum Archysinagogus cum suis:

*Res neganda!*[1]

Hoc fiat pluries. Augustinus incipiat:

*Angelus consilii*
*natvs est de uirgine,*
*sol de stella!*

Respondeant Prophete:

*Sol occasum nesciens,*
*stella semper rutilans,*
*semper clara!*

Dicat Augustinus:

*Cedrus alta Libani*
*conformatur ysopo*
*ualle nostra!*

Dicant Prophete:

*Verbum ens altissimi*
*corporali passum est*
*carne sumpta!*

Postea dicat Augustinus:

*Ysaias cecinit,*
*synagoga meminit;*
*nunquam tamen desi⟨n⟩it*[2]
*esse ceca!*

Respondeant Prophete:

*Si non suis uatibus,*
*credant*[3] *uel gentilibus*
*sibillinis uersibus*
*hec predicta!*

Postea dicat Augustinus cum Prophetis omnibus:

*Infelix, propera,*
*crede uel uetera!*
*Cur dampnaberis, gens misera?*
*Natum considera,*
*quem docet littera;*
*ipsum genuit puerpera!*

Postea Augustinus solus cantet:

*Discant nunc Iudei, quomodo de Christo consentientes nobiscum amplexari debent noui partus nouum gaudium, noue spem salutis ipsum expectantium! Nunc uenturum credant et nasciturum expectent nobiscum dicentes: Rex nouus erit salus mundo!*[4]

Inter cantandum omnia ista Archysinagogus[5] obstrepet mouendo corpus

[1] For this utterance no music is provided.
[2] desi⟨n⟩it] Emend. D; desiit (S.F).
[3] credant] credat (emend. D).
[4] This speech may have been modelled on the liturgical antiphon *Dicant nunc Judæi*. See above, i, 255.
[5] Archysinagogus] archysanag*ogus* (MS).

et caput, et deridendo predicta. Hoc conpleto, detur locus Prophetis, uel ut recedant, uel sedeant in locis suis propter honorem ludi. Deinde Angelus appareat Marie operanti muliebriter, et dicat:

*Aue Maria, gratia plena! Dominus tecum!*[1]

Et iterum:

*Ecce, concipies | et paries*,

et cetera. Illa stupefacta dicat:

*Quomodo fiet istud, quia uirum non cognosco?*

R*espondeat* Angelus:

*Spiritus Sanctus superueniet*,

et cetera. Versus:

*Ideoque quod nascetur*,

et cetera. R*espondeat* Maria:

*Ecce, ancilla Domini*,

et cetera. Deinde Maria uadat casualiter, nichil cogitans de Elisabeth uetula Iohanne inpregnata, et salutet eam; et dicat ⟨Elisabeth⟩:

*Vnde hoc mihi*,[2]

et cetera. Et cantabit:

*Ex quo facta est uox salutationis*,

et cetera. Eadem dicat:

*Benedicta tu in mulieribus*,

et cetera.

*Tu que portabis p. h. et añ geñ.*[3]

R*espondeat* Maria:

*Magnificat anima mea Dominum.*

Deinde recedat Elysabeth, quia amplius non habebit locum hec persona. Deinde Maria uadat in lectum suum, que iam de Spiritu Sancto concepit, et pariat Filium. Cui assideat Ioseph in habitu honesto et prolixa barba. Nato Puero, appareat stella, et incipiat chorus hanc antiphonam:

*Hodie Christus natus est, ⟨hodie salvator apparuit; hodie in terra canunt angeli, lætantur archangeli; hodie exultent justi dicentes: Gloria in excelsis Deo, alleluia.⟩*[4]

[1] plena . . . tecum] p. do. te. (MS), without music. For parallels to the Annunciation scene see below, pp. 245 sqq.

[2] For this speech no music is provided.

[3] Tu que . . . geñ] Has no musical notation. No previous editor has interpreted this passage, nor can I do more than report the suggestions of generous friends. Dom Wilmart calls my attention to a sequence beginning as follows (Chevalier, *R. H.*, no. 1879, printed in Daniel, *Thesaurus*, ii, 92; Villetard, *Corbeil*, pp. 100, 149):

Ave Maria, gratia plena,
Dominus tecum, virgo serena;
benedicta tu in mulieribus,
que peperisti pacem hominibus
et angelis gloriam.

The original of the passage in the play may have been related in some way to lines 4 and 5 of this sequence. Monsignor Ryan gives me the interesting suggestion that *Tu que portabis* may be the beginning of a liturgical piece, and that what follows may be a rubric such as *Post hoc et antiphona generalis*. Without reference to any known liturgical piece Dom Beyssac mentions the following as a possible expansion: *Tu que portabis pacem hominibus et ante gentes*.

[4] See Hartker, p. 51.

Qua finita, Stella appareat. Qua uisa, tres Reges a diuersis partibus mundi ueniant et ammirentur de apparitione talis Stelle, quorum primus dicat:

*Per curarum distrahor*
*frequenter quadruuium,*
*rationis paciens*
*et mentis naufragium,*
*cum hanc stellam uideo*
*portantem inditium,*
*quod ipsius nouitas*
*nouum portet nuntium!*

*Cursus ego didici*
*et naturas siderum,*
*et ipsorum memini*
*perscrutari numerum;*
*sed cum hanc inspicio,*
*ego miror iterum,*
*quia non conparuit*
*aput quemquam ueterum!*

*Quando luna patitur,*
*et sol*[1] *obscurabitur,*
*quem effectum habeat*
*Stilbon comes Ueneris,*
*in quo gradu maxime*
*Mars nociuus diceris,*
*michi fecit cognitum*
*lingua | secte ueteris.*

*Sed elinguem efficit*
*hic me stelle radius!*
*Quid portendat, nescio,*
*sed querens attentius*
*hoc unum conjicio,*[2]
*quod est natus filius,*
*cui mundus obediet,*
*quem timebit amplius!*

Hoc dicat primus semper inspiciendo Stellam, et disputet de illa. Dicat secundus:

*Mea iam precordia*
*dulce uestit gaudium;*
*michi uie factum* ⟨*est*⟩
*non parum compendium.*

[1] sol] sol quando (MS. S.F).

[2] conjicio] conitio (MS. F).

*In eo, quod ambigo,*
*se monstrantem dubium*
*et cure participem*
*iam inueni socium!*

*Quando mente uigili*
*planetas inspicio,*
*mea uim cuiuslibet*
*deprehendit ratio*
*de Marte, de Uenere,*
*de Sole, Mercurio,*
*de Iouis clementia,*
*de Saturni senio,*
*que sit uis cuiuslibet*
*in quo domicilio.*[1]
*Sed in hac quam aspicis*
*et quam monstras digito,*
*qualitate cognita*
*de effectu dubito.*
*Sed quid inde sentiam*
*tu mecum accipito,*
*ut fruamur pariter*
*quesiti proposito!*

*Illud*[2] *iubar, quod inspicis*
*et in tantum radiat*
*et planetas ceteros*
*in pallorem uariat,*
*regem natum predicat,*
*quo maior non ueniat,*
*cuius cedens nutui*
*totus orbis seruiat!*

Dicat tercius monstrando et disputando de Stella:

*Questionum nouerat*
*enodare rete*
*ille, per quem habeo,*
*quod, quando comete*
*se producit radius,*
*tunc hebent*[3] *planete,*
*et quorundam principum*
*se presentant mete.*

*Quid sit stella, nouimus,*
*et quid sit planeta;*

[1] que sit . . . domicilio] D proposes omitting.

[2] Illud] Hoc (emend. D).

[3] hebent] habent (MS); latent (emend. S. F); absunt (proposed D). I adopt the emendation of Meyer-Hilka.

*horum hec est neutrum!*[1]
*Sed cum sit cometa,*
*inungamur gaudio,*
*sit mens nobis leta;*
*magni enim principis*
*uerus est propheta!*

*Vide, stelle claritas*
*quanta propagatur;*
*in planeta quolibet*
*splendor | hebetatur;*[2]
*quod ei, qui natus est,*
*satis adaptatur,*
*cuiusuis potentia*
*per hunc obscuratur!*

*Ergo cum muneribus*
*una procedamus,*
*et quo stella duxerit,*
*gressus dirigamus,*
*ut, quando uiderimus*
*quem natum speramus,*
*nostra ei munia*[3]
*reges offeramus!*

Modo procedant Reges usque in terram Herodis, querendo de Puero et cantando:

*Vbi est, qui natus est,*

et cetera.[4] Quibus occurrant Nuntii Herodis dicentes:

*Vos, qui regum habitus*
*et insigne geritis,*
*nobis notum facite,*
*quare sic inceditis,*
*uel si notum*[5] *aliquid*
*reserandum noscitis,*
*Iudeorum quod ad aures*
*regis ferre queritis.*[6]

*Nos Herodis uernule*
*sumus et uicarii,*

[1] horum . . . neutrum] Istud sidus est neutrum; Hoc sidus est neutrum (emend. proposed D).

[2] Beginning with *hebetatur*, the text lacks musical notation through l. 509.

[3] munia] munera (emend. S).

[4] See Matt. ii, 2.

[5] notum] noturum (MS); secretum (emend. S); latens, clausum, tectum (proposals D).

[6] Iudeorum . . . queritis] quod ad aures regis ferre queritis (MS); quod ad aures regias vos deferre queritis (emend. S); Judææ quod ad aures regis ferre quæritis (emend. D). I adopt the emendation of Meyer-Hilka.

*ad quem*[1] *sepe transuolant*
*ex diuersis nuntii.*
*Nulla nobis clausa sunt*
*secreta palatii;*
*ergo scire poscimus*[2]
*uestri rem negocii.*

R*espondeant* Reges:

*Sepelire nolumus*[3]
*quod a nobis queritur;*
*ipsum stella reserat,*
*que a nobis cernitur!*
*Regem natum querimus,*
*de quo stella loquitur,*
*quod eius inperium*
*nullo fine clauditur!*

R*espondeant* Nuntii:

*Felix istud ueniet*
*Herodi preconium,*
*et libenter audiet*
*hoc de rege nuntium,*
*ut hinc ergo primitus*
*per nos sumat gaudium,*
*uos nostrum sequimini*
*⟨paulatim⟩*[4] *uestigium!*

Postea Nuntii festinent ad Herodem dicentes:

*Rex Herodes, accipe*
*quiddam ammirandum,*
*iam a tribus regibus*
*tibi reserandum:*
*ipsi natum asserunt*
*regem uenerandum,*
*cui esse non ambigunt*
*orbem subiugandum!*

Respondet Herodes cum magna indignatione:

*Cur audetis talia*
*regi presentare?*
*No|lite, uos consulo,*
*falsum fabricare!*
*Nam*[5] *Herodes ego sum*
*potens subiugare*
*quicquid mundus continet,*
*celum, terra, mare.*

[1] quem] quos (emend. D).
[2] poscimus] possumus (MS). I follow Meyer-Hilka. [3] nolumus] uolumus (MS).
[4] Emend. S and D.
[5] Nam] num (MS. S. D. F). I follow Meyer-Hilka.

Post hec Herodes maxime indignatus uocari faciat Archysinagogum cum Iudeis suis dicens:

*Huc Iudea ueniat*
*fecunda consilio,*
*ut nobiscum disserat*[1]
*super hoc negocio.*
*Ego*[2] *uos precipiam*
*exponi suplicio,*
*si uos esse deuios*
*conprobabit ratio!*

Modo ueniat Archisynagogus cum magna superbia et Iudeis suis, cui dicat Herodes:

*Te, magister, alloquor,*
*et aduertant alii!*
*Nostra mordet uiscera*
*duri fama nuntii.*
*Huc tres magi ueniunt*
*non astrorum inscii,*
*qui ad ortum properant*
*prepotentis filii.*

R*espondeat* Archisynagogus cum magna sapientia et eloquentia:

*Ne curarum, domine,*
*uerseris in biuio.*
*Tres huc reges ueniant*
*querendo de filio,*
*quibus te consilies*
*diligenti studio,*
*et eis sic loquere*
*sub amoris pallio:*

*'Reges estis, uideo,*
*quod prophetat habitus;*
*uester michi gratus est*
*factus ad nos transitus!*
*Sed quid uos huc traxerit,*
*reserate penitus,*
*nam uobis*[3] *ad omnia*
*rex erit expositus.'*

R*espondeant* Reges:

*Stella noua radiat*
*eius ortus nuntia,*
*cui mundus obediet,*
*et qui reget omnia,*

[1] disserat] differat (MS). [2] Ego] et ego (MS). [3] uobis] nobis (D).

*et nil stare poterit*
*absque huius gratia.*
*Nos ad illum tendimus*
*hec ferentes munia!*

Herodes respondet:

*Ne sim uos inpediens*
*ad vie propositum.*
*Ite, ad nos postea*
*maturantes reditum,*
*ut et ego ueniens*
*munus feram debitum*
*ei, cui non ambigo*
*mundum fore subditum.*

Ab Herode discedant tres Magi pau|latim, inspicientes Stellam et disputantes de illa. Interim Angelus appareat Pastoribus et dicat:

*Magnum uobis gaudium,*
*pastores, annuntio:*
*Deus se circumdedit*
*carnis uestre pallio,*
*quem ⟨mater⟩*[1] *non peperit*
*carnali conmercio;*
*immo uirgo permanens*
*mater est ex filio!*

Pastoribus euntibus dicat Diabolus:

*Tu ne credas talibus*
*pastorum simplicitas!*
*Scias esse friuola,*
*que non probat ueritas.*
*Quod sic in presepio*
*sit sepulta deitas,*
*nimis est ad oculum*
*reserata falsitas.*

Iterum Pastoribus ad negocium suum redeuntibus dicat Angelus:

*Pastores, querite*
*natum in*[2] *presepio,*
*et uotum soluite*
*matri cum filio;*
*nec mora ueniat*
*isti consilio,*
*sed uos huc dirigat*
*mentis deuotio.*

Iterum Pastoribus abeuntibus dicat Diabolus ad aures eorum:

*Simplex cetus, aspice,*

[1] Emend. D and Meyer-Hilka; S proposes ⟨*mulier*⟩.

[2] in] D suggests omitting.

*qualis astucia*
*eius, qui sic fabricat*
*uero contraria;*
*utque sua fallare⟨n⟩t*
*nugis mendatia,*
*in ritmis conciliat,*
*que profert omnia!*

Mirentur Pastores, et unus dicat ad alterum:

*Nunquid, frater, colligis*[1]
*ea que audio?*
*Quedam uox insinuat*
*de nato filio*
*uerum in contrarium;*
*ab hoc suscipio,*
*quod audita resident*
*iuncta mendatio!*

Dicat iterum Angelus ad Pastores:

*Cur non aures uertitis*
*ad hunc ueri nuntium?*
*Quis est iste subdolus*
*uertens uos in deuium?*
*Ne uos error induat*
*propter aduersarium.*
*Ite, nam quod predico,*
*monstrabit presepium.*

Dicat iterum euntibus Diabolus:

*O gens simplex nimium*
*et in sensu uulnerata!*
*Fer*[2] *fenum et pabulum,*
*que bubus non ingrata;* |
*in presepi comedat*
*deitas reclinata.*
*Debacharis nimium,*
*cum putas ista rata!*

Iterum Pastores ad socios suos:

*Audi, frater, iterum,*[3]
*qualis repugnantia.*
*Inde quedam audio,*
*hinc horum contraria;*
*meus simplex animus,*
*mea mens non sobria*
*ignorat, que potior*
*sit horum sententia.*

[1] colligis] colligit (MS). [2] Fer] fert (MS). [3] iterum] verum (S).

Postea simul conueniant Angeli, et simul cantent:

*Gloria in excelsis Deo, et in terra pax hominibus bone uoluntatis, alleluia, alleluia.*[1]

Qua uoce audita, dicat Pastor ad socios suos:

*Ad hanc uocem animi*
*produco suspirium;*
*ex hac intus habeo*
*citharizans gaudium!*
*Procedamus igitur*
*simul ad presepium,*
*et curuatis genibus*
*adoremus filium!*

Deinde procedant Pastores ad Presepe cantando hanc antiphonam:

*Facta est cum angelo multitudo celestis* ⟨*exercitus laudantium et dicentium: Gloria in excelsis Deo, et in terra pax hominibus bonæ voluntatis, alleluia*⟩.[2]

Quo cantato, adorent Puerum. Deinde reuertantur Pastores ad officia sua, quibus occurrant tres Magi dicentes:

*Pastores, dicite quidnam uidistis, et annuntiate Christi natiuitatem?*[3]

Respondeant Pastores:

*Infantem uidimus pannis inuolutum et choros angelorum laudantes saluatorem.*

Postea Reges uadant ad Presepe, et primo adorent Puerum, et postea offerant ei munera sua: primo aurum, postea thus, tercio mirram. Deinde modicum procedant, et tunc dormiant; et Angelus appareat eis in somnis dicens:

*Nolite redire ad Herodem,*

et cetera.[4] Postea non reuertentibus ad Herodem sic dicat:

*Gens Iudea properet,*
*ut Herodem*[5] *audiat,*
*et prestet consilium*
*de re que me*[6] *sauciat.*
*Rex Herodes anxius*
*ignorat quid faciat,*
*cum a tribus regibus*
*se lusum inspiciat.*

Veniat Archisy|nagogus cum suis, cui dicat Herodes:

*Tu, magister, aperi*
*prophetarum edita,*
*si qua sunt de puero*

[1] For this antiphon see Hartker, p. 51.

[2] For this antiphon see Hartker, p. 50.

[3] This speech and the one succeeding constitute an antiphon found in Hartker, p. 51.

[4] Cf. Matt. ii, 12. For ll. 527–43 there is no music.

[5] Herodem] heredem (S).

[6] me] hunc (emend. suggested D).

*a prophetis tradita;*
*nam a te fideliter,*
*re michi exposita,*
*se monstrabunt proprii*
*cordis abscondita!*

R*espondeat* Archisynagogus:

*Tu Bethlehem, terra Iuda,*

et cetera.[1] Deinde Herodes iratus dicat ad Milites suos:

*Ite, ite pariter*[2]
*manu iuncta gladio;*
*etas adhuc tenera*
*nulli parcat filio!*
*Immo mater quelibet*
*nudo fleat gremio,*
*ut de nato puero*
*michi detur ultio!*

Vadant Milites et interficiant Pueros, quorum Matres sic lugeant et lamententur:

*Heu, heu, heu!*
*Mens Herodis effera*
*cur in nostra uiscera*
*bella mouet aspera?*
*Heu, heu, heu!*
*Que etas adhuc*[3] *tenera*
*⟨matris⟩*[4] *sugens ubera*
*perpetrauit scelera?*
*Heu, heu, heu!*
*Iste dolor anxius,*
*dum transegit inpius*
*innocentes gladius!*
*Heu, heu, heu!*
*Proles adhuc tenera,*
*per te mater misera*
*descendet ad infera!*
*Heu, heu, ⟨heu!⟩*
*Michi uite gaudium,*
*fili, nunc supplicium,*
*mortis eris ostium!*

Postea Herodes corrodatur a uermibus, et excedens de sede sua mortuus accipiatur a Diabolis multum congaudentibus. Et Herodis corona inponatur Archelao filio suo. Quo regnante, appareat in nocte Angelus Ioseph dicens:

*Accipe matrem et filium, et uade in Egiptum.*[5]

[1] For this antiphon see Hartker, p. 37.

[2] pariter] parete (emend. D). For ll. 545–75 there is no music.

[3] adhuc] tam (suggested D).

[4] Emend. S. D suggests ⟨*adhuc*⟩.

[5] See Matt. ii, 13.

Precedens Maria asinum dicat:

*Omnia dura pati uitando pericula nati*
*Mater sum presto; iam uadam, tu comes esto.*[1]

The opening part of the play may be regarded as a prologue, presenting the general theme of the *Ordo Prophetarum*. Before the chair of Augustine, in the nave of the church,[2] are stationed, at his right, Isaiah, Daniel, the Sibyl, Aaron, and Balaam, and on his left, the chief of the Synagogue and a group of Jews. Isaiah and Daniel begin the action by rising and singing prophecies, the general tenor of which is familiar to us from the plays of the preceding chapter. The Sibyl then sings her verses, moving about with considerable gesticulation, and gazing at the star suspended above her. Aaron is ceremoniously introduced by a choral piece, and brings with him his flowering rod. Balaam rides his ass, and, before singing his prophecy, is challenged by an angel.

At the conclusion of the prophecies Archisynagogus becomes aggressively obstreperous, striking his companions, shaking his head, stamping his feet, acting like a Jew generally (*imitando gestus Judæi in omnibus*), and ridiculing the prophecies concerning the birth of a child from a virgin. Interceding as a sort of chorus, the Boy Bishop assures us that the drunken inanities of the Jews will be refuted through the intellectual prowess of Augustine. Then ensues an animated debate in which the hilarious arguments of Archisynagogus are solemnly demolished by Augustine and his prophets. At the end of this the prophets are permitted either to withdraw, or to remain in their assigned places, *propter honorem ludi*. Archisynagogus, as we shall see, has a further part to play.

Now begins the real action of the piece, with the Annunciation and the visit to Elisabeth, which are presented with notable fidelity to the Biblical narrative. After Elisabeth has withdrawn, Mary reclines upon her bed, with Joseph seated beside her, conceives of the Holy Spirit, and gives birth to her Son. At this moment the star appears, and the chorus sings the antiphon *Hodie Christus natus est*.

The scene of the Magi, which follows, is highly elaborate. The

[1] Here ends the preserved text of the present play. For what follows in the MS see Notes, p. 463.

[2] To the interpretation of the phrase *in fronte ecclesie*, as meaning 'in the front part of the church,' rather than 'in front of the church,' I recur below, p. 196.

Magi, now called kings, enter one by one, from different points of the compass, each uttering four stanzas of learned bewilderment and speculation concerning the new star in the heavens. This display of erudition is agreeably humanized by the opening stanza of the second king, in which he confesses his relief in acquiring a companion for the long journey. When they reach the environs of Jerusalem, the kings are challenged by the messengers of Herod, who inform him of the strange visit. In his indignation over the situation, Herod takes counsel with Archisynagogus, and is advised to control his anger and receive the kings with an appearance of good will. The monarch acquiesces, and, after a brief interview with them, allows them to depart towards Bethlehem.

At this point the shepherds first appear upon the scene, and listen, on the one hand, to an angel's persistent urging that they visit the new-born king, and, on the other hand, to the intermittent dissuasion of a devil. When the angelic chorus sings *Gloria in excelsis*, however, their perplexity is dissolved, and they proceed to the manger and adore the Child. On the way home from Bethlehem they encounter the three kings, and announce to them what they have seen. The kings complete their journey to the *præsepe*, make their offering, lie down to sleep nearby, and are eventually roused by an angel and speeded homeward by a route which avoids Jerusalem.

When the Magi fail to re-appear at Jerusalem, Herod resorts again to Archisynagogus for advice, and being assured that a new king is to arise from Bethlehem, angrily commands his soldiers to slaughter the children. This order, the stage-direction assures us, is executed with dreadful efficacy. Then additional horror follows in the pantomimic death of Herod, who is gnawed by worms, carried dead from his throne, and gleefully received by devils. His crown is transferred to his son, Archelaus.

At this point an angel warns Joseph of danger, and the Holy Family set out for Egypt. Thus ends the play with which we are now concerned.[1]

When we inquire as to the sources of the main divisions of the composition, we observe that, although in literary detail they show considerable freedom and originality, in essential content they reflect the influence of dramatic pieces of the sort which we have reviewed in the preceding chapters of this study. The

[1] For what follows in the MS see below, p. 463.

prologue, for example, is, as has been said, merely a modification of the *Ordo Prophetarum*.[1] The most conspicuous changes are the reduction of the number of prophets to five, the omission of the summoning of these speakers, the versifying of their utterances, and the addition of a debate between Augustine, representing the Church, and Archisynagogus, representing the whole body of unbelieving Jews. The five prophecies include the gist of the pronouncements uttered by the same personages in the pseudo-Augustinian sermon or in one or another of the prophet plays.[2] Each prophecy, however, is not only given a fresh literary form, but is also extended through the addition of passages not seen in any version of the *Ordo Prophetarum* considered above. Of these additions the most notable are the four stanzas on the theme of the *nova progenies* which the Sibyl sings, on behalf of Virgil, as it were,[3] and the responsory *Salve, nobilis virga*, sung by the chorus as a processional for Aaron.

The disputation between Augustine and Archisynagogus is instigated by the Boy Bishop, who strays from the liturgical revels of Innocents' Day into the present play for no other purpose than to suggest that Archisynagogus' ridicule of the paradox of the virgin mother can be adequately met only by the great Church father.[4] The prominence given to Augustine here arises, no doubt, from his reputed authorship of the sermon from which the preceding scene of the prophets derives. The debate itself was probably composed under the direct, or indirect, influence of another pseudo-Augustinian composition, *De Altercatione Ecclesiæ et Synagogæ Dialogus*.[5] This dialogue, like the sermon *Vos inquam*, studied in the preceding chapter, was inspired by medieval anti-Semitism, and had an influence upon literature and art parallel to that of the sermon. It was not, however, incorporated into the Roman liturgy, and its bearing upon dramatic literature, at least, was very much less conspicuous than that of the other pseudo-Augustinian text.[6] Since the subject of debate in

[1] See above, chapter xxi.

[2] For the prophecies of Isaiah, Daniel, the Sibyl, Aaron, and Balaam respectively see above, for example, pp. 126, 140, 130, 157, 150. See also Duriez, p. 157.

[3] See above, for example, p. 164.

[4] In regard to the *Episcopus Puerorum* see above, i, 106 sqq.

[5] *Sancti Aurelii Augustini . . . Opera*, viii, Paris, 1688, Appendix, col. 19–24, reprinted in Migne, *P.L.*, xlii, 1131–40. On the deficiencies of this text see G. Morin, *Études, Textes, Découvertes*, i, Maredsous and Paris, 1913, p. 30; Morin, in *Revue d'Histoire ecclésiastique*, i (1900), 270–3.

[6] The *Dialogus* and its relation to the drama are discussed especially by Weber, *Kunst*, pp. 28–30, 58–81. See also Walther, pp. 27–8, 99–105; Chambers, ii, 64.

the *Dialogus* is not the paradox of virginal motherhood, but the authority of the Church as the bride of Christ, the influence of the piece upon the dramatic scene before us is only formal and general.[1] The metrical vivacity, the vehement hilarity of Archisynagogus, and Augustine's crowning analogy of the sheet of glass unharmed by the penetrating ray of light are all peculiar to the present play.

At the close of the disputation Augustine and the prophets alternate in singing sentences from St Bernard's sequence *Lætabundus exultet fidelis chorus*.[2] The suitability of this poem for use here is obvious. It refers to the maternal virginity of Mary, and mentions the prophecy of Isaiah and the Sibylline verses as evidences for converting the Jews. By adding to the sequence the rhyming refrain *Res neganda*, the playwright enables Archisynagogus to prolong his recalcitrancy.

The scenes of the Annunciation and the visit to Elisabeth, with which the play proper begins, follow the text of the Vulgate closely, and thus resemble scenes upon the same subjects considered in a later part of this study.[3] Then follows a pantomimic representation of the Nativity itself, the details of which are left to speculation. At the arrival of the Child a star appears, and the chorus sings the liturgical antiphon *Hodie Christus natus est.*

With the rising of the star begins appropriately the scene of the Magi, or Three Kings, which differs very substantially from any dramatization of this subject which we have seen hitherto. In place of the brief exclamations with which the versions of the *Officium Stellæ* normally open,[4] we have versified speeches of the kings which are somewhat appalling in their prolixity and pedantry. In the subsequent interview between Herod and the visitors, the role of adviser to the king, usually assigned to the scribes, is assumed by Archisynagogus.[5] He gives Herod wily counsel, and on the king's behalf addresses to the Magi a formal inquiry as to their errand. Having heard their explanation, Herod sends them on their way with false representations as to his own interest in the object of their quest.

The succeeding scene of the shepherds is unique in the presence of *diabolus*, who after each speech of the angel, attempts to corrupt the listeners with false doctrine. This situation recalls that in

[1] For a suggestion as to the source of the disputation in the play see Notes, p. 468.

[2] For the complete text see below, p. 450.

[3] See below, pp. 245 sqq.

[4] See above, for example, pp. 43, 53–4.

[5] See above, for example, pp. 61, 65.

which the devil besets the wayward Mary Magdalen in the Passion play from the same monastery of Benediktbeuern, and points forward to an arrangement frequent in the vernacular moral plays, whereby the human representative is solicited alternately by good and evil agents.[1] New also in the present play is the liturgical antiphon *Facta est cum angelo*, sung by the shepherds as they proceed to Bethlehem. As they return from adoring Jesus at the manger, they meet the Magi, in a scene similar to what we have observed in several versions of the *Officium Stellæ*.[2]

The remaining scenes in which Herod and the Magi are concerned follow the order of events in such a play as the *Officium Stellæ* from Laon,[3] but in versified speeches found nowhere else. When the Magi fail to return to Jerusalem, Herod—somewhat tardily—bids his adviser, Archisynagogus, consult the prophetic books; and when he hears the prophecy that a king of Israel is to arise from Bethlehem, he vehemently commands that the male children be slaughtered. The lament of the mothers over the bodies of their slain offspring resembles the parallel utterances in the *Ordo Rachelis* in content; in metrical expression, however, the passage before us is unique.[4]

Similarly unmatched in other Christmas plays is the hideously realistic representation of the death of Herod. The violent circumstances of his ending are described in detail by Flavius Josephus,[5] and were kept before the minds of medieval readers by such passages as the following in Bede's *Martyrology*:[6]

Bethlehem Judææ natale sanctorum Innocentum, quos Herodes, cum Christi nativitatem Magorum indicio cognovisset, tricesimo quinto anno regni sui interfici jussit, qui anno tricesimo sexto morbo intercutis aquæ, et scatentibus toto corpore vermibus, miserabiliter et digne mortuus.

Further details are communicated by Peter Comestor:[7]

Dehinc variis affligebatur languoribus. Nam febris non mediocris erat, prurigo intolerabilis in omni corporis superficie, assiduis vexabatur colli tormentis, pedes intercutaneo vitio tumuerant, putredo testiculorum

[1] See above, i, 535; and, for example, W. R. Mackenzie, *The English Moralities from the Point of View of Allegory*, Boston, 1914, pp. 39 sqq.

[2] References are given above, p. 22.

[3] For the Laon play see above, p. 103.

[4] See above, chapter xx.

[5] See *Antiquitates Iudaicæ*, Lib. xvii, cap. vi, 5, in *Flavii Iosephi Iudæi Opera Omnia*, iv, Leipzig, 1850, pp. 99–102; Sondheimer, pp. 133–5; Duriez, p. 275.

[6] Migne, *P.L.*, xciv, 1144.

[7] *Petri Comestoris Historia Scholastica in Evangelia*, cap. xvi, in Migne, *P.L.*, cxcviii, 1546.

vermes generabat, creber anhelitus et interrupta suspiria, quæ ad vindictam Dei ab omnibus referebantur.

For the grim pantomine, then, the playwright was supplied with ample details. His own contribution was merely the courage necessary for putting so offensive an incident upon the stage.

The scene of the flight of the Holy Family into Egypt is probably fragmentary. It is, in any case, briefer than the same part of the *Ordo Rachelis* from Freising. The two hexameters of Mary are the same in the two plays, but in the Benediktbeuern version the speeches of Joseph are lacking.[1]

In its general structure the play before us is sufficiently orderly. In one or two instances, to be sure, the chronological order of the Scriptural narrative is violated. The Nativity is not announced to the shepherds, for example, until after the Magi have departed from Jerusalem for Bethlehem; and the flight of the Holy Family into Egypt occurs only after the Innocents have been slaughtered and Herod has died. Otherwise the sequence of scenes is acceptable, and the transitions are usually smooth. Occasional variations in literary form effect agreeable dramatic contrasts. After the ponderous stanzas of the disputation between Augustine and Archisynagogus, the scene closes with the lyrical *Lætabundus exultet fidelis chorus*; and this, in turn, is followed by the serenely simple representation of the Annunciation. The heavier style reappears in the scenes of the Magi and Herod, and again, somewhat inappropriately perhaps, in the speeches of the shepherds.

This literary sophistication, and the formal learning of which it is made the vehicle, testify to the scholastic authorship of the play. It may be that it was composed by the pupils of the monastery, who put their heads together for a display of their grammatical, scientific, and philosophical attainments;[2] or, more probably, it may belong to the stock of the *vagantes*, whose compositions form the body of the manuscript in which the play is preserved. The ascription of it to the wandering scholars is suggested by the element of worldly learning, and by the possibilities of humour in the role of Archisynagogus.[3] In general, however, the play maintains its tone of learned gravity, supported by quotations from the Vulgate and by not a few liturgical pieces. Noticeably restrained is the use of the Boy Bishop, who

[1] See above, p. 118.

[2] See Sepet, *Drame*, p. 105.

[3] See Creizenach, i, 93. The amount of comedy in the play seems to me to be somewhat exaggerated by Jacobsen, pp. 87–9.

exhibits none of the liturgical antics commonly associated with his name, but, in his brief role, actually lends encouragement to one of the more serious elements in the composition.

As to the circumstances under which the play was performed we have no information. The text itself bears no evidence of direct attachment to the liturgy, but, on the other hand, it contains nothing inappropriate to a performance within the church building. The opening rubric *Primo ponatur sedes Augustino in fronte ecclesiæ* has usually been interpreted as locating the platforms, or *sedes*, of the actors outside the structure—'in front of the church'.[1] There is, however, no obstacle to our understanding the phrase *in fronte ecclesiæ* as meaning 'in the front part of the church', and as referring to the nave, or, more precisely, to the west end of it. That the play was presented within the building is rendered somewhat more likely, perhaps, by the indications that the liturgical chorus participated.

Wherever it may have been produced, the most noteworthy theatrical aspects of the play are its pageantry and its realism. The defile of prophets, Archisynagogus and his band of Jews, the court of Herod, and the adoration of the Magi all furnished opportunities for brilliance of costume and of processional movements. The realism prescribed by the rubrics of the text surpasses anything that we have seen hitherto in its daring, particularly in representing the *accouchement* of Mary, and the loathesomeness of the death of Herod. Concerning the means by which such ambitious effects were produced we can only speculate. So difficult do they seem, indeed, that at least one critic infers that the text could never have been intended for actual use upon the stage, but was merely an academic literary exercise, in which the writer gave rein to his learning and his fancy for realism, without consideration for the practical limitations of theatrical performance.[2] My own surmise is that the play was written for actual performance, but that such occurrences as the death of Herod were represented in a conventional sort of pantomime, which reminded the spectators of a well-known traditional story, without the use of intensely realistic detail.[3]

[1] See, for example, Sepet, *Drame*, p. 112; Michael, iv, 419; K. Francke, *Personality in German Literature before Luther*, Cambridge, 1916, p. 117. Chambers (ii, 79) lists this among the plays 'certainly intended for the open'.

[2] See A. Schönbach, in *Zeitschrift für deutsche Philologie*, iv (1873), 366.

[3] Sondheimer (p. 162) regards the play as a stage-piece, but is uncertain as to whether the death of Herod was represented physically.

# PLAYS UPON OTHER SUBJECTS FROM THE BIBLE AND FROM LEGENDS

# CHAPTER XXIII

# PLAYS FROM THE NEW TESTAMENT

## THE RAISING OF LAZARUS—THE CONVERSION OF SAINT PAUL

THE plays reviewed thus far may be said to fall into two large groups centring, respectively, in the Nativity and the Resurrection, and within the confines of these two themes, indeed, will be found the greater proportion of the extant dramatic pieces composed for the use of the Church. This concentration about the two *foci* of Christmas and Easter was, no doubt, inevitable and praiseworthy. We may reasonably infer, however, that from the life of Christ and the early history of Christianity as recounted in the New Testament a considerable number of other subjects were chosen for independent dramatic treatment. Two of these, in any case, were used to form well-wrought plays which are still preserved: the Raising of Lazarus, and the Conversion of St Paul.[1]

### The Raising of Lazarus

A brief dramatic scene representing the raising of Lazarus is found in the Passion play from Benediktbeuern, discussed in an earlier chapter.[2] We are now to consider two independent treatments of this occurrence which are both ample in scope and somewhat careful in their literary finish.

### I

The dramatization of this subject in the play-book from the monastery of Fleury is as follows:[3]

#### Incipiunt Uersus de Resuscitacione Lazari

In primis adducatur Simon cum quibusdam Iudeorum, et resideat in domu sua. Post h*ec* ueniat Ihesus in plateam,[4] cum Discipulis cantantibus:

*In sapiencia disponens omnia*,[5]

[1] For bibliography relating to these plays see Notes, p. 469.

[2] See above, i, 524.

[3] Orleans, Bibl. de la Ville, MS 201 (*olim* 178), Miscellanea Floriacensia sæc. xiii, pp. 233–43, previously edited by Monmerqué, in *Mélanges*, vii, 197–213; Wright, pp. 45–53; Du Méril, pp. 213–25; Coussemaker, pp. 220–34. Only Coussemaker includes the music. For a description of the MS see above, i, 665.

[4] plateam] palateam (MS).

[5] Concerning the complete text of this sequence see Notes, p. 469.

et cetera, uel:

*Mane prima sab⟨b⟩ati.*[1]

Et[2] tunc ueniat Simon ad Ihesum, inuitans eum in domum suam, dicens:

*⟨T⟩u dignare*[3] *per inmundiciam*
*mee carnis tuam potenciam*
*declarare;*
*nobis optatum dones gaudium,*
*et digneris nostrum hospicium*
*subintrare.*|

Ihesus dicat ad Discipulos:

*Audit, fratres, uestra dilectio*
*quid amici petat deuocio;*
*audiatur.*
*Subintremus eius hospicium,*
*atque suum iam desiderium*
*compleatur.*

Tunc Simon inducat Iesum in domum suam, et, posita mensa, ueniat Maria in habitu per plateam meretricio, et cadat ad pedes Domini. Vnde Simon indignans secum suauiter dicat:

*Si hic homo esset a Deo,*

et cetera. Require in Evangelio.[4] Tunc Ihesus dicat ei:

*Loqui tecum, O Simon, habeo*
*namque tuos aperte uideo*
*cogitatus.*

Simon:

*Nunc, Magister, quod placet loquere;*
*auscultando quicquid uis dicere*
*sum paratus.*

Ihesus:

*Debitores uir duos habuit:*
*alter minus, alter plus debuit*
*creditori.*
*Non ualenti referre creditum,*
*condonauit utrique debitum*
*debitori.*
*Nunc demonstret*[5] *tuum iudicium:*
*Quis hunc uirum debet debencium*
*plus amare?*

Simon:

*Credo causam maiorem habuit*

[1] For the complete text of this sequence see above, i, 234–5.

[2] Et] Reading uncertain. MS may have *E⟨t⟩*.

[3] dignare] Crossed out in the MS, but obviously needed for the metre and meaning.

[4] Evangelio] Because of correction, the second letter is not clearly legible. See Luke vii, 39 sqq.

[5] demonstret] demonstent (MS).

*diligendi uir qui plus debuit,*
*doctor care.*

Iesus:

*Equus iudex fuisti nimium;*
*istud tuum, Simon, iudicium*
*nequit[1] frangi.*
*Tecum dicis si hanc mulierem*
*cognouissem, me non permitterem* |
*ab hac tangi.*
*Hospes meus,[2] in hoc hospicio,*
*pedes aqua uel capud oleo*
*non suffudit;*
*pedes meos rigauit lacrimis,*
*caput meum unguentis optimis*
hec *perfudit.*

Tunc dicat Ihesus ad Mariam:

*Dilexisti multum, o femina;*
*tui fletus tua peccamina*
*diluerunt;*
*illud enim oris confessio*
*atque illa cordis compunctio*
*meruerunt.*

His factis, surgat Maria, et ibi resideat. Tunc Ihesus cum Discipulis inde discedat, et abeat quasi in Galileam; et sit ex aduerso preparatus quidam locus ubi resideat. Postea recedant Iudei in quendam alium locum quasi in Ierusalem, ut inde in competenti loco uenia⟨n⟩t consolari duas Sorores. Domus uero ipsius Simonis, ipso remoto, efficiatur quasi Betthania; et tunc ad⟨d⟩ucatur Martha. Lazarus autem tunc incipiat infirmari; quo infirmante, sic dicat Martha:

*Cara soror, hunc miserabilem*
*esse reor inmedicabilem*
*morbum fratris.*
*Ut germano reddatur sanitas,*
*est oranda summa benignitas[3]*
*nostri Patris.*

*Ipse solus nostra protectio,*
*nostra solus est consolacio,*
*sed nunc abest.*
*Abest quidem, sed corporaliter,*
*qui ubique potencialiter*
*presens adest.*

[1] nequit] nequid (MS).
[2] meus] deus (MS).
[3] benignitas] Correction by a later hand from *benitas*.

Maria respondeat:

*Transmit|tamus ei iam nuncium*
*et rogemus eius auxilium,*
*et dabitur.*
*Si re⟨s⟩ciscat hec infortunia,*
*mox per ipsum nostra tristicia*
*sedabitur.*

*Quamuis eum nil prorsus lateat,*
*nostrum tamen legatum uideat*
*actualem,*
*qui imploret eius clemenciam;*
*nobis suam monstret presenciam*
*corporalem.*

Maria loq*uitur* ⟨ad⟩ Nuncios sic:

*Hinc ad Ihesum, legati, pergite,*
*et presenti presentes dicite*
*hoc mandatum:*
*Nos rogamus ut nos exaudiat,*
*et germanum sanare ueniat*
*infirmatum.*

*Per uos noscat quanta tristicia*
*sit repleta sua familia*
*Pater bonus,*
*ut uirtute sue potencie*
*iam recedat tante tristicie*
*tantum onus.*[1]

Nuncii ad Ihesum:

*Aue, Ihesu, Redemptor omnium!* |
*Ad te quoddam portamus nuncium,*
*et hoc audi;*
*anularum dolorem respice,*
*et earum iam uota suscipe*
*et exaudi.*

*Harum frater iacet in lectulo,*
*magno morbi constrictus uinculo;*
*sed soluatur.*
*Te presentem eis ex⟨h⟩ibeas,*
*atque morbum abire iubeas;*
*hoc rogatur.*

Ihesus ad Nuncios:

*Ibo quidem, sed nondum tempus est;*

[1] onus] honus (MS).

*hic nequaquam ad mortem morbus est;*
*sat euadet.*
*Cum egroto dabo remedium,*
*admirandus stupor astancium*
*cor inuadet.*

Idem ad Discipulos:

*Quod sit eger, propter uos gaudeo,*[1]
*quos tamdiu esse condoleo*
*non credentes.*
*Iamiam uestri cordis duriciam*
*deponetis,*[2] *Christi potenciam*
*admirantes.*

Iudei uenientes consolari Sorores, in itinere dicant:

*Iam Mariam et Martham pariter*
*conquerentes lamentabiliter*
*adeamus,*
*et dolori fratrem merencium*
*iuxta nostrum posse solacium*
*conferamus.*

Iam presentibus Iudeis et moriente Lazaro, dica⟨n⟩t Maria et Martha:

*Iam moratur, et plus quam nimium,*
*ille qui est solus refugium*
*nostre spei.*
*Heu! heu! Frustra hunc expectauimus;*
*quod sanetur non esse cernimus |*
*uelle Dei.*

*Ecce noster germanus moritur!*
*Iam fraternum corpus dissoluitur*
*lege mortis;*
*miserarum hic uicem gerimus,*
*cum tam grauem excessum*[3] *cernimus*
*dire sortis.*

*Care frater, frater carissime,*
*legem mortis iam passus pessime,*
*nos liquisti.*
*Propter primi peccatum hominis*
*generalis tormentu⟨m⟩ criminis*
*iam sensisti.*

Iudei consolantes dicant:

*Non uos sternat hoc infortunium!*
*Inter tantos casus solacium*
*est habendum.*

[1] gaudeo] Inserted in MS by a later hand.
[2] deponetis] deponentis (MS).
[3] excessum] excelsum (MS).

*Hac de causa uobis*[1] *congemimus,*
*sed defunctum non esse credimus*
*sic deflendum.*

*Moriemur et nos similiter;*
*omnes gentes aduncat*[2] *pariter*
*mortis hamus.*
*Tali lege intramus seculum,*
*ut quandoque carnis ergastulum*
*exeamus.*

*Pro dilecti fratris interitu*
*ne ploretis; in eius*[3] *exitu*
*est gaudendum.*
*Liberatus multis sup⟨p⟩liciis*
*iam euasit quod restat aliis*
*paciendum.*

It*eru*m Sorores:

*Quam lugubres et mestas | ⟨h⟩odie*
*nos relinquis, frater egregie,*
*nequit*[4] *dici.*
*Crebros in nos assultus facient,*
*bona nostra nobis subripient*
*inimici.*

*Care frater, dilecte Lazare,*
*nostro cetu iam facto dispare*
*te deflemus;*
*morti que te nobis subripuit,*
*nec nos tecum mori sustinuit,*
*inuidemus.*

It*eru*m Iudei:

*Si iam contra assultus hostium*
*nobis ferre desistat clipeum*
*uester frater,*
*non uos linquit*[5] *sine consilio;*
*imo uestra fiet protectio*
*summus Pater.*

*Satis,*[6] *scitis, sic Deo placuit,*
*ipse uestrum germanum uoluit*
*sic obire;*

[1] uobis] nobis (MS).

[2] aduncat] Preceded by the erasure of a word.

[3] eius] eis (MS).

[4] nequit] nequid (MS).

[5] linquit] linquid (MS).

[6] Satis] Preceded by a hole in the parchment and also by a blank space adequate for a considerable rubric; but there is no sign of an entry.

*uoluntati sue potencie*
*prohibetur*[1] *nostre miserie*
*contra ire.*

*Est rogandum nobis humillime,*
*ut germani donetur anime*
*uera dies;*
*sit in celi locatus solio,*
*ubi semper est exultacio*
*atque quies.*

Interea Ihesus promouet se ad iter. Dicat Discipulis:

*In Iudeam eamus iterum,*
*dormientem a sompno Lazarum*
*excitemus,*
*et sorores eius doloribus*
*iam depressas et multis fletibus*
*confortemus.*

Discipuli ad Ihesum:

*In Iudeam quare uis | tendere?*
*Ut te perdant sat noscis querere*
*te Iudeos.*
*Anne placet ut hii et alii*
*gratulentur se homicidii*
*esse reos?*

Iesus ad illos:

*Non est uestrum me redarguere;*
*imo uestrum est acquiescere*
*uerbis*[2] *meis.*
*Uirtus Dei, que adhuc tegitur*
*per Iudeos, manifestabitur*
*in Iudeos.*

Thomas:

*Insequamur eius uestigia,*
*adimpleri sua consilia*
*permittamus.*
*Festinemus cum eo pergere*
*in Iudeam, et ibi uiuere*
*desistamus.*

Ihesu adueniente, quidam ex Nunciis precurrens dicat[3] Marthe:

*Ecce, uestrum aduentat gaudium;*
*ecce, uenit*[4] *Saluator gencium*
*expectatus.*[5]

[1] prohibetur] peribetur (MS).
[2] uerbis] Unintelligibly written in MS.
[3] dicat] dicacat (MS).
[4] uenit] Partly because of a preceding erasure, the reading of this word is uncertain.
[5] expectatus] expectamus (MS).

*Iamiam uester dolor sedabitur,*
*et per eum iam liberabitur*
*infirmatus.*

Tunc Martha occurrens Ihesum procidat ad pedes eius et dicat:

*Quem mors ausa fuit inuadere,*
*si hic esses, nunc scirem uiuere*
*fratrem meum;*
*tuam enim uirtutem noscimus,*[1]
*et te corde perfecto credimus*
*esse Deum.*

*Sed et scimus quicquid poposceris,*
*imo quicquid esse uolueris,*
*dabit Deus;*
*si sic uel*is *esse percipere,*
*a defunctis potest resurgere*
*frater meus.*

Ihesus ad illam:

*Ne desperes |fratrem resurgere;*
*illum debes et potes credere*
*surrecturum;*
*nullum scias qui in me credere*
*atque mihi uult acquiescere*
*moriturum.*

Martha:

*Hoc in meo fixum est animo,*
*quod resurget die nouissimo,*
*die illa,*
*qua supremum fiet iudicium,*
*in qua caro resurget gencium*
*ex fauilla.*

Ihesus:

*Ego uestra sum resurreccio.*
*Nulla potest hos desperacio*
*subintrare,*
*quibus cura cum summo studio*
*Patris mei sese seruicio*
*prorsus dare.*

*Vade, uoca Mariam concito;*
*ad sepulcrum post me deducito*
*tui fratris;*
*fiet enim manifestissima*
*coram multis uirtus altissima*
*mei Patris.*

[1] noscimus] nescimus (MS).

Tunc ueniens Martha ad Sororem susurret[1] ei in aure:

*Magister te uocat.*[2]

Et Maria tacite a domo egrediente, dicant Iudei:

*Sunt commota Marie uiscera,*
*causa flendi petit hec misera*
*monumentum;*
*non debemus illam permittere*
*tanto fletu, tantum incurrere*
*detrimentum.*

H*oc* dicentes Iudei seq*uantur* eam; ipsa uero, corruens multociens ad pedes Domini, dicat:

*Pietatis fons clementissime,*
*contristate nostre sunt anime*
*fratris causa.*
*Te | absente, mors huc accedere*
*atque fratrem nostrum obruere*
*fuit ausa.*[3]

*Miserere nostri, te petimus;*
*a te solo nos expectauimus*
*confortari.*
*Miserere iam nostrum omnium,*
*miserere*[4] *cuius est proprium*
*consolari.*[5]

Ihesu⟨s⟩, fremens et lacrimans in se, dicat:

*Ad sepulcrum me iam deducite,*
*atque mihi locum ostendite*
*sepulture;*
*iam me mouet uestra miseria;*
*iam me mouent uestra suspiria,*
*uestre cure.*

Tunc quidam de Iudeis circumstantibus quasi ammirando dicat:

*Hic qui ceci lumen aperuit,*
*nonne mortem demere potuit*
*ab egroto?*
*Hic qui gentes ad preces instituit,*[6]
*cur sororum abesse uoluit*
*pio uoto?*

Ihesus t*ransiens* ante[7] monumentum dicat:

*Uelox huius saxi remocio,*

[1] susurret] susurtet (MS).
[2] This speech has, of course, no music.
[3] ausa] causa (MS).
[4] miserere] miserei (MS).
[5] consolari] MS seems to read *et solari.*
[6] One is tempted to mend the metre of this line by omitting the first word.
[7] transiens ante] The reading *intrans in* of the previous editors cannot be supported from the MS.

*et spelunce fiat apertio*[1]
*sine mora.*
*Qua debetis miranda cernere*
*atque Dei nomen extollere*
*hec est hora.*

Martha:

*Per bis duos dies iam iacuit;*
*dat fetorem caro que putruit*
*tumulati.*

Ihesus:

*Ne desperes, uidebis*[2] *gloriam*
*Dei Patris atque potenciam |*
*sui nati.*

Ihesus, eleuatis oculis in celum, sic oret et dicat:

*Deus, cuius uirtus et filius*
*eternalis, non temporaneus,*
*credor esse,*
*tuum natum ut honorifices,*
*atque meum nomen glorifices*
*est necesse.*

Ad Lazarum:

*Tibi dico iam uoce publica:*
*Exi foras atque letifica*
*cor parentum.*
*Tu sis dolor insidiantibus*
*atque certum sis dubitantibus*
*argumentum.*

Iam Lazaro sedente, dicat Ministris:

*Suscitatum confestim soluite,*
*et solutum abire sinite.*
*Quid stupetis?*
*Omne Deo esse possibile*
*per* hoc *patet satis credibile*
*quod uidetis.*

Et chorus: *Te Deum laudamus.* Sic finiatur.

At the opening of the Fleury play, after Simon, with certain Jews, has taken his position at his *domus*, Jesus and his disciples appear before the place, the disciples singing a sequence—either *In sapientia disponens omnia* or *Mane prima sabbati.* Jesus accepts Simon's invitation to a meal in his house, during which the courtesan, Mary Magdalen, appears and falls at the Master's

[1] apertio] operacio (MS). [2] uidebis] uidebitis (MS).

feet. As a reproof to Simon for his scorn of Mary, Jesus recounts to him the parable of the two debtors, and pronounces his forgiveness of the erring woman. At the close of this scene Mary remains behind while Jesus withdraws to a *locus* representing Galilee, and the Jews take their position at another place representing Jerusalem.

The action is resumed at Bethany, where Lazarus lies mortally ill, with his sisters beside him. In response to Martha's lamenting the absence of Jesus, Mary promptly dispatches messengers to summon him. When Jesus receives the message in Galilee, he gives his promise to come, after a little time, and show his power. Meanwhile at Bethany Lazarus dies, and his friends come from Jerusalem to comfort the grieving sisters.

As Jesus advances from Galilee towards Bethany, his disciples warn him against the hostile Jews; but he reassures them, and persuades them to follow him. Upon his arrival at the place which represents the village, Martha hastens to meet him, lamenting his delay, but expressing her faith in his power. Jesus promises that Lazarus shall rise again. After Mary has repeatedly fallen at Jesus' feet, begging for consolation, he gives way to tears, and asks to be shown the tomb. As the grave is opened, Martha warns Jesus that Lazarus has been dead four days; but he promises her that she shall soon see God's might and glory. After praying for aid from heaven, he calls upon the dead man to come forth; and as Lazarus sits erect, with his grave-cloths upon him, Jesus bids the bystanders unbind him, and witness the infinite power from on high. At the close of the action the chorus sings the *Te Deum*.

It is clear that in sequence and structure the play faithfully follows the narrative of the Gospel, the scene at the house of Simon deriving from the account of St Luke, and the remainder of the action following the account of St John.[1] Nothing significant is omitted, and nothing alien is introduced. The most notable amplifications of the Biblical text are the laments of the sisters and the condolences of their friends. Although the opening scene is obviously unessential, its presence is natural in the light of the traditional identification of the courtesan of St Luke's narrative as Mary Magdalen and as the sister of Lazarus.[2]

In its general literary form, and in certain details, the play

[1] See Luke vii, 36–48; John xi, 1–44.

[2] See John xi, 2; and above, i, 534.

discloses a learned origin.[1] The very opening rubric *Incipiunt versus* might indicate that the play is a rhetorical exercise from the monastic school. One observes, for example, the didactic and theological, rather than personal and dramatic, touch in the laments of the sisters:

Abest quidem, sed corporaliter,
qui ubique potentialiter
præsens adest.

. . .

Quamuis eum nil prorsus lateat,
nostrum tamen legatum videat
actualem,
qui imploret ejus clementiam;
nobis suam monstret præsentiam
corporalem.

. . .

Propter primi peccatum hominis
generalis tormentum criminis
jam sensisti.

The stanzas of the consoling friends, however, contain passages of a certain poetical feeling:

Moriemur et nos similiter;
omnes gentes aduncat pariter
mortis hamus.

. . .

Si jam contra assultus hostium
nobis ferre desistat clipeum
vester frater,
non vos linquit sine consilio.

The stanzaic regularity of the play is, no doubt, monotonous; but it must be admitted that the style achieves a sustained elevation and gravity worthy of the pathetic subject.

For the staging of the performance are required four *sedes*, or *loca*—representing the house at Bethany, Galilee, Jerusalem, and the tomb—arranged in the choir or some other part of the church. A single *sedes* appears to have served both as the house of Simon and that of Lazarus and his sisters. For the tomb may have been used the Easter sepulchre, for as we have already observed, this structure at Fleury was sufficiently large to allow a person to enter.[2]

[1] For observations on literary aspects of the play see especially Sepet, *Origines*, pp. 34–45 *passim*; Petit de Julleville, i, 54–5.

[2] See above, i, 395. Chambers (ii, 60) conjectures this use of the Easter sepulchre.

The play may, or may not, have been designed for use among the services of the choir. The closing *Te Deum*, to be sure, points toward a performance at Matins.[1] From the presence of the Easter sequence *Mane prima sabbati*, at the beginning, several critics have inferred that the play was designed for performance during the Easter season.[2] This inference, however, is far from secure, for the sequence was used, probably, not because of its Easter associations, but because in it is celebrated the *beata peccatrix*, Mary Magdalen, who appears in the opening scene.[3] It is possible that the play was intended for the feast of St Lazarus (December 17), who was honoured in numerous communities of Southern and Central France.[4]

## II

From the anonymous composition written at the monastery of Fleury we pass with especial satisfaction to a play concerning Lazarus to which we can attach—our first opportunity of this kind—the name of the author. He is the wandering scholar, Hilarius, known to us only through meagre biographical disclosures in the one slender manuscript of his extant writings.[5] This little volume of some sixteen leaves exhibits astonishing literary variety. Here are two student songs, a versified *vita*, a poem in praise of a resort of learning, eight verse-letters to women and boys, and three highly significant plays. In this agreeable *mélange* are expressed sly merriment, outspoken anger, equivocal amorousness, pious laudation, and dramatic tension.

Although Hilarius addresses certain poems to English persons, we have no assurance that he was himself an Englishman. He certainly studied in France under Abelard, whose pupil he calls himself, and to whom he addressed a poem at the time, apparently, of the master's retirement to the oratory of the Paraclete near Nogent-sur-Seine in 1125 or thereabouts. Since he writes also about persons associated with Angers and its neighbourhood, we easily surmise that at some period in his life he sojourned in those parts.

[1] Coussemaker (p. 333) regards the play as 'tout à fait liturgique', and Sepet (*Origines*, p. 31), as 'semi-liturgique'.

[2] See Sepet, *Origines*, pp. 31–6, 47–54 *passim*; Petit de Julleville, i, 55; Chambers, ii, 59. The combining of the Lazarus play with a scene at the house of Simon suggests to Sepet (pp. 35–6) that the composition before us was originally part of a larger Passion play performed at Eastertide.

[3] See the text of the sequence above, i, 234.

[4] See Coffman, *New Theory*, pp. 67–70; and below, p. 469.

[5] For bibliography see Notes, p. 471.

Such is the shadowy biography of the author of the following play:[1]

### SVSCITACIO LAZARI

Ad quem ⟨ludum⟩ iste persone sunt necessarie:

Persona Lazari
⟨Personæ⟩ duarum Sororum
⟨Personæ⟩ quatuor Iudeorum
⟨Persona⟩ Ihesu Christi
⟨Personæ⟩ duodecim Apostolorum, uel vi ad minus.

In primis, Lazaro lang⟨u⟩escente, due sorores, Maria et Martha, cum quatuor Iudeis se maxime affligentes, aduenient, et as⟨s⟩istentes eius lectulo, cantabunt hos uersus:

*O sors tristis! O sors dura,*
*cuius grauis est censura!*
*Nam per tua modo iura*
*languet frater, nostra cura.*

*Languet frater, et nos uere*
*facit sibi condolere;*
*sed tu, Deus, miserere,*
*cuique*[2] *potes tu medere.*

Ad earum consolacionem dicent Iudei:

*Karissime, flere desinite,*
*nec adstantes ad fletum cogite;*
*immo preces ad Deum mittite,*
*Lazaroque salutem poscite.*

Quibus ille dicent:

*Ite, fratres, ad summum medicum;*
*ite citi regem ad unicum;*
*fratrem nostrum narrate languidum,*
*ut ueniat et reddat ualidum.*

Illi autem, cum uenerint ad Ihesum, dicent:

*Quia ⟨quem⟩ tu diligis*
*infirmatur grauiter,*
*ad te iussi*[3] *fuimus*
*uenire celeriter.*

[1] Paris, Bibl. Nat., MS lat. 11331, Hilarii Versus et Ludi sæc. xii, fol. $9^{r}$–$10^{v}$, previously edited by Champollion-Figeac, pp. 24–33; Du Méril, pp. 225–32; Fuller, pp. 75–86. For Young's review of Fuller's edition see *Speculum*, v (1930), 112–4. The text of Champollion-Figeac is reprinted, with modifications, by Gaselee, pp. 99–106. The MS provides no music. Several emendations from Paul von Winterfeld are reported by P. S. Allen, in *M.P.*, ix (1911–2), 427. For remarks upon the MS see Fuller, pp. 3–6. Opposite the heading of the play, in the left margin, a relatively modern hand has inserted in the MS the word *Ludus*, which requires no explanation. For the other two plays of Hilarius see below, pp. 276, 337.

[2] cuique] quique (MS).

[3] iussi] iuxi (MS).

*Qui summus es medicus,*
*egrum nostrum uisita,*
*ut tibi deseruiat,*
*sospitate reddita.*

Ihesus respondet:

*Morbus iste, fratres mei,*
*non ad mortem erit ei;*
*sed euenit ut per eum*
*manifestem uobis Deum.*

Interim, cum illi redierint, Lazaro iam mortuo, duo ex illis Mariam ducent ad eum; cui illa cantabit:

*Ex culpa ueteri*
*damnantur*[1] *posteri*
*mortales fieri.*|
*Hor ai dolor,*
*hor est mis frere morz;*
*por que gei plor.*

*Per cibum uetitum,*
*nobis interitum*
*constat inpositum.*
*Hor ai dolor,*
*⟨hor est mis frere morz;*
*por que gei plor.⟩*

*Facta sum misera*
*et soror altera,*
*per fratris funera.*
*Hor ai dolor,*
*⟨hor est mis frere morz;*
*por que gei plor.⟩*

*Cum de te cogito,*
*frater, et merito*
*mortem afflagito.*
*Hor ai ⟨dolor,*
*hor est mis frere morz;*
*por que gei plor⟩.*

Tunc duo Iudei consolantes eam dicent:

*Cesset talis gemitus,*
*cesset meror penitus,*
*cessentque suspiria.*
*Talis lamentacio,*
*talis eiulacio*
*non est necessaria.*

[1] damnantur] dannatur (MS).

*Non per tales lacrimas*
*uisum fuit animas*
*redisse corporibus.*
*Cessent ergo lacrime,*
*que defunctis minime*
*proderunt hominibus.*

Post hec ueniet Martha cum aliis duobus Iudeis cantans:

*Mors execrabilis!*
*Mors detestabilis!*
*Mors mihi flebilis!*
*Lase, catiui!*
*Des que mis frere est morz,*
*porque sue uiue?*[1]

*Fratris interitus*
*grauis et subitus*
*est causa gemitus.*
*Lase, chatiue!*
*Des que ⟨mis frere est morz,*
*porque sue uiue⟩?*

*Pro fratre mortuo*
*mori non abnuo,*
*nec mortem metuo.*
*Lase, chatiue!*
*⟨Des que mis frere est morz,*
*porque sue uiue?⟩*

*Ex fratris funere*
*recuso uiuere.*
*Ue mihi misere!*
*Lase, chatiue!*
*⟨Des que mis frere est morz,*
*porque sue uiue?⟩*

Duo Iudei ad eius solacium dicent:

*Tolle fletum, quesumus;*
*nichil enim possumus*
*per fletum proficere.*[2]
*Insistendum fletibus*
*esset, si quis talibus*
*posset reuiuiscere.*

*Quare non consideras*
*quia, dum te macheras,*
*nichil prodes mortuo?*

[1] In the left margin, opposite the French refrain, a modern hand has written *Lase chetiue Des que mi frere est morz pour que sui viue.*

[2] proficere] profiscere (MS).

*Quare tu non respicis*
*quia nichil ⟨proficis⟩*[1]
*ut iam uiuat denuo?*

Ihesus ad Di⟨s⟩cipulos dicet:

*In Iudeam iterum*
*nos oportet pergere,*
*vbi quiddam paululum*
*decreui peragere.*

Cui Dis⟨ci⟩puli dicent:

*Te nuper lapidibus*
*uolebant obruere,*
*et uis tamen iterum*
*in Iudeam tendere!*

Et Ihesus ad illos:

*Ecce dormit Lazarus |*
*quem decet ut uisitem;*
*uadam illuc igitur,*
*ut a somno*[2] *excitem.*

Discipuli iterum:

*Pos⟨t⟩quam dormit, saluus erit;*
*salus enim somnum*[3] *querit.*

Ihesus iterum ad illos:

*Non*[4] *est sicut creditis;*
*inmo iam defunctus est;*
*sed in Patris nomine*
*nobis suscitandus est.*

T⟨h⟩omas uero dicet:

*Ergo nos proficiscamur*
*et cum illo moriamur.*[5]

Postea Martha dicet ad Ihesum:

*Si uenisses primitus,*
*dol en ai,*
*non esset hic gemitus.*
*Bais frere, perdu uos ai!*

*Quod in uiuum poteras,*
*dol en ai,*
*hoc defuncto conferas.*
*Ba⟨i⟩s frere, perdu uos ai!*

*Petis Patrem quid libet,*
*dol en ai,*

[1] Emendation of Champollion-Figeac.
[2] somno] sunno (MS).
[3] somnum] su*m*nu*m* (MS).
[4] Non] Nu*n* (MS).
[5] Champollion-Figeac and Du Méril propose transposing this speech and its rubric to a position immediately after line 108.

*statim Pater ex⟨h⟩ibet.*
*Bais frere, perdu uos ai!*

Ihesus dicet:

*Nunc comprimas*
*has lacrimas*
*et luctum qui te urget.*
*Frater tuus*
*est mortuus,*
*sed facile resurget.*

Et illa ad eum:

*Resurgere*[1]
*et uiuere*
*fratrem meum affirmo.*
*Tunc denique*
*cum utique*
*resurget*[2] *omnis homo.*

Et Ihesus iterum:

*Immo, soror, non despera,*
*nam sum ego uita uera;*
*et quicumque credet ita*
*uiuet in me, qui sum uita.*

*Et qui uiuens in me credet,*
*mors ad illum non accedet.*
*Credis, Martha, fore uerum*
*quod sit talis ordo rerum?*

Martha uero respondet:

*Te Christum, Dei Filium,*
*ad hoc nostrum exilium*
*uenisse in a⟨u⟩xilium*
*ego credo.*

Martha, nuncians Marie Ihesum aduenisse, dicet:

*Ihesus adest, soror carissima;*
*cesset luctus, et cesset lacrima;*
*ipsum prece flectas humillima,*
*ut redeat ad fratrem anima.*

Tunc Maria ad Ihesum dicet:

*Nullius solacio*
*mea desolacio*
*ualet umquam auferri.*
*Sed credo consilium*
*per te, Dei Filium,*
*posse mihi conferri.*

[1] Resurgere] Rexurgere (MS). [2] resurget] rexurget (MS).

*Tu ergo qui potens es,*
*qui mitis*[1] *et clemens es,*
*ad tumulum uenito;*
*fratrem meum suscita,*
*quem mors | carni dedita*
*surripuit tam cito.*

Et Ihesus ad illam:

*Volo, soror, uolo multum*
*me deduci ad sepultum,*
*ut in uitam reuocetur*
*qui a morte detinetur*

Illa autem, ducens Ihesum ad sepulcrum, dicet:

*Hic eum posuimus;*
*ecce locus, Domine;*
*quem in Patris poscimus*
*suscitari nomine.*

Ihesus ad circumstantes:

*Sustollatis lapidem*
*qui superest tumulo,*
*ut resurgat*[2] *Lazarus*
*coram omni populo.*

Illi dicent:

*Fetorem non poteris*
*sustinere mortui;*
*namque fetens*[3] *grauiter*
*funus est quatridui.*

Tunc Ihesus, suspiciens in celum, sic orabit ad Patrem:

*Pater, Uerbum tuum clarifica,*
*Lazarumque, precor, uiuifica;*
*sic Filium mundo*[4] *notifica,*
*Pater, in hac hora.*

*Nec hoc dixi ex dif⟨f⟩idencia,*
*sed pro gentis huius presentia,*
*vt de tua certi potencia*
*credant absque mora.*

Tunc dicet ad mortuum:

*O Lazare, foras egredere;*
*aure dono uitalis utere;*
*in paterne uirtutis munere,*
*exi foras, et uita fruere!*

[1] mitis] mittis (MS).
[2] resurgat] rexurgat (MS).
[3] fetens] ferens (MS)—emended by P. von Winterfeld, in *M.P.*, ix (1911–2), 427.
[4] mundo] mondo (MS).

Tunc pos⟨t⟩quam surrexerit Lazarus, dicet Ihesus:

*Ecce uiuit! Nunc ipsum soluite,*
*et solutum abire sinite.*

Lazarus solutus dicet astantibus:

*Ecce que sunt Dei magnalia,*
*uos uidistis, et hec et alia.*
*Ipse celum fecit et maria;*
*mors ad eius tremit inperia.*

Et conuersus ad Ihesum dicet:

*Tu magister, tu rex, tu Dominus,*
*tu populi delebis facinus.*
*Quod precipis, illud fit protinus.*
*Regni tui non erit terminus.*

Quo finito, si factum fuerit ad Matutinas, Lazarus incipiat *Te Deum laudamus*; si uero ad Uesperas, *Magnificat anima mea Dominum.*[1]

In its general arrangement and content Hilarius' play does not differ essentially from the Fleury version. Both compositions follow the narrative of the Gospel with striking fidelity. In the present play the most noticeable additions are the highly developed laments, and the assigning to Lazarus of a speaking part after his resurrection. The laments of Mary and Martha are somewhat formalized in that each of the sisters is allowed four stanzas for the expression of her grief, and is attended by two friends who utter two stanzas of condolence. Within this formal arrangement the two women contrive to utter genuine human grief which contrasts somewhat sharply with the frigid exhortations of their comforters. The boldest and happiest addition to the content of the play is the participation of Lazarus at the end. His address to the bystanders and his tribute to Christ provide an impressive conclusion.

In literary detail Hilarius' play is decidedly more interesting than that from Fleury. The verse shows far more freedom and variety, and the speeches are more flexible. The result is a play of less sustained elevation, but of greater freshness and animation. This effect is due in some measure, no doubt, to the refrains in French. Although these passages in the vernacular must certainly have brought moments of agreeable relief to an audience ignorant of Latin, they do not, it appears, represent an attempt to interpret the dialogue to the unlettered. The French sentences are not translations or paraphrases of the Latin which precedes

[1] The play ends at the very bottom of fol. $10^{v}$. At the top of fol. $11^{r}$ begins the play of St Nicholas printed below, pp. 338 sqq.

them, but lyrical additions expressing genuine emotion. Similar vernacular refrains are found among the non-dramatic poems of the same author.[1]

From the literary sophistication of the play one might infer that it was written for performance, not in conjunction with the liturgy, but under more worldly circumstances. One critic, for example, appears to regard it as designed for use 'au théâtre'.[2] Nothing, however, could be clearer than the closing rubric assigning it either to Matins or to Vespers.[3]

## The Conversion of Saint Paul

Hardly less striking than the story of Lazarus in its theatrical possibilities is the second New Testament miracle to be considered here: the conversion of St Paul. Of this event we have only the following dramatization from the play-book of Fleury:[4]

Ad representandum[5] Conuersionem Beati Pauli Apostoli paretur in competenti loco, quasi Ierusalem, quedam sedes, et super eam Princeps Sacerdotum. Paretur et alia sedes, et super eam iuuenis quidam in similitudine[6] Sauli; habeatque secum Ministros armatos. Ex alia uero parte, aliquantulum longe ab his sedibus, sint parate quasi in Damasco due sedes, in altera quarum sedeat uir quidam nomine Iudas, et in altera Princeps Sinagoge Damasci. Et inter has duas sedes sit paratus lectus, in quo iaceat uir quidam in similitudine Annanie. His ita paratis, dicat Saulus Ministris suis:

*Propalare uobis*[7] *non ualeo*
*quam ingenti michi sint odio*
*Christicole, qui per fallaciam*
*totam istam seducunt patriam.*

*Ite ergo, ne tardaueritis,*
*et quoscunque tales poteritis*
*inuenire, ui comprehendite;*
*comprehensos uinctos adducite.*

[1] See the poems *Ad Petrum Abælardum* and *De Papa Scolastico*, Champollion-Figeac, pp. 14, 41; Fuller, pp. 63, 96. See Ilvonen, pp. 23–4. Literary aspects of the play are considered by Sepet, *Origines*, pp. 37–40, and Petit de Julleville, i, 57; Gaselee, p. 226; Fuller, pp. 30–3.

[2] See Coussemaker, p. 333.

[3] See Petit de Julleville, i, 57; Sepet, *Origines*, p. 38. From the option allowed between Matins and Vespers Chambers (ii, 58) regards the attachment to the liturgy as 'almost accidental'.

[4] Orleans, Bibl. de la Ville, MS 201 (*olim* 178), Miscellanea Floriacensia sæc. xiii, pp. 230–3, previously edited by Monmerqué, in *Mélanges*, vii, 189–94; Wright, pp. 42–4; Du Méril, pp. 237–41; Coussemaker, pp. 210–9. Only the last of these includes the music. The text of Coussemaker is reprinted by Adams, pp. 51–4. For observations on the MS see above, i, 665. See also plate xix.

[5] representandum] The previous editors have emended, unnecessarily, to *representandam*. See Nunn, p. 95.

[6] similitudine] similitudi*nem* (MS).

[7] uobis] nobis (MS).

Hoc audientes Ministri abeant, et, cum redierint, duos sumptos ad Dominum suum conducant dicentes:

*Christicolas multos inuenimus,*
*et ex illis ⟨hos⟩ retinuimus;*
*in Damascum fugerunt alii*
*seductores huius consorcii.*

Tunc Saulus quasi iratus surgat, et ad Principem Sacerdotum eat; cumque ad eum ueniat, dicat:

*Uestre mihi dentur epistole*
*in Damascum, ubi Christicole*
*blandis uerbis sue fallacie*
*gentes*[1] *huius seducunt patrie.*

Tunc Princeps Sacerdotum det ei aliquid breue sigillatum, et dicat:

*Trado uobis meas epistolas*
*in Damascum contra Christicolas,*
*euadere ne dimiseritis*
*Christicolas quos inueneritis.*|

⟨Tunc vox ex alto:⟩[2]

*Saule! Saule! Quid me persequeris?*
*Vidi mala que meis feceris.*
*Quem dilexi cur noces populo?*
*Recalcitres nequaquam stimulo.*

Hoc audito, Saulus, quasi semimortuus in terram cadat, et iam non cadens, dicat:

*Quid*[3] *sic faris? Quis es tu, Domine?*
*Cur me meo priuasti lumine?*
*Quando tuum afflixi populum?*
*Quis es, et quod tibi uocabulum?*[4]

Dominus:

*Ihesus uocor, quem tu persequeris,*
*cuius sepe seruos afflixeris.*
*Surgens tamen urbem ingredere,*
*et audies que debes facere.*

Tunc resurgat Saulus, cumque homines sui uideri⟨n⟩t eum excecatum,[5] apprehendant eum et ducant in Damascum ad domum Iude. Tunc ueniat Dominus ad Annaniam, et dicat:

*Annania, surge quam propere,*
*atque Iude domum ingredere.*
*Te expectat uir, Saulus nomine;*
*dices ei que debet facere.*

[1] gentes] gẽs (MS); but the *e* may be expunged. Previous editors print *gentem*.

[2] The emendation is Monmerqué's. At the foot of p. 230 of the MS ample space is left for a rubric.

[3] Quid] Corrected by a later hand from *Qui* (MS).

[4] uocabulum] Written by a considerably later hand over the expunged word *filium* (MS).

[5] excecatum] excacatum (MS).

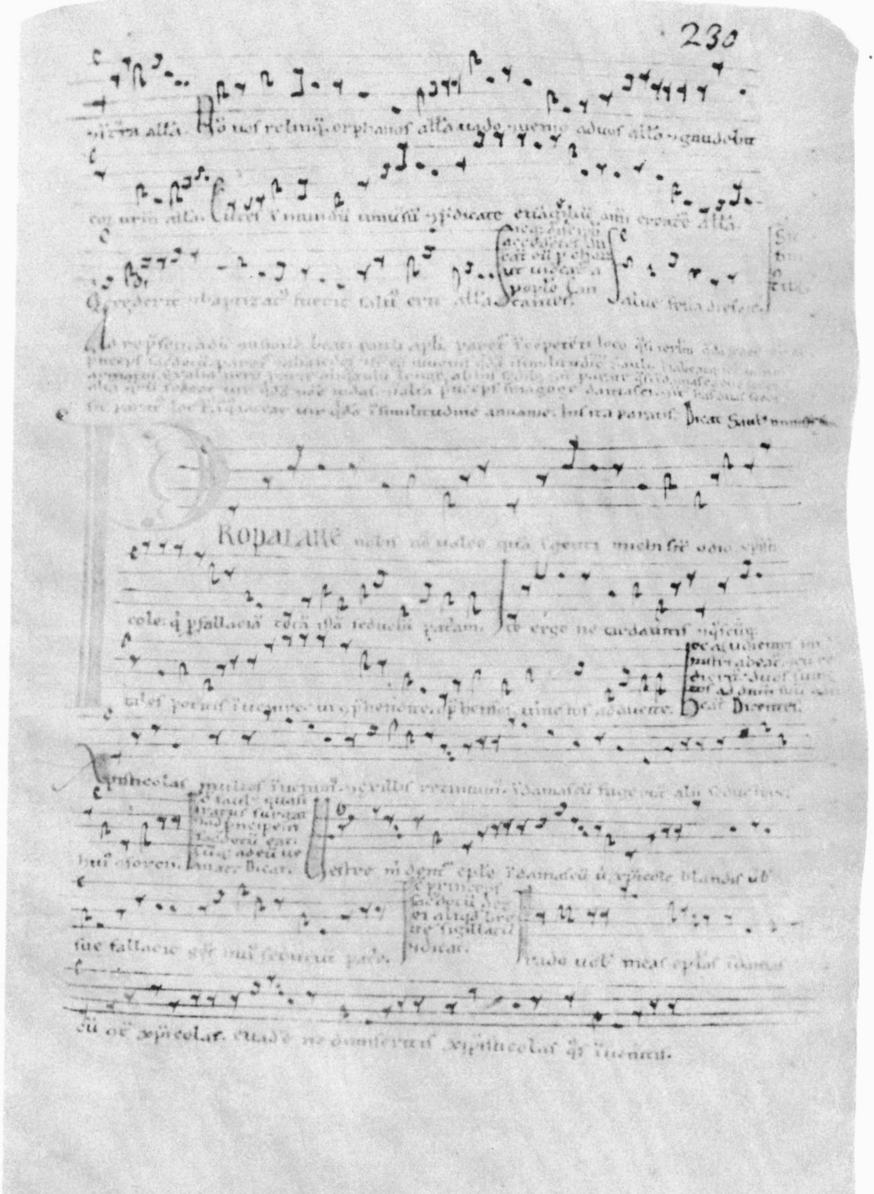

xix. Play of the Conversion of St Paul, from the Fleury Play-book, in Orleans, Bibliothèque de la Ville, MS 201 (178), p. 230

Annanias:

*De hoc Saulo audiui plurima;*
*fecit tuis mala quam maxima.*
*Si quem uidet qui tibi seruiat,*
*semper furit ut eum destruat.*

*Hic principis*[1] *habet epistolas*
*ut occidat omnes Christicolas.* |
*His de causis hunc Saulum timeo;*
*ad hu⟨n⟩c Saulum ire non audeo.*

Item Dominus:

*Annania, surge uelociter;*
*quere Saulum fiducialiter:*
*ecce*[2] *enim orat ut uenias,*
*et ut eum uidere facias.*

*Hunc elegi meo seruicio;*
*hunc elegi nostro consorcio;*
*hunc elegi ut de me predicet*[3]
*et ⟨ut⟩ nomen meum clarificet.*

Tunc surgens Annanias domum Iude introeat, et, cum uiderit Saulum, dicat:

*Ad te, Saule, me misit Dominus*
*Ihesus, Patris excelsi Filius,*
*qui in uia tibi ap⟨p⟩aruit;*
*ut uenirem ad te me monuit.*

*Predicabis coram principibus*
*nomen eius, et coram gentibus;*
*ut sis ciuis celestis patrie,*
*multa feres*[4] *pro Christi nomine.*

Tunc surgat Saulus et quasi iam credens, et predicans alta uoce, dicat:

*Cur, Iudei, non resipiscitis?*
*Ueritati cur contradicitis?*
*Cur negatis Mariam | uirginem*
*peperisse Deum et hominem?*

*Ihesus Christus, Marie filius,*
*et Deus est, et homo carneus,*
*deitatem a Patre retinens,*
*et a matre carnem suscipiens.*

H*ec* audiens, Princeps Sinagoge Damasci Ministris suis armatis dicat:

*Custodite urbis introitus,*
*conseruate uiarum exitus,*

[1] principis] princeps (MS).

[2] ecce] Inserted by a considerably later hand (MS).

[3] predicet] prodicet (MS).

[4] feres] ferres—apparently with first *r* expunged (MS).

*et, quam cito Saulum uideritis,*
*mortem eius ne distuleritis.*

Tunc Ministri eant et quera⟨n⟩t Saulum. Quo comperto, Saulus cum Discipulis suis in sporta ab aliquo alto loco, quasi a muro, ad terram demittatur. Cum autem uenerit in Iherusalem, occurret ei uir unus in similitudine Barnabe, qui, cum uiderit Saulum, ei dicat:

*Te elegit Marie filius,*
*ut sis fratrum nostrorum socius.*
*Nunc, ut laudes nobiscum Dominum,*
*ueni, uide nostrum collegium.*

⟨Ad Apostolos⟩:

*Gaudeamus, fratres, in Domino;*
*colletemur de tanto socio;*
*qui nunc erat lupus seuissimus,*
*nunc est agnus mansuetissimus.*

Omnes Apostoli incipiant *Te Deum laudamus*. Sic finiatur.[1]

At the beginning of the play Saul is represented as being in Jerusalem, proclaiming his hatred of the Christians, and dispatching soldiers to capture and bind them. Presently his emissaries return with two Christian captives, reporting that the rest of the sect have fled to Damascus. Obtaining from the high priest letters authorizing him to lay hands upon the refugees, Saul sets out from Jerusalem. On the journey he hears a voice from heaven saying, 'Saul, Saul, why persecutest thou me?' Prostrate upon the ground and blinded Saul replies, 'Who art thou, Lord?' When Jesus charges him to proceed to Damascus and await commands there, Saul's escort lead him on to the house of Judas. The Lord now appears to Ananias in Damascus, commanding him to find Saul at Judas's house and to give him counsel. As soon as he has received guidance from Ananias, Saul begins preaching to the Jews the virgin birth and divinity of Christ. This preaching arouses the anger of the high priest of the synagogue in Damascus, and Saul is forced to flee from the city, his adherents lowering him from the wall in a basket. Upon his arrival in Jerusalem, Barnabas promptly introduces him into the company of the apostles, and bids them rejoice in the conversion of a baneful enemy into a humble Christian. The apostles then conclude the play appropriately by singing the *Te Deum*.

Like the dramatizations of the story of Lazarus, the play before

[1] Followed by the rubric *Incipiunt uersus de resuscitacione Lazari*, introducing the play printed above, pp. 199 sqq.

us, in its general content, adheres closely to the Biblical account.[1] A few aspects of the narrative are somewhat amplified. The opening scene, for example, representing Saul's commands to his attendants and their fetching of Christian prisoners, is developed from a mere brief reference in the Vulgate: *Saulus autem adhuc spirans minarum et cædis in discipulos Domini.*[2] Likewise original with the playwright are the speaking part given to the high priest at Jerusalem, and the enunciation of the dogma of the virgin birth by the converted Saul. In view of these amplifications one is surprised at certain omissions and abbreviations. In the play, for instance, no use is made of the touching circumstance that when the converted Saul returned to Jerusalem and wished to ally himself with the disciples of Christ, 'they were all afraid of him, and believed not that he was a disciple'.[3] One would expect, moreover, that a playwright bent upon creating dialogue would gladly use everything of this sort in the Biblical text. It appears, however, that in the passage between Saul and the voice from heaven some five utterances are compressed into three.[4]

As a literary composition the play is by no means distinguished. The uniform ten-syllable quatrains lend to the action a simple gravity, but they lack elevation and animation. Even the variety that would arise from the occasional use of a liturgical piece is entirely absent.

For its lack of literary distinction the text before us in some measure atones through the generosity of its rubrics concerning the staging.[5] In this respect it surpasses all the plays previously considered. One side of the playing-space is to be regarded as Jerusalem, and here is the *sedes*, or platform, of the high priest, and near it, that of the young Saul, with his armed attendants. The other side of the *platea* represents Damascus, with the platforms of Judas and the chief of the synagogue, and between them, the bed upon which Ananias reclines. The realism implied in this last stage-property is present in far more spectacular form in the scene in which Saul is lowered in a basket *ab aliquo alto loco, quasi a muro*. From such details we infer a somewhat elaborate stage equipment for the performance as a whole. As to the part of the church building in which the play may have been

[1] See Acts ix, 1–27.
[2] Acts ix, 1.
[3] Acts ix, 26.
[4] See Acts ix, 4–7.
[5] See Cohen, *Théâtre*, pp. 17–8.

performed we have in the text no hint. The space required was considerable.

The performance could have been given appropriately only on the feast of the Conversion of St Paul, January 25th. The only liturgical element in the piece is the *Te Deum* sung at the close. This conclusion points, somewhat indecisively, to Matins as the service with which the play was associated.

CHAPTER XXIV

# PLAYS OF THE BLESSED VIRGIN MARY

## THE PRESENTATION IN THE TEMPLE—THE ANNUNCIATION—THE PURIFICATION—THE ASSUMPTION

SEVERAL of the plays representing New Testament subjects reviewed in the preceding chapters contain scenes which assign a significant role to the Blessed Virgin Mary. In some instances she has been found to have a salient speaking part,[1] in others, her brief utterances are scarcely noticeable in the general progress of the dialogue,[2] and in certain of these scenes she is entirely silent.[3] In none of these plays does the Virgin Mary herself assume a dominating position.

The dramatic ceremonies of the later Middle Ages to be considered in the present chapter are of a different order. Here the honouring of the Blessed Virgin is the primary purpose of the representations, and each of the dramatic observances is the most notable liturgical act of a feast-day dedicated especially to her. Although in most instances she does not participate in the speaking, she takes a prominent part in the mimetic action, and is always the centre of interest.

### The Presentation of the Blessed Virgin Mary in the Temple

The feast of the Presentation of the Virgin Mary in the Temple, celebrated on November 21st, arose from a story in the apocryphal Gospels.[4] In fulfilment of a promise made by her parents, the tradition runs, Mary, at the age of three years, accompanied them to the temple, ascended the steps unaided, and after making a vow of virginity, remained in the temple to be brought up with other virgins. During her years there she rejoiced in daily visits from angels, and in celestial visions. When she reached her fourteenth year, the high priest wished to send her home, in order that she might marry; but she interposed her vow of virginity. After divine consultation, the high priest summoned

[1] See above, i, 516, 530; ii, 180.

[2] See above, pp. 118, 190.

[3] See above, pp. 15, 188.

[4] For the texts see Tischendorf, *Evangelia*, pp. 14–7, 115–9. For bibliography and comment see Holweck, *Calendarium*, pp. 386–7; Holweck, *Fasti*, pp. 267–9; Kellner, pp. 265–6; Vigouroux, iv, 782–4; Rohault de Fleury, *Vierge*, i, 47–53; Hirn, pp. 203, 262 sqq., 421, 423. The dramatic performance is edited, with additional commentary and bibliography, by Young, *Presentation*.

the youths of the house of David, and promised Mary as a wife to him whose rod should blossom, and to whom the Holy Spirit should descend in the form of a dove. Under these conditions the choice fell upon Joseph.

The feast based upon this tradition originated in the East, to which for some centuries the observance of it was exclusively confined. Although there are some evidences of its existence as early as the seventh or eighth century, writers generally agree that it was fully and officially recognized for the first time in a Constitution of the Emperor Manuel Comnenus, in the year 1166.[1] Of the liturgical offices used for the Presentation in oriental churches we have no precise information; and, happily, for our present purpose our ignorance upon this point is not embarrassing.[2]

Concerning the introduction of this liturgical observance into the West, however, and concerning its nature thereafter, our knowledge is abundant and detailed, thanks especially to the pious activity and literary diligence of the distinguished French nobleman, Philippe de Mézières (1326 or 1327–1405).[3] It was during his various sojourns in the Orient that this diplomat, crusader, and religious enthusiast became acquainted with the feast of the Presentation and formed his project for introducing it into Western Europe. Of the progress and outcome of his undertaking we have virtually complete information through Philippe's own manuscript containing the liturgical offices for the feast, a letter of his concerning their reception into Italy and France, the text of a dramatic performance, and a note relating to it.[4]

Philippe's letter, just referred to,[5] written after November 21st, 1372, informs us that the *Festum Præsentationis Beatæ Mariæ Virginis* had been celebrated 'temporibus antiquis' by the Eastern Church on November 21st, and was still observed, in his own time, in the kingdom of Cyprus by a special office. It appears, moreover, that in Venice, several years earlier,[6] Philippe himself had brought about a solemn observance of this feast, in which promi-

[1] See Holweck, *Calendarium*, p. 386; Holweck, *Fasti*, p. 267; Kellner, p. 266.

[2] For bibliography see Young, *op. cit.*, pp. 183–4, 232–3.

[3] The most notable biography of this personage is that of N. Jorga, *Philippe de Mézières*, Paris, 1896 (*Bibliothèque de l'École des Hautes Études*, Fascicule 110). A convenient short account is given by A. Molinier, *Les Sources de l'Histoire de France*, iv, Paris, 1904, pp. 112–6.

[4] The MS is in Paris, Bibl. Nat., MS lat. 17330. For a description see Notes, p. 472.

[5] This letter is found in MS lat. 17330, fol. 4ʳ–5ᵛ. For the full text see Notes, p. 473.

[6] Concerning Mézières' visits to Venice see Jorga, *op. cit.*, pp. 236–44, 402–4.

nence was given to some sort of dramatic ceremony.[1] Pope Gregory XI (1370–8) regarded the new *festum* with favour, received from Mézières' hand the book containing the liturgical offices of the day, and submitted it to a learned body of ecclesiastics for their approval. With the approbation of all, the Pope committed the arrangements to Mézières, and the feast was given its first official celebration in the West on November 21st, 1372, in the church of the Friars Minor at Avignon.

Although Philippe de Mézières does not mention the matter specifically, we naturally infer that this celebration on November 21st, 1372, included the *repræsentatio figurata* which had previously been performed at Venice. In any case, we have a record of a dramatic performance, before Mass on the feast of the Presentation, at Avignon in 1385.[2] According to this, Mary is impersonated by a little girl three or four years of age, and is accompanied by fourteen other young girls of similar size, by older persons costumed as Joachim and Anna, and by several persons representing angels. To the music of various instruments, these personages all move in procession to the altar, where Mary readily ascends fifteen wooden steps, and is presented by her parents to a cleric costumed as a Jewish high priest. After Mary, Joachim, Anna and the angels have sung certain *laudes* and psalms, Mass proceeds, Mary occupying a stall next to the cardinals.

This record may not describe the exact form of dramatic observance used at Avignon in 1372, and at an earlier date in Venice; and we cannot be sure that it describes fully even the performance of 1385. Our knowledge of the dramatic office is not confined to descriptive records, however, for in the manuscript before us, immediately after the note outlined above, is the following complete text of the *repræsentatio figurata* in the form that must have had the approval both of Philippe de Mézières himself and of the hierarchy at Avignon:[3]

Quibusdam deuotis personis Matris illius qui dat sapientiam sapientibus et scientiam intelligentibus disciplinam, qui reuelat profunda et abscondita et nouit in tenebris constituta, cum quo lux est reuelans misteria que ventura sunt, a quo omne donum optimum et perfectum

[1] In preclara ciuitate Venetiarum, aliquibus electis deuote Virginis ipsius ciuitatis adiuuantibus, solempniter celebrari fecit cum representatione figurata et deuotissima (MS lat. 17330, fol. 4$^{v}$, printed below, p. 474).

[2] For the text, from MS lat. 17330, fol. 17$^{v}$, see Notes, p. 478.

[3] MS latin 17330, fol. 18$^{r}$–24$^{r}$, previously edited by Young, *Presentation*, pp. 202–28. See plate xx, and below, pp. 472–3.

descendit, reuelare placuit ut xxj[a] die Nouembris pro.commemoratione diei illius quo eius eterni uerbi Mater per carnales parentes in templo Domini extitit presentata, vt sibi cui seruire regnare est in perpetuum assisteret, immaculata secundum eorum vota aliquam[1] ordinauerunt solempnitatem cum representationibus quibusdam deuotissimis verbis nouisque actibus et signis ornatis ex quibus omnibus in Christo credentibus declararent quod per hanc humillime Virginis presentacionem in templo omnia catholica fundamenta incepta sunt, ex quibus etiam a carne mens agrauata tamquam per visibilia signa et opera secundum apostoli doctrinam ad cognitionem inuisibilium visibiliumque misteriorum Dei peruenire valerent, vt in sequentibus lucide declaratur.

Et primo de xxij. personis et nominibus ipsarum pro representatione fienda.

Secundo de indumentis ipsarum et ornamentis diuersis.

Tercio qualiter pro representationibus omnibus locus ordinetur.

Quarto de[2] processione fienda et ordine ipsius.

Quinto de representatione fienda[3] et laudibus Marie.

Sexto de Presentatione Marie solempni Missa celebranda et breui sermone.

Primo namque erit quedam virgo iuuencula et pulcherrima circiter trium aut iiij[or] annorum, que representabit Mariam, et cum ea alie due Virgines pulcherrime eiusdem etatis. Deinde erunt Ioachim et Anna; ceterum erunt duo angeli, Gabriel et Raphael. Deinde erunt nouem Angeli representantes nouem ordines angelorum. Postea erit quedam mulier pulcherrima etatis circiter xx. annorum, que vocabitur Ecclesia, et representabit ecclesiam. Deinde erit quedam mulier prouecte etatis, que vocabitur Synagoga, et representabit legem Moÿsi et Vetus Testamentum. Ceterum erunt duo iuuenes cum instrumentis pulsantes. Deinde erit Michael archangelus et Lucifer. Vltimo erit episcopus cum dyacono et subdiacono.

Dicto de nominibus personarum pro representatione fienda, dicendum est de indumentis et ornamentis ipsarum.

Maria vero tunicam habebit indutam albissimam de cendato, sine aliquo artificio superfluo, cum plicatura parua eiusdem tunice exterius apparente circa inferiorem partem tunice in circulo, et tunica lata erit ubique exceptis manicis, que erunt adiacentes, nec super tunicam se cinget. Postea habebit quendam mantellum etiam albissimum de cendato aut panno serico, apertum ante in longitudinem corporis cum cordula de frizello aureo in firmatione mantelli ante pectus secundum formam mantelli sponsarum, et circa collare tunice et aperturam mantelli in longitudine apponetur paruus frizellus aureus, et in circulo man|telli inferius erit etiam plicatura apparens exterius ipsius mantelli. Capud

[1] aliquam] Preceded by *nouisque actibus*, crossed out (MS).

[2] de] Written twice; second writing crossed out (MS).

[3] fienda] Preceded by *marie*, crossed out (MS).

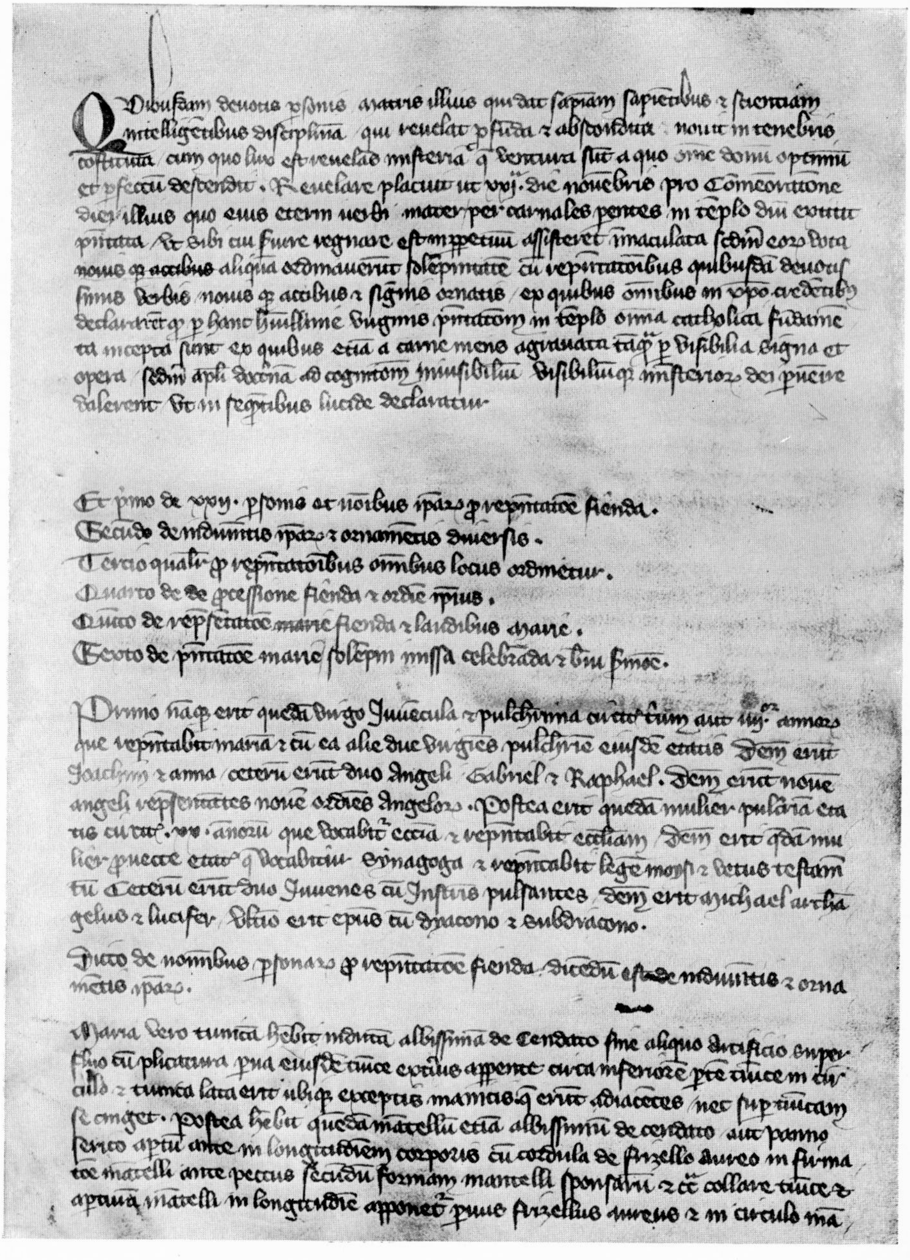
Quibusdam devotis personis matris illius qui dat sapientiam sapientibus et scientiam intelligentibus disciplinam qui revelat profunda et abscondita novit in tenebris constituta cum quo lux est revelato mysteria que ventura sunt a quo omne donum optimum et perfectum descendit. Revelare placuit ut xxj. die novembris pro commemoratione diei illius quo eius eterni verbi mater per carnales parentes in templo domini extitit presentata et sibi cum fuerit regnare est imperium assisteret immaculata secundum eorum vota novis quoque actibus aliqua ordinaverunt solempnitate cum representationibus quibusdam devotissimis verbis novis quoque actibus et signis ornatis ex quibus omnibus in corpore credentibus declaratur quod per hanc humillime virginis presentationem in templo omnia catholica fundamenta incepta sunt ex quibus etiam a carne mens adiuvata tanquam per visibilia signa et opera secundum apostoli doctrinam ad cognitionem invisibilium visibiliumque misteriorum dei pervenire valerent ut in sequentibus lucide declaratur.

Et primo de representatione personis et nominibus ipsarum que representatione fienda.
Secundo de indumentis ipsarum et ornamentis diversis.
Tertio qualiter pro representatoribus omnibus locus ordinetur.
Quarto de de processione fienda et ordine ipsius.
Quinto de representatione marie fienda et laudibus marie.
Sexto de presentatione marie solempni missa celebranda et bini sermone.

Primo namque erit quedam virgo iuvencula et pulcherrima circiter etatis trium aut iiij^or annorum que representabit mariam et cum ea alie due virgines pulchre eiusdem etatis. Item erit Joachim et anna. Ceterum erunt duo angeli Gabriel et Raphael. Item erunt novem angeli representantes novem ordines angelorum. Postea erit quedam mulier pulcra etatis circiter xx. annorum que vocabitur ecclesia et representabit ecclesiam. Item erit quedam mulier provecte etatis que vocabitur synagoga et representabit legem moysi et vetus testamentum. Ceterum erunt duo iuvenes cum instrumentis pulsantes. Item erit michael archangelus et lucifer. Ultimo erit episcopus cum dyacono et subdyacono.

Dicto de nominibus personarum que representatione fienda, dicendum est de indumentis et ornamentis ipsarum.

Maria vero tunicam habebit indutam albissimam de cendato sine aliquo artificio superfluo cum plicatura pura eiusdem tunice extrinsecus apparente circa inferiorem partem tunice in circuitu et tunica lata erit ubique exceptis manicis que erunt adiacentes nec super tunicam se cinget. Postea habebit quoddam mantellum etiam albissimum de cendato aut panno serico aptum ante in longitudinem corporis cum cordula de firzello aureo in summitate mantelli ante pectus secundum formam mantelli sponsarum et cum collare tunice et apertura mantelli in longitudine apponetur purus firzellus aureus et in circulo ma

xx. Philippe de Mézières Dramatic Office for the Feast of the Presentation of the Blessed Virgin Mary in the Temple, in Paris, Bibliothèque Nationale, MS lat. 17330, fol. 18r

autem Marie nudum[1] erit, et capilli extensi retro super humeros; habebit autem super capud quemdam circulum aureum de argento deaurato in latitudine modici digiti cum diademate rationabilis latitudinis de argento deaurato subtili firmato in circulo in posteriori parte capitis. Hoc erit ornamentum capitis Marie, nec anulos nec zonam nec aliquid aliud super se habebit nisi album et aureum, puritatem et virginitatem Marie demonstrans et caritatis claritatem ipsius.

Due autem Virgines associantes Mariam: vna induetur de cerico seu cendato viridi, figurante[2] humilitatem Marie, et alia de colore blauio seu celestino, fidem et spem Marie figurante;[2] nam secundum apostolum conuersatio nostra, sed pocius Marie, in celis est. Iste due Virgines mantellum non portabunt sicut Maria, sed tunicas latas habebunt cum plicatura inferiori, ut supra dictum est; nec etiam ornentur[3] super tunicas. Super capud vero nudum portabunt vnum circulum de argento sine diademate in latitudine prius declarata; et capilli extensi retro, ut supra de Maria.

Ioachim vero, pater Marie, induetur alba sacerdotis desuper cinctus velud sacerdos cum stola ad collum, et ante pectus in cruce procedente ut sacerdos, et desuper induetur quodam pluuiali antiquo non fracto, et in capite habebit quoddam velum subtile et aliquantulum longum et, si inuenietur, aliqualiter laboratum, cum quo inuoluet capud et collum et duas extremitates veli qualibet longitudine duarum palmarum et modicum plus proiciet super humeros super pluuiale a dextris et a sinistris; habebit ante prolixam amplam et albam barbam procedentem super pectus, et tenebit in manu extra pluuiale vnum vas mediocre vitreum plenum[4] vino rubeo.

Anna vero induetur de lino albo, tam in corpore quam in capite ad modum antique honeste matrone, et portabit in manu vnum pannum rotundum albissimum et satis magnum.

Duo autem angeli induti erunt, Gabriel et Raphael, cum amictibus albis cincti desuper cum stola ad collum et in cruce ante pectus. Super capud uero portabunt quasdam barretas adiacentes in capite super aures, et in circulo capitis desuper habebunt formam triangularem aut quadrangularem non nimis latas, cum duabus fanis retro velud in mitra episcopi. Et erunt iste barrete de cendato albo seu panno sericeo aut de papiro seu de pergamento cum quodam frizello in circulo barreti de pictura aliqua et floribus seminatis picture super barretam, et qui voluerit, poterit ponere in circulo barretarum paruas fringias de cerico diuersi coloris. Habebunt etiam duo angeli quilibet duas alas, et portabunt in manu dextra quilibet vnam virgam rubeam.

Nouem Angeli induentur sicut Gabriel et Raphael, excepto quod tres qui representabunt superiorem ordinem angelorum, scilicet cherubim

[1] nudum] Preceded by *telli* crossed out (MS).
[2] figurante] figurantem (MS).
[3] ornentur] orngentur, with *g* expunged (MS).
[4] plenum] pleno (MS).

et cetera, habebunt barretas suas rubeas de pictura, ut dictum; tres vero secundi ordinis angelorum habebunt barretas blauias seu cele-|stini coloris; et tres tercij ordinis angelorum, albas barretas. Habebunt omnes nouem lilium super quandam virgam subtilem viridis coloris, et lilium primi ordinis deauratum erit, et lilium secundi ordinis celestini coloris, et tertium argentei coloris.

Ecclesia vero erit quidem pulcerrimus[1] iuuenis circa xx. annos sine barba, et induetur[2] totum de auro in habitu diaconi, capillis pulcerrimis mulieris extensis super humeros; et super capud portabit quandam coronam auream cum lilijs et lapidibus preciosis. Contra pectus vero erit firmatus cum cordula quidam calix argenteus et deauratus sine patena, qui calix significabit Nouum Testamentum; et in manu sinistra portabit quandam crucem longam latitudine corporis, et capitis cuius crucis virga rubea erit latitudine pollicis magni, et crux tota deaurata erit sine aliquo artificio. In manu vero dextra portabit quoddam pomum rotundum totum deauratum significans vniuersalem dominationem ecclesie.

Synagoga vero induetur ad modum antique vetule cum tunica talari inueterata alicuius panni simplicis coloris, et mantello nigro et rupto. Capud vero ad modum vetule ornatum de aliquo velo obscuri coloris, et coram oculis et facie habebit velum nigrum, per quod tamen possit videre. In manu vero sinistra portabit quoddam vexillum rubeum cuius hasta nigra fracta apparebit, vexillo inclinato super humeros suos. In quo quidem vexillo rubeo scribentur litere de auro: S. P. Q. R., que sunt arma Romanorum. Et in manu dextera portabit duas tabulas lapideas inclinatas versus terram, in quibus tabulis lapideis erunt scripte litere quasi litere Hebreorum significantes legem Moysi et Vetus Testamentum.

Duo Iuuenes qui pulsabunt instrumenta dulcia induti erunt sicut Angeli, excepto quod non portabunt stolas neque alas, sed bene barretas viridis coloris.

Deinde erit Michael archangelus, qui armatus erit armis pulcerrimis de pede usque ad capud, et super galeam seu bachinetum seu barbutam habebit quandam coronam deauratam in signum militis victoriosi et in signum Christi triumphantis. In manu autem dextra[3] tenebit Michael gladium nudum fulgentem et erectum versus celum; et in sinistra manu tenebit quandam cathenam ferream, cum qua[4] Lucifer in collo ligatus retro sequetur Michaelem.

Lucifer autem ornetur tali ornamento sicut eidem decet turpissimo et abhominabili, cum cornubus, dentibus et facie horribili. Et cum manu dextra tenebit Lucifer quendam trocum seu vncum ferreum portando

[1] pulcerrimus] pulcerrius (MS).
[2] induetur] Preceded by *inditir*, indistinctly crossed out (MS).
[3] dextra] dextra autem (MS).
[4] qua] quo (MS).

super humerum; et cum sinistra manu tenebit cathenam, quasi rebellare vellet Michaeli.

Qualiter pro representatione fienda locus ordinetur.

In ecclesia namque inter portam magnam occidentalem et portam chori canonicorum seu fratrum in medio ecclesie, aliquantulum tamen magis prope portam chori quam prope portam occidentalem, vt ab omnibus partibus ecclesie lucidius videri possit, construetur quoddam edificium de lignis seu | stacio in altitudine vj. pedum desuper, vero erit tabulatum ad modum solarij, quod quidem solarium in transuerso ecclesie, scilicet de aspectu partis septentrionalis ad partem australem habebit x. pedes in longitudine, et de aspectu partis orientalis ad occidentalem solarium habebit in latitudine viij. pedes; et contra medium solarij versus portam occidentalem erunt gradus tot quot esse poterunt de pauimento ecclesie usque ad solarium, et similiter erunt similes gradus in opposito porte chori, ad descendendum de solario, ita quod quilibet gradus in se longitudinem circiter trium pedum, vt minus occupet solarium quam fieri poterit, et isti gradus ab utraque parte clausi erunt cum tabulis seu lignis ita quod nemo ascendere valeat nisi cum ordine ad representationem faciendam. Desuper vero solarium in via inter vtrosque gradus via plana erit; sed ad partem septentrionalem erit quoddam scampnum ad sedendum protensum supra solarium de parte occidentali ad partem orientalem, et istud scampnum ita longum erit ut Ioachim et Anna in capitibus scampni et Maria in medio sedere valeant, ita tamen quod sedes Marie tantum eleuetur, ut, sedentibus ipsis tribus, capud Marie sedentis in medio in equalitate altitudinis cum patre et matre inueniatur. Et inter scampnum et extremitatem solarij versus partem septentrionalem dimittetur spacium pro Gabriele et Raphaele, qui ibidem stabunt retro Mariam in pedibus. Ad partem autem australem super solarium vltra viam graduum erunt due sedes ita alte sicut scampnum predictum, super quibus sedebunt Ioachim et Anna, quarum sedium vna erit posita ad partem orientalem solarij et alia ad partem occidentalem, super quibus sedebunt Ecclesia et Synagoga respicientes Mariam, ita quod ascendendo gradus in solarium ascendens ire possit libere inter Ecclesiam et Synagogam ad extremitatem partem solarij uersus partem australem. In quatuor vero cornibus solarij stabunt in pedibus ad cornua septentrionalia Gabriel et Raphael, et ad cornua partis australis stabunt in pedibus duo iuuenes pulsatores. Solarium vero in circuitu suo munietur quodam ligno subtili altitudinis a solario duorum pedum per modum appodiationis, ut dictum solarium magis aptum appareat ad representationem fiendam, et ne illi qui super solario erunt a solario leuiter cadere possint. Istud solarium, scampnum et sedes co⟨o⟩perientur de tapetis. Fiat igitur edificium seu solarium de lignis fortissimis et bene ligatis ne propter pressuram populi astantis aliquomodo cadere valeat.

Insuper inter sedes canonicorum seu fratrum et altare maius ad partem septentrionalem contra parietem seu pilare in loco eminenti construetur aliud solarium de lignis magnis, tamen paruum, videlicet in altitudine vij. uel viij. pedum. Solarium namque desuper erit quadratum sex pedum, in qualibet quadratura et in circulo etiam munietur quodam ligno subtili vnius pedis altitudinis a solario. Et cooperietur solarium de tapetis, et super tapetum quasi in medio solarij ponetur paruum scabellum coopertum de aliquo panno pulcro serico cum cussino paruo serico ad apodiandam Mariam audiendo Missam. Et recte in medio solarij super tapetum ponetur cussinus maior de serico ad sedendum Mariam, et scabellum predictum immediate ante Mariam.

Ordinabitur etiam de aliquo loco prope ecclesiam, sicut de quadam camera per terram sufficienti[1] ad recipiendum omnes personas pro representatione ordinandas seu induendas, qui locus forte poterit esse capitulum fratrum, clausum tamen ante cum cortinis de aliqua domo prope ecclesiam | ad hoc sufficienti, in qua Maria nostra dulcissima cum societate sua parabitur et parata et ornata ut supra declaratum est expectabit processionem.

De processione fienda et ordine ipsius.

Episcopus namque seu archiepiscopus Missam celebraturus indutus pontificalibus cum baculo pastorali, diacono et subdiacono precedentibus cum omni clero, sacerdotibus indutis pluuialibus seu reliquijs de altari maiori, incipiet processionem cantando alta voce *Salue Regina*, et ibit processio recta via versus locum vbi Maria erit, semper cantando. Et cum tota processio transierit locum seu capitulum, episcopo immediate transacto, aperientur cortine seu porta. Et primo exibit vnus de ordine Angelorum cum virga alba in manu sua dextra, quasi ad ostendendum et parandum viam, et sequetur iste Angelus immediate episcopum quasi ad duos passus prope eum, ita tamen quod nulla persona se interponat inter episcopum et Angelum; Angelus autem sequendo episcopum proportionaliter cum virga sua a dextris et a sinistris parabit viam. Et post Angelum seq*uen*tur alij octo Angeli, vnus post alterum gradiendo secundum ordinem suum, et ierarchiam cherubim et cheraphim retrogradientibus quilibet portando in manu sua sinistra lilium supra declaratum. Post nouem Angelos immediate sequetur Synagoga, capite dimisso, et portando vexillum suum et tabulas lapideas, ut supra declaratum est. Et post Synagogam sequetur Ecclesia formosa cum sua cruce, calice in pectore et pomo aureo in manu dextra. Post Ecclesiam immediate sequentur duo iuuenes Pulsatores gradientes insimul et pulsantes instrumenta. Post Pulsatores sequentur duo Virgines gradientes insimul, et illa que induta erit colore viridi portabit in manu dextra vnam candelam tercie partis libre viridis coloris, et alia Virgo similem candelam celestini coloris.

[1] sufficienti] sufficipienti (MS).

Post duas Virgines immediate sequetur nostra dulcissima Maria portando in manu sua dextra similem candelam in pondere albissimam tamen, et in manu sua sinistra portabit quandam columbam albissimam ad pectus suum; et ad latus Marie dextrum gradietur Gabriel cum virga sua rubea eleuata; et ad latus sinistrum Marie simili modo Raphael gradiens in equalitate cum Maria reuerenter, nec nimis appropinquantes ad personam Marie, sed eam semper respicientes.

Post Mariam, Gabrielem et Raphaelem gradientur simul Ioachim et Anna respicientes continue Mariam, et portantes panem et vinum, ut supra declaratum est. Et post ipsos veniet Michael archangelus armatus cum gladio fulgenti et erecto in manu dextra, et cum sinistra per cathenam vnius passus ducendo trahet Luciferum cachinnantem et aliquando vlulantem, et quasi inuitum[1] incendentem.

Maria autem exeunte de capitulo seu loco ubi ipsa processiones exspectabat, subito vnus de Angelis ponet se inter duos Pulsatores eundo processionaliter et alta voce inchoabit quandam cantilenam per modum rondelli instrumentis pulsantibus de Beatissima Virgine, et hec in vulgari ad excitandum populum ad deuotionem. Et omnes Angeli cum Ecclesia, Gabrieli et Raphaeli et Pulsatoribus respondebunt. Clerus vero qui ante cantabat *Salue Regina*, quando audiet Angelum canentem,[2] tacebit, et omnes tacebunt exceptis Angelis qui continue dictum rondellum cantabunt, vno inchoante et alijs respondentibus processionaliter eundo usque ad solarium in medio ecclesie constructum.

Et post Michaelem et Luciferum gra|dientur nobiles et persone autentice vulgares, et postea populus vtriusque sexus. Ibit autem[3] processio per claustrum usque ad portam que ducit ad plateam que est ante valuas magnas ecclesie occidentales. In qua quidem platea processio faciet quendam circulum circuiendo plateam et reuertendo ad magnam portam ecclesie gradiendo et cantando ut supra usque ad solarium predictum. Et notandum est quod quelibet persona de clero eundo processionaliter portabit vnam candelam accensam in manu, et si nobiles persone autentice et populus portare uoluerint candelas in processione illius noui luminis ex vtero postea illuminantis vniuersum orbem, ab ipso lumine non dubito premiabitur. Cum autem Maria de capitulo cum societate sua exibit, erunt ordinati certi homines iuuenes et robusti qui hastas lancearum cum fune in transuerso inuicem ligatas in manibus tenebunt in longitudine ab episcopo usque ad Luciferum inclusiue, et hoc duplici ordine gradiendo processionaliter, vt videlicet Maria cum sua societate adornata eundo inter hastas a pressura populi non molestetur et habeat viam expeditam; ita tamen quod homines tenentes hastas in manibus in transuerso extra hastas versus populum ab utraque parte gradientur sustinendo populum cum hastis

[1] inuitum] inuitus (MS). [2] canentem] canentum (MS).
[3] autem] Written twice (MS).

ne aliquis inter duos[1] ordines hastarum intrare valeat nisi Maria et societas sua, exceptis duobus tribus aut quatuor seruientibus aut clientibus iusticie qui inter hastas esse poterunt ad sedandum pressuram populi, ne Maria et societas sua a populo opprimi valeant.

Intrante autem processione in ecclesiam, Episcopus cum clero suo transiet iuxta solarium et ibit ad altare maius, ibique in cathedra sua expectabit cum clero representationem fiendam super solarium, et postea Presentationem Marie ad ipsum Episcopum fiendam. Et Maria cum societate sua inter hastas coram solario constructo firmiter stabit inter solarium et magnam portam ecclesie occidentalem, Angelis semper cantantibus tantum quod Episcopus ad cathedram suam peruenire valeat et totus populus in ecclesiam intrauerit. Et nota quod processio valde mane circa solis ortum incipi debeat, quia misterium representationis prolixum est et deuotissimum, et dies tunc breues sunt.

De Representatione fienda et Laudibus Marie.

Representatio talis est. Gabriel et Raphael cum Maria, Ioachim et Anna et duobus Pulsatoribus pulsantibus et preeuntibus ad pedem graduum solarij properabunt, alijs Angelis, Ecclesia, Synagoga, Michaele et Lucifero in ordine suo firmiter stantibus et exspectantibus. Per seruientes autem armorum seu clientes ascensus graduum solarij solicite custodiatur, ne aliqui ascendere presumant nisi ad representationem fiendam ordinati. Tunc Gabriel primus in solarium ascendet, et cum virga sua voluendo se ad omnem plagam nutu non verbo omnibus silencium inponet cum virga. Et subito Maria sola sine adiutorio aliquo per gradus in solarium hylari facie ascendet, et si non poterit portare candelam suam ascendendo, Raphael eam candelam portabit, et Maria columbam suam coram pectore suo ascendendo portabit, instrumentis pulsantibus. Et quando Maria erit super solarium erecta facie uersus altare maius, statim Raphael ascendet et vna cum Gabriele Mariam ponent in sedem suam superius declaratam versus septentrionalem partem. Et tunc Gabriel et Raphael insimul cum profunda reuerentia adorabunt Mariam et ibunt retro ipsam, Gabriel in cornu solarij versus orientem pedibus stando Mariam semper respiciendo et virga erecta, et sic Raphael in alio cornu solarij retro Mariam virga erecta. Maria autem tenebit cum ambabus manibus columbam in gremio suo ipsam aliquando osculando et ponendo ad pectus suum. Et candela Marie ponetur per Raphaelem super vnum candelabrum coram Maria; et sic ponentur due candele duarum Virginum, quando ascense erunt, | in solario super duo candelabra in equalitate candelabri Marie. Tunc ascendent due Virgines insimul tenentes candelas suas, et ponent se ad pedes Marie sedendo. Et postea duo Pulsatores ascendent et ponent se in cornubus solarij versus australem partem, quilibet in vno cornu solarij, respicientes Mariam et pulsantes. Statim post ascensionem

[1] duos] duas (MS).

Pulsatorum ascendent Ioachim et Anna, et capite modicum inclinato quasi reuerendo Mariam, sedebunt super scampnum superius declaratum, Maria in medio versa facie versus partem australem, Ioachim ad sinistram Marie uersus orientem, et Anna uersus dextram Marie uersus occidentem sedendo. Et statim ascendent Synagoga primo et post eam Ecclesia, et sedebunt super scabella sua prius declarata, scilicet Synagoga ad partem orientalem et Ecclesia ad partem occidentalem, respicientes Mariam et tenentes in manibus Synagoga vexillum et tabulas, et Ecclesia crucem et pomum, ut supra declaratum est. Et sic remanebit via expedita in solario inter duos gradus inter ascensum solarij occidentalem et descensum ipsius orientalem inter Mariam, Ioachim et Annam equaliter sedentes, Gabriele et Raphaele retro in cornubus solarij partis septentrionalis stantibus et pulsantibus inter Synagogam et Ecclesiam, Pulsatoribus retro in cornubus solarij partis australis stantibus et pulsantibus.

Nunc autem veniendo ad Laudes Marie primo silentio inposito per Gabrielem et Raphaelem cum virgis suis, primus Angelus qui tenebit virgam albam in manu dextra et lilium suum in manu sinistra ascendet in solarium virga erecta; et cum venerit ante Mariam, ponet virgam suam super tapetum et profunde Mariam inclinabit, et statim ponet se inter Synagogam et Ecclesiam et Pulsatores facie erecta uersus Mariam tenentibus instrumentis et omnibus de Ecclesia tenendo lilium erectum in manu sinistra et cum manu dextra uersus Mariam alta voce quasi cantando incipiet dicere:

> *Que est illa que ascendit per desertum sicut virgula fumi ex aromatibus mirre et thuris? Estne illa virga que egredietur de radice Iesse, et flos de radice eius ascendit et requiescit super eum spiritus Domini, spiritus sapientie et intellectus, spiritus scientie et concilij, spiritus pietatis et fortitudinis, et spiritus timoris Domini?*

Quo dicto, pulsabuntur instrumenta, et dictus Angelus veniet coram Maria, et inclinando se coram ea accipiet virgam suam et descendet de solario per gradus partis orientalis, et tenebit se inter gradus et hostium chori, ubi erunt iuuenes homines robusti tenentes hastas in transuerso duplici ordine, ut prius declaratum est, ad recipiendum et Angelos et Mariam quando descendent de solario, et ibunt per chorum ad altare maius ad presentandum Mariam Episcopo. Primo autem Angelo descendente de solario, pulsantibus instrumentis, secundus Angelus ascendet in solarium per gradus occidentales, et cum lilio suo in manu sinistra profunde Mariam inclinabit et ponet se in loco vbi fuerat Angelus inter Ecclesiam, Synagogam et pulsatores, et simili modo tenendo lilium erectum in manu sinistra, et dextram extendendo[1] ad Mariam alta voce dicet:

> *Ecce appropinquat gaudium nostrum,*

[1] extendendo] Preceded by *ascend* (MS).

cum manu a dextris et a sinistris vertendo, et reducendo ad Mariam dicet:

*Considerate et videte speciosam virginem, Deo placentem, claritate refulgentem, angelos letificantem, in honestate perseuerantem, et mundum decorantem. Dies immense leticie et magne exultationis omnibus creaturis, quia ecce archa Domini, vasculum diuine sapientie, et conseruatio | naufragantis nature, que hodie in templo presentatur, Deo dedicatur et in perpetuum ad honorem omnipotentis Dei obligatur.*

Quo dicto, instrumenta pulsentur et Angelus inclinet se coram Maria et descendat cum primo Angelo, stetque in ordine suo exspectando. Tercius autem Angelus in loco vbi supra dicet:

*Virgo ascendit in templum, et angeli descendunt ad eam. Hec ancilla vocatur et domina erit; humilis dicitur et Deum humiliabit; virginitatem vouet et Deum generabit. Tu es virgo, exemplum virginum, mulier decus mulierum, domina regula dominarum, benedicta tu quia per te virgines decorabuntur, mulieres benedicentur, et omnes sancti per te premiabuntur.*

Quartus Angelus dicet:

*Ecce virginitas, ecce humilitas, ecce mansuetudo, ecce puritas,*[1] *ecce innocentia, ecce perfecta caritas, in qua habitabit immensa bonitas, et ecce illa que fiet sponsa, mater, et templum Dei.*

Et notandum est quod omnes Angeli in eodem loco dicent et cantabunt versus suos seu carmina, et in ascendendo in solarium stando cantando inclinando coram Maria, descendendo de solario et exspectando inter gradus solarij orientales et hostium chori tenebunt illum ordinem qui superius declaratus est de duobus primis Angelis. Quintus Angelus cantabit dicens:

*O grande edificium in quo sustentabitur humana fragilitas, super quod edificabitur vniuersa fidelitas, a quo inchoatur perfecta virginitas, et in quo terminabitur immensa bonitas; a te, per te, et in te laudabitur summa diuinitas.*

Sextus Angelus cantabit et dicet:

*O admirabilis Domina in conspectu hominum, in conspectu angelorum, et in presentia Dei! Quis te digne laudabit, quis te digne invocabit, cum in mundo sis sine exemplo, et in natura sine macula, et in celo eris cum immensa gloria?*

Septimus Angelus cantabit et dicet:

*Aue, Domina nostra, aue reparatio humane nature, aue mediatrix diuine iusticie et in qua misericordia Dei ostendetur, quia tu mater et virgo eris, Deus et homo, fides et cor humanum. Certe mirabilis puelle ascendentis ascensio, sed mirabilior sapientia puelle operantis, sed mirabilissima destorsio Dei descendentibus, que sanctis Patris erit gaudium et omnibus Deum diligentibus, quia cum ea apud Deum semper gaudebimus per infinita seculorum secula.*

Octauus Angelus dicet seu cantabit:

*Aue, Maria, gratia plena, Dominus tecum; et plus tecum quam in celo, enim*

[1] ecce puritas] Written twice (MS).

*in te habitabit assumens de te carnem; tecum erit et cum omnibus qui tecum sunt, qui te diligunt, qui te honorant; tecum creator erit. O creatura Dominus, O ancilla sponsus, O admirabilis sponsa, nos te benedicimus, nos te laudamus, nos te adoramus per infinita seculorum secula.*

Nonus Angelus e cherubin cantabit dicens:

*O inestimabilis amor! O immensa dilectio! O infinita caritas!*

seipsum cum manu propria ostendendo; deinde Mariam cum manu ostendendo dicet:[1]

*Ecce illa cui dabitur precium humane redemptionis, donum infinite estimationis, et premium summe perfectionis! Hec est illa Virgo, Mater Filij Dei humilis, que a Spiritu Sancto obumbrabitur, ancilla elec|tissima vocabitur, et cum Deo Patre in eternum premiabitur.*

Pulsantibus autem instrumentis, et ix. Angelis in ordine suo, secundum quem gradiebantur in processione, in terra exspectantibus, inter solarium et hostium chori, Anna mater Marie surget et stando pedibus in loco suo, instrumentis tacentibus, leuabit ambas manus suas ad celum cum pane in sinistra, et voce grossa mulieris vidue et prouecte dicet:

*Audite, filij Israel, exultantes mecum, quia mirabilia Dei narrabo: Sterilis facta est mater* (seipsam ostendendo cum manu),[2] *et genuit exultationem in Israel. Ecce potero offerre munera Domino, et non poterint me prohibere inimici mei. Dominus Deus exercituum factus est memor uerbi sui, et visitauit populum suum visitatione sua sancta.*

Quo dicto et osculata Maria, sedebit in loco suo, ut prius, et instrumenta pulsabuntur modicum. Tunc Ioachim surget in pedibus stando in loco suo, et similiter leuabit manus ad celum cum vino in sinistra, et vertendo se a dextris et sinistris cum manibus annuendo grossa voce dicet:

*Gaudete omnes mulieres, quia delebitur opprobrium vestrum; et vos omnes homines, quia Deus homo ex ea nascetur* (ostendendo Mariam cum manu; deinde ad Angelos uertendo se);[2] *et vos omnes angeli, quia sedes vestre reparabuntur.*

Deinde uertet se circumquaque et dicet:

*Et vos omnes creature, quia per eam decorabimini.*

Et cum manibus ad celum eleuatis, genuflectendo,[3] facie ad partem australem sicut sederat, concludet dicens:

*Gaudeamus ergo omnes et exultemus, et Patrem et Filium et Spiritum collaudemus.*

Et tunc surget et, osculata Maria, sedebit in loco suo sicut prius, et pulsabuntur instrumenta modicum. Tunc surget Ecclesia de scabello suo, et stando in pedibus respiciendo Mariam cantabit alta voce dicens:

*Letentur celi et exultet terra! Ecce appropinquat redempcio nostra, ecce appropinquat congregatio filiorum Dei!*

[1] seipsum . . . dicet] Underlined in black (MS).

[2] Marks of parenthesis are the editor's, the first of the two passages enclosed being underlined in black in the MS.

[3] genuflectendo] genuflectando (MS).

Et ostendendo seipsam cum manu dextra tenendo pomum aureum dicet:[1]

*Ecce noua mater vbertate plena non legis sed gracie, non timoris sed amoris, non seruitutis sed libertatis, quia ecce illa virgo* (demonstrando Mariam)[2] *que concipiet et pariet filium, qui saluum faciet populum suum a peccatis eorum. Gloria Patri et Filio et Spiritui Sancto; sicut erat in principio, et nunc et semper, et in secula seculorum.*

Et omnes angeli respondebunt[3] *Amen.* Et remanebit Ecclesia in loco suo sedendo super scabellum suum sicut prius. Et post modicam pulsationem surget Synagoga in pedibus stando in loco suo, facie inclinata ad partem sinistram, quasi tristis vertet se circumquaque, et quasi flendo cantabit dicens:

*Quis*[4] *dabit fontem lacrimarum oculis meis, ut plorem miserabilem desolationem meam. Ecce illa* (ostendendo Mariam),[5] *per quam verificabitur illa veritas: Cum venerit sanctus sanctorum, cessabit vnctio vestra.*[6]

Et tunc subito venient Gabriel et Raphael, et quasi cum indignatione expellentes Synagogam de solario per gradus occidentales; et tunc Synagoga descendendo proiciet vexillum et tabulas | a dextris et a sinistris in templo extra solarium, et sic erecta fugiet plorando et murmurando extra ecclesiam, nec amplius apparebit. Et Gabriel et Raphael non descendent de solario, sed[7] reuertentur in loco suo; et pulsabuntur instrumenta modicum, et tantum quod populus quietetur a risu propter Synagogam expulsam. Pulsando uero instrumenta, Michael ascendet solarium et ducet secum Luciferum quasi inuitum incedentem et vlulantem, et post inclinationem Michaelis ad Mariam ponet se ubi Angeli cantabunt carmina sua, et Lucifer erit iuxta Michaelem, sed cum transibit coram Maria, finget se timorosum et trementem, et dimittet se cadere in faciem suam. Et Michael eum quasi vi trahet ad locum prius dictum, scilicet vbi Angeli dixerunt versus suos. Tunc Michael, facie versa ad Mariam, in altum tenendo gladium fulgentem et in sinistra tenendo cathenam Luciferi genuflectentis alta voce dicet:

*Aue, altissima Domina, cui celi, terra, mare, abyssi et omnes creature obediunt, precipe et ego obediam tibi.*

Et cum puncto gladij ostendendo Luciferum dicet:[8]

*Ecce rebellator Dei, scandalum angelorum, et inimicus humane nature. Tu enim a Deo accepisti potestatem conculcandi, repellendi et cruciandi eum ex parte omnipotentis Dei. Tue damnationi supponitur, tue uoluntati traditur, et sub pedibus tuis vinculatur.*

Et tunc Michael Luciferum sic ligatum et ululantem sub pedibus Marie

[1] Et . . . dicet] Underlined in black (MS).

[2] Marks of parenthesis are the editor's, the words enclosed being underlined in black in the MS.

[3] Et . . . respondebunt] Underlined in black (MS).

[4] Quis] Preceded by *quis*, crossed out (MS).

[5] Marks of parenthesis are the editor's, the words enclosed being underlined in black in the MS.

[6] Cum . . . vestra] See Daniel ix, 24, and below, p. 305.

[7] sed] sede (MS).

[8] Et . . . dicet] Underlined in black (MS).

ponet, que ipsum cum pedibus verberabit, ipsumque a se expellet; et statim per Michaelem, Gabrielem et Raphaelem de solario per gradus occidentales proiciatur in terram, nec amplius in festo appareat, et pulsabuntur instrumenta. Et Michael ponet se ubi erat Synagoga, respiciendo semper Mariam. Post modicum autem interuallum surget Ecclesia de loco suo, et inclinabit se coram Maria, et descendet de solario cum Angelis stando in ordine suo, et post Ecclesiam descendent duo Pulsatores pulsantes instrumenta sua, et immediate post ipsos descendent due Virgines portantes in manibus candelas suas. Et Maria cum candela sua in manu statim post eas, in medio Gabrielis et Raphaelis, modicum tamen ante ipsos sine interuallo descendet de solario in societate Angelorum[1] in ordine suo prius declarato. Et postea immediate descendent Ioachim et Anna, et ultimo Michael quasi regens processionem,[2] eundo per chorum ad altare maius, vbi Episcopus exspectat indutus casula pro Missa celebranda cum dyacono suo ⟨et⟩ subdyacono, vnum a dextris et alium a sinistris erecti apodiantes se ad altare, versa facie ad Mariam venientem. Cum autem Michael descenderit de solario cum Maria et societate sua, inter duos ordines hastarum erit parata ad gradiendum versus altare, subito duo de Angelis alta voce incipient:

*Veni creator spiritus.*

Et omnes Angeli respondebunt *Mentes tuorum uisita*, totum versum; et finito versu, duo Angeli iterum incipient *Qui paraclitus*, et cetera. Et alij respondebunt sicut prius. Et eundo ad altare lento gradu complebitur totus hymnus.[3] Quando vero Maria inueniet se coram altari, Angeli coram altari diuident se a dextris et sinistris Marie, Maria remanente in gradu altaris coram Episcopo inter Ioachim et Annam, Gabriele et Raphaele in medio retro Mariam remanentibus cum virgis suis quasi custodiendo Mariam, et due Virgines a dextris et sinistris. Ioachim et Anna erecti stabunt; Ecclesia autem ponet se ad dextrum cornu altaris, versa facie ad Mariam uel ad populum. Et sic faciet Michael in cornu sinistro altaris. Hymno completo, duo Angeli cantatores incipient:

*Emitte spiritum tuum et creabuntur.*[4]

Et alij respondebunt:

*Et renouabis faciem terre.*[5]

Tunc Episcopus alta voce dicet:

*Deus, qui corda ⟨fidelium sancti Spiritus illustratione docuisti, da nobis in eodem Spiritu recta sapere, et de ejus semper consolatione gaudere⟩.*[6]

Et postquam *Veni creator* incipietur, instrumenta amplius non pulsabunt. Vnum notandum est, | quod quando Maria cum societate sua peruenerit

[1] Angelorum] Preceded by *sua*, crossed out (MS).

[2] processionem] possessionem (MS).

[3] For the text of *Veni creator, spiritus* (Chevalier, *R.H.*, no. 21204), see *A.H.*, l, 193.

[4] Emitte . . . creabuntur] Underlined in black (MS).

[5] Et . . . terre] Underlined in black (MS).

[6] For this prayer, and the preceding verse and response, see *Missale Romanum Mediolani*, 1474, ed. R. Lippe, ii (*Henry Bradshaw Society*, xxxiii), London, 1907, p. 308.

coram altari[1] et Angeli diuident se, ut dictum est, illi iuuenes robusti qui portabunt hastas duplici ordine coram altari facient vnum magnum quadrangulum de hastis suis in quo quadrangulo Maria et societas sua sine pressura erunt, nec permittent seruientes armorum quod aliqua persona intret nisi sit de societate Marie, vt videlicet misterium Presentationis Marie ab omnibus videri possit sine inpedimento.

Nunc autem ad Presentationem Beate Marie in Templo sciendum est quod omnia supra figurata in signis, dictis, factis et representationibus satis lucide declarant ascensionem graduum Marie Presentationemque eius; et quante uirtutis sit apparet in Laudibus ipsius et carminibus sepe replicatis et fundamentum catholicum et iocundum nostre redemptionis et reparationis. Nunc vero ad Presentationem Marie que Presentatio letantibus angelicis et Matris Dei deuotis exultantibus hodie in ecclesia Dei non immerito a fidelibus celebratur. Anna vero erecta cum pane eleuato in manu sinistra et cum dextra brachium sinistrum Marie tenendo alta voce dicet:

> *Accipe, Domine, fructum nostrum per te ab eterno ordinatum, a te benedictum, per angelum tuum annunciatum, mirabiliter conceptum, gloriose natum, per te gubernatum, et a te in habitaculum tuum electum.*

Tunc Ioachim[2] erectus manu dextra cum vino eleuata, et cum sinistra tenendo brachium dextrum Marie eleuatum cum candela, alta voce etiam dicet:

> *Benedictus Dominus Deus Israel, quia visitauit nos in prole, et preparauit redempcionem plebi sue. Accipe, Domine, votum nostrum, fructum sterilitatis nostre, quia consolatus es senectutem nostram, qui mandas salutos[3] Iacob. Veni cito, et descende in eam, ut prophete tui fideles inueniantur, et genus humanum a Babilonica seruitute per eam redimatur.*

Quo dicto, Ioachim et Anna capitibus in terram inclinatis modicum orabunt, Maria in pedibus remanente. Et statim surgent, et ducent Mariam tenentem candelam et columbam coram Episcopo, ipsamque eidem presentabunt genibus flexis. Tunc Episcopus alta voce dicet in personam Dei Patris:

> *Veni amica mea, veni columba mea, quia macula non est in te. Veni de Lybano electa ab eterno, ut te accipiam sponsam dilecto filio meo.*

Et tunc Episcopus eam accipiet in vlnis suis, vertendo se a dextris et sinistris, et faciet ipsam osculari altare et deponet eam in terram. Ioachim vero et Anna offerent supra altare panem et vinum osculando altare dimittentes Mariam coram altari cum duabus Virginibus, que etiam osculabuntur altare, et descendent cum Angelis. Tunc Gabriel et Raphael in medio ipsorum ducent Mariam in solarium preparatum inter altare et sedes chori ad partem septentrionalem superius declaratum. Et due Virgines etiam ascendent in solarium cum Maria, in quo

[1] altari] alteri (MS).
[2] Ioachim] Iohacim (MS).
[3] salutos] For *solutos*? Reading of the MS clear, but unintelligible.

solario paruo nullus remanebit nisi Maria cum duabus Virginibus, Gabriele et Raphaele retro Mariam in pedibus cum virgis suis erectis remanentibus quasi ad custodiam Marie. Ante vero scabellum paruum Marie, super quo apodiabit se audi|endo Missam, erunt tria candelabra, quibus ponentur candele Marie et Virginum, et super scabellum erit quidam libellus paruulus pulcer, cuius folia Maria reuoluet quasi dicendo horas suas, et quandoque sedebit super cussinum maiorem, et Virgines prope eam super tapetum. In evvangelio surget Maria et Virgines, et tenebunt candelas in manibus, et tenebit se Maria in Missa mature et deuote, Gabriele et Raphiele eam instruentibus. Missa namque incepta, Maria columbam permittet euolare. Et notandum quod quando Maria erit super istud solarium paruum, Ioachim, Anna, Ecclesia, Michael, ix Angeli, Pulsatoribus pulsantibus, quilibet in gradu suo Angeli primi, Ecclesia, Pulsatoribus, Ioachim et Anna et Michaele retrogradientibus inclinatis capitibus coram Episcopo et altari et postea profunde coram Maria, recedent processionaliter, instrumentis pulsantibus, et ibunt ad locum ubi parauerant se, et deponent vestimenta sua et ornamenta, que omnia ornamenta sollicite custodiantur pro representatione anni futuri.

Predictis autem recedentibus a facie Episcopi et Marie, Episcopus incipiet *Confiteor*, et cantores chori incipient *Gaudeamus*,[1] officium Presentationis, Maria in solario remanente usque ad finem Misse, facie uersa ad partem australem, et Virgines et duo Angeli quasi continue respicient Mariam. Et si videbitur quod possit fieri sermo breuis de solempnitate in Missa, et quod tempus patiatur, fiat. Sed quia misteria prolixa fuerunt et deuota, arbitrio dominorum relinquatur, ita tamen quod aut in Missa aut post prandium tanta solempnitas Regine celi sermone seu predicatione nullo modo careat.

Missa autem finita, Maria cum Angelis suis et Virginibus de solario descendet, et osculando altare candelam suam offeret, et Virgines etiam. Et statim aderunt Pulsatores, qui recesserunt,[2] et ipsis precedentibus et pulsantibus, Maria in medio Gabrielis et Raphaelis, Virginibus recedentibus, associata multitudine dominarum nobilium maxime puellarum et puerorum sexus vtriusque, ad domum vbi prandere velut portabitur per aliquem hominem procere stature seu equitando super palefridum; et Angeli etiam super duos equos, Maria in medio faciendo modicum circuitum per ciuitatem, si tempus fuerit serenum. In prandio autem Maria in habitu suo in loco sublimiori et cathedra regali ponatur, associata Virginibus quam plurimis in mensa, Gabriele et Raphaele vsque ad finem prandij diligenter sollicite et cum profunda reuerentia seruientibus.

Et qui dulcissimam Virginem Mariam feruentius et ardentius seruire

[1] For the introit *Gaudeamus* see *Missale Romanum Mediolani*, 1474, *supra cit.*, ii, 251.

[2] recesserunt] Preceded by *pulsauerunt*, crossed out (MS).

poterit et ipsius Laudes dignissimas recensendo replicare et annunciare valuerit, mihi manum adiuratione, exoro, porrigat, quia ueraciter merito non frustrabitur. Et notandum quod carmina de Laudibus Virginis suprascripta, que per Angelos et personas alias suprascriptas alta voce cantabuntur seu proferentur, deuotissima sunt ac certe lacrimabilia pre deuotione maxime fidelibus gramaticam intelligentibus; sed quia vulgaris populus gramaticam non intelligit, si videbitur expediens et nostra Maria dulcissima in cordibus deuotorum suorum per gratiam inspirauerit, translatari poterunt sepetacta carmina in vulgari dictamine et vulgariter simili modo dictari poterunt. Istud relinquo fiendum uel non fiendum deuotis intemerate Virginis presentem representationem pie legentibus. Istam autem solempnitatem Presentationis Beate Marie Virginis in Templo nouiter choruscantem de partibus orientalibus ad partes occidentales, quomodo Beata Virgo voluit ipsam solempnitatemin dictis partibus celebrari, debere quomodo fuit celebrata in Ytalia, et postea in Curia Romana, per quem et quante virtutis et deuotionis ipsa solempnitas existat, in epistola de Presentatione Marie in Templo et nouitate eius ad partes occidentales legenti lucidius | apparebit, que quidem epistola ante principium Officij Presentationis poni debet;[1] vnde deuoto Marie legenti epistolam, officium, et presentem representationem humiliter exoro ut in tanta deuotione noua Virginis pro anima mea misera apud ipsam Inperatricem celi empyrei et anchoram spei mee intercedere dignetur. Amen.

This astonishing *ordo* provides us, in the first place, with the names, and a description of the costumes, of twenty-two personages, representing Mary, two small maidens, Joachim, Anna, Gabriel, Raphael, nine angels, Ecclesia, Synagoga, two musicians, Michael, and Lucifer. The accurate details regarding costume leave us in no doubt as to the appearance of these characters—who are, to be sure, sufficiently conventional. Noteworthy, however, are the symbols of Ecclesia, and the splendid dignity of Michael leading the unwilling Lucifer by an iron chain.

Still more exact are the data regarding the dimensions and arrangements of the two platforms, or stages. The larger of these, erected in the nave of the church, is rectangular, measuring ten feet from north to south, and eight feet from east to west, and stands six feet high. This stage is approached on the east and west by steps three feet long, and is provided with a light railing, two feet high, extending round the top. Upon the stage a bench, extending from east to west, provides a seat for Mary in the middle and seats for Joachim and Anna on the child's left and

[1] See the *epistola* printed below, pp. 473 sqq.

right respectively. Opposite Joachim is placed a stool for Synagoga, and opposite Anna, one for Ecclesia. On the north-east corner Gabriel is to stand, on the north-west, Raphael, and on the other two corners, the musicians. The platform and the seats are covered with carpets.

The smaller stage is erected against the north wall of the choir, between the choir-stalls and the main altar. It is seven or eight feet high and six feet square, and is provided with a railing one foot high. This platform is furnished with a seat for Mary, and with a cushion upon which she may kneel during Mass.

These two stages are the goal of the procession and the setting of the main action.

Although certain details relating to the procession are not entirely clear, the general procedure is easily followed. After the vesting and costuming of the personages in the chapter-house, the procession moves in a stately course through the cloister to the west portal of the church, and enters the nave. The order of the personages in the procession is as follows: the clergy, the deacon and subdeacon, the bishop, the nine angels, Synagoga, Ecclesia, the two musicians, the two maidens, Mary, Gabriel (on Mary's right), Raphael (on Mary's left), Joachim and Anna, Michael, Lucifer, and a company of approved laymen. The procession advances with singing, protected on either side by a line of able-bodied men carrying spears.

When the procession has entered the church, the bishop proceeds down the nave, past the main stage, to his *cathedra* beside the altar. Then the chief personages of the action ascend the steps of the main stage and take their places, as already indicated. With a gladsome countenance Mary mounts the steps unaccompanied, carrying her dove close to her bosom with one hand, and, if possible, her candle in the other hand. After all have arranged themselves on the stage in due order, and after the lights have been put in place before Mary, everything is ready for the *Laudes Mariæ*.

The *laudes* are delivered with the greatest precision. Each of the nine angels in turn ascends the west steps of the stage, makes obeisance before Mary, utters a verse of praise, and descends by the east steps to the pavement between the stage and the door of the choir. Then Anna, Joachim, and Ecclesia offer their praise, one at a time. Synagoga, however, after a tearful lament, is pushed down the west steps of the stage by Gabriel and Raphael, lets fall her banner and the tables of the Old Law, and flees crying from the church. After the laughter of the people has subsided (*tantum quod populus quietetur a risu*), Michael ascends the platform leading the howling and unwilling Lucifer (*inuitum incedentem et ululantem*). After Michael has delivered his verse of praise, and has humbled Lucifer to the extent of making him Mary's footstool, Michael, Gabriel, and Raphael unite in thrusting *rebellator Dei* to the ground by way of the west steps.

The principal personages now group themselves in procession once more, and, during the singing of a hymn, pass from the main stage through the choir to the main altar. Here Joachim and Anna, with suitable words and action, deliver Mary into the arms of the bishop,[1] representing by this act the *Præsentatio Beatæ Virginis Mariæ in Templo*. Mary is presently set upon the pavement again and led by Gabriel and Raphael to the smaller stage, already mentioned, set against the north wall of the choir between the choir stalls and the high altar. Upon this stage Mary remains during Mass. At the beginning of the office she lets her dove fly away, and to each part of the Mass she gives reverent attention. At the end of the office Mary descends from the platform, kisses the altar, and offers her candle. With the carrying of Mary from the church, in the arms of a strong man or upon a palfrey, the dramatic office is concluded.

This careful *ordo*, written down in Philippe de Mézières' own service-book, describes, we may presume, the dramatic ceremony which he arranged primarily for the celebration at Avignon on November 21st, 1372. Its importance for the history of medieval *mise en scène* could not easily be exaggerated. In few records of the stage are costume, setting, text, and action prescribed in such detail. From the copious rubrics it is clear that we have before us not a mere piece of dramatic liturgy, but rather, a true play. The story is completely presented in the form of action, and the characters concerned in it are elaborately impersonated. The close attachment of the play to the Mass fixes it firmly within the domain of liturgical drama, where it appears to be unique. Had an enthusiast such as Philippe de Mézières promoted this dramatic performance in Western Europe a century or two earlier, we may be sure that it would have been adopted or imitated in numerous churches during the formative

[1] According to the record concerning the performance of 1385, the bishop wears the vestments of a Jewish high priest (*habitu summorum pontificum Iudeorum*). See below, p. 479.

period of church drama. From the historical circumstances, however, it happens that for the wider acceptance of this theme into the drama of the West we must look to the dramatic literature developed in the vernaculars, outside the auspices of the Church itself.

### The Annunciation

In considering the dramatic manifestations associated with the feast of the Annunciation one has to recall, in the first place, that in different localities and periods this commemoration occurred on two widely separated dates. At a very early period the Roman Church assigned it to March 25th, and has always retained this date. The Spanish church, however, objecting to the presence of this feast in Lent, chose December 18th, in Advent, as being more appropriate, and during a long period observed both dates. After the eleventh century certain other churches celebrated the Annunciation on the Wednesday of Ember Days in December—the Wednesday after December 13th.[1] The dramatic ceremonies with which we are concerned usually attached themselves to the celebration on one of the dates in December.[2]

These ceremonies developed especially at the reading of the liturgical gospel,[3] either in the Mass or in Matins, the censing of the gospel-book, or of the altar, having suggested, perhaps, the descent of the Holy Spirit or of a celestial messenger. Durandus, in any case, assures us that the deacon who reads the gospel represents the Angel Gabriel making his announcement to Mary, and that the censing of the altar symbolizes the descent upon her of the Holy Spirit.[4] At Salisbury and at Bayeux, when the deacon read the gospel in Matins on Wednesday of Ember Days in December, he held a branch of palm in his hand, as an angelic symbol.[5] At Parma, in the Mass, artificial figures of the Angel Gabriel and Mary were used at the pulpit where the gospel was read. The figure of Gabriel was lowered from an opening in the roof.[6]

[1] Concerning Ember Days (*Quatuor tempora*) see L. Fischer, *Die kirchlichen Quatember*, Munich, 1914. In regard to the dates for the feast of the Annunciation see Holweck, *Calendarium*, pp. 60–1, 417; Holweck, *Fasti*, pp. 45–7, 291–3, 300; Kellner, pp. 231–4; Beissel, pp. 326–7; Wordsworth, *Notes*, pp. 196–7, 273.

[2] For a dramatization of the Annunciation as a scene in the Christmas play from Benediktbeuern see above, p. 180.

[3] Luke i, 26–38.

[4] See Durandus, fol. cxlviii$^{v}$: Dyaconus euangelium pronuncians est angelus annuncians Virgini quod conciperet. Altaris thurificatio est Spiritus Sancti ipsi Virgini obumbratio.

[5] See *Sarum Breviary*, i, p. cxv; Martene, iii, 30.

[6] See Notes, p. 479.

The most elaborate ceremony of this sort comes to us from the later Middle Ages under the name of *Aurea Missa*, or Golden Mass, the word *aurea* designating no material accompaniment, but merely implying a belief in the special efficacy of the observance.[1] It is said to have been established at Tournai as early as 1231,[2] is reported as existing at Hildesheim in the thirteenth century, was widespread in Germany in the fourteenth, and was found in many places in Belgium and Holland during the fifteenth.[3]

From Tournai we have a full description of this ceremony as arranged there by Pierre Cotrel in the sixteenth century.[4] This was performed on Ember Wednesday in December. During Matins two boys are to be costumed as Mary and the angel, and after the seventh lesson they are to mount their respective curtained platforms. At the beginning of Mass, which follows Matins, the curtains of Mary's *sedes* are opened, showing her in a kneeling posture. Gabriel is not disclosed until the singing of the *Gloria in excelsis*. When the deacon sings the gospel, Mary and Gabriel themselves utter the words assigned to them in the text. In singing the words *Ave, gratia plena*, Gabriel bows to Mary thrice. At the words *Spiritus Sanctus superveniet in te*, the image of a dove is made to descend to a position before the platform of Mary, and there it remains until after the *Agnus Dei*, when it is drawn aloft again. After the *Ite, missa est*, Mary and Gabriel leave their platforms, and with lights preceding them, go to the vesting-room.

This is obviously a genuine dramatization of the gospel of the day. Mary and Gabriel are adequately impersonated, and they sing their proper sentences. The deacon retains much of his normal liturgical function as reader of the gospel, serving dramatically as a sort of chorus, or narrator.

Similar dramatic performances were established in each of the two cathedral churches of Besançon in 1452,[5] and in the collegiate church of Saint-Omer about the middle of the sixteenth century.[6] At Besançon the part of Mary was taken by a young girl ten or

[1] The *Aurea Missa* is comprehensively discussed by B. Kruitwagen, in *De Katholiek*, cxxx (1906), 438–66; cxxxi (1907), 158–88, 394–420, 464–90. I am acquainted with this study only through the summary of it in *Analecta Bollandiana*, xxvii (1908), 90–1. See also Beissel, pp. 323–7; Chambers, ii, 66–7; Bartholomaeis, pp. 153–6, 531–2; Fischer, *op. cit.*, pp. 97–8.

[2] See Holweck, *Fasti*, p. 300.

[3] See Beissel, pp. 324–6.

[4] For the text see Notes, p. 480.

[5] See F. I. Dunod de Charnage, *Histoire de l'Église, Ville et Diocèse de Besançon*, i, Besançon, 1750, pp. 262–3; Martene, iii, 30.

[6] See Notes, p. 482.

twelve years of age; and in the gallery from which the dove descended was stationed an elderly man to represent God.

Somewhat earlier in date, and more comprehensive in scope, than these ceremonies is the one for which the following text was provided at the cathedral of Cividale in the fourteenth century:[1]

In Annunciatione Beate Marie Virginis Representatio

Angelus:

*Ave, Maria, gratia plena, Dominus tecum; benedicta tu in mulieribus.*

Angelus:

*Ne timeas, Maria; inuenisti gratiam apud Dominum. Ecce concipies in utero, et paries filium, et uocabis nomen eius Yhesum. Hic erit magnus, et Filius Altissimi uocabitur; et dabit illi Deus sedem Dauid, patris eius, et regnabit in domo Iacob in eternum; et regni eius non erit finis.*|

Maria:

*Qvomodo fiet istud, Angele Dei, quia uirum in concipiendo non pertuli?*

Angelus:

*Avdi, Maria, Uirgo Cristi: Spiritus Sanctus superueniet in te, et uirtus Altissimi obumbrabit tibi. Ideoque et quod nascetur ex te sanctum, uocabitur Filius Dei. Et ecce Helisabeth, cognata tua, et ipsa concepit filium in senectute sua; et hic mensis est sextus illi que uocatur sterrilis, quia non erit impossibille apud Deum omne uerbum.*|

Maria:

*Ecce ancilla Domini; fiat michi secundum uerbum tuum.*

⟨Elisabeth:⟩

*Salue cara, Deo grata,*
*te saluto, sis beata;*
*tecum sitque Dominus.*

*Benedicta tu in mulieribus et benedictus fructus uentris tui. Et unde hoc michi ut ueniat mater Domini mei ad me? Ecce enim ut facta est uox salutationis tue in auribus meis, exultauit in gaudio infans in utero meo. Et beata es que credidisti, quoniam perficientur ea que dicta sunt tibi a Domino.*|

⟨Maria:⟩

*Magnificat anima mea Dominum, et exultauit spiritus meus in Deo, salutari meo, quia respexit humilitatem,*

et cetera. Hoc completo, corarij intonent *Te Deum laudamus*, usque ad ecclesiam.

In view of the meagreness of the rubrics in this text, it is fortunate that two relevant *ordines* are available, one from the manuscript which contains the play, and the other from the same

[1] Cividale, Reale Museo Archeologico, MS CII, Process. Cividalense sæc. xiv, fol. 69ᵛ–71ʳ, previously edited by Coussemaker, pp. 280–4 (with the music), and reprinted from him by Bartholomaeis, p. 531. Coussemaker refers to the MS as 'Processionale C.'

church.[1] From these it appears that the dramatic performance occurs, not in the church, but in a public place (*forum*) outside, the responsory *Gaude, Maria virgo*[2] being sung as the procession leaves the church, and the *Te Deum* as it returns. The presence of the *Te Deum* may, or may not, indicate an association with Matins. There is, in any case, nothing to show that the performance is attached directly to the Mass.

From the *ordines* it is clear also that the speeches of Mary, Elisabeth and the angel in the dramatic text above do not constitute all that is spoken. The purely narrative part of the Gospel account is intoned by the deacon in the usual way (*diaconus legat evangelium in tono*), and at each passage of direct discourse, his reading is interrupted by the appropriately impersonated character, who sings his own part. This arrangement is accurately described in the sentence *Cantatur evangelium cum ludo*. In scope the play extends somewhat beyond the liturgical gospel of the Annunciation,[3] and dramatizes also the visit to Elisabeth, ending with Mary's singing of the *Magnificat*.[4] The speeches of the three impersonated characters are, in general, faithful to the text of the Vulgate, the only creative touch appearing in the brief verses of salutation sung by Elisabeth.

A play of similar scope is described in more vivid detail in an *ordo* of the fourteenth century from the cathedral of Padua:[5]

In die Annuntiationis post prandium hora consueta pulsetur campana magna, et interim clerici conueniant ad ecclesiam, et[6] in sacristia maiori preparent se aliqui de clericis cum pluuialibus et alijs necessarijs. Et in dicta sacristia stent Maria,[7] Elisabeth, Ioseph et Ioachin preparati cum diacono et sub|diacono portantes in manibus libros argenteos. Et hora debita exeant processionaliter de sacristia, et pergant ad loca eis preparata. Hijs dimissis, processionaliter pergant ad baptisterium, et ibi stet puer preparatus in modum Gabrielis super cathedram; et ⟨de⟩ baptisterio eleuetur et feratur in ecclesiam a latere platee, et portetur super scalam uersus chorum. Et clerici stent per medium ecclesie[8] in modum cori; et interim subdiaconus incipiat prophetiam, scilicet

[1] For the texts see Notes, p. 483.

[2] For the text of this responsory see Hartker, p. 118, and above, p. 113.

[3] Luke i, 26–38 (*Missus est Angelus . . . secundum verbum tuum*).

[4] See Luke i, 39–55.

[5] Padua, Bibl. Capit., MS C. 56, Process. Patavinense sæc. xiv, fol. 35$^v$–38$^r$, described by Dondi Orologio, pp. 46–7, and, from him, by Bartholomaeis, pp. 154–6. The text itself is now published, I think, for the first time. For the speeches the MS provides square musical notation on four lines.

[6] et] Possibly *etiam* was the scribe's original intention. There is a marginal correction, of uncertain meaning.

[7] Maria] Followed by the word *Ioseph*, crossed out (MS).

[8] ecclesie] eccc̄lie (MS).

*Locutus est Dominus ad Achac*,[1] *dicens.* Finita prophetia, diaconus incipiat euangelium, scilicet *Missus est angelus Gabriel*, usque ad locum *Et ingressus angelus ad eam dixit.* Postea[2] Gabriel, flexis[3] genibus, duobus digitis manus dextre[4] eleuatis, alta uoce incipiat infrascriptam antiphonam:

*Ave, Maria, gratia plena, Dominus tecum; benedicta tu in mulieribus.*

Finita antiphona, diaconus ultra prosequitur in euangelio usque *Et ait angelus ei.* Hoc finito, Angelus iterum stando manu dextra eleuata tota aperta incipiat infrascriptam antiphonam:

*Ne timeas, Maria; inuenisti gratiam apud Dominum. Ecce conci|pies et paries filium.*

Finita antiphona, diaconus ultra prosequ*i*tur usque *Dixit autem Maria ad angelum.* Hoc finito, Maria plana uoce respondeat infrascripta antiphona:

*Qvomodo fiet istud, Angele Dei, quia uirum in concipiendo non pertuli?*

Finita antiphona, diaconus ultra prosequ*i*tur *Et respondens angelus dixit ei;* et Angelus iterum incipiat infrascriptum versum:

*Avdi, Maria, Cristi Uirgo, Spiritus Sanctus superueniet in te, et uirtus Altissimi obumbrabit tibi.*

Sed cum peruenerit ad locum, scilicet *Spiritus Sanctus superueniet in*, tunc columba aliquantulum ostendatur. Finito versu, | iterum diaconus prosequatur usque *Dixit autem Maria ad angelum.* Hoc finito, Maria ⟨se⟩ eleuet, et stando brachijs apertis alta uoce incipiat *Ecce ancilla.* Ante finem dicte antiphone columba dimittatur, et Maria recipiat dictam sub clamide. Antiphona:

*Ecce*[5] *ancilla Domini; fiat michi secundum uerbum tuum.*

Hijs finitis, diaconus ultra prosequ*i*tur in alio euangelio, scilicet *Tunc exurgens Maria abijt in montana*, usque *Et exclamauit uoce magna, et dixit.* Interim Maria descendat de loco suo et uadat a⟨d⟩ locum Helisabeth et Ioachin, et ambo sus⟨c⟩ipiant Mariam sicut scriptum est in euangelio. Hoc facto, Helisabeth genibus flexis tangendo corpus Marie cum ambabus manibus humili uoce incipiat infrascriptam antiphonam:

*Benedicta tu in mulieribus, et benedictus fructus uentris tui.*

Finita antiphona, Elisabeth erigit se, et stando iterum incipiat infrascriptam antiphonam:

*Et unde hoc michi ut ueniat mater Domi|ni*[6] *mei ad me? Ecce enim ut facta est uox salutationis tue in auribus meis, exultauit in gaudio infans in utero meo. Et beata es, Maria, que credidisti; perficientur in te que dicta sunt tibi a Domino.*

Hijs finitis, iterum diaconus prosequatur *Et ait Maria.* Et Maria uertat se uersus populum, et alta uoce cantet in octauo tono infrascriptos tres versus:

[1] Achac] The last letter has been modified, probably with the intention of producing *z* (MS). For the passage see Isaiah vii, 10.

[2] Postea] posteat (MS).

[3] flexis] Partly illegible through rubbing.

[4] digitis manus dextre] digiptis manv dextre (? MS).

[5] Ecce] Eccce (MS).

[6] Domini] Domimini (MS).

*Magnificat anima mea Dominum, | et exultauit spiritus meus in Deo, salutari meo, quia respexit humilitatem ancille sue; ecce enim ex hoc beatam me dicent omnes generationes.*

Hijs finitis, cum organo respondeatur unus versus, et a choro aliud sic ultra prosequendo usque ad finem. Et hijs finitis, omnes reuertantur ad sacristiam.[1]

This ceremony occurs after dinner. The chief personages concerned are Mary, Elisabeth, Joseph, Joachim, and Gabriel. The first four costume themselves in the main sacristy, whence they pass directly to their assigned places within the church. Then the boy impersonating Gabriel is carried in from the baptistery on a chair.[2] After the subdeacon has read the epistle of the day—here called the prophecy[3]—the deacon begins the gospel *Missus est angelus*. At the appropriate places in the narrative Gabriel and Mary, with suitable gestures, utter their own speeches. At Gabriel's words *Spiritus Sanctus superveniet in te*, a dove is let down over Mary, and as she says *Ecce ancilla Domini*, she receives it under her cloak, thus symbolizing her conception. Then occurs a representation of the visit to Elisabeth. Mary proceeds to the place where Elisabeth and Joachim are stationed, and after listening to the prescribed addresses, sings the *Magnificat*. Finally all return to the sacristy.

This observance at Padua appears to illustrate the fullest development of the theme within the church itself.[4]

## The Purification

The Feast of the Purification of the Blessed Virgin Mary, on February 2nd, celebrates the presentation of Jesus in the Temple forty days after the Nativity, as recounted in the Gospel of Luke.[5] This commemoration was brought to the West from the Orient in the fifth century, and in the Western Church it assumed the character of a feast of Christ rather than of his Mother. As early as the seventh century the liturgy of the day at Rome included

[1] Followed by the rubric *In Sabbato sancto*.

[2] Although the language of the *ordo* is not entirely clear, I infer that Gabriel makes a separate entrance.

[3] Isaiah vii, 10–5.

[4] For further bibliography see Notes, p. 484.

[5] Luke ii, 22–38. In regard to the feast see Holweck, *Calendarium*, pp. 28–9; Holweck, *Fasti*, pp. 18–20; Thalhofer, i, 681–2, 686–9; *Catholic Encyclopedia*, iii, 245–6; Franz, *Benediktionen*, i, 442–4; Hirn, pp. 380–1. The treatment of dramatic ceremonies of the Purification in the present chapter follows closely an article by the present writer in *Speculum*, v (1930), 97–102. Craig (*Modern Philology*, x [1912–13], 475, note 4) points to a scene in which Simeon appears, near the end of the *Ordo Prophetarum* of Laon (see above, p. 150), as being the most primitive known form of play on this theme.

a procession, and throughout the Middle Ages this ceremony gave prominence to the carrying into the church of lighted candles, symbolizing the entering there of Christ, the *lumen ad revelationem gentium.*[1] In some communities symbolism was carried farther. A twelfth-century *ordo* from the cathedral of Augsburg, for example, prescribes that the latter part of the procession shall proceed as follows:[2]

Et cum appropinquauerint foribus ecclesie, stent per ordinem,| et distincte moroseque cantent antiphonam istam:

> *Responsum accepit Symeon a Spiritu Sancto, non uisurum se mortem nisi uideret Christum Domini. Et cum inducerent puerum in templum, accepit eum in ulnas suas, et benedixit Deum, et dixit: Nunc dimittis, Domine, seruum tuum in pace.*

Et interim unus senior ex presbyteris in uice Sancti Symeonis accipiat plenarium in ulnas, et portet in ecclesiam pro puero Christo. Et ingrediendo imponat antiphonam *Cum inducerent puerum Ihesum.* Psalmus *Benedictus Dominus, Deus Israel.*[3]

In this ceremony, during the singing of an appropriate antiphon, a priest representing Simeon carries into the church a gospel-book as a symbol of Christ.[4]

A service-book of later date from the same church describes the action thus:[5]

Fit statio sub porticu, et quando chorus cantat de ipso responsorio vnam clausulam, tunc duo deputati sacerdotes simul cantant neuma, quod tamen apud alios non est necesse seruari:

> *Responsum accepit Symeon ą Spiritu Sancto, non visurum se mortem nisi videret Christum Domini. Et cum inducerent puerum in templum, accepit eum in vlnas suas, et benedixit Deum, et dixit: Nunc dimittis, Domine, seruum tuum in pace,*

et cetera. Finita hac antiphona, ingreditur in templum, vbi obuiam se prebet dignior quidam sacerdos, indutus pluuiali, tenens in vlnis suis ante se Imaginem Pueri super puluinar, circumstantibus eum duobus ceroferarijs, et locans se ad locum aptum, vt tota processio pretereat eum, quam postea vltimus insequitur. Introeundo templum canitur antiphona:

[1] See Luke ii, 32.

[2] Munich, Staatsbibl., MS lat. 3909, Ordin. Augustense sæc. xii, fol. 153$^{r}$–153$^{v}$, cited by Hoeynck, p. 203, and now printed from the MS. The MS provides music. For a previous printing see Young, *Purification*, pp. 98–9.

[3] The procession proceeds with a verse, response, and prayer, and then leads directly into the Mass of the day.

[4] The *plenarium*, or *pleonarium*, is either the gospel-book or some other service-book containing the liturgical gospels.

[5] *Obsequialis secundum diocesis Augustensis morem*, Augsburg, 1487, fol. vi$^{v}$. Part of this passage is quoted by Hoeynck, p. 203, and all of it by Young, *Purification*, p. 99.

*Cum inducerent puerum Ihesum parentes eius, accepit eum Symeon in vlnas suas, et benedixit eum dicens: Nunc dimittis, Domine, seruum tuum in pace,* et cetera.

In this instance the last person to enter the church is a senior priest in a cope, carrying on a cushion an effigy of the infant Jesus. Sometimes the object especially honoured in such processions was an effigy of the Virgin Mary, along with the *pleonarium*, or gospel-book.[1] Presumably the *ymago Beatæ Mariæ*, in such instances, represented the Mother with the Child in her arms.

In such ceremonies as these, however, one discerns no evidence of impersonation on the part of the participants, and hence nothing that can be called a play. Noticeable also is the fact that the Virgin Mary is either absent altogether or is represented only by a plastic figure. In searching for an example in which the Virgin is actually impersonated, one finds at least a partial satisfaction in the following description from the so-called certificate of the Gild of St Mary, at Beverley, written at some time between November 1st, 1388, and February 2nd, 1389:[2]

Ordinatum est quod singulis annis in festo Purificationis Beate Marie, incipiendo hoc proximo festo Purificationis, conueniant omnes fratres et sorores eiusdem gilde in loco certo honesto ad hoc assignato a dicta ecclesia distante; eritque ibi ordinatus quidam de gilda qui ad hoc aptior inuenietur, nobilissime et decenter vestitus et ornatus vt Regina Virgo instar gloriose Virginis Marie, habens quasi Filium in vlnis suis; eruntque ibi alij duo assimulantes Ioseph et Simeonem; eruntque duo Angeli portantes candelabrum formam cratis habens et super se xxiiij$^{or}$ grossos cereos cum aliis magnis et grossis luminaribus precedentibus. Et sic cum omni melodia et exultacione dicta Virgo cum Filio suo et Ioseph et Simeon sequentur dicta luminaria in processione versus dictam ecclesiam; sequenturque tunc inmediate dictam Virginem omnes sorores dicte gilde, et postremo omnes fratres quilibet omnium habens in manu sua vnum cereum ponderis dimidie libre; ibuntque ibidem bini et bini in ordine sobrio et moderato gressu sic processionando ad dictam ecclesiam. Et cum ibi peruentum fuerit, offeret ibi dicta Virgo

[1] See Arens, pp. 33–5.

[2] London, Public Record Office, Chancery Miscellanea, Bundle xlvi, no. 448, referred to by Toulmin Smith, *English Gilds*, London, 1870, p. 149, as Miscellaneous Rolls, Tower Records, CCCVIII. 104. The document itself, in Latin, has not been published; but a digest of it, in English, is given by Smith, pp. 149–50. See also H. F. Westlake, *The Parish Gilds of Mediæval England*, London, 1919, p. 233. I print here only the part of the original document which concerns the procession on the feast of the Purification. For an earlier printing of this part see Young, *Purification*, p. 100.

Filium suum Simeoni ad[1] summum altare instar Purificationis gloriose Virginis Marie, et sic consequenter singuli sorores et fratres offerent cereos suos cum vno denario in vnoquoque cereo de suis propriis. Hiis itaque cum omni solempnitate sic gestis, regredientur vnusquisque cum gaudio ad propria.

This ordinance requires that on the feast of the Purification the whole gild shall make a procession to the church of the Blessed Virgin, carrying lighted candles, and that the defile shall be led by persons costumed realistically to represent Joseph, Simeon, two angels, and Mary, with an effigy of Jesus in her arms. Within the church, at the high altar, Mary is to present the figure of Jesus to Simeon. What was said or sung during this action is not mentioned. The description, then, is obviously incomplete, but the use of impersonation assures us that what we have before us is, in some measure, a true play.

The most ambitious dramatic ceremony of this sort, within the knowledge of the present writer, is that described in a service-book of the fourteenth century formerly used in the cathedral of Padua:[2]

In die Purificationis inmediate post prandium pulsetur canpana magna, et interim scolares conueniant ad ecclesiam, et in sacristia maiori preparent se quatuor sacerdotes in modum Prophetarum, et duo clerici cum[3] dalmaticis, qui cantare debent *Aue, gratia plena*. Et predicti exeant cum cruce, cereis, et alijs necessarijs processionaliter, et pergant ad Templum preparatum post altare sanctorum Fabiani et Sebastiani. Postea processionaliter sacerdotes et clerici uadant ad baptisterium, et ibi sint duo clerici preparati in modum Angelorum, et alter preparatus in modum Marie cum Puero in ulnas, Ioseph asociate calato portanti super humerum, et alter preparatus | in modum Angeli super cathedram; et post Mariam pergit alter clericus preparatus in modum Anne prophetisse cum carta magna in manu. Et ita processionaliter exeant de baptisterio a latere platee, et intrent ecclesiam, Angelis cum Maria et Anna precedentibus, post sequente[4] Angelo qui est super cathedram. Peruentis in ecclesia, posterior Angelus remaneat super scalam uersus chorum cum duobus cereis et cruce. Interim[5] sacerdotes et scolares stent per medium ecclesie in modum chori, et Maria cum Angelis preceden-

[1] ad] Written twice (MS).

[2] Padua, Bibl. Capit. MS C. 56, Process. Patavinense saec. xiv, fol. $14^{r}$–$16^{v}$, described by Dondi Orologio, pp. 44–6, and, from the data of Dondi Orologio, by Bartholomaeis, pp. 156–7. The complete text was printed first, I believe, by Young, *Purification*, pp. 101–2. The antiphons and other spoken parts are furnished with musical notation on four lines.

[3] cum] con (MS).

[4] sequente] sequentes, with final *s* crossed out (MS).

[5] Interim] Followed by a single superfluous stroke (MS).

tibus Puerum[1] in ulnis portante, plane pergant uersus Templum. Et interim duo pueri qui sunt ad Templum induti dalmaticis incipiant cantare infrascriptam antiphonam:

*Ave, gratia plena, Dei genitrix uirgo, ex te enim ortus est sol iusticie illuminans que in tenebris sunt letare. Tu senior iuste, suscipiens in ulnis liberatorem animarum nostrarum,| donantem nobis resur⟨r⟩eccionem.*[2]

Hijs finitis, Maria cum pueris, Anna et Ioseph Puerum[3] in ulnis portante, ascendant ad Templum et offerant Puerum cum pul⟨l⟩is columbarum.[4] Interim pueri dalmaticis induti cantent infrascriptum responsorium, *Obtulerunt*, Symeone cum Puero garulante:

*Obtulerunt pro eo domino par turturum aut duos pullos columbarum.*[4]

Finito responsorio,[5] Symeon accipiat pullos, et uersus populum respiciat sub allas, si boni sunt. Hoc facto, Angelus qui stat uersus chorum incipiat infrascriptam antiphonam:

*Ecce positus est hic in ruinam et in resur⟨r⟩e⟨c⟩tionem multorum; et in si|gnum cui contradicetur; et tuam ipsius animam pertransibit gladius.*

Finita suprascripta[6] antiphona, duo Angeli qui sunt ad Templum cum Maria cantent infrascriptam antiphonam:[7]

*Responsum accepit Symeon a Spiritu Sancto, non uisurum se mortem nisi uideret Dominum.*

Finita suprascripta antiphona, iterum pueri cantent infrascriptum versum:

*Svscipiens Symeon puerum Ihesum in manibus exclamauit dicens.*[8]

Hijs finitis, Symeon alta uoce incipiat *Nunc dimittis*, in sexto tono, sine *Gloria Patri*. Postea cum organo decantetur *Gloria*, et chorus respondeat *Sicut erat*. Hijs uero finitis, processionaliter reuertantur ad maiorem sacristiam.[9]

At Padua the chief characters impersonated are Mary, with her Child in her arms, Joseph bearing a basket on his shoulders, Anna the prophetess, with a large sheet of parchment in her hand, four prophets, and three angels. The main action occurs at a representation of the Temple, arranged behind the altar of Saints Fabian and Sebastian. As Mary passes in procession from the baptistery into the church and toward the Temple, two choristers there sing the antiphon *Ave, gratia plena, Dei genitrix virgo*. Then Mary offers her child to Simeon, along with two young doves, while the choir-boys sing *Obtulerunt pro eo*. When

[1] Puerum] puero (MS).

[2] Here follows in the MS a repetition of the text of this antiphon ($15^r$–$15^v$), with a different melody.

[3] Puerum] puero (MS).

[4] columbarum] colunbarum (MS).

[5] responsorio] responsorium (MS).

[6] Finita suprascripta] Finito supra (MS).

[7] antiphonam] Followed by a single stroke and point, which may indicate the numeral *primam* (MS).

[8] Here follows in the MS a repetition of the text of this verse ($16^r$–$16^v$), with a different melody.

[9] Followed by the rubric *Dominica in Palmis*.

Simeon receives the doves, he inspects them, 'to see if they are in good condition'. Then the angel over by the choir sings the antiphon *Ecce positus est*, and this is followed by an antiphon from two angels stationed at the Temple, and by a verse from the choir-boys. Finally Simeon begins the *Nunc dimittis*, at the conclusion of which all return to the sacristy.

The observance at Padua, then, may be characterized as a genuine play, in the form of an elaborate dumb-show, in which the action is accompanied by the singing of appropriate liturgical pieces. Although such a performance is highly formalized and restrained, it is by no means negligible as an effort toward realistic drama.

### The Assumption

In comparison with the dramatizations of other events in the life of the Virgin Mary, the ceremonies of this kind provided for the feast of the Assumption, on August 15th, were limited in scope, and have left only meagre records. In view of the fact that this feast and its procession were established in Rome as early as the eighth century, and that the legends of the Assumption were widely distributed in the West throughout the Middle Ages, the relative absence of dramatic celebrations is not easily explained.[1]

The sort of wanton observance which may have occurred in numerous churches is imperfectly reflected in certain prohibitions from the end of the Middle Ages at Rouen.[2] The celebration there seems to have taken place particularly in a chapel of the cathedral known as Notre-Dame-du-Jardin, at the west corner of the south transept. Here the brotherhood of the Assumption arranged a garden, with figures and grotesques representing the twelve apostles and a devil, and conducted some sort of procession and dramatic performance. The acts of the chapter for the years 1460, 1506, and 1521, however, disclose the fact that the antics of the *confrérie* on this occasion were somewhat scandalous.

We are not to infer, of course, that dramatic celebrations of the Assumption were always of this indecorous nature. Completely

[1] In regard to the history of the feast see Holweck, *Calendarium*, pp. 267–8; Holweck, *Fasti*, pp. 170–3; Cabrol and Leclercq, i, 2995–3001. Concerning the legends see Duriez, *Apocryphes*, pp. 69–72, where are given references to the essential texts. See also Hirn, pp. 193, 428 sqq. For observances in Spain see Mérimée, pp. 8–9.

[2] These are described by Le Verdier, i, pp. xl-xlii, and texts are given by Gasté, pp. 76–9.

reverent, in any case, is the ceremony described in the following *ordo* of the sixteenth century from Halle:[1]

Finita Nona, exibunt de sacristia ad summum altare tali modo: primo precedent cammerarij, pueri cum vexillis, et alij duo pueri cum candelis; deinde isti duo cum thuribulis, prepositus; deinde decanus et cantor cum feretro. Et fiet processio per ecclesiam et ambitum cum responsorio *Vidi spe|ciosam*,[2] et compulsabitur sub exitu processionis cum omnibus campanis. Ordinabitur autem ita processio: primo precedent cammerarij, et portabuntur duo alba minima vexilla damascena; postea chorales et succentor; iterum duo alba damascena vexilla, et sequentur vicarij et domini; iterum duo alba vexilla; postea pueri cum cereis; deinde isti cum thuribulis, prepositus; postremo decanus et cantor cum feretro. In reditu ad ecclesiam habetur statio ante chorum, et cantabitur antiphona *Tota pulchra es*, vt in primis Vesperis de festo habetur. Statio ita erit ordinata: cammerarij et duo vexilla prima, chorales, succentor, vicarij et domini contra orientem manebunt diuisi linealiter ex vtroque latere. Sub hiatu autem vel foramine testudinis debebit esse positum scamnum rubeo sammitto tectum, in quo ponetur Imago Beate Virginis; et mox post demissionem tabernaculi, quod tunc emittetur, accendentur omnes candele apud Imaginem. Et ex vnoquoque latere erit vnus puer, vna candela, vnum vexillum et vnum thuribulum. Prepositus autem stabit prope Imaginem. Finita antiphona, senior sinistri chori imponet antiphonam *Assumpta est Maria in celum*, et non vltra. Succentor incipiet solenniter *Benedictus*, quod continuabitur solenniter in organo et choro per totum. Ad *Gloria Patri* prepositus solus thurificabit Imaginem Beate Virginis. Sub *Sicut erat* decanus et cantor innectent diligenter funes Imagini, eius facie versa ad orientem, et permittent euehi in altum. Et iubilabunt interim in organis ecclesie et tubicines uel fistulatores ciuitatis super testudinem, et dum amplius Imago non videbitur. Isti duo dabunt thuribula subcustodi, et mox duo pueri bene vociferati super testudinem cantabunt antiphonam *Que est ista que progreditur*, et cetera. Et chorus respondebit cantando *Ista est speciosa*. Post hanc antiphonam succentor solenniter incipiet antiphonam *Hodie Maria Virgo celos ascendit*. Et interim processio redibit ad chorum. Finita antiphona, prepositus dicit versum *Exaltata es*, et collectam *Veneranda nobis*, et redibit cum decano, cantore et alijs, eo ordine quo exiuerunt, ad sacristiam. Ibidem deponent cappas, et fiet sermo ad populum. Obmittentur autem hic effusiones aquarum et alie leuitates sub Assumptione.[3]

This observance, after None, consists of an elaborate pro-

[1] Bamberg, Staatsbibliothek, MS lit. 119 (Ed. VI. 3), Ordin. Hallense anni 1532, fol. 166v–167r, previously edited by Müller, *Geschichte*, p. 523.

[2] For the choral pieces in this text see Hartker, pp. 296, 298, 299, 300, 385.

[3] Followed by the rubric *In secundis Vesperis*. In connexion with the levities mentioned in the last sentence see above, i, 487.

cession about the church, at the conclusion of which an effigy of the Virgin Mary, resting upon a platform in front of the choir, is drawn up through an opening in the roof, to the accompaniment of festal music. The officiants are in the usual liturgical vestments, and the choral utterances are regular liturgical pieces. Since there is no impersonation, the performance cannot be called a play. Nor is there at hand any other evidence that during the Middle Ages the liturgy of the Assumption included true drama.

## CHAPTER XXV

# PLAYS ON SUBJECTS FROM THE OLD TESTAMENT

## ISAAC AND REBECCA—JOSEPH AND HIS BRETHREN—DANIEL

OF the plays centring in personages from the Bible there still remain for examination a small collection representing events narrated in the Old Testament. Dramatic pieces of this kind, it would appear, were never numerous. A few scenes treating such subjects have, to be sure, already come into view in our study of the *Ordo Prophetarum*. In one version or another of this play are found not only impersonations of the Old Testament prophets themselves, but also at least two brief scenes representing salient occurrences associated with Balaam and Nebuchadnezzar.[1] It is quite possible, moreover, that other prophets in the *Ordo* were centres of similar scenes, and that personages from other parts of the Old Testament were included in the prophet play and treated in the same way. One critic, as we have seen, has conjectured that some of these individual dramatizations may have attained considerable dimensions, and may have eventually detached themselves altogether from the *Ordo Prophetarum*, and have become independent pieces. This critic, indeed, inclines to the belief that all plays on subjects from the Old Testament originated in this way.[2] The present chapter, however, does not undertake to support this doubtful hypothesis. Although attention will be given to certain evidence pointing to an original connexion between one play and the procession of prophets,[3] the dramatic pieces now before us will be treated, in general, as independent compositions.

### ISAAC AND REBECCA

In accordance with Biblical chronology, our attention falls first upon a dramatization of the story of Isaac and his sons, of which we have the following fragment, of uncertain provenance, from the end of the twelfth century:[4]

[1] See above, pp. 150, 159, 164.

[2] See the observations on Sepet's argument above, pp. 170–1.

[3] See below, p. 304.

[4] The text is found on two sides of a sheet of vellum formerly pasted to the front cover of MS 223 in the Chorherrenstift at Vorau, in Steiermark, Austria. MS 223 contains sermons of Johannes Geuss de Teining, of the fifteenth century. The sheet with which we

## Ordo de Ysaac et Rebecca et Filiis eorum Recitandus

Tria tabernacula disparatim disponenda *sunt* cum lectis et aliis ornatibus[1] prout facultas erit, vnum Ysaac, secundum Iacob et Rebecce, tercium Esau. Coquine Esau et Iacob, vbi delicate dapes cum pane et uino promte sint. Capreolus, si esse p*otest.* Duo hedi. Tece manuum pilose. Pellis, que tegat collum, pilosa. Pillea Iudaica Ysaac et filiis, et coloribus uariata; cetera simplicia aptentur. Vestes prout decentiores prouideantur. Arcus cum pharetris. Cuique predictorum plurimi clare uestiti assistant cum cantoribus suis, qui in singulis locis historie allegorias dulciter canant. Hoc cantu producendus est Ysaac usque ad lectum honorifice dispositum:

*Ecce rugis exaratus*
*Ysa⟨a⟩c, uisu priuatus,*
*sedulo reficiendus*
*cibis lectoque fouendu⟨s⟩.*
*Ecce quanta clientela*
*tibi defert obsequela;*[2]
*fessos artus placet quies,*
*senem grauat nox*[3] *et dies.*

Ysaac in lecto recepto, pueri ambientes lectum clare uestiti all*egoriam* cantent:

*Ysaac uite senectus*
*mundi designat defectus;*
*sed oculi*[4] *caligantes*
*fidem Christi exsufflantes*[5]
*lumenque religionis*
*in noua superstitionis*
*preostendunt conuertendum*

are concerned was originally folded so as to form four pages. Pp. 1 and 2 are occupied by the dramatic fragment now under consideration, written in a hand of the late twelfth century; p. 3 contains the end of a Latin homily; p. 4 is blank. The dramatic fragment was published by Otakar Kernstock, in *Anzeiger für Kunde der deutschen Vorzeit*, 1877, no. 6, June, col. 170–3 (K). Part of the text in the MS is provided with musical notation in the form of neums. In the lower margin of p. 1, in a coarse hand of the fifteenth century, is written *Ordo seu ludus*. Under these words, in a similar hand, is written, and partly cut away, an entry which may be read, doubtfully, as follows: *Omelia super librum Geneseos*. The text now printed is made possible through photographs from the original sheet of vellum, and through the aid of a collation of the original generously made for me by the Reverend Pius Fank, Novice Master and Librarian of the Monastery of Vorau. Illegible or destroyed passages in the MS are indicated by two devices: (1) dots, representing passages for which no restorations are offered; and (2) pointed brackets, enclosing passages that may be restored with reasonable probability. The defects of the MS are so serious that a satisfactory text is impossible. For observations upon the content of the play see Creizenach, i, 68; Weber, *Praefigurationen*, pp. 17–20.

[1] ornatibus] hornatibus (?MS)—reading of first letter uncertain. Clearly *h* was not the letter written originally. The correct reading may be ɔ, for *cum*.

[2] obsequela] obsequia (MS).

[3] In the left margin, opposite the line beginning with nox is written *or*.

[4] oculi] occuli (MS).

[5] exsufflantes] exfuflantes (MS).

*uobis, quod est precauendum.*
*Ysaac fert formam patris,*
*Rebecca gracie matris,*
*gentis Esav timentis*
*legem, Iacob diligentis.*

Tunc eleuatus Ysaac manibus astantium[1] repetensque excreationes et suspiria ut senes ad quosdam de astantibus sibi can⟨tet⟩:

*Pro Esau properate,*
*ut ueniat indicate;*
*nulla restet occasio*
*que uos tardet cum filio.*

Abeuntibus missis, pueri all*egoriam* cant*ent*:

*Quod natus maior uocatvr*
*synagoga designatvr,*
*prior pressa sub onere*
*non spiritus sed littere.*
*Maior lege precedentem,*[2]
*minor fid⟨e⟩ subsequentem*
*populum notat uocatum*
*et in Christo adunatvm.*
*Ysaac Seyr amaui⟨t⟩,*
*se uenatu cuius pauit;*
*sic Devs primo Iudevm,*
*hostiis dum colit eum.*
*Rebecce Iac⟨ob⟩ placebat,*
*nam gratia preuidebat*
*de gentibus adoptandos*
*et Iudeos confutandos*

Missi intrantes ad Esau c*antent*:

*Ysaac euigilauit*
*et ut uenias rogauit,*
*uult uerter⟨e⟩ colloquia*
*tecum*[3] *nescimus qualia.*

Procedens Esau multis comitatus[4] et ueste clar⟨a⟩ in itinere c*antet*:

*Letvs ad patre⟨m ambulo;*
*eius⟩ me fouet uisio,*
*et mutua colloquia;*
*sic res pelletur anxia.*[5]

Esav ueniente ad patrem, Rebecca interesse⟨t⟩ uerbis illorum relatura omnia Iacob; et ipse stans c*antet*:

*En tuus presto sum natvs*

[1] astantium] affantium (MS).
[2] precedentem] precedemtem (MS).
[3] tecum] terum (MS); rerum (K).
[4] comitatus] commitatus (MS).
[5] Procedens Esau . . . anxia] Inserted in the lower margin, with a reference mark in the text above.

*ad parendum ⟨nunc⟩ paratus;*
*que iubes, licet grauia,*
*feram pro patris gratia.*

Ad h*ec* Ysaac:

*Esav ⟨fi⟩li, parentis*
*preces ne spernas petentis,*
*cui primogeniture*
*decus dedit ius ⟨na⟩ture.*
*Lustra saltus et nemora*
*cinctvs arcu cum pharetra,*
*et quod uenatu capies,*
*⟨bonos⟩ in cibos facies.*
*Pastus senum sunt mollia*
*mixta dulci cibaria,*
*raritas quos m⟨olenti⟩um*
*compellit ad sorbicium.*
*Vt prius te benedicat*
*mori quem status indicat*
*. . . ras egredere*
*comple, que scis me petere.*[1]

All*egoriam* pueri c*antent*:

*Venatores misit*[2] *⟨Deus⟩,*
*per quos captus homo revs*
*armis uerbi iaculatvs,*
*cibus factus Deo gratus.*
*Promis⟨sa be⟩nedictio*
*est sacri uerbi fusio*
*soliique spes futuri,*
*quo sunt sabbatizaturi.*

Mo⟨x abe⟩at Esau et more uenantium arcu et pharetra cum comitibus accinctus, buccina perstre⟨pente⟩, hinc inde dum ad horam discurrerint edum uel aliud animal sagittis occis⟨um pe⟩tat, et inde quod placet faciat; sed ante prefatos cibos ad manus habean⟨t⟩, | quos post exitum Iacob a patre in uasis argenteis ad Ysaac cum pane et uino deferat. At Rebecca egressa post Esau ab eo loco, vbi uerba Ysaac de uenatu cum filio audierat, Iacob sic narrans c*antet*:

*Tuo clam astabam patri,*
*cum mandasset ⟨tuo fratri⟩,*
*ut quot fe⟨ret uenatio⟩*
*sibi foret refectio*
. . . . .[3]

[1] At this point the musical notation ceases.

[2] misit] Preceded by *metu*, crossed out (MS).

[3] From one to three lines of verse are quite illegible here; and the reading of the preceding lines of this speech is far from certain.

*felicem semper uiuere,*
*prius quam cedat ⟨hora grata*
*ma⟩tris ergo fac mandata.*
*Duos hedos fer electos,*
*quos instaurem ⟨ut⟩ porrectos,*
*Ysaac te benedicat,*
*mors quem iam sibi uendicat.*

. . . [1] all*egoriam* pueri cantent:

*Quod Iacob aduexit hedos*
*homines designat fedos,*
*quorum Christus incarnatv⟨s*
*amans⟩ soluerat reatus.*
*At in binis designatur*
*esu Devs quo letatvr*
*duple⟨x⟩ g⟨ratie⟩ assumptio*
*et earum correctio.*
*Teneri quod assumuntur*
*docibiles describuntur*
*et innocentes anime*
*se. tollentes in sublime.*[2]

Ad h*ec* quasi ualde stupefactus Iacob r*espondeat*:

*Muliebri consilio*
*torqueri uis supplicio,*
*mater, quem amas filium*
*ut illusorem m⟨axim⟩um.*
*Nosti lenis quod sim, mater,*
*et pilosus natvs frater;*
*timens pater s⟨i⟩ me tractet,*
*maledictum in me iactet.*

Ad h*ec* Rebecca:

*Quos gessere mei artvs*
*numquid prodam tales partus?*
*In me sint hec maledicta;*
*tantum affer, que ⟨s⟩unt dicta.*

Iacob r*espondeat*:

*Inter spem et timorem*
*licet sic et sic laborem*
*exitus sit anxius,*
*matri parebo filius.*[3]

Tunc abeunte Iacob ⟨et⟩ reportante ⟨he⟩dos c*antet*:

*Ecce tuli que iussisti;*

[1] The brief illegible word may begin with *Q*.

[2] sublime] Over the final *e* and the point following it is written *a*, for which I have no explanation.

[3] Here is written a symbol of reference, presumably to a marginal insertion now lost.

*adaptentur ut dixisti;*[1]
*grata si fit refectio,*
*⟨ce⟩ssabit indignatio.*

Interim, dum mater protegit manus et collum Iacob pellibus pilosis ⟨et ues⟩tibus optimis domi Esau relictis aromatizantibus uestit eum, pueri all*egoriam* c*antent*:

*Seyr ⟨u⟩estes precios⟨e*
*relic⟩te domi ociose*
*decalogus est tabularum*
*a Iudeis relictarum.*
*. . . ata plebs gentium,*
*pii actus edulium*
*offert Deo cum panibus*
*uerbum ⟨de⟩signantibus.*
*Bene cibat ille Deum,*
*qui per dicta, facta reum*
*mactat, ut . . . ⟨pe⟩reat,*
*et esus Christo placeat.*

Tunc assumptis Iacob ferculis cum panibus et uino ⟨cum sequen⟩tibus seru⟨is⟩ intrans ad Ysaac sic eum cantans salutat:

*Pater mi, pater mi, pater*
*tu, frater . . . et mater,*
*tot gradus in te nescio,*
*quo colam beneficio.*
*Pietas hoc uult . . . um,*
*parentum iussa suorum*
*explicari uiriliter,*
*nec inmorari segniter.*

⟨Post hoc expl⟩orans quis sit Ysaac r*espondeat*:

*Quis es, fili, quem audio,*
*quo urgeris negotio?*
*⟨Ut men⟩tem turbes senis*
*carne, neruis lassum, uenis?*

Iacob quasi mentem ha . . . r*espondeat*:

*Tuus sum primogenitus,*
*pater; uenatu concitus*
*cibos tuli quos ⟨iussisti⟩,*
*. . . me ut uouisti.*

Ammirans de uelocitate uenationis Ysaac r*espondeat*:

*⟨O mir⟩anda prosperitas,*
*quod siluestris captiuitas*

[1] dixisti] A blurred space between *s* and *t*—possibly the erasure of two or three letters—raises doubt as to the reading.

*tam festine se ingessit*
*et in ⟨part⟩es has digessit.*

Iacob r*espondeat*:

*Dei fuit uoluntate,*
*quod tanta celeritate*
*. . . occurreret placitum*
*et propter tuum meritum.*

All*egoriam* pueri c*antent*:

*. . . quod tam concitum*
*miratur nati reditum*
*expeditam . . . ium*
*fidem demonstrat gentium.*

Ad hec Ysaac:[1]

. . . . .

Although the textual and stylistic obscurities of this text are extreme, they do not conceal the general course of the dramatic action. At the opening of the first scene, as Isaac totters to his platform, a chorus sings some verses describing his decrepitude, fatigue and hunger. After he has lain down upon his bed, the choristers sing an 'allegory,' in which they somewhat darkly interpret Isaac's physical weaknesses as prefigurings of Christian realities. Then Isaac querulously demands that Esau be summoned. As the messengers depart, an allegory is sung explaining that Esau symbolizes the Jews, and Jacob, the Christians. When Esau is brought before Isaac, the father asks for food, and straightway sends his son off to the hunt. After another allegory has been sung, the hunting expedition of Esau is represented in dumb-show. Meanwhile Rebecca proposes to Jacob a plan whereby he shall outwit Esau and obtain Isaac's blessing. The chorus then allegorizes the two kids which Jacob kills by way of deceiving his father. Prodded and aided by his mother, Jacob clothes himself in the skins of the goats, and in garments left at home by Esau. The choral allegory explains, among other things, that the garments left behind by Esau symbolize the decalogue abandoned by the Jews. In his disguise Jacob represents himself to his blind father as Esau, and offers him food. When Isaaç expresses surprise at Esau's so speedy return from hunting, Jacob attributes it to God's help. With another allegory, hardly intelligible, the fragment ends.

The play clearly undertakes to represent the Biblical story of

[1] The second page ends here. In the lower margin may be entries no longer legible.

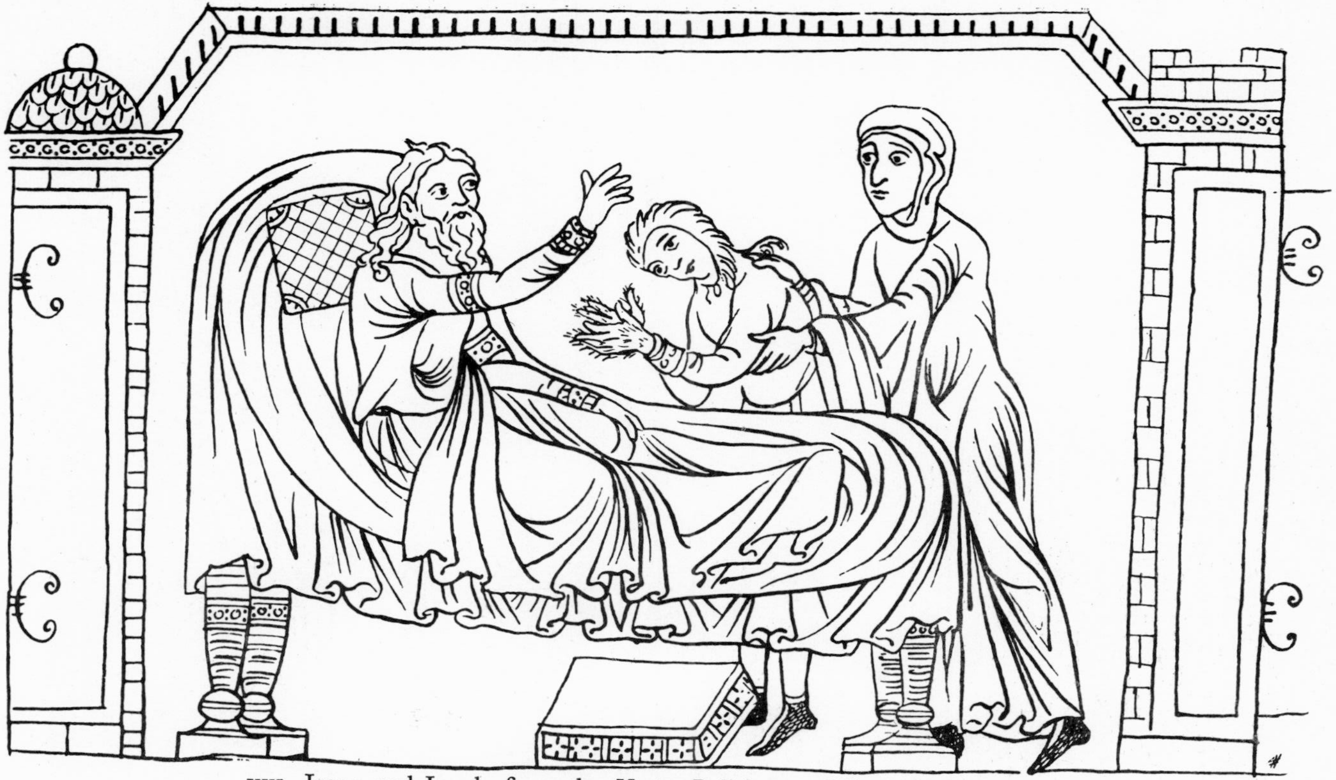

xxi. Isaac and Jacob, from the *Hortus Deliciarum* of Herrad of Landsberg

Jacob and Esau with realistic thoroughness.[1] The playing-space is set with three main 'mansions,' or *tabernacula*, one for Jacob and Rebecca, and one each for Esau and Isaac. The mansions are provided with beds and such other furnishings as can be supplied. Kitchens are arranged for both Esau and Jacob. The stage equipment includes also a roe-buck, two kids, hairy coverings for the hands and neck of Jacob, a bow and arrows, and suitable Jewish hats and other garments for all. Whether or not all this realism was effected within the church building we cannot tell. The text, in its present fragmentary state, bears no evidence of attachment to the liturgy.

The unusual interest of this play, however, arises not from the ambitious detail of its staging, or from the strained rhetoric enclosed in its octosyllabic trochaic couplets, but in the allegories copiously distributed throughout the action. These passages illustrate that method of Scriptural exegesis which theologians have called figurative, or typological, in that it regards persons, things and occurrences recorded before the earthly life of Christ as prefigurings of similar matters recorded in the Gospels.[2] It assumes a mysterious harmony between the Old Testament and the New, the 'types' of the former anticipating and conforming to the 'antitypes' of the latter. The application of the method and the meaning assumed for the word *allegoria* are conveniently indicated by Peter Comestor in the prologue to his *Historia Scholastica* as follows:[3]

> Allegoria paries superinnitens, quæ per factum, aliud factum figurat ... Sumitur allegoria quandoque a persona, ut Isaac significat Christum; etiam David quandoque hoc modo significat Christum. Quandoque a re quæ non est persona, ut vervex occisus humanitatem passam significat, et lapis duritiem cordis.

This form of exegesis, enormously amplified and systematized during the Middle Ages, may be said to have originated in the New Testament itself. St Matthew, for example, repeatedly interprets events in Christ's life as fulfilments of the Hebrew prophecies;[4] St Paul refers to Christ as the new Adam;[5] and

[1] Although the fragment covers only Genesis xxvii, 1–20, the play probably treated all, or most, of the chapter.

[2] For accounts of medieval typology see Perdrizet, pp. 110–3; Mâle, *XIII^e Siècle*, pp. 162–74; Taylor, ii, 41–59; Weber, *Praefigurationen*, pp. 1–16. As to the use of 'Präfigurationen' in later religious drama see Creizenach, i, 227.

[3] Migne, *P.L.*, cxcviii, 1053–4.

[4] See Matt. i, 22–3; ii, 15; iv, 14–6; viii, 17; xiii, 35; xxi, 4–5; xxvii, 35.

[5] See 1 Cor. xv, 22.

Christ Himself draws comparisons between occurrences in His own life and those recorded in the Old Testament.[1] Among the most eminent of those who used the typological method during the Middle Ages are St Augustine, Isidore of Seville, Bede, Walafrid Strabo, Hugh of St Victor, and Durandus of Mende. From the writings of such men are drawn the allegories obscurely versified in the play before us. As his immediate source the playwright may have used an anthology of *allegoriæ*, or he may have resorted eclectically to several typological writers.[2] The beginning of the first allegory, for example, appears to reflect an interpretation such as the following:[3]

Senectus Isaac, consummationem mundi; oculi caligantes periisse fidem de mundo, et religionis lumen neglectum esse, significant.

The remaining allegories of the play reflect the kind of prefigurings found abundantly in the *Glossa Ordinaria* of Strabo, and in the *Allegoriæ in Vetus Testamentum* often attributed to Hugh of St Victor.[4] In view of the frequency with which the medieval allegorists borrowed from one another, we need not expect to discover the precise source from which the playwright drew each, or all, of his figures.[5] The significance of his using the device lies not in his immediate sources, but in his attempt to apply dramatically a universally esteemed form of Biblical interpretation. In so doing he contributes toward establishing the conventional figure of the expositor familiar in later medieval drama.[6] The result in the play before us is a series of obscure and laboured verses, and a somewhat irksome interrupting of the dramatic action.

## JOSEPH AND HIS BRETHREN

From a play in which Jacob is a central figure we pass to the dramatization of a narrative concerning his son, Joseph. Of this the only known text is the following incomplete one of the thirteenth century from the cathedral of Laon:[7]

[1] See, for example, Matt. xii, 40.

[2] For an attempt to derive the *allegoriæ* of the present play largely from Rupert of Deutz (†1135) see Weber, *Praefigurationen*, pp. 17–20, and below, p. 485.

[3] *Walafridi Strabi . . . Glossa Ordinaria*, i, 27, in Migne, *P.L.*, cxiii, 149.

[4] See Notes, p. 484.

[5] For classified lists of Biblical 'allegories' and 'figures' in patristic writings see Migne, *P.L.*, ccxix, 123 sqq.

[6] See, for example, Venzmer, pp. 17–22.

[7] Laon, Bibl. de la Ville, MS 263, Troparium-Hymnarium Laudunense sæc. xiii, fol. 151r–153v, previously edited by Young, in *M.L.N.*, xxvi (1911), 33–7, where the MS is described. For this play the MS provides no music. The text before us is immediately preceded in the MS by the *Ordo Stelle* printed above, pp. 103 sqq. For references to other plays presenting the subject of Joseph see Notes, p. 485.

## Ordo Ioseph

*Letetur hodie*
*chorus fidelium;*
*quiescant fabule,*
*crescat silentium.*

*Sequantur homines*
*Ioseph consilium;*
*vitent mulieres*
*nature uitium.*

*Iam recitabitur*
*grauis inuidia,*
*quom Ioseph pertulit*
*fratrum nequitia.*

*Si fratri nocuit*
*fraternum odium,*
*fratribus profuit*
*Ioseph dominium.*

*Si scire placeat*
*que sint exordia,*
*de Iacob Moysi|*
*narrat historia.*

*Audite pariter*
*que causa fuerit,*
*cur domus Israel*
*mare transierit.*

Iacob uocat Ioseph et dicit:

*Ioseph, nate*
*mi dilecte,*
*scire uolo, propera*
*circa fratres*
*atque greges,*
*si sint cuncta prospera.*

Ille, accepto baculo, uadit. Fratres eum uidentes dicunt:

*Ecce uenit*
*somniator;*
*nobis datur copia.*
*Occidamus,*
*uideamus,*
*si quid prosint somnia.*

Ruben eum uolens liberare dicit:

*Non est bonum*
*ut fraternum*

*effundamus sanguinem;*
*sed exutum*
*recondamus*
*in cisternam ueterem.*

*Vestem eius*
*in edinum*
*polluamus sanguinem,*
*atque patri*
*per ignotum*
*remittamus hominem.*

Exuunt illum et ponunt in cisternam. Apparent Hismaelite, quos uidens Iudas dicit ad Fratres:

*Mercatores*
*Hismaelis*
*veniunt de finibus;*
*venundetur*
*transmarinis*
*et ignotis partibus.*
*Viuat puer,*
*impollutis*
*et nos simus manibus.*

Iudas extrahit eum de lacu, et ducens secum ad Mercatores dicit:

*State, queso.*
*Uobis uendo*
*puerum egregium;*
*vos bis denos*
*mihi nummos*
*dabitis in pretium.*

Unus de Mercatoribus ad socios[1] dicit:

*Festinate, socii,*[2]
*soluite marsupium;*
*donentur argentei,*
*bonum est commercium.*

Iudas, acceptis argenteis, redit et diuidit inter Fratres. Hismaelite Ioseph splendida ueste indutum ducunt, et uenientes ante Pharaonem dicunt:

*Viuat rex in eternum.*

Et transeuntes | Futiphar Eunucum dicunt:

*Puerum de nobili*
*genitum prosapia,*
*quem ostendit nobilem*
*facies eximia,*

[1] socios] sotios (MS). [2] socii] sotii (MS).

*Regali seruitio*
*uolumus relinquere,*
*emptum graui precio,*
*si plus uelis emere.*

Phutifar, uocato consilio, intuens Puerum dicit:

*Ex aspectu pueri*
*bonam spem concipio.*
*Nostro bene poterit*
*seruire palatio.*
*Date quod exigitur*
*pretium pro puero.*

Consiliarij surgunt, et leti de Puero dicunt ad Dominum suum:

*Libenter agimus*
*tuum imperium;*
*gratanter addimus*
*nostrum consilium.*

*Videtur utilis*
*ista mercatio;*
*dimittant puerum,*
*accepto pretio.*

Mercatores, parata statera, ponderant argentum, et inclinantes Regi, in partem uadunt. Ruben reuersus ad puteum et non inueniens Puerum dicit:

*Querens non inuenio;*
*quo me uertem nescio.*
*Qui pro nobis exiit,*
*per nos frater periit.*

Interim Peregrinus quidam iuxta Fratres Ioseph transiens uocatur. Dant illi tunicam Ioseph et dicunt:

*Redde patri*
*vestem nati,*
*defunctumque nuntia.*
*Si tristatur,*
*illum nostra*
*leuabit presentia.*

Vadit Peregrinus ad Iacob, excitat illum, osendit tunicam, et dicit:

*Vide, uestis*
*an sit ista*
*Ioseph tui filij?*
*Eius quippe*
*credens esse,*
*reportare uolui.*

Iacob pauefactus surgit. Tunicam agnoscens dicit:

*Ioseph, fili,*

*cur te misit*
*paterna stultitia!*
*Te crudelis*
*deuorauit*
*et insana| bestia!*

Quo dicto, cadit pasmatus. Accedunt Filij eius et leuantes eum dicunt:

*Care pater,*
*ne te tanti*
*vis doloris superet,*
*cum profecto*
*uitam nemo*
*mortuus recuperet.*

Iacob iterum clamat:

*Ioseph, fili,*

vt supra. Iterum Filij eius consolantur eum et dicunt:

*Audi, pater,*
*liberorum*
*preces et solatia;*
*certe nosti*
*quia multos*
*occidit tristitia.*

Quiescit Iacob; sedent Filij eius circa eum. Iterum uxor Phutifar diligens Ioseph uocat eum secreto. Ioseph non concedit consilio, quo uolente discedere, illa clamidem rapit. Ioseph dimisit et fugit. Illa festinat ut innocenti culpam[1] imponat. Ante dominum suum uenit, clamidem secum ferens; clamorem in hec uerba facit:

*Ioseph ille*
*cui tantam*
*dedisti potentiam,*
*nos offendit*
*atque summam*
*maiestatem regiam!*

*Me lasciuus*
*in conclaui*
*uoluit opprimere!*

Et ostendens clamidem dicit:

*Ecce clamis*
*quam amisit*
*cum uellet discedere!*

Facto clamore, discedit. Eunucus ad Famulos:

*Hic Ebreus*
*quasi reus*
*seruetur in carcere;*

[1] culpam] culpat (MS).

*qui dilectam*
*nobis sponsam*
*uoluit opprimere.*

Ioseph in carcerem uadit. Rex recordatus Pistoris et Pincerne produci iubet e carcere. Pistor exit cum nebulis et cophino, et Pincerna cum uite et racemis; quibus ante Regem presentatis, Pincerna ait:

*Ioseph nobis sapiens*
*reuelauit somnia,*
*quod haberem gratiam*
*et pistor suspendia.*

Pistor ad Regem:

*Parce tuo | famulo,*
*Rex inuicte, Pharao!*
*Si recusas parcere,*
*fiat tua iussio.*

Rex ait de Pistore:

*Hic dampnetur.*

De Pincerna:

*Et hic suo*
*reddatur officio.*[1]
*Sic de illis*
*curialis*
*ordinauit ratio.*

Iterum Rex mittit, et, Ioseph de carcere educto et uenienti ante se, dicit:

*Non ignoro*
*quanta tui*
*cordis sit prudentia,*
*qui tam mire*
*uisionis*
*reuelasti somnia.*

Et porrigens ei sceptrum dicit:

*Per te bona*
*regni nostri*
*disponantur omnia.*

Ioseph, osculata dextera, et genu inclinans Regi sessum uadit. Surgunt Filij Iacob, et excitantes Patrem dicunt:

*Audi, pater,*
*nos instanter*
*fames urget ualida.*
*Nobis dictum*
*in Egiptum*
*quod sit ingens copia.*
*Vis eamus*

[1] officio] offitio (MS).

*uel mittamus*
*comparandi gratia.*

Iacob dans eis argentum dicit:

*Hoc argento*
*de frumento*
*quod est necessarium*
*comparate,*
*reportantes*
*ad uite subsidium.*
*Beniamin exiguum*
*habebo solatium.*
*Hic mecum remaneat,*
*in uia ne pereat.*

Vadunt in Egyptum, et uenientes ante Ioseph dicunt:

*Te, ministrum tanti regis,*
*qui sub rege cuncta regis,*
*salutantes ueneramur,*
*ne superbi uideamur.*

Ioseph ad Fratres:

*Scire uolo*
*que sit uobis*
*ueniendi ratio.*
*Enarrate*
*qui uos estis,*
*et que uestra natio.*

Respondent Fratres et adeuntes Iosep⟨h⟩ dicunt:

*Procurator*
*et saluator*
*totius prouincie,*[1]
*regnum regis*
*Pharaonis*
*subintramus hodie*
*vt argento*
*comparatis*
*onerati frugibus.* |

Ioseph suscipit argentum, dat eis in saculis frumentum, et cum frumento reponit argentum. Et Fratres discedunt securi. Et Ioseph uocat Famulos et mittit post illos dicens:

*Que mora iam nostros*
*detinet famulos?*
*Currite citius,*
*soluite saculos.*

[1] prouincie] prouintie (MS).

*Frumentum deferunt*
*atque pecuniam;*
*pati non possumus*
*talem iniuriam.*

Famuli ad Fratres:

*Fultum fecistis; tormenta pati meruistis.*
*Procuratori si placet, ite mori.*

Reducuntur Fratres; inuenta est pecunia in saculis; confusi uerecundia tacent. Dicit eis Ioseph:

*Furti quidem conscij*
*omnes estis socij.*
*Sed unum de fratribus*
*tenebo pro omnibus.*
*Carcer hunc custodiat*
*donec ille ueniat*
*quem pater retinuit,*
*qui plus ei placuit.*

Vnus tenetur captus; alij discedunt inter se dicentes:

*Merito grauissimam*
*patimur iniuriam.*
*Talis retributio*
*est pro fratre uendito.*

Venientes ad Patrem deponunt sacculos et dicunt:

*Pater dilectissime,*
*nobis male contigit.*
*Pro nobis in laqueum*
*frater noster incidit.*

*Quolibet euadere*
*pretio non poterit,*
*nisi prius Beniamin*
*princeps ille uiderit.*

Iacob amplexatus Beniamin exclamat:

*Eya, fili Beniamin,*
*fili mi, quid faciam?*
*Quo te fratres distrahunt*
*ad innotam patriam.*

*Deus te reliquerat*
*pro Ioseph solatium;*
*quod te perdam, fili mi,*
*mortis est inditium.*

Iudas ad Patrem:

*Esto, queso, patiens,*

*sicut pater sapiens.*
*Me seruum pro puero.*[1]

The play opens with a prologue in which are set forth the scope and moral of the piece. The action, it appears, is not to extend beyond the actual story of Joseph and his brethren (Genesis, xxxvii–l). If we wish to learn of the later experiences of the children of Israel in Egypt, we are directed to the story in the Book of Exodus. The moral of the piece appears in the second stanza:

Sequantur homines
Joseph consilium;
vitent mulieres
naturæ vitium.

The action begins with Jacob's sending his favourite, Joseph, to inspect the flocks of his other sons. The latter so heartily resent this discrimination that they are dissuaded from killing Joseph only by Reuben's proposal that they make him prisoner in a cistern. Presently they sell Joseph to some passing Midianite merchants, who take him off to Egypt, and dispose of him in the household of Potiphar. Meanwhile, having dipped Joseph's coat in the blood of a kid, the brothers send it to Jacob with a message that the unfortunate youth is dead.

Now occurs, in pantomime, the attempt of Potiphar's wife to seduce Joseph, at the unsuccessful conclusion of which she hastens to her husband with Joseph's coat, and reports that she has been assaulted. Joseph is clapped into jail, and while there —as we are to infer—he interprets the dreams of the king's baker and cup-bearer. Presently Pharaoh summons these servants forth, condemns the baker to death, restores the cup-bearer to his office, and exalts Joseph to a high place in the kingdom.

Famine having arisen in the land of Canaan, Jacob dispatches his sons to Egypt for food, retaining Benjamin at home. In Egypt they present their request to Joseph, and are sent homeward with grain and money in their bags. After they have departed, however, Joseph summons them back, discloses the money that they have carried away, and accuses them of hostile designs. Retaining one brother as a hostage, he dismisses them again,

[1] Thus end the page and the fragment. At the top of fol. $154^{r}$ is the rubric *In aduentu Domini hymnvs*.

commanding that on their return they bring Benjamin with them. With a scene in which the brothers are persuading Jacob to relinquish Benjamin the fragmentary text ends.

From this outline of the action it appears that the play departs from the narrative of Genesis in no striking way.[1] The dreams of Joseph and Pharaoh, naturally enough, assume less prominence in the dramatic performance than in the narrative; but nothing of primary importance is omitted. A few re-arrangements appear to have been made for purposes of dramatic motivation or condensation. In proposing that Joseph be imprisoned in the cistern, for example, Reuben adds the suggestion that his coat be dipped in the blood of a kid, whereas in the narrative this latter procedure is proposed neither by Reuben nor at this moment in the story.[2] In the Biblical account, moreover, when the brothers come to interview Joseph concerning food, he immediately accuses them of being spies.[3] In the play he makes this accusation only after it has been motivated by his finding the money in the sacks.

In literary detail the composition is noteworthy less for felicity of expression than for variety of metrical form. Here are found, for example, stanzas containing iambic verses of six syllables, and trochaic verses of seven or eight syllables.[4] What would ordinarily appear as trochaic verses of fifteen syllables fall here into three shorter lines, through the frequent occurrence of internal rhymes.[5] So far as one can tell from the text before us, the writer versified the play throughout, without recourse to liturgical pieces in either verse or prose.

As to the circumstances under which the play was produced we have no information. The part of the text which is lost may, or may not, have contained evidence of its connexion with the services of the church. The staging, in any case, is not elaborate beyond the possibility of a performance in such circumstances. The *sedes* for Jacob, Potiphar, and Pharaoh, and the cistern and prison, could all have been provided, along with the other stage-properties somewhat carefully mentioned in the rubrics. As to the day on which the performance may have been given we have no satisfactory information. Although the narrative of Joseph's being sold by his brethren was a traditional liturgical

[1] See Genesis xxxvii, xxxix–xlv.
[2] See Genesis xxxvii, 31.
[3] See Genesis xlii, 16.
[4] See, for example, ll. 1–4, 69–76, 186–9.
[5] See, for example, ll. 25–30, 58–63.

lesson for Wednesday of the second week in Lent,[1] there is no certainty that the play was used on that day.

## Daniel

From the fragmentary *Ordo de Isaac et Rebecca* and *Ordo Joseph* we advance, across a long tract of Old Testament history, to a play representing events in the life of the prophet Daniel. Of this we are fortunate in possessing two versions, both complete, and both marked by literary distinction.

### I

It is convenient to consider first the composition preserved under the name of the wandering scholar, Hilarius, whose career and play of Lazarus have been reviewed in an earlier chapter.[2] The story of Daniel he dramatizes as follows:[3]

#### ⟨H⟩istoria de Daniel Representanda

In cuius prima parte he persone sunt necessarie:
  Rex unus sub persona Baltasar
  Regina
  Daniel
  Quatuor Milites
  Quatuor Seniores
In secunda uero parte:
  Rex unus sub persona Darii
  Idem Daniel
  Milites et Seniores qui et in prima
  Angelus unus in lacu leonum
  Abacub
  Angelus alius, qui deferat Abacub ad lacum
  Angelus tercius, qui cantet *Nuncium uobis fero*.

In primis cum uenerit Baltasar cum ponpa sua, sederitque in trono suo, cantabunt Milites coram eo hanc prosam:[4]

*Resonent unanimes cum plausu populari*
*Et decantent principis potenciam preclari!*
*Cuius ⟨s⟩ceptrum maxime debemus uenerari;*

[1] See A. Wilmart, in *Revue bénédictine*, xxxiv (1922), 30. Jenney (p. 61) speaks of 'the probably pure origin of the plays of Joseph in the Matin lessons and responses and in the many sermons of the Lenten period'.

[2] See above, pp. 211 sqq.

[3] Paris, Bibl. Nat., MS lat. 11331, Hilarii Versus et Ludi sæc. xii, fol. 12v–16r, previously edited by Champollion-Figeac, pp. 43–60 (C); Du Méril, pp. 241–54 (D); Fuller, pp. 98–117 (F). The MS provides no music. As to further observations on the MS see above, p. 212.

[4] prosam] After this word, and extending into the right margin, is written the rubric *IORDANUS*.

*Nam late diffunditur in terris et in mari;*
*Cuius pater potuit de hoste gloriari,*
*Uasa de dominico diripiens altari;*
*Qui percussit gladio Ierusalem letali,*
*Et adduxit miseros cum ponpa triumphali.*
*Teque summum principem et filium uictoris,*
*Quem non esse credimus potencie minoris;*
*Cuius dat intuitus iudicium tremoris,*
*Collaudandus citaris et uocibus sonoris;*
*Qui, sequens in omnibus exenpla genitoris,*
*Subiugas*[1] *rebellia | dominio*[2] *uigoris.*

Quo finito, dicet Rex ad Milites suos:

*Adsint ad opus prandii*
*⟨hec⟩ uasa sanctuarii,*
*que pater ⟨meus⟩*[3] *habuit,*
*Ierusalem*[4] *cum diruit.*

Tunc Milites uas⟨a⟩ afferentes taliter cantabunt:

*Iubilemus hodie*
*maiestati regie,*
*vim cuius potencie*
*tremunt gentes uarie!*
*Hic est cuius potencia*
*domat que sunt rebellia!*
*Hic est cuius potenciam*
*tremunt qui colunt Asiam!*

*Vt sit in memoria*
*paterna uictoria,*
*uideas presencia*
*Ierusalem spolia!*
*Hic est cuius potencia*
*domat que sunt rebellia!*
*Hic est cuius ⟨potenciam*
*tremunt qui colunt Asiam⟩!*

*Hostis per te domitus,*
*et orbis perterritus,*
*sicut patri primitus*
*sic est tibi subditus.*
*Hic est cuius potencia*
*⟨domat que sunt rebellia!*
*Hic est cuius potenciam*
*tremunt qui colunt Asiam⟩!*

[1] subiugas] subiugat (MS).
[2] dominio] d*omi*no (MS).
[3] Emendations in this stanza are from D.
[4] Ierusalem] ieł̄im (MS).

*Tu patri simillimus*
*et rex regum maximus,*
*⟨h⟩eres strenuissimus,*[1]
*deus es, ut credimus.*
*Hic est cuius potencia,*

et cetera. Postea ap⟨p⟩arebit quedam dextera super capud Regis scribens: Mane, Techel, Phares. Quo uiso, Rex conturbatus dicet ad Milites suos:

*Querite quantocius*
*regni magos istius,*
*qui sciant dissoluere*
*quis sit sensus litere.*

Tunc uenient quatuor, ad quos Rex dicet:[2]

*Sapientes Babilonis,*
*sensum mee uisionis,*
*sapientes enim estis,*
*enarrate,*[3] *si potestis,*
*et quid dicat litera.*

*Quedam manus quam uidebam,*
*quid ⟨s⟩cribebat nesciebam,*
*videbatur se mouere,*
*nec licebat plus uidere*
*manus quidem dextera.*

*Scribens manus se mouebat;*
*sed ignoro quid scribebat.*
*Vos scripturam si legatis*
*et quid dicat exponatis,*
*multa dabo munera.*

Quatuor autem Seniores secedent in partem, et paulo post reuertentes Regi dicent:

*Ne scripturam dextere,*
*neque sensum littere*
*scimus tibi soluere.*|

Tunc Rex publice dicet:

*Cognoscat ergo regio*
*quod meo fit inperio:*
*torque dictatus aureo,*
*uestimento purpureo,*
*mecum sit regno tercius,*
*qui declarabit certius.*[4]

[1] strenuissimus] trenuissimus (MS); D and F emend the line to *ære⟨ere⟩ strenuissimus*.

[2] In the right margin, opposite the beginning of the speech which follows, is written *Hugo*, crossed by a line of rubrication.

[3] enarrate] enarrare (MS).

[4] declarabit certius] declabit cercius (MS). The *t* of *declabit*, however, is not clearly formed.

Regina ueniente[1] ad consulendum Regem, quatuor Milites ante eam sic cantabunt:

*O coniunx,[2] aue, regia,*
*super omnes egregia,*
*summa cuius prudencia*
*nouit que sunt latencia,*
*mulierum omnium es gloria;*
*ergo ueni regis ad palacia,*
*vt in nostri principis presencia*
*tua mira nota sit sciencia.*
*Veni cito,*
*ut marito*
*prebeas consilia.*

*O mulierum[3] omnium*
*sola non habens uicium,*
*et ad cuius eloquium*
*mens stupet sapiencium,*
*in te dignum regis est consorcium;*
*permirandum etenim ingenium,*
*sola regis illius inperium;*
*ergo regem consolare dubium*
*veni cito,*
*ut marito*
*prebeas consilium.*

Que astans Regi dicet:

*Ne turberis, Baltasar, propter uisum subitum,*
*adest ⟨enim⟩[4] Daniel cui nil est incognitum.*
*In hoc, ut cognouimus,*
*est deorum spiritus,*
*multa namque uidimus*
*que predixit primitus.*
*Vt queratur Daniel igitur, Rex, inpera,*
*per quem tam dif⟨f⟩icilis exponatur littera.*

Tunc Rex ad Milites suos:

*Inquiratis igitur Danielem, famuli,*
*eius ut consilio mihi possit consuli.*

Milites adducentes Danielem sic cantabunt:

*Omnis absit hodie mesticia,*
*nunc est enim congrua leticia.*

[1] ueniente] ueniens (MS).

[2] coniunx] cu*n*iuns (MS). In the left margin, opposite the opening words of this speech is written *Hilarius*, crossed by a line of rubrication.

[3] mulierum] muelierum (MS).

[4] Emendation of F, which produces a better verse than D's *Adest Daniel cui n⟨ih⟩il est incognitum.*

*Danieli referatur gracia,*
*cuius sapiencia,*
*futurorum prescia,*
*scit que sunt latencia;*
*cui certa sunt et cognita*
*cum futuris preterita;*
*per quem erit exposita*
*uisio regis subita.*

*Illi per quem exponetur littera*
*infinita rex promisit munera,*
*principatum, purpuram et cetera.*
*Sed in Babilonia |*
*nulla sunt ingenia*
*que sciant hec dubia.*
*Regis ergo palacio*
*hunc presentabit concio,*
*per quem iam sine dubio*
*regis soluetur uisio.*

Postea dicet Rex Danieli:

*Si sunt uera que nos audiuimus,*
*certus erit uisus quem uidimus;*
*nam est in te deorum spiritus,*
*quia noscis cuncta diuinitus.*

*Ne cuncteris ergo persoluere*
*quis sit sensus istius litere;*
*que⟨m⟩ si mihi uelis exponere,*
*diues multo iam fies munere.*

Daniel ad Regem:

*Tolle, Princeps, munera non curanda;*
*namque gratis proferam hec miranda.*
*Tuis habes usibus uasa Dei;*
*sed te causa destruet huius rei.*
*Hoc testatur litera de qua queris,*
*quia mane crastino rex non eris.*
*Techel signat regimen*[1] *ponderatum,*
*inuenitur itaque minoratum.*
*Phares ⟨tandem⟩*[2] *indicat iam diuisum;*
*constat hoc a Domino sic prouisum.*

Tunc Rex, induens eum pulcherrimis indumentis et secum residere faciens, dicet:

*Qui sic nobis hanc exponit literam*
*purpuram accipiet,*[3] *ut dixeram,*

[1] regimen] regnum (C); regnum ⟨nunc⟩ (D).

[2] Emendation of D.

[3] accipiet] Emended to *accipiat* (D.F).

*sedeat⟨que⟩*[1] *principis ad dexteram;*
*mecum*[2] *regnet etiam,*[3]
*ob suam periciam,*
*partem regni terciam.*

Et conuersus ad Milites dicet:

*Propter uaticinium uatis huius ueri*
*nostro decet a conspectu uasa remoueri;*
*in contemtum non habebo uasa velud ante;*
*nolo quod sint mihi causa cladis tante.*

Milites uero, uasa reportantes et Reginam reducentes, cantabunt ante eam:[4]

*Gaude, coniux regia,*
*Babilonis gloria,*
*que precellis omnia*
*Regi necessaria*
*domina.*

*Cuius sapiencia*
*regi dat consilia,*
*et dando solacia*
*uincis muliebria*
*agmina.*

*In cuius consilio*
*tota pendet regio,*
*et pre sensu nimio*
*te laudat cum gaudio*
*concio.*

*triplex est | laudacio,*
*forma, pudor, racio,*
*que uix adsunt alio;*
*digna es consorcio*
*regio.*

Postea Darius, rex Persarum et Medorum, adueniens cum exercitu suo, et quasi interficiens Baltasar, et auferens ei coronam, inponet capiti suo. Qui cum sederit in trono suo, cantabitur hec laus coram eo:[5]

*Ad honorem tui, Dari,*
*quia decet ⟨nos⟩*[6] *letari,*
*omnes ergo mente pari*
*gaudeamus;*
*laudes tibi debitas referamus!*

[1] sedeat⟨que⟩] Emend. F; ⟨et⟩ sedeat (D).
[2] mecum] Etec̄ (MS).
[3] etiam] ectiam (MS).
[4] In the right margin, opposite the opening words of the speech which follows, is written *Iordanus*, crossed by a line of rubrication.
[5] In the left margin, opposite the opening words of the speech which follows, is written *Hilarius*, crossed by a line of rubrication.
[6] D's emendation. See Meyer, p. 57.

*Cuius iugum timent Perse*
*nec non gentes uniuerse,*
*quia summi minimique*
*sibi subsunt et ubique,*
*gaudeamus;*
*laudes tibi debitas referamus!*

*Cuius iram satis sensit*
*quisquis sibi non consensit;*
*cum rex ergo tam potens sit,*
*gaudeamus;*
*Laudes sibi debitas ⟨referamus⟩!*

*Cuius regno sunt aclines*
*tam remoti quam af⟨f⟩ines;*
*ergo regi as⟨s⟩istentes,*
*regis gesta recolentes,*
*gaudeamus;*
*Laudes sibi debitas ⟨referamus⟩!*

Postea quidam intimantes ei de sapiencia Danielis dicent:

*Potencior Rex omni principe,*
*Danielem inquiri precipe*
*doctissimum;*
*quem peritum fore didicimus,*[1]
*et Baltasar fuisse nouimus*
*carissimum.*

Milites ad Populum dicent:[2]

*Audiant principes qui sunt in curia*
*quod iuxit fieri potestas regia,*
*nec debent respui regis inperia:*
*Est uir incognitus in Babilonia,*
*qui, cunctis preminens mira sciencia,*
*predixit Baltasar regni discidia.*
*Nos ergo petimus eius suffragia;*
*queratur ut intret nostra palacia,*
*vt sit domesticus regi per omnia.*

Tunc qui Danielem adducent sic cantabunt:[3]

*Referatur hodie*
*Danieli gratia,*
*cuius sapientie*
*cuncta sunt patencia!*

[1] didicimus] didiscimus (MS).

[2] In the right margin, at the end of this rubric, is written *IORDANUS*, crossed by a line of rubrication.

[3] In the right margin, opposite the opening words of the speech which follows, is written *HILARIUS*, crossed by a line of rubrication.

*Adest illi spiritus*
*quo prenoscit omnia,*
*et futura penitus,*
*tanquam sint presentia.*
*Regnet ut securius*
*rex eius scientia.*[1]

*Ipsum ergo ducimus*
*ad regis | palacia,*
*per quem nobis credimus*
*conferri solacia.*

Cum Daniel Regi astabit, dicet ad eum Rex:

*Tua sapiencia,*
*que nouit latencia,*
*in mea presencia*
*est hodie laudata.*

*Si mihi consilia*
*conferas utilia,*
*sub tua potencia*
*regna dabo regenda.*

Et Daniel ad eum;

*Tua, Princeps, dona non sicio;*
*sed si meo tibi seruicio*
*opus erit, ecce prenuncio;*
*gratis fiet et sine precio.*

Tunc Rex faciet eum secum assidere.[2] Videntes Inuidi eum esse in amicitia[3] Regis, et uolentes eum inimicare Regi, nec inuenientes causam, nisi in lege dei sui, uenientes ad Regem dicent:[4]

*Precipe decreta, Rex, seruari,*
*que dedere principes preclari.*
*In decretis principum habetur,*
*preter te ne deus adoretur.*
*Tu solus es deus super deos,*
*qui regis gentiles et Caldeos.*
*Conuenit*[5] *ut solus adoreris,*
*populos et regna dum tueris.*
*Si quis querat preter te patronum,*
*subiacebit unguibus leonum.*

Et Rex dicet:

*Mea sunt inperia;*

[1] Regnet . . . scientia] F conjectures that, preceding these two lines, two other lines have been lost; D conjectures, apparently, that the loss is *after* the two lines in the text.

[2] assidere] asedere (MS).

[3] amicitia] amicicia (MS).

[4] dicent] After this rubric, and extending into the right margin, is written *SIMON*, crossed with a line of rubrication.

[5] Conuenit] Cūuenit (MS).

*rata fient omnia*
*que decreuit curia.*

Tunc Daniel, occulte discedens, orabit Deum suum. Quo uiso, Inuidi ad Regem dicent:

*O Rex, cui sunt subdita   regna Babylonia,*
*iussa fiunt irrita   que decreuit curia;*
*nam decreuit dierum per triginta spacia*
*adorari numina   te quasi celestia;*
*ac*[1] *si quis ⟨s⟩perneret precepta regalia,*
*sentiret ex merito leonum consorcia.*

Et Rex subiunget:

*Vere iuxit me timeri quasi deum,*
*et a cunctis exaltari numen meum.*

Iterum illi Inuidi:

*Danielem nos uidimus*
*pronum suis numinibus.*
*Esca detur leonibus,*
  *quia spreuit*
*quod Babilonis Darius*
  *rex decreuit.*|

Rex ad illos:

*Si legem pati, quam dederam, noluit,*
*iras leonum senciat, ut meruit.*

Illi ducent Danielem ad lacum. Tunc Rex iratus, ueniens o⟨b⟩uiam ei, a⟨d⟩ consolandum dicet:[2]

*Ne desperet seruus Dei*
*quod hec pena datur ei;*
*sed in suo fidat Deo,*
*quia parcet sibi leo.*

Et Daniel intrans lacum sic orabit:

*Deus terre, Deus poli,*
*me commendo tibi soli;*
*defensorem mihi trade,*
*qui me seruet ab hac clade.*

Tunc ap⟨p⟩arebit Angelus Domini in lacu, habens gladium, qui concludat ora leonum. Postea alius Angelus ueniet ad Abacub deferentem prandium messoribus suis, ad quem sic dicet Angelus:[3]

*Abacub, celi fero nuncium:*
*Danieli quod habes prandium,*
*vade, defer in Babilonia,*
*cui leonum parcit seuicia.*

[1] ac] at⟨que⟩ (F).

[2] After this rubric, and extending into the right margin, is written *HILARIUS*, crossed with a line of rubrication.

[3] After this rubric, and at the end of the space normally occupied by a line of text, is written *SIMON*, crossed with a line of rubrication.

Respondens Abacub dicet:

*Nouit Deus quod lacum nescio,*
*neque locum de quo fit mencio.*

Angelus uero ducet eum ad lacum capillo; qui astans Danieli dicet:

*O uir bone, quem Deus diligit,*
*quem nec ira leonum tetigit,*
*nunc in terris te Deus eligit;*
*ergo sume quod tibi dirigit,*
*care frater.*

Tunc Daniel, gratias persoluens Deo, dicet:[1]

*Nunc patuit*
*quod uoluit*
*me Dominus seruare,*
*qui prandium*
*per nuncium*
*dignatus est donare.*

*Quin etiam*[2]
*seuiciam*
*compescuit leonum;*
*nam tribuit*
*ut decuit*
*angelicum patronum.*

Darius iratus uisitabit Danielem dicens:

*Numquid putas, o uir bone,*
*quod te posset a leone*
*Deus tuus liberare,*[3]
*quem non cessas adorare?*

Et Daniel ad eum:

*Misit meus*
*mihi Deus*
*defensorem bonum,*
*per quem uere*
*cessauere*
*fremitus leonum.*

Rex subiunget:

*Ergo quia nil peccauit,*
*iustus | extra⟨h⟩atur;*
*sed qui iustum accusauit*
*intus detrudatur.*

Tunc Inuidi mittentur in lacum, ut deuorentur a leonibus. Postea rex

[1] After this rubric, and at the end of the space normally occupied by a line of text, is written *HILARIUS*, crossed with a line of rubrication.

[2] etiam] ectiam (MS).

[3] liberare] adorare. o liberare (MS).

accipiens Danielem per manum ducet eum ad tronum suum et sibi faciet assidere.[1] Deinde dicet ad Milites suos:

*Edicatur*
*ut colatur*
*Danielis Dominus;*
*quod decretum*
*si sit spretum,*
*uindicetur protinus.*

Et illi ad Populum:

*Audiatis*
*ne ⟨s⟩pernatis*
*que a rege iuxa sunt;*
*iubet coli*
*regem poli,*
*per quem cuncta facta sunt.*

*Quem rex uolet*
*si non colet*
*quisquam temerarius,*
*sciat dire*
*se perire*
*sicut iuxit*[2] *Darius.*

Tunc Daniel prophetabit hoc modo:[3]

*Exultet hodie fidelis concio;*
*Iudee regibus instat confusio.*
*Nascetur Dominus cuius inperio*
*cessabit regimen et regum unctio;*
*quem qui crediderit cum rege Dario,*
*remunerabitur perenni gaudio.*

Et tunc ap⟨p⟩arebit Angelus, alta uoce canens:

*Nuncium uobis fero,*

et cetera.[4] Quo finito, si factum fuerit ad Matutinas, Darius incipiat *Te Deum laudamus;* si uero ad Uesperas, *Magnificat anima mea Dominum.*[5]

Clearly in the general course of the action this play follows conscientiously the narrative of the Bible.[6] As Belshazzar enters and ceremoniously ascends the throne, his soldiers sing a prose recalling his father's conquest of Jerusalem and removal of the vessels from the temple. This introduction leads naturally to the king's command that these sacred vessels be brought forth

[1] assidere] asedere (MS).

[2] sicut iuxit] sic juxit (C); sic edixit (Winterfeld).

[3] After this rubric, and at the end of the space normally occupied by a line of text, is written *IORDANVS*, crossed with a line of rubrication.

[4] For the complete text see below, p. 433.

[5] Followed by an unrelated passage, in a later hand, beginning *In hoc nomine Iehrusalem ista tria inueniuntur*.

[6] See Daniel v, 1–vi, 27.

for use in the present banquet. The soldiers obey Belshazzar's order, singing an elaborate processional in celebration of his power. During this singing, we may assume, the revelling of the king and the defiling of the sacred vessels proceed riotously. When the words *Mane*, *Thecel*, *Phares* have appeared on the wall, and the king's counsellors have failed to interpret them, the queen is formally ushered in, and advises that Daniel be summoned. The prophet appears, and after he has given his interpretation, the king assigns him a seat of honour, the vessels are removed, and the queen, with a military escort, departs. The withdrawal of Daniel also, although not mentioned, must be assumed.

What we may regard as the second part of the play begins with a pantomine representing a battle, in the course of which Darius kills Belshazzar, and assumes his crown. Having ascended the throne amid general rejoicing, Darius, advised by some of his counsellors, summons Daniel and gives him a share in governing the kingdom. This act of favour arouses the envy of certain courtiers, who contrive to convince Darius of Daniel's religious disloyalty, and persuade the king to send him to the den of lions. During his sojourn there Daniel experiences a form of consolation recounted only in an apocryphal addition to the Old Testament narrative. Here we are told that after an angel has closed the mouths of the lions, a second angel visits Habakkuk as he is carrying a meal to his mowers, and leads him by the hair to Daniel, with the food.[1] The next morning—or after six days, according to the apocryphal story—Darius visits Daniel and hears his testimony as to God's miraculous care; whereupon the king frees Daniel, gives him a seat beside the throne, sends the prophet's accusers to the lions, and proclaims Daniel's God as his own. Daniel then utters his prophecy of the coming of Christ, and the play concludes with the angel's singing of the Christmas hymn *Nuntium vobis fero*, and Darius' beginning of either the *Te Deum* or the *Magnificat*.

In the general content of the play the only notable departure from the canonical narrative of the Bible, aside from the episode of Habakkuk, is the introducing of Daniel's prophecy (ll. 331–6), of which something will be said below. We need pause here merely to observe one dramatic alteration in characterization. In both the canonical and the apocryphal accounts of Daniel's

[1] See Daniel xiv, 32–8.

imprisonment we are told that the king condemns him most reluctantly, grieves sincerely over his imminent death, and when visiting the prisoner, calls to him 'with a lamentable voice'.[1] In Hilarius' play, on the other hand, Darius condemns Daniel without hesitation, and is moved by anger when he commits him to the lions' den and when he visits him there. In the light of this shift in characterization we must interpret the king's consoling of Daniel as ironical, for we can scarcely draw the subtle inference that the anger is assumed for deceiving the envious accusers.[2] We may, perhaps, more safely surmise that the personality of Darius reflects the influence of the angry Herod of the Epiphany plays.[3]

In richness of literary quality the play surpasses all the compositions examined hitherto. The metres are varied with marked success. The processional pieces, or *conductus*, which mark the entrance of important personages, produce an effect of stateliness, and provide effective comment upon the turns in the action. In their unbridled eloquence these pieces may, at times, approach a certain tumidity, as in the lines to the queen (ll. 87 sqq.),

O! mulierum omnium
sola non habens vicium,
et ad cujus eloquium
mens stupet sapientium,
in te dignum regis est consortium;
permirandum etenim ingenium,
sola regis illius imperium.

Such pomposity, however, is scarcely more than the situation demands, and must, in general, be commended for its fluency. The desire for a somewhat inflated style and for a highly ceremonious tone may account for the absence of the vernacular refrains which are found in the other two plays of this author.[4]

There are indications that the variety of verse in this particular play may have resulted, in some measure, from the collaboration of several writers. As is shown in the notes to the text above, four proper names appear in the margins of the manuscript, or at the ends of lines: *Hilarius* five times, *Jordanus* four times,

[1] Daniel vi, 20.

[2] See ll. 268 sqq.

[3] See above, chapter xix.

[4] See the *Suscitatio Lazari* and *Iconia Sancti Nicolai*, above, p. 212, and below, p. 337. Champollion-Figeac (p. xiii) infers that the vernacular is excluded from the play before us by the gravity of the subject and treatment. I do not know how he would explain the presence of the vernacular, then, in the *Suscitatio Lazari*. As to the style of the play before us see Creizenach, i, 66; Fuller, p. 45.

*Simon* twice, and *Hugo* once.[1] These are presumably the names of the persons who wrote the parts of the play opposite and following the entries.[2] They can hardly be the names of actors, for in the majority of instances they are placed opposite, or before, passages sung by groups of persons.[3] If we may assume, then, that we have before us the names of fellow-students who took part in composing the play, we are still in doubt as to the amount written by each. We may conjecture, if we wish, that each writer produced the passage between his name and the next marginal entry. No contributor, in any case, assumed a monopoly of any single form of verse.

Hardly unworthy of the literary elaboration of the piece is the ambitious staging assumed in the spoken text and prescribed in the rubrics. Richness and brilliance of costume must have been provided for the *entourage* of the kings, Belshazzar and Darius. Each has about him his courtiers and military escort. The former enters, we are told, *cum pompa sua*, and wears, of course, a crown. Daniel is eventually clad *pulcherrimis indumentis*. The vessels, brought forth during the singing of an extended processional, shone, presumably, with all the splendour of which the church sacristy and treasury were capable. The battle in which Darius kills Belshazzar may well have presented a notable spectacle. Stage devices of an advanced order must have been employed for producing the handwriting on the wall and for representing the destruction of the detractors of Daniel in the den of lions. These animals, it has been suggested, may have been represented by persons dressed in skins and masks.[4]

Were it not for the specific statement in the text itself, we might well question the possibility of conducting so elaborate a performance in the midst of the liturgy. The closing rubric, however, assures us with the utmost precision that the play was to occur immediately before the *Te Deum* of Matins or the

[1] Fuller (pp. 40–3) discusses these entries at some length, and rightly infers, I think, that the names are later additions.

[2] This is the opinion of Sepet, *Prophètes*, p. 63; Chambers, ii, 58; Pollard, p. xviii. Pollard credits Hilarius with only *two* collaborators.

[3] Du Méril (p. 241) conjectures that the names are of those who, at some performance, led the chorus. In some four instances, however, the names are opposite, or precede, speeches of single individuals. Fuller (pp. 42–3) comes to the following conclusion: 'The text is written by Hilarius. He and his friends, true goliards, staged this play whenever and wherever they had a chance. They themselves, knowing the music, took the leading parts. When this copy of Hilarius was finished, some one who remembered their presentation added from his memory the names to the present manuscript. That would explain some inconsistencies as resulting from faulty memory.'

[4] See Sepet, *op. cit.*, p. 67.

*Magnificat* of Vespers.[1] As to the day on which the piece was performed we are left in uncertainty. From the verses *Nuntium vobis fero*, which the angel sings at the close, and from the apparent relation of the play to the *Ordo Prophetarum*, to be mentioned below,[2] we may infer that it was designed for use during the Christmas season.[3]

## II

About the time when the wandering scholar Hilarius—aided, presumably, by his fellows—was occupied in composing his spectacular dramatization of the story of Daniel, an even more majestic play on this subject was being written by the students of the cathedral school of Beauvais.[4] The text of this *ludus*, the manuscript of which has been recently rediscovered, is as follows:[5]

INCIPIT DANIEL*is* LUDUS

*Ad honorem tui, Christe,*
*Danielis ludus iste*
*in Beluaco est inuentus,*
*et inuenit hunc iuuentus.*

Dum uenerit Rex Balthasar, Principes sui cantabunt ante eum hanc prosam:

*Astra tenenti*
*cunctipotenti*
*turba uirilis*
*et puerilis*
*concio*[6] *plaudit.*

*Nam Danielem*
*multa fidelem*
*et subiisse*
*atque tulisse*
*firmiter audit.*

*Conuocat ad se rex sapientes*
*gramata dextre qui sibi dicant enucleantes;*
*que quia scribe non potuere*
*soluere, regi ilico muti conticuere.*

[1] The hints of Sepet (pp. 59–61) and Chambers (ii, 58), that the connexion of the play with the liturgy was tenuous or accidental, seem hardly cogent.

[2] See p. 304.

[3] See Creizenach, i, 67; Pollard, p. xviii.

[4] Meyer (pp. 55, 56) infers that both the Beauvais play and that by Hilarius were written about 1140.

[5] London, Brit. Mus., MS Egerton 2615, Officium Circumcisionis et Danielis Ludus sæc. xii, fol. $95^r$–$108^r$, previously edited, with the music, by Danjou, pp. 1–32; Coussemaker, pp. 49–82. For a discussion of the play see Charvet, pp. 6–10. For remarks on the MS and further bibliography see Notes, p. 486.

[6] concio] contio (MS).

*Sed Dani|eli scripta legenti mox patuere*
*que prius illis clausa fuere.*
*Quem quia uidit preualuisse*
*Balthasar illis, fertur in aula preposuisse.*
*Causa reperta*
*non satis apta*
*destinat illum*
*ore leonum*
*dilacerandum.*
*Sed, Deus, illos ante malignos*
*in Danielem tunc uoluisti esse benignos.*
*Huic quoque panis,*
*ne sit inanis,*
*mittitur a te*
*prepete uate*
*prandia dante.*

Tunc ascendat Rex in solium, et Satrape ei applaudentes dicant:

*Rex, in eternum uiue!*

Et Rex apperiet os suum dicens:

*Vos qui pa|retis meis uocibus,*
*afferte uasa meis usibus*
*que templo pater meus abstulit,*
*Iudeam grauiter cum perculit.*

Satrape uasa deferentes cantabunt hanc prosam ad laudem Regis:

*Ivbilemus regi nostro magno ac potenti!*
*Resonemus laude digna uoce competenti!*
*Resonet iocunda turba sollempnibus odis!*
*Cytharizent, plaudant manus, mille sonent modis!*
*Pater eius destruens Iudeorum templa*
*Magna fecit, et hic regnat eius per exempla.*
*Pater eius spoliauit regnum Iu|deorum;*
*Hic exaltat sua festa decore uasorum.*
*Hec sunt uasa regia quibus spoliatur*
*Iherusalem et regalis Babylon ditatur.*
*Presentemus Balthasar ista regi nostro,*
*Qvi sic suos perornauit purpura et ostro.*
*Iste potens, iste fortis, iste gloriosus,*
*Iste probus, curialis, decens et formosus.*
*Ivbilemus regi tanto uocibus canoris;*
*Resonemus omnes una laudibus sonoris.*
*Ridens plaudit Babylon, Iherusalem plorat;*
*Hec orbatur, hec triumphans Balthasar ad|orat.*
*Omnes ergo exultemus tante potestati,*
*Offerentes regis uasa sue maiestati.*

Tunc Principes dicant:

*Ecce sunt ante faciem tuam.*

Interim apparebit dextra in conspectu Regis scribens in pariete: *Mane, Thechel, Phares*; quam uidens Rex stupefactus clamabit:

*Vocate mathematicos*
*Caldeos et ariolos;*
*auruspices inquirite,*
*et magos introducite.*

Tunc adducentur Magi, qui dicent Regi:

*Rex, in eternum uiue!*
*Adsumus ecce tibi.*

Et Rex:

*Qvi scripturam hanc legerit*
*et sensum aperuerit,*
*sub illius potentia*
*subdetur Baby|lonia,*
*et insignitus purpura*
*torque fruetur aurea.*

Illi uero nescientes persoluere dicent Regi:

*Nescimus persoluere nec dare consilium*
*Que sit superscriptio, nec manus inditium.*

Conductus Regine uenientis ad Regem:

*Cum doctorum*
*et magorum*
*omnis adsit concio,*[1]
*secum uoluit,*
*neque soluit,*
*que sit manus uisio.*
*Ecce prudens,*
*styrpe cluens,*
*diues cum potentia;*
*in uestitu*
*deaurato*
*coniunx adest regia.*
*Hec latentem*
*promet uatem*
*per cuius indicium*
*rex describi*
*suum ibi*
*no|uerit exitium.*
*Letis ergo*
*hec uirago*
*comitetur plausibus;*

[1] concio] contio (MS).

*cordis, oris*
*que sonoris*
*personetur uocibus.*

Tunc Regina ueniens adorabit Regem dicens:

*Rex, in eternum uiue!*
*Vt scribentis noscas ingenium,*
*Rex Balthasar, audi consilium.*

Rex audiens hec, uersus Reginam uertet faciem suam, et Regina dicat:

*Cum Iudee captiuis populis*
*prophetie doctum oraculis*
*Danielem a sua patria*
*captiuauit patris uictoria.*
*Hic sub tuo uiuens imperio,*
*vt mandetur, requirit racio.*
*Ergo | manda ne sit dilatio,*
*nam docebit quod celat uisio.*

Tunc dicat Rex Principibus suis:

*Vos Danielem querite,*
*et inuentum adducite.*

Tunc Principes, inuento Daniele, dicant ei:

*Vir propheta Dei, Daniel, vien al Roi.*
*Veni, desiderat parler a toi.*
*Pauet et turbatur, Daniel, uien al Roi.*
*Vellet quod nos latet sauoir par toi.*
*Te ditabit donis, Daniel, uien al Roi,*
*Si scripta poterit sauoir par toi.*

Et Daniel eis:

*Multum miror cuius consilio*
*me requirat regalis iussio.*
*Ibo tamen, et erit cogni|tum*
*per me gratis quod est absconditum.*

Conductus Danielis uenientis ad Regem:

*Hic uerus Dei famulus,*
*quem laudat omnis populus;*
*cuius fama prudentie*
*est nota regis curie.*
*Cestui manda li Rois par nos.*

Daniel:

*Pauper et exulans enuois al Roi par uos.*

Principes:

*In iuuentutis gloria,*
*plenus celesti gratia,*
*satis excellit omnibus*
*uirtute, uita, moribus.*
*Cestui manda li Rois par nos.*

Daniel:

*Pauper et exulans enuois al Roi par uos.*

Principes:

*Hic est | cuius auxilio*
*soluetur illa uisio*
*in qua scribente dextera*
*mota sunt regis uiscera.*
*Cestui manda li Rois par nos.*

Daniel:

*Pauper et exulans enuois al Roi par uos.*

Veniens Daniel ante Regem, dicat ei:

*Rex, in eternum uiue!*

Et Rex Danieli:

*Tune Daniel nomine diceris*
*huc adductus cum Iudee miseris?*
*Dicunt te habere Dei spiritum*
*et prescire quodlibet absconditum.*
*Si ergo potes scripturam soluere,*
*immensis muneribus ditabere.*

Et Daniel Regi:

*Rex, tua nolo | munera;*
*gratis soluetur litera.*
*Est autem hec solutio:*
*instat tibi confusio.*
*Pater tuus pre omnibus*
*potens olim potentibus,*
*turgens nimis superbia*
*deiectus est a gloria.*
*Nam cum Deo non ambulans,*
*sed sese Deum simulans,*
*vasa templo diripuit*
*que suo usu habuit.*
*Sed post multas insanias*
*tandem perdens diuitias,*
*forma nudatus hominis,*
*pastum gustauit graminis.*
*Tu quoque eius filius,*
*non ipso minus impius,*
*dum patris | actus sequeris,*
*uasis eisdem uteris;*
*quod quia Deo displicet,*
*instat tempus quo uindicet.*
*Nam scripture indicium*
*minatur iam supplitium,*

*et mane, dicit Dominus,*
*est tui regni terminus.*
*Thechel libram significat*
*que te minorem indicat.*
*Phares, hoc est diuisio,*
*regnum transportat alio.*

Et Rex:

*Qvi sic soluit latentia*
*ornetur ueste regia.*

Sedente Daniele iuxta Regem, induto ornamentis regalibus, exclamabit Rex ad Principem militie:

*Tolle uasa, princeps militie,*
*ne sint | michi causa miserie.*

Tunc, relicto palatio, referent uasa Satrape, et Regina discedet. Conductus Regine:

*Soluitur in libro Salomonis*
*digna laus et congrua matronis.*
*Precium est eius si quam fortis*
*procul et de finibus remotis.*
*Fidens est in ea cor mariti*
*spolijs diuitibus potiti.*
*Mulier hec illi comparetur*
*cuius rex subsidium meretur.*
*Eius nam facundia uerborum*
*arguit prudentiam doctorum.*
*Nos quibus occasio ludendi*
*hac die conce|ditur sollempni,*
*demus huic preconia deuoti,*
*ueniant et concinent remoti.*

Conductus referentium uasa ante Danielem:

*Regis uasa referentes*
*quem Iudee tremunt gentes,*
*Danieli applaudentes,*
*gaudeamus;*
*laudes sibi debitas referamus!*

*Regis cladem prenotauit*
*cum scripturam reserauit,*
*testes reos comprobauit,*
*et Susannam liberauit.*
*Gaudeamus;*
*laudes ⟨sibi debitas referamus⟩!*

*Babylon hunc exulauit*
*cum Iudeos captiuauit,*

*Balthasar quem honorauit.*
*Gaudeamus;* |
*⟨laudes sibi debitas referamus!⟩*

*Est propheta sanctus Dei,*
*hunc honorant et Caldei*
*et gentiles et Judei.*
*Ergo iubilantes ei,*
*gaudeamus,*

et cetera. Statim apparebit Darius rex cum Principibus suis, uenientque ante eum Cythariste et Principes sui psallentes hec:

*Ecce rex Darius*
*uenit cum principibus*
*nobilis nobilibus.*
*Eius et curia*
*resonat leticia,*
*adsunt et tripudia.*
*Hic est mirandus,*
*cunctis uenerandus.*
*Illi imperia*
*sunt tributaria.*
*Regem honorant*
*omnes et adorant.*
*Illum Babylonia*
*metuit et patria.*
*Cum armato agmine*
*ruens*[1] | *et cum turbine*
*sternit cohortes,*
*confregit et fortes.*
*Illum honestas*
*colit et nobilitas.*
*Hic est Babylonius*
*nobilis rex Darius.*
*Illi cum tripudio*
*gaudeat hec concio,*[2]
*laudet et cum gaudio*
*eius facta fortia*
*tam admirabilia.*
*Simul omnes gratulemur; resonent et tympana;*
*Cythariste tangant cordas; musicorum organa*
*resonent ad eius preconia.*

Antequam perueniat Rex ad solium suum, duo precurrentes expellent

[1] Cum . . . ruens] Repeated in a late cursive hand in the lower margin.
[2] coneio] contio (MS).

Balthasar quasi interficientes eum. Tunc sedente Dario Rege in maiestate sua, Curia exclamabit:|

*Rex, in eternum uiue!*

Tunc duo flexis genibus secreto dicent Regi ut faciat accersiri Danielem, et Rex iubeat eum adduci. Illi autem alijs precipientes dicent hec:

*Avdite, Principes regalis curie,*
*qui leges regitis tocius patrie.*
*Est quidam sapiens in Babylonia,*
*secreta reserans deorum gratia.*
*Eius consilium regi complacuit,*
*nam prius Balthasar scriptum aperuit.*
*Iste uelociter, ne sit dilatio,*
*nos uti uolumus eius consilio.*
*Fiat, si uenerit, consiliarius*
*regis, et fuerit in regno tercius.*

Legati, inuento Daniele, dicent hec ex parte Regis:|

*Ex regali uenit imperio,*
*serue Dei, nostra legatio.*
*Tua regi laudatur probitas,*
*te commendat mira calliditas.*
*Per te solum cum nobis patuit*
*signum dextre quod omnes latuit.*
*Te rex uocat ad suam curiam,*
*vt agnoscat tuam prudentiam.*
*Eris, supra ut dicit Darius,*
*principalis consiliarius.*
*Ergo ueni, iam omnis curia*
*preparatur ad tua gaudia.*

Et Daniel:

*Genuois al Roi.*

Conductus Danielis:

*Congaudentes celebremus natalis sollemp|nia;*
*Iam de morte nos redemit Dei sapientia.*
*Homo natus est in carne, qui creauit omnia,*
*Nasciturum quem predixit prophete facundia.*
*Danielis iam cessauit unctionis copia;*
*Cessat regni Judeorum contumax potentia.*
*In hoc natalitio,*
*Daniel, cum gaudio*
*te laudat hec concio.*[1]
*Tu Susannam liberasti de mortali crimine,*
*Cum te Deus inspirauit suo sancto flamine.*[2]
*Testes falsos comprobasti reos accusamine.*

[1] concio] contio (MS).

[2] flamine] Preceded by the superfluous letters *fla* (MS).

*Bel draconem peremisti   coram ple|bis agmine.*
*Et te Deus obseruauit   leonum uoragine.*
*Ergo sit laus Dei uerbo   genito de uirgine.*

Et Daniel Regi:

*Rex, in eternum uiue!*

Cui Rex:

*Quia noui te callidum,*
*totius regni prouidum,*
*te, Daniel, constituo,*
*et summum locum tribuo.*

Et Daniel Regi:

*Rex, michi si credideris,*
*per me nil mali feceris.*

Tunc Rex faciet eum sedere iuxta se; et alij Consiliarij Danieli inuidentes, quia gratior erit Regi, alijs in consilium ductis ut Danielem interficiant, dicent Regi:

*Rex, in eternum uiue!*

Item:

*Decreuerunt in tua | curia*
*principandi quibus est gloria,*
*vt ad tui rigorem nominis*
*omni spreto uigore numinis,*
*per triginta dierum spatium*
*adoreris ut Deus omnium.*
*O Rex!*

*Si quis ausu tam temerario*
*renuerit tuo consilio,*
*vt preter te colatur deitas,*
*iudicij sit talis firmitas,*
*in leonum tradatur foueam,*
*sic dicatur per totam regiam.*
*O Rex!*

Et Rex dicat:

*Ego mando*
*et remando*
*ne sit spretum*
*hoc decretum.*
*O hez.*

Daniel hoc audiens ibit in domum suam, | et adorabit Deum suum; quem Emuli uidentes accurrent et dicent Regi:

*Nunquid, Dari,*
*obseruari*
*statuisti omnibus*
*qui orare*

*uel rogare*
*quicquam a numinibus,*[1]
*ni te Deum,*
*illum reum*
*daremus leonibus,*
*hoc edictum*
*sic indictum*
*fuit a principibus.*

Et Rex nesciens quare hoc dicerent, respondet:

*Vere iussi me omnibus*
*adorari a gentibus.*

Tunc illi adducentes Danielem, dicent Regi:

*Hunc Judeum*
*suum Deum*
*Danielem uidimus*
*adorantem*
*et precantem,*
*tuis spretis legibus.*

Rex uolens liberare Danielem dicet:

*Nunquam uobis con|cedatur*
*quod uir sanctus sic perdatur.*

Satrape hoc audientes ostendent ei legem, dicentes:

*Lex Parthorum*
*et Medorum*
*iubet in annalibus*
*vt qui spreuit*
*que decreuit*
*rex, detur leonibus.*

Rex hoc audiens uelit, nolit, dicet:

*Si spreuit legem quam statueram,*
*det penas ipse quas decreueram.*

Tunc Satrape rapient Danielem, et ille respiciens Regem dicet:

*Heu! heu! heu! quo casu sortis*
*uenit hec dampnatio mortis?*
*Heu! heu! heu! scelus infandum!*
*Cur me dabit ad lacerandum*
*hec fera turba feris?*
*Sic me, Rex, perdere queris!|*
*Heu! qua morte mori*
*me cogis! parce furori.*

Et Rex non ualens eum liberare, dicet ei:

*Deus quem colis tam fideliter*
*te liberabit mirabiliter.*

[1] numinibus] muminibus (MS).

Tunc proicient Danielem in lacum. Statimque Angelus tenens gladium comminabitur leonibus ne tangant eum, et Daniel intrans lacum dicet:

*Huius rei non sum reus;*
*miserere mei, Deus,*
*eleyson!*
*Mitte, Deus, huc patronum*
*qui refrenet uim leonum;*
*eleyson!*

Interea alius Angelus admonebit Abacuc prophetam ut deferat prandium quod portabat messoribus suis Danieli in lacum leonum, dicens:

*Abacuc, tu senex pie,*
*ad lacum Babylonie*
*Danieli fer prandium;*
*mandat ti|bi Rex omnium.*

Cui Abacuc:

*Nouit Dei cognitio*
*quod Babylonem nescio,*
*neque lacus est cognitus*
*quo Daniel est positus.*

Tunc Angelus, apprehendens eum capillo capitis sui, ducet ad lacum, et Abacuc Danieli offerens prandium, dicet:

*Surge, frater, ut cibum capias;*
*tuas Deus uidit angustias;*
*Deus misit, da Deo gratias,*
*qui te fecit.*

Et Daniel, cibum accipiens, dicet:

*Recordatus es mei, Domine;*
*accipiam in tuo nomine,*
*alleluia!*

His transactis, Angelus reducet Abacuc in locum suum. Tunc Rex, descendens de solio suo, ueniet ad lacum, dicens lacrimabiliter:

*Tene, putas, Daniel,| saluabit, ut eripiaris*
*A nece proposita, quem tu colis et ueneraris?*

Et Daniel Regi:

*Rex, in eternum uiue!*

Item:

*Angelicum solita misit pietate patronum,*
*Quo Deus ad tempus conpescuit ora leonum.*

Tunc Rex gaudens exclamabit:

*Danielem educite,*
*et emulos immittite.*

Cum expoliati fuerint et uenerint ante lacum, clamabunt:

*Merito hec patimur, quia peccauimus*

*in sanctum Dei, iniuste egimus,*
*iniquitatem fecimus.*

Illi proiecti in lacum statim consumentur a leonibus; et Rex uidens hoc dicet:

*Deum Danielis qui regnat | in seculis*
*adorari iubeo a cunctis populis.*

Daniel in pristinum gradum receptus prophetabit:

*Ecce uenit sanctus ille, sanctorum sanctissimus,*
*Quem rex iste iubet coli potens et fortissimus.*
*Cessant phana, cesset regnum, cessabit et unctio;*
*Instat regni Iudeorum finis et oppressio.*

Tunc Angelus ex inprouiso exclamabit:

*Nuntium uobis fero de supernis:*
*Natus est Christus, Dominator orbis,*
*in Bethleem Iude, sic enim propheta*
*dixerat ante.*[1]

His auditis, cantores incipient *Te Deum laudamus*. Finit Daniel.[2]

It is obvious that in general content and sequence of action the play from Beauvais closely resembles that written by Hilarius. This similarity includes not only the parts of the two plays drawn from the canonical story in the Vulgate, but also the apocryphal incident of the fetching of Habakkuk, the prophecy of Daniel and the angel's message at the end, and the presence of a concluding liturgical piece. In a few details of arrangement, however, and especially in certain disclosures of psychology, the play now before us makes some claims of its own. The summarizing of the action of the piece in the opening chorus of the princes, in the manner of a prologue, for example, has no parallel in Hilarius' composition. The animation of the action, moreover, is somewhat increased by the invention of dialogues between Daniel and the courtiers whom both Belshazzar and Darius send to summon him.[3] Still more arresting are the fresh revelations of character in several of the personages. Darius' reluctance in condemning the upright Daniel is disclosed in the lines (332–3),

Nunquam vobis concedatur
quod vir sanctus sic perdatur.

and in the words *velit*, *nolit*, of the rubric which presently follows. Clearly the Darius of this play is quite the opposite of the irate

[1] Concerning this hymn see above, p. 35.

[2] Followed by the rubric *In Pascha Domini euangelium ad Missam secundum Marchum.*

[3] See ll. 112 sqq., 257 sqq.

personage invented by Hilarius. The personality of Daniel is enriched through the dignity of his address to Belshazzar, and through his very human appeal to Darius for mercy, and his *eleyson* in prison.[1] Even Daniel's accusers assume an additional mild reality through being allowed a tardy confession of their sin.[2]

In literary detail the play of the Beauvais students differs from that of Hilarius most noticeably in the dignity and gusto of the choral pieces, and in the presence of a certain number of sentences and phrases in French. Although the choruses in Hilarius' play are by no means lacking in amplitude and dignity, those now before us show a still higher degree of splendour and enthusiasm. These qualities appear, for example, in the verses with which Darius is received upon the stage. In the stanzas of Hilarius is nothing equal to the abandon and resonance of the lines (238–45),

> Illi cum tripudio
> gaudeat hæc concio,
> laudet et cum gaudio
> ejus facta fortia
> tam admirabilia.
> Simul omnes gratulemur; resonent et tympana;
> Cytharistæ tangant cordas; musicorum organa
> resonent ad ejus præconia.

We are to remember also that the singing of such lines was unquestionably accompanied by the melody and clangour of musical instruments.[3]

As has been remarked above, the absence of French from the *Daniel* of Hilarius is noteworthy, in view of his use of it in his two other plays.[4] The employment of it in the Beauvais play, in any case, is after Hilarius' manner.[5] The French passages are not translations for the benefit of an audience, but literary flourishes, or refrains, of a self-conscious writer. Possibly their chief purpose is to lend formality to the summons brought to Daniel by the emissaries of the king. They are, in general, neither undignified nor essential.

In the arrangements of its staging the Beauvais play must

[1] See ll. 342 sqq., 354, 357.

[2] See ll. 380 sqq. Danjou (p. 73) detects a sarcasm—which escapes me—in the chorus *Regis vasa referentes* (ll. 195 sqq.), sung before Daniel.

[3] See Coussemaker, p. 326.

[4] See above, p. 288.

[5] See ll. 112–7, 126–7, 132–3, 138–9, 269.

have resembled that of Hilarius; but from the larger number of actors, the variety of personages accompanying the two kings, and the specific mention of musical instruments, we may infer that the play now before us was decidedly the superior in the brilliance of its pageantry.[1]

That this performance occurred at some time during the Christmas season appears from the angelic announcement at the end, and from such a passage as the following in the midst of the play (ll. 270–3):

> Congaudentes celebremus natalis solempnia;
> Jam de morte nos redemit Dei sapientia.
> Homo natus est in carne, qui creavit omnia,
> Nasciturum quem prædixit prophetæ facundia.

As the date on which these lines were sung one critic has suggested either the feast of the Circumcision (January 1) or the preceding day.[2] This arrangement would bring the play into close association with the feast of Fools, and from the famous Prose of the Ass attached to those revels an echo has been discerned in the exclamation *O hez*, uttered by Darius.[3] Although there is no apparent obstacle to the play's having been given on the eve of the Circumcision, we have no certainty of it. Whatever the day, the closing *Te Deum* of the text points to Matins as the part of the liturgy to which the performance was attached.[4]

Although, as we have seen, the play written by the students of Beauvais must be adjudged more striking than that of Hilarius and his associates, the two compositions are so similar in general structure, and even in certain literary details, as to raise the question of their possible interdependence. Both were written in France as the work of professed scholars, and there appears to be no reason why one may not have served as the model of the other. As a possible avenue of communication between Hilarius and Beauvais can be mentioned a certain Raoul, who taught at the cathedral school of Beauvais in the twelfth century. Both he and Hilarius appear to have been pupils of Abelard.[5]

[1] Sepet (*Prophètes*, pp. 77, 78) conjectures that the angel who protected Daniel in the lions' den appeared from behind a curtain, and that the *Nuntium vobis fero*, at the end of the play, was sung from the triforium. For an additional observation on staging see Notes, p. 486.

[2] See Desjardins, pp. 121, 122. Chambers observes (ii, 60), 'It was perhaps intended for performance on the day of the *asinaria festa*.'

[3] See l. 311; Sepet, *Prophètes*, p. 76; and above, i, 105, 551.

[4] Meyer (p. 56) speaks of the play's having been performed at Matins or Vespers on some minor feast of the Christmas season; but again (p. 65) he seems to deny that this is a liturgical play at all.

[5] See Maitre, p. 101. As to our lack of

The similarity of the two plays in detail may be seen most pointedly, perhaps, in the use by both of the choral refrain,

Gaudeamus;
laudes tibi (sibi) debitas referamus.[1]

From such a resemblance one is almost forced to infer either that the writer of one of these passages had before him the other passage, or that the two writers used a common source. The critic who has considered this matter most attentively thinks it very probable that Hilarius borrowed directly from the Beauvais text.[2] My own inference is that, if the two plays are related directly, rather than through a common source, the students of Beauvais were probably the borrowers. It seems unlikely that if Hilarius had had the Beauvais version before him, he and his collaborators would have so generally renounced its superior dramatic and literary qualities.

In parting from the plays on the subject of Daniel we must inquire finally as to the evidence of their having arisen originally from the *Ordo Prophetarum*.[3] In the pages above I have mentioned the debatable possibility of such an origin for the plays of Isaac and Rebecca and of Joseph. Sepet would, no doubt, hold that these two pieces arose within the limits of an enlarged procession of prophets.[4] Since, however, both of these plays are preserved in a fragmentary state, we lack the evidences, negative or positive, which fuller texts might have afforded. In considering the two plays of Daniel we are left in no such uncertainty, for their texts are complete. The most pointed indication of a relationship between them and the play of the prophets is Daniel's prophesying at the end of the performance. In the version of Hilarius this prophecy runs thus (ll. 331–6),

Exultet hodie fidelis concio;
Judææ regibus instat confusio.
Nascetur Dominus cujus imperio
*cessabit* regimen et regum *unctio*;
quem qui crediderit cum rege Dario,
remunerabitur perenni gaudio.

In the play from Beauvais it takes the following form (ll. 385–8):

Ecce venit *sanctus ille*, *sanctorum sanctissimus*,
Quem rex iste jubet coli potens et fortissimus.

information concerning the cathedral school of Beauvais see Notes, p. 486.

[1] See Hilarius, ll. 179 sqq., and Beauvais, ll. 198 sqq. For further details see Meyer pp. 56–7.

[2] See Meyer, p. 57.

[3] See above, p. 171.

[4] See Sepet, p. 53.

Cessant phana, cesset regnum, *cessabit et unctio*;
Instat regni Judæorum finis et oppressio.

These utterances appear certainly to contain paraphrases of Daniel's prophecy in the several extant versions of the *Ordo Prophetarum*,

Sanctus sanctorum veniet,
et unctio deficiet;[1]

and this prophecy originates not from any passage in the Vulgate, but from the testimony of Daniel in the pseudo-Augustinian sermon,

Cum venerit Sanctus Sanctorum, cessabit unctio.[2]

These resemblances in themselves are, no doubt, decided indications of a relationship between the plays of Daniel and the tradition of the *Ordo Prophetarum*. Of the exact nature of this relationship, however, we cannot be entirely certain. The most convenient inference would be that the plays were originally merely scenes in the *Ordo*, which were gradually amplified, dissociated themselves eventually from the prophet play, and were then, through skilled hands, put into the literary form now before us.[3] On the other hand it must be admitted that the prophecy in the Daniel plays has no very close relationship with the dramatic action which precedes; and at least one critic regards the presence of this prophecy as no evidence at all that these plays arose from the *Ordo Prophetarum*.[4] All we can say with assurance is that the form of prophecy in the Daniel plays must derive either from the pseudo-Augustinian sermon or from the prophet plays themselves. It may have been borrowed by itself, and have been attached as a sort of conclusion to plays composed quite independently of the *Ordo Prophetarum*. It may, on the other hand, have come from the *Ordo* along with the

[1] See above, pp. 140, 147, 158.

[2] See above, p. 126. The nearest parallel in the Book of Daniel (ix, 24) is scarcely relevant: *Septuaginta hebdomades abbreviatæ sunt super populum tuum, et super urbem sanctam tuam, ut consummetur prævaricatio, et finem accipiat peccatum, et deleatur iniquitas, et adducatur justitia sempiterna, et impleatur visio, et prophetia, et ungatur Sanctus sanctorum.*

[3] See Sepet, *Prophètes*, pp. 49–52.

[4] See Meyer, pp. 55–6. Meyer points also to the fact that even briefly amplified scenes within the *Ordo Prophetarum* are known to us only in MSS of the thirteenth and fourteenth centuries (see the versions of Laon and Rouen in chapter xxi), whereas the highly developed Daniel play of Hilarius was written during the first half of the twelfth century. Hence Meyer seems to incline to the opinion that the two plays of Daniel have no connexion with the *Ordo Prophetarum*. Against Meyer, however, one should observe that there may have been highly developed scenes in versions of the *Ordo* earlier than the thirteenth and fourteenth centuries.

dramatic action which precedes it. Even though the latter be the true case, however, we need not infer that the texts of the Daniel plays now before us are in the form in which they left the frame-work of the prophet play. Whatever their origin, these compositions received their final shape through the talent of accomplished scholars. Though the dramatic actions may have been used first as part of a comprehensive *Ordo Prophetarum*, the literary distinction of the two extant dramatizations of the story of Daniel is the achievement of Hilarius and his collaborators, and of the students of Beauvais.

CHAPTER XXVI

# THE MIRACLE PLAYS OF SAINT NICHOLAS

ALL the dramatic pieces treated in the preceding chapters represent personages known to us through the Bible or the apocrypha. Although some of the incidents brought upon the stage are not to be found in sacred writings, these additions may be regarded as mere dramatic amplification. The kind of play which we are now to consider, on the other hand, has virtually no association with Scriptural tradition, and is so peculiarly medieval in its content that, in dramatic history, it has been given a distinctive name of its own. The miracle play, or *miraculum*, may be described as the dramatization of a legend setting forth the life or martyrdom or miracles of a saint.[1] Possibly, however, for our present purpose this definition should be somewhat narrowed in its application. Among the medieval saints, for example, are reckoned various persons who have a place in the narrative of the New Testament, such as the Blessed Virgin Mary, Mary Magdalen, Lazarus, and Paul, all of whom appear in plays considered in earlier chapters of this treatise. But in those plays the actions of the personages represent, in general, not miraculous accretions of the Middle Ages, but merely scenes from Biblical biography. Thus the Virgin Mary who appears in the Passion play, for example, is regarded as the Mother of Christ, and not as the wonder working saint of later centuries; and the Lazarus who figures in the play of Hilarius is the friend of Jesus according to Scripture, and not the miraculous saint who is legendarily credited with a journey to France, and who became the centre of a somewhat nebulous medieval cult.[2] By the expression, 'life or martyrdom or miracles of a saint,' therefore, I shall mean the non-Biblical legends which accumulated about the names of hallowed and canonized persons during the long period of the Middle Ages.

The number of such legends is very large and the body of plays which they inspired during the late medieval period in

[1] This is the definition of Manly, *Literary Forms*, p. 585, accepted by Coffman, *New Theory*, p. 7. See also Coffman, *Nomenclature*, pp. 448–65; Manly, *Miracle Play*, pp. 133–7. For further bibliography see Notes, p. 487; and for a note on the term *miraculum* see below, p. 503.

[2] See below, p. 469.

the European vernaculars was enormous.[1] The range of appropriate subjects was as wide as the register of the saints themselves, and as the multiplicity of their *acta*; and of these sources the playwrights made voluminous use. During the earlier centuries, however, the number of miracle plays designed for use in churches appears to have been relatively small. The only saint, in fact, whose legends are treated in Church plays that are extant and complete is Nicholas;[2] and of the numerous occurrences narrated in his *vita* we have dramatizations of only four.

Of St Nicholas, 'the most popular saint in Christendom,' virtually all we know historically is that he was bishop of Myra, in Lycia, in the fourth century.[3] The legends recount that he was born at Patara, in Lycia, of affluent parents, and that even during his earliest years he disclosed marvellous traits. In his very cradle he practised fasting, refusing to take his mother's milk more than once on Wednesdays and Fridays; and even in childhood he performed miracles. After a pilgrimage through the Holy Land and Egypt, he was chosen bishop of Myra, in the year 325. He became esteemed especially for acts of benevolence, and was famed for a succession of supernatural deeds. He gave money to the needy, protected the health of children, saved sailors in danger at sea, obtained the release of persons unjustly imprisoned, and served generally as the friend of the oppressed. It is reported that he suffered imprisonment during the persecution of Diocletian. After his death and burial at Myra he accomplished further miracles, through coming to the relief of persons in distress, and through providing a healing oil in a continuous flow from his tomb.

History records the fact that in the year 1087 Italian merchants laid hands upon the body of St Nicholas and brought it to Bari, in Southern Italy. This translation of the relics seems to have given a special impulse to his cult, for although he had previously been honoured in certain places in Western Europe for several centuries, the real florescence of this devotion began in the eleventh century.[4] The shrine at Bari soon became the goal of numerous pilgrimages, and parts of the relics themselves found

[1] For France, for example, see Petit de Julleville, ii, 221 sqq.; 466 sqq.; Weydig, pp. 23 sqq.

[2] Concerning the lost miracle play of St Catherine performed at Dunstable see Coffman, *New Theory*, pp. 72–8; Catherine B. C. Thomas, *The Miracle Play at Dunstable*, in *M.L.N.*, xxxii (1917), 337–44; Motter, p. 223; appendix D below, p. 541.

[3] For bibliography see Notes, p. 487.

[4] For the evidence see Coffman, *New Theory*, pp. 45–51.

their way beyond the Alps. Although the cult spread widely, it prospered especially in the northern, central, and eastern parts of France. In this region the *vita* of St Nicholas was especially esteemed, and here, and in the related centres, probably about the twelfth century, at least four of his legends were given dramatic form: namely, the dowry legend, or *Tres Filiæ*, the story of the resuscitating of three young scholars, or *Tres Clerici*, the miracle of the image, or *Iconia Sancti Nicolai*, and the rescue of the son of Getron, or *Filius Getronis*.[1]

Concerning the process through which such legends became drama we have no explicit information. One is, of course, attracted by the apparent possibility that, like the plays of Easter and Christmas Day, the dramatic *miracula* of St Nicholas arose directly from those kinds of literary embellishment of the liturgy ordinarily known as tropes.[2] The liturgy of the feast of St Nicholas on December 6th, in any case, was amply provided with this sort of adornment, the material for which was in large measure drawn from the traditional *vita*. Thus among the tropes of the Mass we find an elaborate version of the *Kyrie* containing references to three of the legends with which we are especially concerned.[3] Likewise at least two published tropes of the epistle contain, in the midst of allusions to various legends, clear references to the story *Tres Filiæ*.[4] These tropes of the *Kyrie* and the epistle, however, show nothing dramatic in form or in suggestion.

A nearer approach to drama is to be found in the special class of tropes of the Mass known as sequences. Of these a generous number were composed for the feast of St Nicholas, and among them are references to most of the well-established legends.[5] Occasionally a sequence includes a bit of continuous narrative from this or that legend, and sometimes brief passages of direct discourse, such as appear in the following narrative from the legend of the endangered sailors:[6]

[1] See Coffman, *New Theory*, pp. 49–51, 61, 63–5.

[2] See above, for example, i, chapters vi–viii.

[3] See *A. H.*, xlvii, 212–3.

[4] See *A. H.*, xlix, 199–201. The MSS are of the twelfth century. Coffman (*New Theory*, pp. 13–7) discusses the theory that the farced, or troped, epistle was an influence in the formation of the miracle play. I fully concur in his conclusion that neither the Latin nor the vernacular tropes of the epistle are among the essential origins of this type of play.

[5] See *A.H.*, viii, 194–5; ix, 230–32; x, 272–8; xxxiv, 242–4; xxxix, 245; xl, 257–8; xlii, 265–70; xliv, 226–8; liv, 95–9; lv, 296–302.

[6] *A.H.*, liv, 96. For the complete sequence see above, i, 186–7.

1. Quidam nautæ navigantes
et contra fluctuum
sævitiam luctantes
navi pæne dissoluta,

2. Iam de vita desperantes
in tanto positi
periculo clamantes
voce dicunt omnes una:

3. 'O beate Nicolae,
nos ad portum maris trahe
de mortis angustia;

4. Trahe nos ad portum maris,
tu qui tot auxiliaris
pietatis gratia.'

5. Dum clamarent nec incassum,
ecce, quidam dicens: 'Assum
ad vestra præsidia.'

Although such a passage is ripe for dramatic use, we have no evidence that this sequence, or any other trope of the Mass, ever developed into a play of St Nicholas.[1]

Similar amplifications of the authorized liturgical text are found in the Canonical Office for this feast. Any of the responsories of Matins, for example, was likely to be adorned by a trope, and any of the antiphons of the day might assume metrical form.[2] The musical skeleton of the *cursus*, thus embellished, was called a *historia*.[3] For their texts, the *historiæ* drew, necessarily, upon the *vita*, and in one or another of the antiphons, responsories or tropes almost every legendary incident was briefly touched upon. We have no evidence, however, that these liturgical treatments of the subject ever developed into drama.[4]

In so far, then, as we can judge from the extant miracle plays, they rest not upon short and summary references to the *vita* such as are found in liturgical embellishments, but directly upon the complete forms of the legends themselves. The plays represent the incidents of the traditional narratives with substantial fidelity, and they appear to have arisen through the application of the dramatic treatment directly to these stories.[5] As to the precise channel through which a particular playwright acquired his knowledge of the legends we cannot, and need not, decide. He might have heard the narratives read as lessons in Matins, or as less formal recitations in the office of Prime;[6] or he might have

[1] A vague hint that sequences of St Nicholas developed into drama is uttered by Monmerqué and Michel, p. 159. See also Crawford, *Nicholas*, p. 17.

[2] For an example of a versified antiphon see *Copiose caritatis* below, p. 357.

[3] The *historiæ* of St Nicholas are discussed and illustrated at some length by Young, *Miracle Play*, pp. 254–68. See also *Sarum Breviary*, iii, 23–40; R. Delamare, in *Revue Mabillon*, x (1914), 88–95.

[4] For further bibliography bearing upon this matter see Notes, p. 488.

[5] For a similar opinion see Manly, *Literary Forms*, pp. 585–6.

[6] See C. Horstmann, *Altenglische Legenden*, Neue Folge, Heilbronn, 1881, pp. xiii–xxiii. Concerning the lessons of Matins and the martyrology in Prime see above, i, 53, 69.

read the whole *vita* for himself privately, or, as a school-boy, he might have been assigned this or that prose legend for versifying.[1]

To account for the fact that the plays are in verse and are set to music we need only refer to the general activity of the monasteries of Western Europe, during the tenth, eleventh, and twelfth centuries, in composing thousands of rhythmical and versified musical pieces for the unofficial embellishment of their daily liturgy, and in giving verse-form to the *vitæ* of patron saints.[2] About the year 1100 Raoul Tortaire was teaching versification to novices in the monastery of St-Benoît-sur-Loire, at Fleury, and was himself putting into verse the legends of St Benedict and St Maur.[3] Naturally enough, then, at this same monastery about the same period, or soon after, the adornment of verse was bestowed also upon the legends of St Nicholas—such verse as is seen in the St Nicholas plays in the Fleury play-book of the thirteenth century.[4]

## The Dowry, or 'Tres Filiæ'

In considering the plays themselves it is appropriate to begin with a dramatization of one of the oldest, and perhaps the most widely esteemed, of the legends. This is the so-called 'dowry' story, or *Tres Filiæ*, recounting how St Nicholas, by timely gifts of gold to an indigent father, rescues the three daughters from careers of prostitution, and provides the dowries required for their marriages.[5]

### I

Of this legend we have two dramatic treatments, the oldest and simplest being the following, of the eleventh or twelfth century, from Hildesheim:[6]

[1] Concerning such exercises of school-boys see F. A. Specht, *Geschichte des Unterrichtswesens in Deutschland*, Stuttgart, 1885, p. 113; Gröber, ii, part i, 395. Weydig (pp. 44–6) seems to declare with confidence that the earliest St Nicholas plays were school exercises; but Coffman, although admitting this possibility (*New Theory*, pp. 17–9), justly observes that Weydig's assertion has not been proved.

[2] See above, chapter vi; Coffman, *New Theory*, pp. 37–44.

[3] See E. de Certain, *Raoul Tortaire*, in *Bibliothèque de l'École des Chartes*, xvi (1855), 495–8; *Les Miracles de Saint Benoît*, ed. E. Certain, Paris, 1858, p. xv.

[4] See below, pp. 316, 330, 343, 351. For bibliography bearing upon this MS and upon the monastery at Fleury see above, i, 665.

[5] For a text of the legend see Notes, p. 488.

[6] London, Brit. Mus., Add. MS 22414, Miscellanea Hildesiensia sæc. xi–xii, fol. $3^v$–$4^r$, previously edited by E. Dümmler, in *Z.f.d.A.*, xxxv (1891), 402–5 (D). The text begins at the top of fol. $3^v$ without a heading, the preceding page being irrelevant. There is no music, and no spaces are left for the rubrics supplied editorially in the text printed here. For bibliography see Notes, p. 490.

⟨Pater:⟩

*Cara mihi pignora, filie,*
*opes patris inopis unice*[1]
*et solamen mee miserie,*
*michi mesto tandem consulite.*
*Me miserum!*

*Olim diues et nunc pauperrimus,*
*luce feror et nocte anxius;*[2]
*et quam ferre non consueui⟨mus⟩,*
*paupertatem grauiter ferimus.*
*Me miserum!*

*Nec me*[3] *mea tantum inopia*
*quantum uestra uexat penuria,*
*quarum olim lasciua*[4] *corpora*
*modo domant lo⟨n⟩ga geiunia.*
*Me miserum!*

⟨Prima Filia:⟩

*Care pater, lugere*[5] *desine,*
*nec nos lugens lugendo promoue,*
*et quod tibi ualeo dicere*
*consilium, hoc a me su⟨s⟩cipe,*
*care pater.*

*Vnum nobis restat auxilium,*[6]
*per dedecus et per obprobrium,*
*ut nostrorum species corporum*
*uictum nobis lucretur puplicum,*
*care pater.*

*Et me primam, ⟨pater,⟩ si*[7] *iubeas,*
*dedecori submittet pietas,*
*ut sentiat primam anxietas*[8]
*quam contulit primam natiuitas,*
*care pater.*

⟨Pater:⟩[9]

*Consilium hoc miserabile*
*mihi prebet cor lamentabile:*[10]
*corpus tuum tam uenerabile*
*meum frangit senio debile*
*suspirando.*

[1] unice] hunice (MS).
[2] anxius] anctius (MS).
[3] me] Written above the line by a contemporary hand.
[4] lasciua] latiua (MS).
[5] lugere] lucere (MS).
[6] auxilium] ausilium (MS).
[7] ⟨pater⟩ si] si ⟨modo⟩ (D).
[8] anxietas] anctietas (MS).
[9] ⟨Pater⟩] ⟨Responsum⟩ (D).
[10] lamentabile] lammentabile (MS).

Secunda Filia:

*Noli, pater, noli, caris⟨s⟩ime,*
*doloribus dolores addere,*
*ne pro damno uelis inducere*
*periculum irreparabile,*
*care pater.*

*S⟨c⟩imus quidem quod fornicantibus*
*obstrusus est celorum aditus;*
*care, ergo te nos deposcimus*[1]
*ne nos uelis addere talibus,*
*care ⟨pater⟩.*

*Ne⟨c⟩ te uelis nec nos infamie*
*submittere, pater, perpetue,*[2]
*nec ab ista labi pauperie*
*in eterne lacu⟨m⟩ miserie,*
*care pater.*

R*esponsio*:[3]

*Tuum, nata, placet consilium,*
*et exemplum placet egregium;*[4]
*sed paupertas augetur nimium,*
*que me grauat quem domat senium,*
*heu frequenter!*

Tertia Filia:

*Meum quoque, pater, perpetue*
*consilium audire*[5] *sustine*
*adque finem breuiter collige:*
*Deum, pater, time et dilige,*
*care ⟨pater⟩.*

*Nichil enim deesse nouimus*
*per scripturas Deum timentibus,*
*et omnia*[6] *ministrat omnibus*
*omnipotens se diligentibus,*
*ca⟨re pater⟩.*

*Neu desperes propter inopiam,*
*Deo esse quam scimus placidam;*
*Iob respice, pater, penuriam*
*et deinde secutam copiam,*
*care pater.*

[1] deposcimus] depotimus (MS).
[2] perpetue] perdetue (MS).
[3] Responsio] Responsum (D).
[4] placet egregium] palcet egreguum (MS).
[5] audire] MS seems to have *audice* or *audite*.
[6] omnia] Followed by an erasure of several letters.

⟨Pater:⟩

*Siste gradum, quisquis es, Domine;*
*siste gradum, et qui sis exprime,*
*qui dedecus tolles infamie,*[1]
*onus quoque leuas inopie.*
*Me beatum!*[2]

⟨Sanctus Nicolaus:⟩

*Nicolaum me uocant nomine.*
*Lauda Deum ex dato munere,*
*et non uelis ulli ascribere*
*largitatis laudes dominice.*
*Deum lauda.*

⟨Pater:⟩

*Iam iam mecum gaudete, filie,*
*paupertatis elapso tempore;*
*ecce enim in auri pondere*
*quod sufficit nostre miser⟨i⟩e.*
*Me beatum!*[3]

Although this text is defective at the end, the amount of the play which has been lost is small, and the general action of the piece is not obscured. A father who has suddenly fallen from affluence into poverty is complaining to his three daughters of their ill fortune, and is asking them for counsel. The eldest daughter proposes that the three girls gain a livelihood for the family through prostitution, and offers herself as the first victim. This proposal the father rejects. The second daughter opposes following the counsel of the eldest, pointing to the inevitable damnation that would ensue. To this view the father assents, though referring to the increasing pinch of poverty and to his weight of years. The third daughter advises that they love God in fear, drawing from the Bible the assurance that God ministers to those who love Him, and recalling the example of Job. Although the text provides no rubric, we must infer that at this point in the dialogue St Nicholas casts gold in at the window

[1] infamie] infamine (MS).

[2] Here ends the page; but in the lower margin a later hand has written the first two lines of the play: *Care mihi pignora, filie, opes patris inopis unice.*

[3] The MS proceeds, unintelligibly, as follows: *Gror̄ g̊pe hospes gaudeto pacemque salutis habeto. R̄ hospitis Vobis letisiā Ds̄ eximiā* ⟨blank space for six or eight letters⟩ *o filie te deū.* Then follows the play *Tres Clerici*, beginning *Hospes care, tres sumus socii.* See below, p. 325. I infer that the words *Te Deum* mark the end of the play now before us, but that part of the preceding words are related in some way to the play *Tres Clerici*. Dümmler prints the close of the present play as follows:

*Gr . . . hospes gaudeto*
*pacemque salutis habeto . . .*

Responsum hospitis:

*Vobis letis iam Deus eximiam*
*. . . o filie . . .*
*Te Deum.*

and hastens away. The father overtakes the benefactor and demands his name. St Nicholas declares himself, but charges them all to render their thanks to God. The father calls upon his daughters to rejoice with him. After words of praise from the family, and, apparently, after a blessing from St Nicholas, the play ends with the *Te Deum*, sung, presumably, by a chorus.

In comparing the play with a standard medieval form of the legend, one observes especially the fortunate change whereby the playwright makes clear that the proposal of prostitution is made by one of the daughters. In the traditional narrative the situation—distressing enough in any case—is particularly revolting through the apparent possibility that the proposal emanates from the father.[1] Noteworthy also in the three speeches invented for the young women is their adequacy in variety of thought and sentiment.

The taste of the Hildesheim writer, however, clearly exceeds his talent for theatrical vivacity. He has reduced to the minimum both the number of the roles and the opportunities for activity on the stage. He combines the three separate visits of St Nicholas into one, and ignores the problem of the marriage of the daughters. The resulting brevity and compactness give the piece almost too quiet a dramatic tenor.

This simplicity of structure is reflected in the evenness and monotony of the metrical form. The piece is composed throughout in a uniform stanza of four rhymed lines of ten syllables, with a refrain of four syllables. Each speech contains one or more of these simple stanzas, and none of the speeches ends within a stanza. This regular succession of unbroken staves makes the impression of a hymn-like poem rather than of a play.[2] Although the line of ten syllables is not normal for early medieval hymns, the general influence of hymnody seems to be shown in the succession of uniform stanzas.[3]

From this hymn-like aspect of the composition, and from the almost complete absence of rubrics, one might infer that it was not intended for actual dramatic performance. Certainly there is no explicit indication of impersonation or scenery. That the play was acted, however, seems probable from the demands of mere intelligibility. The sequence of the incidents immediately

[1] For a text of the legend see below, p. 488.

[2] See Weydig, pp. 59, 70, 75.

[3] For relevant observations on the metrical forms of hymns see, for example, F. A. March, *Latin Hymns*, New York, 1874, pp. 321–8; Meyer, *Abhandlungen*, i, 174–333; M. Britt, *The Hymns of the Breviary and Missal*, New York, &c., 1924, pp. 25–31.

after the speech of *Tertia Filia* can scarcely be understood except upon the supposition that at this point is actually represented the throwing in of St Nicholas' gift at the window.[1]

For the staging of this play only the simplest arrangements are necessary: a room and an open space beside it. Although the text does not require that St Nicholas toss his gift specifically through a window, we may assume that this traditional arrangement is intended. A space beside the house must be provided for the action of the father in rushing out to seize the benefactor.[2]

From the fact that the text appears to have ended with the *Te Deum*, we may conjecture that the play was attached to the liturgy, and was performed at the end of Matins.

## II

The simplicity and uniformity of the Hildesheim play is brought into relief through a comparison of it with the dramatization of the same legend in the play-book from the monastery of St Benedict at Fleury:[3]

⟨Pater:⟩
*In lamentum et merorem uersa est leticia*
*quam prebebat olim nobis rerum habundancia.*
*O rerum[4] inopia!*
*Heu! heu! perierunt huius uite gaudia.*[5]
*Forma, genus, morum splendor, iuuentutis gloria,*
*cumprobatur[6] nichil esse, dum desit pecunia.*
*O rerum inopia!*
*Heu! ⟨heu! perierunt huius uite gaudia.⟩*
⟨Filiæ simul:⟩
*Finis opum, dum recedunt, luctus et suspiria.*
*Eia! pater ipse lugens opes lapsas, predia,*
*tractat secum, ut speramus, dampnorum socia.*[7]
*O rerum inopia!*

[1] See Weydig, pp. 59, 75–6.

[2] See Weydig, p. 76.

[3] Orleans, Bibl. de la Ville, MS 201 (*olim* 178), Miscellanea Floriacensia sæc. xiii, pp. 176–82, previously edited by Monmerqué, in *Mélanges*, vii, 91–9 (M); Wright, pp. 3–7 (W); Du Méril, pp. 254–62 (D); Coussemaker, pp. 83–99 (C). Only Coussemaker publishes the music. For observations on the MS see above, i, 665. The text of the play begins, without heading, at the top of p. 176. The content of the preceding page of the MS is irrelevant. In arranging the stanzas for the first two speeches I have had the assistance of Dr. Otto E. Albrecht.

[4] rerum] reron (MS).

[5] D infers that after this verse a line is lost.

[6] cumprobatur] cum probatur (MS. M).

[7] D comments upon the defective sense and metre in this line, and proposes two emendations: (1) *tractat secum, ut speremus quæ bonorum socia;* (2) *tractat secum, ut damnorum nobis parcat socia.*

*Heu! heu! perierunt huius uite gaudia.*|
*Adeamus; audiamus que capit*[1] *consilia.*

Pater conquerens ad Filias:

*Cara michi pignora, filie,*
*opes patris inopis unice*
*et solamen mee miserie,*
*michi mesto tandem consulite.*
*Me miserum!*

*Olim diues et nunc pauperrimus,*
*luce fruor et nocte anxius,*
*et quam ferre non consueuimus,*
*paupertatem grauiter ferimus.*
*Me miserum!*

*Nec me mea tantum inopia*
*quantum uestra uexat*[2] *penuria,*
*quarum primum*[3] *la⟨s⟩ciua corpora*
*longa modo dampna⟨n⟩t ieiunia.*
*Me miserum!*

Prima Filia ad Patrem:

*Care pater, lugere desine,*
*nec nos lugens lugendum* | *promoue,*[4]
*et quod tibi ualeo dicere*
*consilium, hoc a me recipe,*
*care pater.*

*Vnum nobis restat auxilium,*
*per dedecus et per obprobrium,*
*ut nostrorum species corporum*
*nobis uictum lucretur publicum,*
*care pater.*

*Et me primam, pater, si iubeas,*
*dedecori submittet pietas,*
*ut senciat prima anxietas*
*quam contulit prima natiuitas,*
*care pater.*

Proiecto auro, Pater hilarius ad Filias:

*Iam iam mecum gaudete, filie,*
*paupertatis elapso tempore;*
*ecce enim in auri pondere*
*quod suf⟨f⟩icit nostre miserie.*
*Me beatum!*

[1] capit] capet (MS). M and D suggest the emendation *cepit*.

[2] uexat] uexit (MS).

[3] primum] primus (MS).

[4] D proposes an emendation: *nec nos, lugens, ad lugendum move.*

Filie stantes dicant:|

*Graciarum ergo preconia*
*offeramus et laudum munera*
*uni Deo, cui in secula*
*laus et honor, uirtus et gloria,*
*care pater.*

Gener ad Patrem:

*Homo,*[1] *fame note preconio,*
*natam tuam quesitum uenio;*
*quam legali ducam con⟨n⟩ubio,*
*si dederis.*

Pater ad primam Filiam:

*Dic, filia, si tu uis nubere*
*huic iuueni, uenusto corpore*
*et nobili.*

Filia ad Patrem:

*In te mea sita sunt consilia,*[2]
*fac ut lubet*[3] *de tua filia,*
*care pater.*

Pater ad Generum:

*Ergo tue committo fidei;*
*uos coniungant legales laquei*
*et gracia.*

Iterum plang*ens* se Pater ad Filias:

*Cara michi ⟨pignora, filie,*
*opes patris inopis unice*
*et solamen mee miserie,*
*michi mesto tandem consulite.*
*Me miserum!⟩*

*Olim diues ⟨et nunc pauperrimus,*
*luce fruor et nocte anxius,*
*et quam ferre non consueuimus,*
*paupertatem grauiter ferimus.*
*Me miserum!⟩*[4]

Secunda Filia ad Patrem:

*Noli, pater, noli, carissime,*
*doloribus dolores addere,*
*nec per dampnum uelis in|ducere*
*periculum inreparabile,*
*care pater.*

[1] Homo] honor (MS).

[2] D comments upon the superfluousness of *sunt* in this line.

[3] lubet] The *u* is written over the expunction of an *i*.

[4] After this stanza M and W insert the entire stanza *Nec me mea . . . ieiunia me miserum* found above (ll. 25–9); but there is no rubric or *incipit* suggesting the addition.

*Scimus enim quod fornicantibus*
*obstrusus sit celestis additus;*
*pater, ergo cauere poscimus*
*ne nos uelis addere talibus,*
*care pater.*

*Nec te uelis et nos infamie*
*submittere, pater, perpetue,*
*nec ab ista labi pauperie*
*in eterne lacum miserie,*
*care pater.*

Proiecto auro, Pater ad Filias:

*Iam iam mecum gaudete, ⟨filie,*
*paupertatis elapso tempore;*
*ecce enim in auri pondere*
*quod sufficit nostre miserie.*
*Me beatum!⟩*

Filie ad Patrem:

*Graciarum ergo preconia*
*⟨offeramus et laudum munera*
*uni Deo, cui in secula*
*laus et honor, uirtus et gloria,*
*care pater⟩.*

Secundus Gener ad Patrem:

*Homo,*[1] *fame note preconio,*
*⟨natam tuam quesitum uenio;*
*quam legali ducam connubio,*
*si dederis.⟩*

Pater ad secundam Filiam:

*Dic, filia, si tu ⟨uis nubere*
*huic iuveni, uenusto corpore*
*et nobili⟩.*

Filia ad Patrem:

*In te mea sita sunt consilia;*
*⟨fac ut lubet de tua filia,*
*care pater.⟩*

Pater ad Generum:

*Istam tue committo fidei;*
*uos coniungant legales laquei*
*et gracia.*

Iterum plang*ens* se ad terciam Filiam:|

*Carum michi pignus, o filia,*
*non me*[2] *mea tantum inopia*

[1] Homo] honor (MS).

[2] me] Inserted by a later hand (MS).

*quantum tua uexat penuria;*
*tantum michi restas miseria.*
*Me miserum!*

Tercia Filia ad Patrem:

*Meum quoque, pater carissime,*
*consilium audire sustine,*
*atque finem breuiter collige:*
*Deum time, pater, et dilige,*
*care pater.*

*Nichil enim Deum timentibus*
*per scripturam deesse notamus;*
*et omnia ministrat omnibus*
*omnipotens se diligentibus,*[1]
*care pater.*

*Ne desperes propter inopiam,*
*nunc quam esse scimus*[2] *fallaciam;*
*Iob respice,| pater, penuriam*
*ac deinde secutam copiam,*
*care pater.*

Proiecto auro tercio a Sancto Nicholao, Pater prostratus ad pedes eius dicat:

*Siste gradum, quisquis es, Domine;*
*siste, precor, et quis sis exprime,*
*qui, dedecus tollens infamie,*
*onus*[3] *quoque leuas inopie.*
*Me beatum!*

Nicholaus ad Patrem:

*Nicholaum me uoca⟨n⟩t nomine.*
*Lauda Deum ex dato munere;*
*hanc ne michi uelis ascribere*
*largitatis laudem dominice,*
*queso, frater.*

Pater aduersus ad terciam Filiam:

*Nata, tibi sit uox leticie,*
*paupertatis elapso tempore;*
*ecce enim ⟨in auri pondere*
*quod sufficit nostre miserie.*
*Me beatum!⟩*

Filia ad Patrem:

*Graciarum ergo ⟨preconia*
*offeramus et laudum munera*

[1] diligentibus] diligencius (MS).
[2] nunc quam esse scimus] nunquam esse secutus (M.W); nunquam esset secus (D.C).
[3] onus] honus (MS).

*uni Deo, cui in secula*
*laus et honor, uirtus et gloria,*
*care pater⟩.*

Tercius Gener ad Patrem:

*Homo, fame note ⟨preconio,*
*natam tuam quesitum uenio;*
*quam legali ducam connubio,*
*si dederis⟩.*

Pater ad Filiam suam:

*Dic, filia, si tu uis ⟨nubere*
*huic iuveni, uenusto corpore*
*et nobili⟩.*

Filia ad Patrem:

*In te mea sunt sita consilia;*
*⟨fac ut lubet de tua filia,*
*care pater.⟩*

Pater ad Generum:

*Istam tue*[1] *committo ⟨fidei;*
*uos coniungant legales laquei*
*et gracia⟩.*

Et chorus omnis sic dicat:

*O Christi pietas, ⟨omni prosequenda laude, qui sui famuli Nicholai merita longe lateque declarat, nam ex tumba ejus oleum manat, cunctosque languidos sanat.⟩*[2]

This version of the play opens with a soliloquy, in which the father laments the loss of his fortune. When his three daughters join him, *Pater* continues his complaint, and helplessly turns to them for counsel. The eldest daughter proposes that she and her sisters support the household through prostitution, and offers to take the lead. Before the father can reply to this proposal, however, gold is thrown in at the window, and all rejoice at their rescue from disgrace and poverty. With astonishing promptitude a suitor now appears, asking for the hand of the eldest daughter. After receiving her docile assent, the father cheerfully delivers her in marriage. Having exhausted his resources in providing a dowry for this occasion, *Pater* is again

[1] tue] tibi (MS).

[2] The text ends at the foot of p. 182, half of the last line being blank. The first words at the top of p. 183 are *Nos quos causa*, with which begins the play *Tres Clerici*, printed below, pp. 330 sqq. For the antiphon *O Christi pietas* see *Sarum Breviary*, iii, 38, where it is attached to the *Magnificat* in Second Vespers of the feast of St Nicholas, Dec. 6. See also Chevalier, *Bayeux*, p. 193. For the less frequent position of this antiphon, at the *Benedictus* of Lauds, see, for example, Chevalier, *Laon*, p. 207.

reduced to poverty, and addresses to the remaining two daughters the same lament that he used at the outset.[1] The second daughter, having in mind the proposal of the eldest, who is now married, argues against prostitution, urging the misery that must follow upon such a sin. At this juncture gold is once more thrown in at the window, and once more *Pater* and *Filiæ* rejoice and give thanks in language previously employed. Through a similar repetition, a second suitor presents himself instantly, and is accepted. Left in poverty for a third time, *Pater* vents his sorrow upon the remaining daughter. She counsels that they fear and love God, drawing from the Bible the assurance that He will minister to them, and recalling the example of Job. St Nicholas now casts in gold for a third time and hastens away. When *Pater* overtakes him and demands his name, the saint discloses himself, but charges that the thanks be given to God. After gratitude has been rendered in language substantially like that used twice before, a third suitor appears, and repetitiously wins the third daughter. The chorus ends the play with the antiphon *O Christi pietas*.

Although the Hildesheim and Fleury plays are, in large part, textually identical, the latter somewhat enlarges the roles common to the two pieces, and greatly increases the liveliness of the theme through the invention of new characters.[2] The enlargement of common roles is seen, for example, in the first two speeches, containing the introductory laments of the father and the daughters. These speeches provide against the sort of abruptness felt at the opening of the Hildesheim play.[3]

The more striking difference between the versions, however, is the presence in the Fleury play of the theme of matrimony. In the traditional legend this element is of capital importance, and the *generi* are clearly implied.[4] For his effort toward developing this implication the playwright is, of course, to be commended, but his result is flat. The regularity with which the *generi* appear in turn, and the repetition of language for the several appearances, are drearily mechanical.[5] One longs, indeed, for the courage to infer that the alacrity with which the suitors scent the dowries, and the uniformity of their wooings, are intended

[1] That is to say, he repeats at least two of the three stanzas, and possibly, all three. See Weydig, p. 51.

[2] See Weydig, pp. 53–6, 58.

[3] I do not share the opinion of Weydig (p. 55), that the opening speeches of the Fleury play are superfluous.

[4] See the legend printed below, p. 488.

[5] See Sepet, *Origines*, p. 65; Coussemaker, p. 328.

for comic effect! The solemnity of the plodding author's intention, however, is all too obvious.

There are, moreover, other dramatic effects in which the Fleury author is not altogether happy. The arrival of the first gold from St Nicholas, for example, is so abrupt as to forestall a response from the father to his eldest daughter's revolting proposal. We should have expected from him a protest of the sort found in the Hildesheim play. Another ineptitude may, perhaps, be felt in the absence of an unequivocal pecuniary provision for the father at the end. As the play stands, one is moved to inquire whether, after the marriage of the third daughter, *Pater* is left in the destitution in which he began, and into which he relapsed after the first and second marriages.[1] Upon this point, to be sure, the legend itself is not entirely clear; but a satisfying dramatic ending through the removal of this uncertainty would seem to have been a fair charge upon the playwright.

The notable increase in stage activity in the Fleury play is almost inevitably reflected in the variety of the verse.[2] Whereas the Hildesheim play proceeds in uniform and unbroken stanzas, the version now before us shows several stanzaic arrangements. The opening lament consists of rhyming lines of fifteen syllables, broken into groups of two or three by a refrain of seven syllables. The conversation between the father and daughters is conducted prevailingly in ten-syllable lines, rhymed in stanzas of four verses, each stanza ending with a refrain of four syllables—the arrangement noted above in the Hildesheim play. The *generi* use a three-line stanza concluded with a refrain of four syllables. In the more animated movement of the betrothals, the father and daughters use stanzas of two lines concluded with the usual short refrains.

In so far as we can tell from the text, the stage-setting for the Fleury play might well be of the simple sort inferred for the Hildesheim play on the same subject.[3] The stage need represent only a room and an open space outside. Since the play ends with the choral singing of the antiphon *O Christi pietas*, the presumption is that the dramatic performance occurred during Vespers or Lauds on St Nicholas' day, in which this liturgical piece is commonly found.[4]

[1] See Weydig, pp. 56–8.
[2] See Weydig, p. 59.
[3] See Weydig, pp. 59, 76–7.
[4] See above, p. 321.

Before leaving the two plays now before us we must recur to the fact that some fifteen of the nineteen stanzas of the Hildesheim piece are found also in the Fleury version. To put the matter broadly, the greater part of the Hildesheim play could be formed by extracting parts from the Fleury play. Is the former composition, then, merely an excerpt from the latter?[1] Or is the latter an elaboration of the former? Or, if the two plays are not related so directly, which of the two represents the earlier dramatic tradition? Since the Hildesheim play is the simpler in content, one easily assumes that it is also the earlier, unless evidence appears to the contrary.[2] This assumption seems to be supported by the mechanical fashion in which the roles of the sons-in-law are attached to the main theme in the Fleury play, and by the general improbability that after the part of the *generi* had once been dramatized, it would be dropped out. We need not infer, however, that the dowry legend was certainly dramatized first in Germany and then elaborated in France. The use of the line of ten syllables points to the play's having originated in France, and having appeared in Germany through adoption.[3] We are permitted to conjecture, therefore, that a simple form arose first in France, that this passed to Hildesheim without substantial change, and that at Fleury it was eventually enlarged, somewhat clumsily, through the addition of new roles.[4]

## THE THREE CLERKS, OR 'TRES CLERICI'

In the next legend with which we are concerned, St Nicholas is brought into direct relationship with the class of scholars, or *clerici*, who probably had most to do with producing plays in his honour. Although, as we shall see, there is some uncertainty as to the date at which this saint came to be regarded explicitly as the patron of scholars, he is dramatized in this role as early as the eleventh or twelfth century.

### I

The simplest, and probably the oldest, extant dramatization of this kind is the following from Hildesheim:[5]

[1] Creizenach (i, 99) regards the Hildesheim play as 'eine abgekürzte Fassung des Texts von Fleury'.

[2] This is the assumption of Schröder (*Z.f.d.A.* xxxvi [1892], 239–40), Weydig (pp. 47, 56), and Coffman (*New Theory*, pp. 61, 64).

[3] See Coffman, *New Theory*, pp. 64–5; Meyer, p. 118.

[4] As to intercommunication between Fleury and Hildesheim see Coffman, *op. cit.*, p. 65.

[5] London, Brit. Mus., Add. MS 22414, Miscellanea Hildesiensia sæc. xi–xii, fol. 4$^r$,

⟨Primus Clericus:⟩

*Hospes care, tres sumus socii*[1]
*litterarum*[2] *quos causa studii*[3]
*cogit ferre penas exilii,*
*nos sub tui tectis hospitii*
*hospitare.*

Secundus ⟨Clericus⟩:

*Fessi sumus longo itinere,*
*tempus esset iam nos quies⟨c⟩ere;*
*nobis uelis amoris federe*
*hospitium noctu concedere*
*quo egemus.*

Tertius ⟨Clericus⟩:

*Summo*[4] *⟨mane⟩ cras, hospes, ibimus.*
*Non de tuo uiuere querimus,*
*quia uictum nobiscum gerimus;*
*hospitium tantum depos⟨c⟩imus*
*causa Dei.*

R*espondeat* Hospes:

*Cum uos ita fessos conspiciam,*[5]
*propter summam Dei clementiam*
*uos hic intus noctu su⟨s⟩cipiam,*
*uobis ignem cum lecto faciam;*
*ite sessum.*

⟨Hospes ad Uxorem⟩:

*Vxor,*[6] *audi meum consilium:*
*isti censum*[7] *gerunt eximium;*
*inpendamus eis exitium,*
*ut eorum tesauri pretium*
*habeamus.*

⟨Uxor:⟩

*Tantum nefas, coniux, si fiere⟨t⟩,*
*creatorem nimis offendere⟨t⟩;*
*et si quisquam forte percipere⟨t⟩,*
*nos per orbis spatium gere⟨ret⟩*
*infamia.*

previously edited by Dümmler, in *Z.f.d.A.*, xxxv (1891), 405–7 (D). For comment upon the MS, and for bibliography, see below, p. 490. In regard to what immediately precedes the present text in the MS see above, p. 314. For the rubrics supplied editorially no spaces are left in the MS itself.

[1] socii] sotii (MS).

[2] litterarum] Corrected from *letterarum* (MS).

[3] studii] Followed by an erasure covering seven or eight letters.

[4] Summo] so*m*mo (MS).

[5] conspiciam] conspitiam (MS).

[6] Vxor] Voxor (MS).

[7] censum] scensum (MS). The scribe wrote *gerunt scensum*, but entered symbols reversing the order of the two words.

R*espondeat* ⟨Hospes⟩:

*Frustra times, bene celabitur;*
*nemo s⟨c⟩iet ⟨si⟩ pertractabitur.*
*Horum nobis morte parabitur*[1]
*in manticis qui clauditur*[2]
*opum census.*

Vxor r*espondeat:*

*Fiat quod uis, ego consentiam;*
*que proposse tibi subueniam,*
*tam infeste cladis nequitiam*
*caute tecum coniunx*[3] *incipiam*
*vxor*[4] *tua.*

Verba Sancti Nicol⟨a⟩i:

*Ad te gradu*[5] *nocturno uenio*
*tuo pauper a⟨d⟩motus hostio;*
*hic exoro frui hospitio;*
*faue mihi pro Dei Filio.*
. . .[6]

⟨Hospes:⟩

*Precor, hospes, intra hospitium*
*ut per noctis istius spatium*
*meum tibi prosit auxilium;*
*quod exigis habe remedium;*
*vade sessum.*

Nicolaus:

*Noue carnis si quidquam habeas,*
*inde mihi parumper tribuas,*
*quam si mihi prebere ualeas,*
*adiuro te per Deum nequeas.*[7]
. . .

R*esponsio*:[8]

*Que tu poscis,*[9] *hospes, non habeo,*
*nec hanc tibi prebere ualeo;*
*non sum diues, sed pauper maneo,*
*multis enim semper indigeo*
*diutius.*

Sanctus Nicolaus:

*Falsum refers atque*[10] *mendacium,*
*nuper enim per infortunium*

[1] parabitur] parantur (MS).
[2] D observes the lack of two syllables in this line.
[3] coniunx] coniuns (MS).
[4] vxor] Vuxor (MS).
[5] Ad te gradu] Atte gradum (MS).
[6] For the missing words, here and in the next speech of Nicolaus (there is no vacant space or erasure), D suggests *care hospes*.
[7] nequeas] D's collaborator suggests emending to *prebeas*.
[8] Responsio] Responsum (D).
[9] poscis] possis (MS).
[10] atque] adque (MS).

*peregisti opus nefarium,*
*clericorum fundens ex⟨it⟩ium*
*per corpora.*

*Ergo prece mentis sollicite*
*nostro simul pectora tundite*[1]
*et Dominum mecum deposcite*[2]
*indulgere uobis illi⟨ci⟩te*
*crimen mortis.*

Oratio Sancti Nicolai:

*Misere⟨re⟩ nostri, Rex glorie;*
*nobis locum concede uenie,*
*et clericis perem⟨p⟩tis impie*[3]
*per uirtutem ⟨tue⟩ potentie*
*redde uitam.*

⟨Chorus:⟩

*O Christi pietas, ⟨omni prosequenda laude, qui sui famuli Nicolai merita longe lateque declarat, nam ex tumba ejus oleum manat, cunctosque languidos sanat.⟩*[4]

Angelus:

*Nicolae, uita*[5] *fidelibus*
*reddita est a Deo precibus.*[6]

This play opens, somewhat abruptly, with the arrival of three wandering scholars at an inn, each one in turn appealing to the host for shelter. He grants their request promptly, and, we must assume, the scholars immediately go to bed. The host now proposes to his wife that they murder their guests for their money. At first the woman rejects this proposal as being offensive to God, and dangerous; but after her husband has assured her of secrecy, she assents. Although the text is silent, we infer that at this juncture the murder is represented in pantomime. Now appears St Nicholas as a poor wanderer asking in Christ's name for hospitality. After being admitted to the inn, the new guest asks for fresh meat, and when the host replies that he

[1] tundite] tondite (MS).

[2] deposcite] depossite (MS).

[3] impie] Followed by the words *redde uitam* almost completely erased.

[4] For the text of this antiphon see *Sarum Breviary*, iii, 38, where it is attached to the *Magnificat* of Second Vespers of the feast of St Nicholas, Dec. 6. See above, p. 321.

[5] uita] Followed by an erasure of three or four letters—possibly of the word *uita*.

[6] precibus] Preceded in the MS by the letters *uis* or *ius*. D prints *⟨t⟩uis*, and observes that this word enlarges the line beyond the norm by two syllables. The fragment and the MS page end abruptly with the word *precibus*. The closing speeches appear to be disarranged, for one would expect the play to end with the antiphon *O Christi pietas*. See above p. 321. In the lower margin of fol. $4^r$ are written in isolation the words *nobis in exilio proscripti*, which I am unable to include in either of the dramatic texts on fol. $3^v$–$4^r$.

cannot provide it, the saint accuses him of having murdered the three guests and charges him to pray to God for pardon. St Nicholas leads in a prayer for forgiveness, and for the raising of the dead scholars. After the singing of the antiphon *O Christi pietas*, an angel reports that the murdered clerks have returned to life.

The nature of the source of this play cannot be determined, for the story represented is not found among the established early narrative legends of the saint,[1] and we have no version of it older than the play itself. We may be reasonably sure that the Hildesheim playwright did not invent it, however, for references to it in a service-book of the late eleventh century would seem to show that by that date it had considerable currency.[2] Not long after the writing of the Hildesheim manuscript, Wace (c. 1150) records the scholars' legend thus in his *Vie de Saint Nicholas*:[3]

Trei clerc aloent a escole,
N'en ferai mie grant parole.
Lor ostes par nuit les oscit,
Los cors muscea, l'avoir enprit;
Saint Nicholas par Deu le sout,
S'empres fu la si cum Deu plout.
Les clers al oste demanda
N'es pout muscier, si li mostra.
Seint Nicholas par sa priere
Les ames mist el cors ariere.
Por ceo que as clers fist tiel honor,
Font li clerc feste a icel jor
De bien lirre, de bien chantier,
E de miracles recitier.

In this passage, unfortunately, Wace throws no light upon the earlier history of the legend. His Latin source may have been some isolated narrative as old as the Hildesheim play, or older; possibly it was a dramatic version similar to the one before us.[4] If the last four lines of Wace's narrative are to be accepted in their obvious sense, it would appear that the story of the *tres clerici* had been an established legend well before the middle of

[1] See Bohnstedt, p. 38.

[2] See Young, *Miracle Play*, pp. 261, 263.

[3] N. Delius, *Maistre Wace's St Nicholas*, Bonn, 1850, p. 8, lines 216–29. For a text from another MS see Crawford, *Nicholas*, pp. 77–8.

[4] Concerning the source of his poem as a whole Wace writes thus (ll. 1519–21):

Ci faut li livres mestre Guace
Qu'il ad de seint Nicholas fait,
De latin en romanz estrait.

the twelfth century, and that this account of St Nicholas' favour toward the *clerici* was the reason for their observing his feast-day by reading, singing and reciting his miracles. We have, however, no decisive evidence that Nicholas was regarded as the saint specifically of scholars at an earlier period than the date of the Hildesheim manuscript.[1]

Returning to the dramatic text in hand we observe that the action is slight. Since, indeed, so little of theatrical activity is explicitly indicated, and since the rubrics prescribe nothing in the way of impersonation, one might surmise that the piece was not intended for actual stage performance at all. Such an inference, however, cannot be allowed, for certain passages would be unintelligible without the accompaniment of mimetic action. We must assume, for example, that after the fourth stanza the *clerici* are represented as going to bed, and that after the eighth stanza occurs a physical representation of the murder.[2]

Concerning the literary form of the play nothing need be added to what has been said above about the version of *Tres Filiæ* from the same manuscript.[3] The stanza form is the same in the two plays, and in neither do the divisions of the dialogue occur within the stanzas.

The staging of the play seems to have been very simple, for the text demands the actual representation of only one room, the main apartment of the inn.[4] At the opening of the action the three *clerici* are already at the door of this room, and we infer that, after being received by the host, they pass from the open stage as if entering an adjoining sleeping-chamber. As to their re-appearing upon the stage we are left in some uncertainty. If we may assume that the murder is committed off stage, it may be that the raising of the *clerici* is merely reported by *Angelus* at the end. It is entirely possible, however, that *Angelus* conducts the resuscitated persons back to the open room to take part in the singing of the closing antiphon *O Christi pietas*. It may be, on the other hand, that the stage undertook to represent both the general room of the inn and the sleeping apartment, in two separate *sedes*, and that all the action implied by the text was performed in full view of the spectators.

From the presence, at the end, of the antiphon *O Christi pietas*

[1] For an examination of the evidence bearing upon this matter see Coffman, *New Theory*, pp. 19–23; and Notes, p. 490.

[2] See Weydig, p. 62.

[3] See above, p. 315.

[4] See Weydig, pp. 77–9.

we may surmise that the play was attached to Vespers or Lauds of the feast of St Nicholas.[1]

## II

A somewhat more ambitious dramatization of the scholars' legend is to be seen in the following composition from the Fleury play-book:[2]

⟨Primus Clericus:⟩

*Nos quos causa discendi literas*
*apud gentes transmisit exteras,*
*dum sol adhuc extendit radium,*
*perquiramus nobis hospicium.*

Secundus Clericus:

*Iam sol equos tenet in litore,*
*quos ad presens merget sub equore.*
*Nec est nota nobis hec patria;*
*ergo queri debent hospicia.*

Tercius Clericus:

*Senem quemdam maturum moribus*
*hic habemus coram luminibus;*
*forsan, nostris compulsus precibus,*
*erit hospes nobis hospitibus.*

Insimul omnes ad Senem dicant:

*Hospes care, querendo studia*
*huc relicta uenimus patria;* |
*nobis ergo prestes hospicium*
*dum durabit hoc noctis spacium.*

Senex:

*Hospitetur uos factor omnium,*
*nam non dabo uobis hospicium;*
*nam nec mea in hoc utilitas,*
*nec est ad hoc nunc op⟨p⟩ortunitas.*

Clerici ad Uetulam:

*Per te, cara, sit impetrabile*
*quod rogamus, etsi non utile.*
*Forsan propter hoc beneficium*
*uobis Deus donabit puerum.*

Mulier ad Senem:

*Nos his dare, coniux, hospicium,*

[1] See above, p. 321.

[2] Orleans, Bibl. de la Ville, MS 201 (*olim* 178), Miscellanea Floriacensia sæc. xiii, pp. 183–7, previously edited by Monmerqué, in *Mélanges*, vii, 103–7 (M); Wright, pp. 8–10 (W); Du Méril, pp. 262–6 (D); Coussemaker, pp. 100–8 (C). Coussemaker's text is reprinted by Adams, pp. 59–62. Only Coussemaker publishes the music. For observations on the MS see above, i, 665. The text of the play begins, without introductory rubric, at the top of p. 183.

*qui sic uagant querendo studium,*
*sola saltem compellat karitas;*
*nec est dampnum, nec est utilitas.*

Senex:

*Acquiescam tuo consilio,*
*et dignabor istos hospicio.*

Senex ad Clericos:

*Accedatis, scolares, | igitur;*
*quod rogastis uobis conceditur.*

Senex, Clericis dormientibus:

*Nonne uides quanta marsupia?*
*Est in illis argenti copia;*
*hec a nobis absque infamia*
*possideri posset pecunia.*

Vetula:

*Paupertatis onus*[1] *sustulimus,*
*mi marite, quamdiu uiximus;*
*hos si morti donare uolumus,*
*paupertatem uitare possumus.*

*Euagines ergo iam gladium,*
*namque potes morte iacencium*
*esse diues quamdiu uixeris;*
*atque sciet nemo quod feceris.*

Nicholaus:

*Peregrinus, fessus itinere,*
*ultra modo non possum tendere;*
*huius ergo per noctis spacium*
*michi prestes, precor, hospicium.*

Senex ad Mulierem:|

*An dignabor istum ⟨h⟩ospicio,*
*cara coniux, tuo consilio?*

Vetula:

*Hunc persona*[2] *commendat nimium,*
*et est dignum ut des hospicium.*

Senex:

*Peregrine, accede propius.*
*Uir uideris nimis egregius;*
*si uis, dabo tibi comedere;*
*quidquam uoles temptabo querere.*

Nicholaus ad mensam:

*Nichil ex his possum comedere;*[3]
*carnem uellem recentem*[4] *edere.*

[1] onus] honus (MS).
[2] persona] personam (MS).
[3] comedere] commedere (MS).
[4] recentem] resecentem, with second *e* expunged (MS).

Senex:

*Dabo tibi carnem quam habeo,*
*namque carne recente*[1] *careo.*

Nicholaus:

*Nunc dixisti plane mendacium;*
*carnem habes recentem*[2] *nimium;*
*et hanc habes magna | nequicia,*
*quam mactari fecit pecunia.*

Senex et Mulier dixerunt:

*Miserere nostri, te petimus,*
*nam te sanctum Dei cognouimus.*
*Nostrum scelus abhominabile*
*non est tamen incondonabile.*

Nicholaus:

*Mortuorum afferte corpora,*
*et contrita sint uestra pectora.*
*Hi*[3] *resurgent per Dei graciam;*
*et uos flendo queratis ueniam.*

Oracio Sancti Nicholai:

*Pie Deus, cuius sunt omnia,*
*celum, tellus, aer et maria,*
*ut resurgant isti precipias,*
*et hos ad te clamantes audias.*

Et post omnis chorus dicat *Te Deum laudamus.*[4]

At the beginning of this version we find the three scholars wandering in an alien land. The first and second call attention to the need of finding shelter before night-fall, and the third points to an aged man who may be persuaded to receive them. In unison, then, they present their request to the host of the inn. Being repulsed by him, they address his wife, suggesting that if she will grant them shelter, God may give her a son. The wife now argues with her husband that, although such a deed can bring neither advantage nor disadvantage, sheer pity dictates relieving the homeless visitors. Yielding to this appeal, the host invites the scholars in, and they go to bed. During the night the host leads his wife to where the scholars are sleeping and points to their purses, with the suggestion that the money may be stolen with impunity. The wife promptly assents, and urges her husband to murder the three sleepers. After the crime

[1] recente] rescente (MS).
[2] recentem] rescentem (MS).
[3] Hi] hii (MS).
[4] The text ends at the bottom of p. 187. At the top of p. 188 a rubric begins *Aliud miraculum*, introducing the play printed below, pp. 344 sqq.

has been accomplished, St Nicholas appears at the door, asking for shelter. With the encouragement of his wife, the host receives the pilgrim cordially, invites him to sit at table, and consults his wishes concerning food. St Nicholas asks for fresh meat, and when the host explains that he has none, the saint accuses him of murder. The husband and wife now recognize their guest as one of God's saints, and beg for mercy. St Nicholas charges them to fetch the dead bodies and to repent. In a prayer to God the saint begs for the raising of the dead scholars and for the pardon of the murderers. Then the choir sings the closing *Te Deum*.

Obviously the present play provides a considerably larger variety of action than does the version from Hildesheim. In the Fleury play we see for the first time such elements as the following: the first three utterances of the *clerici*, spoken among themselves on the road outside the inn; the host's preliminary refusal of hospitality, and the successful appeal of the *clerici* to his wife; the host's consultation with his wife as to the propriety of their receiving St Nicholas when he appears as an unknown *peregrinus*; and the final confession of the two criminals to the saint.

This variety in the action is naturally accompanied by a certain development in characterization. Although the *clerici* show no substantial increase in vitality, the host and his wife have personalities of considerably more distinctness than can be discerned in the play of Hildesheim. The host shows a marked deference to his wife, and she in turn has a fresh vigour. The Hildesheim version has no parallel to the bitterness and energy with which she assents to the crime. One observes also the touching quality of the prayer of St Nicholas at the end.[1]

The verse takes the ten-syllable form found in the piece from Hildesheim. The stanzas have four lines; but whereas in the Hildesheim play the lines have one rhyme throughout, in the Fleury version they usually follow the formula *aabb*. The succession of uniform stanzas inevitably suggests a narrative rather than a dramatic action. A certain lack of fertility is disclosed by the somewhat frequent repetition of rhyme-words, and by the occasional repetition of parts of the lines themselves. Thus, for example, the couplet (ll. 15–6),

> Nobis ergo præstes hospitium
> dum durabit hoc noctis spatium

[1] See Coussemaker, p. 329. In regard to dramatic details see also Weydig, pp. 65–9.

resembles the later passage (ll. 47–8),

Huius ergo per noctis spatium
mihi præstes, precor, hospitium.

From the dramatic point of view the most interesting aspect of the Fleury stanza is the mild evidence of flexibility in the use of it. In the conversations between the host and his wife, and between the host and St Nicholas, stanzas are freely divided into speeches of two lines.[1]

Between the Fleury and Hildesheim plays there appears to be no direct literary relationship. Such verbal resemblances as may be discerned—between the first stanza of the Hildesheim version, for example, and the fourth stanza of the Fleury play—are insufficient for establishing interdependence.[2] The Fleury writer, indeed, creates a certain literary tone of his own through introducing into a Christian play the pagan suggestiveness of such lines as the following (5–6):[3]

Iam sol equos tenet in litore,
quos ad præsens merget sub æquore.

As in versification, so also in staging the Fleury play seems to be superior to the version from Hildesheim. The text of the latter apparently requires the representation of only one room, the murder probably being acted off stage. The Fleury play, on the other hand, requires, in the first place, a representation of the highway, for on their first appearance the *clerici* are represented as being at some distance from the inn. In addition to the general room of the inn, the stage may have represented also a sleeping-chamber. This arrangement is suggested by the fact that the conversation of the prospective criminals seems to occur in the room in which the *clerici* are sleeping, and by the circumstance that after St Nicholas has entered the inn and has vainly asked for meat, he orders the bodies of the *clerici* to be brought to him as from a separate apartment. It may well be, then, that the stage was arranged as a *platea* and two *sedes*, the *platea* for the street, and the two *sedes* for the two rooms.[4]

The ending of the text with the *Te Deum* seems to indicate that the play was performed at the end of Matins, presumably on the feast day of St Nicholas.[5]

[1] For observations on the verse see Weydig, pp. 69–71; Coussemaker, p. 329.

[2] See Weydig, pp. 69–70; Coffman, *New Theory*, pp. 61–4.

[3] See Petit de Julleville, i, 71; Weydig, p. 79.

[4] This is the general view of Weydig, pp. 77–9.

[5] See Sepet, *Drame*, p. 219.

## III

The dramatic interest aroused by the legend of the young scholars is further evidenced by the following fragment of the twelfth century from Einsiedeln:[1]

⟨Nicolaus peregrinus ad Hospitem:⟩
*Obsecro per Dominum, tu suscipe me peregrinum,*
*Meque tua patere paulisper in ede manere.*
⟨Hospes ad Uxorem:⟩
*Cara mihi merito dic uxor fida marito:*
*Estne repellendus peregrinus, an excipiendus?*
⟨Uxor:⟩
*Rem tibi, dilecte, iustam persuadeo recte:*
*Pande fores isti, peregrinum suscipe Christi.*
⟨Hospes ad Nicholaum:⟩
*Qui requiem queris, intres, sedeas, epuleris.*
⟨Nicolaus:⟩
*O dapifer, uesci desidero carne recenti.*
⟨Ad Mulierem:⟩
*Hec ut mittatur, dominus tuus, oro, petatur.*
⟨Uxor ad Hospitem:⟩
*Inclyte noster here, noua fercula querit habere*
*Qui uespertinus ad nos uenit peregrinus.*
⟨Hospes ad Uxorem:⟩
*Gressu festino remeans refer hec peregrino:*
*Tempore presenti nos carne carere recenti.*
⟨Uxor ad Nicolaum revertens:⟩
*Quod tibi mandat herus index ego nuntio uerus:*
*Quam petis ut demus nos carne recente caremus.*
⟨Nicolaus ad ambos⟩:
*Uir, mulier, dapifer, mecum uia corripiatur*
*Ut quesita recens caro cautius inueniatur.*
⟨Intrant cubiculum ubi Juvenes occisi jacent:⟩
*Nunc est inuenta caro cruda recensque cruenta!*
*Esca placet talis bruti caro non animalis!*
*Est mihi gratorum dulcedo reperta ciborum!*

[1] Einsiedeln, Stiftsbibl., MS 34, Miscellanea sæc. x–xii, fol. $2^v$–$3^r$ (sæc. xii), previously edited by Gall Morel, in *Anzeiger für Kunde der deutschen Vorzeit*, Neue Folge, vi (1859), 207–8 (M). I have retained, in brackets, the rubrics successfully invented by Morel. By his failure to make clear that these rubrics are not in the MS Morel appears to have misled Coffman (*New Theory*, p. 64). The fragment with which we are concerned is immediately preceded in the MS by the following irrelevant verses:
Disce libens et quere frequens, utriusque memor sis.
Dilige doctorem simul et metuas monitorem.
He claues quinque tibi pandunt claustra sophie.

*Pro*[1] *dolor! O mentem nimium feritatis habentem!*
*Quod scelus egisti, qui tres mucrone petisti,*
*Hospes eos leto dans, summo iudice spreto!*

⟨Ad Uxorem:⟩

*Nec bene nupsisti, que conscia facta*[2] *fuisti*
*Tam magni sceleris, quia consensisse uideris*
*Horrifico sceleri; nec conuenit hoc mulieri.*

⟨Mulier ad Nicolaum:⟩

*Sancte pater, quid agam? Peccati lugeo plagam.*
*Sana lugentem, refoue peccasse fatentem.*
*Uir pie, uir celebris, compunctio te muliebris*
*His tantisque malis moneat quod sis uenialis.*|

⟨Nicolaus:⟩

*Qui regit omne quod est, cui crimina soluere fas est,*
*Uestri placatus dissoluat uincla reatus.*
*Ex ope diuina que gaudia fert inopina*
*Mors iuuenum fugiat, uiteque reuersio fiat.*

⟨Ad Occisos:⟩

*Participes uite, iuuenes, de morte redite;*
*Lausque Deo detur, cui mors obstare uereturs.*[3]

This fragment preserves only the latter part of the play, representing the events that follow the murder of the three *clerici*. When the lonely wanderer, St Nicholas, asks for shelter, the host follows the advice of his wife and invites the saint to enter and take food. At the guest's request for fresh meat, the hostess withdraws to take counsel with her husband, and returns to report to St Nicholas that she cannot satisfy his desire. The visitor now accuses them of murder, denounces their sin, and especially condemns the wife for her part in the crime. After she has begged forgiveness, the saint commends her to God's mercy. He then brings the dead *clerici* back to life, and renders thanks to God.

The present play advances beyond the version from Fleury both in variety of action and in characterization. The host shows an increased subservience to his wife, the stage movements connected with the ordering of the food are more decided, and the speeches of St Nicholas are longer and more numerous. The saint enlarges upon the horrors of the murder, and the host's wife makes an uncommonly desperate appeal for mercy.

[1] Pro] Pie (M).

[2] facta] facti (M).

[3] Followed immediately by irrelevant leonines, of which the first reads: Roma tenens morem nondum saciata priorem.

Thus the characters are developed with noticeably greater subtlety than in the other two compositions on the subject.

This superiority is probably due in some measure to sheer metrical form. It can be urged, for example, that the leonine hexameter allows a wider range of dramatic expression than do the quatrains of the two related plays. The freedom with which the playwright uses the hexameter is seen in the varying number of lines assigned to the several speakers, and in the successful resort to alliteration in such a line as,

Nunc est inventa caro cruda recensque cruenta.[1]

The stage demands and the liturgical attachment of the Einsiedeln play are probably not substantially different from those of the piece from Fleury. The fragment before us seems to assume the representation of two rooms, and the lost part of the play may well have required a *platea*, for use as a high-way.[2] The attachment of the play to the liturgy cannot be affirmed with assurance, but the words *Lausque Deo detur* in the last line would provide a graceful transition to the *Te Deum*.[3]

## The Image of Saint Nicholas, or 'Iconia Sancti Nicolai'

With the next play to be considered, the *Iconia Sancti Nicolai*, we return to the early and more widely-accepted traditions of this saint. The story concerns a heathen, or Jewish, tax-collector, who, relying upon the magical powers of an image of St Nicholas in his possession, entrusts it with the protection of his house and valuables while he is away on a journey.[4]

### I

One of the extant dramatizations of this legend is preserved among the writings of the wandering scholar, Hilarius:[5]

[1] Line 18. For observations on the style see Weydig, p. 75; Coffman, *New Theory*, p. 64.

[2] See Weydig, pp. 77–9.

[3] See Weydig, p. 75; Coffman, *op. cit.*, p. 62. For extended comparisons of the three dramatizations of the scholars' legend see Weydig, pp. 65–79; Coffman, pp. 61–4. It may well be that the Fleury writer was indebted to some such simple piece as the Hildesheim version. Coffman (p. 61) is, perhaps, unwarrantably precise in his conclusion that 'the author of the Einsiedeln play evidently employed both the Hildesheim and Fleury compositions as models'.

[4] For a text of the legend see Notes, p. 491.

[5] Paris, Bibl. Nat., MS lat. 11331, Hilarii Versus et Ludi sæc. xii, fol. 11r–12r, previously edited by Champollion-Figeac, pp. 34–9 (C); Du Méril, pp. 272–6 (D); Fuller, pp. 87–93 (F). The text of Champollion-Figeac is reprinted by Adams, pp. 55–8. I assume that the text of Pollard (pp. 162–5) is also from Champollion-Figeac. The MS provides no music. See plate xxii. For observations upon the MS see Champollion-

## Lvdus svper Iconia Sancti Nicolai

⟨A⟩d quem he persone sunt necessarie:
Persona Barbari qui commisit ei tesaurum
Persona Iconie
⟨Personæ⟩ IIII^or vel sex Latronum
⟨Persona⟩ Sancti Nicholai.

In primis Barbarus, rebus suis congregatis, ad Ichoniam ueniet et, ei res suas conmendans, dicet:

*Nicholae, quidquid possideo,*
*hoc in meo misi teloneo;*
*te custodem rebus ad⟨h⟩ibeo;*
*serua quę sunt ibi.*
*Meis, precor, adtende precibus;*
*vide, nullus sit locus furibus.*
*Preciosis aurum cum uestibus*
*ego trado tibi.*

*Proficisci foras disposui;*
*te custodem rebus inposui;*
*reuertenti redde quę posui*
*tua sub tutela.*
*Iam sum magis securus solito,*
*te custode rebus inposito;*
*reuertenti uide ne merito*
*mihi sit querela.*

Illo autem profecto, Fures transeuntes, cum uiderint hostium apertum et nullum custodem, omnia diripient. Barbarus uero rediens, non inuento tesauro, dicet:

*Grauis sors et dura!*
*Hic reliqui plura,*
*sed sub mala cura.*
*Des! quel domage!*
*Qui pert la sue chose, pur que nenrage?*

*Hic res plus quam centum*
*misi, et argentum;*
*sed non est inuentum.*
*Des! quel domage!*
*Qui pert ⟨la sue chose, pur que nenrage⟩?*

*Hic reliqui mea;*
*sed hic non sunt ea;*
*est imago rea.*

Figeac, pp. v–xiv; Fuller, pp. 3–6. For the other two plays of Hilarius, and a sketch of his career, see above, pp. 211 sqq., 276 sqq. See also Kressner, pp. 35, 48–50.

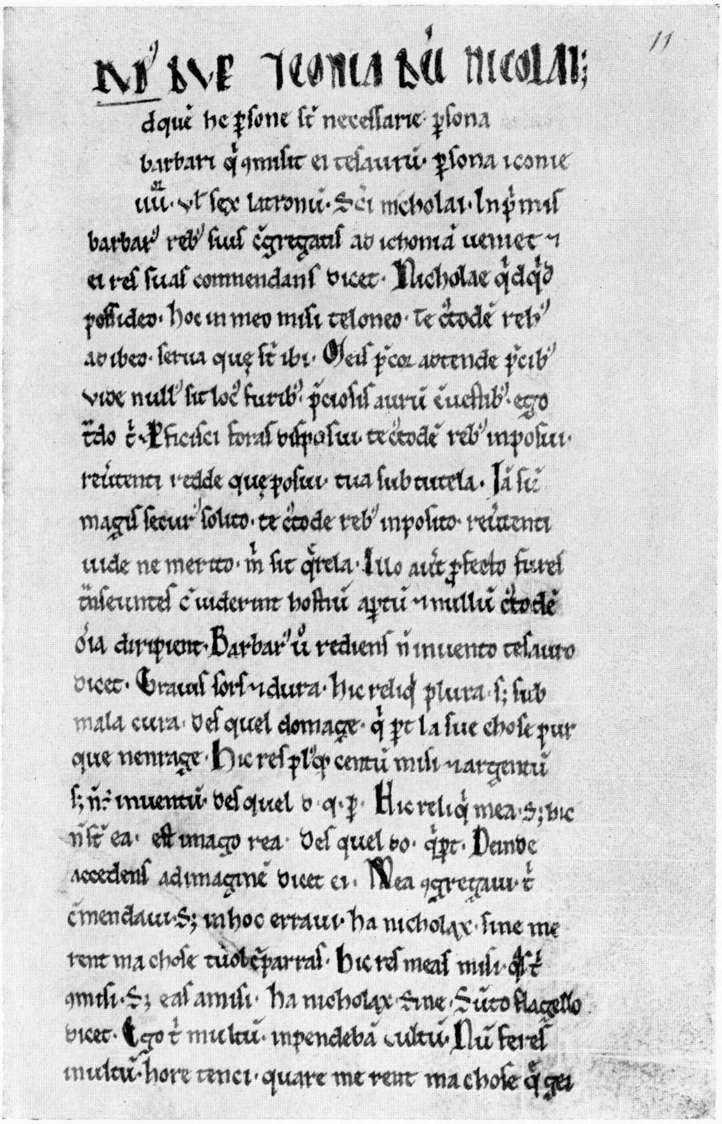

XXII. Play of the Image of St Nicholas, by Hilarius, in Paris, Bibliothèque Nationale, MS lat. 11331, fol. 11r

*Des! quel domage!*
*Qui pert* ⟨*la sue chose, pur que nenrage*⟩*?*

Deinde accedens ad Imaginem, dicet ei:

*Mea congregaui,*
*tibi commendaui;*
*sed in hoc erraui.*
*Ha! Nicholax!*
*Si ne me rent ma chose, tu ol comparras.*

*Hic res meas misi,*
*quas tibi commisi;*
*sed eas amisi.*
*Ha! Nicholax!*
*Si ne* ⟨*me rent ma chose, tu ol comparras*⟩.

Sum⟨p⟩to flagello, dicet:

*Ego tibi multum*
*inpendebam cultum;*
*non*[1] *feres inultum.*
*Hore ten ci,*
*quare me rent ma chose que gei | mis ci.*

*Tuum testor Deum:*
*te, ni reddas meum,*
*flagellabo reum.*
*Hore ten ci,*
*quare* ⟨*me rent ma chose que gei mis ci*⟩.

Tunc sanctus Nicholaus, ueniens ad Latrones, dicet eis:

*Miseri, quid facitis?*
*Non longa*[2] *deperditis*
*erunt uobis gaudia.*
*Custos eram positus,*
*uosque sum intuitus*
*cum portatis omnia.*

*Flagella sustinui,*
*cum ea non potui,*
*ut debebam, reddere.*
*Verba passus aspera,*
*cumque uerbis uerbera,*
*ad uos ueni propere.*

*Reportate, miseri,*
*gressu quidem celeri*
*reportate perdita.*
*Erant enim omnia*

[1] non] nū (MS). [2] longa] longua (MS).

*sub mea custodia*
*quę portasti⟨s⟩ posita.*

*Quod si non feceritis,*
*suspensi cras eritis*
*crucis in patibulo.*
*Vestra namque turpia,*
*uestra latrocinia,*
*nunciabo populo.*

Latrones timentes omnia reportabunt. Quibus inuentis, Barbarus dicet:

*Nisi uisus fallitur,*
*io en ai,*
*tesaurus hic cernitur.*
*De si grant merueile en ai.*

*Rediere perdita,*
*io en ai,*
*nec per mea merita.*
*De si grant meruegle en ai.*

*Quam bona custodia,*
*io*[1] *en ai,*
*qua redduntur omnia!*
*De si grant ⟨merueile en ai⟩.*

Tunc accedens ad Imaginem et sup⟨p⟩licans, dicet:

*Sup⟨p⟩lex ad te uenio,*
*Nicholax;*
*nam per te recipio*
*tut icei que tu gardas.*

*Sum profectus peregre,*
*Nicholax;*
*sed recepi integre*
*tut ice que tu gardas.*

*Mens mea conualuit,*
*Nicholax;*
*nichil enim defuit*
*de tut cei que tu gardas.*

Postea ap⟨p⟩arens ei, beatus Nicolaus dicet:

*Sup⟨p⟩licare mihi noli,*
*frater, inmo Deo soli;*
*ipse namque factor poli,*
*factor maris atque soli,*
*restaurauit perditum.*

[1] io] ioe (MS).

*Ne sis ultra quod fuisti,*
*solum laudes nomen Christi;*
*soli Deo credas isti,*
*per quem tua recepisti;*
*mihi nullum meritum.*

Cui respondens, Barbarus dicet: |

*Hic nulla consultacio,*
*nulla erit dilacio,*
*quin ab erroris uicio*
*iam recedam.*
*In Christum, Dei Filium,*
*factorem mirabilium,*
*ritum linquens gentilium,*
*ego credam.*

*Ipse creauit omnia,*
*celum, terram, et maria;*
*per quem erroris uenia*
*mihi detur.*
*Ipse potens et Dominus*
*meum delebit facinus;*
*cuius regnum ne terminus*
*consequetur.*[1]

The central personage here is a certain pagan who has become possessed of an image of St Nicholas, in the magical properties of which he has learned to trust. Setting out on a journey, *Barbarus* leaves the image as guard over the treasure in his house. During his absence robbers come, and finding the door open and no appearance of a guard, they steal all the goods. When the traveller returns, he first laments the loss of the property, and then denounces and beats the image. Meanwhile St Nicholas, in his own person, visits the robbers, and, with threats of disclosing their crime, charges them to return the plunder. When the robbers have carried out this command, *Barbarus* joyfully and penitently gives thanks to the image. St Nicholas himself now appears, bidding *Barbarus* transfer his gratitude to the Almighty. Accordingly the penitent renounces his past errors, and declares his belief in Christ, the Son of the one God.

A comparison of the play with the legend shows that the playwright has been fairly faithful to his narrative source.[2] The

[1] Followed by the rubric *Ad Pvervm Anglicvm*, introducing verses irrelevant to the play.

[2] For a text of the legend see below, p. 491.

central figure remains the *barbarus* of the tradition; he has not been transformed into the *Judæus* whom we shall encounter in the parallel play from Fleury. Through omitting matters connected with the origin of the image and with the conversion of the family of the heathen, Hilarius has successfully concentrated attention upon the most dramatic element in his material. And this element he has expanded by adding one substantial incident: the appearing of St Nicholas in the presence of *Barbarus* after the return of the treasure.[1] This addition is a natural one, and it gives an appropriate religious emphasis to the conversion of the pagan. From the point of view of stagecraft, however, the most notable aspect of the play is the restriction in the number of speakers. Seven (or nine) actors are prescribed, but only two, St Nicholas and *Barbarus*, have speaking parts. Although the robbers have ample opportunities for mimetic action, their silence eliminates certain obvious possibilities of characterization and theatrical variety.

Since *Barbarus* does most of the speaking, his part provides a fair opportunity for psychological disclosures through varied verse-forms.[2] For each of his principal speeches he uses a special form of stanza, thus appropriately differentiating his several moods: confidence in the image, rage over his loss, glee over the recovery, and a convert's penitence at the end. And even within a single speech he can expose the several facets of his emotion through variations of vernacular refrain. Thus in his outburst after the loss of his fortune he first enforces his selfish and frantic sorrow through repeating (ll. 20–1),

Des! quel domage!
Qui pert la sue chose, pur que nenrage!

Then he turns to the image, bitterly placing the blame there (ll. 35–6),

Ha! Nicholax!
Si ne me rent ma chose, tu ol comparras.

Finally as his rage mounts to threats of personal violence, he uses a third refrain (ll. 45–6),

Hore ten ci,
quare me rent ma chose que gei mis ci.

A similar use of vernacular refrain is apparent in the speech of

[1] See Weydig, p. 86. [2] See Sepet, *Origines*, pp. 171–6; Weydig, p. 86.

rejoicing after *Barbarus* has recovered his property (ll. 76–87). And it will be observed that in both speeches the refrains are used, not as paraphrases or expositions of the Latin text, but as independent forms composed for literary variety and emotional emphasis.[1]

Likewise worthy of note is the literary effectiveness of the final speech of *Barbarus*. This valedictory of a Christian convert, expressed in a stanza-form seen nowhere else in the play, contributes a pleasant elevation of tone. The effect of this conclusion deserves emphasis in view of a general judgement passed upon the play by a certain eminent critic. Justly impressed by suggestions of *esprit gaulois* in the theme and treatment of the piece, Petit de Julleville concludes, 'On peut dire qu'avec Hilarius le drame liturgique cesse même d'être religieux'.[2] This opinion, I assume, must give way before the religious earnestness with which the play ends.

The staging of the piece seems to require two *sedes*, one representing the interior of the house of *Barbarus*, and one representing the headquarters of the robbers. Concerning stage properties and costuming the text provides no definite information.

Although the play bears no direct evidence of attachment to the liturgy, we may conjecture that it was performed at some point in the Canonical Office. Since the closing rubrics of the two religious plays by Hilarius in the same manuscript clearly attach them either to Matins or to Vespers, we should expect a similar liturgical association for the play before us. It may be that in copying the *Iconia Sancti Nicolai* the scribe omitted a closing rubric of liturgical significance.[3]

## II

To the play of Hilarius a significant contrast, in several particulars, is found in the dramatization of the same legend in the play-book from the monastery at Fleury:[4]

[1] For an interpretation of these passages as comic see Gayley, *Comedies*, p. xv; Gayley, *Forefathers*, pp. 63–5; Ilvonen, pp. 24–5; Petit de Julleville, i, 74; Fuller, p. 34. Adams (p. 55) infers that, 'since Barbarus, a foreigner, is made to use French, the present play may have been designed for an English rather than a French audience'. This inference is scarcely supported by Hilarius' use of French elsewhere. See above, p. 218.

[2] Petit de Julleville, i, 74.

[3] See above, pp. 218, 286. It is fair to remark that the MS itself gives no hint of such an omission. Petit de Julleville (i, 74) feels sure that the performance was not 'partie intégrante de la liturgie'. Fuller (pp. 12, 35) infers that the absence of direct evidence of liturgical association 'shows beyond doubt that the play was not meant for the church'.

[4] Orleans, Bibl. de la Ville, MS 201 (*olim*

Aliud miraculum de Sancto Nicholao et de quodam Iudeo, qui Imaginem Sancti apud se absconditam pro posse suo cotidie uenerabatur. Hic autem, cum esset[1] diues, apud rus tendens, Sanctum Nicholaum et Imaginem eius custodem sue domus sine sera reliquit.[2] Interim Fures cuncta que habebat furati sunt. Que Sanctus Nicholaus ei post modum restituit, Furibus iussu Sancti omnia referentibus. Iudeus ad Sanctum Nicholaum:[3]

*Si que dicta*
*sunt ascripta*
*tibi, Dei famule,*
*re testantur,*
*ceu uulgantur*
*te post bustum uiuere,*[4]
*non est sane*
*quod non plane*
*tuis credam meritis.*
*Quidnam miri*
*quod non uiri*
*de te dant Christicole?*
*Qui carentes*
*sensu,*[5] *mentes*
*astruunt componere?*
*Quo qui luce*
*carent duce*
*uisum dicunt sumere;*
*tuque morti*
*datos sorti*
*uiuos reddis pristine.*

*Aure surdos,*
*uoce mutos,* |
*atque claudos gressibus,*
*tu confirmas*
*res infirmas,*
*quasque reddens uiribus.*

*Quem sic bonum*
*me patronum*

178), Miscellanea Floriacensia sæc. xiii, pp. 188–96, previously edited by Monmerqué, in *Mélanges*, vii, 111–8 (M); Wright, pp. 11–4 (W); Du Méril, pp. 266–71 (D); Coussemaker, pp. 109–22 (C). Only Coussemaker publishes the music. For observations on the MS see above, i, 665. The text printed here begins at the top of p. 188. See also Kressner, pp. 35, 50.

[1] esset] essed (MS).

[2] reliquit] aliquid (MS).

[3] The Jew is, of course, addressing not St Nicholas himself, but the *image*.

[4] W infers here the loss of 3 lines, or 15 syllables. Likewise D observes the absence of a rhyme for *meritis*.

[5] Qui carentes sensu] Que carentes sese (MS)

*delegisse gaudeo,*
*in quo uitam*
*mei sitam*
*et sistendam flagito.*
*Ergo rerum*
*te mearum*
*seruatorem statuo.*
*Tuque bonus,*
*presens domus,*
*excuba dum abero.*
*Ad quam, seram*
*nunquam feram,*
*te custode credito.*
*Non est multi*
*tanta fulti*
*gestorum potencia.*
*Huic si presit,*
*ne quid desit*
*tecto cum substancia.*
*Sed me mei*
*causa rei*
*rus compellit egredi.*
*Nec, ut credo,*
*fas habebo,*
*mox quod | mallem, regredi.*
*Iamque uale,*
*nec quid male*
*nos tra⟨c⟩tent malefici.*
*Vigil cura,*
*ne iactura*
*domus adsit censui.*

Interim ueniant Fures, et post recessum eius dicant omnes insimul:

*Quid agemus?*
*Quo tendemus?*
*Que*[1] *captamus consilia?*
*Oporteret*
*ut impleret*
*nostra quisquam*[2] *marsupia.*

Ad h*ec* dicat unus ex eis:

*Audite, socii, mea consilia:*
*uir hic est Iudeus, cuius pecunia,*
*si uultis, iam erit nostra penuria*
*releuata.*

[1] que] quo (MS).

[2] quisquam] Emendation *quis* or *quid* proposed (D).

Alius:

*Eamus propere; pellantur ocia;*
*tollantur ianue, frangantur hostia.*
*Iudei forsitan huius incuria,*
*iam esse poterit nostra pecunia*
*augmentata.*[1]

Et cum cicius inceperint ire, dicat tercius:

*O mei comites, | ite suauius,*
*uosque prospicite nunc diligencius;*
*uir talis caucius seruat quam alius*
*rem de qua metuit, et uigilancius*
*est seruata.*

Cum uenerint ad locum ubi furari debent, sit ibi arca patrata, quam curueant. Primus dicat:

*Arcam istam hinc tollite,*
*si potestis, quam concite;*
*quod si nequitis, frangite;*
*que sunt in ea capite.*

Quo dicto, fingant[2] se non posse leuare archam; et dicat secundus:

*Nos oportet hanc archam frangere;*
*quam nequimus integram tollere.*

Tunc ueniens tercius et inueniens seram non firmam, dicat:

*O quanta exultacio!*
*Hec archa, magno gaudio,*
*se reserari uoluit*
*et se*[3] *nobis aperuit!*

Hoc dicto, capto quod fuerit in archa, abeant.[4] Et tunc ueniens Iudeus et comperiens furata, dicat:

*Vah! perii! nichil est reliqui*[5] *michi! cur esse cepi?*
*Cur, mater, cur, | seue pater, fore me tribuisti?*
*Heu! quid proferri michi profuit aut generari?*
*Cur, Natura parens, consistere me statuebas,*
*Que luctus michi, que gemitus hos prospiciebas?*
*Quod querar in tantam mihi crimen obesse ruinam?*
*Qui modo diues eram, uix aut nullius egebam.*
*Pollens argento, preciosis uestibus, auro,*
*Sum miser, idque mei moles est pauperiei.*
*Nam latet ex habitu me post modo quo fruar usu.*
*Quod leuius ferrem, si ferre prius didicissem.*
*Sed, ni decipior, ego sane desipiebam.*
*Sic ego, quod nomen Nicho|lai*[6] *mane colebam.*

[1] augmentata] agmentata (MS. D. C). C erroneously reports that the MS has *argumentata*.

[2] fingant] fugiant (MS).

[3] se] Inserted by a later hand (MS).

[4] abeant] habeant (MS).

[5] reliqui] Over an erasure the MS seems to read *reliqii*.

[6] Nicholai] The scribe wrote *Nicholaus*; but the partial erasure of the last two letters

*Quidni noxa? Fides nocuit michi Christicolarum,*
*Que probat, et sine*[1] *sic te, Nicholae, uigere?*
*Id michi tristandi causam dedit et lacrimandi.*
*Nec solus flebo, nec inultus, credo, dolebo:*
*Tu meritis subdare probris tondere flagellis.*
*Sed fessus cedam, noctis tibi tempora credam.*
*Quod nisi mane mea repares tibi credita causa,*
*Primo flagellabo te, postque flagella cremabo.*

Nicholaus ad Fures furtum diuidentes:

*Quid, prophani? Quid nota reconditis?*
*Quid, dementes, ut uestra diuiditis?*
*Interi⟨i⟩stis.*
*Quid, | perditi, geritis*[2] *hominum?*
*Vos uobis abduxit fraus demonum.*
*Occubuistis.*
*Vos an transit, omnium miserrimi,*
*his abductis,*[3] *finis teterrimi,*
*quem meruistis?*[4]
*Non me late⟨n⟩t, inpudentissimi,*
*que sunt michi commissa*[5] *domui,*
*que rapuistis.*
*Has argenti marchas, his uestibus,*
*hanc auri massam insignibus*
*continuistis.*
*Michi autem sunt probra, turpium*
*michi quidem et causa uerberum,*
*que perpetrastis.*
*Quod si noctis huius presencia*
*festin⟨at⟩e refertis omnia,*
*id deuitatis.*
*Ne deprensi mane a populo,*
*me indicante, dignas*[6] *patibulo |*
*penas soluatis.*[7]

Recedente Sancto, dicat unus ex eis:

*Quanta mors est has gazas reddere!*
*Si laudatis, uolo diuidere.*

Alius:

*In isto negocio,*

may indicate a correction to *Nicholai*, as the four previous editors inferred.

[1] sine] sine te, the second word being expunged (MS).

[2] geritis] geris (MS).

[3] his abductis] hos abductus (MS).

[4] For these three defective lines D proposes this emendation:

An transeunt vos, o miserrimi,
his abductis, fines teterrimi,
quos meruistis?

[5] commissa] commisse (MS).

[6] indicante dignas] Emendation *testante digni* proposed (D).

[7] soluatis] soluaris (MS).

*egemus consilio;*
*nunquam letus fuero*
*si hec sic reddidero.*

Tercius:

*Est melius hec nobis reddere*
*quam sic uitam pendendo perdere.*

Omnes insimul:[1]

*Redeamus,*
*et reddamus.*

Iudeus, rebus inuentis suis, dicat alta uoce:

*Congaudete michi, karissimi,*
*restitutis cunctis que perdidi.*
*Gaudeamus!*
*Que mea dispersit incuria,*
*Nicholai resumpsi gracia.*
*Gaudeamus!*
*Conlaudemus hunc Dei famulum;*
*abiuremus obcecans*[2] *idolum.*
*Gaudeamus!*
*Vt, errore sublato | mencium,*
*Nicholai*[3] *mereamur consorcium.*
*Gaudeamus!*

Omnis chorus dicat:

*Statuit ei Dominus ⟨testamentum pacis, et principem fecit eum, ut sit illi sacerdotii dignitas in æternum.* Psalmus: *Memento, Domine, David, et omnis mansuetudinis ejus⟩.*[4]

Finitur miraculum.[5]

The opening rubric of this version informs us that a certain Jew has been accustomed to venerate an image of St Nicholas hidden in his house, and that he has become rich. As the play opens the Jew is setting out upon a journey, leaving his possessions in an unlocked chest under the protection of the image. After his departure three robbers arrive, and finding the chest unlocked, carry off the contents. Upon his return the Jew laments the loss of his riches, deplores his past confidence in St Nicholas, and promises the image a beating on the morrow. Meanwhile St Nicholas visits the robbers and threatens them with criminal punishment if they do not return the stolen goods to the owner that night. After St Nicholas has withdrawn, the

[1] insimul] simul (C.D)

[2] obcecans] obscecans (MS).

[3] Nicholai] Substitution *ejus* proposed (D).

[4] Introit of the Mass for the feast of St Nicholas. See *Sarum Missal*, p. 234.

[5] Followed immediately in the MS by the rubric *Ad representandum quomodo Sanctus Nicholaus*, introducing the play *Filius Getronis*, printed below, pp. 351 sqq.

robbers take counsel with one another as to his threat. Two of them propose retaining the loot, but the third robber persuades his companions to return it. At the restoration of his possessions the Jew rejoices, and calls upon the bystanders to give praise to St Nicholas.[1] The chorus closes the play with the singing of the introit *Statuit ei Dominus*.

A comparison of the Fleury play with that of Hilarius discloses relatively few important differences in the action. Somewhat more of the narrative legend is reflected in the former play through the opening speech of the Jew, in which he reviews the miraculous powers attributed to the image by the Christians. This account of the Christian origin of the image has no parallel in the version of Hilarius. The effect of activity upon the stage is, no doubt, increased in the Fleury play through the fact that the robbers have speaking parts. In one respect, however, the Fleury version provides less action than the other: in that St Nicholas does not appear a second time, at the end.

In characterization the Fleury writer proceeds with a freer hand. In the first place, *Barbarus* of Hilarius and of the legend becomes *Judæus*, with special new traits.[2] In his long opening address, for example, the Jew shows a characteristic scepticism as to the powers of the image. He scoffs at the credulity of the Christians, and commits his treasure to the image with a hesitant warning. The Jew is characterized also by one of the robbers who, in the following lines, credits him with the special talent of knowing how to keep his money safe (ll. 76–80):

O mei comites, ite suavius,
vosque prospicite nunc diligentius;
vir talis cautius servat quam alius
rem de qua metuit, et vigilantius
est servata.

Another distinctive bit of characterization appears in his denunciation of the Christians for misleading him into a false confidence in the image.[3] The lament in which this denunciation occurs, although it shows a narrower range of emotion than does the parallel part of Hilarius' play, discloses a laudable

[1] I assume that the persons addressed are the members of the *conventus* in the choir. See Sepet, *Origines*, p. 169.

[2] See Sepet, *Origines*, pp. 168–71, 176; Weydig, pp. 85–6.

[3] See ll. 102–6.

naturalness in that the Jew decides to postpone beating the image until the next day, because of sheer weariness (l. 109)—

Sed fessus cedam, noctis tibi tempora credam.

This effect of naturalness, attained through omitting the flagellation, may have resulted merely from a desire to reduce the comic tendency of the story in the interests of monastic decorum.[1]

The parts of the robbers also are developed with considerable skill. It is, indeed, surprising that the play-book which shows such ineptitude in managing the three *generi* in the dowry play should show so much flexibility in the treatment of the *fures* here.[2] The agitation of the three robbers is to some extent shown in the metres. Noteworthy are the short opening interrogations (ll. 61–3),

Quid agemus?
Quo tendemus?
Quæ captamus consilia?

A similar agitation is apparent in the impulsive words in which, under threat of death, the three in unison express their eagerness to return the stolen treasure (ll. 144–5),

Redeamus,
et reddamus!

It will be noted also that in a special canniness and caution the third robber stands apart from the others as an individual. It is he who at the outset warns his companions of the Jew's vigilance;[3] and when, in spite of St Nicholas' threats, the other two are amusingly intent upon retaining their booty, it is the third robber who soberly brings them to their senses (ll. 142–3):

Est melius hæc nobis reddere
quam sic vitam pendendo perdere.

The variety of versification seen in the roles of the robbers is characteristic of the play throughout. Although it is by no means clear that each kind of verse is fitted to the speaker with complete propriety, the variety in itself has a certain interest. Possibly this particular form of virtuosity may seem somewhat forced, as Sepet felt when he remarked, 'On sent trop l'exercice scolaire d'une matière développée tellement quellement en vers latins'.[4] Striking are the internal rhymes applied to the fifteen-

[1] See Creizenach, i, 98.
[2] See above, p. 322.
[3] See ll. 76–80, quoted above.
[4] Sepet, *Origines*, p. 168.

syllable units of the Jew's opening speech, the hexameters of his second speech,[1] the 'student refrain' of the Jew's closing address,[2] and the general variety in stanzaic arrangements.[3]

The general arrangements of the stage required for this play are probably not essentially different from those for the version of Hilarius. Two *sedes* seem to be needed: one for the house of the Jew, and one for the retreat of the robbers. The rubrics provide a few meagre suggestions as to properties and incidental action. The struggle of the robbers with the chest in the house of the Jew is explicitly indicated, as is also their gleeful dividing of the spoils in their own dwelling.

Although the literary variety of this play effaces any liturgical or hymn-like aspect such as we have seen in the plays from Hildesheim, the present piece may still be attached in some way to the liturgy. The closing rubric, in any case, directs the choir to sing the introit of the Mass of St Nicholas, *Statuit ei Dominus.*

## The Son of Getron, or 'Filius Getronis'

The only other legend of St Nicholas extant in dramatic form is usually entitled *Filius Getronis.* It recounts the abduction of the Christian lad, Deodatus, his captivity among heathen enemies, and his restoration to his parents through the miraculous power of the benevolent saint.[4] Of this story the only known dramatization is that preserved in the play-book from Fleury:[5]

Ad representandum quomodo Sanctus Nich⟨o⟩laus Getron⟨is⟩ Filium de manu Marmorini, Regis Agarenorum, liberauit, paretur in competenti loco cum Ministris suis armatis Rex Marmorinus in alta sede, quasi in regno suo sedens. Paretur et in alio loco Excoranda, Getronis ciuitas, et in ea Getron, et cum Consolatricibus suis, uxor eius, Eufrosina, et Filius eorum Adeodatus. Sitque ab orientali parte ciuitatis Excorande ecclesia Sancti Nicholai, in qua puer rapietur. His itaque

[1] See ll. 91 sqq. Sepet (p. 169) surmises that this speech is written in imitation of Plautus.

[2] See ll. 146 sqq. Concerning this *Gaudeamus* Monmerqué writes (*Mélanges*, vii, 117): 'Ce mot est le commencement de l'*Introit* de la messe de Saint-Nicolas, dans certains missels.' The usual introit for the Mass of St Nicholas is *Statuit ei Dominus.* As used here the word *Gaudeamus* seems to be merely a jubilant refrain, rather than the *incipit* of an introit.

[3] See Petit de Julleville, i, 71; Weydig, p. 85.

[4] For a text of the legend see Notes, p. 492.

[5] Orleans, Bibl. de la Ville, MS 201 (*olim* 178), Miscellanea Floriacensia sæc. xiii, pp. 196–205, previously edited by Monmerqué, in *Mélanges*, vii, 121–30 (M); Wright, pp. 15–20 (W); Du Méril, pp. 276–84 (D); Coussemaker, pp. 123–42 (C). Only Coussemaker publishes the music. The text of Coussemaker is reprinted by Adams, pp. 63–9. For observations on the MS see above, i, 665. As to what immediately precedes in the MS see above, p. 348. See also Kressner, pp. 56–7.

paratis, ueniant Ministri Marmorini Regis coram eo, et dicant omnes, uel primus ex eis:

*Salue, Princeps, salue, Rex optime!*
*Que sit tue uoluntas anime*
*seruis tuis ne tardes dicere;*
*sumus que uis parati facere.*

Rex dicet:

*Ite ergo, ne tardaueritis,*
*et quascunque gentes poteritis*
*imperio meo subicite;*
*resistentes uobis occidite.*

Interim Getron et Eufrosina, cum multitudine Clericorum, ad ecclesiam Sancti Nicholai, quasi ad eius sollempnitatem celebrandam, Filium suum secum ducentes, eant. Cumque Ministros Regis armatos illuc uenire uiderint, Filio suo pre timore oblito, ad ciuitatem suam confugiant. Ministri uero Regis, puerum rapientes, coram Rege ueniant, et dicant omnes, uel secundus ex eis:

*Quod iussisti, Rex bone, fecimus;*
*gentes multas uobis subegimus,*
*et de rebus quas adquisiuimus*
*hunc | puerum uobis adducimus.*

Omnes dicant, uel tercius:

*Puer iste, uultu laudabilis,*
*sensu prudens, genere nobilis,*
*bene debet, nostro iudicio,*
*subiacere uestro seruicio.*[1]

Rex:

*Apolloni qui regit omnia*
*semper sit laus, uobisque gracia,*
*qui fecistis michi tot patrias*
*subiugatas et tributarias.*

Rex Puero:

*Puer bone, nobis edissere*
*de qua terra, de quo sis genere,*
*cuius ritu*[2] *gens tue patrie:*
*sunt gentiles, siue Christicole?*

Puer:

*Excorande principans populo,*
*pater meus, Getron uocabulo,*
*Deum colit, cuius sunt maria,*
*qui fecit nos et uos et omnia.*

[1] seruicio] Preceded by *imperio*, deleted by underlining (MS).

[2] cuius ritu] D suggests emendation *cujus ritus*, or *de quo ritu*.

Rex:

*Deus meus Apollo; deus est*
*qui me | fecit; verax et bonus est;*
*regit terras, regnat in ethere.*[1]
*Illi soli debemus credere.*

Puer:

*Deus tuus mendax et malus est;*
*stultus, cecus, surdus et mutus est;*
*talem deum non debes colere,*[2]
*qui non potest seipsum regere.*

Rex:

*Noli, puer, talia dicere;*
*deum meum noli despicere;*
*nam si eum iratum feceris,*
*euadere nequaquam poteris.*

Interea Eufrosina, comperta obliuione Filii, ad ec⟨c⟩lesiam Nicholai redit; cumque Filium suum quesitum non inuenerit,[3] lamentabili uoce ⟨dicat⟩:[4]

*Heu! heu! heu! michi misere!*
*Quid agam? Quid queam dicere?*
*Quo peccato merui perdere*
*natum meum, et ultra uiuere?*

*Cur me pater infelix genuit?*
*Cur me mater infelix abluit?*
*Cur me nutrix lactare debuit?*
*Mortem michi quare non prebuit?*

Consolatrices exeant et dicant: |

*Quid te iuuat hec desolacio?*
*Noli flere pro tuo filio.*
*Summi Patris exora Filium,*
*qui*[5] *conferat ei consilium.*

Eufrosina, quasi non curans consolacionem earum:

*Fili care, fili carissime,*
*fili, mee magna pars anime,*
*nunc es nobis causa tristicie*
*quibus eras causa leticie!*

Consolatrices:

*Ne desperes de Dei gracia,*
*cuius magna misericordia*
*istum tibi donauit puerum;*
*tibi reddet aut hunc aut alium.*

[1] ethere] etthere (MS).

[2] colere] Written by a later hand over *credere*, which has been deleted by underlining (MS).

[3] inuenerit] inueniret (MS).

[4] Some of the letters in this rubric, and in the succeeding one, are indistinct at the edge of the page.

[5] qui] quo (MS).

Eufrosina:

*Anxiatus est in me spiritus.*
*Cur moratur meus interitus?*
*Cum te, fili, non possum*[1] *cernere,*
*mallem mori quam diu uiuere.*

Consolatrices:

*Luctus, dolor et desperacio*
*tibi nocent, nec prosunt filio;*
*sed pro eo de tuis opibus*
*da clericis atque pauperibus.*

*Nicholai roga clemenciam,*
*ut exoret | misericordiam*
*summi Patris pro tuo filio;*
*nec fal⟨l⟩etur tua peticio.*

Eufrosina:

*Nicholae, pater sanctissime,*
*Nicholae, Deo carissime,*
*si uis ut te colam diucius,*
*fac ut meus redeat filius!*

*Qui saluasti multos in pelago,*
*et tres uiros a mortis uinculo,*
*preces mei*[2] *precantis audias,*
*et ex illo me certam facias.*

*Non comedam carnem diucius*
*necque uino fruar ulterius,*
*nullo modo letabor amplius,*
*donec meus redibit filius.*

Getron:

*Cara soror, lugere desine;*
*tue tibi nil prosunt lacrime;*
*sed oretur pro nostro filio*
*summi Patris propiciacio.*

*In crastino erit festiuitas*
*Nicholai, quem Christianitas*
*tota debet | deuote colere,*
*uenerari et benedicere.*

*Audi ergo mea consilia:*
*adeamus eius sollempnia;*
*conlaudemus eius magnalia;*
*deprecemur eius suffragia.*

[1] possum] Inserted by a later hand (MS). [2] mei] mee (MS).

*Dei forsan est inspiracio*
*que me monet pro nostro filio;*
*est oranda cum Dei gracia*
*Nicholai magna clemencia.*

Tunc resurgant; ad ecclesiam Sancti Nicolai eant, in quam cum introierint, tendat manus suas ad celum Eufrosina, et dicat:

*Summe ⟨Pater⟩,*[1] *regum Rex omnium,*
*Rex unicorum remoriencium,*[2]
*nostrum nobis fac redi filium,*
*uite nostre solum solacium!*

*Audi preces ad te clamancium,*
*qui in mundum misisti filium,*
*qui*[3] *nos ciues celorum faceret*
*et inferni claustris eriperet!*

*Deus Pater, cuius potencia*
*bona bonis ministrat omnia,*
*peccatricem | me noli spernere,*
*sed me meum natum fac cernere!*

*Nicholae, quem sanctum dicimus,*
*si sunt uera que de te credimus,*
*tua nobis et nostro filio*
*erga Deum prosit oracio!*

His dictis, exeat ab ecclesia, et eat in domum suam, et paret mensam, et super mensam panem et uinum, unde Clerici et Pauperes reficiantur. Quibus uocatis et comedere incipientibus, dicat Marmorinus Ministris suis:

*Dico uobis, mei carissimi,*
*quod ante hanc diem non habui*
*famem tantam quantam nunc habeo;*
*famem istam ferre non ualeo.*

*Uos igitur quo uesci debeam*
*preparate, ne mortem subeam.*
*Quid tardatis? Ite velocius;*
*quod manducem parate cicius.*

Ministri euntes afferant cibos et dicant Regi:

*Ad preceptum tuum parauimus*
*cibos tuos, et huc adtulimus;*
*nunc, si uelis, poteris propere*
*qua grauaris famem extinguere.*

[1] Emendation of D.
[2] unicorum remoriencium] Emendations: vivorum et morientium (M.W.C); unicus et spes mortalium (D).
[3] qui] quo (MS).

His dictis, afferatur aqua, et lauet manus suas Rex, et incipiens comedere,[1] dicat: |

*Esuriui et modo sicio;*
*uinum michi dari precipio;*
*quod afferat michi quam cicius*
*⟨servus⟩*[2] *meus Getronis filius.*

Puer itaque, h*ec* audiens, suspiret grauiter et secum dicat:

*Heu! heu! heu! michi misero!*
*Uite mee finem desidero;*
*uiuus enim quamdiu fuero,*
*liberari nequaquam potero.*

Rex Puero:

*Pro qua causa suspiras taliter?*
*Suspirare te uidi fortiter.*
*Quid est pro quo sic suspiraueris?*
*Quid te nocet, aut unde quereris?*

Puer:

*Recordatus mee miserie,*
*mei patris et mee patrie,*
*suspirare cepi et gemere,*
*et intra me talia dicere:*

*Annus unus expletur ⟨h⟩odie*
*postquam seruus factus miserie,*
*potestati subiectus regie,*
*fines huius intraui patrie.*

Rex:

*Heu! miselle, quid ita cogitas?*
*Quid te iuuat cordis anxietas?*
*Nemo potest te | michi tollere*
*quamdiu te non uelim perdere.*

Interea ueniat aliquis in similitudine Nicholai; Puerum, ciphum cum recentario tenentem, ap⟨p⟩rehendat, ap⟨p⟩rehensumque ante fores componat, et quasi non compertus, recedat. Tunc uero unus de Ciuibus ad Puerum dicat:[3]

*Puer, quis es, et quo uis pergere?*[4]
*Cuius tibi dedit largicio*
*cyp⟨h⟩um istum cum recentario?*

Puer:

*Huc uenio, non ibo longius;*
*sum Getronis unicus filius.*

[1] comedere] commedere (MS).
[2] Emendation of M, W, and D.
[3] Some of the letters in this rubric are indistinct at the edge of the page.
[4] D notes the lack of a line to rhyme with this one.

*Nicholao sit laus et gloria,*
*cuius hic me reduxit gracia.*

Quo audito, currat Ciuis ille ad Getronem et dicat:

*Gaude, Getron, nec fleas amplius;*
*extra fores stat tuus filius.*
*Nicholai laudat magnalia,*
*cuius eum reduxit gracia.*

Cumque huiusmodi nuncium audierit Eufrosina, ad Filium suum currat; quem sepius deosculatum amplexetur et dicat:[1]

*Deo nostro sit laus et gloria,*
*cuius magna misericordia,*
*luctus nostros uertens in gaudium,*
*nostrum nobis reduxit filium!*

*Si⟨n⟩tque patri nostro perpetue*
*Nicholao lau|des et gracie,*
*cuius erga Deum oracio*
*nos adiuuit in hoc negocio.*

Chorus omnis:

*Copiose karitatis,* ⟨*Nicholae pontifex,*
*Qui cum Deo gloriaris* *in cœli palatio,*
*Condescende, supplicamus,* *ad te suspirantibus,*
*Ut exutos gravi carne* *pertrahas ad superos.*⟩[2]

Hic finit.[3]

The action of this ambitious play opens with a scene in which the heathen king, Marmorinus, orders his soldiers to go forth and subdue as many nations as possible. Meanwhile, in the city of Excoranda, Getron and Euphrosina have taken their boy Adeodatus to a feast of St Nicholas in the church dedicated to this saint. When the army of Marmorinus attacks this church, the parents of Adeodatus flee, leaving their son a captive. The boy is led off to king Marmorinus, who after giving victorious thanks to Apollo, questions Adeodatus as to his parentage and religion. In his straightforward response the lad declares with especial vigour his allegiance to the Christian deity, and his contempt for the god of Marmorinus. Meanwhile, in Excoranda, Euphrosina is lamenting the loss of her son, while her women try in vain to console her. At their suggestion she prays to St Nicholas, reminding him of his previous miracles, and vowing

[1] A few letters in this rubric are indistinct at the edge of the page.

[2] For the text of this antiphon see *Sarum Breviary*, iii, 37; Chevalier, *R.H.*, no. 3864.

[3] Followed immediately in the MS by the rubric *Incipit ordo ad representandum Herodem*, introducing the version of the *Officium Stellæ* printed above, pp. 84 sqq.

to fast until the return of Adeodatus. After enduring unhappiness for a year, Getron persuades his wife to join him in celebrating the returning feast of St Nicholas at the church. Having offered her prayer to God and her patron saint, Euphrosina returns home and serves a generous meal to the clergy and the poor. Meanwhile at the city of Marmorinus this king is ordering a sumptuous meal for himself. When he commands that Adeodatus shall serve his wine, he overhears the boy sighing, and, through questioning, finds that Adeodatus is pining for his parents and home. Marmorinus indignantly declares that no one shall remove the boy against the will of his captor. At this utterance, however, St Nicholas appears, wafts Adeodatus to the gates of Excoranda, and disappears. To one of the citizens the boy explains his parentage and the manner of his rescue. The citizen reports to Getron, and at the close of the action Euphrosina is embracing her son, and giving thanks to God and St Nicholas. At the conclusion the chorus sings the versified antiphon *Copiose caritatis*.

A glance at the traditional legend discloses the fact that although the dramatist follows the outline of the story faithfully, he shows a certain discrimination in the selection of material.[1] He omits from consideration, for example, the first part of the narrative, in which we are told of the parents' desire for a son, of their preserving relics of St Nicholas and erecting a church to honour him, and of their receiving, in recognition of their piety, a child significantly named *A-deo-datus*. At the opening of the play this boy is represented as being already well grown. The omission of introductory considerations undoubtedly makes for a desirable concentration, but it leaves certain aspects of the play unexplained—the name Adeodatus, for example, and the unusual attachment of the parents to the particular saint.[2]

More important than the playwright's independence in selection, however, is his tact in characterization. This talent is shown particularly in the role of the boy, Adeodatus.[3] Attributable to the dramatist, for example, is the first conversation between King Marmorinus and the boy, in which the spirited retorts of the latter reveal a genuine individuality.[4] Further individualization appears in a later conversation, in which the boy confesses his homesickness.[5] The personality of the king

[1] For a version of the legend see below, p. 492.

[2] See Weydig, p. 94.

[3] See Sepet, *Origines*, pp. 68–9; Petit de Julleville, i, 75; Weydig, pp. 94–5.

[4] See ll. 33 sqq.

[5] See ll. 141 sqq.

himself is also developed considerably beyond any suggestion found in the legend. Since the peremptoriness of Marmorinus' manner and the regal ceremonial of his court are in the tradition of the Herod of Church drama, we may infer here the influence of the well-known plays of Epiphany.[1] A similar influence from other plays may be inferred for the lament of Euphrosina. Although the legend itself provides her with a sufficient expression of grief, the presence of the *consolatrices* and the general form of their dialogue with Euphrosina seem to show that the writer has profited from his acquaintance with the scenes of Rachel in the *Ordo Rachelis*.[2]

The playwright is obviously alert also to the realistic and spectacular aspects of his subject. He appears to have visualized the details of the meal set before King Marmorinus, and of the collation which Euphrosina sets forth in pantomime at her house, for the poor and the clergy. Spectacular, certainly, are the military assault upon the church at Excoranda, the abduction of Adeodatus, and the rescue of the boy by St Nicholas.[3]

In contrast to such a play as the *Iconia Sancti Nicolai* from the same monastery, however, the present play shows surprisingly little variety in versification. With slight exceptions, the form used throughout is a quatrain, rhyming usually *aabb*, and occasionally *aaaa*; and the quatrains are never broken by the dialogue. Such a succession of unbroken stanzas produces the hymn-like lyrical effect which we have observed in the plays from Hildesheim.[4]

In staging, this play is considerably more ambitious than any of the other plays of St Nicholas; and possibly the theatrical demands imposed by the nature of the legend account for the fact that only a single dramatization of it is known. Fortunately the rubrics describe the *mise en scène* rather generously.[5] At one side of the playing-space is the *sedes* of King Marmorinus. At this place the king occupies a raised throne, surrounded by his courtiers and soldiers. On the other side of the space is represented the city of Excoranda, in which reside the family of Getron and the *consolatrices* of his wife, Euphrosina. Near this *sedes* (*ab orientali parte civitatis Excorandæ*) is the church of

[1] See above, especially chapter xix.

[2] See above, chapter xx. Compare, for example, Euphrosina's *Anxiatus est in me spiritus* (l. 61) and Rachel's *Anxiatus est in me spiritus meus* (see above, p. 113).

[3] See Sepet, *Origines*, pp. 70–2.

[4] See above, pp. 311, 324.

[5] For remarks on staging see Weydig, pp. 96–7.

St Nicholas from which the boy, Adeodatus, is abducted. The amount of action upon the playing-space was considerable. The soldiers of King Marmorinus pass from the court of the king to the church of St Nicholas and back; the family of Getron and the clerics pass back and forth between the city of Excoranda and the church; and finally St Nicholas conveys the boy from the court of Marmorinus back across the stage to Excoranda. This last bit of action raises the question as to whether the stage properties included some sort of mechanical aid to realism.

The activity upon the stage draws attention to one other aspect of the play: the violation of the 'unities'.[1] The place changes from one city to another, and the captivity of Adeodatus is represented as enduring for a full year.[2] This year must be assumed to pass between the last speech in Euphrosina's lament (ll. 73–84) and the immediately succeeding speech of Getron. For this need the text scarcely makes adequate provision.

In spite of its theatrical demands, the play may have been attached directly to the liturgy. The performance ends, in any case, with the choral singing of the antiphon *Copiose caritatis*, which is most often found accompanying the *Benedictus* of Lauds.[3] It is possible, therefore, that the play was given at this point in the liturgy of St Nicholas' day, or at some other moment in the *cursus* at which this antiphon was used.[4]

[1] See Sepet, *Origines*, p. 72.

[2] See l. 145.

[3] See, for example, the *historia* published by Young, *Miracle Play*, p. 263; Chevalier, *Bayeux*, p. 193; *Sarum Breviary*, iii, 37.

[4] For the use of *Copiose caritatis* at the *Magnificat* of Second Vespers of St Nicholas' day see Chevalier, *Laon*, p. 209. From certain words of Getron in the play (ll. 89–90, *In crastino erit festivitas Nicholai*), Creizenach infers (i, 99—following Monmerqué, in *Mélanges*, vii, 125) that the performance occurred on the vigil, December 5. Concerning the structure of Lauds and Vespers see above, i, 64, 71.

## CHAPTER XXVII

# PLAYS ON SUBJECTS FROM ESCHATOLOGY

## THE WISE AND FOOLISH VIRGINS—ANTICHRIST

THE prominence given in the New Testament and in patristic writings to prophecies and parables concerning the 'last things', or the events associated with the general end of the world, could not fail to arouse in the medieval worshipper a profound feeling of apprehension.[1] The fear inspired by the mere conception of a Last Judgement was intensified by the Christian assurance that one could know neither the day nor the hour when it should come.[2] This undertone of anxiety is betrayed in repeated, but unauthorized, attempts to predict the final date, and it finds rich expression in ecclesiastical eloquence and plastic art. It inevitably moved the playwrights of the Church also to present the terrifying themes of eschatology upon the stage. The number of these plays must have been considerable, if we may judge from the popularity of such subjects in the vernacular religious drama of the later Middle Ages. Of early plays in Latin, however, only two are preserved. One briefly dramatizes the parable of the wise and foolish virgins recounted by Christ in his general discourse to the disciples concerning his second coming and the end of the world.[3] The other play treats elaborately the theme of Antichrist, referred to frequently in the New Testament, and liberally expounded by medieval commentators.

### The Wise and Foolish Virgins

The play upon the theme of the wise and foolish virgins is found, under the title *Sponsus*, in a manuscript of the eleventh or twelfth century from the monastery of St Martial at Limoges:[4]

[1] For a general discussion of eschatology, with a noteworthy bibliography, see J. A. MacCulloch, in Hastings, *Encyclopædia*, v, 373–91.

[2] See Matt. xxv, 13.

[3] See Matt. xxv, 1–13.

[4] Paris, Bibl. Nat., MS lat. 1139, Trop. Martialense sæc. xi–xii, fol. $53^r$–$55^v$, critically edited by W. Cloetta, in *Romania*, xxii (1893), 177–229 (C). It is expected that a new critical edition by L.-P. Thomas will appear in the series *Classiques français du Moyen Âge* (Paris, Champion). The Romance dialect used in the play has been systematically studied by Cloetta (pp. 177–220), who assigns it to St-Amant-de-Boixe, some ten miles north of Angoulême, and about fifty miles west of Limoges. In preparing the present text I have been most generously aided by my colleague, Professor Raymond T. Hill. He must, however, be absolved from responsibility for the use which I have made of his guidance. I hardly need say that I do not undertake to present the immense body of textual commentary accumulated by previous editors. I aim to record the actual

## Sponsus

⟨Chorus:⟩

*Adest Sponsus, | qui est Christus, uigilate, uirgines!*
*Pro aduentu cuius gaudent et gaudebunt homines.*

*Venit enim liberare gentium origines,*
*Quas per primam sibi matrem subiugarunt demones.*

*Hic est Adam qui secundus per propheta⟨m⟩ dicitur,*
*Per quem scelus primi Ade a nobis diluitur.*

*Hic pependit ut celesti patrie nos redderet,*
*Ac de parte inimici liberos nos traheret.*

*Venit Sponsus qui nostrorum scelerum piacula*
*Morte lauit atque crucis sustulit patibula.*

⟨Accedant⟩ Prvdentes, ⟨et dicat Gabriel:⟩

*Oiet, uirgines, aiso que uos dirum.*
*Aiseet presen que uos comandarum.*
*Atendet un espos, Ihesu*[1] *Saluaire a nom,*
*Gaire noi | dormet!*
*Aisel espos que uos hor atendet.*

*Uenit en terra per los uostres pechet,*
*De la uirgine en Betleem fo net,*
*E flum Iorda lauet e bateet,*[2]
*Gaire ⟨noi dormet!*
*Aisel espos que uos hor atendet⟩.*

*Eu fo batut, gabet*[3] *e laideniet,*
*Sus e la crot batut e claufiget,*
*Eu*[4] *monumen desoentre pauset,*
*Gaire ⟨noi dormet!*
*Aisel espos que uos hor atendet⟩.*

*E resors es, la scriptura o dii.*
*Gabriels soi, eu ⟨m'a⟩ trames aici.*
*Atendet lo, que ia uenra praici,*
*Gaire ⟨noi dormet!*
*Aisel espos que uos hor atendet⟩.*

Fatve:

*Nos uirgines que ad uos uenimus,*
*Negligenter oleum fundimus;*

readings of the MS always, and to retain these readings in the text itself when they can be considered admissible. The result is a text which shows, no doubt, less literary finish than do some of the highly emended editions, but which is, I hope, faithful to the MS. For further bibliography see Notes, p. 495. See also plate xxiii.

[1] Ihesu] Omitted by C, for metrical reasons. A more radical emendation of the line is proposed by Thomas, *Versification*, pp. 20–4.

[2] bateet] buteet, *or* luteet (?MS). See Thomas, *Versification*, pp. 35–7.

[3] gabet] gablet (MS).

[4] Eu] Deu (MS).

*Ad*[1] *uos orare, sorores, cupimus,*
*Ut ad*[2] *illas quibus nos credimus.*
*Dolentas, chaitiuas, trop i auem dormit!*

*Nos co|mites huius itineris*
*Et sorores eiusdem generis,*
*Quamuis male contigit miseris,*
*Potestis nos reddere superis.*
*Do⟨lentas, chaitiuas, trop i auem dormit⟩!*

*Partimini lumen lampadibus,*
*Pie sitis insipientibus,*
*Pulse ne nos simus a foribus,*
*Cum uos Sponsus uocet in sedibus.*
*Dole⟨ntas, chaitiuas, trop i auem dormit⟩!*

Prvdentes:[3]

*Nos precari, precamur, amplius*
*Desinite, sorores, ocius.*[4]
*Uobis enim nil erit melius*
*Dare preces pro hoc ulterius.*
*Dolentas, ⟨chaitiuas, trop i auet dormit!⟩*

*Ac ite nunc, ite celeriter,*
*Ac uendentes rogate dulciter*
*Ut oleum uestris lampadibus*
*Dent equidem uobis inertibus.*
*Do⟨lentas, chaitiuas, trop i auet dormit⟩!*

⟨Fatuæ:⟩

*A! misere, nos hic quid facimus?*
*Uigilare numquid po|tuimus?*
*Hunc laborem, que⟨m⟩ nunc perferimus,*
*Nobis nosmet ipsæ*[5] *contulimus.*
*Dol⟨entas, chaitiuas, trop i auem dormit⟩!*

*Et de⟨t⟩ nobis mercator ocius*[6]
*Quas habeat merces, quas socius;*[7]
*Oleum nunc querere uenimus,*
*Negligenter quod nosmet fudimus.*[8]
*Dol⟨entas, chaitiuas, trop i auem dormit⟩!*

⟨Prudentes:⟩

*De nostr'oli queret nos a doner.*
*No'n auret pont, alet en achapter*

[1] Ad] C omits, for metrical reasons.

[2] ad] et (MS). C transposes l. 34 to a position between ll. 31 and 32.

[3] Prudentes] Opposite this word, in the extreme left margin, is written *prudē*—probably as a reminder to the rubricator.

[4] ocius] otius (MS).

[5] nosmet ipsæ] nosmed (MS).

[6] ocius] otius (MS).

[7] socius] sotius (MS).

[8] nosmet fudimus] nosme fundimus (MS).

*Deus merchaans que lai ueet ester.*

. . . . . . .

*Dol⟨entas, chaitiuas, trop i auet dormit⟩!*[1]

Mercatores:

*Domnas gentils, no uos couent ester,*
*Ni loiamen aici a demorer.*
*Cosel queret, nou uos poem doner;*
*Queret lo Deu, chi uos pot coseler.*

*Alet areir a uostras sinc seros,*
*E preiet*[2] *las per Deu lo glorios*
*De oleo fasen socors a uos;*
*Faites o tost, que ia uenra l'espos.* |

Fa⟨tuæ⟩:[3]

*A! misere, nos ad quid uenimus?*
*Nil est enim illut quod querimus.*
*Fatatum est, et nos uidebimus;*
*Ad nuptias numquam intrabimus.*
*Dol⟨entas, chaitiuas, trop i auem dormit⟩!*

Modo veniat Sponsus.[4] ⟨Fatuæ dicant:⟩

*Avdi,*[5] *Sponse, uoces plangentium:*
*Aperire fac nobis ostium*
*Cum sociis*[6] *⟨ad dulce prandium;*
*Nostræ culpæ⟩ prebe remedium!*
*⟨Dolentas, chaitiuas, trop i auem dormit!⟩*

Christus:[7]

*Amen dico, uos ignosco, nam caretis lumine,*
*Quod qui perdunt*[8] *procul pergunt huius aule limine.*[9]
*Alet, chaitiuas, alet, malaureas!*
*A tot iors mais uos so penas liureas;*
*En*[10] *efern ora seret meneias!*

Modo accipiant eas Demones, et precipitentur in infernum.[11]

[1] ll. 66–70 C transposes to a position between ll. 55 and 56. The order of the MS is defended by Thomas, *Strophes*, p. 75. The fourth line of the stanza has been omitted from the MS.

[2] preiet] preiat (MS).

[3] This rubric is not written in the body of the text, but is indicated by the letters *fa* in the extreme left margin.

[4] In the extreme left margin opposite l. 84 are written the words *modo veniat sponsus*—presumably as a guide to the rubricator. In the body of the text, however, this rubric is written only over *Christus*, before l. 89.

[5] Avdi] Mvdi (?MS).

[6] sociis] sotiis (MS). I follow C in using the conjectural restoration of ll. 86–7 suggested by Gaston Paris.

[7] Opposite this rubric, in the extreme left margin, is written an abbreviation for *Christus*—presumably as a guide to the rubricator.

[8] perdunt] pergunt (MS).

[9] limine] lumine (MS).

[10] En] E en (C)—an attractive metrical emendation.

[11] Followed immediately in the MS by the verses *Omnes gentes, congaudentes*, beginning the version of the *Ordo Prophetarum* printed above, pp. 138 sqq.

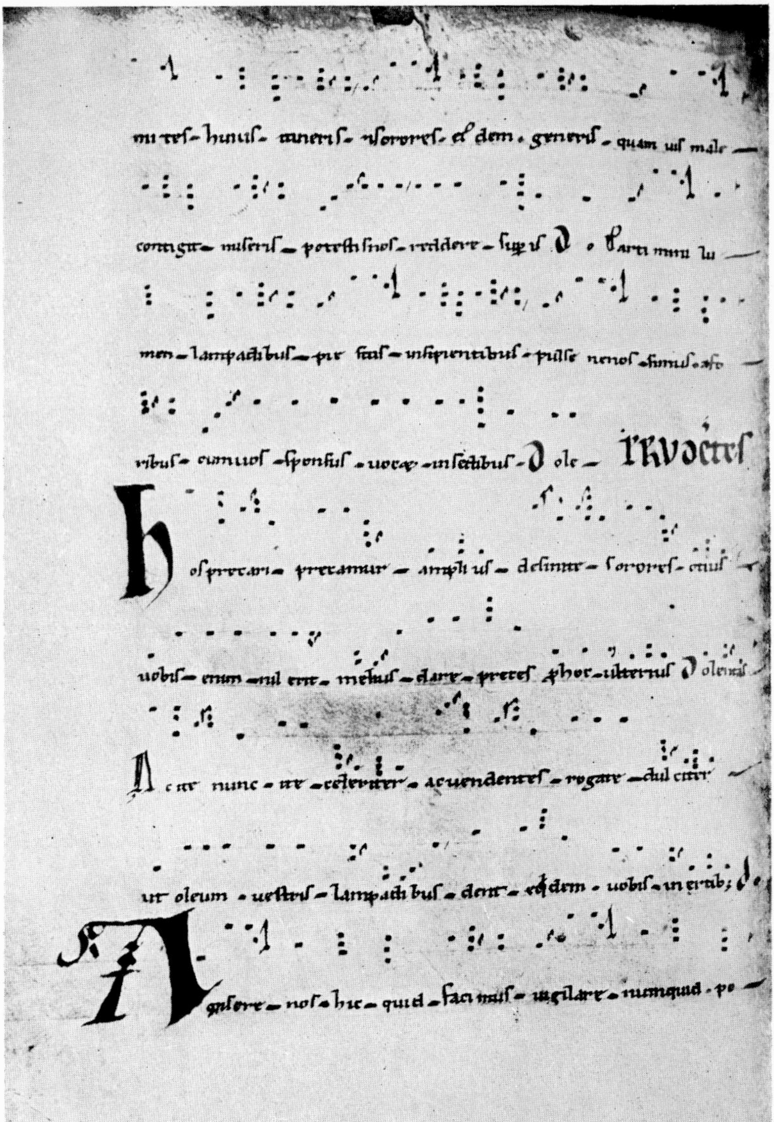

XXIII. Play of the Wise and Foolish Virgins (*Sponsus*), from Limoges, in Paris, Bibliothèque Nationale, MS lat. 1139, fol. 54v

The qualities of this stirring little play will be more readily discernible if we have before us the parable which inspired it.[1]

1. Tunc simile erit regnum cœlorum decem virginibus, quæ accipientes lampades suas exierunt obviam sponso et sponsæ.

2. Quinque autem ex eis erant fatuæ, et quinque prudentes.

3. Sed quinque fatuæ, acceptis lampadibus, non sumpserunt oleum secum.

4. Prudentes vero acceperunt oleum in vasis suis cum lampadibus.

5. Moram autem faciente sponso, dormitaverunt omnes et dormierunt.

6. Media autem nocte clamor factus est: Ecce sponsus venit, exite obviam ei.

7. Tunc surrexerunt omnes virgines illæ, et ornaverunt lampades suas.

8. Fatuæ autem sapientibus dixerunt: Date nobis de oleo vestro, quia lampades nostræ extinguuntur.

9. Responderunt prudentes, dicentes: Ne forte non sufficiat nobis et vobis, ite potius ad vendentes, et emite vobis.

10. Dum autem irent emere, venit sponsus; et quæ paratæ erant, intraverunt cum eo ad nuptias, et clausa est janua.

11. Novissime vero veniunt et reliquæ virgines, dicentes: Domine, Domine, aperi nobis.

12. At ille respondens ait: Amen dico vobis, nescio vos.

13. Vigilate itaque, quia nescitis diem neque horam.

From a comparison of the play with this narrative it appears that the most original aspect of the dramatic version is the centring of interest upon the foolish virgins, and the emphasis, not so much upon the failure of the *fatuæ* to provide themselves with oil, as upon their sleeping too long.[2] This emphasis is enforced by the *vigilate* of the opening line of the play, and by the refrains *Gaire noi dormet* and *Dolentas, chaitivas, trop i avem dormit.*[3] The Biblical motif of the neglected oil is, of course, adequately represented in the play; but it is made to appear that the chief delinquency of the *fatuæ* is their failure to be awake. From the dramatic text as it stands, indeed, one would infer that the wise virgins obey precisely the injunction *vigilate*, and that only the *fatuæ* sleep at all. In the absence of rubrics we may assume, if we wish, that the foolish ones fall asleep immediately after the opening speech, and that they continue in their slumber throughout Gabriel's address to the *prudentes*.[4]

[1] Matt. xxv, 1–13.

[2] See Fischer, pp. 11–5; Morf, p. 388.

[3] The command *Vigilate* is, of course, found in the closing verse of the parable (Matt. xxv, 13).

[4] Schwan (p. 470) infers that the *fatuæ* do not appear at all until they speak in l. 31.

It is possible, to be sure, that both the *prudentes* and the *fatuæ* are awake during the first two speeches, and that both then lie down for a brief slumber, and presently rise together. The refrain *trop i avem dormit*, of the third speech, might then imply not that the *fatuæ* have slept longer than the *prudentes*, but that the former, being unprovided with oil, could less well afford to sleep at all.[1] The first interpretation seems to fit the situation more adequately. Whatever arrangement of the action may be intended by the text, the play obviously departs from the parable in the salience given to the need of remaining awake.

The dramatic prominence of the foolish virgins is further emphasized by their extended laments. Although these recall the sorrowings of the Marys in the Easter plays, and of Rachel in the *Ordo Rachelis*, we may safely enough assume that the present author invented them to meet his own immediate needs.[2] Similarly the *mercatores* of the present play have a parallel in the *unguentarius* who sells spices to the Marys in the Easter play.[3] Presumably, however, the merchants now before us owe their existence not to imitation of other plays, but to the plain suggestion of the Biblical source.[4]

Likewise original in the play is the vigour of the *dénouement*. The closing words of Christ, consigning the foolish virgins to Hell, and the alacrity of the devils in executing this command, are not mere amplifications of what is found concerning the *fatuæ* in the Gospel, but are additions of the playwright. This enlargement may have been inspired by passages concerning the Last Judgement such as the following from the latter part of the chapter which contains the parable of the wise and foolish virgins:[5]

[1] Morf (p. 388) infers that both the *fatuæ* and the *prudentes* are to be represented as asleep at the opening of the play, that the *prudentes* awake after the first speech, and that the *fatuæ* rise only after the second speech. Fischer (pp. 11–2) thinks that the *vigilate*, rather than *surgite*, of the opening line precludes this arrangement. Cloetta (*Époux*, p. 226) infers that the *fatuæ* fall asleep and awake between the second speech and the third. He does not explain whether he regards the *prudentes* as having behaved similarly.

[2] See above, for example, i, 385, 393, 398. Beckers (p. 39) appears to regard as imitations of the Easter plays not only these laments, but also several other features of the present play, such as the opening speech.

[3] See above, for example, i, 405, 423, 435.

[4] See Matt. xxv, 9–10; Fischer, p. 19. Borrowing from the Easter plays is rendered improbable also by considerations of chronology.

[5] Matt. xxv, 41, 46. See Fischer, p. 18. Fischer's suggestion that the *dæmones* in our play are borrowed from the dramatic representations of the Harrowing of Hell in certain plays or dramatic ceremonies of Easter appears to be invalidated by the relatively late date of the latter. See Rudwin, *Teufel*, p. 2, and above, chapter v, and i, 425, 430.

Discedite a me, maledicti, in ignem æternum, qui paratus est diabolo et angelis ejus.

Et ibunt hi in supplicium æternum.

Whatever the origin of the devils who here make their *début* in the drama of the Church, they are, in the present instance, employed not comically, but with grim seriousness.[1]

As to the relation between the present bilingual text and a hypothetical original Latin play, or between the Romance and the Latin passages of the play as preserved, a diversity of conjectures is possible.[2] It has been inferred, for example, that the original Latin play may be disclosed by simply withdrawing all the vernacular passages, the latter being merely enlargements and paraphrases unessential to the fundamental structure.[3] One critic who takes this general view regards the French speeches as attempts to aid the unlettered congregation through making intelligible to them merely the most significant moments in the action. Accordingly the vernacular parts are regarded not as translations of Latin, but as general expository summaries or additions.[4] Another critic looks upon the Latin lines as preserving completely the original liturgical play, but regards the vernacular amplification as somewhat fragmentary in the extant text. Thus lines 66 to 68 are considered to be a misplaced remnant of an original exchange of speeches between *Prudentes* and *Fatuæ*.[5] The boldest view is that of Stengel, who holds that the extant text is fragmentary throughout. He surmises that the play consisted originally of the following four successive dialogues: *Gabriel* and *Prudentes*, *Fatuæ* and *Prudentes*, *Fatuæ* and *Mercatores*, and *Fatuæ* and *Sponsus*. Each dialogue consisted, he thinks, of two Latin speeches, the pair of speeches being followed by a vernacular translation.[6]

Probably no one of these views will be accepted universally. In some of its details the extant text must be regarded as fragmentary or disordered. The second speech of the *prudentes* (ll. 66–70), for example, seems clearly to indicate incompleteness

[1] See Fischer, p. 9; Rudwin, *Teufel*, pp. 7–8.

[2] In speaking of the Romance passages I mean to include the occasional Latin words imbedded therein. See, for example, ll. 11, 16, 17, 26. Thomas (*Versification*, pp. 47 sqq.) holds that originally the Romance text contained a still larger number of Latin words.

[3] See Beckers, pp. 38–9.

[4] See Schwan, pp. 471–2. This is the general view of Thomas (*Strophes*, pp. 72 sqq., 104 sqq.), who examines in detail the devices employed by the vernacular reviser.

[5] See Morf, pp. 385–90.

[6] See Stengel, pp. 235–7.

or displacement; and the rubric *Prudentes*, standing by itself before the second speech of the play (ll. 11–30), is hardly intelligible. It is obvious also that the vernacular parts differ as to the closeness with which they follow the related Latin passages. The first vernacular passage (ll. 11–30) shows certain resemblances to the Latin which precedes; and the refrain *Gaire noi dormet! Aisel espos que vos hor atendet* might be regarded as a general rendering of the opening line of the play.[1] In the final speech of Christ, on the other hand, the Romance passage contains none of the sense of the Latin lines, and introduces into the action a fresh notion.[2]

The text before us bears no evidence of attachment to the liturgy, or of having developed from liturgical pieces.[3] The play may, or may not, have been performed within the church. As to the day on which the performance occurred we are also left in uncertainty. Most critics have assigned it to the season of Advent or Christmas;[4] but from the reference to the Passion and Resurrection in Gabriel's second speech some have inferred that it belongs to the cycle of Easter.[5] The passage of the Gospel recounting the parable was used liturgically on a variety of days throughout the year in various communities, but chiefly on feasts of holy virgins.[6] In view of these facts one cannot confidently attach the play to a specific liturgical season.

The closing rubric concerning the devils is our only explicit evidence as to *mise en scène*. If the playing-space was provided with some practical representation of the mouth of Hell, we may infer that it was equipped also with stage devices of other kinds, such as a booth for the merchants, and a door to the wedding-apartment.[7] Probably the characters were impersonated with some care; Gabriel, no doubt, had his wings, and the virgins, their vessels for oil.[8]

[1] See Sepet, *Origines*, p. 112; Cloetta, p. 224.

[2] See Schwan, p. 472.

[3] See Heyne, pp. 25–7.

[4] See Chambers, ii, 62; Sepet, *Drame*, p. 120; Petit de Julleville, i, 27; Cloetta, *Époux*, p. 177.

[5] See Morf, pp. 390–1; Reuschel, p. 3. Morf seems to be unduly impressed by the fact that in the MS the play is immediately preceded by the Easter dialogue, *Quem quæritis in sepulchro?* See above, i, 212. Equally significant, as a matter of fact, is the circumstance that the play is immediately followed by a version of the *Ordo Prophetarum* of the Christmas season. Liuzzi (*Vergini*, p. 108) assigns the play to Holy Week.

[6] See Heyne, pp. 27–30. For a symbolical representation of the five wise virgins in the liturgy of All Saints' Day see Notes, p. 496.

[7] Morf (p. 388) suggests that for this last the entrance to the sacristy may have been used.

[8] For conjectures as to staging see especially Sepet, *Drame*, pp. 24–9, 113–20; Petit de Julleville, i, 30–4.

The inadequacies of the extant text do not obscure the general dramatic excellence of the play. The verses are vivid, and the refrains impressive. The distress of the foolish virgins is expressed with genuine feeling, and the fatal conclusion arrives with relentless force. The piece is thoughtfully conceived and carefully phrased.

## Antichrist

The simple parable of the wise and foolish virgins, and the brief dramatization of it from Limoges, produce a relatively modest impression when compared with the awesome legend of Antichrist, and the pretentious play on this subject written, perhaps at Tegernsee, in the Bavarian Alps, in the twelfth century.

According to the common understanding of the medieval Church, Antichrist was the false Messiah, or adversary and complete opposite of Christ, who was expected to appear upon earth to deceive and corrupt the faithful before the second coming of the Redeemer and the Last Judgement.[1] Although the name, Antichrist, is found first in Christian writings,[2] the conceptions associated with this word, and especially the notion of an enemy of God ruling during the last days of the world, run back into the pre-Christian period. The chief theme associated with this legend probably rests ultimately upon the general speculative notion of a battle between God and the devil at the end of time. From an original conception of a contest between God and a dragon-like monster may have arisen that of a contest of God with a human adversary in whom the devil resided. The conception of this adversary as an actual person, identifiable with one historical figure or another, can be traced back to the second century before Christ, particularly in the Book of Daniel, where it is prophesied that the great enemy shall come as a king with armies, shall persecute and destroy, and shall set up in the temple the 'abomination of desolation'.[3]

From Judaism Christianity adopted the legend in its fulness, as may be seen in the reflections of it in the New Testament.[4]

[1] Concerning the legend of Antichrist see especially H. Preuss, *Die Vorstellungen vom Antichrist im späteren Mittelalter, bei Luther und in der konfessionellen Polemik*, Leipzig, 1906, pp. 10–82; W. Bousset, *The Antichrist Legend*, London, 1896; Bousset, in Hastings, *Encyclopædia*, i, 578–81; Wadstein, pp. 81–137.

[2] See, for example, 1 John ii, 22; iv, 3; 2 John 7.

[3] See Hastings, *Encyclopædia*, i, 578; and, for example, Daniel vii, 8, 19–25; viii, 9–13; xi, 21–45; xii, 11.

[4] See Matt. xxiv, 15; Mark xiii, 14; 2 Thess. ii, 4; Rev. xiii.

In accepting the tradition, however, Christian writers altered it somewhat radically by transforming the mighty enemy of God into a more seductive personage who should seek, not so much a conquest through force, as a recognition of his divinity by means of signs and wonders. Thus Antichrist becomes definitely a false Messiah, and the direct adversary of Christ. By the fourth century was introduced into the legend a fresh element of great importance to our present consideration: namely, the Sibylline prophecy that the last emperor of Rome before the advent of Antichrist should obtain dominion over the whole world, and at the end of his reign should go to Jerusalem and lay down his crown. This became a persistent part of the tradition, and it is the most striking feature of a *sermo* of Pseudo-Methodius, available in Greek and Latin from the eighth century onwards.[1]

Of all the writings concerning Antichrist, however, the most significant for our present study is the so-called *Libellus de Antichristo* written about the middle of the tenth century by the monk, Adso, in the form of a letter to Queen Gerberga of France.[2] The essential content of Adso's treatise may be sketched as follows:

Antichrist will be in all respects the opposite of Christ—arrogant, an expert in crime, and a perverter of the Gospel. He will be born of the Jews, and at his conception the devil will enter his mother's womb. His birthplace will be Babylon, and the magicians and evil spirits who educate him will teach him wickedness, falsehood, and skill in magic. He will come to Jerusalem, will torment those whom he cannot corrupt, will proclaim himself the son of God, and will occupy a throne in the Temple. He will send his emissaries throughout the world, will convert kings and princes, and will perform miracles, such as causing trees to grow, reversing the courses of rivers, and raising the dead. He will deceive Christians, Jews, and heathen, and, after winning them to his cause, will put his sign on their foreheads. His three chief means for corrupting the faithful will be terror, gifts, and miracles. The time of his coming will be shortly before the Last Judgement, and he will reign over the world for three years and a half. Just before his advent, the

[1] For the text of the prophecy of the Tiburtine Sibyl, and for the Latin text of Pseudo-Methodius, see Sackur, pp. 60–96, 177–87.

[2] For the text of Adso see Sackur, pp. 104–13, or Migne, *P.L.*, ci, 1291–8. Sackur's text is reprinted in Notes, pp. 496 sqq.

Roman Emperor, after having brought the kingdoms of the world under his rule, will surrender his imperial authority at Jerusalem. Eventually the prophets, Enoch and Elijah, will come, will expose the falsehood of Antichrist, and will exhort the faithful to resist his authority. The prophets, and those who believe them, will be put to death, but, through the power of the Lord, will rise again after three days. Antichrist's reign of three years and a half will be ended by his death through divine intervention.

This form of the legend, which we may regard as standard for the Middle Ages, is dramatized in the following play of the twelfth century from Tegernsee:[1]

Templum Domini et vii sedes regales primum collocentur in hunc modum: Ad orientem templum Domini; huic[2] collocantur sedes Regis Hierosolimorum et sedes Sinagogę. Ad occidentem sedes Imperatoris Rom*anorum*;[3] huic[2] collocantur sedes Regis Theotonicorum et sedes Regis Francorum. Ad austrum sedes Regis Grecorum. Ad meridiem sedes Regis Babilonię et Gentilitatis. His ita ordinatis, primo procedat Gentilitas cum Rege Babiloni⟨e⟩ cantans:

*Deorum immortalitas*
*est omnibus colenda,*
*eorum et pluralitas*
*ubique metuenda.*

*Stulti sunt et uere fatui,*
*qui deum unum dicunt,*
*et*[4] *antiquitatis ritui*
*proterue contradicunt.*

*Si enim unum credimus*
*qui presit uniuersis,*
*subiectum hunc concedimus*
*contrarie diuersis,*

[1] Munich, Staatsbibl., MS lat. 19411, Miscellanea Tegirinsensia sæc. xii–xiii, pp. 6–15 (old pagination), most authoritatively edited by Meyer, *Abhandlungen*, i, 150–70 (M). This edition by Meyer supersedes his earlier one in *Sitzungsberichte der philosophisch-philologischen und historischen Classe der k. b. Akademie der Wissenschaften zu München* (1882), i, 1 sqq. A considerable amount of reconstruction is attempted in the edition by F. Wilhelm, *Der Ludus de Antichristo* (*Münchener Texte*, ed. F, Wilhelm, i), Munich, 1912 (W). See the review of this edition by S. Aschner in *Münchener Museum für Philologie des Mittelalters und der Renaissance*, i [1911–12], 355–62. In the present text I am under large obligations to Meyer, whose emendations I adopt usually, and whose line-numbering I follow throughout. For references to earlier editions, and for further bibliography, see Notes, p. 500.

[2] huic] hinc (emend. M).

[3] Romanorum] Romani (M).

[4] et] quia (MS); et (emend. M. W).

*Cum hinc bonum pacis foueat*
*clementi pietate,*
*hinc belli tumultvs moueat*
*seua crudelitate.*

*Sic multa sunt officia*[1]
*diuersaque deorum,*
*quę nobis sunt indicia*[2]
*discriminis eorum.*

*Qui ergo*[3] *tam multifariis*
*unum dicunt preesse,*
*illorum ⟨deum⟩*[4] *contrariis*
*est affici necesse.*

*Ne ergo unum subici*
*contrariis dicamvs,*
*et his diuinam affici*
*naturam concedamus,*

*Ratione hac decernimus*
*deos discriminare,*
*officia*[5] *quorum cernimus*
*ab inuicem distare.*

Quod etiam debet cantare per totum ludum in temporibus; et sic ipsa et Rex Babilon*ie* ascendunt[6] in sedem suam. Tunc sequitur Sinagoga cum Iudeis cantans:

*Nostra salvs in te, Domine;*[7]
*nulla uitę spes in homine;* |
*error est in Christi nomine*
*spem salutis estimari.*
*Mirum si morti subcubuit,*
*qui uitam aliis tribuit.*
*Qui se saluare non potuit,*
*ab hoc quis potest saluari?*
*Non hunc, sed qui est Emmanuel,*
*Deum adorab*is *Israel.*
*Ihesum sicut deos Ismahel*
*te iubeo detestari.*

Quod et ipsa cantab*it* in singulis temporibus[8] et sic ascendat tronum suum. Tunc Ecclesia in muliebri habitu procedit induta thoracem et coronata, assistente sibi Misericordia cum oleo ad dextram et Iustitia cum libra et gladio ad sinistram utrisque muliebriter indutis. Sequentur

[1] officia] offitia (MS).
[2] indicia] inditia (MS).
[3] ergo] igitur (MS).
[4] Emend. M. W.
[5] officia] offitia (MS).
[6] ascendunt] asscendunt (MS).
[7] See Jeremiah iii, 23: *Vere in Domino Deo nostro salus Israel.*
[8] temporibus] in temporibus (MS).

etiam eam Apostolicvs a dextris cum clero et Imperator Rom*anorum* a sinistris cum Militia. Cantabit autem Ecclesia conductum[1] *Alto consilio*, his qui eam secuntur ad singulos versvs respondentibus:

*Hec est fides, ex qua uita,*
*in qua mortis lex sopita.*[2]
*Quisquis est, qui credit aliter,*
*hunc dampnamus ęternaliter.*

Ascendit autem ipsa cum Apostolico et Clero, Imperatore et Militia sua, eundem tronum. Postea procedunt et alii Reges cum Militia sua, cantantes singuli, quod conueniens uisum fuerit; et sic unvsquisque cum Militia sua ascendet tronum suum, templo adhuc et uno trono uacuis remanentibus. Tunc Imperator dirig*it* Nuntios suos ad singulos Reges, et primo ad Regem Francorum dicens:

*Sicut scripta tradunt hystoriographorum,*[3]
*Totvs mundus fuerat fiscvs Romanorum.*
*Hoc primorum strenuitas elaborauit,*
*Sed posterorum desidia dissipauit.*
*Sub his inperii dilapsa est potestas,*
*Quam nostrę repetit potentię maiestas.*
*Reges ergo singuli privs instituta*
*Nunc Romano soluant inperio tributa.*
*Sed quod in milịtia ualet gens Francorum,*
*armis imperio*[4] *rex seruiat eorum.*
*Huic, ut hominium*[5] *cum fidelitate*
*Nobis in proximo faciat, imperate.*

Tunc Legati uenientes ad Regem Francorum coram eo cantent:

*Salutem mandat Imperator Romanorum*
*Dilecto suo inclito Regi Francorum.*
*Tuę discretioni notum scimus esse,*
*Quod Romano iuri tu debeas subesse.*
*Vnde te repetit sententia tenenda*[6]
*Summi imperii et semper metuenda.*
*Cuius ad seruitium nos te inuitamus*
*Et cito uenire sub precepto mandamus.*

Quibus ille:

*Historiographis si qua fides habetur,*
*Non nos imperio sed nobis hoc debetur.*
*Hoc*[7] *enim seniores Galli possederunt*

[1] conductum] ɔd̄ (MS); condit. (M); conductam (W). No appropriate hymn or trope beginning *Alto consilio* has been found. See Chevalier, *R.H.*, nos. 954, 22889, 22890. *Conductus* is well known as a term for a processional chant. See Villetard, *Corbeil*, p. 75; Gautier, *Tropes*, p. 159.

[2] See Rom. viii, 2.

[3] hystoriographorum] hystoriograuorum (MS).

[4] imperio] Corrected from *inperio* (MS).

[5] hominium] hominum (MS); hominium (emend. M. W).

[6] tenenda] M conjectures *tremenda*, which W adopts.

[7] Hoc] Illuc (MS); hoc (emend. M. W).

*Atque suis posteris   nobis reliquerunt.*
*Sed hoc inuasoria   ui nunc spoliamur.*
*Absit, inuasoribus   ut nos obsequamur.*

Tunc Legati | redeuntes ad Imperatorem cantent coram eo:

*Ecce Franci super te*[1]   *nimium elati*
*Proterue se opponunt   tuę maiestati.*
*Immo et imperii   tui ius infirmant*[2]
*Illud inuasorium   ⟨esse⟩*[3] *dvm affirmant.*
*Digna ergo pena   correpti resipiscant,*
*Ut per eos alii   obedire discant.*

Tunc Imperator cant*at*:

*Corda solent ante   ruinam*[4] *exaltari.*
*Superba stultos loqui   nolite mirari.*[5]
*Quorum nos superbiam   certe reprimemus*
*Ac eos sub pedibus   nostris conteremus.*[6]
*Et qui nunc ut milites   nolunt obedire,*[7]
*Tanquam serui postmodvm   cogent*ur *seruire.*

Et statim aciebus uadit ad expugnandum Regem Francorum. Qui sibi occurrens congreditur cum eo, et superatvs captiuus reducitur ad sedem Imperatoris. Et sedente Imperatore, stat coram eo cantans:

*Triumphi gloria   est parcere deuictis.*
*Victvs ego tuis   nunc obsequor edictis.*
*Vitam meam simul   cum regni dignitate*
*Positam fateor   in tua potestate.*
*Sed si me pristino   restitues honori,*
*Erit honor uicti   laus maxima uictori.*

Tunc Imperator eum suscipiens in hominem et concedens sibi regnum cant*at*:

*Viue per gratiam   et suscipe honorem,*
*Dum me recognoscis   solum imperatorem.*

Et ille cum honore dimissvs reuertitur in regnum suum cant*ans*:

*Romani nominis   honorem ueneramur,*
*Augusto Cesari   seruire gloriamur,*
*Cuius imperii   uirtus est formidanda,*
*Honor et gloria   maneant ueneranda.*
*Omnium rectorem,   te solum profitemur;*
*Tibi tota mente   semper obsequemur.*

Tunc Imperator dirigens Nuntios suos ad Regem Grecorum cant*at*:

*Sicut scripta tradunt   hystoriographorum,*

1 super te] M conjectures *superbi*, which W adopts. See Rom. i, 30: *superbos elatos*; 2 Tim. iii, 2: *elati superbi*.

2 infirmant] *in*firmat*ur* (MS).

3 Emend. M.W.

4 ruinam] riuam (MS); ruinam (emend. M.W). See Prov. xvi, 18: *ante ruinam exaltatur spiritus*.

5 See Ecclesiasticus xiii, 26: *locutus est superba*; 2 Peter ii, 18: *superba enim vanitatis loquentes*.

6 See Lam. of Jer. iii, 34: *ut conteret sub pedibus suis*.

7 obedire] ut milites obedire (MS).

*Quicquid habet mundus, fiscvs est Romanorum.*
*Hoc primorum strenuitas elaborauit,*
*Sed posterorum desidia dissipauit.*
*Sub his imperii dilapsa est potestas,*
*Quam nostrę repetit potentię maiestas.*
*Reges ergo singuli prius instituta*
*Nunc Romano soluant imperio tributa.*
*Hoc igitur edictum Grecis indicate*
*Et ab ipsis debitum censum reportate.*

Qui uenientes ad Regem cant*ant* coram eo:

*Salutem mandat,* 110a

et cetera, ibi mutantes,

*Cuius ad seruitium ⟨nos⟩*[1] *te inuitamus*
*Et tributvm dare sub precepto mandamus.*

Quos ille honeste suscipiens cant*at*:

*Romani nominis honorem ueneramur,*
*Tributum Cesari reddere gloriamur,*

et cetera. Eosque cum honore dimittens ipsemet ascendet[2] ad imperium cantans:

*Romani | nominis,* 114a

et cetera. Qui eum in hominem suscipiens et regnum sibi concedens cant*at*:

*Viue per gratiam,* 114b

et cetera. Tunc ille, suscepto regno, reuertitur cant*ans*:

*Romani nominis,* 114c

et cetera. Tunc iterum dirigit Nuntios suos Imperator ad Regem Ierosolimorum dic*ens*:

*Sicut scripta tradunt,* 114d

et cetera. Qui uenientes ad Regem coram eo c⟨antant⟩:

*Salutem mandat Imperator Romanorum*
*Dilecto suo regi Ierosolimorum,*

et cetera. Quibus ille honeste susceptis cant*at*:

*Romani nominis,* 116a

et cetera. Et ascendens ad imperium cant*at* hoc ipsum iterans:

*Romani nominis,* 116b

et cetera. Quo ille suscepto concedit sibi regnum. Ipso itaque reuerso in sedem suam cum iam tota ecclesia subdita sit imperio Romano, consurg*it* Rex Babylonis in medio suorum cant*ans*:

*Ecce superstitio nouitatis uanę,*
*Quam error adinuenit sectę Christianę.*
*Fere ⟨iam⟩*[3] *destruxit ritvm antiquitatis*
*Et diis subtraxit honorem deitatis.*
*Quorum cultum prorsvs deleri ne sinamus,*

[1] Emend. M.W. [2] ascendet] ascendens (MS). [3] Emend. M.W.

*Nomen Christianum  de terra deleamus.*
*Quod ab eo loco  debemus inchoare,*
*Unde primo cepit  hec secta pullulare.*

Et ordinans acies suas uadit ad obsidendam Ierosolimam. Tunc Rex Ierosolimę dirig*it* Nuntios suos ad imperium cant*ans*:

*Ite, hec ecclesię  mala nuntiantes,*
*Nobis auxilium  ab ipsa postulantes.*
*Hec dum cognouerit  Romanvs Imperator,*
*Ipse noster erit  ab hoste liberator.*

Qui uenientes ad imperium cant*ant* coram eo:

*Defensor ecclesię  nostri miserere,*
*Quos uolunt inimici  Domini delere.*
*Venerunt gentes in  Dei hereditatem,*[1]
*Obsidione*[2] *tenent  sanctam ciuitatem.*
*Locvm, in quo sancti  eius pedes steterunt,*[3]
*Ritu spurcissimo  contaminare querunt.*

Quibus ille:

*Ite, uestros propere  fratres consolantes,*
*Ut nostrum auxilium  lęti postulantes*
*Nos pro certo sciant  in proximo uenire,*
*Ne de ipsis ualeant  hostes superbire.*

Qui reuersi stant coram Rege cantantes:

*Viriliter agens*[4] *ab hoste sis securus,*
*Adpropinquat enim  ab hoc te redempturvs.*
*Quem debes in prelio  constans prestolari,*
*Per hunc te gaudeb*is  *in breui liberari.*

Interim dum Imperator colligit exercitum, Angelus Domini subito apparens c⟨antat⟩:

*Iudea*[5] *et Ierusalem  nolite timere*
*Sciens te auxilium  Dei cras uidere.*
*Nam tui fratres assunt,  qui te liberabunt*
*Atque tuos hostes  potenter superabunt.*

Tunc chorus:

*Iudea*[6] *et Ierusalem.*

[1] See Ps. lxxviii, 1: *Deus, venerunt gentes in hereditatem tuam.*

[2] Obsidione] obsidione*m* (MS).

[3] See Ps. cxxxi, 7: *ubi steterunt pedes ejus.*

[4] See 1 Chron. xxviii, 20: *Viriliter age.* For additional Biblical references see W, p. 10.

[5] Iudea] Iuda (emend. M); Juda (emend. W). See 2 Chron. xx, 17: *O Juda et Jerusalem, nolite timere, nec paveatis; cras egrediemini contra eos.*

[6] Iudea] Iuda (emend. M); Juda (emend. W). For the responsory see Hartker, p. 7: *Judea et Jerusalem, nolite timere; cras egrediemini, et Dominus erit vobiscum.* Versus: *Constantes estote; videbitis auxilium Domini super vos.* The fact that the playwright means to use this liturgical piece is shown not only by the word *responsorio* in the succeeding rubric, but also by identity of the musical notation over the three words in the dramatic text and the notation over the same words in Hartker. It appears also that ll. 143–4 are probably based upon the responsory, and not upon the passage from the Vulgate cited in the preceding note. Hence the emendation *Iuda*, or *Juda*, of M and W is unnecessary. Musical

Interim Imperator cum suis procedat ad prelium, et, finito responsorio, prelio[1] congrediatur cum Rege Babylonis; quo superato et fugam ineunte, Imperator cum suis intret templum, et postquam ibi adorauerit, tollens coronam de capite et tenens eam cum sceptro et imperio[2] ante altare cantet:

*Suscipe quod offero, nam corde benigno*
*Tibi Regi regum imperium resigno,*
*Per quem | reges regnant, qui solus*[3] *Imperator*
*Dici potes et es cunctorum gubernator.*

Et eis depositis super altare, ipse reuertitur in sedem antiqui regni sui, Ecclesia, quę secum descenderat Ierosolimam, in templo remanente. Tunc cum Ecclesia et Gentilitas et Synagoga uicissim cantant ut supra, procedant Ypocritę sub silentio et specie humilitatis inclinantes circumquaque et captantes fauorem laicorum. Ad ultimum omnes conueniant ante Ecclesiam et sedem Regis Ierosolime, qui eos honeste suscipiens ex toto se subdet eorum consilio. Statim ingreditur Antichristus sub aliis[4] indutus loricam comitantibus eum Ypocrisi a dextris et Heresi a sinistris, ad quas ipse cantat:

*Mei regni uenit hora;*[5]
*per uos ergo sine mora*
*fiat, ut conscendam regni solium.*[6]
*Me mundus adoret et non alium.*
*Vos ad ⟨hoc⟩*[7] *aptas cognoui,*
*uos ad hoc hucusque foui.*
*Ecce labor uester et industria*
*nunc ad hoc sunt mihi necessaria.*
*En Christum gentes honorant*
*uenerantur et adorant.*
*Eius ergo delete memoriam*[8]
*in me suam transferentes gloriam.*

Ad Ypocrisin:

*In te pono fundamentum.*

Ad Heresim:

*Per te fiet incrementum.*

Ad Ypocrisin:

*Tu fauorem laicorum exstrue.*

notation is found nowhere else in the dramatic text.

[1] responsorio prelio] prelio responsorio (MS).

[2] et imperio] imperiali (emend. suggested M).

[3] solus] solis (W). See Prov. viii, 15: *Per me reges regnant.*

[4] sub aliis] M conjectures *sub albis*, which W adopts.

[5] See John ii, 4: *nondum venit hora mea.* For additional Biblical references see W, p. 14.

[6] See Gen. xli, 40: *regni solio.* For additional Biblical references see W, p. 14.

[7] Emend. M.W.

[8] See Exod. xvii, 14: *delebo enim memoriam Amalec.*

Ad Heresim:

*Tu doctrinam clericorum destrue.*

Tunc ille:

*Per nos mundus tibi credet;*
*nomen Christi tibi cedet.*

Ypocrisis:

*Nam per me fauorem dabunt laici.*

Heresis:

*Et per me Christum negabunt clerici.*

Tunc precedent eum, ipso paulatim sequente. Et postquam uenerint ante sedem Regis Ierosolimę, Ypocrisis insusurret Ypocritis annuntians eis aduentum Antichristi. Qui statim occurrunt sibi cantantes:

*Sacra religio iam diu titubauit;*
*Matrem ecclesiam uanitas occupauit.*
*Vt quid perditio*[1] *per uiros faleratos?*
*Deus non diligit seculares prelatos.*
*Ascende culmina regię potestatis;*
*Per te reliquię mutentur uetustatis.*

Tunc Antichristus:

*Quomodo fiet hoc? ego sum uir ignotvs.*[2]

Tunc ipsi:

*Nostro consilio mundus fauebit totus.*
*Nos occupauimus fauorem laicorum.*
*Nunc per te corruat doctrina clericorum.*
*Nostris auxiliis hunc tronvm occupabis;*
*Tu tuis meritis cetera consummabis.*

Tunc Antichristus ueniens ante sedem Regis Ierosolime cantat ad Ypocritas:

*Quem sub ecclesię*[3] *gremio concepistis,*
*Longis conatibus me tandem genuistis.*
*Ascendam igitur et regna subiugabo,*
*Deponam uetera, noua iura dictabo.*

Tunc exuentes ei superiora indumenta ascendunt expositis gladiis, et deponentes Regem Ierosolimis coronant Antichristum cantantes:

*Firmetur manus tua, et exaltetur d⟨extera⟩ t⟨ua⟩.*[4]

Tunc Rex Ierosolimis ascendit ad Regem Teotonicorum solus cantans:

*Deceptvs fueram per speciem bonorum.*
*Ecce destituor fraude simulatorum.*
*Regni fastigia putabam beata,*[5]
*Si essent talium | edictis ordinata.*
*Romani culminis dum esses aduocatus,*

[1] See Matt. xxvi, 8: *Ut quid perditio hæc?*

[2] See Luke i, 34: *Quomodo fiet istud, quoniam virum non cognosco?*

[3] ecclesie] ecclesia (emend. suggested M).

[4] See Ps. lxxxviii, 13: *Firmetur manus tua, et exaltetur dextera tua.*

[5] putabam beata] putaveram firmata (emend. suggested M).

*Sub honore uiguit   ecclesię statvs.*
*Nunc tuę patens est   malum discessionis;*
*Uiget pestiferę   lex superstitionis.*

Interim Ypocrite conducunt Antichristum in templum Domini ponentes ibi tronum suum. Ecclesia vero quę ibi remanserat multis contumeliis et uerberibus affecta redibit ad sedem Apostolici. Tunc Antichristus dirig*it* Nuntios suos ad singulos Reges, et primo ad Regem Grecorum dicens:

*Scitis diuinitus   ad[1] hoc me uobis datum,*
*Ut per omnes habeam   terras principatum.*
*Ad hoc idoneos   ministros uos elegi,[2]*
*Per quos totus mundus   subdatur nostrę legi.*
*Hinc primo terminos   Grecorum occupate.*
*Grecos terroribus   aut bello subiugate.*

Qui uenientes ad Regem Grecorum cantant coram eo:

*Rex, tibi salus sit   ⟨dicta⟩[3] a saluatore*
*Nostro, regum et totius[4] orbis rectore.*
*Qui sicut ex[5] scripturis   mundo fuit promissvs,*
*Descendit de cęlis   ab arce Patris missus.[6]*
*Ille semper idem   manens in deitate*
*Ad uitam sua nos   inuitat pietate.*
*Hic se uult a cunctis   ut Deum uenerari*
*Et a toto mundo   se iubet adorari.*
*Huius edicti formam   si tu preteribis,*
*In ore gladii[7]   cum tuis interibis.*

Quibus ille:

*Libenter exhibeo   regi famulatum,*
*Quem tanto dicitis   honore sublimatum.*
*Honor est et gloria   tali obedire;*
*Huic tota mente   desidero seruire.*

Et hoc iterans uenit ad presentiam Antichristi et stans coram eo cant*at*:

*Tibi profiteor   decus imperiale;*
*Quo tibi seruiam   ius postulo regale.*

Et flexo genu offert ei coronam.[8] Tunc Antichristus depingens primam

[1] ad] Corrected from *ab* (MS).

[2] See 2 Cor. iii, 6: *qui et idoneos nos fecit ministros novi testamenti*.

[3] dicta] Emend. M. For the couplet W prints the following:
*Rex tibi salus sit   a nostro saluatore*
*rege regum et totius orbis rectore.*

[4] totius] tocius (MS). M prints the line as follows:
*nostro, regum et orbis   totius rectore.*

[5] ex] Omitted (emend. M.W).

[6] See the following responsory (Hartker, p. 45; Migne, *P.L.*, lxxviii, 734): *Descendit de cœlis missus ab arce Patris; introivit per aurem Virginis in regionem nostram, indutus stolam purpuream, et exivit per auream portam lux et decus universæ fabricæ mundi.* Versus: *Tanquam sponsus, Dominus procedens de thalamo suo.* The hymn *Pange, lingua, gloriosi*, of Venantius Fortunatus, contains the following lines (*A.H.*, l, 71, stanza 4):
*Quando venit ergo sacri   plenitudo temporis,*
*Missus est ab arce Patris   natus orbis conditor*
*Atque ventre virginali   carne factus prodiit.*

[7] See Num. xxi, 24: *in ore gladii*. See, further, W, p. 17.

[8] coronam] Preceded by *munera*, crossed out (MS).

litteram nominis sui Regi et omnibus suis in fronte, et coronam ei in capite reponens cant*at*:

*Viue per gratiam  et suscipe honorem,*
*Dum me recognoscis  cunctorum creatorem.*

Tunc ille reuertitur ad sedem suam. Iterum Antichristus dirig*it* Ypocritas ad Regem Francorum cum muneribus dicens:

*Hec munera regi  Francorum offeretis,*
*Quem cum suis ad nos  per illa conuertetis.*
*Hi nostro ritui  formam adinuenere,*
*Nostro aduentui  uiam preparauere.*[1]
*Horum subtilitas  nobis elaborauit*
*Tronum conscendere  quem uirtvs occupauit.*

Tunc Ypocritę, acceptis muneribus, uadunt[2] ad Regem Francorum, et stantes coram eo cant*ant*:

*Rex tibi salvs sit,*

et cetera, vltimam clausulam ista commutantes,

*Sed de tui regni  certvs deuotione*
*Rependit tibi uicem  uoluntatis bonę.*

Tunc Rex, acceptis muneribus, cant*at*:

*Libenter exhibeo,*

et cetera. Et hoc iterans uenit ad presentiam Antichristi, et flexo genu offert ei coronam cant*ans*:

*Tibi profiteor,*

et cetera. Antichristus, eo suscepto, in osculvm signans eum et suos in frontibus et imponens ei coronam cant*at*:

*Viue per gratiam,*

et cetera. Tunc iterum dirigit Ypocritas ad Regem Teotonicorum cant*ans*:

*Excellens est in armis  uis*[3] *Teotonicorum,*
*Sicut testantur experti robur*[4] *eorum.* |
*Regem muneribus  est opus mitigari;*
*Est cum Teotonicis  incautum preliari.*
*Hi secvm pugnantibus  sunt pessima pestis;*
*Hos nobis subicite  donis si potestis.*

Tunc Ypocritę, acceptis muneribus, transeunt ad Regem cantantes coram eo:

*Rex, tibi salus sit,*

et cetera, ultimum uersum iterum isto commutantes:

*Et his te honorans  muneribus absentem*
*Amicum cernere  desiderat presentem.*

[1] See Isaiah lxii, 10: *præparate viam populo.* See, further, W, p. 18.
[2] uadunt] aiadunt (MS).
[3] uis] ius (? MS).
[4] experti robur] robur experti (emend. M.W).

Tunc Rex Teotonicorum cantat:

*Fraudis uersutias   compellor experiri,*
*Per quas nequitia   uestra solet mentiri.*
*Sub forma ueritas   uirtutis putabatur;*
*Osten*dit *falsitas,   quod forma mentiatur.*
*Per uos corrupta est   fides Christianorum;*
*Per me contereretur   regnum simulatorum.*
*Plena sunt fraudibus   munera deceptoris;*
*Iniquus*[1] *corruet   per gladium ultoris.*
*Secum pecunia   sit in perditionem,*[2]
*Grauem iniuria   exspectat*[3] *ultionem.*

Tunc Ypocritę confusi redeunt, et stantes coram Antichristo c*antant*:

*O regni gloria,   caput totius mundi,*
*Offensa⟨m⟩ aspice   populi furibundi.*[4]
*Certe predictum est   per fidem antiquorum,*
*Quod tu subities   ceruices superborum.*
*Si uirtute tua   totvs orbis subsistit,*
*Qua ui Teotonicus*[5] *furor tibi resistit?*
*Tuam*[6] *G⟨er⟩mania   blasphemat dicionem,*
*Extollit cornua   contra religionem.*
*Respice ⟨igitur⟩*[7] *nostram confusionem,*
*In ea iudica   tuam offensionem.*
*Tuam potentiam   iniuria testatur,*
*Cuius imperio   ruinam comminatur.*[8]

Tunc Antichristus:

*Consummabo uere   gentem perditionis*
*Pro tanto scandalo   sanctę religionis.*
*Ecce superbiam   humanę potestatis*
*Teret potentia   diuinę maiestatis.*

Tunc dirig*it* singulos Nuntios ad Reges[9] dicens eis:

*Ite, congregantes   facultates regnorum;*
*Conculcent impetu   furorem superborum.*

Nuntii vero uenientes coram Regibus c⟨antant⟩:

*Ecce noster dominus   et deus deorum*[10]
*Per nos exercitvm   conuocauit suorum.*
*Vt per hos*[11] *Teotonicum   condempnet furorem,*
*In bello martyrum   consignabit crvorem.*

[1] iniquus] in quos (MS); iniquus (emend. M.W).
[2] See Acts viii, 20: *Pecunia tua tecum sit in perditionem.*
[3] exspectat] exspectet? (M).
[4] furibundi] Corrected from *furibunda* (MS).
[5] Teotonicus] teotonicorum (MS); Teotonicus (emend. M.W).
[6] Tuam] Igitur tuam (MS); Tuam (emend. M.W).
[7] Emend. M.W.
[8] comminatur] *cominatur* corrected from *comutatur* (MS).
[9] Reges] singulos reges (emend. suggested M).
[10] See Dan. ii, 47: *Vere Deus vester Deus deorum est.* See, further, W, p. 21.
[11] hos] eos (MS); hos (emend. M.W).

Tunc Reges conueniunt ante tronum Antichristi, quibus ille:

*Consummabo uere,* 266a

et cetera.

*Ite, Germanię terminos inuadetis,*
*Superbum populum cum rege conteretis.*

Tunc omnes cant*ant*:

*Deus nobiscum est,*[1] *quos tuetur potenter.*
*Pro fide igitur pugnemus confidenter.*

Et disponentes acies suas in occursum Teotonicorum congrediuntur cum eis et superatur exercitus Antichristi. Tunc Rex Teotonicorum rediens et sedens in trono suo cant*at*:

*Sanguine patrię honor est retinendus,*
*Virtute patrię est hostis expellendvs.*
*Ius dolo perditum est sanguine uenale;*
*Sic retinebimvs decus imperiale.*

Tunc Ypocrite adducunt Claudum coram Antichristo, quo sanato, Rex Teotonicorum hesitabit in fide. Tunc iterum adducunt Leprosum, et illo sanato, Rex plus dubitabit. Ad ultimum important feretrum, in quo iacebat[2] quidam simulans se in prelio occisum. Iubet itaque Antichristus ut surgat dicens:

*Signa semper querunt rudes et infideles.*[3]
*Surge*[4] *uelociter, quis sim ego, reueles.*

Tunc ille de feretro cantat:

*Tu sapientia supernę ueritatis |*
*Uirtus inuicta es diuinę maiestatis.*

Et Ypocritę secum c⟨antant⟩:

*Tu sapientia,* 278a

et cetera. Tunc Rex Teotonicorum uidens signum seducitur dicens:

*Nostro nos impetu semper periclitamur,*
*Aduersvs Dominum incauti preliamur.*
*In huius nomine mortui suscitantur*
*Et claudi ambulant ⟨et⟩*[5] *leprosi mundantur.*
*Illius igitur gloriam ueneremur.*[6]

Tunc Rex ascend*it* ad Antichristum hoc idem cantans.[7] Cum autem uenerit coram eo, flexo genu offert ei coronam c⟨antans⟩:

*Tibi profiteor,* 284a

et cetera. Tunc Antichristus signans eum et suos in frontibus et imponens ei coronam c⟨antat⟩:

*Viue per gratiam,* 284b

[1] See Joshua xxii, 31: *nobiscum sit Dominus*. See, further, W, p. 21.

[2] iacebat] iacebit (emend. M.W).

[3] See Matt. xii, 39: *Generatio mala et adultera signum quærit*.

[4] Surge] surge surge (MS). See Acts xii, 7: *Surge velociter*.

[5] Emend. M.W. See Matt. x, 8: *Infirmos curate, mortuos suscitate, leprosos mundate*; Matt. xi, 5: *claudi ambulant, leprosi mundantur*.

[6] M and others have noted the loss of a line after this one.

[7] cantans] cantat (MS); cantans (emend. M.W).

et cetera. Tunc committit sibi expeditionem ad gentes dicens:

*Vobis credentibus conuertimur ad gentes.*

Et dato sibi gladio, c⟨antat⟩:

*Per te disponimus has fieri credentes.*

Tunc Rex ueniens ad tronum Gentilitatis et mittens Legatum[1] ad Regem Babylonis, qui cantat coram eo:

*Potestas Domini maneat in ęternum,*[2]
*Quę adoranda quasi*[3] *numen sempiternum*
*Condempnat penitus culturam idolorum.*[4]
*Precip*it *abici ritvs simulacrorum.*

Tunc Gentilitas ad Legatum:

*Finx*it *inuidia hanc singularitatem,*
*Ut unam coleret homo diuinitatem.*
*Ille iure deus cupidus estimatur,*
*Qui spretis*[5] *ceteris uult, ut solvs colatur.*
*Nos ergo*[6] *sequimur ritum antiquitatis,*
*Diis discrimina reddimus deitatis.*

Tunc Nuntivs:

*Vnus est dominus, quem iure ueneramur,*
*Qui solvs deus est.*

Et deiciens simulacrum c⟨antat⟩:

*Ydolum detestamur.*

Statim Gentiles concurrunt et preliantur cum exercitu Antichristi; et superatvs Rex Babylonis ducitur captiuus ad Antichristum. Tunc Rex genu flexo offert[7] coronam Antichristo d⟨icens⟩:

*Tibi profiteor,* 298a

et cetera. Tunc Antichristus signans eum et suos in frontibus et imponens coronam ei c⟨antat⟩:

*Viue per gratiam,* 298b

et cetera. Statim redeunt ad sedes suas omnes cantantes:

*Omnium rectorem te solum profitemur.*
*Tibi tota mente semper obsequemur.*

Tunc Antichristus dirigens Ypocritas ad Synagogam c⟨antat⟩:

*Iudeis dicite Messiam aduenisse*
*Et me in gentibus tributum accepisse.*
*Iudeis dicite: En ego sum Messyas;*
*Ego sum promissvs eis per prophetias.*[8]

[1] Legatum] lengatum (MS).

[2] See Heb. vii, 24: *quod maneat in æternum, sempiternum habet sacerdotium.*

[3] quasi] est quasi (MS); quasi (emend. M.W).

[4] See 1 Cor. x, 14: *idolorum cultura.*

[5] spretis] spiritus (MS); spretis (emend. M.W).

[6] ergo] igitur (MS); ergo (emend. M.W).

[7] offert] Followed by *ei*, crossed out (MS).

[8] prophetias] prophetas (MS); prophetias (emend. M.W).

Tunc Ypocrite ad Synagogam:

*Regalis generis gens es*[1] *peculiaris,*
*Fidelis populus ubique predicaris.*[2]
*Pro tuenda lege iam dudum exulasti,*
*Procul a patria Messiam exspectasti.*
*Hec exspectatio reddet hereditatem,*
*Iocunda nouitas mutabit uetustatem.*
*Ecce mysterium tuę redemptionis;*[3]
*Rex enim natus est auctor religionis.*
*Hic est Emmanuel, quem testantur scripture,*
*Per cuius gratiam tu regnabis secure.*
*Erexit humiles et superbos deiecit:*
*Potenter omnia sub pedibus subiecit.*[4]
*Surge, Ierusalem, surge, illuminare,*[5]
⟨*Et*⟩[6] *captiua diu Synagoga lętare.*

Tunc Synagoga:

*Hec consolatio diuinę bonitatis*
*Laborem respicit nostrę captiuitatis.*
*Eamus igitur obuiam saluatori;*
*Dignum est reddere gloriam redemptori.*

Tunc Synagoga | surgens uadit ad Antichristum et cantat:[7]

*Ades, Emanuel, quem semper ueneramur,*
*In cuius gloria nos quoque gloriamur.*

Tunc uenientem suscipit Synagogam signans eam et dicens:

*Per me egredere uectem confusionis;*
*Tibi restituo terram promissionis.*
*In tuo lumine en gentes ambulabunt,*[8]
*Et sub pacis tuę lege reges regnabunt.*

Tunc, Synagoga redeunte, intrant Prophetę dicentes:[9]

*Verbum Patris habens diuinitatem*
*In uirgine sumpsit humanitatem.*
*Manens Deus effectus est mortalis,*
*Semper Deus factus est temporalis.*
*Non naturę usu sic testante*[10]
*Hoc factum est sed Deo imperante.*

[1] es] est (MS); es (emend. M.W). See Deut. vii, 6: *populus peculiaris*; 1 Peter ii, 9: *genus electum, regale sacerdotium, gens sancta.*

[2] predicaris] predicans (MS); predicaris (emend. M.W).

[3] See 1 Cor. xv, 51: *Ecce mysterium vobis dico.*

[4] See 1 Cor. xv, 26: *omnia enim subjecit sub pedibus ejus.*

[5] See Isaiah lx, 1: *Surge, illuminare, Jerusalem.*

[6] Emend. M.W.

[7] cantat] cetera (MS); cantat (emend. M.W).

[8] ambulabunt] ambulant (MS); ambulabunt (emend. M.W).

[9] This speech of the *Prophetæ* contains numerous echoes from the Apostles' Creed and the Athanasian Creed.

[10] sic testante] sibi constante (emend. M.W).

*Nostram ⟨Christus⟩*[1] *sumpsit infirmitatem,*
*Ut infirmis conferret firmitatem.*
*Hunc Iudei mortalem cognouerunt,*
*Immortalem quem esse nescierunt.*
*Nec sermoni nec signis credidere;*
*Sub Pilato Christum crucifixere.*
*Moriendo mortem mortificauit;*
*A Gehenna credentes liberauit.*
*Hic surrexit uere non moriturus;*
*Regnat semper in proximo uenturus.*
*Hic seculum per ignem iudicabit,*
*Uniuersos in carne suscitabit.*
*A reprobis saluandos separabit;*
*Malos dampnans bonos glorificabit.*
*Vere scitis quid scripturę loquantur;*
*Enoch*[2] *uiuum et Heliam testantur.*

Tunc Synagoga:

*Vbinam sunt?*

Helias:[3]

*Illi nos sumus uere*
*In quos fines seclorum*[4] *deuenere:*
*Iste Enoch, et ego sum Helias,*
*Quos hucusque seruauerat Messias.*
*Qui iam uenit et adhuc est uenturus,*
*Per nos primum Israel redempturus.*
*Ecce uenit homo perditionis*[5]
*Magnę consummans muros*[6] *Babylonis.*
*Non est Christus ⟨sed mendax Antichristus⟩.*[7]

. . . . . . .

Tunc tollunt ei uelum. Statim Synagoga conuertitur ad uerba Prophetarum dicens:

*Seducti fuimus*[8] *uere per Antichristum,*
*Qui mentitur ⟨esse⟩*[9] *se Iudeorum Christum.*
*Certa indicia*[10] *sunt nostrę libertatis*
*Helyas et Enoch prophetę ueritatis.*

*Tibi gratias damus, Adonay, Rex glorię,*

[1] Emend. M.W.

[2] Enoch] Enooh (MS).

[3] Helias] Illi (MS); Helias (emend. M.W). In the MS *Illi* is written as a rubric.

[4] seclorum] *seculorum* (MS); seculorum (emend. M.W), for metrical reasons. See 1 Cor. x, 11: *in quos fines sæculorum devenerunt.*

[5] See 2 Thess. ii, 3: *homo peccati, filius perditionis.*

[6] consummans muros] muros consummans (emend. M.W). See Rev. xviii, 2: *Cecidit Babylon magna, et facta est habitatio dæmoniorum.*

[7] Emend. M, who infers the loss of a complete line after this one. W does not adopt the emendation.

[8] fuimus] sumus (MS); fuimus (emend. M.W).

[9] Emend. M.W.

[10] indicia] iudicia (MS).

*Personarum trinitas*[1] *eiusdem substantię.*
*Vere pater Deus est, cuius unigenitus*
*Deus est. Idem*[2] *Deus est amborum spiritus.*

Interim Ypocritę uenientes ad Antichristum c⟨antant⟩:

*O culmen regium diuinę maiestatis,*
*Tibi subtrahitur honor diuinitatis.*
*Intrauere senes doctores uanitatis,*
*Qui blasphemant tuę honorem potestatis.*
*Iudeis predicant tenore scripturarum*
*Te, rex omnipotens, caput ypocritarum.*

Tunc Antichristus ad Ypocritas:

*Cum me totvs orbis studeat adorare,*
*Ius mei nominis*[3] *quis audeat negare?*
*Synagogam et senes mihi presentate.*[4]
*Reos conueniam super hac leuitate.*

Tunc Ministri uenientes ad Prophetas et Synagogam c*antant*:

*Testes mendatii, precones falsitatis,*
*Uos tribunal uocat diuinę maiestatis.*

Tunc Prophete:

*Non seducet homo iniquitatis*
*Seruos Christi ministris*[5] *falsitatis.*

Tunc Nuntii adducunt Prophetas et Synagogam ad Antichristum, quibus ille:

*Fert in insaniam proprietatis*[6]
*Uos, quos | decipiunt uultus auctoritatis.*
*Sanctis promissvs sum redemptio futura;*
*Uere Messias ⟨sum⟩,*[7] *ut testatur scriptura.*
*De me suscipite formam religionis;*
*Sum infidelibus lapis offensionis.*[8]

Tunc Prophetę:

*Tu blasphemvs auctor iniquitatis,*
*Radix mali, turbator ueritatis.*
*Antichristus, seductor pietatis,*
*Uere mendax sub forma deitatis.*[9]

Tunc Antichristus commotus dic*it* Ministris:

*Ecce blasphemias meę diuinitatis*
*Ulciscatur manus diuinę maiestatis.*
*Qui blasphemant in me diuinam pietatem,*

[1] trinitas] trinitatis (MS); trinitas (emend. M.W).

[2] Idem] item (emend. suggested M).

[3] nominis] numinis (emend. suggested M).

[4] presentate] representate (MS); presentate (emend. M.W).

[5] ministris] ministri (emend. suggested M).

[6] proprietatis] M conjectures that this word is a corruption of some such subject of the verb *fert* as *doctrina vanitatis*.

[7] Emend. M.W.

[8] See Isaiah viii, 14: *in lapidem autem offensionis*.

[9] deitatis] pietatis (MS); deitatis (emend. M.W).

*Diuini numinis gustent seueritatem.*
*Pereant penitus oues occisionis*[1]
*Pro tanto scandalo sanctę religionis.*

Tandem Synagoga c*antat* confessionem istam:

*Nos erroris penitet, ad fidem conuertimur;*
*Quicquid nobis inferet persecutor, patimur.*

Tunc Ministri educunt eos et occidunt. Interim vero dum occiduntur, Ecclesia c⟨antat⟩:

*Fasciculvs mirrę dilectus meus mihi.*[2]

Tunc, Ministris reuersis, Antichristus dirigit Nuntios suos ad singulos Reges c⟨antans⟩:

*Reges conueniant et agmina sanctorum;*[3]
*Adorari uolo a gloria regnorum.*
*Cuncta diuinitus manus ima*[4] *firmau*it,
*Suos diuinitas hostes exterminau*it.
*Pace conclusa sunt cuncta iura regnorum;*
*Ad coronam uocat suos deus deorum.*

Tunc omnes Reges conueniunt undique cvm suis usque ad presentiam Antichristi ⟨cantantes⟩:

*Cuncta diuinitus,*

et cetera. Quibus Antichristus:

*Ista predixerunt mei predicatores,*
*Uiri mei nominis et iuris cultores.*
*Hec mea gloria, quam diu predixere,*
*Qua fruentur mecum, quicunque meruere.*
*Post eorum casum, quos uanitas illusit,*
*Pax et securitas*[5] *uniuersa conclusit.*

Statim fit sonitus super caput Antichristi, et, eo corruente et omnibus suis fugientibus, Ecclesia cant*at*:

*Ecce homo qui non posuit Deum adiutorem suum.*
*Ego autem sicut oliua fructifera in domo Dei.*[6]

Tunc omnibus redeuntibus ad fidem, Ecclesia ipsos suscipiens incipit:

*Laudem dicite Deo nostro.*[7]

In order to follow the action of the play conveniently, one must first fix clearly in mind the arrangement of the *sedes* explained in the opening rubric.[8] The playing-space, it appears, represents virtually the whole of the inhabited part of the earth.

[1] See Ps. xliii, 22: *oves occisionis.*

[2] See Song i, 12: *Fasciculus myrrhæ dilectus meus mihi.*

[3] sanctorum] suorum (emend. M.W).

[4] ima] mea (emend. suggested M).

[5] See 1 Thess. v, 3: *pax et securitas.*

[6] See Ps. li, 9–10: *Ecce homo qui non posuit Deum adjutorem suum . . . Ego autem, sicut oliva fructifera in domo Dei.*

[7] See Rev. xix, 5: *Laudem dicite Deo nostro.* What follows in the MS is irrelevant to the play.

[8] In regard to the arrangement of the *sedes* see especially Michaelis, pp. 79–81; Scherer, pp. 450–1; Vetter, p. 286; Meyer, *Abhandlungen*, i, 140; Creizenach, i, 74.

On the borders of the *platea* are eight structures, or platforms, one for the Temple of the Lord (*Templum Domini*), and seven for particular personages.[1] The Temple is on the east side, and near it are the *sedes* of the King of Jerusalem and that of Synagoga. On the west side are three platforms, for the Roman Emperor, the German king, and the French king respectively; and on the south are two *sedes*: one for the king of the Greeks, and the other for the king of Babylonia and for *Gentilitas*, the personification of heathendom.[2] Since by this arrangement the north border of the *platea* is left free of stage-structures, one infers that the spectators occupied this side.

The performance begins with a kind of prologue providing for the entrance of the principal personages. First enters *Gentilitas*, accompanied by *Rex Babiloniæ*, declaring her faith in polytheism. Then follows *Synagoga*, with a company of Jews, asserting the errors of Christianity. The next group is led by *Ecclesia*, accompanied by Mercy, Justice, the Pope and his clergy, and the Roman Emperor with his soldiers—all of whom may be assumed to ascend the *sedes* of the Roman Emperor. Finally the 'other kings'—presumably of Jerusalem, of Greece, and of France—enter and take their appropriate scaffolds. At the end of the prologue, the *Templum Domini* and the *sedes* of *Rex Theotonicorum* are temporarily left vacant.

The action proper opens with the Emperor's proclaiming that all the kings of the earth shall again pay tribute to the Roman Empire, and by his dispatching messengers to demand obeisance. The king of the Franks yields only after a battle, but the kings of the Greeks and of Jerusalem offer no resistance. The king of Babylonia, however, straightway undertakes the complete destruction of Christianity through a military assault

[1] Scherer (p. 450) finds an inconsistency between the 'vii sedes regales' mentioned at the opening of the rubric and the eight, as he supposes, mentioned subsequently. He is also troubled by the fact that the *sedes* of the German king is distinct from that of the Roman Emperor, whereas in the action of the play the Emperor after laying down his imperial crown becomes the German king. Scherer, therefore, infers that *Rex Theotonicorum* is an interpolation. See also Vetter, p. 286. I do not observe the alleged inconsistency, nor do I perceive a difficulty in the presence of separate *sedes* for *Rex Theotonicorum* and *Imperator Romanorum*. I infer that the *sedes* of the German king is vacant at the opening of the play, but is later occupied by the Emperor, after he has laid down his crown. The *sedes* originally occupied by the Emperor is, I suggest, eventually occupied by *Ecclesia*, after she has been ejected from the Temple by Antichrist.

[2] A difficulty has sometimes been felt in the fact that the expression *ad austrum* is used for the *sedes* of the king of the Greeks, and *ad meridiem* for that occupied by the king of Babylonia and *Gentilitas*. See especially Michaelis, pp. 79–81. I see no serious obstacle to our accepting two different expressions meaning 'south'.

XXIV. Antichrist seducing the Kings by Gifts, from the *Hortus Deliciarum* of Herrad of Landsberg

upon the king of Jerusalem, and the city is saved only through the timely arrival of the Emperor and his forces. When he has routed the king of Babylonia, the Emperor enters the empty Temple, and deposits his crown and imperial insignia before the altar, declaring that Christ alone is the true imperial ruler. Then he who was Roman Emperor returns to the seat of his former kingdom—presumably the *sedes regis Theotonicorum*—while Ecclesia, who had accompanied him to Jerusalem, remains in the Temple accompanied, probably, by the Pope.

Now begins the part of the play dominated by Antichrist. While *Ecclesia*, *Gentilitas*, and *Synagoga* are repeating their doctrinal assertions, the hypocrites enter sanctimoniously and win the favour of the laymen and of the king of Jerusalem. Then Antichrist himself appears, accompanied by Hypocrisy and Heresy, whom he charges with the responsibility of corrupting the laity and clergy. Presently Antichrist overcomes the king of Jerusalem, assumes the crown, and ascends the throne in the Temple. Meanwhile the king of Jerusalem flees to the king of the Teutons, and *Ecclesia*, after suffering abuse and indignity, is driven from the Temple, and apparently returns, along with the Pope, to the platform which she had originally shared with the Pope and the Roman Emperor (*ad sedem Apostolici*).

Antichrist now undertakes to subjugate all the kings of the earth, and sends out messengers to demand submission. The kings of the Greeks and the Franks he subdues easily through threats and gifts, receiving their homage and putting his mark on their foreheads. With the sturdy king of the Teutons, however, he has serious difficulties. Since this king rejects his gifts and overcomes his army, Antichrist is forced to resort to performing miracles. After witnessing the healing of a lame man and of a leper, the king is still uncertain as to Antichrist's authority; but by the raising of a dead soldier he is completely convinced, bends his knee to the wonder-worker, and receives Antichrist's brand on his forehead. The Teuton king now leads Antichrist's army against Gentilitas and the king of Babylonia, and conquers them. Finally, through the agency of the hypocrites, *Synagoga* submits to Antichrist, and thus completes his domination of the world.

The final stage in the career of Antichrist begins with the arrival of the prophets, Enoch and Elijah, who declare the truths of Christianity, convert *Synagoga*, denounce the deceits of the usurper, and are promptly put to death, along with the converted *Synagoga*. Antichrist then summons all the kings and their followers into his presence, in order that they may acknowledge him as the true God. As he is declaring his omnipotence, however, thunder crashes over his head, he collapses, and all his followers flee. *Ecclesia*, however, summons them all back to the Christian faith, and the play ends with praises to God.

There has never been any doubt that the chief source of the play is the *Libellus* of Adso.[1] The Roman emperor's conquest of the world, his resigning his authority at Jerusalem, the mission of Enoch and Elijah, the manner of Antichrist's coming, his use of terror, gifts, and miracles, his putting his sign upon his converts—all these principal elements of the action appear to have been drawn from the Latin treatise. The features of the play arising from other sources are all subordinate. A few details in the action, and a few phrases, appear to have been borrowed from Pseudo-Methodius.[2] The influence of the Vulgate and of the liturgy is, of course, unmistakable.[3] The opening scene of the play seems to reflect the popular theme of the *Altercatio Ecclesiæ et Synagogæ*,[4] and the presence of the prophets as opponents of Antichrist suggests the possibility that the author may have known some version of the *Ordo Prophetarum*.[5]

Whatever the range of his sources, the author obviously manipulated them with great freedom. Although in the main action he follows essentially the tradition expounded by Adso, in the complication of incidents and especially in the emphasis upon German hegemony in the first part of the play he is unquestionably original.[6] In this individuality of treatment critics have usually discerned a political intention, and they have virtually all agreed that the piece was written for performance at some important moment in the career of Frederick I, or Frederick Barbarossa, who became emperor in 1155, and died on the Third Crusade, in 1189.[7] As to the precise date with

[1] See Meyer, *Abhandlungen*, i, 139–45; Michaelis, pp. 68–75; Chambers, ii, 64; Creizenach, i, 72. For the text of Adso see below, p. 496. Michael (iv, 433–6) differs somewhat from other critics in emphasizing the possibility of influence from the chronicle of Otto of Freising.

[2] See Michaelis, pp. 68–75.

[3] See the footnotes to the text above; Michaelis, pp. 68, 74–5.

[4] See above, p. 192; Chambers, ii, 64.

[5] See above, chapter xxi; Michaelis, p. 69; Chambers, ii, 64.

[6] See, for example, Creizenach, i, 74; Golther, p. 170.

[7] The career of Frederick Barbarossa is elaborately surveyed by Giesebrecht, vols. v and vi, and is summarized in *The Cambridge Medieval History*, v, New York, 1926, pp. 381–453; and, very briefly, by Vetter, pp. 279–85.

which the play should be associated, however, there has been no general unanimity of opinion. The event of which one is most immediately tempted to see a reflection in the dramatic text is the Reichstag held at Mainz at Easter of 1188. At that time the emperor was making his preparations for the Third Crusade. He summoned the kings of Western Europe to join the holy expedition, and sent a warning to Saladin; he wrote to the king of Hungary, the emperor of Constantinople, and the Sultan of Iconium demanding the right of unmolested passage through their dominions. At the Reichstag at Mainz, when Frederick and his nobles met with great ceremony to take up the Cross, the emperor performed a striking gesture: he declined to occupy the throne, saying that it belonged to Christ alone, the true leader of the crusade.[1] To this act certain critics have discerned a reference in the scene of the play in which the Roman emperor lays down his crown and imperial insignia in the *Templum Domini* at Jerusalem.[2] It is to be observed, however, that the resemblance between drama and history here is much less impressive than that between the play and its recognized literary source. There is no reason to suppose that the dramatic author has in mind anything beyond the text of Adso, which he is following closely.[3] It can scarcely be proved, then, that the play mirrors the events immediately preceding the Third Crusade; and had the dramatist intended to indicate a period after the Crusade, he might have been expected to include some recognizable reference to this unfortunate expedition. One critic, to be sure, sees in the latter half of the play a picture of the general disillusionment of the years 1190 and 1191, after Frederick's death;[4] but this effect appears to the present writer to arise primarily from Adso's account of Antichrist.

The great majority of those who have considered the possible historical bearings of the play find its most likely associations, not with the Third Crusade, but with events during the earlier years of Frederick's reign, between his imperial coronation, in 1155, and crowning of his son Henry as king of the Germans, in 1169.[5] This latter terminus is suggested by the fact that at the opening

[1] Concerning these scenes see Giesebrecht, vi, 184, 677.

[2] See ll. 147 sqq.; Zezschwitz, pp. 123–30; Froning, pp. 203–4.

[3] See Vetter, p. 282, and the text of Adso below, pp. 496 sqq.

[4] See Aschner, pp. 359–60.

[5] See Meyer, *Abhandlungen*, i, 145–8; Golther, p. 169; Chambers, ii, 64; Gundlach, iii, 838–40; Scherer, pp. 452–5; Wilhelm, pp. vii–viii; Creizenach, i, 75–8.

of the play the throne of the German king (*sedes Regis Theotonicorum*) is left vacant.[1] By this arrangement seems to be intended a period before the coronation of Henry. The general political situation of the years 1155 to 1169 seems to be reflected in the play in several particulars. The strained relations between the Emperor and the Pope is probably shown by the silence imposed upon the latter throughout the action.[2] The historical enmity between the Emperor and the French king is abundantly represented. The threatening of Jerusalem by the infidels may be said to appear in the dramatic beleaguering of that holy place by the king of Babylonia.

Another reason sometimes adduced for placing the play within the period now under consideration is the possible reference to our play by Gerhoh of Reichersberg. In his *De Investigatione Antichristi*, written during the years 1161 and 1162, this prelate speaks of a dramatic representation of Antichrist as follows:[3]

Et sacerdotes, qui dicuntur, jam non ecclesiæ vel altaris ministerio dediti sunt sed exercitiis avaritiæ, vanitatum et spectaculorum, adeo ut ecclesias ipsas, videlicet orationum domus, in theatra commutent ac mimicis ludorum spectaculis impleant. Inter quæ nimirum spectacula adstantibus ac spectantibus ipsorum feminis interdum et antichristi, de quo nobis sermo est, non ut ipsi æstimant imaginariam similitudinem exhibent sed in veritate, ut credi potest iniquitatis ipsius mysterium pro parte sua implent. . . . Quid ergo mirum, si et isti nunc antichristum vel Herodem in suis ludis simulantes eosdem non, ut eis intentioni est, ludicro mentiuntur sed in veritate exhibent, utpote quorum vita ab antichristi laxa conversatione non longe abest?. . . . Contigit, ut comperimus, aliquando apud tales, ut eum quem inter ludicra sua quasi mortuum ab Elisæo propheta suscitandum exhiberent peracta simulatione mortuum invenirent. Alius item antichristo suo quasi suscitandus oblatus intra septem dies vere mortuus, ut comperimus, et sepultus est. Et quis scire potest, an et cetera simulata antichristi scilicet effigiem, dæmonum larvas, Herodianam insaniam in veritate non exhibeant? . . . Exhibent præterea imaginaliter et Salvatoris infantiæ cunabula, parvuli vagitum, puerperæ virginis matronalem habitum, stellæ quasi sidus flammigerum, infantum necem, maternum Rachelis ploratum. Sed divinitas insuper et matura facies ecclesiæ abhorret spectacula

[1] See the rubric before l. 49.

[2] As Meyer observes (*Abhandlungen*, i, 146), however, this silence may be due in part to the fact that Adso and Methodius provide no role for the Pope.

[3] Scheibelberger, i, 25–8. The chapter from which the present excerpts are made may be seen in Appendix C, pp. 524 sq. Concerning the date and intention of Gerhoh's *De Investigatione Antichristi* see Giesebrecht, v, pt. i, 267; vi, 302–3; Wadstein, p. 144.

theatralia, non respicit in vanitates et insanias falsas, immo non falsas sed jam veras insanias, in quibus viri totos se frangunt in feminas quasi pudeat eos, quod viri sunt, clerici in milites, homines se in dæmonum larvas transfigurant.

The general argument of the chapter in which this passage occurs is that the clergy who promote plays within the churches are carrying out the work of that very Antichrist whom they represent upon the stage. There are some who discern in this charge a direct reference to the play from Tegernsee, and who infer that 'Gerhoh has been stung by the lampooning of his party as the *Hypocritæ* in the pro-imperialist *Antichristus*'.[1] The critics who take this view have, of course, a means for dating the play before 1162.[2] It can scarcely be maintained, however, that Gerhoh's description applies to the dramatic text with irresistible exactitude.[3]

From the historical and personal references in the play, then, we can hardly hope to date the play with precision.[4] We may, however, confidently assign it to the time of the Emperor Frederick Barbarossa, and safely admit that its political content conforms more exactly to the earlier than to the later part of his reign. It would be conservative to say that the play was probably written about the year 1160, when the Emperor Frederick's relations with the Pope and with the king of France were none too friendly, and when the Saracens were threatening Jerusalem. As to the ecclesiastical loyalties of the playwright we can draw at least a general inference from the following lines spoken by the *Hypocritæ* (ll. 171–4):

Sacra religio iam diu titubavit;
Matrem ecclesiam vanitas occupavit.
Ut quid perditio per viros faleratos?
Deus non diligit seculares prælatos.

From the fact that this disparagement of the secular clergy is uttered by the Hypocrites, it would appear that the author himself must have been of the party represented as being censured, and that the Hypocrites must represent the ecclesiastical reformers and adherents of the Pope, such as Gerhoh of Reichersberg.[5]

[1] See Chambers, ii, 98–9.
[2] See Reuschel, pp. 36–7.
[3] See Michaelis, p. 86; Gundlach, iii, 838–9.
[4] See Scherer, p. 453; Vetter, p. 285; Gundlach, iii, 838.
[5] This summary conforms, in general, to the view of Chambers, ii, 64. See also Meyer,

As to the actual circumstances under which the play was performed we have no information. There is nothing to show that it was acted in association with the liturgy, or even within a church.[1] It contains one or two liturgical pieces, and includes choral repetitions suggestive of liturgical singing;[2] but these do not establish it as related directly to the services of the Church. It could, no doubt, have been acted within a church building;[3] but a *mise en scène* of the amplitude described above, and a dramatic action involving large movements and many persons, could have been most conveniently accommodated out of doors.[4] It is a pleasant, but idle, fancy that the background of the *platea* may have been, on one or more occasions, one of the portals of the church at Tegernsee itself. As to the season of the year at which the play may have been presented we are again left to mere conjecture. Most of the critics have declared for Easter, but without mentioning substantial reasons for their preference.[5] For its effectiveness, however, the play is not dependent upon the external circumstances of its performance, for it contains within itself elements of ample dramatic impressiveness. Among these one of the most remarkable is the characterization of certain conspicuous personages.[6] The author's thorough devotion to the notion of a German world empire, for example, appears in the traits assigned to the monarch who is at first the Emperor and later the German king. In the earlier part of the play, his power appears especially by way of contrast to the impotence of his opponents, particularly the king of France. When commanded to pay homage to the Emperor the French king makes a spirited show of resistance (ll. 69–74):

*Abhandlungen*, pp. 147–8; Wilhelm, pp. vii–viii; Creizenach, i, 73–8; Haskins, p. 175. Michaelis (pp. 81–6) stands apart from the other critics in denying to the play any political bearing at all. He sees in it reflections of the preaching of St Bernard (1090–1153), and would place it chronologically before the unfortunate conclusion of the Second Crusade. Speculation as to the author's having been the Tegernsee monk, Werinherus, or Werinhere, is summarized by Zezschwitz, pp. 133–7. See also Froning, pp. 204–5. Both critics reject this ascription.

[1] Reuschel (p. 2) vaguely conjectures a liturgical origin for the play.

[2] See Gundlach, iii, 814.

[3] Chambers (ii, 63) remarks, 'It must have taken up the whole nave of some great church'.

[4] See Zezschwitz, p. 131; Vetter, p. 286; Golther, p. 171.

[5] See Froning, p. 200; Vetter, p. 297; Reuschel, p. 3; Hase, p. 14. Chambers (ii, 62) says that the play 'was almost certainly performed at Advent', and cites an Italian *lauda* on the same subject mentioned by D'Ancona (i, 141) as occurring 'In Dominica de Adventu'. Creizenach (i, 70) associates our play with 'the last Sunday of the church year'. The responsory *Judæa et Jerusalem* sung by the chorus in the course of the action (l. 146a) is from the liturgy of the eve of Christmas.

[6] See Froning, pp. 202–3; Meyer, *Abhandlungen*, i, 149; Gundlach, iii, 841, 843; Creizenach, i, 74.

Historiographis si qua fides habetur,
Non nos imperio sed nobis hoc debetur.
Hoc enim seniores Galli possederunt,
Atque suis posteris nobis reliquerunt.
Sed hoc invasoria vi nunc spoliamur.
Absit, invasoribus ut nos obsequamur.

In the battle which immediately follows, however, this French pretentiousness comes to naught. The same Gallic impotence appears after the advent of Antichrist. Whereas the German monarch spurns the latter's threats and gifts, the French accepts offerings, does obeisance without delay, and submits to the final degradation of being the only ruler whom Antichrist kisses. It is to the fine-spun and demoralizing scholasticism of the French, indeed, to which Antichrist attributes no small measure of his success (ll. 221–4):

Hi nostro ritui formam adinvenere,
Nostro adventui viam preparavere.
Horum subtilitas nobis elaboravit
Tronum conscendere quem virtus occupavit.

Very different is Antichrist's tribute to the German power of resistance (ll. 227–30):

Excellens est in armis vis Teotonicorum
Sicut testantur experti robur eorum.
Regem muneribus est opus mitigari;
Est cum Teotonicis incautum prœliari.

From such utterances it is clear that the author is determined to express his conception of a contrast in national character. Further variety in the way of stage figures appears in the allegorical personages, such as *Hæresis*, *Hypocrisis*, *Misericordia* and *Justitia*, who in this play make, possibly, their first appearance upon the medieval stage.

The author's literary style can scarcely be said to show marked distinction. Although the language is forcible and free from learned obscurities, the verses, as a whole, do not move fluently. Of the four hundred lines or so, some three hundred—in which the regular dialogue is conducted—are lines of thirteen syllables, rhyming in couplets. The individual verses show a considerable variety of internal movement, but only a moderate amount of literary grace.[1]

[1] The verse is analysed in detail by Meyer, *Abhandlungen*, i, 334–8; and Meyer's findings are re-examined, with considerable adverse criticism, by Vetter, pp. 301–11. To Vetter

Whatever the author's limitations may be in his form of expression, one must commend the orderly and harmonious structure of his play as a whole. The wide sweep of the action is presented with lucidity and animation. Religious feeling, traditional legend, political opinion, and German patriotism are effectively combined in a composition which may fairly be regarded as the best literary product of German ecclesiastical life in the twelfth century.[1]

the lines seem smoother than to any previous critic, and he pronounces the dramatist (p. 310) 'ein tüchtiger Verskünstler'.

[1] Concerning the influence of this play, and the treatment of its theme, during the succeeding centuries, in various countries, see Vetter, pp. 297–300; Reuschel, pp. 37 sqq.

# CONCLUSION

THE survey of the drama of the medieval Church presented in the chapters above may be regarded as fairly complete both in its scope and in its exhibition of the texts of the plays themselves. Although additional examples will undoubtedly come to light, we cannot confidently hope for the disclosure of important new types of liturgical drama not represented in some fashion in the present collection. It seems fitting, therefore, that this treatise should close with a brief general characterization of the dramatic pieces now before us, and with a gathering together of a few of the incidental comments which have accompanied the various texts. In such a summary one may appropriately consider the scope and content of the plays, the means employed for performing them, and their literary and dramatic values. Here must be recorded also the estimate placed upon them by the hierarchy of the Church itself, and their eventual departure from ecclesiastical precincts and control.

## I

These plays appear to have achieved their essential development between the tenth century and the thirteenth. Not far from the year 900 arose a small Easter dialogue apt for dramatic treatment and destined to become, before the end of the century, a true play provided with attentive impersonation and adequate setting.[1] By the end of the thirteenth century had been composed all the more highly elaborated pieces known to the Church, such as the most ambitious versions of the Easter and Epiphany plays,[2] the longer Passion play found among the *Carmina Burana*,[3] the studied dramatizations of subjects from the Old Testament,[4] the *miracula* of St Nicholas,[5] and striking treatments of subjects from eschatology.[6] With the year 1300, to be sure, ecclesiastical performances did not cease. A few dramatic ceremonies, indeed, such as those for the feast of the Presentation of the Blessed Virgin Mary and for the Assumption, seem to have come into existence only toward the end of the medieval period,[7] and simple

[1] See the trope *Quem quæritis* considered in chapter vii, and the *Visitatio Sepulchri* from the *Regularis Concordia* of St Ethelwold printed above, i, 249.

[2] See chapters xiii, xiv, xix.

[3] See above, i, 518.

[4] See chapter xxv.

[5] See chapter xxvi.

[6] See chapter xxvii.

[7] See chapter xxiv.

forms of the *Visitatio Sepulchri* continued to be revived or devised even during the sixteenth and seventeenth centuries.[1] By the opening of the fourteenth century, however, the more important themes of Church drama had received full and characteristic treatment.

The range of subjects treated in the plays was broad, and it may have extended over the whole course of sacred history. Of dramatizations inspired by the Old Testament, to be sure, very few examples remain, and the earliest narrative treated is that of Isaac and his sons. Probably, however, other Old Testament plays once existed, and some of these may have reached back to the story of Adam and his progeny.[2] The final events of history, as conceived in medieval belief, are represented in dramatizations of themes associated with the Last Judgement and the end of the world.[3] Within these limits most attention was given, inevitably, to the life of Christ, especially to the Nativity and the Resurrection. Subsequent Christian events are treated in plays concerning the conversion of St Paul, the life of the Virgin Mary, and the miracles of St Nicholas. From the texts still preserved, then, and from others whose existence may be reasonably inferred, we must conclude that the Church dramatized sacred history with generous inclusiveness.

In the general nature of their content and of their attachment to the liturgy the plays differ greatly. One kind of performance is essentially a dramatization of an established liturgical ceremony, and hence is not only liturgical in content, but also an indispensable part of public worship. This is true, for example, of the Epiphany play from Besançon, which virtually appropriates the gospel in the Mass, and in which the impersonated *reges* participate in reading, or intoning, the liturgical gospel itself.[4] Slightly different is the bearing of the Epiphany play from Limoges, for though this is clearly a dramatization of the offertory of the Mass, the utterances of the *reges* do not include the established liturgical text.[5] Somewhat similar is the intrusion of Mary and John into the liturgical ceremony of the Adoration of the Cross at Regensburg.[6] A further variation is shown by the

[1] For bibliography see Notes, p. 501.

[2] See above, pp. 170–1.

[3] See chapter xxvii.

[4] See above, pp. 37 sqq. See also the participation of Mary and Gabriel in the singing of the gospel of the Annunciation, above, pp. 246 sqq. In supporting my statements in the present chapter I do not undertake to exhaust the evidences contained in the body of the treatise and in the Notes.

[5] See above, pp. 34 sqq.

[6] See above, i, 503 sqq. See also the rela-

*Ordo Prophetarum*, which seems to have arisen as a dramatization of an authorized *lectio* in Matins, but which, as a play, became extra-liturgical, or detachable, and took varying positions on the periphery of the main liturgical structure.[1]

In general, however, the plays arose not as dramatizations of essential parts of the liturgy, but as deliberate additions to it. The earliest dramatic germ, from which developed the plays of Easter, was a brief dialogue inspired by the Gospel narratives of the Resurrection, but composed with freedom, and attached to the true liturgical text as an avowed embellishment. This dialogue was gradually extended, for dramatic purposes, through the addition of liturgical pieces from the choir-books, of passages from the Bible, and, eventually, of verses composed imaginatively.[2] A parallel, though limited, development can be traced for the *Officium Pastorum* of Christmas,[3] and possibly other plays had a similar history.[4] Most of the more elaborate plays, however, seem to have been composed in their extant forms in a spirit of literary and dramatic independence, and to have been attached to the liturgy as appendages, rather than as intimate accompaniments of central acts of worship.[5] This is true, for example, of the longer Magi plays, and of the plays on Lazarus, St Paul, and St Nicholas.[6]

As to the general method of staging the plays we can be fairly certain, since a considerable number of texts describe the arrangements in detail.[7] The principle was that of a group of 'places' or 'structures' (*loca*, *loci*, *sedes*, *domus*) distributed about a central, open playing-space (*platea*). Each of these *sedes*, whether or not it was furnished with realistic 'properties', was the centre of a scene. The simplest Easter play required only one specific *sedes*: namely, some sort of representation of a *sepulchrum*. Here the angel was stationed for his dialogue with the Marys, and with this dialogue the action began and ended. For a more elaborate Easter play, such as that from Klosterneuburg,

tion of the *Peregrinus* to the *Processio ad Fontes* in Easter Vespers, above, i, 456 sqq.

1 See chapter xxi.

2 The development of the Easter play is traced in chapters vii–xiv.

3 See chapter xvii.

4 See, for example, the *Ordo Rachelis*, chapter xx.

5 Some texts, of course, bear no evidence of direct liturgical attachment. See, for example, the Benediktbeuern Passion play and Christmas play, and the plays on subjects from eschatology, chapters xvi, xxii, and xxvii. The rubrics of two plays of Hilarius allow an option between two widely separated liturgical positions. See above, pp. 218, 286.

6 See chapters xix, xxiii, xxvi.

7 For observations see, for example, Creizenach, i, 79–80; Sepet, *Prophètes*, pp. 69–70; Wilken, pp. 190–208; Chambers, ii, 79; Cohen, *Théâtre*, pp. 16–8; Cohen, *Mise en Scène*, pp. iii–x.

would be needed several separate *sedes*, for all, or some, of the following: Pilate and his soldiers, the *pontifices*, the *specionarius*, the *sepulchrum*, Peter and John and the other apostles, Christ and Mary Magdalen, and *Infernus*.[1] A similar arrangement of the action among a number of *sedes* is assured, or may be inferred, for any of the more highly developed plays, such as the Norman *Officium Stellæ*,[2] the *Suscitatio Lazari* and *Conversio Sancti Pauli* of the Fleury play-book,[3] or the *Antichristus* from Tegernsee;[4] and in a fair proportion of such pieces the passing of actors, and the progress of the action, from one *sedes* to another are indicated explicitly.[5] This plan of staging obviously presents the possibility of representing action at two separate *sedes* simultaneously, and this procedure seems occasionally to have been followed.[6]

Although for most plays, probably, the structures and stage-properties required at the various *sedes* were relatively simple, in some instances the structural and mechanical provisions must have been fairly ambitious. The greater part of the Easter plays may have required merely the simplest sort of *sepulchrum*: the altar itself, or a small edifice formed of books arranged upon the altar table, or a niche in the wall of the choir. Some sepulchres, however, were ample spaces enclosed by curtains, elaborately carved monuments, or even spacious imitations of the Holy Sepulchre at Jerusalem.[7] Likewise the simplest Christmas plays required only a small *præsepe* furnished with one or more images;[8] but in the more highly developed compositions of Epiphany the *sedes* for Herod and his *entourage* must have shown considerable elaboration.[9] Examples of the more elaborate structures, stage-properties, and mechanisms in other plays are the following: the representation of the *castellum* with its supper-table in some versions of the *Peregrinus*;[10] the contrivance for raising the *imago Christi* in the dramatic ceremony of the Ascension;[11] the tree for Zacchæus, the tomb for Lazarus, the room for the Last Supper, the *sedes* for Mount Olivet, and the

[1] See above, i, 421 sqq. One or more of the personages or groups might, of course, act their parts upon the central *platea*, and enter and withdraw without using special *sedes* of their own. For Pilate a specific *locus* is provided, but none is mentioned for the *pontifices*.

[2] See above, p. 68.

[3] See above, pp. 199, 219.

[4] See above, p. 371.

[5] See, for example, the *Officium Stellæ* of Rouen (above, p. 43), and the Fleury *Conversio Sancti Pauli* and *Filius Getronis* (above, pp. 219, 351).

[6] See the shorter Passion play from Benediktbeuern above, i, 514; Creizenach, i, 85; Cohen, *Théâtre*, p. 17.

[7] The *sepulchrum* is discussed in Appendix A.

[8] See above, pp. 10 sqq.

[9] See especially the plays in chapter xix.

[10] For examples see chapter xv.

[11] See above, i, 488.

cross for the Crucifixion, in the Passion play from Benediktbeuern;[1] the furnace of Nebuchadnezzar, and the ass of Balaam, in the *Ordo Prophetarum* of Rouen;[2] the device for lowering Saul from the wall of Damascus, in the *Conversio Sancti Pauli*;[3] the carefully-erected stages for the ceremony of the Presentation of the Blessed Virgin Mary;[4] the kitchens and other *sedes* in the play of Isaac and Rebecca;[5] the *lacus* for lions, and the arrangements for *regalia*, battles and pageantry in the plays of Daniel;[6] the church, and the contrivance for transporting Adeodatus, in the miracle play *Filius Getronis*;[7] and the impressive deploying of platforms in the Antichrist.[8] With the increase in the number, size and elaborateness of the *sedes*, probably the playing-space was extended from the choir of the church into the nave; and some plays, such as the *Ludus de Antichristo*, if played within the building, must have taxed its entire resources.[9]

For information as to costuming and the other means employed for impersonation we must rely upon the texts of the plays themselves, and these are not uniformly communicative. Silence concerning such matters is particularly noticeable in the rubrics of some of the longer and more elaborate pieces, in which we should expect impersonation to be provided for most carefully. In the highly spectacular dramatic ceremony for the Presentation of the Blessed Virgin Mary, to be sure, the meticulous descriptions of costume leave nothing to be desired;[10] but we have no assurance that the details in this late medieval invention are applicable to the plays of the preceding centuries. For our facts, then, we must resort chiefly to the uncommonly generous rubrics in the many versions of the Easter play.[11] In these, it would appear, the costumes were usually the ordinary vestments of the sacristy, often slightly rearranged and sometimes supplemented by realistic or symbolical objects, through an earnest effort toward accuracy of impersonation.[12] Thus in the *Visitatio*

[1] See above, i, 518 sqq.

[2] See above, pp. 154 sqq.

[3] See above, p. 222.

[4] See above, pp. 227 sqq.

[5] See above, p. 259.

[6] See above, pp. 276 sqq.

[7] See above, pp. 351 sqq.

[8] See above, p. 371.

[9] See above, p. 394; Chambers, ii, 79. Even in some of the simpler versions of the *Visitatio Sepulchri* the action ranged outside the choir. At Aquileia (see below p. 510) and Essen (see i, 335) the *sepulchrum* was in the western end of the church, and in a play from Würzburg (see i, 258) it was in the crypt. In regard to the doubtful possibility that plays such as the St Nicholas ones from Fleury were acted in the cloister or the refectory see Creizenach, i, 96–9.

[10] See above, pp. 228 sqq.

[11] See chapters ix–xiv, and the Notes thereto. From the abundant evidence in these chapters I cite here only a few examples.

[12] Liturgical vestments are expounded in

*Sepulchri* of Rouen the three Marys appear as follows: *Tres dyaconi canonici, induti dalmaticis, et amictus habentes super capita sua ad similitudinem Mulierum, vascula tenentes in manibus.*[1] Here the three deacons undertake to impersonate women by shifting amices from their shoulders to the tops of their heads, and by carrying vessels in their hands. This arrangement is sufficiently typical. It is not significant that the dalmatics are sometimes replaced by copes or albs, and that the objects carried may be vases or boxes or pyxes. Of some interest is the occasional attempt to indicate individuality through a difference in costume, such as is shown by the following rubric from the Easter play of Fécamp: *Tres fratres in specie Mulierum, quorum unus in capa rubea portet thuribulum inter duos alios, et ceteri duo ex utroque latere ejus in dalmaticis candidis portent vasa in modum pissidarum.*[2] A normal vesting of the cleric who takes the role of Christ is described in the following rubric from the *Visitatio Sepulchri* from Nuremberg: *Mox ex improviso Dominica Persona adveniens, quæ sit vestita dalmatica, casulamque complicatam super humeros habeat, coronamque capiti superimpositam, nudis pedibus incedat.*[3] Similarly liturgical is the costume of the angel in the *Visitatio* from the *Regularis Concordia* of the tenth century: *Quatuor fratres induant se, quorum unus alba indutus acsi ad aliud agendum ingrediatur, atque latenter Sepulchri locum adeat, ibique manu tenens palmam quietus sedeat.*[4]

Realism is increased when the angels are provided with wings,[5] and when the clerics impersonating the Marys are costumed *ad modum mulierum*, or *vestibus puellaribus*, or *vestibus mulieribus*.[6] A further advance is illustrated by a device such as the staff set with ten candles borne by the angels, in the *Visitatio* from Coutances, as a representation of the *aspectus sicut fulgur* which struck dumb the guards at the sepulchre.[7] That realism in gesture was also carefully cultivated is shown by rubrics such as *pedetemptim*, *vultibus submissis*, *lamentabili voce*, and *Petro claudicante*,[8] and by the directions for the behaviour of Archisynagogus in the Christmas play from Benediktbeuern, and of the participants in the *Planctus Mariæ* from Cividale.[9]

many manuals, and notably by J. Braun, *Die liturgische Gewandung im Occident und Orient*, Freiburg, 1907.

[1] See above, i, 370.

[2] See above, i, 264.

[3] See above, i, 399.

[4] See above, i, 249. For a discrimination between the costumes of the two angels at the sepulchre see above, i, 435.

[5] See above, i, 290, 294.

[6] See above, i, 257, 294, 296.

[7] See above, i, 408; Matt. xxviii, 3.

[8] See above, i, 249, 363, 370; ii, 353.

[9] See above, p. 175; i, 507; Mantzius, ii, 5–7; Herrmann, pp. 241–3.

A certain emancipation from liturgical tradition in costume appears in the life-like habiliments of some of the prophets in the *Ordo Prophetarum* from Laon, and of the chief personages in the ceremony of the Presentation of the Virgin Mary.[1]

As to the status of the actors, the texts of the more elaborate plays seldom give us any information. The more ample rubrics supplied for the various versions of the *Visitatio Sepulchri* indicate that in these plays, at least, the roles were usually assumed by members of the clergy in major orders, or by *pueri*, *fratres*, or *clerici*.[2] Dignitaries such as bishops or heads of monastic houses seem not to have taken part in the acting, but they may be assumed to have presided over performances, and they are frequently spoken of as having taken up the singing of the *Te Deum* at the close.[3] In nunneries the roles of the Marys seem sometimes to have been assumed, very appropriately, by women.[4] Probably the practices associated with the plays of Easter apply also to other dramatic performances.[5] It is entirely possible, however, that in the more ambitious pieces, such as those from Benediktbeuern, the plays of Daniel and the *Ludus de Antichristo*, some of the actors were *clerici vagantes*, or schoolboys, or other outsiders.

The plays themselves, as we have had ample opportunity to observe, are not free from dramatic ineptitudes. One of these is the presence in some speeches of bits of narrative or exposition inappropriately assigned to the speakers themselves. Thus in an early Easter play from Reichenau the Marys say, *Et dicebant ad invicem: Quis revolvit nobis lapidem ab ostio monumenti?* and in a later one from Einsiedeln Mary Magdalen exclaims, *Rabbi! quod dicitur magister*.[6] Likewise Peter and John are sometimes called upon to say the antiphon *Currebant duo simul*, recounting their own action.[7] Usually, however, this antiphon, and the other narrative and explanatory passages introducing, accompanying, or concluding the dialogue, are sung by the chorus;[8] and these

[1] See above, pp. 145, 228.

[2] For illustrations see, for example, the texts printed above, i, 244, 249, 264, 310, 370, 381.

[3] See above, for example, i, 250, 262.

[4] See the texts from Barking and Troyes above, i, 381, 603. At Essen the Marys were *tres canonicæ*, and at Brescia, *tres dominæ*. See above, i, 221, 333. See also Brooks, *Sepulchre*, p. 48.

[5] The versions of the *Officium Pastorum* associated with Rouen seem to have been acted by *pueri* and *clerici*. See above, pp. 14 sqq.

[6] See above, i, 259, 391. In the text from Tours (see above, i, 449) Thomas begins by saying, *Thomas dicor Didymus*.

[7] See above, i, 354, 356.

[8] As to *Currebant duo simul* see the abundant examples in chapters xi and xii. For other examples of choral utterances see above, i, 400, 464, 523, 524.

choral utterances are the precursors of the role of the 'expositor' or 'doctor' in the later religious drama in the vernaculars.[1] Sometimes, in the Church plays, the chorus usurps a place in the dialogue itself, as, for example, when one or more choristers address *Dic nobis* to Mary Magdalen or the other Marys in the Easter plays;[2] and occasionally a purely narrative choral passage is imperfectly adapted to the dialogue which it accompanies, as is the responsory *Dum transisset sabbatum*, mentioning three women, when only two appear in the action.[3]

Sometimes associated with choral singing is another practice which could result in theatrical awkwardness: namely, the preliminary stationing of the *dramatis personæ* at their several *sedes*, with or without the accompaniment of a formal procession.[4] This procedure is illustrated by the opening rubric of the *Conversio Sancti Pauli* from Fleury:[5]

Ad repræsentandum Conversionem Beati Pauli Apostoli paretur in competenti loco, quasi Jerusalem, quædam sedes, et super eam Princeps Sacerdotum. Paretur et alia sedes, et super eam juvenis quidam in similitudine Sauli; habeatque secum Ministros armatos. Ex alia vero parte, aliquantulum longe ab his sedibus, sint paratæ quasi in Damasco duæ sedes, in altera quarum sedeat vir quidam nomine Judas, et in altera Princeps Synagogæ Damasci. Et inter has duas sedes sit paratus lectus, in quo jaceat vir quidam in similitudine Ananiæ.

From these directions one infers that the personages of the play, including Ananias lying on his bed, take their positions in full view of the spectators at the outset, and thus preclude the possibility of pleasurable surprise at appropriate moments in the subsequent action. Presumably this maladjustment was sometimes remedied by hanging before a *sedes* a curtain which could conceal the character until his cue arrived;[6] and in some instances a principal character was kept from the stage altogether until his presence was actually required. In this manner Antichrist and his associates enter *in medias res* in the *Ludus de Antichristo*.[7]

[1] See Venzmer, pp. 17–21. As this critic explains (pp. 3–6), the use of the chorus in the Church plays is not an inheritance from ancient classical drama. See also above, p. 266.

[2] See above, for example, i, 281, 284.

[3] See above, for example, i, 315, 325.

[4] See Creizenach, i, 80, and above, i, 518; ii, 351–2, 371.

[5] See above, p. 219.

[6] This possibility is suggested by the curtain in the *Visitatio Sepulchri* of the *Regularis Concordia* (see above, i, 249), in the Rouen *Officium Stellæ* (see above, p. 44), and in the dramatic ceremony of the Annunciation (see above, p. 246, and below, p. 480). See the curtains used for some of the 'scaffolds' in the English Hegge Plays (see K. S. Block, ed., *Ludus Coventriæ*, London, 1922, pp. 245, 254, 283).

[7] See above, p. 377.

More precisely literary are the faults arising occasionally from clumsy sequence and from monotonous repetition. In the great majority of versions of the *Visitatio Sepulchri*, for example, the invitation *Venite et videte*, spoken by the angel, is placed awkwardly in the general progress of the action; and in a good many of these same Easter plays the position of *Victimæ paschali* causes dramatic difficulties.[1] Monotony appears in such matters as the uniformity of the stanzas in the Hildesheim miracle plays, and the identical dialogues accompanying the actions of the three suitors in the *Tres Filiæ* from Fleury.[2]

It is fair to say, however, that blemishes of this sort are fewer than they might have been, and that they do not seriously impair the impressiveness of the plays as a whole. This impressiveness arises, no doubt, chiefly from the subjects presented, and from the striking effects inherent in the narratives dramatized. No representation of the Crucifixion or the Harrowing of Hell or the coming of Antichrist could fail to convey somewhat of the majesty or awesomeness associated with these themes; nor could the oriental ceremoniousness of the Daniel plays and of the longer versions of the *Officium Stellæ* fall short of spectacular pageantry, or the appearances of Christ to Mary Magdalen and the mourning disciples lack pathos. To achieve his effect the playwright had only to let the Gospels or the legends take visible form, and often without greatly modifying the speeches of the personages as recorded in the Vulgate or established in passages of the liturgy.[3] Usually, however, he resorted to verse, the greater part of which shows no poetic distinction, but which sometimes has a mild creative significance, such as is seen in *Planctus ante nescia*,[4] in the laments of Rachel,[5] in the consolation uttered to the sisters of Lazarus,[6] in the opening lines of the longer *Peregrinus* from Sicily,[7] and in the sonorous lines accompanying the pageantry of the Daniel plays.[8]

In the portrayal of the chief sacred personages in these plays we should not expect to find striking subtlety or originality. Such psychological disclosures and discriminations of personality as are attempted are often attached to characters concerning

[1] See above, i, 247, 336. For defective sequence see also above i, 301–2.

[2] See above, pp. 312 sqq., 318 sqq.

[3] See the simpler forms of Easter play (chapters ix and x), the *Peregrinus* (chapter xv), and parts of the Passion plays from Benediktbeuern (chapter xvi).

[4] See above, i, 496 sqq.

[5] See above, chapter xx.

[6] See the Fleury play above, p. 210.

[7] See above, i, 477.

[8] See above, pp. 279, 291.

whom the Scriptures have little to say, or who are dramatic inventions. Outbursts of remorse, or anger, or terror are exhibited in the penitent Mary Magdalen of the Benediktbeuern Passion play,[1] in the blustering Herod of the Magi plays,[2] and in the desperate *fatuæ* of the *Sponsus*.[3] More delicate shades of feeling appear, for example, in the subdued reverence of the apothecary in the Easter play from Origny,[4] in the shifting moods of Darius in the play of Daniel from Beauvais,[5] and in the self-assurance of the boy, Adeodatus, in the *Filius Getronis*.[6] Discrimination of character upon a more ample scale is shown in the *Ludus de Antichristo* in the contrasted temperaments of the French and German kings.[7]

How far characterization proceeded in the direction of the comic is not easy to estimate, in the general absence of direct indications in the rubrics of the plays themselves. That the Church could tolerate a substantial amount of buffoonery in association with the liturgy is apparent from the history of the Feast of Fools and of the Boy Bishop;[8] and there is evidence enough that popular horse-play sometimes attached itself, in an external way, to sober dramatic ceremonies such as those representing the Ascension and the Assumption.[9] We are told explicitly, moreover, that the spectators were expected to laugh at the discomfiture of *Synagoga* in the highly decorous ceremony of the Presentation of the Virgin Mary;[10] and the gestures prescribed for Archisynagogus in the Christmas play from Benediktbeuern seem clearly to have been aimed at a comic effect.[11]

In many instances, however, we are left in doubt as to how a medieval congregation felt toward certain figures which in the modern world would evoke only laughter. Thus critics differ as to the dramatic effect intended by the devil who tempts Mary Magdalen in the Passion play from Benediktbeuern, and by the *dæmones* who snatch away the Foolish Virgins at the close of the *Sponsus*.[12] Undoubtedly the Germanized *diabolus* of the Middle Ages in Western Europe was an object of derision

[1] See above, i, 522, 524.
[2] See above, for example, pp. 98 sqq.
[3] See above, p. 364.
[4] See above, i, 420.
[5] See above, p. 301.
[6] See above, p. 358.
[7] See above, p. 395.
[8] See above, i, 104 sqq.
[9] See above, i, 489; ii, 256. See also below, p. 504.
[10] See above, p. 238.
[11] See above, p. 175.
[12] See above, i, 535; ii, 364. Wilmotte (pp. 112–3, 118–20) regards these roles as comic; Creizenach (i, 71) refers to the *dæmones* of the *Sponsus* as 'gewiss noch keine trivialen Spassmacher'.

as well as of fear, but in a particular dramatic situation we may not be able to say confidently which effect was intended or achieved.[1] In the examples mentioned I infer that the motives of the playwright were essentially serious; but this inference is not indisputable. Similar uncertainties arise in other cases. Whereas the gibberish of two of the Magi in the Norman *Officium Stellæ* is by some regarded as comic,[2] it seems rather to have represented an effort toward a mild sort of realism.[3] It may be hard for us to believe that the long ears and restive movements of Balaam's ass in the *Ordo Prophetarum* failed to arouse merriment, and yet the texts of the play and the ecclesiastical tradition associated with this animal give no encouragement to such an interpretation.[4] As nuclei for comic action one would naturally cite also such possibilities as the bustling retinue of Herod in the plays of Epiphany,[5] the soldiers and the *unguentarius* of the Easter plays,[6] and the Mary Magdalen *in gaudio* of the Benediktbeuern Passion play;[7] and beyond all doubt such figures were treated with levity in the later religious drama in the vernaculars.[8] But for the Latin plays of the Church such developments are to be claimed only with caution. One might even hesitate to say at precisely what point in its expansion the rage of *Herodes iratus* himself came to be felt as purely ludicrous.

Whatever the degree of levity or seriousness intended in a particular play or scene, the distinction does not appear in the nomenclature attached to the texts themselves. We are never guided by such designations as *tragœdia* and *comœdia*.[9] In many instances the plays are referred to by mere liturgical expressions, such as *Ordo Processionis Asinorum*, *Festum Asinorum*, *Ordo ad Peregrinum*, *Ordo Rachelis*, *Ordo ad visitandum Sepulchrum*, and *Ordo*

[1] For a discussion of the nature of the devil in medieval religious drama see Rudwin, *Teufel*, pp. 1–14.

[2] See Wilmotte, pp. 107–8.

[3] See above, p. 70.

[4] See the plays from Laon and Rouen above, pp. 150, 159. In regard to the ecclesiastical tradition of the ass see Cabrol and Leclercq, i, 2041–68.

[5] See above, for example, pp. 53, 82; Wilmotte, p. 100.

[6] See above, for example, i, 431, 437.

[7] See above, i, 521.

[8] See Creizenach, i, 199–209; Chambers, ii, 90–1; below, p. 422.

[9] The prophet play performed at Riga in 1204 is called *ludus . . . quem Latini Comœdiam vocant* (see appendix D, p. 542); but probably this learned reference is merely a contribution of the chronicler. See Chambers, ii, 103, 210. Probably a chronicler is again responsible for the designation *comœdia sacra* applied to the play produced by the English bishops at Constance in 1417. See below, p. 419. In regard to medieval conceptions of *comœdia* and *tragœdia* see above, i, 6. The medieval designations applied to Church plays in general are reviewed by Chambers, ii, 103–5; and particular designations are considered above, i, 411, 576, 684, 688.

*Stellæ*.[1] Likewise liturgical in tone is the use at Rouen of the designations *Officium Sepulchri*, *Officium Peregrinorum*, *Officium Pastorum*, *Officium Regum Trium*, and *Officium Stellæ*.[2] Again the designation may be a mere description of the theme of the play, as in the following: *Visitatio Sepulchri*,[3] *Suscitatio Lazari*,[4] *Versus de Resuscitatione Lazari*,[5] *Angelica de Christi Resurrectione*,[6] *De Peregrino*,[7] and *Ad Interfectionem Puerorum*.[8]

A closer approach to a distinctively dramatic designation appears in such rubrics as *Versus ad Herodem faciendum*[9] and *Tunc fit Visitatio Sepulchri*;[10] and particularly in the use at Fleury of the noun *similitudo* (*Ad faciendam similitudinem Dominici Sepulcri*; *Ad faciendam similitudinem Dominicæ Apparitionis in specie Peregrini*).[11] Probably the most normal term for a dramatic performance is *repræsentatio*, frequently found in expressions like *Repræsentatio Sepulcri*,[12] *Repræsentatio Herodis*,[13] *In Annuntiatione Beatæ Mariæ Virginis Repræsentatio*,[14] *Post repræsentationem Mariarum*,[15] *Annuntiationis Repræsentatio*,[16] *Repræsentatio Peregrinorum*,[17] and *Repræsentatio Pastorum . . . Resurrectionis . . . Peregrinorum*.[18] Occasionally one finds the word *ludus*, a designation rendered generally ambiguous through its common association with popular revelling, but clearly dramatic in the following uses: *Ludus breviter de Passione*,[19] *Incipit Danielis ludus*,[20] and *Ludus super Iconia Sancti Nicolai*.[21] In one instance this word is coupled with *exemplum* (*Incipit ludus, immo exemplum, Dominicæ Resurrectionis*),[22] and at least once this latter term is used alone (*Incipit exemplum apparitionis Domini Discipulis suis juxta Castellum Emaus*).[23] The text of the *Iconia Sancti Nicolai* from Fleury twice employs the significant

[1] See above, i, 467, 664; ii, 103, 117, 154.

[2] See above, i, 370, 693; ii, 14, 43, 432. Chambers (ii, 103) may well be right in his inference that '*officium* may be taken to denote the thing itself, the special service or section of a service; *ordo* rather the book, the written directions for carrying out the *officium*'. *Officium* is also used in the meaning of 'role' or 'part' (see above, i, 327, 355: *Dyaconus . . . acturus officium Angeli*).

[3] See above, for example, i, 333, 354.

[4] See above, p. 212.

[5] See above, p. 199.

[6] See above, i, 587.

[7] See above, i, 459.

[8] See above, p. 110.

[9] See above, p. 59; and also above, i, 477, and below, p. 439.

[10] See above, i, 331; and also above, i, 453.

[11] See above, i, 393, 471.

[12] See above, i, 606.

[13] See above, p. 99.

[14] See above, p. 247.

[15] See above, i, 616.

[16] See below, p. 479.

[17] See above, i, 694.

[18] See below, p. 522. See also above, i, 658, 690. For uses of the related verb see, for example, *Ad repræsentandum Conversionem Beati Pauli* (above, p. 219), *Ordo ad repræsentandum Herodem* (above, p. 84), and *Historia de Daniel repræsentanda* (above, p. 276).

[19] See above, i, 514.

[20] See above, p. 290.

[21] See above, p. 338. Concerning *ludus* see also above, i, 684.

[22] See above, i, 432.

[23] See above, i, 463.

word *miraculum*: in the expression *Aliud miraculum de Sancto Nicholao et de quodam Judæo*, where it might denote merely the legend dramatized, and in the closing rubric *Finitur miraculum*, where it seems pretty clearly to mean the dramatization itself.[1]

Of all the recorded designations the most instructive in its relationships is *misterium*, or *mysterium*, which can be cited from at least two texts of the fourteenth century, and from another which represents the usage of that period. The expression *Resurrectionis mysterium* from a decree of the Synod of Worms in 1316 refers to the ceremony of the *Elevatio Crucifixi* on Easter morning, and can hardly be shown to indicate anything specifically dramatic in this ceremony.[2] In this instance *mysterium* may mean no more than 'ceremonial act', 'service', or 'office', and may thus conform to an established liturgical use in the sense of *officium ecclesiasticum*.[3] The same interpretation, perhaps, is to be given to the terms *misterium repræsentationis* and *misterium Præsentationis Mariæ* referring to the elaborate dramatic office of the Presentation of the Blessed Virgin Mary.[4] It is hard to believe, however, that in the expression *misterium repræsentationis* the first word implies nothing dramatic. This meaning seems to become specific, in any case, in the following *ordo* of the fourteenth century from the monastery of Mont-Saint-Michel:[5]

Die sabbati in vigilia Palmarum cantor precipiet fratribus ut dicant Passiones: scilicet succentori illam de Dominica, et aliis fratribus Passiones de feria tertia, quarta et sexta. Et precipiet vni qui faciat Deum ad *misterium* Matutini Pasche, et vni iuueni qui faciat Angelum desuper altare, et tribus aliis iuuenibus ut faciant tres Mulieres, et duobus aliis fratribus vt faciant Angelos de Sepulchro. Et die Veneris in Parasceue in choro preparatur habitaculum ad modum Sepulcri. Et postquam Crux in illa die adorata fuerit, abbas dicat ad altare antiphonam *Super omnia*. Et post eat ad illud habitaculum et ponat ibi Crucem cantando antiphonam *In pace*. Et sit ibi Crux usque ad duodecimam horam noctis ante Matutinum Pasche, in qua hora abbas veniet et fratres in albis, et leuabit eam et deferat super altare, et incipiet *Christus resurgens*.

I have quoted liberally in order to make clear the fact that whereas the play of the three Marys at the tomb, with its provision for impersonation, is called *misterium*, the liturgical

[1] See above, pp. 344, 348. Concerning *miraculum* see also below, p. 503.

[2] See above, i, 553. The *Depositio* and *Elevatio* are treated in chapters iv and v.

[3] See Du Cange, v, 424.

[4] See above, pp. 234, 240.

[5] Avranches, Bibl. de la Ville, MS 214, Ordin. monasterii Sancti Michaëlis sæc. xiv, p. 236, printed above, i, 575. I italicize the word under discussion.

ceremonies, *Depositio* and *Elevatio*, are not so designated.[1] Here, then, we seem to have, in the fourteenth century, an example of the use of *misterium* meaning 'dramatic performance'; and this word with this meaning would seem to be the acceptable parent of the word *mystère*, or *mistère*, which arose in France late in the fourteenth century, and flourished during the century following.[2]

## II

This summary description of ecclesiastical drama, drawn chiefly from evidences in the texts of the plays themselves, raises a natural query as to how these dramatic performances were regarded during the Middle Ages by persons charged with the intimate guidance of the faithful, and by the authorities responsible for general Church government. The answers to this question have not always been free from confusion. That the *ludi* of the folk, the liturgical buffoonery of the *clerici*, and the disorderly conduct of spectators were widely condemned there can be no doubt. The succession of utterances upon these matters from Church councils and dignitaries is a long one.[3] By no means so numerous, however, and by no means so uniform in their character, are the responsible pronouncements upon the serious dramatizing of sacred subjects. It is with these alone that we are concerned here.[4]

As to the reverent intention of the clerics who composed and performed the plays we are fairly assured. The tropes, or literary embellishments, from which the first dramatic representations arose were inserted into the liturgy for the serious purpose of adornment and exposition, and they were eventually dramatized in a manifest desire to convey edifying instruction. In speaking of the dramatic ceremonies at the Easter sepulchre, for example, the authors of the *Regularis Concordia* declare that they are designed 'to fortify the faith of the unlearned vulgar and of neophytes';[5] and the devout motive of the abbess, Katherine of Sutton, in arranging an Easter play at Barking in the fourteenth century is explained thus:[6]

[1] Concerning the fundamental difference between the *Visitatio Sepulchri* and the *Depositio-Elevatio* in dramatic content see above, i, 237. For the text of the *Visitatio Sepulchri* from Mont-Saint-Michel see above, i, 372.

[2] For further observations on this etymological development see Notes, p. 501.

[3] See, for example, D'Ancona, i, 49–51, 53–7; Chambers, i, 90–102, 276–9, 292 sqq.; ii, 290–306; and above, i, 489; ii, 256.

[4] For bibliography see Notes, p. 502.

[5] See above, i, 133.

[6] See above, i, 165.

Quoniam populorum concursus temporibus illis videbatur deuocione frigessere, et torpor humanus maxime accrescens, venerabilis Domina Katerina de Suttone, tunc pastoralis cure gerens vicem, desiderans dictum torporem penitus extirpare et fidelium deuocionem ad tam celeb⟨r⟩em celebracionem magis excitare, vnanimi consororum consensu instituit ut statim post tertium responsorium Matutinarum die Pasche fieret Dominice Resur⟨r⟩exionis celebracio.

Although the texts of the plays are seldom accompanied by declarations so explicit as these, we may assume that a similar didactic purpose was general among the playwrights.[1]

It hardly need be said, however, that an exalted intention on the part of those who brought the plays forth was not inevitably accompanied by the sanction of ecclesiastical authority. The dramatic compositions, and the general liturgical embellishment from which they developed, were not a project of the Church hierarchy as a whole, but the gradual and irregular achievement of various separate communities, which imitated and emulated one another in accordance with local desires and resources.[2] Hence, in performing plays, the separate communities took a variety of risks, and the accredited moralists and disciplinarians might be expected to express a variety of judgements. Gerhoh of Reichersberg (1093–1169), a firm supporter of the papacy, for example, condemned comprehensively all those who interested themselves in dramatics. He expressed contempt for the monks of Augsburg who, when he was *magister scholæ* there (c. 1122–3), occupied the dormitory or used the refectory only on occasions when a representation of Herod or of the slaughter of the Innocents, or some other *ludus*, provided an incentive to conviviality:[3]

Cohærebat ipsi ecclesiæ claustrum satis honestum, sed a claustrali religione omnino vacuum, cum neque in dormitorio fratres dormirent, neque in refectorio comederent, exceptis rarissimis festis, maxime, in quibus Herodem repræsentarent Christi persecutorem, parvulorum interfectorem seu ludis aliis aut spectaculis quasi theatralibus exhibendis comportaretur symbolum ad faciendum convivium in refectorio, aliis pene omnibus temporibus vacuo.

That Gerhoh's hostility to Church plays continued throughout his life appears from his treatise *De Investigatione Antichristi*,

[1] See below, p. 479; Brinkmann, pp. 115, 142.

[2] See D'Ancona, i, 53.

[3] *Gerhohi Præpositi Reicherspergensis Commentarium in Psalmos*, in Migne, *P.L.*, cxciv, 890.

written about the year 1161. Here he devotes a chapter (*De spectaculis theatricis in ecclesia Dei exhibitis*) to the contention that those who use a church as a theatre for representing the deeds of Antichrist or the rage of Herod are themselves guilty of the vices of the personages portrayed:[1]

Quid ergo mirum si et isti nunc antichristum vel Herodem in suis ludis simulantes eosdem non, ut eis intentioni est, ludicro mentiuntur sed in veritate exhibent, utpote quorum vita ab Antichristi laxa conversatione non longe abest?

His condemnation includes, moreover, the plays of the Nativity cycle as a whole, and, as we may assume, dramatizations of all sacred events in which clerics undertake impersonation, be it of women, soldiers or devils:[2]

Exhibent præterea imaginaliter et Salvatoris infantiæ cunabula, parvuli vagitum, puerperæ virginis matronalem habitum, stellæ quasi sidus flammigerum, infantum necem, maternum Rachelis ploratum. Sed divinitas insuper et matura facies ecclesiæ abhorret spectacula theatralia, non respicit in vanitates et insanias falsas, immo non falsas sed jam veras insanias, in quibus viri totos se frangunt in feminas quasi pudeat eos, quod viri sunt, clerici in milites, homines se in dæmonum larvas transfigurant.

Far more discriminating than the attitude of Gerhoh is that taken, toward the end of the twelfth century, by Herrad of Landsberg. As abbess of the monastery of Hohenburg (1167–95) she prepared for the edification of her nuns a generous compilation of religious and literary lore, which, from its rich variety and profuse pictorial illustration, was aptly entitled *Hortus Deliciarum*. The author's counsel concerning Church plays is conveyed in the following passage:[3]

Denique multa mala exempla de bonis orta sunt. Quod ab ecclesiæ rectoribus ex antiquo sancta intentione quæsitum inventum ad posteritatem erudiendam permissum est quod pro augenda fide vel religione Christiana in misticis exemplaribus ad meliora positum et decretum est a successoribus eorum vel eorum subditis et modernis aut immutatum aut ordine incompetentiori diversificatum vel certe penitus obliteratum est de his exemplum adiciendum est.

Postquam Deus homo factus est et mundo apparuit qui in forma Dei semper invisibilis fuit oblatam gratiam primitivus ecclesiæ populus tanto

[1] Scheibelberger, p. 26. For the entire chapter see Appendix C. See also Creizenach, i, 94; Chambers, ii, 98–9.

[2] Scheibelberger, p. 27.

[3] Wilmart, pp. 95–7. Concerning the text see Notes, p. 502.

amoris fervore suscepit de ordine illo divino id est de gradibus susceptæ humanitatis Christi vel scriptis vel exemplis transmittere posteritati poterat modis omnibus intenderet ut si deessent alicubi scripta ad fidem secula secutura firmarent vel exempla.

Igitur de Nativitate Christi, de eius manifestatione et Magorum mysticis muneribus, de circumcisione, de eius in laude populi et palmis virentibus Hierosolimam itinere in asino et de duobus in Emaus[1] discipulis quædam imitandi vestigia ecclesia præfixit per exempla quæ in quibusdam iuxta traditionem antiquorum digna veneratione celebrantur ecclesiis, in quibusdam aut pro voluntate aut pro necessitate vel mutata sunt vel neglecta. Et ut superiora repetamus quo sepe ex honorum exemplorum radice mali fructus prodierunt oportet ostendi de paucis excessum et neglectum cognoscamus in multis. De sancta die vel octava Epiphaniæ ab antiquis patribus religio quædam imaginaria de Magis stella duce Christum natum quærentibus, de Herodis sævitia et eius malitia fraudulenta, de militibus parvulorum obtruncationi deputatis, de lectulo Virginis et angelo Magos ne redirent præmonente et de ceteris diei illius appendiciis præfinita est per quam fides credentium augeretur gratia divina magis coleretur et in ipsa spiritali officio etiam incredulus ad culturam divinam excitaretur. Quid nunc? Quid nostris agitur in quibusdam ecclesiis temporibus? Non religionis formula non divinæ venerationis et cultus materia sed irreligiositatis dissolutionis exercetur iuvenilis lascivia. Mutatur habitus clericalis, incohatur ordo militaris, nulla in sacerdote vel milite differentia, domus Dei permixtione laicorum et clericorum confunditur, commessationes, ebrietates, scurrilitates, ioci inimici ludi placesibiles armorum strepitus, ganearum concursus omnium vanitatum indisciplinatus excursus. Huc accedit quod aliquo discordiæ genere semper turbatur hoc regnum et si aliquo modo pacifice incohatur vix sine dissidentium gravi tumultu terminatur. Hæccine vos o genus electum, regale sacerdotium, gens sancta, populus acquisitionis religio divinis placebit obtutibus, ubi clericalis ordo Deus exhonoratur proximus non edificatur, incredulus scandalizatur. Nonne multo melius esset tale penitus exemplum intermitti, quam in hoc transgressibili cultu offensionem pro gratia promereri? Excessus proprii ordinis, defectus sanctæ religionis est et spes mercedis vacuetur ubi proprietatis cultu vanitas exercetur. Beatos igitur ecclesiæ principes spiritales dixerim qui talia prohibenda malunt evangelica lectione quæ in ortu Christi gesta sunt ad memoriam revocare quam huiusmodi spectaculis fundamenta fidei resolvere. Quid quod in Cena Domini in conventu canonicorum ipsi sumus experti, quod multis coram positis personis laicalibus religiosis peracta iuxta mandatum Domini pedum lavationem miræ magnitudinis panis circumferatur ex quo singuli sumptis partibus suis coram facie altaris comedunt et bibunt. Hoc ritu cenam

[1] in Emaus] amans (MS). The emendation is Walter's.

Dominicam memoriæ posteritatis repræsentare quod aliud est quam quadragesimæ vel ieiunii sermone accepto cibo vacare. Figuram inquiunt Cenæ Dominicæ causa religionis exercemus, non corporali indigentiæ satisfaciamus, sicut a patribus accepimus in omnibus huiusmodi legibus locus dandus est rationi quia minus erudita antiquitus secula multa posteris observanda transmiserunt. Igitur vivendum est ecclesiæ filiis qua religionis forma Christum imitetur ut siue in verbis seu rationabilibus exemplis Christi gloria semper dilatetur nec cultor veritatis mercede privetur.

In this utterance the abbess correctly asserts that the Church plays were invented to strengthen the belief of the faithful, and to convince the sceptical. She regretfully observes, however, that the performances have become occasions for buffoonery and general disorder;[1] hence she opines that those in spiritual authority are well-advised in prohibiting the plays, admirable though they be in themselves. Not the least interesting of Herrad's observations is her appeal to the symbolic ceremonies of the liturgy itself—the *Mandatum* of Holy Thursday, for example—as supplying the need for visual instruction.[2]

Church plays, presumably, are included in the general condemnation of religious drama expressed in the Wycliffite *Tretise of miraclis pleyinge* of the late fourteenth century.[3] The *miraclis* to the representation of which the writer objects are the works, and particularly the marvellous achievements, of God, Christ, and the saints. Although the composing of the *Tretise* may have been animated chiefly by the performance of vernacular plays outside the church, the hostile arguments apply quite as well to plays associated with the liturgy. The contention of those who favour such representations are set forth candidly: that they are part of man's worship of God; that they often convert men to good living; that by the sight of the sufferings of Christ and the saints men are moved to tears; that some men can be reached only 'by gamen and pley'; that human nature requires recreation; and that, since the miracles of Christ and the saints may be delineated in painting, they may appropriately be imitated also in action. These arguments the reformer answers thus:

(1) The purpose of those who act the plays is 'more to ben seen of

[1] For examples of disorder and clownery in association with representations of the Ascension and of Herod see above, i, 489; ii, 99.

[2] See above, i, 98.

[3] Edited by E. Mätzner, *Altenglische Sprachproben*, i, part 2, Berlin, 1869, pp. 222 sqq.

the world and to plesyn to the world thanne to ben seen of God or to plesyn to hym';

(2) Since the plays take the name of God in vain, they necessarily violate God's law and pervert Christian belief;

(3) The weeping of men and women at plays is not for their sins, but merely because of the moving story represented; and Christ, moreover, reproved even the women who wept over his Passion;

(4) Men who are not converted by God's sacraments will not be truly converted by plays;

(5) The recreation provided by plays is false and worldly, whereas one's refreshment 'shulde ben in the werkis of mercy to his neyebore, and in dilityng hym in alle good comunicacioun with his neybore';

(6) Painted pictures have religious value only when they merely tell the plain truth, as books do, whereas the plays 'ben made more to deliten men bodily than to ben bokis to lewid men'.

This brief summary conveys only feebly the thoughtful precision of what is, perhaps, the most careful and energetic challenge to the religious drama uttered during the Middle Ages.

The vehement denunciations of Church plays uttered by reformers during the sixteenth century concern us only slightly. These writers were assaulting the very constitution of the Roman Church itself, and were commenting only incidentally upon such compositions as the *Visitatio Sepulchri* and such dramatic ceremonies as the procession of Palm Sunday, the *Depositio* and *Elevatio*, and the symbolic observances of Ascension and Whitsuntide. Conspicuous among such controversial publications are the *Regnum Papisticum* (1553), of Thomas Kirchmayer ('Naogeorgus'), translated by Barnabe Googe as *The Popish Kingdome, or reigne of Antichrist* (1570), and the satire of Philipp van Marnix ('Isaac Rabbotenu'), issued in 1569, and turned into English by George Gilpin as *The Bee hiue of the Romishe Churche* (1579). The contemptuous tone of these assailants may be illustrated by the following from *The Popish Kingdome*:[1]

In some place solemne sightes and showes, and Pageants fayre are playd,
With sundrie sortes of maskers braue, in straunge attire arayd,
As where the Maries three doe meete, the sepulchre to see,
And Iohn with Peter swiftly runnes, before him there to bee.
These things are done with iesture such, and with so pleasaunt game,

[1] This passage, along with substantial extracts from Kirchmayer, Googe and Gilpin, may be seen below, Appendix C. For evidences of a milder reforming spirit in England see Notes, p. 502.

That euen the grauest men that liue, woulde laugh to see the same.

. . .

Thou seest how they with Idols play, and teach the people to,
None otherwise then little gyrles with Puppets vse to do.

When we pass from the opinions of individuals of restricted authority, and seek pronouncements from the Roman See itself, we find that the genuine plays of the medieval Church seem never to have elicited an official papal utterance. It has often been asserted, to be sure, that Innocent III (1198–1216) condemned them in the course of a letter of January 8th, 1207, to Henry, archbishop of Gnesen, in Poland—a communication which was incorporated among the *Decretals* of Pope Gregory IX (1227–41), where the relevant part of it stands as follows:[1]

> Interdum ludi fiunt in eisdem ecclesiis theatrales, et non solum ad ludibriorum spectacula introducuntur in eis monstra larvarum, verum etiam in aliquibus anni festivitatibus, quæ continue natalem Christi sequuntur, diaconi, presbyteri ac subdiaconi vicissim insaniæ suæ ludibria exercere præsumunt, per gesticulationum suarum debacchationes obscœnas in conspectu populi decus faciunt clericale vilescere, quem potius illo tempore verbi Dei deberent prædicatione mulcere. Quia igitur ex officio nobis iniuncto zelus domus Dei nos comedit, et opprobria exprobrantium ei super nos cadere dignoscuntur, Fraternitati vestræ per apostolica scripta mandamus, quatenus, ne per huiusmodi turpitudinem ecclesiæ inquinetur honestas, . . . prælibatam vero ludibriorum consuetudinem vel potius corruptelam curetis a vestris ecclesiis taliter extirpare, quod vos divini cultus et sacri comprobetis ordinis zelatores.

From the text itself it is reasonably clear that the *ludi theatrales*, *ludibria*, *larvæ* and *spectacula* mentioned by Pope Innocent are either the usual *festum stultorum* of the Christmas season, or other popular disorders, and are not the reverential liturgical plays with which we are primarily concerned. This interpretation, indeed, seems to be definitively established by the following gloss attached to the prohibition during the course of the thirteenth century:[2]

> Non tamen hoc prohibetur representare presepe Domini, Herodem, Magos et qualiter Rachel plorat filios suos, et cetera, que tangunt

[1] A. Friedberg, *Corpus Iuris Canonici*, ii, Leipzig, 1922, col. 452. For information concerning this decree see A. Potthast, *Regesta Pontificum Romanorum*, i, Berlin, 1874, p. 253, no. 2967.

[2] *Compilatio Decretalium Domini Gregorii Pape Noni*, Nuremberg, 1482, sig. t 10 verso.

festiuitates illas de quibus hic fit mentio, cum talia potius inducant homines ad compunctionem quam ad lasciuiam vel voluptatem, sicut in Pasca sepulchrum Domini et alia representantur ad deuotionem excitandam.

This annotation not only removes from condemnation such plays as the *Officium Pastorum*, *Officium Stellæ*, *Ordo Rachelis* and *Visitatio Sepulchri*, but even commends them as aids to religion.[1]

This approving distinction between the earnest plays of the Church itself and the disorderly *ludi* of the folk and of the wayward clergy is maintained in later opinions of devotional writers and councils. It appears, for example, in William of Wadington's *Manuel des Pechiez*, written not far from the year 1300, and freely translated into English by Robert of Brunne in his *Handlyng Synne* (1303). The relevant passages from these two works are as follows:[2]

Vn autre folie apert
Vnt les fols clercs cuntroué,
Qe 'miracles' sunt apelé;
Lur faces vnt la deguisé
Par visers, li forsené,
Qe est defendu en decrée;
Tant est plus grant lur peché.
Fere poent representement,—
Mes qe ceo seit chastement
En office de seint eglise
Quant hom fet la Deu seruise,—
Cum Ihesu Crist la fiȝ dée
En sepulcre esteit posé,
E la resurrectiun,
Pur plus auer deuociun.
Mes, fere foles assembleȝ
En les rues des citeȝ,
Ou en cymiters apres mangers,
Quant venent les fols volunters,—

Hyt is forbode hym, yn þe decre,
Myracles for to make or se;
For, myracleṣ ȝyf þou bygynne,
Hyt ys a gaderyng, a syght of synne,
He may yn þe cherche þurgh þys resun
Pley þe resurreccyun,—
þat ys to seyë, how God ros,
God and man yn myȝt and los,—
To make men be yn beleuë gode
þat he ros with flesshe and blode;
And he may pleye withoutyn plyght
Howe God was bore yn ȝolë nyght,
To make men to beleue stedfastly
þat he lyght yn þe vyrgyne Mary.
ȝif þou do hyt yn weyys or greuys,
A syght of synne truly hyt semys.
Seynt Ysodre,[3] y take to wyttnes,
For he hyt seyþ þat soþe hyt es;

[1] For correct interpretations of Pope Innocent's prohibition and the accompanying gloss see D'Ancona, i, 53–4; Creizenach, i, 94; Chambers, ii, 99–100. Certain misinterpretations are referred to by Chambers, ii, 99, note 2.

[2] Lines 4292–322 of the French, and ll. 4637–60 of the English, in *Robert of Brunne's 'Handlyng Synne'*, ed. by F. J. Furnivall, part i (*Early English Text Society*, Original Series, no. 119), London, 1901, pp. 154–5. See Chambers, ii, 100–1; Coffman, *Nomenclature*, pp. 452–6.

[3] Seynt Ysodre (Seint Isidre of the French text) is Isidore of Seville (†636), and the reference is to his *Etymologiæ*, xviii, 59 (*De horum ⟨spectaculorum⟩ exsecratione*), where he condemns the Roman *spectacula*. For the passage see Notes, p. 503.

Tut dient qe il le funt pur bien,—
Crere ne les deueȝ pur rien
Qe fet seit pur le honur de Dée,
Einȝ del deable, pur verité,
Seint Ysidre me ad testimoné
Qe fu si bon clerc lettré;
Il dist qe cil qe funt sepectacles
Cume lem fet en miracles,
Ou ius qe nus nomames einȝ,
Burdiȝ ou turneinens,
Lur baptesme vnt refuseȝ,
E Deu de ciel reneieȝ.

þus hyt seyþ, yn hys boke,
þey forsakë þat þey toke—
God and herë crystendam—
þat make swyche pleyys to any man
As myracles and bourdys,
Or tournamentys of grete prys.

The 'decree' mentioned in the two texts seems pretty clearly to be the letter of Innocent III as embodied in the Gregorian *Decretals*, with its accompanying gloss. The poems, in any case, conform to the glossed decretal in condemning wanton representations and disguisings, and in permitting the usual liturgical plays, within the church building, at Christmas and Easter.[1] A similar distinction between forbidden revels and approved dramatic performances appears in a decree of the provincial council of Sens of 1460:[2]

Item cum per choreas, et ludos theatrales, ludificationes, et insolentias, soleant templa Domini profanari, et sacra in vilipendium deduci, in virisque ecclesiasticis talibus se immiscentibus scandala et opprobria generari, ludos, et choreas, et tales insolentias, in sacris ecclesiis et locis de cætero fieri prohibemus. Quod si ad memoriam festivitatum, et venerationem Dei ac sanctorum, aliquid juxta consuetudines ecclesiæ, in Nativitate Domini, vel Resurrectione, videantur faciendum, hoc fiat cum honestate et pace, absque prolongatione, impedimento, vel diminutione servitii, larvatione, et sordidatione faciei, ex speciali permissione Ordinarij, et beneplacito ministrorum ipsius ecclesiæ. Ut autem hæ insolentiæ ludorum, circa festum præsertim Innocentium, in aliis nostris provincialibus statutis prohibitæ, et quam prohibitionem iterum renovamus, penitus arceantur, Constitutionem sacri Basiliensis concilij observandam, et huic nostro præsenti statuto duximus inserendam, cujus tenor sequitur, et est talis:

'Turpem etiam illum abusum in quibusdam frequentatum ecclesiis, quo certis annis nonnulli cum mitra, baculo, ac vestibus pontificalibus, more episcoporum benedicunt; alij ut reges et duces induti, quod festum

[1] The English author seems to condemn all plays, even the reverential ones, when performed outside the church, in the streets or cemeteries. In regard to the use of the word *miracle* in the passages before us see Notes, p. 503.

[2] P. Labbé, ed., *Sacrosancta Concilia*, xiii, Paris, 1672, col. 1728.

fatuorum vel Innocentium, seu puerorum, in quibusdam regionibus nuncupatur; alij larvales et theatrales iocos, alij choreas ac tripudia marium ac mulierum facientes, homines ad spectanda et cachinnationes movent; alij comessationes et convivia ibidem præparantes. Hæc Synodus detestans, statuit et jubet, tam ordinariis, quam ecclesiarum decanis et rectoribus, sub pœna suspensionis omnium proventuum ecclesiarum, trium mensium spatio, ut hæc aut similia ludibria, etiam mercantias, seu negotiationes nundinarum, in ecclesia, quæ domus orationis debet esse, et etiam cœmeteriis, exercere amplius non permittant; transgressoresque per censuram ecclesiasticam, aliaque juris remedia, punire non negligant.'

Meanwhile, in the general spirit of these favouring opinions, religious plays were sometimes given under particularly august ecclesiastical auspices. Thus a performance of January 24th, 1417, arranged by the English bishops at the council of Constance is recorded, along with the report of an eye-witness, Eberhardus Dacher, as follows:[1]

*Robertus Archiepiscopus Sarisberiensis*, Episcopus Londoniensis, aliique Angliæ Episcopi plures, Legati Regii, præter splendidum convivium, quo Constantiensem senatum exceperunt, *comœdia sacra*, *de Mariæ partu*, *Magorum in natum Jesum devotione*, *Herodis in Magos insidiis ejusdemque infanticidio*, novo et admirabili exemplo, Constantiam reddidere illustriorem.

Quem actum scenicum, verbis *Dacherii*, spectatoris, oculati testis, ob novitatem facinoris, hic delineare[2] fas fuerit: *Am* 24*ten tag des Monats Januarii, das war auff Timotheus tag, da luden die Bischöff aus Engeland, der Bischoff Salisburgensis, der Bischoff von Londen, und demnach fünff Bischoff von Engeland, alle Räht zu Costniz und sonst viel ehrbar Bürger daselbst, in Burchart Walters Haus, das man vorzeiten nennt zu dem Burgthor, itzt zu dem gulden Schwert, allernächst bey S. Laurenz. Und gab ihnen fast ein köstlich mahl, ie* 3. *Gericht nach einander, jedes Gericht besonder mit* 8. *Essen: Die trug man allweg eins mahl dar, deren alweg waren* 4. *verguld oder versilbert. In dem mahl, zwischen dem Essen, so machten sie solch bild und geberd, als unser Frau ihr Kind unsern Hern und auch Gott gebahr, mit fast kostlichen Tuchern und Gewand. Und Joseph stelten sie zu ihr. Und die heiligen* 3. *Könige, als die unser Frauen die Opffer brachten. Und hatten gemacht einen lauteren guldnen Stern, der ging vor ihnen, an einem kleinen eisern Drat. Und machten Konig Herodem, wie er den drey Konigen nachsandt, und wie er die Kindlein ertodtet. Das machten sie alles*

[1] H. von der Hardt, *Magnum Oecumenicum Constantiense Concilium*, iv, Frankfort and Leipzig, 1699, pp. 1088–9. See Chambers, ii, 101–2. Concerning a repetition of the performance before the Emperor Sigismund on January 31 see Von der Hardt, iv, 1091; J. Lenfant, *Histoire du Concile de Constance*, ii, Amsterdam, 1727, p. 21; J. Lenfant, *The History of the Council of Constance*, ii, London, 1730, p. 25. For further bibliography see Paetow, pp. 301, 304.

[2] delineare] declineare (Print).

*mit gar kostlichen Gewand, und mit grossen guldenen und·Silbernen Gurteln, und machten das mit groster Gezierd, und mit grosser Demuht.*

This performance appears to have consisted of several separate scenes representing the Nativity, the visit of the Magi, and the slaughter of the Innocents. Although the text may have been in Latin, it seems not to have been recited in association with the liturgy.

The decorous patronage of the play at Constance gives no assurance that dramatic performances in churches would always be under similar careful supervision; and in the next century, at any rate, special provision was made for careful oversight. Such precaution appears, for example, in the following decree of the council of Seville of 1512:[1]

Sumus informati, quod in quibusdam ecclesiis nostri Archiepiscopatus, et Provinciæ permittitur fieri nonnullas repræsentationes Passionis Domini nostri Jesu Christi, et alios actus, et memoriam Resurrectionis, Nativitatis Salvatoris nostri, vel alias repræsentationes. Et quia ex talibus actibus orta sunt, et oriuntur plura absurda, et sæpe sæpius scandala in cordibus illorum, qui non sunt bene confirmati in nostra sancta Fide Catholica, videntes confusiones, et excessus, qui in hoc committuntur; propterea, sacro Concilio approbante, statuimus, et mandamus omnibus Parochis nostri Archiepiscopatus, et Provinciæ, omnibusque aliis Presbyteris, et Regularibus personis, ut non faciant, nec dent locum, ut in suis ecclesiis, et Monasteriis fiant dictæ repræsentationes, nec aliquæ illarum absque nostra speciali facultate, et mandato. sub pœna unius floreni applicandi modo supradicto, Presbyteris contrafacientibus, et laicis, ut sint excommunicati.

The implication of such a regulation is not that the plays are evil in themselves, but that they are too frequently accompanied by disorder, and hence can be allowed only through special permission. The same general intention is expressed in the following passages from decrees of the council of Compostella of 1565:[2]

Missarum proinde solennia, aliaque Divina Officia graviter, ac devote peragantur; nulli actus, sive repræsentationes, nec tripudia, aut choreæ in ecclesia fieri permittantur, dum Sacra peraguntur, quæ perturbari, aut interpellari nefas est, sed aut ante, aut post illud tempus, secundum

[1] J. Saenz de Aguirre, ed., *Collectio Maxima Conciliorum Omnium Hispaniæ et Novi Orbis*, v, Rome, 1755, p. 370. See Chambers, ii, 102.

[2] Saenz de Aguirre, v, 450, 560. See Chambers, ii, 102. In regard to disorder accompanying Easter plays at Gerona see Notes, p. 503.

quod Episcopo loci, aut ejus Vicario visum fuerit; nulli etiam actus, sive sacræ historiæ, sive profanæ in his, aut aliis solennitatibus admittantur, nisi mense uno antequam agantur, ab Episcopo, vel ejus Vicario lecti fuerint, gratisque approbati. . . .

Cum hebdomadæ sanctæ tempore Dominicæ Passionis memoriam Ecclesia recolat, et Unigeniti mortem lugeat, nulli actus, aut repræsentationes illis diebus permittantur, nisi talia sint, quæ aguntur, ut devotionem potius, quam tumultum excitare possint.

On the whole, then, it is clear that the hierarchy of the medieval Church discriminated effectually between its own edifying dramatic performances and the *ludi* of secular entertainers and louts who lurked within ecclesiastical boundaries. As a sound historian has observed, 'Such opposition to the religious drama as can be traced after the thirteenth century came not from the heads of the Church but from its heretics'.[1] We may assume, then, that the removal of literary and dramatic interpolations from the Roman service-books legalized by the council of Trent (1545–63), and the gradual disappearance of such intrusions from local uses, were inspired less by hostility to religious drama than by a fundamental determination to return in all things to the purer and simpler liturgical tradition of the early Middle Ages.[2]

## III

Even though the Roman hierarchy was essentially friendly to Church plays during the closing centuries of the Middle Ages, this period actually witnessed the gradual transference of religious drama from ecclesiastical to secular auspices. The change came about not through peremptory legislation, but, if we may judge by the results, through the natural desire of both playwright and audience for an increase in the scope of the performances, for an enrichment of content, and for the use of the vernacular.

So long as the plays remained closely attached to the liturgy, they were restricted in all these respects, and were capable of causing embarrassment to all concerned. However useful they may have seemed as aids to instruction, they were, in the nature

[1] Chambers, ii, 102.

[2] The revision of service-books under the authority of the council of Trent is recounted by Bäumer, ii, 160–233; Batiffol, chapter v; K. Weinmann, *Das Konzil von Trient und die Kirchenmusik*, Leipzig, 1919, pp. 21–39, 59–74; Fortescue, *Mass*, pp. 206–8. The treatise of C. Dejob, *De l'Influence du Concile de Trente sur la Littérature et les Beaux-Arts chez les Peuples catholiques*, Paris, 1884, does not bear upon the plays of the Church.

of the case, intrusions into the liturgical system, and could not be permitted to develop indefinitely. The tendency toward the expansion of single plays, or toward the combination of several of them into comprehensive compositions, is apparent in the longer Easter plays, and in such pieces as the *Officium Stellæ* of Laon and the Christmas and Passion plays from Benediktbeuern.[1] Nor were the activities of the impersonated characters always confined within the limits of the dramatic texts. That these personages sometimes usurped the duties of the regular liturgical officiants is shown by the *reges* who share in reading the gospel in the Mass of Epiphany at Besançon, or take part otherwise in the office of this day at Rouen, or by the Marys who assume a place in Lauds of Easter at Rouen.[2] As to the length possible for a play without prohibitive disturbance to regular worship we can only draw uncertain inferences. Although the outcome may have depended somewhat upon the exact position of the performance within the liturgical structure,[3] this consideration did not always govern. The *Visitatio Sepulchri* and the *Officium Stellæ*, for example, though performed on the periphery of Matins, seem not to have expanded more amply than the *Lazarus* and *Daniel* of Hilarius, which were to be acted either at the end of Matins or before the *Magnificat* in the very midst of Vespers.[4] Without the support of definite evidence, then, we can only infer that those who were especially ambitious for the development of the religious drama must eventually have desired a larger freedom for literary and theatrical expansion than could be tolerated within the confines of authorized worship.

Particularly important in the general dramatic expansion, no doubt, was the impulse toward increasing the worldly appeal of the plays through the comic element.[5] Although the germs of comedy are present in several of the liturgical plays, the hearty development of these suggestions was possible only in secular surroundings.[6] Even the friendly clerical opinions of the drama reviewed above disclose sufficient evidence of an ecclesiastical vigilance discouraging to an easy gaiety. The impulse toward the comic, and its results when the plays were secularized, are particularly discernible in Germany. Here the willing hand of

[1] See above, i, 514, 518; ii, 103, 172.
[2] See above, i, 661; ii, 37, 44–5.
[3] See above, i, 223; ii, 398.
[4] See above, pp. 218, 286.
[5] See Wirth, pp. 144–8; Chambers, ii, 90–1; Jacobsen, pp. 85–101.
[6] See above, pp. 406–7.

the *clerici vagantes* is to be inferred. Their talents are to be seen, no doubt, in the Latin plays from Benediktbeuern, and probably they were operative also in some of the vernacular compositions which are clearly derived from the plays of the Church.[1] If not through the *vagantes*, then it was through similar worldly agencies that a fresh hilarity was associated with certain relatively inoffensive personages of the Latin plays, such as Pilate and his *entourage*, the *unguentarius*, the devils, and Mary Magdalen.[2] For a figure such as Herod, this expansiveness was abundantly encouraged by the traditions of the Church stage itself. Although the growth of the comic element is more readily traced in Germany than in France and England, this development undoubtedly occurred also in these latter countries.[3]

As the drama relinquished its close association with established worship, it gradually abandoned also the Latin of the liturgy in favour of the language of ordinary life.[4] The presence of passages in the vernacular, indeed, has already been observed in a fair number of the Latin plays themselves. In some instances these passages are short, and seem to have been intended as literary ornaments rather than as aids to an unlettered audience.[5] Again the vernacular parts are of substantial length, and serve either as translations of accompanying Latin passages, or as independent dramatic units.[6] The result of these uses of the speech of the populace is a body of transitional plays in each of which one of the vernaculars is either prominent or predominant, but in which elements inherited from Church plays are still conspicuous.[7] From Germany the most striking example of such a composition is the Easter play in a fourteenth-century manuscript at Treves.[8] Here the Latin speeches of a complete version of the *Visitatio Sepulchri* are accompanied by translations and verse-paraphrases in German. Likewise transitional in its general character is the celebrated Anglo-Norman fragment, *Adam*, of the twelfth century.[9] Although the greater part of the

[1] See Wirth, pp. 144 sqq.

[2] See Wirth, p. 148.

[3] See Creizenach, i, 205–9; Cohen, *Pèlerins*, pp. 109 sqq.

[4] See Creizenach, i, 100–60 *passim*; Chambers, ii, 88–90.

[5] See the *Lazarus* and *Iconia Sancti Nicolai* of Hilarius (above, pp. 218, 342), and the Easter plays from Klosterneuburg and Benediktbeuern (above, i, 431, 434).

[6] See the Easter play from Origny-Sainte-Benoîte (above, i, 413), the Passion play from Benediktbeuern (above, i, 521), and the *Sponsus* (above, p. 362). For an *ordo* permitting the use of the *dictamen vulgare* in the dramatic office of the Presentation of the Virgin Mary see above, p. 242.

[7] See Creizenach, i, 100 sqq.; Chambers, ii, 89–90.

[8] For the text see Froning, pp. 49–56. See also Creizenach, i, 103–5; Wirth, pp. 235–7.

[9] Edited by P. Studer, *Le Mystère d'Adam*,

text is in Norman-French, it provides for the reading *in choro* of the Pseudo-Augustinian *lectio, Vos, inquam, convenio, o Judæi*, and for the summoning of the prophets after the manner of the liturgical *Ordo Prophetarum.*[1] The prophecies themselves are recited first in Latin, and then in versified forms in the vernacular. For England the classical illustration of the passage of the drama from the language of the Church into the native speech is the so-called Shrewsbury Fragments, found in a manuscript of the early fifteenth century.[2] These pieces preserve only the parts spoken by one or two of the actors, and a few choral passages, in an *Officium Pastorum*, a *Visitatio Sepulchri*, and a *Peregrinus*. Although the texts are predominantly in English, Latin passages from liturgical plays clearly establish the parentage of the fragments as a whole.

Transitional pieces of this sort were eventually succeeded by vernacular religious plays of increasing scope, and often of prodigious length. The ultimate outcome was dramatic compositions covering the whole range of sacred history, from the Creation to the Last Judgement, and sometimes requiring several days for the performance.[3] Plays of this magnitude are, of course, not to be related directly to simple originals produced in association with the liturgy of the Church, and they disclose their ultimate ancestry only incidentally or by accident.[4] Although among their subjects are inevitably found most of those treated also in the Church plays, these repeated themes, like the ones which are not paralleled in the extant Church texts, are presented in the vernacular with immensely greater breadth, from a wealth of additional sources in Scripture, history, legend, theological treatise and learned commentary; and even these ample sources are supplemented from popular story and from the realities of contemporary life.

For the production of a lengthy play out of doors before huge crowds, a requirement of capital importance was the good

Manchester, 1918. See Creizenach, i, 127–32; Chambers, ii, 89–90; Mantzius, ii, 8–15.

[1] See above, chapter xxi, and Studer, pp. xii–xvii.

[2] These are printed and discussed in Appendix B.

[3] The vernacular religious plays produced during the closing century or two of the Middle Ages are surveyed by Creizenach, i, 224–343.

[4] Liturgical elements in some of the longer plays are noticed by Creizenach (i, 107–27, 174, 220), and by some of the editors of separate texts. A study of the literary relationships between the liturgical plays and those in the vernacular is being made by another investigator. The insufficiencies of Cargill's treatment of this matter are indicated by the reviewers mentioned above, i, 542.

weather of late spring and early summer. Since such a composition treated a wide variety of subjects, and was therefore more or less appropriate to a considerable number of separate feast-days, the choice of any one day, or group of days, was increasingly a matter of indifference, and might fall upon any great ecclesiastical festival which would naturally bring together large numbers of people. The times most favoured were Pentecost, or Whitsuntide, and Corpus Christi.[1] This latter festival, promulgated by Pope Urban IV in 1264, and brought into active liturgical use and given processional splendour during the first half of the fourteenth century, was brought into contact with the drama most prominently in Spain and England.[2] In the dramatic histories of this latter country, indeed, the procession of Corpus Christi has probably been given an importance hardly justified by the known facts. Although the popularity of the feast and the elaborateness of the procession undoubtedly gave encouragement to the acting of plays, and influenced the methods of staging them, we are not to infer that the very existence of long religious plays in England during the fourteenth and fifteenth centuries was due primarily to the institution of a new festival.[3]

Of all the changes brought about through the secularizing of the plays, the most far-reaching and impressive is the transforming of them from a cosmopolitan product into a variety of national developments.[4] During the period when the religious drama belonged exclusively to the Church, and was written in the ecclesiastical language, it was, like the Church itself, essentially international. Among the Latin plays, to be sure, we have observed a few national and regional differences, and some achievements of individual talent; but in a survey of the whole body of Church plays one is impressed less by the rise of special forms from particular places than by the international likenesses in form and content. From the fourteenth century

[1] See Chambers, ii, 94–6.

[2] The rise of the procession in the fourteenth century is briefly surveyed in an anonymous article, *La Procession de la Fête-Dieu*, in *Revue du Chant grégorien*, xxix (1925), 140–2. See also Chambers, ii, 95. It appears that the nature of this procession during the fourteenth and fifteenth centuries has not been thoroughly investigated.

[3] The conjectural derivation of the English cyclical plays from the Corpus Christi procession is clearly and cautiously stated by Chambers, ii, 95–6. A sceptical re-examination of the matter has been made by Merle Pierson, *The Relation of the Corpus Christi Procession to the Corpus Christi Play in England*, in *Transactions of the Wisconsin Academy of Sciences, Arts and Letters*, xviii, part i (1915), 110–65.

[4] See Creizenach, i, 359–63; Chambers, ii, 91–4.

onward, however, although a few types of Latin play continued in general circulation, the chief dramatic developments assumed an unprecedented significance nationally. All had a background in the cycle of plays produced by the Church itself, and all drew upon common sources in Scripture, legend, and ecclesiastical exegesis; but the several countries of Western Europe showed significant variations in literary form, in choice of themes, and in methods of performance. To the study of these national differences a treatise such as the present one may, perhaps, serve as an appropriate introduction.

# NOTES

## CHAPTER XVII

## THE SHEPHERDS AT THE HOLY MANGER

**Page 3, note 1.** The dramatic pieces treated in this chapter are the subject of a special study by Young, *Officium Pastorum: A Study of the Dramatic Developments within the Liturgy of Christmas*, in *Transactions of the Wisconsin Academy of Sciences, Arts and Letters*, xvii, part 1 (1912), 299–396. See also Böhme, pp. 2–46; Bartholomaeis, pp. 147–8, 525–6; Anz, pp. 34–42; Creizenach, i, 52–4; Chambers, ii, 41–4; Chasles, pp. 169–81; Hirn, pp. 358 sqq.; Gayley, *Forefathers*, pp. 24–8; Köppen, *passim*. Böhme (pp. 44–6) conceives a highly speculative theory as to the development of the *Officium Pastorum*. For his neglect of the first study mentioned above he is censured by Brinkmann, p. 128.

**Page 4, note 3.** There appears to be no reason for printing here the texts, similar to the one in Paris MS lat. 887, found in the following places: Paris, Bibl. Nat., MS lat. 13252, Trop. Sammaglorianum sæc. xii, fol. 3$^{r}$; *ibid.*, MS lat. 903, Trop. Sancti Aredii Lemovicensis sæc. xi, fol. 147$^{v}$; *ibid.*, MS lat. 1119, Trop. Sancti Augustini Lemovicensis sæc. xi, fol. 4$^{r}$; *ibid.*, MS lat. 1121, Trop. Martialense sæc. xi, fol. 2$^{r}$–2$^{v}$; *ibid.*, MS lat. 9449, Trop. Nivernense sæc. xi, fol. 7$^{r}$; *ibid.*, MS lat. 1084, Trop. Martialense sæc. xi, fol. 53$^{v}$–54$^{r}$; *ibid.*, Nouvelles Acquisitions, MS lat. 1235, Grad.-Trop. Nivernense sæc. xii, fol. 183$^{v}$–184$^{r}$; *ibid.*, Nouv. Acq., MS lat. 1871, Trop. Moissiacense sæc. xi, fol. 4$^{r}$ (fragment); *ibid.*, MS lat. 909, Trop. Martialense sæc. xi, fol. 9$^{r}$; Huesca, Bibl. Capit., MS 4, Trop. Oscense sæc. xi–xii, fol. 124$^{r}$; Modena, Bibl. Capit., MS O. 1. 7, Trop. Ravennatense sæc. xi–xii, fol. 6$^{v}$–7$^{r}$ (fragment); Piacenza, Bibl. Capit., MS 65, Trop.-Hymnarium Placentinum sæc. xii, fol. 229$^{v}$ (fragment); Vercelli, Bibl. Capit., MS 146, Trop. Vercellense sæc. xi, fol. 107$^{r}$; *ibid.*, MS 161, Trop. Vercellense sæc. xii, fol. 118$^{v}$; *ibid.*, MS 162, Trop. Vercellense sæc. xii, fol. 187$^{r}$–187$^{v}$; Vich, Archiv. Capit., MS 32, Trop. Rivipullense (?) sæc. xii–xiii, fol. 30$^{r}$; *ibid.*, MS 124, Process. Vicense (?) sæc. xiii–xiv, fol. A$^{v}$–B$^{r}$. These texts are all printed or mentioned by Young, *op. cit.*, pp. 300–7. Concerning one or more of these texts, and the general type, see Gautier, *Tropes*, pp. 215, 218; Chambers, ii, 41; Anz, pp. 37–42; *A. H.*, xlix, 8–9. I have not seen the texts to be found as follows: Volterra, Bibl. Commun., MS 13 (5700), Trop. Volaterranense sæc. xi, fol. 3$^{v}$–4$^{r}$, published by G. Pisani, *Illustrazione di un Codice liturgico-musicale di Volterra*, Volterra, 1909; Rome, Bibl. Vatic., MS lat. 10645, from which the trope is published by Bartholomaeis, p. 525; Pistoia, Bibl. Capit., MS 70, Trop. Pistoriense sæc. xi–xii, fol. 14$^{v}$. Especially noteworthy is the absence of the trope *Quem quæritis in præsepe?* from the service-books of St Gall.

**Page 6, note 1.** With the trope from Ivrea MS 60 is to be associated the following from Paris, Bibl. Nat., MS lat. 1118, Trop. Lemovicense sæc. xi–xii, fol. 8$^{v}$–9$^{r}$, reproduced, in part, in facsimile by Gautier, *Tropes*, p. 215, and previously printed by Young, *op. cit.*, pp. 303–4:

IN DIE *Natale* DOMINI STACIO AD SANCTUM PETRVM.

Incipivnt tropus[1] antequam dicatur officium:
*Qvem queritis in presepe, pastores, dicite?*
R*espondent*: *Saluatorem, Christum Dominum, infantem pannis inuolutum, secundum sermonem angelicum.*
R*espondent*: *Adest hic paruulus cum Maria, matre sua, de qua dudum uatizinando Isaias dixerat propheta: Ecce uirgo concipiet et pariet filium; et nunc euntes dicite quia natus est.*
R*espondent*: *Alleluia, alleluia! Iam uere scimus Christum natum in terris, de quo canite omnes cum propheta dicentes.*
A*ntiphonas*[2] son*i*: *Puer natus.*
Ad psalmum: *Cantate Domino canticum nouum; eia dic, dompne, eia!*[3]

**Page 12, note 2.** Montpellier MS H. 304 is described by Young, *Rouen*, pp. 201 sqq., and by Delamare, pp. xxxii sqq. Of the nine separate pieces in the codex, we are concerned with no. 6 (fol. $28^r$–$42^v$), which may be entitled 'Fragmentum operis de Ratione Divini Officii incerti auctoris'. Although the author of this fragmentary treatise is unknown, it may be assigned to the ecclesiastical province of Rouen, and in many respects it resembles the eleventh-century *Liber de Officiis Ecclesiasticis* of Jean d'Avranches. In a supplement at the end of the fragment are two plays; the *Officium Pastorum* (fol. $41^r$–$41^v$) now under consideration, and the *Officium Stellæ* (fol. $41^v$–$42^v$), printed above, pp. 68 sqq.

**Page 14, note 4.** Bibliography concerning the Rouen MSS containing the *Officium Pastorum* is given by Young, *Rouen*, pp. 224–7. The text in Rouen MS 384 is found also, in Paris, Bibl. Nat., MS lat. 1213, Ordin. Rothomagense sæc. xv, pp. 17–8, and in Rouen, Bibl. de la Ville, MS 382 (*olim* Y. 108), Ordin. Rothomagense sæc. xv, fol. $23^r$–$23^v$. The text of the first of these two MSS, with complete variants from the second, is published by Young, *Officium Pastorum*, pp. 387–90. Part of the variants from Rouen MS 382 are printed by Gasté, pp. 25–32. A somewhat eclectic text of the liturgical sequel to the *Officium Pastorum* in Rouen MSS 382 and 384 is given by Mme Chasles (pp. 179–81), with comment (pp. 170–2) on the Rouen *Officium Pastorum.* I give here the text from Paris MS lat. 1213 (A), with the variants from Rouen MS 382 (B):

Finito *Te Deum laudamus*,[4] peragatur Officium Pastorum hoc modo, secundum vsum Rothomagensem.[5] Presepe sit paratum retro altare, et ymago Sancte Marie sit in eo posita. In primis quidam puer ante chorum in excelso in similitudinem Angeli Natiuitatem[6] Domini nuncians[7] ad quinque canoni-

[1] As to the bewildering variety of ways in which *tropus* is spelled and declined see Gautier, *Tropes*, pp. 49–50. In this rubric, *officium* means 'introit'.

[2] This rubric I am unable to interpret. I am told that the nominative singular *antiphonas* is found in Limoges MSS of the eleventh and twelfth centuries, and that *sonus* is used in the sense of *tonus*.

[3] Followed by the rubric *Alios*, introducing a fresh rubric of the introit.

[4] laudamus] Omitted (B).

[5] vsum Rothomagensem] Rothomagensem vsum (B).

[6] Natiuitatem] natiuitatis (A).

[7] nuncians] annuncians (B).

cos quindecim marcharum et librarum, uel ad eorum[1] vicarios de secunda sede, Pastores intrantes per magnum | ostium chori per medium chorum transeuntes, tunicis et amictis ⟨indutos⟩,[2] hunc versum ita dicens: *Nolite timere*,[3] vsque *In presepio*. Sint plures pueri in uoltis ecclesie quasi Angeli, qui alta voce incipiant: *Gloria in excelsis Deo*, et cantent vsque *Voluntatis*. Hoc audientes Pastores ad locum in quo paratum est Presepe accedant cantantes[4] hunc versum: *Pax in terris*, totum. Quod dum intrauerint, duo presbyteri dalmaticati[5] quasi Obstetrices, qui ad Presepe fuerint dicant: *Quem queritis*, vsque *Dicite*. Pastores respondeant: *Saluatorem Christum*, vsque *Angelicum*. Item Obstetrices cortinam aperientes Puerum demonstrent[6] dicentes: *Adest hic paruulus*, vsque *Ysaias dixerat propheta*. Hic ostendant matrem Pueri dicentes: *Salue, Virgo singularis*,[7] vsque *Frui natus visione*.[8] Deinde vertant se ad chorum, redeuntes et dicentes: *Alleluia, alleluia, iam vere scimus*, vsque *Cum propheta dicentes*.[9] Hoc finito, incipiatur Missa, et Pastores regant chorum.

**Page 20, note 5.** The words of the antiphon *Quem vidistis, pastores?* form the first part of a responsory of Christmas Matins, which has, I think, no essential bearing upon the present survey. This responsory is discussed by Young, *Officium Pastorum*, pp. 344 sqq. Referring to that discussion, Gougaud arrives at the astonishingly erroneous conclusion that this responsory is the germ of all dramatic ceremonies at the *præsepe*. His statement is as follows (p. 28): 'Le germe de toute cette littérature dramatique paraît se trouver dans le répons *Quem vidistis, pastores?* du premier nocturne de l'office de la Nativité.'

**Page 21, note 2.** The use of the liturgical *Pastores, dicite* before the first Mass of Christmas is seen in the following from Oxford, Bibl. Bodl., MS Douce 222, Trop. Novaliciense sæc. xi, fol. $4^v$–$5^r$, previously printed by Young, *Officium Pastorum*, p. 351:

TROPUS IN MEDIA NOCTE

*Pastores, dicite, quidnam uidistis, et annunciate Christi natiuitate⟨m⟩.*

iii.[10] *Infantem uidi|mus pannis inuolutum, et choros angelorum laudantes Saluatorem.*

iii.[10] *Dominus dixit.*

The word *tropus* in the heading seems to mean merely that what follows is an interpolation in the official liturgy.

**Page 24, note 2.** The history of the *præsepe*, or *præsepium*, is treated in detail by Young, *Officium Pastorum*, pp. 334–44, with somewhat extensive bibliography. Of particular importance are the following: G. Hager, *Die Weihnachtskrippe*, Munich, 1902; H. Usener, *Das Weihnachtsfest* (*Religions-*

[1] eorum] eos (A).
[2] ⟨indutos⟩] inductos (B).
[3] timere] timere ecce enim (B).
[4] accedant cantantes] accendant cantores (A).
[5] dalmaticati] dalmatici de maiori sede (B).
[6] demonstrent] demonstrant (B).
[7] singularis] Omitted (B).
[8] natus visione] natus Tunc eo viso inclinatis ceruicibus adorent puerum et salutent dicentes Salue Virgo singularis vsque frui natus visione (B).
[9] dicentes] ducentes (A).
[10] The meaning of this numeral is unknown to me. *Tres*, *ter*, and *tertius modus* are all impossible.

*geschichtliche Untersuchungen*, i), Bonn, 1889, pp. 279–93; F. Bianchini, *De Sacris Imaginibus . . . dissertationes duæ*, Rome, 1727, pp. 1–14; P. Lafond, *La Crèche de la Cathédrale Sainte-Marie d'Oloron*, in *Réunion des Sociétés des Beaux-Arts des Départements*, xxi (1901), 567–72; M. Schmid, *Die Darstellung der Geburt Christi in der bildenden Kunst*, Stuttgart, 1890, pp. 82–7; Evelyn M. Cesaresco, *Puer Parvulus*, in *Contemporary Review*, lxxvii (1900), 117–23; L. Gougaud, *La Crèche de Noël avant Saint François d'Assise*, in *Revue des Sciences religieuses*, ii (1922), 26–34; Böhme, pp. 2–5; Rietschel, *Weihnachten*, pp. 51–61, 157; Cabrol and Leclercq, iii, 3021–9. The most remarkable collection of plastic representations of the Crib is that in the Bayerisches Nationalmuseum in Munich. Upon this collection is based the work of R. Berliner, *Denkmäler der Krippenkunst*, Augsburg, 1926 sqq.

**Page 27, note 1.** The following is Bonaventura's account of the *præsepe* of St Francis, from *Acta Sanctorum*, Oct., ii, Paris and Rome, 1866, p. 770:

Contigit autem anno tertio ante obitum suum, ut memoriam nativitatis pueri Jesu ad devotionem excitandam apud Castrum Græcii disponeret agere, cum quanto majori solemnitate valeret. Ne vero hoc levitati posset adscribi, a summo Pontifice petita et obtenta licentia, fecit præparari præsepium, apportari fœnum, bovem et asinum ad locum adduci. Advocantur fratres, adveniunt populi, personat silva voces, et venerabilis illa nox luminibus copiosis et claris, laudibusque sonoris et consonis, et splendens efficitur et solennis. Stabat vir Dei coram præsepio, pietate repletus, respersus lachrymis, et gaudio superfusus. Celebrantur Missarum solennia super præsepe, levita Christi Francisco sacrum Euangelium decantante. Prædicat deinde populo circunstanti de nativitate Regis pauperis, quem cum nominare vellet, *Puerum de Bethlehem* præ amoris teneritudine nuncupabat. Miles autem quidam virtuosus et verax, qui, propter Christi amorem seculari relicta militia, viro Dei magna fuit familiaritate conjunctus, dominus Joannes de Græcio se vidisse asseruit puerulum quendam valde formosum in illo præsepio dormientem; quem beatus pater Franciscus ambobus complexans brachiis, excitare videbatur a somno. Hanc siquidem devoti militis visionem non solum videntis sanctitas credibilem facit, sed et designata veritas comprobat, et miracula subsecuta confirmant. Nam exemplum Francisci consideratum a mundo excitativum est cordium in fide Christi torpentium; fœnum præsepii, reservatum a populo, mirabiliter sanativum fuit brutorum languentium, et aliarum repulsivum pestium diversarum, glorificante Deo per omnia servum suum, sanctæque orationis efficaciam evidentibus miraculorum prodigiis demonstrante.

**Page 27, note 2.** The following is Thomas of Celano's account of the *præsepe* of St Francis, from *Acta Sanctorum*, Oct., ii, pp. 706–7:

Summa ejusdem intentio, præcipuum desiderium supremumque propositum ejus erat, sanctum Evangelium in omnibus et per omnia observare, ac perfecte omni vigilantia, omni studio, toto desiderio mentis, toto cordis fervore, Domini nostri Jesu Christi doctrinam sequi, et vestigia imitari. Recordabatur assidua meditatione verborum ejus et sagacissima consideratione ipsius opera recolebat: præcipue incarnationis humilitas et caritas passionis ita ejus memoriam occupabant, ut vix valeret aliud cogitare. Memorandum proinde ac reverenti memoria recolendum, quod tertio anno ante gloriosi obitus sui diem apud castrum, quod Grecium dicitur, fecit in die natalis Domini nostri Jesu Christi. Erat in terra illa vir quidam, nomine Joannes, bonæ famæ, melioris vitæ, quem beatus Franciscus amore præcipuo diligebat; quoniam, cum in terra sua et honorabilis plurimum extitisset, carnis nobilitate calcata, nobilitatem animi est sequutus. Hanc vero beatus Franciscus, sicut sæpe solebat, per quindecim dies ante Nativitatem Domini fecit ad se vocari, et dixit ei: Si desideras, ut apud Grecium præsentem festivitatem Domini celebremus, festina præcedere, et quæ, tibi dico, præpara diligenter. Volo enim illius Pueri memoriam agere, qui in Bethlehem natus est, et infantilium necessitatum ejus incommoda, in præsepio reclinatus, et quomodo, astante bove atque asino, super fœnum positus extitit, utcumque corporeis oculis pervidere. Quod audiens vir bonus atque fidelis, cucurrit citius, et omnia in prædicto loco, quæ Sanctus dixerat, præparavit.

Appropinquavit autem dies lætitiæ, tempus exultationis advenit. E pluribus locis vocati sunt Fratres, viri et mulieres[1] terræ illius secundum posse suum, exultantibus animus,[2] cereos et faces præparant ad illuminandam noctem, quæ scintillanti sydere dies omnes illuminavit et annos. Venit denique Sanctus Dei, et inveniens omnia præparata, vidit et gavisus est. Et quidem præparatur præsepium, apportatur fœnum: bos et asinus adducuntur, honoratur ibi simplicitas, exaltatur paupertas, humilitas commendatur, et quasi nova Bethlehem de Grecio facta est. Illuminatur nox ut dies, et hominibus atque animalibus deliciosa extitit. Adveniunt populi, et ad novum mysterium novis gaudiis adlætantur. Personat sylva voces, et jubilantibus rupes respondent. Cantant Fratres, Domino laudes debitas persolventes, et tota nox jubilatione resultat. Stat Sanctus Dei coram præsepio suspiriis plenus, pietate constrictus, et mirabili gaudio superfusus. Celebrantur Missarum solennia persæpe, et nova fruitur consolatione sacerdos.

Induitur[3] leviticis ornamentis, quia levita erat, et voce sonora Euangelium cantat. Et quidem vox ejus vox vehemens, vox dulcis, vox clara, voxque sonora, cunctos invitans ad præmia summa. Prædicat deinde populo circumstanti, et de nativitate pauperis Regis, et Bethlehem parvula civitate melliflua eructat. Sæpe quoque, cum vellet Jesum Christum nominare, amore flagrans nimio, eum *Puerum de Bethlehem* nuncupabat, et more balantis ovis *Bethlehem* dicens, os suum sic magis dulci affectione totum implebat; et labia sua, cum Puerum de Bethlehem vel Jesum nominaret, quasi lingebat lingua, felici palato degustans, et deglutiens dulcedinem verbi hujus. Multiplicantur ibi dona Omnipotentis, et a quodam viro virtutis mirabilis visio cernitur. Videbat enim in præsepio puerulum unum jacentem exanimem, ad quem videbat accedere sacerdotem Dei, et eumdem puerum quasi a somno suscitare. Nec inconveniens visio ista, cum puer Jesus in multorum cordibus oblivioni fuerit datus, in quibus, ipsius gratia faciente, per servum suum sanctum Franciscum resuscitatus est, et impressus memoriæ diligenti. Finiuntur deinde solemnes excubiæ, et unusquisque cum gaudio ad propria remeavit.

[1] mulieres] mulieris (Print). [2] animus] animis? [3] induitur] induiter (Print).

Conservatur fenum in præsepio positum, ut per ipsum jumenta et animalia salva faciat Dominus, quemadmodum multiplicavit misericordiam suam sanctam. Et revera sic actum est, ut animalia diversos morbos habentia per circum adjacentem regionem, manducantia de hoc feno, a suis sint ægritudinibus liberata. Imo et mulieres, partu gravi et longo laborantes, de prædicto feno sibi superimponentes, partu pariunt salutari, atque a diversis cladibus utriusque sexus concursus desideratam ibidem obtinent sanitatem. Consecratus est denique locus præsepii templum Domino, et in honorem beatissimi patris Francisci supra præsepe altare construitur, et ecclesia dedicatur, ut ubi animalia quandoque feni pabulum comederunt, ibi de cætero ad sanitatem animæ et corporis manducent homines carnes Agni immolati Jesu Christi, Domini nostri, qui summa et ineffabili caritate dedit seipsum nobis, cum Patre et Spiritu sancto vivens et regnans Deus æternaliter gloriosus per cuncta sæcula sæculorum. Amen.

## CHAPTER XVIII

## THE COMING OF THE MAGI

**Page 29, note 1.** The most thorough study of the plays of Epiphany is by H. Anz, *Die lateinischen Magierspiele*, Leipzig, 1905, which supersedes the survey by Köppen, pp. 9–28. For important treatments of the subject see also Chambers, ii, 44–52; Böhme, pp. 18–9, 47–105; Chasles, pp. 258–66, 297–307; Kehrer, *Literatur*, i, 55–63; Sondheimer, pp. 1–135, 158–9; Meyer, pp. 38–44; K. Schiffmann, in a review of Anz, in *Anzeiger für deutsches Altertum und deutsche Litteratur*, xxxi (1907), 12–7. In adopting the term *Officium Stellæ* I have the support of Jean d'Avranches (see Migne, *P.L.*, cxlvii, 43) and of the Norman play (see p. 68). The MSS of the plays give a variety of other designations: *Officium Regum Trium* (see p. 43), *Ordo Stellæ* (see p. 103), *Versus ad Herodem faciendum* (see p. 59), *Ordo ad repræsentandum Herodem* (see p. 84), and *Stella* (see below, p. 439). In objecting to the designation *Officium Stellæ* for a play in many versions of which Herod is the dominating figure, Böhme (p. 126) appears to have neglected part of the evidence.

**Page 34, note 1.** In regard to ceremonies at the offertory see also Böhme, pp. 50–1; Tolhurst, i, 45; ii, 371. Martene (iii, 44) records the custom of announcing the date of Easter after the reading of the gospel in the Mass of Epiphany, and speaks thus of an offering made by the kings of France in association with this ceremony:

Denuntiato Paschatis die, sequitur oblatio in qua olim Francorum reges exemplo Magorum aurum, thus et myrrham ad altare offerebant.

An Epiphany offering made by King Charles V of France in 1378, during a visit from Charles, Emperor of Rome, is described thus:[1]

[1] P. Paris, ed., *Les Grandes Chroniques de France*, vi, Paris, 1838, pp. 382–3.

Et quant ce vint à l'offrande, le roy avoit fait appareillier trois paires des offrandes, d'or, d'encens et de mirre, pour offrir pour luy et pour l'empereur ainsi qu'il est acoustumé. Et fist demander le roy à l'empereur s'il offreroit point, lequel s'en excusa en disant qu'il ne povoit aler né soy agenoillier né aucune chose tenir pour la goute, et qu'il pleust au roy offrir et faire selon son acoustumance; si fu l'offrande du roy tèle qui s'ensuit: Trois chevaliers, ses chambellans, tenoient hautement trois bèles coupes dorées et esmaillées; en l'une estoit l'or, en l'autre l'encens, et en la tierce le myrre, et alèrent tous trois par ordre, comme l'offrande doit estre bailliée, devant le roy et le roy après, qui s'agenoillièrent, et il s'agenoilla devant l'arcevesque, et la première offrande qui fu de l'or, luy bailla celuy qui la tenoit et il l'offri et baisa la main. La seconde, qui est de l'encens, bailla le secont chevalier qui la tenoit au premier, et il la bailla au roy, et il l'offri en baisant la main de l'arcevesque. La tierce, qui est de myrre, bailla le troisième chevalier qui la tenoit au deuxiesme, et le deuxiesme au premier, et le premier la bailla au roy, et en baisant la main dudit arcevesque tierce fois l'offri. Ainsi parfist son offrande dévotement et honorablement.

**Page 35, note 2.** The hymn *Nuntium vobis fero de supernis*, by Fulbert of Chartres, is printed as follows in *A.H.*, l, 283:

1. Nuntium vobis fero de supernis:
   Natus est Christus, dominator orbis,
   in Bethlem Judæ, sic enim propheta
   dixerat ante.

2. Hunc canit lætus chorus angelorum,
   stella declarat, veniunt eoi
   principes digno celebrare cultu mystica dona.

3. Tus Deo, murram trocletem humando,
   bratheas regi chryseas decenter,
   dum colunt unum, meminere trino
   tres dare terna.

4. Gloriam trinæ monadi canamus,
   cum Deo divæ genitore proli,
   flamini nec non ab utroque fuso
   corde fideli.

**Page 37, note 4.** Concerning the dramatic ceremony of the Three Kings in the church of St John at Besançon, Crombach gives the following summary description 'ex veteri consuetudine' (p. 732):

In basilica Metropolitana S. Ioannis Bisonticensis ex veteri consuetudine in codice rituum adnotata inter Missarum solennia clerici tres personati cum coronis et ornatu regio totidem ministris in vasis auro conspicuis regia munera præferentibus, alijs etiam è clero cum baculis argenteis, cum cereis accensis cum thuribulo comitantibus è sacrario egressi supplicabundi omnes egregia pompa per aliquot stationes, quibus inseritur Euangelium, varios ad mysterium versus accinunt, tandemque Stella duce progressi, munera sua altari imponunt.

Crombach appears not to have been acquainted with any complete description of this ceremony as it was performed in the church of St Stephen. A description in French is found in the *Liber Cæremoniarum et Officiorum divinorum quæ fiunt in ecclesia Sancti Stephani Bisuntini*, written by Francis Guenard, a priest of St Stephen's, in 1629 (Besançon, Bibl. de la Ville, MS 109, pp. 44–6).[1] This passage, previously edited by Young, *Trois Rois*, pp. 81–3, is as follows:

POUR LA PROCESSION DES TROIS ROIS

Pendant que l'on dit Tierce on habille trois petits garcons à la mode de pages de Perses auec habillements a ce propres, l'un desquelz on doibt noircir par le visage et les mains, qui represente le Roy more, et tous trois tiennent en main vne coupe, et apres l'Epistre les deux sieurs Altaristes auec les deux sieurs Choristes s'en vont au reuestiaire ensemble du sieur Surchantre, pour s'habiller en Roys scauoir les deux sieurs Alteristes et surchantre, auec aulbes, Tunicques, et pluuiales toutes de diuerses couleurs auec les ceintures et Chapeaux coronnez a ce propres ayant chascun la palme en main et chascun vn liburet où est noté et escript ce qui doîbuent fere et chanter: Estans ainsi habillez, le plus jeune Choriste va deuant l'autel de nostre Dame et les Choriaux portantz les Chandeliers et cierges allumez, puis lesdit trois Roys, et les pages apres eux chascun à l'endroit de son maistre, le plus anciens Choriste va le dernier, et là estans Ilz chantent a haulte voix *Nouæ genituræ* qui est la premiere pause. Dez là Ilz s'en vont au droit de la chapelle du Saint Suaire, et font la seconde pause chantans le second verset, la troizieme pause se faict à lendroit de la sepulture de fut monsieur Baldoux, la quatriesme | se faict en la Chapelle ou Cymitiere des Comtes. La cinquieme au milieu de la nefz, la sixieme soub le Jube. Nota que le plus jeune Choriste et les Choriaux se doibuent retourner vers lesdits trois Rois pendant qu'ilz chantent lesdits versetz.

Apres cela, Ilz montent tous sur le Jube pour y chanter l'Euangile *Cum natus esset*. Le diacre commence, [2]estant a las droicte,[2] le soubdiacre suyt, [3]qui est au milieu des trois,[3] puis le Surchantre qui est a la gauche, et la chantent comme elle est notée dedans ces petits liburetz, et la musicque respond, et quand Ilz arriuent a ces parolles icy, *Aurum, Thus, et Myrrham*, les pages qui demeurent dernier[4] les trois Rois, presentent leur couppes chascun a son maistre, le premier Roy commence a chanter *Aurum*, monstrant et leuant ladite couppe, le second chante *Thus*, faisant comme le premier, le troiziesme chante *Et myrrham*, faisant comme les deux autres, les pages reprennent lesdites couppes.

L'Euangile dict, le premier Roy chante *Ecce stella*, la monstrant au doibt, ou auec la main ouuerte, laquelle Estoille doibt estre arrestée au droit du pulpite qu'est au choeur, le second Roy et le troizieme font de mesme, et immediatement tous trois ensembles chantent[5] *In oriente præuisa iterum præcedet nos lucida*.

Puis ilz descendent du Jubé et s'en vont tous au milieu du choeur deuant le grand Chandelier, et là chantent le verset de la septieme station, comme elle est dedans ces petits libures, et de là s'en vont deuant le grand autel, et là

[1] No mention of the *Officium Stellæ* is made in any of the following: Besançon MS 99, Rituale Bisuntinum sæc. xv in.; Besançon MS 101, Ordin. Bisuntinum sæc. xv; *Cérémonial du Diocèse de Besançon*, Besançon, 1682; *Cérémonial du Diocèse de Besançon*, Besançon, 1707.

[2–2] Supplied from left margin.

[3–3] Supplied from left margin.

[4] dernier] Preceded by *derriere*, which is crossed out.

[5] chantent] Preceded by *Ilz*, which is crossed out.

estants à genoux ilz chantent le huictieme verset. Les pages leur donnent leur couppes à chascun la sienne, et les offrent au sieur[1] qui dit la grande Messe, le premier Roy chantant tout seul *Jus in auro regium*, presentant[2] sa couppe et sa coronne, le second chante *Thure sacerdotium*, presentant aussi sa couppe et sa corone, le troizieme chante *Myrrha munus tertium* | *mortis est indicium*, puis tous trois ensembles Ilz repetent *Mortis est indicium*. Cela faict le Sieur qui dit la grande Messe commence a chanter *Credo in vnum Deum*. Ce pendant les Rois sen vont, le premier par la porte Saint Agapit, le second par la porte du choeur, et le troizieme par la porte du costé de nostre Dame; et tous trois se rendent au vestiaire pour mettre bas leurs habillementz, et les pages suyuent leur maistre. Les deux Sieurs Altaristes s'en retournent au grand autel, et les Choristes au Choeur.[3]

Although the liturgical text for which this ceremonial is provided differs in no substantial detail from the Latin text given above (pp. 38 sqq.) from the church of St John, in indications as to impersonation and dramatic action the French text is somewhat more generous. The office here consists of three parts: (1) a procession, (2) a singing of the gospel, and (3) the oblation. The *cantiones* used in the procession appear to be the same as those in use at St John's, providing eight stanzas for eight stations. We are told that the boys who served as pages to the kings wore Persian costume, and that one of them had his face and hands blacked for the impersonation of a Moor.[4] The sentences of the gospel are distributed in four parts among the Three Kings and the cantor. At the singing of the words *Obtulerunt ei munera*, the pages handed to the kings their cups, each king raising his cup aloft as he took his part in singing the significant series *Aurum, Thus, et Myrrham*.

**Page 38, note 2.** The song *Novæ genituræ* contains the following fifth stanza, printed in *A.H.*, xx, 63:

Patetque descendens,
lapis est ascendens,
    fulgens flos insignis,
    extra micat ignis
inter rubum splendens,
    non est opus signis
      nato Christo.

**Page 43, note 1.** For discussion above I have chosen the text of the *Officium Stellæ* from Rouen MS 384 because, of all the available texts, it has the most informing rubrics. Less extensive rubrics, but complete speeches and, often, complete liturgical forms, are found in Paris, Bibl. Nat., MS lat. 904, Grad. Rothomagense sæc. xiii, fol. $28^v$–$30^r$, published by Coussemaker, pp. 242–9, and facsimiled by Loriquet, *Graduel*, vol. ii. Facsimiles and text are given also by Chasles, pp. 302–7. Most of the text is printed, with interpolated comments, by Clément, pp. 107–13. I re-edit the text from MS 904:

[1] sieur] Written above *plus*, which is crossed out.

[2] presentant] Preceded by the words *Le second*, which are crossed out.

[3] Followed by the words *Il y a Miserere apres la grande Messe*.

[4] As to the tradition that Balthazar was *fuscus* see Mâle, *XIIIe Siècle*, p. 256, and above, p. 31.

In die Epiphanie, Tercia cantata, tres clerici de maiori sede, cappis et coronis ornati, ex tribus partibus, cum suis famulis tunicis et amictis indutis, ante altare conueniant. Primus stans retro altare, quasi ab oriente ueniens, Stellam baculo ostendat; dicat simplici uoce: |

*Stella fulgore nimio rutilat.*

Secundus a parte dextera ueniens:

*Que regem regum natum demonstrat.*

Tercius a sinistra parte ueniens dicat versum:

*Quem uenturum olim prophecie signauerant.*

Tunc regressi ante altare congregati osculentur simul dicentes uersum:

*Eamus ergo et inquiramus eum, offerentes ei munera: aurum, thus, et mirram.*

Hoc finito, eat processio ut in dominicis, cantore incipiente:

*Magi ueniunt ab oriente, Ierosolimam querentes, et dicentes: Ubi est qui natus est, cuius stellam uidimus, et uenimus adorare Dominum.* Versus: *Cum natus esset Ihesus in Bethleem Iude in diebus Herodis regis, ecce Magi ab oriente uenerunt Ierosolimam dicentes. Ubi est.*

Ad introitum nauis ecclesie Magi ostendentes Stellam cum baculis incipia⟨n⟩t ant*iphonam*, et cantantes pergant ad Altare Crvcis:

*Ecce stella in oriente preuisa iterum precedit nos lucida. Hec inquam stella natum demonstrat, de quo Balaam | cecinerat dicens.* Versus: *Oritur stella ex Iacob, et exurget homo de Israhel, et confringet omnes duces alienigenarum, et erit omnis terra possessio eius.*

Hoc finito, duo de maiori sede dalmaticis induti, in utraque parte altaris stantes, submissa uoce inter se dicant:

*Qui sunt hii qui, stella duce, nos adeuntes inaudita ferunt?*

Tunc Magi respondeant:

*Nos sumus, quos cernitis, reges Tharsis et Arabum et Sabba dona ferentes Christo, Regi, nato Domino, quem, stella deducente, adorare uenimus.*

Tunc duo dalmatic⟨at⟩i operientes cortinam dicant:

*Ecce puer adest quem queritis; iam properate adorare, quia ipse est redempcio mundi.*

Tunc procidentes simul Reges ita salutent Puerum et dicant:

*Salue, Princeps seculorum.*

⟨Tunc primus offerat, ita dicens:⟩[1]

*Suscipe, Rex, aurum.*

Secundus offerens, ita dicens:

*Tolle thus, tu uere Deus.*

Postea tercius offerat, ita dicens:

*Mirram, signum sepulture.*

Tunc orantibus Magis et quasi sompno sopitis, quidam puer alba indutus[2] quasi Angelus ante autem altare illis dicat:

*Impleta sunt omnia que | prophetice dicta sunt. Ite, uiam*[3] *remeantes aliam, ne delatores tanti regis puniendi eritis.*

Finita antiphona,[4] cantor incipiat responsorium ad introitum chori:

*Tria sunt munera preciosa que obtulerunt magi Domino in die ista, et habent in*

[1] The MS repeats here the preceding rubric *Tunc procidentes simul Reges ita salutent Puerum et dicant.* [2] indutus] indutis (MS).

[3] uiam] obuiam (MS).

[4] antiphona] *anī*, with the last letter partly erased (MS).

*se diuina misteria: in auro ut ostendatur regi⟨s⟩ potencia;*[1] *in thure sacerdotem magnum considera; et in mirra dominicam sepulturam.* Versus: *Salutis nostre auctorem magi uenerati sunt in cunabulis, et de thesauris suis misticas ei munerum species obtulerunt. In auro.*[2]

Sequitur Missa, ad quam tres Reges regant chorum, qui cantent *Kyrie fons bonitatis*, et *Alleluia*, et *Agnus*, et *Sanctus* festiue.

The *Officium Stellæ* of Rouen is found also in the following manuscripts: Paris, Bibl. Nat., MS lat. 1213, Ordin. Rothomagense sæc. xv, pp. 34–5 (published by Young, *Rouen*, pp. 220–1); Rouen, Bibl. de la Ville, MS 382 (Y. 108), Ordin. Rothomagense sæc. xv, fol. $35^v$–$36^r$ (published, in part, through variants by Gasté, pp. 49–52); *ibid.*, MS 222 (A. 551), Process. Rothomagense sæc. xiii, fol. $4^r$–$4^v$ (a fragment, published by Young, *op. cit.*, p. 212). Although these three texts add nothing significant to what is found in the texts from Rouen MS 384 and Paris MS 904, for the sake of certain variants in the rubrics I give them all here. The text from Paris MS lat. 1213, pp. 34–5 (A), with variants from Rouen MS 382 (Y. 108), fol. $35^v$–$36^r$ (B), is as follows:

Officium Trium Regum secundum vsum ecclesie Rothomagensis[3] die Epyphanie. Tercia[4] cantata, tres de maiori sede more Regum induti,—et debent esse scripti in tabula,—ex tribus partibus ante altare conueniant, cum suis famulis portantibus Regum oblationes indutis[5] tunicis et amictis; et debent esse de secunda sede scripti in tabula ad placitum scriptoris. Ex[6] tribus Regibus medius ab oriente veniens, Stellam cum baculo ostendens, dicat alte: *Stella fulgore nimio.* Secundus Rex a dextra parte respondeat: *Que*[7] *regem regum.* Tercius Rex a sinistra parte dicat: *Quem venturum olim.* Tunc Magi ante altare sese osculentur, et simul cantent: *Eamus*[8] *et inquiramus.* Hoc finito, cantor incipiat responsorium *Magi veniunt*, et moueat processio. Versus *Cum natus.* Sequatur aliud responsorium, si necesse fuerit, *Interrogabat magos.* Processione in naui ecclesie constituta, stationem faciant.[9] Dum autem processio nauem ecclesie intrare ceperit, corona ante Altare Crucis pendens in modo Stelle, Magi stellam ostendentes ad Ymaginem Sancte Marie super Altare Crucis prius positam cantantes pergant: *Ecce stella*[10] *in oriente.* Hoc finito, duo de maiori sede cum dalmaticis ex vtraque parte altaris[11] stantes suauiter respondeant: *Qui sunt hi qui, stella.*[12] Magi respondeant: *Nos sumus, quos cernitis.* Tunc duo dalmaticati aperientes cortinam dicant:[13] *Ecce puer adest.* Tunc procidentes Reges ad terram simul salutent Puerum, ita dicentes: *Salue, Princeps seculorum.* Tunc vnus a suo famulo aurum accipiat et dicat: *Suscipe, Rex, aurum*, et offerat.[14] Secundus Rex[15] ita dicat et offerat: *Tolle thus, vere.*[16] Tercius dicat et offerat:[17] *Mirram, signum sepulture.*

[1] potencia] potenciam (MS).
[2] auro] aurum (MS).
[3] ecclesie Rothomagensis] Rothomagensem (B).
[4] Tercia] iii^a (A).
[5] indutis] induti (A).
[6] Ex] Et (A).
[7] Que] Quem (B).
[8] Eamus] Eamus ergo (B).
[9] faciant] faciat (B).
[10] stella] stellam (A).
[11] vtraque parte altaris] vtroque altaris parte (B).
[12] stella] stellam (A).
[13] dicant] dicat (A).
[14] et offerat] Omitted (B).
[15] Rex] Omitted (B).
[16] vere] tu vere (B).
[17] dicat et offerat] ita dicat et aufferat (B).

[1]Iterum fiant oblationes a clero et populo.[1] Tunc Magis[2] orantibus et quasi somno[3] sopitis, quidam puer alba indutus et amictu super caput quasi Angelus in pulpito illis dicat hanc antiphonam: *Impleta sunt*[4] *que prophetice*, et cetera. Hoc finito, Reges recedant per alam[5] ecclesie ante fontes, et intrent chorum per ostium[6] sinistrum; et processio intret chorum sicut consuetum est in dominicis, cantore incipiente hoc[7] responsorium *Tria sunt munera*. Versus *Salutis nostre auctorem*, si necesse fuerit.

Ad missam tres Reges regant chorum,[8] qui *Kyrie fons bonitatis*, *Alleluia*, *Sanctus*, et *Agnus* cantent.[9] Officium *Ecce aduenit*. Psalmus *Deus iudicium*. *Kyrieleyson* et *Gloria* festiue. Oratio *Deus qui hodierna die*.[10] Si archiepiscopus cantauerit, memorie pro Domino Papa et Rege tantum; sin autem, nulla memoria fiat. Epistola *Surge, illuminare*. Predicti famuli cantent graduale *Omnes de Sabba*. Versus *Surge, illuminare*. *Alleluia*. Versus *Vidimus stellam*. Sequencia *Epyphaniam Domino*. Euangelium *Cum natus esset Ihesus*. *Credo*. Offertorium *Reges Tharsis*. Deinde offerant Reges, et omnes qui voluerint.[11] Secreta *Ecclesie tue, quesumus, Domine*. Prefatio | *Quia cum Vnigenitus*. *Communicantes, et diem*. Communio *Vidimus stellam*. Post-Communio *Presta, quesumus, omnipotens Deus*. Prefatio et *Communicantes* dicantur per octauam; etiam ad Missam Beate Marie.[12]

The fragment in Rouen MS 222 (A. 551), fol. $4^r$–$4^v$, is as follows:

. . . ⟨pue⟩rum, ita dicentes: *Salue, Princeps seculorum*.

Tunc primus accipiens aurum a ministro suo offerat et dicat: *Su⟨s⟩cipe, Rex, aurum*.

Secundus offerens thus ita dicat: *Tolle thus, tu vere Deus*.

Tercius offerat mirram, et dicat: *Mirram, signum sepulture*.

Orantibus Magis et quasi[13] sopitis, quidam puer, alba et amictu indutus quasi Angelus, ante altare illis dicat hanc antiphonam: *Impleta sunt omnia que prophetice dicta sunt. Ite, uiam redeuntes aliam, ne delatores tanti regis puniendi eritis*.

Finita antiphona, cantor incipiat hoc responsorium, et intret processio chorum, et fiat oblatio a clero et populo: *Tria sunt munera preciosa que obtulerunt magi Domino in die ista, et habent in se diuina misteria: in aurum ut | ostendatur regis potencia, in thure sacerdotem magnum considera; et in mirra dominicam sepulturam*. Versus: *Salutis nostre auctorem magi uenerati sunt in cunabulis, et de thesauris suis misticas ei munerum species obtulerunt. In aurum*.

Sequatur Missa, ad quam tres Reges regant chorum, qui cantent *Kyrie fons*, *Alleluia*. Versum *Vidimus*, *Sanctus*, et *Agnus* festive.[14]

[1–1] Interim fiant oblaciones a clero et populo. Et diuidatur oblacio predictis duobus canonicis (B).

[2] magis] magi (A).

[3] somno] sompno (B).

[4] sunt] sunt omnia (B).

[5] alam] allam (B).

[6] ostium] hostium (B).

[7] incipiente hoc] incipiente ad introitum chori (B).

[8] regant chorum] chorum regant (B).

[9] cantent] festiue cantent (B).

[10] die] Omitted (B).

[11] voluerint] voluerint; et diuidatur oblatio inter famulos predictos (B).

[12] Followed by the rubric *Ad Sextam*.

[13] quasi] After this word is a blank space sufficient for receiving such a word as *somno*, no sign of which appears. In the blank space a hand of a century later has inserted *in*.

[14] Followed by the rubric *Dominica infra octauam*.

For bibliography concerning the liturgical plays of Rouen in general see Young, *op. cit.*, pp. 201, 224–7. In that place are given the reasons why the texts of Le Prévost, Du Cange, Martene, and Du Méril need not be consulted. My observations upon the texts of Du Méril and Le Prévost differ somewhat from those of Böhme, p. 58. The text printed, from an unidentified source, by Martene, iii, 43–4, is expounded by Pearson, ii, 291–3.

**Page 50, note 2.** Essentially similar to the text from Mazarine MS 1708 is the following from Paris, Bibl. Nat., MS lat. 9449, Trop. Nivernense sæc. xi, fol. $17^v$–$18^r$, previously edited by L. Delisle, in *Romania*, iv (1875), 2–3, and by Chasles, pp. 259–61:[1]

VERSUS[2] AD STELLAM FACIENDAM

Versus: *Stella fulgore nimio rutilat,*[3]
*Que*[4] *regem regum natum monstrat,*
*Quem uenturum olim prophecie signauera⟨n⟩t.*
Versus: *Eamus ergo et inquiramus eum, offerentes ei munera: aurum, thus, et mirram.*
Versus: *Vidimus stellam eius in oriente, et agnouimus regem regum esse natum.*
Versus: *Regem quem queritis natum stella, | quo signo*[5] *didicistis?*
*Si illum regnare creditis, dicite nobis.*
Versus: *Illum natum esse didicimus in oriente, stella monstrante.*
Versus: *Ite et de puero diligenter inuestigate,*
*Et inuentum redeuntes mihi renuntiate.*
Versus: *Ecce stella in oriente preuisa*[6]
*Iterum preueniet.*
Versus: *Qui sunt hii qui, stella duce, nos adeuntes*[7] *inaudita ferentes?*
Versus: *Nos sumus, quos cernitis, reges Tarsis et Arabum et Saba dona ferentes Christo, Regi, nato Domino, quem,*[8] *stella deducente, uenimus adorare.*
Versus: *Ecce puer adest quem queritis; iam properate, adorate, quia ipse est redempcio uestra.*
Versus: *Salue, Rex seculorum; suscipe nunc aurum.*
Versus: *Tolle tus, tu uere*[9] *Deus.*
Versus: *Mirram, signum sepulture.*
Versus: *Inpleta sunt omnia que prophetice dicta sunt. Ite, uiam remeantes aliam, ne delatores tanti regis puniendi eritis.*
*Te Deum laudamus.*[10]

It will be observed that, aside from lacking descriptive rubrics, the text in MS 9449 differs essentially from that in Mazarine MS 1708 only as to the position of the passage *Vidimus stellam eius in oriente, et agnouimus regem regum esse natum.* In the former text this constitutes the third speech in the play; in the latter, it forms part of another speech (*Ecce stella*) farther along in the action.

[1] The manner in which this text is presented by Reiners, *Unbekannte Tropen-Gesänge*, p. 33, is not intelligible to me.
[2] Preceded by liturgical pieces for the first Sunday after Christmas.
[3] nimio rutilat] nimium ructilat (MS).
[4] Que] quem (MS).
[5] signo] signum (MS).
[6] preuisa] preuissa (MS).
[7] adeuntes] audientes (MS).
[8] quem] qui (MS).
[9] uere] uerus (MS).
[10] Followed by another sentence of the *Te Deum* and the rubric *In Epiphania Domini*, introducing a trope of the introit.

Madame Chasles (p. 259) appears to regard the text from MS 9449 as a mere succession of verses not yet employed for dramatic performance.

In association with the simpler form of *Officium Stellæ* from the cathedral at Nevers must be printed the following disordered text from the same church, found in Paris, Bibl. Nat., Nouvelles Acquisitions, MS lat. 1235, Grad.-Trop. Nivernense sæc. xii, fol. 198$^{r}$–199$^{v}$, published by L. Delisle, in *Romania*, iv (1875), 3–6, reprinted from Delisle by Anz, pp. 146–7, and republished from the MS by C. Blume, in *A.H.*, xlix, 12–3, and, in part, by Chasles, pp. 259–61, and Reiners, *Unbekannte Tropen-Gesänge*, p. 33:

⟨A⟩[1]

*Sic speciem ueteres stelle struxere parentes,*
*Quatinus hoc pueri uersus psallant duo regi.*

*Credimvs immensum regem cum sidere natum,*
*Eterna cuius uirtute superna reguntur,*
*Cuius et imperio caro subditur omnis ab euo.*

Nvncivs: *Regia uos mandata uocant; non segniter ite.*

Magi: *Hunc regnare fatentes, cum misticis muneribus de terra longinqua adorare venimus.*

Nvncius: *Rex mandat uobis omnis quem terra tremiscit,*
*Protinus et gressum | uestrum dirigatis ad ipsum.*

Magi: *Nunc uenerande tene sceptrum rex imperiale.*

Rex: *Huc, semiste mei,*
*Dissertos pagina ad me properantes uocate.*

Nvncivs: *O, legis periti, a rege uocati cum prophetarum lineis properando uenite.*

Rex: *O, uos scribe, interrogati dicite si quid de hoc puero scriptum uideritis in libris.*

Semiste: *Vidimus, Domine, in prophetarum lineis quod manifeste scriptum est.*

Chorvs: *Bethleem, non eris minima in principibus Iuda, ex te enim exiet dux qui regat populum meum Israhel; ipse enim saluum faciet populum suum a peccatis eorum.*

Rex: *Regem quem queritis.*

Magi: *Illum natum esse.*

Rex: *Si illum regnare.*

Rex: *Ite et de puero.*

Magi: *Ecce stella in oriente.*

⟨B⟩

Aliter.

Magvs dicit primus: *Stella fulgore nimio*[2] *rutilat.*

Et secundus: *Que regem regum natum monstrat.*

[1] The symbols A and B are used as an aid to the subsequent discussion. The text given here is found at the end of a series of tropes for the Mass of the Octave of Christmas, and is immediately preceded by this trope of the communio: Tropos: *Cernere quod uerbum Domini meruere canamus, eya.* Communio: *Viderunt omnes fines.* Ad Comm̄. The closing rubric of this passage, Ad Comm̄., falls at the end of a line; and above the rubric, and extending into the right margin, are written, in a smaller, but contemporary, script the two hexameters (*Sic speciem . . . duo regi*) with which I begin my text. Unlike the rest of the text (except as indicated below), these two hexameters are not furnished with neums. The verse *Credimus immensum* begins the next normal line of the manuscript page. Texts of the communion trope *Cernere quod verbum* are found in *A.H.*, xlix, 354.

[2] nimio] nimium (MS).

Tercius: *Quem uenturum olim prophecie signauerant.*

Magi simvl: *Eamus ergo et inquiramus eum, offe|rentes ei munera: aurum, thus, et mirram.*

Nvncivs: *En magi ueniunt,*
*Et regem regum natum, stella duce, requirunt.*

Rex: *Ante uenire iube, quo possim singula scire*
*Qvi sint, cur*[1] *ueniant, quo nos rumore requirant.*

Nvncivs: *Regia uos.*

Magi: [2]*Nunc uenerande.*[2]

Rex: *Regem quem queritis, natum*[3] *esse quo signo didicistis?*

Magi: *Illum natum*[4] *esse didicimus in oriente stella monstrante.*

Rex: *Si illum regnare creditis, dicite nobis.*

Rex: *Huc, semiste mei.*

Rex: *Ite et de puero diligenter inuestigate,*
*Et inuentum redeuntes michi renunciate.*

Magi: *Ecce stella in oriente preuisa*
*Iterum preuenit nos lucida.*

Obstetrices: *Qui sunt hii qui, stella duce, nos adeuntes et inaudita ferentes?*

Magi simvl respond*ent*: *Nos sumus, quos cernitis, reges Tharsis et Arabum et Saba dona ferentes Cristo, Regi, nato Domino, quem,*[5] *stella deducente, uenimus adorare.*

Obstetrices: *Ecce puer adest quem queritis; iam | properate, adorate, quia ipse est redemptio uestra.*

Magi simvl: *Salue, Rex seculorum.*

Dicit primus: *Suscipe nunc aurum.*

Dicit secundus: *Tolle thus, tu uere*[6] *Deus.*

Dicit tertius: *Myrram, signum sepulture.*

Angelvs excelsa voce: *Impleta sunt omnia que prophetice dicta sunt. Ite, uiam remeantes aliam, ne delatores tanti regis puniendi eritis.*

Magi: *Deo gracias.*
*Te Deum laudamus.*[7]

The peculiar nature of this text has given rise to considerable comment.[8] It obviously falls into two parts, separated by the rubric *Aliter*. The part preceding *Aliter* may be referred to as A, and the other part, as B. Neither A nor B is intelligible by itself. The two parts contain certain passages in common, but in these instances either A or B has only *initia* for certain passages which are complete in the other part.[9] A and B are written by one hand throughout, and in so far as they contain identical passages of words, the accompanying melodies are identical. As to the liturgical position of this dramatic piece (considering A and B together), the evidence of the manuscript is somewhat confusing, since the text stands between the tropes of the Octave of Christmas and those of Epiphany, is immediately preceded by the rubric *Ad Communionem*, and closes with the *Te Deum*.[10] My own inference is

[1] cur] qur (MS).

[2–2] Not furnished with musical notation.

[3] natum] nato (MS).

[4] Illum natum] illuminatum (MS).

[5] quem] qui (MS).

[6] uere] uerus (MS).

[7] Followed immediately in the MS by a trope of the introit of Epiphany, as follows: Tropos in Epiphania Dei: *Ecclesie sponsus, illuminator gencium.*

[8] See especially Anz, pp. 148–51.

[9] See Anz, pp. 148–9.

[10] This last fact is overlooked by Delisle, and hence by Anz.

that the dramatic text has no connexion with the Mass, and that it represents a play, or parts of a play, designed for performance at the end of Matins of Epiphany.

Toward explaining the textual relationship between A and B several attempts have been made. These I briefly summarize.

Hartmann[1] maintains that during his writing of A the scribe was working from an imperfect copy, or from memory, and that when he recognized the futility of his result, he began anew, under the rubric *Aliter*, and, with some one's assistance, produced B. When in the course of writing B he came to passages that were already satisfactory in A, he copied only the *initia*.

In reviewing Hartmann's monograph, Baist[2] accepts the view that A and B belong to a single version, but invents a new explanation of the scribe's procedure. The scribe's copy, he thinks, consisted of six sheets, each bearing writing on only one side. These six sheets the scribe copied in an erroneous sequence. Baist himself admits that his own reconstruction is not completely intelligible.

Rejecting Hartmann's attempt to resolve A and B into *one* continuous text, Köppen[3] holds that A and B are *two* separate pieces, which differ only in their beginnings. A, he thinks, represents the author's unfortunate attempt to depart from his source in favour of his own originality, shown especially in the several hexameters. In B the author follows his source, with the usual beginning *Stella fulgore*, and retains only one of the hexameters (*Nunc venerande . . . imperiale*) which he had created for A. In B the author includes the scene between Herod and the scribes by inserting only the reference words *Huc, semiste mei*.

Blume[4] infers that A and B together represent two versions of the play. The common element in the two is conceived to be the scene of the Magi and *Obstetrices*, which is fully written out in B (Magi: *Ecce stella in oriente . . . Te Deum laudamus*). One version is formed by prefixing to this scene the entire text of A; the other version, by prefixing all that precedes in B.

Anz[5] regards B as representing, in general, the original and basic text, and A as a succession of variants entered, in the first instance, in the margin of a MS, alongside B. The present state of the text results, he thinks, from the blundering of a subsequent copyist, who mistook the marginal entries for the first column of the text itself, and thus copied A and B in their present continuity.

Although in this brief summary I do scant justice to the ingenuities of the critics concerned, I do not, I hope, misrepresent their general positions, to which, in the present treatise, I cannot yield more space. Each of the critics appears to me to fail either through employing an inadmissible degree of speculation or through arriving at indecisive conclusions. Whether or not the disordered text under discussion can ever be completely clarified, however, it is not devoid of interest; for it appears to show at least that, by the twelfth century, clerics at Nevers were sufficiently interested in the Epiphany play to undertake the elaborating of the simpler form of it which we know to have

[1] See Hartmann, *Dreikönigsspiel*, pp. 12–4.

[2] See G. Baist, in *Zeitschrift für romanische Philologie*, iv (1880), 446–7.

[3] See Köppen, pp. 16–7.

[4] See C. Blume, in *A.H.*, xlix, 12–3. This editor was the first to print the liturgical close at the end of B.

[5] See Anz, pp. 148–51.

existed there in the eleventh century. The nature of the attempted elaboration will be clearer to one who examines the more highly developed versions of the *Officium Stellæ* in the later pages of chapter xix.

**Page 53, note 5.** With the *Officium Stellæ* from Compiègne (Paris, Bibl. Nat., MS lat. 16819) may be conveniently associated the fragments of four other plays which provide roles for messengers and scribes. The first fragment is found in Paris, Bibl. Nat., MS lat. 1152, on the upper half of an isolated fly-leaf at the end of the volume. This leaf (from the north-east of France?) is not related to the psalter of Charles the Bald, which forms the body of the MS. The fragment, of the tenth or eleventh century, has been previously edited anonymously in *Bibliothèque de l'École des Chartes*, xxxiv (1873), 657–8, and is now re-edited from the MS:

*⟨S⟩tella fulgore nimio rutilat,*
*Que regem regum natum monstrat,*
*Quem uenturum olim prophetia signaverat.*
*Eamus ergo et inquiramus eum, offerentes ei munera: aurum, tus*[1] *et myrram; quia scriptum didicimus: Adorabunt eum omnes reges, omnes gentes seruient ei.*

Rex: *Lecti oratores, qui sint inquirite reges*
*Affore quos nostris iam fama reuoluit in oris.*
Nuntii Regi: *Sint*[2] *conpleta citum uestra hec precepta peractum.*[3]
Nuntii ad Magos: *Principis edictu, Reges, prescire uenimus*
*Quo sit directus hic uester, et unde profectus.*
Magi: *Regem quesitum duce stella significatum,*
*Munere prouiso properamus eum uenerando.*
Nuntii ad Regem: *En magi ueniunt,*
*Et regem regum natum stella duce requirunt.*
Rex: . . .

The fragment ends in the middle of the page. The opening part of the role of the messenger as provided in the play from Compiègne is here preceded by an exchange of speeches between the messengers and Herod.

The second fragment is from Rome, Bibl. Vatic., MS lat. 8552, a volume from the monastery of Malmédy, in Belgium, containing a version of Josephus' *Antiquitates Judaicæ*. This MS was first made known to me by the late Reverend H. M. Bannister. Fol. 1v contains, in its two columns and margins, the fragment printed below, written in a hand of the eleventh century and furnished with neums of the school of Metz. Through deterioration of the parchment, considerable passages of the text are illegible. These are enclosed within brackets, or indicated by dots. The fragment has been edited previously by Young, *Officium Stellæ*, pp. 70–1:

*Stella*[4] *fulgore nimio ⟨rutilat⟩,*
*⟨Que⟩ reg⟨em⟩ reg⟨um⟩ natum monstrat,*
*Quem uenturum olim prophetie signauerant.*
. . . . . . .[5]

[1] tus] A mark over this word may be a reminder of the missing *h*.

[2] Sint] This word and the last three letters of the preceding *Regi* are written over an erasure.

[3] peractum] The last five letters are written over an erasure.

[4] Preceded, at the top of the first column, by a line or two of illegible text.

[5] Although the written text runs continuously, a lacuna in the sense is obvious.

H⟨erodes⟩: *Regem quem queritis, natum esse quo signo didicistis?*
*Si illum regnare creditis, dicite nob⟨is⟩.*

aurum thus mirram

Magi: Melchus, Caspar, Fadizarda:[1]
*Illum natum esse didicimus, in oriente stella prenunciante.*
*Hunc regnare fatentes, cum misticis muneribus de terra longinqua adorare uenimus.*

Herodes: *O, uos scribe, interrogati dicite si quid de hoc puero scriptum uideretis in libro.*

Scribe: *Vidimus, Domine, in prophetarum lineis nasci Cristum in Betleem, ciuitate Dauid, Isaia sic uaticinante.*

Chorus: *⟨B⟩ethleem, non es minima.*

Rex: *Ite et de puero diligenter inuestigate,*
*Et inuento, redeuntes mihi renunciate.*

Magi: Melchus, Caspar, Fadizarda:[2]
*Eamus ergo inquiramus eum, offerentes ei munera: aurum, thus, et mirram.*
*Ecce stella in oriente preuisa.*
*Iterum precedit nos lucida.*

Obstetrices: *Qui sunt hii qui, stella duce, nos adeuntes inaudita ferunt?*

Magi: *⟨N⟩os sumus, quos cernitis, reges Tharsis et Arabum et Saba dona ferentes Cristo, Regi, nato Domino, quem, stella deducente, adorare uenimus.*

Obstetrices: *Ecce puer adest quem queritis; iam properate et adorate, quia ipse est redemptio uestra.*

Magi: *Salue, Rex seculorum! Suscipe nunc aurum, regis signum.*
*Tolle*[3] *thus, tu uere Deus.*
*Mir⟨ram, signum⟩ sepulture.*

Angelus in somnis: *Impleta sunt omnia que propheticae dicta sunt. Ite, uiam remeantes aliam, ne delatores tanti regis puniendi sitis.*

Gladiator: *Decerne, Domine, uindicari iram tuam, nam uiri Chaldaici, ⟨ius⟩sum tuum transgressi, forte ⟨per uiam⟩ aliam reuersi sunt ⟨in terram su⟩am.*[4]

H⟨erodes⟩: *Bethlem ne . . . ice cautus M . . . ns iugulum quo caedas puer⟨um⟩.*
*Te Deum.*

. . . . . . .[5]

*⟨Ante uenire⟩ iube, ⟨quo possim singula scire*
*Qui sunt,⟩ cur ueniant, quo nos rumore requirant.*

Nuntius ad M⟨agos⟩: *Regia ⟨uos⟩ manda⟨ta⟩ uocant; ⟨non segn⟩iter ⟨ite⟩.*
. . . :[6] *Salue, Prin⟨ceps Iudeorum⟩!*

[1] *Magi* is written in large capitals. Above *Magi* are written, in small capitals, *Melchus Caspar Fadizarda*. Above these three names are written *aurum thus mirram*.

[2] *Magi* is written in large capitals, and above it, in small capitals, the three names.

[3] Tolle] With this word begins the second column. In the upper margin, over the second column, were written, no doubt, several words no longer legible.

[4] The bracketed passages in this speech are offered only tentatively.

[5] Up to this point the text in the MS occupies continuously the first column and part of the second. What follows—written down the right margin of the page and in the lower part of the second column—may have been intended for insertion in the lacuna noted above, after the three lines at the beginning of the text.

[6] At this point the text shifts to the lower part of the second column, beginning with several illegible words.

Rex: *Que sit causa uie, qui ⟨uos, uel unde uenitis⟩?*
*Dic⟨ite nobis⟩.*
Magi: *Rex est causa uie; reges sumus ⟨ex⟩ Arabitis,*
*Huc uenientes.*[1]

A third fragment became known to me through a transcript found among the papers of the late Professor Wilhelm Meyer. The original is inserted over erasures in Munich, Staatsbibl., MS lat. 14477, fol. 1r–1v. The text, of the twelfth century, is accompanied by neums, but unfortunately not by rubrics. With the generous permission of Professor Alfons Hilka, of Göttingen, I print the text from the MS itself:

*Hoc signum magni regis est; eamus et inquiramus eum, et offeramus ei munera: aurum, thus, et mirram.*
*Stella fulgore nimio rutilat,*
*Que regem regum natum monstrat,*
*Quem uenturum olim prophetia signauerat.*
*Salue, rex Iudeorum!*
*En Magi ueniunt,*
*Et regem regum natum stella duce requirunt.*
*Ante uenire iube, quo possim singula scire*
*Qui sint, cur ueniant, quo nos rumore requirunt.*
*Regia uos mandata uocant; non segniter ite.*
*Querimvs hic regem regnantibus imperitantem,*
*Quem natum mundo lactat Iudaica uirgo.*
*Regem, quem queritis, natum esse quo signo didicistis?*
*Illum natum esse didicimus in oriente, stella monstrante.*
*Si illum regnare creditis, dicite nobis.*
*Illum regnare fatentes, cum misticis muneribus de terra longinqua adorare uenimus, trinum Deum uenerantes: auro regem, ture sacerdotem, mirra mortalem.*
*Huc, simiste mei, disertos pagina scribas prophetica ad me uocate.*
*Vos, legis periti, a rege uocati cum prophetarum libris properando uenite.*
*O, uos scribe, interrogati dicite si quid de hoc puero scriptum uideritis in libris.*
*Vidimus, domine, in prophetarum lineis nasci Christum in Betlehem, ciuitate Dauid, propheta sic uaticinante:*
*Bethlehem non es.* |
*Ite et de puero diligenter inuestigate,*
*Et inuento, redeuntes mihi renunciate.*[2]

A fourth fragment, less coherent than the preceding, is printed by K. Schiffmann, in *Anzeiger für deutsches Altertum und deutsche Litteratur*, xxxi (1907), 15–6, to whose text and comment my acquaintance with the matter is confined. The fragment is found on a half-page, cut lengthwise, in a MS preserved in the monastery of Lambach, in Austria. The mutilated page is from an *ordinarium* of the eleventh century, whose provenance may be the valley of the Rhine. From what is preserved, the play appears to represent a stage of development somewhat simpler than that represented by the play

[1] Followed by a considerable blank space at the bottom of the second column.

[2] Immediately followed, on line 3 of fol. 1v, by a passage from Sallust.

from Compiègne, since it appears to contain no scenes in which messengers are employed.

**Page 57, note 1.** From sources of the eleventh century and later the text of the sequence *Quem non prævalent* is given in *A.H.*, liv, 9, as follows:

Quem non prævalent propria magnitudine
Cæli, terræ atque maria amfisæpire,
De virgineo natus utero ponitur in præsæpio;
Ut propheticus sermo nuntiat, stant simul bos et asinus.
Sed oritur stella lucida, præbitura Domino obsequia,
Quam Balaam ex Judaica orituram dixerat prosapia.
Hæc magorum oculos fulguranti lumine præstrinxit providos.
Atque ipsos prævia Christi ad cunabula perduxit vilia.
Illi at exiguis adorant obsitum pannulis
Offerentes regia aurum, tus et myrrham munera.
Ipsa sed tamen mysticis non carent munera figuris:
Aurum ut regi, tus Deo et magno offerunt sacerdoti,
Atque myrrham in sepulturam.

The use of various parts of this composition in the several versions of the *Officium Stellæ* is discussed by Meyer, pp. 42–4; Anz, pp. 15, 46, 51, 79–82, 136. Anz (p. 80) calls attention to verbal likenesses between the text in the Compiègne play and certain liturgical pieces, but without proving the indebtedness of the former to the latter.

## CHAPTER XIX

## THE COMING OF THE MAGI (*continued*)

**Page 64, note 1.** The text of the *Officium Stellæ* printed above from British Museum Additional MS 23922 is immediately preceded in the MS by this passage: In octaua Epiphanie. Antiphona. *O admirabile commercium.* Psalmus. *Laudate pueri*, vt supra. Ymnus. *Hostis Herodes*. Versus. *Reges Tharsis et insulae.* Antiphona. *Fontes aquarum*. Psalmus. *Magnificat*. As shown above, the *Officium Stellæ* is followed in the MS by a rubric introducing liturgical pieces for the feast of St Hilarius. These facts leave us in some doubt as to the liturgical position of the play. From what precedes it, one might infer that it was performed at Vespers on the octave of Epiphany. This inference, however, is not inevitable. Since the MS provides only part of the liturgical pieces for the offices, and not always in the correct order, we need not heed too strictly the order it shows in the present case. We may regard the text of the *Officium Stellæ* as 'floating'.

**Page 75, note 1.** For bibliography bearing upon the *Officium Stellæ* of Bilsen see Cohen and Young, pp. 357–8; Gessler, pp. 10–8. Bollandist MS 299 is a Gospel-book written in the twelfth century. Gessler (p. 16) calls attention to the fact that on fol. 71$^{v}$ the *explicit* at the end of the Gospel of Matthew mentions the year 1130 as the date of the transcription, and shows that it was made at the monastery of Bilsen. On fol. 179$^{v}$ the close of the Gospel of John is marked by the following passage written in capitals: *Explicit Evangelium secundum Iohannem.* Under this *explicit* is written the colophon *Ego Samuhel indignus diaconus scripsi istud Euangelium.* Below the colophon begins the text of the *Officium Stellæ*, with which the MS ends (fol. 180$^{v}$). Clément (pp. 113, 115) regards the passage *Ego Samuhel . . . Euangelium* as the heading for the play which follows; hence he introduces his text with the words, 'Drame des Mages, par le diacre Samuel'. Gessler believes (p. 18) that the deacon, Samuel, copied the four Gospels in the volume, and that he probably copied also the *Officium Stellæ*. He infers that, like the Gospels, the play was copied at Bilsen for use in the monastery there. To me the play appears to have been copied by a hand of the twelfth century other than that which copied the Gospels. The presumption is, however, that the play was copied for use in the monastery of Bilsen.

**Page 80, note 4.** The hymn *Hostis Herodes*, by Sedulius (Chevalier, *R.H.*, no. 8073) is printed by Daniel, *Thesaurus*, i, 147–8, as follows:

1. Hostis Herodes impie,
Christum venire quid times?
Non eripit mortalia
qui regna dat cœlestia.

2. Ibant magi quam viderant
stellam sequentes præviam;
lumen requirunt lumine,
Deum fatentur munere.

3. Lavacra puri gurgitis
cœlestis agnus attigit;
peccata quæ non detulit
nos abluendo sustulit.

4. Novum genus potentiæ:
aquæ rubescunt hydriæ,
vinumque iussa fundere
mutavit unda originem.

5. Summo parenti gloria—*vel*—
Gloria tibi, Domine,
qui natus es de virgine, etc.

**Page 92, note 5.** In connexion with the *Officium Stellæ* from Freising (Munich MS lat 6264$^{a}$) one may conveniently enough present the following fragment from Einsiedeln, Stiftsbibl., MS 366 (*olim* 179), Fragmenta liturgica sæc. xi–xii, p. 53, previously edited in *Pilger*, viii (1849), 401–3; by Schubiger, *Spicilegien*, pp. 45–6 (with music); and by Anz, pp. 152–3:

Pastores: *Infantem uidimus p⟨annis involutum, et choros angelorum laudantes Salvatorem⟩.*

Pveri: *Qui sunt hi quos stella ducit nos adeuntes, inaudita ferentes?*

Magi: *Nos sumus, quos cernitis, reges Tharsis et Arabum et Saba dona offerentes Christo, Regi, nato Domino.*

Pveri: *Ecce puer adest quem queritis; iam properate adorare, quia ipse est redemptio mundi.*

Magi: *Salue, Rex seculorum.*
*Suscipe, Rex, aurum.*
*Tolle thus, tu uere Deus.*
*Mirram, signum sepulture.*

Angelvs: *Impleta sunt omnia que prophetice dicta sunt. Ite, uiam remeantes aliam, ne delatoris tanti regis puniendi eritis.*
Magi: *O regem celi.*
Chorus: *Te Deum lauda⟨mus⟩.*
Internvnt⟨ius⟩: *Delusus es, Domine, magi uiam redierunt aliam.*
Armiger: *Decerne, Domine, uindicare iram tuam, et stricto mucrone querere iube puerum; forte inter occisos occiditur et puer.*
Rex: *Incendium meum ruina eorum extinguam.*
*Indolis eximie, pueros fac ense perire.*[1]

The most interesting aspect of this fragment is the evidence of revision. With the *Te Deum*, it appears, closes a normal version of the play, in which, after being warned by the angel, the Magi depart singing the antiphon *O regem cæli.* The vigorous short scene in which Herod and the soldier determine to slaughter the male children is an addition. As to the position of the fragment among the other dramatic texts in the MS see above, i, 598.

Here I offer also another fragment, known to me only through a transcript preserved among the papers of the late Professor Wilhelm Meyer. The original—which I cannot identify—is a single sheet of parchment described by Meyer as 'Grobe Schrift, deutsch, Ende des XII. Jh., ausgelöst aus Inc. 2072'. A considerable part of the text has been lost through the trimming of all four margins of the sheet. With the generous permission of Professor Alfons Hilka I print Meyer's transcript, restoring the losses in pointed brackets—with more or less assurance—from notes left by Meyer, and from parallel passages in the other extant texts:

*. . . ubi est expectatio gentium nouiter natus rex Iudeorum, ⟨quem signi⟩s celestibus agnitum uenimus adorandum.*
Quos uidens ⟨unus Re⟩gis a satellitibus, quem Internuntium appellamus, debet festinare ⟨et Regi nun⟩tiare, primum hoc modo salutans:
*Viue, rex, in eternum! ⟨Adsunt nob⟩is, domine, tres uiri ignoti ab oriente uenientes, nouiter ⟨natum que⟩ndam regem queritantes.*
Hoc rumore Rex turbatus suorum ⟨alicui vo⟩cari eos ad se iubet dicens:
*Ante uenire iube, quo pos⟨sim singula⟩ scire*
*Qui sint, cur ueniant, quo nos rumore requirant.*
⟨Hæc Internunt⟩ius complens redit ad eos et dicens:
*Regia uos ⟨mandata uo⟩cant; non segniter ite.*[2]
Etsi uelocius ire contempnunt, ⟨antecurri⟩t pro illis dicens:
*Rex uocat,*
*Ut quem queratis regem ⟨a uobis i⟩pse agnoscat.*
Mox illos accedentes aliquis ex circum⟨stantibus oste⟩ndat Regi dicens:
*En magi ueniunt,*
*Et regem natum stel⟨la duce re⟩quirunt.*
Quos Rex dignanter intuens interrogat:
*⟨Quæ sit cau⟩sa uie, qui uos, uel unde uenitis?*[3]
*Dicite.*

[1] Followed immediately by the rubric *Ad Prophetas.*
[2] ite] Item (MS)—written as part of the succeeding rubric.
[3] uenitis] ueniens (MS?).

Magi respon*dent*:

*⟨Regem quem⟩ queritis, natum esse quo signo didicistis?*[1]

Magi:

*Illum ⟨natum esse didi⟩cimus in oriente stella monstrante.*

⟨Rex:⟩[2]

*Si illum ⟨regnare credi⟩tis, dicite nobis.*

⟨Magi:⟩[2]

*Hunc regnare fatentes, ⟨cum mysticis⟩ muneribus de terra longinqua adorare uenimus.*

Et hec ⟨munera profe⟩rant, dicatque primus: *Auro regem.*[3]

Secundus: *Thure sacerdotem.*[4]

⟨Tertius: *Myh⟩rra mortalem.*

Tunc Rex pro his sollicitus uocat suos atque pro . . .[5]

. . . sedentes adeunt Symmiste et dicunt:

*Vos legis perit⟨i, a rege vocati⟩ cum prophetarum libris properando venite.*

Si uero tardent uenir⟨e, Rex iratus⟩ uasalis suis dicat:

*Eia! Quid statis? Celeres non properatis? Scrib⟨as adducite, et⟩ citius ite.*

Quos cum adduxerint, Rex debet eos interroga⟨re:

*O, vos scri⟩be, interrogati dicite si quid de hoc puero scriptum uideritis ⟨in libro.*

Scribæ:⟩

*Vidimus, Domine, in prophetarum lineis nasci Christum in Beth⟨lehem civitate⟩ Dauid, propheta sic uaticinante. Vidimus, Domine, in ⟨prophetarum⟩ lineis quod*[6] *manifeste dictum est.*

Tunc chorus . . . et cantet antiphonam: *Bethleem non es.*

Interea Scribe offerunt ei librum, ⟨quem cum ape⟩ruit, ipse legat. Sed ille longe a se debet eum proicere, et . . . dimittens eos dicens:

*Ite ⟨et⟩ de puero diligenter inues⟨tigate,*
*Et inuen⟩to, redeuntes mihi renuntiate,*
*Ut et ego ueniens adorem e⟨um.*

Tunc Magi in⟩de uersi, uidentes Pastores, sic eos interrogant dicentes:

*⟨Quem vidistis, pastores, di⟩cite.*

Pastores: *Infantem uidimus.*

Magi abeuntes S⟨tellam aspici⟩endo clament:

*Ecce stella in oriente preuisa*
*Iterum ⟨præcedit nos⟩ lucida.*

Qui cum Presepi adpropinquauerint, pueri qui illud cu⟨stodiunt dicant⟩:

*Qui sunt hi quos stella ducit nos adeuntes ⟨inaudita feren⟩tes?*

Magi:

*Nos sumus, quos cernitis, reges Tharsis et A⟨rabum et Saba⟩ dona ferentes Christo, Regi, nato Domino, quem, stella deduc⟨ente, adorare⟩ uenimus.*

Tunc pueri eleuantes de Presepi Puerum ostendi . . .

**Page 97, note 2.** The hymn *Salvete, flores martyrum*, by Prudentius

[1] This speech should, of course, be assigned to *Rex*.

[2] MS leaves blank spaces.

[3] regem] tur. (MS).

[4] sacerdotem] sacerdotum (MS).

[5] What remains of p. 1 ends here. I make no attempt to report several words doubtfully recovered by Meyer at the top of p. 2.

[6] quod] quod Christus quod (MS).

(Chevalier, *R.H.*, no 18344), is printed by Daniel, *Thesaurus*, i, 124–5, as follows:

1. Salvete, flores martyrum,
quos lucis ipso in limine
Christi insecutor sustulit
ceu turbo nascentes rosas.

2. Vos prima Christi victima,
grex immolatorum tener
aram ante ipsam simplices
palma et coronis luditis.

3. Audit tyrannus anxius
adesse regum principem,
qui nomen Israel regat,
teneatque David regiam.

4. Exclamat amens nuncio:
'Successor instat, pellimur;
satelles, i ferrum rape,
perfunde cunas sanguine.

5. Mas omnis infans occidat,
scrutare nutricum sinus,
fraus ne qua furtim subtrahat
prolem virilis indolis.'

6. Transfigit ergo carnifex,
mucrone districto furens,
effusa nuper corpora
animasque rimatur novas.

7. O barbarum spectaculum;
vix interemptor invenit
locum minutis artubus
quo plaga descendat patens.

8. Quo proficit tantum nefas!
Quid crimen Herodem iuvat!
Unus tot inter funera
impune Christus tollitur.

9. Iesu, tibi sit gloria,
qui natus es de virgine, etc.

A somewhat different version in eight stanzas, of which *Mas omnis* is the fourth, is given in *A.H.*., l, 27–8.

**Page 97, note 4.** The sequence *Lætabundus exultet fidelis* (Chevalier, *R.H.*, no. 10012) is given by Daniel, *Thesaurus*, ii, 61–2, as follows:

Lætabundus exultet fidelis chorus,
  Alleluia.
Regem regum intactæ profundit torus,
  Res miranda.
Angelus consilii natus est de virgine,
  Sol de stella.
Sol occasum nesciens, stella semper rutilans,
  Semper clara.
Sicut sidus radium profert virgo filium
  Pari forma.
Neque sidus radio neque mater filio
  Fit corrupta.
Cedrus alta Libani conformatur hyssopo
  Valle nostra.
Verbum ens altissimi corporali passum est
  Carne sumpta.
Isaias cecinit, synagoga meminit, nunquam tamen desinit
  Esse cæca.
Si non suis vatibus credat vel gentilibus, Sybillinis versibus
  Hæc prædicta.
Infelix propera, crede vel vetera, cur damnaberis gens misera.
Natum considera, quem docet littera; ipsum genuit puerpera.

**Page 100, note 4.** In connexion with the texts of the *Officium Stellæ* considered in chapters xviii and xix should be mentioned a few miscellaneous descriptions and records of related performances. For records of a Magi play at Yarmouth, Norfolk, at the end of the fifteenth century and the beginning of the sixteenth, see L. G. Bolingbroke, in *Norfolk Archæology*, xi (1892), 334–5; Chambers, ii, 399. Concerning provisions for a representation of the Three Kings at York in the thirteenth century see below, Appendix D, p. 543; Chambers, ii, 399. Miscellaneous records of the provision of 'stars' for Epiphany ceremonies in various churches are cited by Cox, *Churchwardens' Accounts*, pp. 247–8. For twelfth-century references to a Magi play in the writings of Gerhoh of Reichersberg and Herrad of Landsberg see below, Appendix C, p. 524, and above, p. 413. The following description of a play performed at Milan in 1336 is printed by L. A. Muratori, *Rerum Italicarum Scriptores*, xii, Milan, 1728, col. 1017–8, from *Gualvanei de la Flamma opusculum de rebus gestis Azonis Vicecomitis*:

De Festo Trium Regum

Christi Anno MCCCXXXVI, eminente in Sede Apostolica in Civitate Avinionensi Benedicto Papa, Johanne Vicecomite Episcopo Novariensi gubernante Archiepiscopatum loco Fratris Aycardi Archiepiscopi Mediolanensis, supradictus Ursus Kavistinianus fuit in regimine refermatus. Isto tempore fuit incœptum festum trium Regum in die Epifaniæ in Conventu Fratrum Prædicatorum. Et fuerunt coronati tres Reges in equis magnis, vallati domicellis, vestiti variis cum somariis multis, et familia magna nimis. Et fuit Stella aurea discurrens per aëra, quæ præcedebat istos tres Reges; et pervenerunt ad columnas Sancti Laurentii, ubi erat Rex Herodes effigiatus cum scribis et sapientibus. Et visi sunt interrogare Regem Herodem, ubi Christus nasceretur; et, revolutis multis libris, responderunt quod deberet nasci in civitate Bethleem in distantia quinque milliariorum a Hierusalem. Quo audito, isti tres Reges coronati aureis coronis, tenentes in manibus scyphos aureos cum auro, thure, et myrrha, præcedente Stella per aëra, cum somariis, et mirabili famulatu, clangentibus tubis, et bucinis præeuntibus, simiis, babuynis, et diversis generibus animalium cum mirabili populorum tumultu pervenerunt ad Ecclesiam Sancti Eustorgii. Ubi in latere altaris majoris erat Præsepium cum bove, et asino, et in Præsepio erat Christus parvulus in brachiis Virginis Matris. Et isti Reges obtulerunt Christo munera; deinde visi sunt dormire, et Angelus alatus eis dixit quod non redirent per contratam Sancti Laurentii, sed per portam Romanam; quod et factum fuit. Et fuit tantus concursus populi, et militum, et dominarum, et clericorum, quod numquam similis fere visus fuit. Et fuit ordinatum, quod omni anno istud festum fieret.

For evidence of an *Officium Stellæ* at Aquileia and Ivrea see *Archivio storico per Trieste, l'Istria e il Trentino*, iii (1884–6), 63; Bartholomaeis, pp. 152–3. Hardly more than a reference need be made, finally, to the so-called Epiphany play, printed by Du Méril, pp. 151–2, without its context, and hence misinterpreted by Creizenach, i, 56; Chambers, ii, 51; Anz, pp. 9, 48–9. The complete text of which this short piece is a part has been re-edited from the MS, with commentary, by Young, *The 'Poema Biblicum' of Onulphus*, in

*P.M.L.A.*, xxx (1915), 25–41. The *Poema* is merely a literary exercise in the form of a succession of dialogues in verse. One of these bears the heading *Ad adorandum Filium Dei per Stellam inuitantur Eoy*, and in it the four speakers are named *Stella, Aureolus, Thureolus*, and *Myrreolus*. Since this brief dialogue seems not to have been designed for dramatic performance, it need not be considered further in the present survey.

**Page 101, note 4.** Meyer (pp. 42–4) notes the fondness of the French versions of the *Officium Stellæ* for the sequence *Quem non prævalent* (see above, p. 446), and the absence of it from the German texts. Assuming that the earliest French version would have contained some part of this sequence, he infers that if such a version had arisen first in France, and had been brought thence to Germany, the Germans would never have dropped out so agreeable a composition. He concludes, therefore, that the play arose in Germany, and that *Quem non prævalent* was added in France. This argument Schiffman (*Review*, p. 12) rejects, and to it Anz (p. 125) applies—justly enough—the adjective, 'utopisch'.

## CHAPTER XX

## THE SLAUGHTER OF THE INNOCENTS

**Page 102, note 1.** The plays dramatizing the Slaughter of the Innocents are treated in a separate publication of the present writer entitled *Ordo Rachelis* (*University of Wisconsin Studies in Language and Literature*, no. 4), Madison, 1919. See also Anz, pp. 69–78; Chambers, ii, 44, 50; Böhme, pp. 106–20; Chasles, pp. 403–9; Schubiger, *Spicilegien*, pp. 29–32; Creizenach, i, 54–5, 60–1; Kretzmann, pp. 59–62; Meyer, pp. 44–8. For an allusion by Gerhoh of Reichersberg to plays containing a scene of the Innocents see Appendix C, p. 525.

**Page 108, note 5.** The sequence *Celsa pueri concrepent melodia* (Chevalier, *R.H.*, no. 2747) is edited in *A.H.*, liii, 264–5, as follows:

1. Celsa pueri
concrepent melodia,

| | |
|---|---|
| 2. Pia innocentum<br>canentes tripudia. | 3. Quos infans Christus ho-<br>die vexit ad astra. |
| 4. Hos trucidavit<br>frendens insania. | 5. Herodis fraudis<br>ob nulla crimina |
| 6. In Bethleem ipsius cuncta<br>et per confinia | 7. A bimatu et infra, iuxta<br>nascendi tempora. |
| 8. Herodes rex Christi nati<br>verens infelix imperia | 9. Infremit totus et erigit<br>arma superba dextera; |

10. Quærit lucis
et cæli regem
cum mente turbida,

11. Ut extinguat,
qui vitam præstat,
per sua iacula.

12. Dum non valent intueri
lucem splendidam
nebulosa quærentis pectora,

13. Ira fervet, fraudes auget
Herodes sævus,
ut perdat piorum agmina.

14. Castra militum
dux iniquus aggregat,
ferrum figit in membra tenera;

15. Inter ubera
lac effudit, antequam
sanguinis fierent coagula.

16. Hostis naturæ
natos eviscerat
atque iugulat;

17. Ante prosternit,
quam ætas parvula
sumat robora.

18. Quam beata sunt innocentum
ab Herode cæsa corpuscula!

19. Quam felices existunt matres,
quæ fuderunt talia pignora!

20. O dulces innocentum acies!
O pia lactentum
pro Christo certamina!

21. Parvorum trucidantur milia;
membris ex teneris
manant lactis flumina.

22. Cives angelici
veniunt in obviam.
Mira victoria
vitæ captat præmia
turba candidissima.

23. Te, Christe, petimus
mente devotissima
nostra qui venisti
reformare sæcula,
innocentum gloria

24. Perfrui nos
concedas per æterna.

**Page 108, note 6.** The sequence *Misit Herodes innocentum* (Chevalier, *R.H.*, no. 11620) is edited in *A.H.*, liv, 70–1, as follows:

1. Misit Herodes innocentum
perdere gloriosa corpora,

2. Ad sinus matrum ut ad castra
prosilit rumpens inter ubera.

3. Exitium
felix ipsum,
per quod cæsi coronantur
in cæli patria!

4. Felix dolor,
prosper luctus,
per quæ datur adipisci
superum gaudia!

5. Planctus matrum et Rachelis
æqua sunt suspiria;

6. Nulla quidem consolatur
magna præ tristitia.

7. Adhuc Herodes sævit
et adhuc Rachel plangit
pignora;

8. Dæmon hoc ipsum facit,
quando nostra frangit
pectora.

9. Adhuc nos plangit ecclesia,
nec habet terminum lacrima,

10. Quando nos superant vitia,
nostra sic moritur anima.

**Page 109, note 1.** Paris MS lat. 1139 is described by Monmerqué and Michel, pp. 1–3, by Coussemaker, *Histoire*, pp. 126–7, and by the same author in his *Drames liturgiques*, pp. 311–9. Since it contains the famous *Sponsus*, numerous notes upon this MS have been written by students of Romanic dialects. See below, p. 495. The text of the *Ordo Rachelis*, as printed in the present study, is immediately preceded in the manuscript by a blank space capable of receiving a rubric of a word or two, and this, in turn, is preceded by a trope of the *Deus in adjutorium*.

**Page 116, note 3.** The sequence *Quid tu, virgo, mater* is printed and discussed by P. von Winterfeld, in *Neue Jahrbücher für das klassische Altertum*, v (1900), 353–5, and by C. Beck, *Mittellateinische Dichtung*, Berlin and Leipzig, 1926, pp. 35–6. The text is edited in *A.H.*, liii, 379–80, as follows:

1\. Quid tu, virgo,

2\. Mater, ploras,
Rachel formosa,

3\. Cuius vultus
Iacob delectat?

4\. Ceu sororis
aniculæ

5\. Lippitudo
eum iuvet!

6\. Terge, mater, fluentes
oculos.

7\. Quam te decent genarum
rimulæ?

8\. 'Heu, heu, heu, quid me
incusatis fletus
incassum fudisse,

9\. Cum sim orbata nato,
paupertatem meam
qui solus curaret;

10\. Qui non hostibus
cederet
angustos terminos,
quos mihi
Iacob acquisivit;

11\. Quique stolidis
fratribus,
quos multos, proh dolor,
extuli,
esset profuturus?'

12\. Numquid flendus est iste,
qui regnum possedit cæleste;

13\. Quique prece frequenti
miseris fratribus
apud Deum auxiliatur?

**Page 116, note 4.** The sequence *Festa Christi* (Chevalier, *R.H.*, no. 6111) is edited in *A.H.*, liii, 50–1, as follows:

1\. Festa Christi omnis
christianitas celebret.

2\. Quæ miris sunt modis
ornata
cunctisque veneranda
populis,

3\. Per omnitenentis
adventum
atque vocationem
gentium.

4\. Ut natus est Christus,
est stella
magis visa lucida.

5\. At illi non cassam
putantes
tanti signi gloriam

6\. Secum munera deferunt,
parvulo offerunt
ut regi,
cæli quem sidus prædicat,

7\. atque aureo tumidi
principis lectulo
transito
Christi præsepe quæritant.

8\. Hinc ira sævi
Herodis fervida
Invidi recens
rectori genito

9\. O Christe, quantum
patri exercitum,
iuvenis doctus
ad bella maxima,

Bethleem parvulos
præcipit ense
crudeli perdere.

populis prædicans
colligis, sugens
cum tantum miseris!

10. Anno hominis
trigesimo
subtus famuli
se incliti
inclinaverat
manus Deus
consecrans nobis
baptisma
in absolutionem
criminum,

11. Ecce, spiritus
in specie
ipsum alitis
innocuæ
uncturus sanctis
præ omnibus
visitat semper
ipsius
contentus mansione
pectoris.

12. Patris etiam
insonuit
vox pia veteris
oblita sermonis
'Pænitet me
fecisse hominem':

13. 'Vere filius
es tu meus
mihimet placitus,
in quo sum placatus;
hodie te,
mi fili, genui.'

14. Huic omnes
auscultate, populi,
præceptori!

**Page 116, note 6.** As possible liturgical sources for the speech of the angel (*Joseph, Joseph*) one may cite, for example, the following (see Young, *Ordo Rachelis*, p. 36):

Antiphona: *Revertere in terram Judam, mortui sunt enim qui quærebant animam pueri.* (Hartker, p. 120);

Responsorium: *Tolle puerum et matrem ejus, et vade in terram Judam; defuncti sunt enim qui quærebant animam pueri.* Versus: *Venit angelus Domini ad Joseph in somnis dicens. Defuncti.* (Migne, *P.L.*, lxxviii, 746).

**Page 116, note 7.** Chambers (ii, 50) regards the *Ordo Rachelis* of Fleury as a continuation of the *Officium Stellæ* which directly precedes it in the Fleury play-book, even though the *Officium Stellæ* ends decisively with the words *Te Deum. Sic finit.* He infers that the performance may have extended over two days—presumably Epiphany and the day following. His objection to assigning the *Ordo Rachelis* to Innocents' Day is expressed as follows (ii, 50): 'It is impossible to regard the *Interfectio Puerorum* as a separate piece from the *Herodes*, acted a week earlier on the feast of the Innocents; for into it, after the first entry of the children with their lamb, *gaudentes per monasterium*, come the flight into Egypt, the return of the *nuntius*, and the wrath of Herod, which, of course, presuppose the *Magi* scenes.' The fact that some of the scenes presuppose the visit of the Magi does not seem to me to preclude a performance of the *Ordo Rachelis* on Innocents' Day. We have already seen, for example, that a representation in dumb show of the Flight of the Holy Family was acted as part of the revels on Innocents' Day, without a preceding representation of the Magi. See above, i, 109.

# CHAPTER XXI

## THE PROCESSION OF PROPHETS

**Page 125, note 1.** The basic study of the *Ordo Prophetarum* is that by M. Sepet, *Les Prophètes du Christ*, Paris, 1878—a reprinting from *Bibliothèque de l'École des Chartes*, xxviii (1867), 1–27, 211–64; xxix (1868), 105–39, 261–93; xxxviii (1877), 397–443. This type of play is the subject of a special study by Young, *Ordo Prophetarum*, in *Transactions of the Wisconsin Academy of Sciences, Arts, and Letters*, xx (1922), 1–82. For other discussions see Petit de Julleville, i, 35–41; Weber, *Kunst*, pp. 41–58; Meyer, pp. 50–6; Chambers, ii, 52–5; Chasles, pp. 121–34. Rudwin (*Prophetensprüche*, pp. 5–34) confines his attention almost entirely to the plays in German.

**Page 138, note 1.** For references to descriptions of MS lat. 1139 of the Bibl. Nat., Paris, see above, p. 453. A complete, but faulty, facsimile of the part of the MS with which we are concerned is found in Coussemaker, *Histoire*, plates xviii–xxiii. The text of the *Ordo Prophetarum* as printed above is immediately preceded in the MS by the closing rubric of the *Sponsus*: *Modo accipiant eas Demones, et precipitentur in infernum* (see above, p. 364), which is written in and above the last third of the third line from the bottom of fol. 55v. The first four words of the *Ordo Prophetarum*—*Omnes gentes congaudentes dent*—occupy the first two thirds of the next line, the rest of which is blank. This blank space appears to have been left for an unwritten introductory rubric. Except for one brief passage, indicated in my footnotes, the entire text is furnished with musical notation.

**Page 144, note 3.** Magnin (*Review*, p. 88) conjectures that the *Ordo Prophetarum* of Limoges was performed as follows:

D'abord, les trois premières strophes, qui sont comme le prologue ou l'exposition du mystère, devaient être dites ou chantées par un ecclésiastique élevé en dignité. Ensuite ce personnage appelait à haute voix chacun des acteurs du drame, lesquels s'avançaient et prenaient successivement la parole. Ce principal interlocuteur était, comme nous dirions pour un spectacle profane, le meneur ou le directeur du jeu. Il se tenait probablement debout sur les degrés de l'ambon ou au milieu du jubé, entouré des musiciens. Les autres personnages, prêtres ou moines, vêtus du costume de leurs rôles, étaient assis dans les stalles, attendant le moment de se lever et de venir au milieu du chœur psalmodier ou chanter leur verset.

For a less venturesome conjecture see Sepet, *Prophètes*, pp. 25–6, 40–1.

**Page 144, note 6.** In MS 1139, fol. 58r–58v, immediately after the rubric, ⟨*H*⟩*ic incoant Benedicamus*, is found the following composition, printed without substantial difference by Sepet, *Prophètes*, p. 26:

Letabundi iubilemus,
accurate celebremus
  Christi natalicia
  summa leticia;
  cum gratia

produxit,
gratanter mentibus
fidelibus
inluxit.

Eructauit Pater Uerbum,
perdit hostis ius acerbum,
quod in nobis habuit,
quod diu latuit,
tunc patuit |
Arcanum.
Qui contra gar⟨r⟩iunt
insaniunt
in uanum.

O re⟨s⟩ digna predicari,
cui non ualent conparari
quantauis miracula!
Ferit uirguncula
per secula
rectorem.
Conceptum edidit,
nec perdidit
pudorem.

Now follows the rubric *Alium Benedicamus*, and a fresh trope beginning: *Prima mundi seducta sobole*, printed by Sepet, *Prophètes*, p. 84.

**Page 152, note 4.** The text of the sequence *Epiphaniam Domino canamus* (Chevalier, *R.H.*, no. 5497) is edited in *A.H.*, liii, 47–8, as follows.

1. Epiphaniam Domino
canamus gloriosam,

2. Qua prolem Dei
vere magi adorant;

3. Immensam Chaldæi
cuius Persæque venerantur
potentiam,

4. Quem cuncti prophetæ
præcinere venturum gentes
ad salvandas.

5. Cuius maiestas
ita est inclinata,
ut assumeret servi formam.

6. Ante sæcula
qui Deus et tempora,
homo factus est in Maria.

7. Balaam de quo vaticinans,
exibit ex Iacob rutilans,
inquit, stella,

8. Et confringet ducum agmina
regionis Moab maxima
potentia.

9. Huic magi munera
deferunt præclara:
aurum, simul tus et murram;

10. Ture Deum prædicant,
auro regem magnum,
hominem mortalem murra.

11. In somnis
hos monet angelus,
ne redeant ad regem commotum
propter regna.

12. Pavebat
etenim nimium
regem natum, verens amittere
regni iura.

13. Magi stella
sibi micante prævia
pergunt alacres itinera,
patriam quæ eos ducebat
ad propriam
linquentes Herodis mandata;

14. Qui perculsus
corde nimia præ ira
extemplo mandat eludia
magica non linqui taliter
impunita,
sed mox privari eos vita.

15. Omnis nunc caterva
tinnulum laudibus
iungat organi pneuma,

16. Mystice offerens
regi regum, Christo,
munera pretiosa,

17. Poscens ut per orbem
regna omnia protegat
in sæcla sempiterna.

**Page 170, note 3.** With the versions of the *Ordo Prophetarum* considered above should be associated the following fragment from Einsiedeln, Stiftsbibl., MS 366, Fragmenta liturgica sæc. xi–xii, pp. 53–5, previously edited by Mone, *Schauspiele*, i, 10–2; Schubiger, *Spicilegien*, pp. 46–7; Young, *Ordo Prophetarum*, pp. 72–4:[1]

AD PROPHETAS

Prophete venientes admonent: |

*Gloriosi*
*et famosi*
*Regis festum*
*celebrantes*
*gaudeamus;*

*Cuius ortum,*
*uite portum,*
*nobis datum,*
*predicantes*
*habeamus.*

Chorvs:

*Gloriosi*
*et famosi.*

Prophete:

*Ecce, regem*
*nouam legem*
*dantem orbis*
*circuitu*
*predicamus.*

*Quem futurum*
*regnaturum*
*prophetico*
*ammonitu*
*nunciamus.*

[1] For a description of the MS see Young, p. 72, and above i, 598.

Chorvs:

*Gloriosi*
*et famosi.*

Prophete:

*Sunt impleta*
*que propheta*
*quisque dixit*
*de futuro*
*summo rege.*

*Impiorum*
*Iudeorum*
*corda negant*
*regnaturum*
*sua lege.*

Chorus:

*Gloriosi*
*et famosi.*

Prophete:

*Dilatata*
*iam priuata*
*fit regali*
*potestate*
*plebs Iudea.*

*Et gentiles*
*prius uiles*
*conuertuntur*
*maiestate*
*etherea.*

Chorvs:

*Gloriosi*
*et famosi.*

Prophete:

*Deum uerum,*
*Regem regum*
*confitentes*
*per lauacrum*
*saluabuntur.*

*Sed Iudei*
*facti rei*
*condemnantes*
*sacrum regem*
*damnabuntur.*

Chorus:

*Gloriosi.*

Prophete:

*Floruisse*
*et dedisse*

*nouum fructum*
*dinoscitur*
*radix Iesse.*

*Israheli*
*infideli*
*iam Maria*
*natus scitur*
*⟨hic⟩ adesse*[1]

Chorvs:

*Gloriosi*[2]
. . .
*centurio*
*florem Marie proprio*
*sepeliuit in tumulo.*
*Flos autem die tercio*
*qui floret ab initio,*
*refloruit e tumulo*
*summo mane diluculo.*

In Resvrrectione.

Angelus dicit: *Quem queritis?*[3]

This fragment contains the processional opening of a version of the *Ordo Prophetarum.* At Einsiedeln, it appears, the prophets themselves sang the stanzas of *Gloriosi et famosi*, a practice which may have been followed at Laon, but certainly not at Rouen. The most puzzling aspect of the text before us is the relation of the fragmentary *Ordo Prophetarum* to the fragment of the prose *Hortum prædestinatio*, which follows it in the MS.[4] Since this prose treats the theme of the Resurrection and is sometimes found in conjunction with the *Visitatio Sepulchri*, one's first impulse is to associate it with the dramatic Easter text which immediately follows it here, rather than with the fragmentary *Ordo Prophetarum* which—after a lacuna of unknown length—precedes it.[5] It happens, however, that although the content of *Hortum prædestinatio* is alien to the theme of the play of the prophets, the Rouen *Festum Asinorum* does actually conclude with the singing of this poem;[6] and in the Einsiedeln MS there is nothing to disprove a similar use of it here. Meyer (p. 51) holds that the rubric *In Resurrectione* effectually separates the Easter play from the preceding poem, and that the latter has 'Nichts mit dem Osterspiel zu thun'. My opinion is that, in the present state of our information, the precise dramatic relations of the fragmentary *Hortum prædestinatio* before us must be left undecided.

Of some interest also in connexion with the *Ordo Prophetarum* is the follow-

[1] adesse] This word and *Gloriosi* following have no musical notation.

[2] Here ends p. 54. Although the MS is paged continuously, it is obvious that one or more leaves have been lost between pages 54 and 55.

[3] Here continues the version of the Easter *Visitatio Sepulchri* printed above, i, 598.

[4] The fragment begins in the midst of the prose, with the words, *centurio florem Marie proprio*.

[5] For the text of the prose *Hortum prædestinatio*, and examples of its use in conjunction with the *Visitatio Sepulchri*, see above, i, 575.

[6] See above, p. 165.

ing liturgical text of the fourteenth century, of uncertain provenance, which I reprint from *A.H.*, xlix, 182–3:[1]

IN EPIPHANIA DOMINI.

Lectio Isaiæ prophetæ: Surge, illuminare, Ierusalem, quia venit lumen tuum, et gloria Domini super te orta est.

*Gloriosi*
*et famosi*
*regis festum*
*celebrantes*
*gaudeamus;*

*Cuius ortum,*
*vitæ portum,*
*nobis datum,*
*prædicantes*
*aveamus.*

Quia, ecce, tenebræ operient terram et caligo populos.

*Ecce, regem*
*novam legem*
*dantem orbis*
*circuitu*
*prædicamus.*

*Quem futurum*
*regnaturum*
*prophetico*
*admonitu*
*nuntiamus.*

Super te autem orietur Dominus, et gloria eius in te videbitur.

*Sunt impleta*
*quæ propheta*
*quisquis dixit*
*de futuro*
*summo rege.*

*Impiorum*
*Iudæorum*
*corda negant*
*regnaturo*
*sua lege.*

Et ambulabunt gentes in lumine tuo, et reges in splendore ortus tui.

*Dilatata*
*iam privata*
*fit regali*
*potestate*
*plebs Iudæa.*

*Et gentiles*
*prius viles*
*convertuntur*
*maiestate*
*ætherea.*

Leva in circuitu oculos tuos et vide; omnes isti congregati sunt, venerunt tibi.

*Deum verum*
*Regem regum*
*confitentes*
*per lavacrum*
*salvabuntur.*

*Sed Iudæi*
*facti rei*
*non fatentes*
*regem sacrum*
*damnabuntur.*

Filii tui de longe venient, et filiæ tuæ de latere surgent.

*Omnes gentes*
*congaudentes*
*de cantu lætitiæ,*

*Quia homo*
*sit de domo*
*natus David hodie.*

Tunc videbis et afflues, et mirabitur et dilatabitur cor tuum, quando conversa fuerit ad te multitudo maris, fortitudo gentium venerit tibi.

*Isaias, dic, de Christo quid prophetizas?*

*Est necesse*
*virgam Iesse*
*de radice provehi;*

*Flos deinde*
*surget inde*
*qui est filius Dei*

[1] For a previous reprinting, with somewhat more extended commentary than is given here, see Young, *Ordo Prophetarum*, pp. 77–80.

Inundatio camelorum operiet te, dromedarii Madian et Epha.

| | |
|---|---|
| *O Iudæi,* | *Vestræ legis* |
| *verbum Dei* | *vestri regis* |
| *cur negastis hominem?* | *audite nunc ordinem.* |

Omnes de Saba venient aurum et tus deferentes, et laudem Domino annuntiantes.

| | |
|---|---|
| *Omnes gentes* | *Confunduntur,* |
| *non credentes* | *convertuntur* |
| *peperisse virginem* | *maiestatis æthere.* |

This is a troped form of the epistle for the Mass of Epiphany. Among the sentences of the Vulgate (Isaiah lx, 1–6) are distributed metrical compositions in the nature of embellishments of the orthodox liturgical text. It will be observed that the trope begins with *Gloriosi et famosi*, and consists of stanzas virtually every word of which we have already encountered in one version or another of the *Ordo Prophetarum.* That this trope is in some way related to the prophet-play is further apparent in the intrusive summons *Isaias, dic, de Christo quid prophetizas?* The question arises, then, as to whether this trope is one of the sources of the *Ordo Prophetarum*, or is itself under the influence of the dramatic tradition. That the latter relation is the valid one is suggested, in the first place, by the uniqueness and late date of the text before us. In order to influence the development of the *Ordo Prophetarum* it would have been necessary that this trope of the epistle be in existence and be well known as early as the eleventh or twelfth century, the date of the Limoges *Ordo Prophetarum*, for this dramatic text contains substantial passages that are identical with passages in the trope.[1] The fact that the editors of *Analecta Hymnica* have discovered only one text of the trope, and that the one text is relatively late, seems to show that this composition can scarcely have had sufficient age or repute for serving as a source of the prophet-play of Limoges. The text before us, therefore, may be regarded as an isolated liturgical composition in which certain stanzas and formulæ from the *Ordo Prophetarum* have been adapted, with considerable appropriateness, as a trope of an epistle.

I see no reason for reprinting or discussing here the *Cantio de Mulieribus*, beginning,

Recedite, recedite,
ne mulieri credite!
Dic tu, Adam, primus homo.

In form, this satirical piece may show the influence of the *Ordo Prophetarum.* A new version of this *cantio*, with information concerning versions published previously, is given by L. Suttina, *Una Cantilena medievale contro le Donne*, in *Studi medievali* (ed. F. Novati and R. Renier), ii (1906–7), 457–60. In the same volume (pp. 538–50), Novati, fetching an analogy from the *Ordo Prophetarum*, undertakes to show that the composition is 'un dramma liturgico' for Ash Wednesday. This demonstration I regard as ineffectual. Bartholomaeis reprints the text of the cantio (pp. 536–7), and comments upon it (pp. 213–5).

For references to dramatic representations of prophets at Regensburg in 1194 and Riga in 1204 see Appendix D.

[1] See above, pp. 138 sqq.

# CHAPTER XXII

## THE CHRISTMAS PLAY FROM BENEDIKTBEUERN

**Page 172, note 3.** For general comment upon the Christmas play from *Carmina Burana* see Creizenach, i, 90–2; Chambers, ii, 72–3; Sepet, *Drame*, pp. 105–6, 112; A. Schönbach, in *Zeitschrift für deutsche Philologie*, iv (1873), 366–7; W. Geser, in *Stimmen aus Maria-Laach*, lxiii (1902), 533–48; Michael, iv, 419–25; Sondheimer, p. 162; Weber, *Kunst*, pp. 45–6, 72; Chasles, pp. 409–12.

**Page 190, note 1.** The Benediktbeuern Christmas play in Munich MS 4660 ends on the third line from the bottom of fol. 104$^{v}$. The last three lines and the lower margin of fol. 104$^{v}$, and the upper half (first twelve lines) and lower margin of fol. 105$^{r}$, are occupied by the poem *Pange, vox Adonis* (Hilka and Schumann, no. 6*; Schmeller, no. CCI), which begins in the upper half of fol. 105$^{r}$, and continues in the lower part of fol. 104$^{v}$ and in the lower margin of fol. 105$^{r}$. This poem is written in a hand different from that prevailing in the play which precedes and in the one which follows. See Hilka and Schumann, ii, 56*. On line 13 of fol. 105$^{r}$ begins a dramatic text which continues to the bottom of fol. 106$^{v}$. Although this is written by the hand that copied the Christmas play printed above, it begins with ornamented capitals, and is to be regarded as a separate, though fragmentary, dramatic composition. See Hilka and Schumann, ii, 54*. For convenience this play may be referred to as *Ludus de Rege Ægypti*. It has hitherto been regarded as part of the Christmas play, and has been edited by Schmeller, pp. 91–5 (S); Du Méril, pp. 206–13 (D); Froning, pp. 896–901 (F). The text of Hilka and Schumann will be no. 228. The play is as follows:

⟨Ludus de Rege Ægypti⟩.

Rex Egipti cum Comitatu suo in locum suum producatur cum conductu:
*Estiuali gaudio,*
et cetera.[1]

*Ab estatis foribus*[2]
*nos amor*[3] *salutat;*
*humus picta floribus*
*faciem conmutat.*
*Flores amoriferi*
*iam arrident tempori,*
*perit absque Uenere*
*flos etatis tenere.*

*Omnium principium,*
*dies est uernalis;*
*uere mundus celebrat*
*diem sui natalis.*

[1] For the complete text of this spring-song see Schmeller, no. 53. For no part of the play does the MS provide music.

[2] foribus] floribus (MS); emend. S; D suggests *limine*. For these verses see Schmeller, no. 123. Concerning the use of this poem here see Waddell, pp. 202–3.

[3] nos amor] amor nos (S).

*Omnes huius temporis*
*dies festi Ueneris;*
*regna Jouis*[1] *omnia*
*hec agant sollempnia.*

Et tam iste Comitatus quam Comitatus Regis hec sepius cantent:[2]

*Ad fontem philosophie*
*sicientes currite,*
*et saporis tripertiti*
*septem riuos bibite,*
*uno fonte procedentes*
*non eodem tramite.*

*Quem Pytago|ras rimatus*
*excitauit physice,*
*inde Socrates et Plato*
*honestarunt ethice,*
*Aristotiles loquaci*
*desponsauit logice.*[3]

*Ab hiis secte multiformes*
*Athenis materiam*
*nacte hoc liquore totam*
*irrigarunt Greciam,*
*qui redundans infinite*[4]
*fluxit in Hesperiam.*

*Hec noua gaudia*
*sunt ueneranda,*
*festa presentia*
*magnificanda.*
*Dulcia flumina*
*sunt Babylonis,*
*mollia semina*
*perditionis.*
*Concupiscentia*[5]
*mixti saporis*
*ingerit somnia*
*lenis amoris.*

*Heccine gaudia*
*cupiditatis*
*tribuunt ydola*
*captiuitatis.*
*Dulcia.*

*Apta delitiis*
*caro letatur,*

[1] Jouis] uiuis (MS).

[2] Of the poem from which the next three stanzas (ll. 18–35) are taken, a much longer version will be published by Hilka and Schumann.

[3] logice] loyce (MS).

[4] infinite] infintte (MS).

[5] Concupiscentia] Concupiscentis (emend. suggested S).

*hac ⟨via⟩*[1] *uiciis*
*mens uiolatur.*
*D⟨ulcia⟩.*

*Affectionibus*
*motus tumultus*
*tollit uirtutibus*
*proprios cultus.*
*D⟨ulcia⟩.*

*Ista sunt deuia*
*felicitatis,*
*ocia mollia*
*sunt uoluptatis.*
*D⟨ulcia⟩.*

*Ista negocia*
*plena malorum*
*et desideria*
*flagiciorum.*
*D⟨ulcia⟩.*

Et sepius ṛepetant:

*Deorum inmortalitas*
*⟨est omnibus colenda,*
*eorum et pluralitas*
*ubique metuenda⟩.*

*Stulti sunt ⟨et vere fatui,*
*qui deum unum dicunt,*
*et antiquitatis ritui*
*proterve contradicunt⟩.*[2]

In ingressu Mariæ et Ioseph cum Iesu omnia ydola Egiptiorum corruant. Ministri uero sepius ea restituant, et thura incendant cantantes:

*Hoc est numen salutare,*
*cuius fundat ad altare*
*preces omnis populus.*
*Huius nutu reflorescit,*
*si quandoque conmarcescit,*[3]
*manus, pes uel oculus.*

*Honor Ioui*[4] *cum Neptuno;*
*Pallas, Uenus, Uesta, Iuno*
*mire sunt clementie,*
*Mars, Apollo, Pluto, Phebus,*
*dant salutem lesis rebus,*
*insite potentie.*

Quod quia non proficit, Minister precedat Regem et cantet:

*Audi, rex Egiptiorum,*
*lapsa uirtus ydolorum,*

[1] Emend. S.

[2] For these two stanzas see the *Ludus de Antichristo* above, pp. 371 sqq.

[3] conmarcescit] commarescit (D).

[4] Ioui] Emend. S and D; Iouis (MS).

*destituta uis deorum*
*iacet cum miseria.*
*Iam delubra ceciderunt,*
*simulacra currue|runt,*
*dii*[1] *fugati fugierunt,*
*heu, cum ignominia!*

Quibus Rex mirabili gestu respondeat:

*Scire uolo, que causa rei, uel qualiter ipsa*
*Numina placentur; sapientes ergo uocentur!*

Tunc Armiger uocet Sapientes ad presentiam Regis, et cantet:

*Regia uos mandata uocant; non segniter ite.*[2]

Tunc dicat Rex Sapientibus:

*Scire uolo,*

et cetera.

*Vos date consilium.*

Sapientes respondeant:

*Nostrum est consilium deos honorare,*
*Aras, templa, tripodes, lucos innouare,*
*Thus, storacem, balsamum, stacten concremare,*
*Et humanum sanguinem superis libare;*
*Tali quippe modo uirtute ministeriorum*
*Et prece deuota placabitur ira deorum!*

Tunc Rex preparet se ad immolandum, et cantet:

*Hoc est numen salutare.*

Comitatus respondeat:

*Stulti sunt.*

Tunc, ydolis restitutis, Rex ad locum suum redeat, et ydola iterum corruant. Quo audito, iterum uocentur Sapientes, quibus Rex dicat:

*Dicite, quid nobis et quid portendat Egipto*
*mira mali species prodigiosa quidem!*

Cui Sapientes:

*Rex et regum dominus, Deus Hebreorum,*
*Prepotens in gloria Deus est deorum*
*Cuius in presentia uelut mortuorum*
*Corruit et labitur uirtus ydolorum!*

Tunc Rex cantet:

*Ecce nouum cum matre deum ueneretur Egiptus!*

Et omnia ydola abiciantur. Hic est finis Regis Egipti. Tunc assurget Rex Babilonis. Istius Comitatus sepius repetat:

*Deorum inmortalitas;*
*Stulti sunt;*

et hunc uersum:

*Ille iure cupidus deus estimatur,*
*Qui uult, spretis ceteris,*[3] | *ut solus colatur.*
*Stulti sunt.*

[1] dii] dum (S.F); di (D).

[2] For this speech from the *Officium Stellæ* see above, for example, p. 60.

[3] uult spretis ceteris] Emend. S; spretis ceteris uult (MS).

In conflictu Gentilitatis, Synagoge et Ecclesie, Gentilitas contra eas cantet:[1]

*Deorum inmortalitas*
*est omnibus colenda,*
*eorum et pluralitas*
*ubique metuenda.*

Comitatus suus[2] r*espondeat:*

*Stulti sunt et uere fatui*
*qui deum unum dicunt,*
*et antiquitatis ritui*
*proterue contradicunt.*

Gentilitas:

*Si enim unum credimus,*
*qui presit uniuersis,*
*subiectum hunc concedimus*
*contrarie diuersis.*

Comitatus r*espondeat:*

*Stulti sunt.*

Gentilitas:

*Finxit inuidia   hanc singularitatem,*
*Ut homo coleret   unam diuinitatem.*

Comitatus r*espondeat:*

*Stulti sunt.*

Item Rex Babylonis contra Ypocritas:

*Fraudis uersutias   conpellor experiri,*
*Per quas nequicia   uestra solet mentiri.*
*Sub forma ueritas   uirtutis*[3] *putabatur,*
*Ostendit falsitas,   quod forma mentiatur.*

Item deuicto Rege, cantet in presentia Antichristi:[4]

*Tibi profiteor   decus imperiale,*
*Quod tibi seruiam,   ius postulo regale.*

Comitatus cantet:

*Omnium rectorem   te solum profitemur,*
*Tibi tota mente   semper obsequemur.*

*Egiptus caput omnium*
*est et decus regnorum;*
*calcabit hec inperium*
*regis Ierosolimorum!*[5]

*Ue tibi, Ierosolima!*
*Ue insano tiranno!*
*Deorum*[6] *uos potentia*
*subuertet in hoc anno.*

[1] Ll. 126–41 and the accompanying rubrics D regards as an interpolation, and removes from the text.

[2] suus] Final *s* imperfectly supplied (MS).

[3] ueritas uirtutis] uirtutis ueritas (emend. D).

[4] Antichristi] D conjectures that *Christi* was intended.

[5] calcabit . . . Ierosolimorum] regis calcabit solium hæc Hierosolymorum (emend. D).

[6] Deorum] (Arm)orum (D); . . . rorum (F).

*Egipti princeps nobilis*
*ut deus ueneretur;*[1]
*Herodes sed odibilis*
*ut stultus reprobetur.*

*Intende, tibi canimus*
*quam uilis sis futurus:*
⟨*tu*⟩[2] *roderis a uermibus,*
*per hos*[3] *interiturus.*[4]

*Ingrata gens et perfida,*
*cum fame laborares,*
*Egipto eras subdita,*
*ut uentrem satiares.*[5]

This confused fragment contains the following chief elements: (1) the entering of the king of Egypt, while his retinue sing the two spring songs *Æstivali gaudio* and *Ab æstatis foribus*, and the song *Ad fontem philosophiæ*; (2) the advent of the Holy Family, and the falling of the Egyptian idols; and (3) substantial passages of dialogue from the Tegernsee *Ludus de Antichristo*. The story of the fall of the idols arises from the prophecy of Isaiah mentioned by Peter Comestor as follows:[6]

Cumque ingrederetur Dominus in Ægyptum, corruerunt idola Ægypti, secundum Isaiam, qui ait: 'Ascendet Dominus nubem levem, et ingredietur Ægyptum, et movebuntur simulacra Ægypti.'

Lines 73–80, 113, 121–47 are borrowed from *Ludus de Antichristo*, ll. 1–12, 215–16, 235–8, 291–4, 299–300 (see above, pp. 371 sqq.). In regard to these borrowings see Meyer, p. 21; Vetter, p. 297; Zezschwitz, pp. 242–8; Wilken, pp. 151–2; Michaelis, pp. 62–4. For attempts—confessedly unsuccessful—to discover an orderly intention in the *Ludus de Rege Ægypti* as a whole, see Michael, iv, 424–5; Froning, pp. 868–9; Geser, pp. 546–7.

**Page 193, note 1.** Geser (p. 540) suggests that the germ of the disputation between Augustine and Archisynagogus is to be found in the following epigram of Hildebert of Tours (Migne, *P.L.*, clxxi, 1282):

Virginitas peperit;
sed si quis quomodo quærit,
non est nosse meum,
sed scio posse Deum.

Walther (p. 28) speaks of having seen the text of a debate on this subject between Ecclesia and Synagoga in a MS of the twelfth century, but he omits the reference. Here may be cited the following fragment printed by Mone

[1] ueneretur] reueretur (S.D).
[2] Emend. D.
[3] hos] Largely illegible.
[4] interiturus] tibi interitus (S).
[5] The text ends thus in the middle of the last line on fol. 106$^{v}$, the rest of the line being blank. At the top of fol. 107$^{r}$ begins the Passion play printed above, i, 518 sqq.
[6] *Historia Scholastica in Evangelia*, cap. x, in Migne, *P.L.*, cxcviii, 1543. See Isaiah xix, 1: *Ecce Dominus ascendet super nubem levem, et ingredietur Ægyptum, et commovebuntur simulacra Ægypti a facie ejus, et cor Ægypti tabescet in medio ejus.*

(*Schauspiele*, i, 195–6) from an unidentified Karlsruhe MS of the year 1439, and reprinted by Du Méril (p. 196):

Eva dicit:

*Per esum vanum destruitur genus humanum;*
*Vos moriemini, quia clausi januam cœli.*

Maria respondet:

*Resero nunc æthera, quem nobis clauserat Eva;*
*Per filium meum salvabo quemlibet reum.*

Ecclesia:

*Sanguine dotata sum Christi sponsa vocata;*
*Ad cœlum scandit, qui michi scelera pandit.*

Synagoga:

*Hircorum sanguis me decipit velut anguis;*
*Heu, sum cæcata et a regno Dei separata.*

## CHAPTER XXIII

## PLAYS FROM THE NEW TESTAMENT: THE RAISING OF LAZARUS—THE CONVERSION OF SAINT PAUL

**Page 199, note 1.** Concerning the plays treated in this chapter see Coffman, *New Theory*, pp. 67–71; Sepet, *Origines*, pp. 31–46, 53–4, 75–88; Chambers, ii, 59–60; Petit de Julleville, i, 54–7; Creizenach, i, 69–70. Coffman (pp. 67, 70, 71) treats the plays of Lazarus and St Paul as miracle plays, to be associated with those based upon the legends of St Nicholas (see above, chapter xxvi). For the purposes of the present treatise I have chosen to discriminate between the dramatizations of narratives concerning Lazarus and Paul *in the canonical New Testament* and plays of St Nicholas based upon *medieval legends*. It is entirely possible, of course, that the plays concerning all three personages were written because the playwrights, and their communities, held them in especial honour. Concerning the medieval legends of St Lazarus—which, I repeat, are not directly associated with the plays before us—see *Gallia Christiana Novissima*, ed. J.-H. Albanés and U. Chevalier, ii, Valence, 1899, pp. 2–6; G. Morin, *Saint Lazare et Saint Maximin*, in *Mémoires de la Société Nationale des Antiquaires de France*, lvi (1897), 27–51; Kellner, pp. 309–15; Coffman, pp. 67–8; Holweck, *Dictionary*, pp. 596–7.

**Page 199, note 5.** There are two sequences beginning *In sapientia disponens omnia*. One of these (Chevalier, *R.H.*, no. 8753) is printed by Kehrein (pp. 43–4) from a sixteenth-century source as follows:

1. In sapientia
disponens omnia
æterna deitas

2. Nobis condoluit,
quos diu tenuit
dira calamitas.

3. Mittitur nuncius,
secreti conscius,
e cœli solio,

4. Qui mundo perferat,
quod iam promiserat
Pater de filio.

5. Salutat virginem:
Deum et hominem,
dicens, concipies;

6. Salutem gentium,
rerum principium,
utero paries.

7. Nec diu distulit
sed, Fiat! intulit,
et plena gratiæ

8. Protulit filium,
lumen fidelium,
solem iustitiæ.

9. Lux refulsit pastoribus,
non populis sublimibus.

10. Vili iacet præsepio,
quem nulla claudit regio.

11. Stella fulgens apparuit,
dum virga Jesse floruit.

12. Offerunt reges munera:
thus, myrrham, auri pondera.

13. Circumcidi passus est,
qui pro nobis natus est.

14. Ad Iordanis flumina
nostra lavit crimina.

15. Offert virgo filium,
vitæ sacrificium.

16. Symeonis brachia
sua gestant gaudia.

17. Prima virtus Salvatoris
aqua vinum edidit;

18. Cæcis visum, claudis gressum,
mutis loqui reddidit.

19. Natus est Dei filius,
cœlorum rex, non alius.

20. Regni cœlestis curia
laudes dicat in gloria. Amen.

The greater part of this text is embodied in another sequence (Chevalier, *R.H.*, no. 8754) printed by Kehrein (pp. 44–5) from a twelfth-century source as follows:

1. In sapientia
disponens omnia
superna deitas

2. Nobis condoluit,
quos diu tenuit
dira calamitas.

3. Mittitur nuncius,
secreti conscius,
e cœli solio,

4. Qui mundo proferat,
quæ iam promiserat
Pater de filio.

5. Salutat virginem:
Deum et hominem,
dicens, concipies;

6. Salutem gentium,
rerum principium,
utero paries.

7. Nec diu distulit,
sed, Fiat! intulit,
et plena gratiæ

8. Protulit filium,
lumen fidelium,
solem iustitiæ.

9. Natus est Dei filius,
cœlorum rex, non alius.

10. Regni cœlestis curia
laudem reddit in gloria.

11. Vili iacet præsepio,
quem nulla claudit regio.

12. Lux refulsit pastoribus,
non populis sublimibus.

13. Stella fulgens apparuit,
cum virga Iesse floruit

14. Cum ferunt reges munera:
aurum, thus, myrrham, cetera.

15. Circumcidi passus est,
qui pro nobis natus est.

16. Ad Iordanis flumina
nostra lavit crimina.

17. Offert virgo filium,
vitæ sacrificium.

18. Simeonis brachia
sua gestant gaudia.

19. Prima virtus Salvatoris
aqua vinum edidit;

20. Cæcis visum, claudis gressum
mutis loqui reddidit.

20. Surdus audit, lepra fugit,
et resurgunt mortui.

21. Hostem fugat, febrem curat,
imperatque fluctui.

22. Panes quinque, pisces duo
quinque pascunt millia.

23. Sanguis manet, Chananææ
reddita est filia.

24. Iuxta vaticinium
magnus pastor ovium
immolandus ducitur;

25. Agnus sine macula,
mortis solvens vincula
mortem crucis patitur.

26. Vitam reddens miseris
rediens ab inferis
surgit die tertia;

27. Visus a discipulis,
in rerum miraculis
operante gratia.

28. Sicque victis hostibus,
illis intuentibus,
Ihesus elevatus est;

29. Nostræ carnis gloria
summa cum victoria
in cœlum assumptus est.

30. Angelus consilii
spiritum solatii
mittens, quem promiserat,

31. Dedit dona filiis,
linguis loqui variis,
sibi quos elegerat.

32. Eia! mente fideli
vos nova regi cantica
reddatis, ut redituris
post brevitatem temporis
huius crimina
tollat, gaudia
reddat perdita,
primi sortem parentis.

From the *incipit* in the rubric of the play one cannot determine which of these two versions may have been used in the play. Neither composition is very appropriate here, for in surveying certain events in the life of Christ neither mentions the occurrences that follow in the dramatic text.

**Page 211, note 5.** Virtually the only ultimate source of information concerning Hilarius is the small body of his writings contained in the twelfth-century MS lat. 11331, in the Bibliothèque Nationale, Paris, edited by J. J. Champollion-Figeac, *Hilarii Versus et Ludi*, Paris, 1838, and by J. B. Fuller, *Hilarii Versus et Ludi*, New York [1929]. Upon reasonable grounds, the latter editor (pp. 12–5) accepts as the work of Hilarius the poem *Iudicium de Calumnia Molendini Brisearte*, published by Marchegay in 1876. The most convenient summaries of facts and inferences bearing upon the life of Hilarius are found in the following places: Fuller, pp. 10–6: Champollion-Figeac, pp. v–xv; *Histoire littéraire*, xii, 251–4; xx, 627–30; H. Morley, *English Writers*, iii, London, &c., 1888, pp. 105–13; *D.N.B.*, xxvi, 380.

# CHAPTER XXIV

## PLAYS OF THE BLESSED VIRGIN MARY: THE PRESENTATION IN THE TEMPLE—THE ANNUNCIATION—THE PURIFICATION—THE ASSUMPTION

**Page 226, note 4.** MS lat. 17330 in the Bibl. Nat., Paris, is described in considerable detail by Young, *Presentation*, pp. 186–8. The importance of this MS, and the probability that much of it is still unpublished, prompt me to repeat most of that description here. The official account of it is short: '17330. Office de la Présentation. Fin du xiv s. Cél.'[1] The principal items of the codex are written in a hand of the late fourteenth century, and none of them could have been written later than during the first half of the fifteenth century. The recto of the fly-leaf is blank. Of the entries (and numerous scribblings) on the verso, the following three are the most important:

(1) In a hand of the end of the fourteenth century:

: Ihesus:
Iste liber est Domini Philippi de Maseriis
cancellarii regni Cipri.

(2) In a hand of the beginning of the fifteenth century:

Iste liber est de Conuentu Fratrum Celestinorum de Parisiis. 29. a.[2]

(3) In a hand of the beginning of the fifteenth century:

Tabula contentorum in hoc uolumine.

Primo: Sermo de Presentatione Uirginis Marie a Magistro Johanne de Basilia Doctore in Theologia Generali Fratrum Heremitarum Sancti Augustini.

Item: Epistola Domini Philippi de Maseriis quondam Cancellarii Cipri de Solemnitate Presentationis Beate Marie Uirginis. Fo. 4.

Item: Quiddam miraculum Beate Marie de duobus Iudeis per pedes suspensis quos Beata Uirgo inuocata liberauit, et baptizati fuerunt. Fo. 6.

Item: Officium Presentationis Beate Marie cum nota. Fo. 7.

Item: Historia de Presentatione Beate Marie per sex lectiones pro octaua. Fo. 14.

Item: Missa de eodem festo cum nota. Fo. 15.

Item: Recommendatio solemnitatis Presentationis Beate Marie in Templo. Fo. 17.

Item: De quibusdam actibus representantibus[3] eandem Presentationem Beate Marie in Templo et processione fienda in Missa. Fo. 18.

An inventory, in some respects more detailed, may be constructed as follows:

[1] L. Delisle, *Inventaire des Manuscrits latins de Notre-Dame et d'autres fonds conservés à la Bibliothèque Nationale sous les numéros* 16719–18613, Paris 1871, p. 41.

[2] 29. a. is the mark given the manuscript in the library of the Celestines of Paris. The same mark is found on fol. 24$^r$. The possession of this codex by the Celestines of Paris is explained by the fact that after the death of Charles V (1380), Mézières associated himself with this community for the rest of his life. See N. Jorga, *Philippe de Mézières*, Paris, 1896, pp. 443 sqq.

[3] representantibus] representientibus (MS).

(1) Fly-leaf, recto: Blank.

(2) Fly-leaf, verso: Several entries of the late fourteenth and the early fifteenth centuries as to the ownership and content of the MS.

(3) Fol. $1^r$–$3^v$: ⟨headed⟩ Sermo de Presentatione Marie in Templo . . . ⟨sæc. xiv ex.⟩.

(4) $4^r$–$5^v$: ⟨headed⟩ Epistola de solennitate Presentacionis Beate Marie in Templo et nouitate ipsius ad partes occidentales . . . ⟨sæc. xiv ex. Printed below⟩.

(5) Fol. $5^v$–$6^r$: Appendix (in the same hand) to the Epistola, recounting a miracle of two Jews.

(6) Fol. $6^v$: ⟨headed⟩ Oroison de Monsigneur Saint Joachim, pere de la Vierge Marie . . . ⟨sæc. xv⟩.

(7) Fol. $7^r$–$17^r$: Officium Presentacionis Beate Marie Virginis in Templo, quod festum celebratur uicesima prima die mensis Nouembris ⟨sæc. xiv ex. Cursus = fol. $7^r$–$15^r$; Missa = fol. $15^r$–$17^r$⟩.

(8) Fol. $17^v$: Without heading, a note of the early fifteenth century regarding the *officia* of the Feast of the Presentation of the Virgin. Printed below.

(9) Fol. $18^r$–$24^r$: Without title, in a hand of the late fourteenth century, a dramatic procession for the Mass of the Feast of the Presentation of the Virgin. Printed above, pp. 227 sqq.

(10) Fol. $24^v$: Irrelevant entries of the fifteenth century.

That this MS belonged to Philippe de Mézières himself is sufficiently established by the entries on the fly-leaf, printed above. The date and content of these entries prove their original association with the body of the manuscript. This codex is, then, a thesaurus of information as to the *Festum Præsentationis Beatæ Virginis in Templo*, and in all that relates to the establishment of this feast in Western Europe it is probably the most important of known documents.

**Page 226, note 5.** The letter in MS lat. 17330, fol. $4^r$–$5^v$, previously edited by Young, *Presentation*, pp. 189–98, is as follows:

Epistola de solennitate Presentacionis Beate Marie in Templo et nouitate ipsius ad partes occidentales que celebratur xxi Nouembris.[1]

Uniuersis in Domino fidelibus, maxime Christianis occidentalibus, Philippus de Maiserijs, Picardie miles infimus, regni Cypri indignus cancellarius vocatus, ac gloriose Virginis Marie zelator abortiuus, sentencias irati summi[2] iudicis per Mariam euadere et ad vitam sempiternam peruenire, exclamare plerumque compellitur dolorem communem et mala gentis nostre in lucem ad memoriam reducere. Dicant igitur nunc cum lacrimis qui redempti sunt a Domino Ihesu: Ve nobis Christianis, rubor in facie et liuor infamie, quia non sunt occultata hodie a filijs alienigenarum infidelium qui in circuitu nostro sunt mala inexplicabilia Christianis adeo inflicta peccatis hec inpetrantibus. Quante nempe pestilentie, seditiones, mortalitates, guerre, proditiones, et hereses temporibus nostris insur⟨r⟩exerunt, maxime ad plagam occidentalem, patet intuenti.

[1] A later hand has added *A Magnifico D. Philippo De Maseriis Edita.*

[2] summi] Inserted by a contemporary hand in the right margin. The reviser is presumably Philippe de Mézières.

Flagellauit etenim Deus et continue flagellat Christianos, qui ad mortem, qui ad gladium, qui ad famem et captiuitatem, Ieremia predicente, et vere cum Bernardo ad Ostiensem, Penestrinum, et Tusculanum cardinales scribente, hodie non immerito dici potest: Sapientiam vincit malicia, adduntur ubique cornua inpijs, et exarmatur iusticie zelus, et non est qui facere bonum, non dico velit, sed possit; superbi inique agunt usquequaque, et nullus audet contra mutire, et vtinam uel ignorantia tuta esset, et iusticia ipsa sibimet sufficeret defensioni. Hec ille.

Nec mirum, Patres et Fratres carissimi, quia, cum precibus nostris pulsamus redemptorem, non calescit, quia iratus est nobis; auertit faciem suam, et conturbati sumus. Quid igitur fiendum est desperandum? Absit. Sed in tantis processis, flagellis et periculis secure ad portum salutis festinandum, videlicet ad aduocatam peccatorum, Mediatricem Dei et hominum, Reginam misericordie, et Matrem Dei, intemeratam Virginem Mariam Christiferam cum nouis laudibus vociferando reccurendum, ut videlicet sua pietas sinum sue[1] misericordie nobis adaperiat, et in recensione iocunditatis laudum sue Presentationis deuocius allecta apud benedictum fructum ventris sui, Ihesum filium suum vnigenitum, pro miseria nostra ipsum placando plus solito intercedere dignetur, ut ipsa adiuuante et protegente a malis liberemur, ad viam rectam reducamur, et sine timore de manu inimicorum nostrorum liberati seruiamus illi deinceps in sanctitate et iusticia omnibus diebus nostris.

Cantemus igitur carmen nouum Regine celi, et antiquas laudes Marie Presentationis in Templo de partibus Orientis nouiter coruscantes vniuersis fratribus nostris Christianis in plaga occidentali, australi et septentrionali de gentibus pro antidoto et leticia spirituali annunciemus. Audiant ergo vniuersi Catholici Europe et Affrice, presertim deuoti intemerate Virginis, eius deuotissimam solennitatem utique in ecclesia occidentali nouam ac rutilantem in cordibus zelatorum Virginis, quamuis antiquam in ecclesia orientali, et ad nouam deuotionem excitentur. Temporibus namque antiquis, et, ut creditur, in primitia ecclesia quando ciuitas sancta Iherusalem et Terra Sancta per Christianos detinebatur, ibique in alijs partibus Orientis in quibus vigebat fides catholica, sanctis patribus instituentibus et verisimiliter miraculis declarantibus, festum Beatissime semper Virginis Marie, quando in tercio etatis sue anno in templo per seipsam | quindecim gradibus templi miraculose[2] ascensis, fuit in dicto templo a parentibus suis presentata, die xxi mensis Nouembris deuotissime et solempniter celebrabatur. Et adhuc in regno Cypri deuotissime per fideles Orientis colitur de presenti, et habet officium totum proprium et deuotissimum secundum usum Curie Romane, etiam musice notatum.

Quod quidem festum supramemoratus cancellarius, quamuis indignus et inutilis, pre deuotione Virginis et iocunditate admirans et in corde suo pie extimans indignum quod tanta solennitas partes lateret occidentales, in quibus, protegente Domino, fidei plenitudo consistit, ob reuerentiam ipsius Beatissime semper[3] Virginis, ipsa adiuuante, dictam solempnitatem iam pluribus annis elapsis in aliquibus partibus Ytalie, videlicet in preclara ciuitate Venetiarum, aliquibus electis deuote Virginis ipsius ciuitatis adiu-

[1] sue] Inserted above the line (MS).

[2] miraculose] Inserted in the left margin (MS).

[3] semper] Inserted in the left margin (MS).

uantibus, solempniter celebrari fecit cum representatione figurata et deuotissima, aliquibus signis et visionibus dictam solempnitatem de cetero celebrandam confirmantibus et eam communicantibus, de qua certe noua deuotio et iocunda Matris Dei in cordibus multorum fidelium non mediocriter exorta est.

Adueniente plerumque dicto cancellario ambassiatore serenissimi principis, Petri Iherusalem et Cypri regis iuuenculi filij, quondam armipotentis Machabei victoriosissime ac lacrimabilis memorie sui quondam domini pro factis orientalibus ad pedes Sanctissimi in Christo Patris et Domini Nostri Domini Gregorij Pape xi^mi^, Sacrosancte Romane ac vniuersalis Ecclesie Summi Pontificis, toto nisu anhelante ut solennitas sepetacta Beate Marie semper Virginis ubique terrarum auctoritate apostolica diuulgaretur, et cum illa humilitate qua potuit, non qua debuit, et deuotione qualicumque oracionum tamen fultus multorum deuotorum Virginis utriusque sexus et adiutus non in arcu suo sperans sed in arcu celesti qui diuinam maiestatem inclinauit usque ad uterum virginalem, dicto Sanctissimo Pape Gregorio dictam solennitatem rutilantem noue deuotionis beatitudini sue tunc ignotam minus male annunciauit, ac officium integrum etiam musice notatum humiliter presentauit, supplicando eidem sanctitati, vice deuotorum Virginis, ut tanta solennitas Matris Dei, ab occidentalibus incognita et neglecta, ubique terrarum auctoritate apostolica celebrari mandare dignaretur, aut saltem deuotis volentibus celebrari permitteret. Qui quidem sanctissimus Pater Gregorius sane vigilans in hijs que fidei sunt, et recensione multiplici armonie diuini cultus, uelut alter Dauid ipsius panaye[1] singulariter electus imitator, in summa clementia et mansuetudine in florida castitate et humilitate in zelo fidei et feruenti deuotione Marie, non utique annunciantis linguam balbutientem abhorrens seu leprosum haurientem aquam mundam repellens, sed amore Virginis tactus et inflammatus, libellum officij memorati manibus proprijs dignanter recepit, ac post multa et deuotissima uerba ipsius animam dicti cancellarij fragilem pre deuotione penetrantia, concludendo Sanctissimus Pater in laudem Virginis prorupit dicens: Non est aliquod remedium ita efficax cuicumque[2] peccatori sicut recursum habere in omni necessitate ad Beatam Virginem Mariam, eique adherere sibi seruire et ipsam laudare. Hec ille.

Tandem clementissimus Papa[3] zelator honoris Marie, viso officio in studio proprio, inportunitate dicti cancellarii[4] postea prosequente voluit pie et catholice sepetactum officium per aliquos reuerendissimos patres et dominos cardinales ac magistros in sacra pagina solempnes examinari debere, quod et factum est, nam Episcopus Pamiensis sancte memorie, Vrbani Pape ac Domini Nostri Gregorij Pape confessor, solempnis in theologia magister Ordinis Heremitarum Sancti Augustini, et Guilielmus Romani Ordinis Fratrum Predicatorum etiam in sacra pagina magister Sacri Palacij, primo examinauerunt dictum officium. Deinde Reuerendissimus Pater Dominus Bertrandus Glandatensis, tituli Sancte Prisce, Presbyter Cardinalis, solempnis magister

[1] panaye] A mark over this word refers to the words *grece Marie*, in the margin.

[2] cuicumque] Inserted in the left margin.

[3] clementissimus Papa] Inserted in the left margin to replace the words *sanctissimus pater*, which are crossed out.

[4] dicti cancellarii] Inserted in the left margin to replace the word *mea*, which is crossed out.

in sacra pagina de Ordine Minorum officium prolixe examinauit et aliqua propria manu correxit; deinde etiam Reuerendissimi Patres Dominus Anglicus Albanensis, Episcopus Cardinalis, et Dominus Petrus Hyspalensis, tituli Sancte Praxedis, Presbyter Cardinalis; post istos vero dominos Frater Thomas quondam Minister Generalis Ordinis Beati Francisci, nunc vero Patriarcha Gradensis, Episcopus Cauilonensis, Minister | Francie, Minister Hibernie, et Procurator Ordinis Minorum. Omnes magistri in sacra pagina insimul congregati dictum officium viderunt, et in presentia reuerendissimi dicti Domini Cardinalis Glandatensis non solum dictam sollennitatem et officium approbauerunt sollennizandum, sed etiam ut celebrari debeat a deuotis volentibus ubique instanter intercesserunt. Factaque relatione de omnibus ad sanctitatem Domini Nostri Pape, idem vicarius dignissimus et imitator illius, qui non cessat Matrem honorare in terris quamuis deuotissimus[1] vicarius Matris sui magistri prudentissimus tamen maturius et catholice in hac parte procedere volens, quam plures dominos cardinales ad se vocauit, et inito consilio supplicationeque dicti cancellarij, hic inde ventilata tandem diuina clementia honorem Matris in salutem et consolacionem Christianorum verisimiliter reuelante ac Virgine gloriosa in corde vicarij filij sui inspirante, cui plane interest pro tempore et loco cultum diuinum corrigere, modificare, tollerare, augmentare, et de nouo instituere, celebrandi deinceps publice sollempnitatem Presentationis Beate Marie in Templo a fidelibus pie, sancte et digne tollerantiam seu permissionem misericorditer concessit; et facta est solempnitas Presentationis Beate Marie cum officio suo proprio sepetacto in Curia Romana, Beatissimo Papa Gregorio tollerante ac in sacro palatio suo degente Auinionensi in ecclesia Fratrum Minorum, videlicet die dominica xxi. die mensis Nouembris, anno de Natiuitate Domini m°. ccc°. lxxij., indictione decima pontificatus Domini Nostri Domini Gregorii Pape xi$^{mi}$ anno secundo.

In vigilia namque ipsius dominice Vespere sollemnes, et de nocte Matutine de officio prelibato per Fratres Minores celebrate fuerunt. Et dominica pretacta Missa solempnis et pontificalis in dicta ecclesia Beati Francisci celebrata fuit per Reuerendum Patrem Dominum Episcopum Cortonensem Romanum, magistrum in sacra pagina solempnem de Ordine Predicatorum, cum sermone eiusdem solennitatis ad clerum in Missa et predicatione vulgari in Vesperis Secundis ad populum laudabiliter factis per Fratrem Franciscum de Fabrica, ministrum Assisij solempnem doctorem in theologia.[2] Verumptamen ad honorandam prelibatam solennitatem Beate Marie in Missa interfuerunt deuoti Virginis Reuerendissimi in Christo Patres et Domini[3] Cardinales infrascripti, videlicet Dominus Anglicus Albanensis Episcopus Cardinalis, frater quondam sancte memorie Vrbani Pape Quinti, Dominus Petrus Pampilonensis, tituli Sancte Anastasie, Presbyter Cardinalis et Vicecancellarius Ecclesie Romane, Dominus Guilielmus, tituli Sancti Clementis, Presbyter Cardinalis, consanguineus germanus Domini Nostri Pape, Dominus

[1] deuotissimus] Written twice (MS).

[2] A symbol at this point refers to the following, written in the upper margin in a hand of the seventeenth or eighteenth century: Ad augmentationem uero dictæ solenitatis aśsistentes in dicto officio recitando, idem sanctissimus Papa Gregorius omnibus qui interfuerunt ad dictam solemnitatem tres annos et tres quadragenas de indulgentiis misericorditer concessit.

[3] Domini] Written twice (MS).

Petrus Florentinus, tituli Sancti Laurentij in Damasco, Presbyter Cardinalis, Dominus Iohannes Lemouicensis, tituli Sanctorum Nerey et Achilley, Presbyter Cardinalis, consanguineus Domini Nostri Pape, Dominus Bertrandus Glandatensis, tituli Sancte Prisce, Presbyter Cardinalis, Dominus Iohannes de Turre, tituli Sancti Laurentij in Lucina, Presbyter Cardinalis, Dominus Hugo Sancti Martialis, tituli Sancte Marie in Porticu, Dyaconus Cardinalis, et Dominus Petrus de B*arento*nio, tituli Sancte Marie in Via Lata, Dyaconus Cardinalis. Fuerunt insuper alij domini et prelati ecclesie, Dominus Patriarcha Gradensis, prothonotarij, archiepiscopi, episcopi, abbates, magistri sacri palacij, et alij magistri in theologia diuersarum religionum, regentes in sacra pagina, doctores sollennes vtriusque iuris, ac catholicus populus utriusque sexus, quorum non erat numerus, omnes congregati in laudem nouam Virginis Marie gloriose saciati plerumque nouo spirituali cibo a Virgine exquisito et preparato finaliter in vitam eternam.

Nec mirum, Patres et Fratres karissimi, quia plerumque in ista sancta solempnitate, misterio non carente, mens deuota contemplando quintuplici cibo refici potest et saciari. Primus namque cibus dici potest quedam translatio Marie sanctificate, ymmo sanctissime, trium annorum de domo patris carnalis ad domum eterni Dei Patris, de tenebris cellule parentum ad ostensionem populi Israel et aulam regis viuentium. Si igitur ecclesia sancta de translatione ossium mortuorum tantam celebritatem facit, quid fiendum est de translatione Marie beatissime domus paterne ad Domini Templum? Secundus vero cibus ymaginari potest oculo mentali, videlicet matura ascensio Marie quindecim graduum, de quibus non immerito ecclesia quindecim psalmos graduales in memoriam ascensionis prelibate sibi assumpsit. Ac sancti laudatores Virginis in suis carminibus | quindecim gaudia Virginis Marie deuotius recitarunt. Tercius autem cibus, et in sollennitate nostra principalis, est ipsa Presentatio Beate Marie in Templo ad Deum Patrem. Congruum nempe et conueniens erat, ut illa que ab initio et ante secula ordinata erat ad concipiendum et portandum in vtero pretium humane redemptionis, Deum et hominem, in templo Deo presentaretur, ibique a Spiritu Sancto de diuinis instrueretur et a conuersacione et contubernio mundanorum totaliter abstraheretur. Delectabilis est certe cibus iste contemplantibus preparationem redemptionis nostre in Maria. Sed quartus cibus virgines et mentes castas inebriare debet, Maria plerumque presentata in templo summo pontifici et reducta in contubernio virginum, expectans redemptionem Israel, contra morem humanum a Spiritu Sancto edocta in templo prima virginitatem vouit, quod tantum Deo placuit, ut Mater Filij Dei fieret et virginitatem non amitteret. Quintus plerumque cibus mentem deuotam ab omni corpore releuare certe debet contemplando totam vitam Marie, singulares actus, et virtutes ipsius a presentatione ipsius in templo usque ad annum tredecimum uel quartumdecimum sanctissima vita sua continue ibidem in templo relucente. Quis enim plene contemplari valet diuinam illam dispensationem atque nouitatem, in qua Virgo regia seni Ioseph nuptui traditur, florente virga Ioseph approbante et Iudaico populo admirante?

Omnia etenim ista misteria et preparatoria aduentus Saluatoris in Mariam in templo subsequenter acta sunt, de quibus omnibus sub titulo Presentationis hodie in ecclesia Dei mens deuota sabbatizando in corde iubilat. Igitur sancti patres non sine magno misterio solennitatem istam gloriosam, nec immerito ad laudem Dei et Virginis instituerunt, in qua nobis proponuntur tot misteria principia et fundamenta humane redemptionis nostre, que omnia in carminibus officij prelibate Presentacionis vestre deuocioni lucidius apparebunt.

Istam modicam epistolam incompositam ac sine sale conditam, cum deuotissimo officio Presentationis Marie in Templo, Patres et Domini catholici occidentales, meridionales, et septentrionales, memoratus cancellarius vermiculus vester et zelator abortiuus deuotioni vestre mitti decreuit, ad excitandum corda fidelium maxime deuotorum Regine Celi, necnon ad recensendum ipsius laudes dignissimas, non ut inde ventum[1] humane laudis acquirat, ipsa intemerata Virgine teste, sed ut ipsa inspirante et Filio suo consumante, sequentibus signis in cordibus vestris tanta solennitas non lateat, et quandoque in consistorio contemplacionis vestre solennitatis noue in Mariam rapti et affecti per gratiam pro anima vestri vermiculi uestra deuocio quandoque apud ipsam intercedere dignetur humiliter exorat, vt etiam multiplicatis intercessoribus latas sentencias irati summi iudicis per intercessionem Beate Marie semper Virginis Christiani nostri euadere mereantur, et ad illam beatissimam visionem, cuius, secundum Augustinum, cernere finis est, peruenire valeant. Quod nobis concedere dignetur fructus Marie benedictus qui viuit, regnat, et inperat per infinita secula seculorum. Amen.

A fifteenth-century text of this letter is found in Bibl. Nat., MS lat. 14454, fol. $2^r$–$4^r$, and an incomplete text of the early fifteenth century is found in Bibl. Nat., MS lat. 14511, fol. $182^v$–$183^r$. Jorga (pp. 411–4) quotes sparingly from a text of this letter found in Meurisse, *Lettres de Charles cinquième et de Philippe de Maisières*, Metz, 1638, in –12°, pp. 6 ff. This publication I have not discovered in the Bibliothèque Nationale, in the British Museum, or in the Bodleian Library. In *Historia Universitatis Parisiensis . . . autore Cæsare Egassio Bulæo*, iv, Paris, 1668, p. 441, the opening sentences of this *epistola* are quoted 'ex Epistola Philippi erga B. Virginem toto animo affecti intelligitur, quæ legitur in libello excusso Metis anno 1638'.

**Page 227, note 2.** The following note concerning a dramatic performance at Avignon in 1385 is found in Paris, Bibl. Nat., MS lat. 17330, fol. $17^v$, previously edited by Young, *Presentation*, pp. 200–1:

Item pro refricacione consolacionis deuotorum Beatissime Uirginis Marie qui sepetactam solempnitatem Presentacionis ipsius Uirginis in templo deuote celebrarunt et in futurum iubilando celebrabunt.

Notandum est quod Anno Domini millesimo trecentesimo octogesimo quinto in ciuitate Auinionensi, superius tacto Philippo de Maserijs, regni Cipri cancellario, personaliter procurante apud Dominum Nostrum Summum Pontificem Clementem Septimum, ipso summo pontifice non sine deuocione et reuerencia ipsius Matris Dei non solum permittente sed deuote ordinante pretacta solempnitas Presentacionis ipsius Uirginis a parentibus in templo xxj die Nouembris anni pretacti in ecclesia Fratrum Heremitarum Beati Augustini Auinioni deuotissime ac solempniter celebrata fuit cum

[1] ventum] dentum (MS).

Missa pontificali, vtique presentibus usque ad finem Misse xviij cardinalibus, archiepiscopis, episcopis cum vniuersali clero ipsius ciuitatis Auenionensis totoque populo vtriusque sexus. In qua quidem Missa solempni, ad laudem Uirginis deuocionemque suorum deuotorum, facta fuit quedam representacio xv iuuencularum uirginum trium aut quatuor annorum, quarum vna formosior representabat Mariam associatam a dictis uirginibus, et sic varijs indutis cum processione deuotissima cum Ioachim et Anna figuratis et angelis precedentibus Virginem ac sequentibus, ducta fuit cum instrumentis musicorum ad altare, ibique velox ascendit xv gradus ligneos tendentes ad altare et presentata a parentibus fuit figuraliter, et deuote accepta a summo sacerdote legis Veteri⟨s⟩ Testamenti induto habitu summorum pontificum Iudeorum. Qua presentata ad altare cum laudibus et carminibus dauiticis alta voce per angelos, Ioachim et Annam et ipsam Mariam recitatis, reducta est in medio chori, et cardinalium in loco eminenciori, ut tactum est, associata, ibique expectauit usque ad finem Misse celebrate, in qua quidem Missa hora offertorij de sancta solempnitate Presentacionis Marie in templo predicauit ad dominos cardinales et ad clerum reuerendus et in scientia admirabilis magister Iohannes de Basilia, solempnissimus doctor in theologia Theothonicus nacione ac generalis ordinis Fratrum Heremitarum Beati Augustini, qui quidem generalis de mandato viue vocis Domini Nostri Summi Pontificis, fecit sermonem, nec habuit spacium prouidendi sermonem pretactum nisi tres dies nec completos et tamen ad confirmandum cor deuotum transformatum per gratiam in amorem Uirginis, ut videlicet tanta solempnitas non lateat quin ymo a fidelibus vbique terrarum deinceps celebretur, ipsa Uirgine uirginum in animam ipsius generalis mirabiliter inspirante sequentibus signis toto clero et dominis cardinalibus publice at⟨t⟩estantibus quasi vna voce omnes dicebant quod numquam temporibus ipsorum pulcriorem sermonem de Beata Uirgine audiuerant in Curia Romana. Denique ipse Dominus Noster Papa Clemens Septimus, deuocione Uirginis Marie eiusque deuota solempnitate accensus, in pretacto diuino officio et festiuitate omnibus existentibus tres annos et tres quadregenas indulgenciarum misericorditer concessit, et qui audiuit et narrata vidit testimonium perhibuit, et verum est testimonium eius ad laudem Matris Dei Filijque eius benedicti, qui est benedictus in secula seculorum.

This note is written in a hand of the early fifteenth century seen nowhere else in the MS.

**Page 245, note 6.** The special ceremony for the Annunciation at Parma is described in the following passage from Barbieri, pp. 120–3, reprinted in part by Bartholomaeis, p. 532:

In Annunciatione Virginis Mariæ, cuius Annunciationis repræsentatio in dicta ecclesia Parmensi annuatim, solemnius et devotius quam fieri possit, celebretur, ad inducendum populum Parmæ ad contritionem, et confirmandum ipsum in devotione ipsius Virginis Mariæ, quæ quoscumque eam devote invocantes a periculis omnibus indubie tuetur; in qua ecclesia et merito fieri potest et debet, cum ecclesia Parmensis in nomine ipsius Virginis dedicata fuerit, et ipsa etiam sit Patrona civitatis et populi Parmæ. Quæ repræsentatio, ut alias facta fuit, omnino fiat, in mane, ad Missam Tertiarum, et similiter in Vesperis, videlicet: a fenestris voltarum dictæ ecclesiæ, versus sanctam Agatham, per funes Angelum transmittendo, usque per directum pulpiti super quo evangelium cantatur, in quo fit reverenter et decenter repræsentatio Virginis Mariæ, ipsam angelica salutatione devote annunciaturum cum Prophetis et aliis solemnitatibus opportunis, videlicet: in primis Vesperis, Baionus[1] solemniter cum aliis pulsetur; paramenta alba; et tria luminaria; et adsint dominus Episcopus, piviali albo conditus, atque sex Custodes etiam cum pivialibus solemnibus. In Matutinis quinque luminaria sacristiæ, et omnino luminaria fabricæ; et ardeant etiam cerei grossi, nisi finita Missa Tertiarum nullatenus extinguendi. Quo Matutino finito, et post *Ave Maria*, pro Missa populi pulsetur Baionus, deinde, ut in Nativitate, videlicet: finita Missa magna, pulsetur iterum Baionus pro prædicatione.

**Page 246, note 4.** A description of the *Aurea Missa* as arranged in the sixteenth century by Pierre Cotrel at Tournai is published by L. Deschamps de Pas, in *Annales archéologiques*, xvii (1857), 167–9, from MS 62 in the Bibliothèque de la Ville, at Lille. I give the text of Deschamps de Pas, which is reprinted also by Chambers, ii, 318–21:

Sequuntur ceremonie et modus observandus pro celebratione Misse *Missus est Gabriel Angelus*, etc., vulgariter dicte *Auree Misse* quolibet anno in choro ecclesie Tornacensis decantande feria x[a] ante festum Nativitatis Domini Nostri Jesu Christi, ex fundatione venerabilis viri magistri Petri Cotrel, canonici dicte ecclesie Tornacensis et in eadem archidiaconi Brugensis, de licentia et permissione dominorum suorum decani et capituli predicte ecclesie Tornacensis. Primo, feria tercia, post decantationem Vesperarum, disponentur per carpentatorem ecclesie in sacrario chori dicte ecclesie Tornacensis, in locis, jam ad hoc ordinatis et sibi oppositis, duo stallagia, propter hoc appropriata, que etiam ornabuntur cortinis et pannis cericeis ad hoc ordinatis per casularium jam dicte ecclesie, quorum alterum, videlicet quod erit de latere episcopi, serviet ad recipiendam Beatam Virginem Mariam, et alterum stallagium ab illo oratorio oppositum, quod erit de latere decani, serviet ad recipiendum et recludendum Angelum. Item similiter eodem die deputatus ad descendendum die sequenti[2] columbam, visitabit tabernaculum in altis carolis dispositum, disponet cordas, et parabit instrumentum candelis suis munitum, per quod descendet Spiritus Sanctus in specie columbe, tempore decantationis ewangelii, prout postea dicetur, et erit sollicitus descendere cordulam campanule, et illam disponere ad stallagium Angeli, ad illam campanullam pulsandam suo tempore, die sequenti, prout post dicetur. Item in crastinum, durantibus Matutinis, magistri cantus erunt solliciti quod duo juvenes, habentes voces dulces et altas, preparentur in thesauraria, hostio clauso, unus ad modum Virginis seu Regine, et alter ad modum Angeli, quibus providebitur de ornamentis et aliis necessariis propter hoc, per fundatorem, datis et ordinatis. Item post decantationem septime lectionis Matutinarum, accedent duo juvenes, Mariam videlicet et Angelum representantes, sic parati de predicta thesauraria, ad chorum intrando per majus hostium dicti chori, duabus thedis ardentibus precedentibus: Maria videlicet per latus domini episcopi, in manibus portans horas pulchras, et Angelus per latus

[1] The name of a bell.

[2] sequenti] sequentis (Print).

domini decani, portans in manu dextra sceptrum argenteum deauratum, et sic morose progredientur cum suis magistris directoribus, usque ad summum altare, ubi, genibus flexis, fundent ad Dominum orationem. Qua facta, progredientur dicti juvenes quilibet ad locum suum, Maria videlicet ad stallagium de parte episcopi preparatum, cum suo magistro directore, et Angelus ad aliud stallagium de parte decani similiter preparatum, etiam cum suo alio magistro directore, et ubique cortinis clausis. Coram quibus stallagiis remanebunt predicte thede, ardentes usque ad finem Misse. Item clerici thesaurarie, durantibus octava et nona lectionibus Matutinarum, preparabunt majus altare solemniter, ut in triplicibus festis, et omnes candele circumquaque chorum sacrarum de rokemes, et in corona nova existentes accendentur. Et clerici revestiarii providebunt quod presbyter, dyaconus, subdiaconus, choriste, cum pueris revestitis, sint parati, in fine hymni *Te Deum*, pro Missa decantanda, ita quod nulla sit pausa inter finem dicti himpni *Te Deum* et Missam. Et in fine predicte Misse sit paratus presbiter ebdoma⟨da⟩rius cantandi versum *Ora pro nobis*, et deinde *Deus in adjutorium*, de Laudibus, illas perficiendo per chorum, et in fine psalmi *De profundis* dicendi in fine Matutinarum, more consueto, adjungetur collecta *Adjuva nos*, pro fundatore, ultra collectam ordinariam. Item, cum celebrans accesserit ad majus altare, pro incipienda Missa, et ante *Confiteor* immediate cortine circumquaque oratorium Virginis solum aperientur, ipsa Virgine attente orante et ad genua existente suo libro aperto, super pulvinari ad hoc ordinato, Angelo adhuc semper clauso in suo stallagio remanente. Item cum cantabitur *Gloria in excelsis Deo*, tunc cortine stallagii, in quo erit Angelus, aperientur. In quo stallagio stabit dictus Angelus erectus, tenens in manibus suis suum sceptrum argenteum, et nichil aliud faciens, quousque fuerit tempus cantandi ewangelium, nec interim faciet Virgo aliquod signum videndi dictum Angelum, sed, submissis oculis, erit semper intenta ad orationem. Item cum appropinquarit tempus cantandi dictum ewangelium, diaconus cum subdiacono, pueris cum candelis et cruce precedentibus, progredientur ad locum in sacrario sibi preparatum, et cantabit ewangelium *Missus est Gabriel*, et etiam cantabunt partes suas Maria et Angelus, prout ordinatum et notatum est in libro ad hoc ordinato. Item cum Angelus cantabit hec verba ewangelii, *Ave, gratia plena, Dominus tecum*, faciet tres ad Virginem salutationes; primo ad illud verbum *Ave*, humiliabit se tam capite quam corpore, post morose se elevando; et ad illa verba *gratia plena*, faciet secundam humiliationem, flectendo mediocriter genua sua, se postea relevando; et ad illa verba *Dominus tecum*, quæ cantabit cum gravitate et morose, tunc faciet terciam humiliationem ponendo genua usque ad terram, et finita clausula, assurget, Virgine interim se non movente. Sed dum Maria Virgo cantabit *Quomodo fiet istud*, assurget et vertet modicum faciem suam ad Angelum cum gravitate et modestia, non aliter se movendo. Et dum cantabit Angelus *Spiritus Sanctus superveniet in te*, etc., tunc Angelus vertet faciem suam versus columbam illam ostendendo, et subito descendet ex loco in altis carolis ordinato, cum candelis in circuitu ipsius ardentibus, ante stallagium sive oratorium Virginis, ubi remanebit, usque post ultimum *Agnus Dei*; quo decantato, revertetur ad locum unde descenderat. Item magister cantus, qui erit in stallagio Angeli, sit valde sollicitus pro propria vice pulsare campanam in altis carolis, respondente in initio ewangelii, ut tunc ille qui illic erit ordinatus ad descendendum columbam sit preadvisatus et preparet omnia necessaria, et candelas accendat. Et secunda vice sit valde sollicitus pulsare dictam campanulam, ita quod precise ad illud verbum *Spiritus Sanctus* descendat ad Virginem columbam ornatam candelis accensis, et remaneat ubi descenderit, usque ad ultimum *Agnus Dei* decantatum, prout dictum est. Et tunc idem magister cantus iterum pulsabit pro tercia vice eamdem campanulam, ut revertatur[1] columba unde descenderit. Et sit ille disponendus vel deputandus ad descendendum[2] dictam columbam bene preadvisatus de supra dicta triplici pulsatione, et quid quilibet significabit ne sit in aliquo defectus. Item predicti, diaconus, Maria et Angelus complebunt totum ewangelium in eodem tono prout cuilibet sibi competit, et ewangelio finito, reponet se Maria ad genua et orationem, et Angelus remanebit rectus, usque in finem Misse, hoc excepto, quod in elevatione Corporis Christi ponet se ad genua. Item postea proficietur Missa, Maria et Angelo in suis stallagiis usque in fine permanentibus. Item Missa finita, post *Ite, missa est,* Maria et Angelus descendent de suis stallagiis et revertentur cum reliquiis et revestitis usque ad revestiarium predictum eorum, flambellis precedentibus. In quo revestiario presbiter celebrans cum predictis revestitis Maria et Angelo dicet psalmum *De profundis*, prout in choro, cum adjectione collecte *Adiuva*, pro fundatore. Item fiet Missa per omnia, ut in die Annunciationis Dominice cum sequentia sive prosa *Mittit ad virginem*, cum organis et discantu prout in triplicibus.

**Page 246, note 6.** The *Missa Aurea* was established in the collegiate church of Saint-Omer by the will of Robert Fabri, a cantor of that church, who died in 1535. I reprint the request of his executors, dated Oct. 12, 1543, as published by L. Dechamps de Pas, in *Mémoires de la Société des Antiquaires de la Morinie*, xx (1886–7), 209–10:

Quant au faict du mystere de la messe justaument après matines se fera, si plaist a MM. en la manière que sensieult.

Primes. Lintroite de la messe ass^r *Rorate. Gloria in excelsis Deo.* Lepistre au grand candelabre du coeur; le gradual par deux vicaires, et le *Alleluia, Angelus Domini* par trois chanoines, se chanteront au coeur devant laigle. Prosa *Hæc clara dies*, repetendo *Ave Maria*, au son des orgues.

A lorganiste pour jouer des orgues 11^s; a son assistent xii^d.

Quant au faict de lévangille de la messe, le dyacre assistent de la dicte messe commencera lévangille *Missus est* en la manière que lon chante journelement estant devant le chandelabre ou on chante les evangilles au coeur, jusques au point de la salutation angelicque *Ave gratia.* Lors ung petit enffant de coeur revestu dune aulbe, acoustré en angele comme on faict le jour de la resurrection, instruict du maistre de chant a ce faire et chanter a bon ton et a loisir parellement a tout ce que sensuit en ladite evangille par ledict angele, et ce au costé senestre du grand autel en bas. Pareillement aussi au costé dextre, ung desdictz enffans representant la vierge Marie, estant accoustré comme une pucelle, le plus honestement que

[1] revertatur] revertetur (Print). [2] descendendum] destruendam (Print).

faire se porra, instruict comme dessus est dict chantera bien dévotement comme levangille requiert.

Après levangille, *Credo*. Le reste selon le jour.

Au maistre de chant pour son salaire dinstruire lesdictz enffans $vi^s$.

Item ausdictz enffans ensemble pour servir audict office et prier Dieu pour lame dudict fondateur $vi^s$.

Item a ce faire est requis que le carpentier de leglise fera deux petis passés non empechans, lung du costé dextre et lautre du senestre empres de levangeliaire, correspondantz lung a lautre. Et demourans lesdictz deux enffans ausditz lieux jusques la messe finie. Et pour ce apprester le jour devant et oster le jour de ladicte solennité après vespres ledict carpentier aura tous les ans $vi^s$.

Item au varlet de la fabricque pour assister et ayder ledict carpentier a faire ce que dessus, garder et mettre en lieux honestes les dictz eschaffaulx pour sa peine $iii^s$.

Item au boursier pour sa peine de distribuer les deniers dessus mentionnés in sicca $ii^s$.

Item a une femme pour parer et accoustrer honestement ledict enffant représentant la vierge Marie, pour sa peine $vi^s$.

The following extract from a list of properties used in the *Aurea Missa* at Saint-Omer is from an inventory of the collegiate church dated 1557 (Archives du Chapitre, MS G. 2787) published by L. Deschamps de Pas, in *Bulletin archéologique du Comité des Travaux historiques et scientifiques* (1886), p. 96. I reprint the text of Deschamps de Pas:

Ung coffre de cuir boully où sont encloses les ornementz et parementz qui s'ensuivent, le tout servant à l'office de *Missus, feria* $4^a$ $4^{or}$ *temporum, in Adventu Domini*, fundé par les exécuteurs de feu $Mons^r$ $M^e$ Rober Fabri chantre.

Primes.

244. Huict pendans de cortines et deux voies de toille blanche servans aux deux tabernacles, armoiez des armes dudit $S^r$ Fabri.

245. Deux cielz de mesme, semez de chacun ung soleil millieu, et de plusieurs estolles de taffetas.

246. Huict coupettes de bois doré pour mettre aux pilliers des deux tabernacles.

247. Ung vestement de damas blancq, et ung aultre de toille ouvré de fil d'or, semé de fleurs de soie.

248. Deux mancherons frinchez et ouvrez aussy de fil d'or qui sont les accoustrementz de la Vierge Marie.

249. Ung trousseau de cheveulz, une couronne de bois doré avec une petite croix par devant, ung sceptre de mesme pour l'ange.

250. Ung colomb de bois revestu de damas blancq.

251. Ung livre de papier couvert de parchemin où est escript en nottes l'évangille du jour.

252. Ung caiet en papier où est escript la fondation et l'office dudit jour.

**Page 248, note 1.** The dramatic ceremony at Cividale is elucidated by the following two *ordines*:

(1)[1]

In festo Annuntiationis Beate Marie Virginis fit processio ad forum cantando responsorium *Gaude, Maria Virgo*; versus cum *Gloria Patri* reservatur in foro, et in medio fori fit statium, et in medio chorarii cantant versus cum *Gloria*. Hoc cantato, subito cantatur evangelium cum ludo. Quo finito, revertendo ad ecclesiam, cantatur *Te Deum*.

(2)[2]

In festo Annunciationis Beate Marie Virginis fit processio ad forum cantando responsorium *Gaude, Maria Uirgo* (quere numero vij),[3] et fit stacium in corpore fori, et versus cum *Gloria* cantatur per chorarios. Quibus cantatis, dyaconus legat euuangelium in tono; et fit representacio Angeli ad Mariam. Quibus finitis, cantando *Te Deum laudamus* clerus reuertatur ad ecclesiam.

**Page 250, note 4.** Dramatic commemorations of the Annunciation are recorded for Le Mans, fifteenth century (P. Piolin, in *Revue historique et archéologique du Maine*, xxix [1891], 249–50); Trevigi, 1261 (D'Ancona, i, 114–5); Cività Vecchia, c. 1304 (Coussemaker, pp. 344–5); Saint-Lô, 1521 (Gasté, pp. 79–80); Venice, 1267, 1328 (D'Ancona, i, 92–3; Bartholomaeis, pp. 153–4). A *computus* of 1452–3 from Lincoln Cathedral records an expenditure 'in serotecis emptis pro Maria et angelo ex consuetudine in aurora Natalis Domini' (Wordsworth, *Lincoln*, ii, p. lv). Chambers (ii, 67, 377) infers that this entry refers to an Annunciation play; but I surmise that a play on Christmas morning would be a version of the *Officium Pastorum* (see above, chapter xvii). On the representations of the Annunciation in art in general see Hirn, pp. 271 sqq., 322 sqq. For an Annunciation sequence containing dialogue see above, i, 568.

## CHAPTER XXV

## PLAYS ON SUBJECTS FROM THE OLD TESTAMENT: ISAAC AND REBECCA—JOSEPH AND HIS BRETHREN—DANIEL

**Page 266, note 4.** The following passages from the *Glossa Ordinaria* of Strabo, and from the *Allegoriæ in Vetus Testamentum* attributed to Hugh of St Victor, are relevant to the play of Isaac and Rebecca:

Quia filius major vocatur, acceptio est legis Judæorum. Quia escas ejus et capturam dilexit pater: homines sunt ab errore salvati, quos per doctrinam justus quisque venatur. Sermo Dei, repromissionis benedictio, et spes regni futuri, in quo cum Christo sunt regnaturi, et verum sabbatum celebraturi. Rebecca plena Spiritu Sancto, sciens quod audisset antequam pareret, quia 'major serviet minori': hæc formam gerit Spiritus Sancti, quæ quod futurum

[1] I reprint this *ordo* from Coussemaker (p. 284), who cites it from 'Processional C., p. x'. This MS is now CII in the Reale Museo Archeologico at Cividale.

[2] Cividale, Reale Museo Archeologico, MS CI, fol. 9$^{r}$.

[3] The marks of parenthesis are editorial.

esse noverat in Christo, ante meditabatur in Jacob, loquitur ad filium minorem. 'Vade ad gregem et affer mihi duos hædos optimos:' præfigurans carneum Salvatoris adventum, in quo eos liberaret qui peccatis tenebantur obnoxii. Hædi enim ubique peccatores significant. Duo afferri jubentur, ut duorum populorum assumptio significetur. Teneri scilicet et humani, docibiles scilicet et innocentis animæ. . . . Fuit ⟨Esau⟩ etiam venator, quia per effusionem sanguinis arietum et vitulorum, et hircorum, Deum placabat. . . . Per duos hædos confessionem peccatorum gentilis populi et pœnitentiam possumus accipere. Hædi optimi, quia confessio peccatorum et pœnitentia valde est Deo acceptabilis.[1]

De benedictione Jacob

Nota est historia, quando Jacob Esau benedictione patris supplantavit (*Gen.* xxvii). Isaac significat Deum, a quo descendit benedictio super caput justi. Rebecca significat matrem gratiam, quæ Jacob de paterna benedictione consuluit. Jacob posterior natu, domi remanens, benedictionemque consequens, gentilem designat populum, qui post Israeliticum populum ad cognitionem divinam venit, et intra se cum matre gratia vota nutrit, quæ reddunt laudationes Deo: benedicitur ab eo in mundo per gratiam, in cœlo per gloriam. Esau prior natu, foris venationi deserviens, benedictionem amittens, populum Israel significat qui ad Dei cognitionem venit, qui foris in littera justitiam quærit, et benedictionem cœlestis hæreditatis dimittit. Pelles, quibus Rebecca filium cooperuit, confessionem exprimunt peccatorum. Cibus, sunt virtutes quibus Deus pascitur, dum per gentilem populum cooperante gratia exercetur. Vestes, sunt bona opera legis quibus misericorditer gratia gentilem populum vestit, populo Israelitico foris stante et vagante. Vinum designat gaudium in Spiritu Sancto. Quo vino Dominum potamus, dum nos in Spiritu Sancto exsultamus. Isaac igitur Deus; Rebecca, gratia; Esau, Judaicus populus; Jacob, gentilis; venatio Esau forinseca, carnalium observationum custodia, et carnalis inscriptionis intelligentia. Pelles hædorum, confessio peccatorum; cibus, virtutum exercitatio; vinum, gaudium in Spiritu Sancto; vestimenta, bona opera; ager, cui benedixit Dominus, sancta Ecclesia, in qua redolet, testante beato Gregorio, flos uvæ per prædicationem, flos lilii per castitatem, flos violæ per humilitatem, flos spicæ per maturitatem bonorum operum, flos olivæ per misericordiam, flos rosæ per patientiam. Odivit Esau Jacob; odio habent populum Christianum ex gentibus collectum Judæi, videntes eum dominari sibi.[2]

Weber (*Praefigurationen*, pp. 17–20) undertakes to derive the allegories of the play largely from chapter xv of *De Trinitate et Operibus ejus Libri XLII*, by Rupert of Deutz, printed by Migne, *P.L.*, clxvii, 460. It is obvious that chapters xiii–xx of that work apply to the matter under discussion, but no more precisely, I think, than do parts of the other treatises cited above.

**Page 266, note 7.** A play upon the subject of Joseph and his brethren in the monastery of Heresburg in the year 1264 is recorded in the so-called *Annales Antiqui Corbeiæ Saxonicæ* as follows (G. W. Leibnitz, *Scriptorum Brunsvicensi Illustrantium Tomus secundus*, Hanover, 1710, p. 311):

[1] *Glossa Ordinaria*, i, 27, in Migne, *P.L.*, cxiii, 149–50.

[2] *Allegoriæ in Vetus Testamentum*, ii, 11, in Migne, *P.L.*, clxxv, 649.

MCCLXIV. Iuniores FF. in Heresburg sacram habuere comœdiam de Iosepho vendito et exaltato, quod vero reliqui Ordinis nostri Prælati male interpretati sunt.

This was, presumably, a play in Latin, but not necessarily for use in the church of the monastery. See Creizenach, i, 69; Chambers, ii, 60; Wright, p. xii. R. Masters (*A History of Corpus Christi . . . Cambridge*, Cambridge, 1753, part i, 5) records that, about the year 1350, William de Lenne and Isabel his wife, on joining the guild of Corpus Christi at Cambridge, 'expended *in ludo filiorum Israelis* half a mark'. Masters does not identify the 'entry-book' of the Corpus Christi guild from which he derives this record. Probably Creizenach (i, 69) is right in his inference that this was a vernacular play performed by laymen. See also Chambers, ii, 344. We are hardly concerned here with the non-dramatic *Versus de Ioseph* printed by E. Dümmler, in *Z.f.d.A.*, xl (1896), 375 sqq., and discussed by A. Wilmart, in *Revue bénédictine*, xxxiv (1922), 30–1.

**Page 290, note 5.** During the last decades of the nineteenth century Egerton MS 2615 was lost from the view of students of the drama, and its whereabouts were rediscovered by Chambers about the beginning of the present century. The MS is described by Chambers, i, 284–5, ii, 60; Danjou, pp. 70–1; Coussemaker, p. 322. The investigator should be warned that Danjou's text of the Beauvais play occupies 32 pages (1–32) which are inserted after p. 96 of the volume containing his monograph. The MS was written during the first half of the twelfth century, and probably within the period 1127–34.

**Page 303, note 1.** From an inventory of the treasury of the cathedral of Beauvais made in 1464 Desjardins (pp. 119, 169–70) cites the following description of a costume which, he infers, may have been used in the play of Daniel:

*Item* ung tissu noir de soye à usage de homme ferré tout autour d'argent lequel avoir au bout une petite chaenne laquelle estoit d'argent.

**Page 303, note 5.** Illuminating information concerning the cathedral school of Beauvais for the twelfth and thirteenth centuries seems not to be available. It is not found, for example, even in such likely places as the following: H. Omont, *Recherches sur la Bibliothèque de l'Église cathédrale de Beauvais*, in *Mémoires de l'Institut National de France: Académie des Inscriptions et Belles-Lettres*, xl (1916), 1–93; G. Robert, *Les Écoles et l'Enseignement de la Théologie pendant la première Moitié du xii^e^ Siècle*, Paris, 1909, pp. 10–5; Morel, *Les Écoles dans les anciens Diocèses de Beauvais, Noyon et Senlis*, in *Bulletin de la Société historique de Compiègne*, vii (1888), 39–197; Delettre, *Histoire du Diocèse de Beauvais*, 3 vols., Beauvais, 1842–3; Dejardins, pp. 113 sqq.; Charvet, pp. 3–10.

## CHAPTER XXVI

## THE MIRACLE PLAYS OF SAINT NICHOLAS

**Page 307, note 1.** The general background for the miracle plays treated in this chapter is supplied by G. R. Coffman, *A New Theory concerning the Origin of the Miracle Play*, Menasha, 1914, and by the same writer, *A New Approach to Mediaeval Latin Drama*, in *M.P.*, xxii (1924–5), 239–71. A corrective to one aspect of the first of these studies is attempted by Young, *Concerning the Origin of the Miracle Play*, in *The Manly Anniversary Studies in Language and Literature*, Chicago, 1923, pp. 254–68. See also Creizenach, i, 97–9; Chambers, ii, 58–60; Sepet, *Origines*, pp. 63–74, 168–75; Sepet, *Drame*, pp. 218–24; Weydig, pp. 7–20, 40–87, 94–7; Gayley, *Forefathers*, pp. 61–6; L. V. Gofflot, *Le Théâtre au Collège du Moyen Âge à nos Jours*, Paris, 1907, pp. 15–20; Crawford, *Nicholas*, pp. 7–17. The studies by Coffman, *Nomenclature*, and Manly, *Miracle Play*, are concerned chiefly with plays in the vernacular. The miracle plays of Fleury are discussed by Cuissard, pp. 290–9, and a thorough-going study of them by Dr. Otto E. Albrecht is in process of publication.

**Page 308, note 3.** A summary *vita* of St Nicholas, with references to authorities, is given by Holweck, *Dictionary*, p. 741. A noteworthy bibliography is provided by E. Marin, *Saint Nicolas, Évêque de Myre*, Paris, 1917, pp. ix–xvi. A convenient list of the texts of the legends of this saint is given by Bohnstedt, pp. 34–44. A survey of these, and of their inter-relations, is made by K. Fissen, *Das Leben des heiligen Nikolaus in der altfranzösischen Literatur und seine Quellen*, Göttingen, 1921, pp. 10–5, and by Marin, pp. 16–40. See also Weydig, pp. 42–4; Coffman, *New Theory*, p. 45; Ermini, *Nicola*, pp. 110–12; Kressner, pp. 34–5. I have not seen Ida del Valle de Paz, *La Leggenda di S. Nicola nella Tradizione poetica in Francia*, Florence, 1921. A useful collection of legends from all periods and authors is that of N. C. Falconius, *Sancti Confessoris Pontificis et celeberrimi Thaumaturgi Nicolai Acta Primigenia*, Naples, 1751. Some literary and historical consideration is given to the legends by E. Schnell, *Sanct Nicolaus, der heilige Bischof und Kinderfreund*, 6 vols., Brünn, 1883–6—especially in ii, 48–78. The work of N. Putignani, *Vindiciæ Vitæ et Gestorum S. Thaumaturgi Nicolai Archiepiscopi Myrensis*, Naples, 1753, does not bear essentially upon our present study. Unfortunately the *Acta Sanctorum* of the Bollandists has not yet reached Dec. 6, the feast of St Nicholas. For representations of the legends in plastic art see Künstle, pp. 459–64; Cahier, i, 92, 145, 303–4, 354, 409; ii, 449, 652; Mâle, *XIIIe Siècle*, pp. 385–8. As representing the basic sources of the plays treated here I use the ninth-century *Vita a Iohanne Diacono Neapolitano* as first printed in the fifteenth-century compilation of Boninus Mombritius. There can be no doubt that this *vita* records the legends in forms typical for Western Europe during the period just preceding the date of the first miracle plays, and its versions of *Tres Filiæ*, *Iconia Sancti Nicholai*, and *Filius Getronis* are as near to the plays in content as are any of the other narrative versions. For the text of Mombritius I use the Solesmes edition, *Boninus Mombritius: Sanctuarium seu Vitæ Sanctorum*, 2 vols., Paris, 1910. In my citations, however, I alter the punctuation.

**Page 310, note 4.** Reference may be made to several vague or unsupported conjectures as to the manner in which miracle plays arose. Gaston Paris (*La Littérature française au Moyen Âge*, Paris, 1905, p. 265) expresses his opinion in this indefinite form: 'Ils ⟨les *miracles*⟩ sont sortis des chants en l'honneur des saints ou des lectures sur leur vie qu'on faisait dans les églises.' Sepet (*Origines*, pp. 17–8) surmises that the miracle play may have arisen from a reciting in dialogue of parts of the *legenda* used as *lectiones* in Matins on saints' days: 'Il ne serait peut-être pas trop téméraire de chercher aussi dans les leçons et dans le procédé de récitation liturgique qui leur fut appliqué à l'époque susdite, la toute première origine des *Miracles* des saints et de la Sainte Vierge *par personnages*.' But no such dialogued *lectiones* for saints' days have been found. Other discredited theories of origin are treated by Coffman (*New Theory*, pp. 9–12) and Weydig (p. 40). Crawford (*Nicholas*, p. 17) seems to regard the plays as derivatives from tropes, sequences or other liturgical pieces. Ermini (*Nicola*, p. 117) infers that such miracle plays as those from Fleury arose as dramatic epilogues to *lectiones*.

**Page 311, note 5.** The dowry legend, or *Tres Filiæ*, is given as follows in Mombritius, ii, 297–9:

Talia eo cogitante, accidit ut quidam conuicaneus eius nimium locuples ad tantam ueniret inopiam, ut nec necessaria uitæ haberet. Quid plura? Ingruente inedia, tres uirgines, quas habebat filias, quarum nuptias etiam ignobiles uiri spernebant, fornicari constituit, ut earum saltem infami commercio infelicem ageret uitam. Proh pudor! Extemplo fama tanti mali, qua non uelocius ullum mobilitate uiget, totam pertulit urbem, et multiplici omnes sermone replebat. Quod ubi sanctus Nicolaus reperit, condoluit miserrimo homini, atque uirginum execrans stuprum decreuit omnino ex suis abundantiis earum supplere inopiam, ne puellæ nobilibus ortæ natalibus lupanari macularentur infamia. Sed cum nollet alium in suis factis nisi Christum habere contemplatorem, cœpit explorare temporum uices, quo id sic operaretur ut etiam eos lateret quibus benefaceret. Taliaque secum uoluens aiebat: Eia, famule Dei, exime pauperiem patris, exime filiarum scortum! Tellus, tuæ mentis hactenus sancto exculta uomere, duplum subito prorumpat in fructum, et ex uno famelici satietur ingluuies, et ex alio uirginum redimatur incœstus. Non occultes serentis Christi fruges, quæ carent zizania. Aperi thesaurum tuum, ubi pietatis gazæ resultant, nec paueas adulationis fomitem, quia non exurit flamma uiciorum diuitias quas approbat Christus. Non timet illa ædificatio ignem æternum quæ fabricatur opifici summo. Rumpe morulas omnes! Opus perfice bonum, ut uideant, imo sentiant homines et glorificent patrem tuum qui in cælis est. Inuenta ergo cuiusdam noctis hora, sumens non modicum aurum ligansque in panno, perrexit domum uiri. Qui undique circumspiciens, per fenestram, quæ competens uidebatur, clam introiecit, clam discessit. O nouam Iacob stropham! Ille commentatus est qualiter Laban mercedem non amitteret; hic autem ut cælestibus non priuaretur commodis. Ille in cannalibus decorticatas ponebat uirgas, ut uaria quæque acciperet; hic ut helyšiis uaria oblectamenta quiuerit adipisci, ædis inter claustra ligatum proiciet obrizum. Hic est, Iesu, magister bone, tuus non surdus auditor, qui iussis obtemperans tuis duo impleuit præcepta:

et miseratus est hominem mendicum, et opus sic prodidit dexteræ ut ignoraret sinistra. Mane itaque facto, cum surrexisset homo aurumque reperisset illud, diriguit primum ac tunc quanto gestiuit gaudio, quantasque Deo gratias egit, si quis uelit, ex huberibus eius lachrymis, quas magnitudo letitiæ fuderat, aduertere potest. Tamen aliquantisper sciscitandus est uir iste de inopinata sua exultatione. Dic, age, rogo te, homo, cur tanto exultas gaudio? Hactenus enim lugubrem uultum tuum ostendebas, nunc te hilarem cerno. Bene, inquit, lætari me uides, quia dominus clæmens nescio per quem præstitit uitæ meæ subsidium quo carere queam infamia quam inuitus incurrebam. Cui ergo ascribis impensam tibi benignitatem? Forsitan fidei tuæ? Prorsus illi, O temeraria lingua uiri! Ante paululum tantæ te ostendisti infidelitatis, ut temptatus non gratias Deo ageres, sed prostibulum esse decerneres templum Spiritus Sancti! Et nunc te astruis hoc dignum fuisse! Quale, inquis, templum Dei dicis? Vis? Nosce quale! Audi! Uas electionis clare illud commendet. Omnis, ait, qui caste uiuit templum est Dei, et sedes Spiritus Sancti. Si ita est, immo quia ita est, quamobrem tu filias tuas fornicari mandabas? Quia, inquis, inedia opprimebar. Et cur non laborabas manibus propriis sicut apostoli fecerunt, qui non tantum pro se, sed ut etiam haberent unde tribuerent necessitatem pacienti laborasse comprobantur. Nobilitas, ait, mea renuebat aliquod opus facere! Infelix! Si te illustrem consyderabas, cur puellas ex te genitas pomposo lenonum ministerio ignobilitari malebas? Disce ergo, miser, disce non tribuere fidei tuæ quæ sententiam meruit apostoli dicentis: Qui templum Dei uiolauerit, disperdet illum Deus. Sed large Dei clæmentiæ, qui non est passus diu contegi famuli sui lucernam sub modio, ne lux lateret in tenebris, sed ut posita super candelabrum[1] luceret omnibus qui sunt in domo Domini. Tu tantum reuoca filias. Esto pronubus copulæ iustæ, non leno commixtionis iniustæ. Trade maritis quas prosternebas fornicatoribus. Lætentur coniugio iusto, non deformentur concubitu iniusto. Præsto est, crede mihi, qui tibi dotem ministrat ut omnes connubio stabili iungere possis. Celebratis igitur ex more primogenitæ filiæ suæ nuptiis, cœpit homo diligenter inquirere quis esset qui inopiæ suæ tantam præstitisset humanitatem. Cumque diu talia moliretur, Nicolaus, Christi seruus, haud multo post triduo quo prius simile peregit opus. O uirum omni imbutum peritia omnique instructum scientia, qui, ut se utrumque testamentum suscipere profiteretur, non est contentus lege litteræ, sed annectit euangelicam gratiam ut duobus fluminibus uno ex meatu profluentibus arentis fidei ortulum bene irrigaret, ne ultra sentes falce pietatis incisæ lolio infande uisionis lætam ualerent atterere frugem. Vbi uero reddita est dies, et homo prosiliuit de stratu suo, inuenitque fului pondo metalli prioris æquale, tanto exultauit gaudio ut, si Homeri aut Maronis adesset facundia, loquacitas in tantarum magnitudine laudum exprimenda, puto, succubuisset. Sed nos non nulla orationis eius prosequentes cætera sagaci lectori melius sub silentio ad intelligendum relinquere quam indigare elegimus. Orauit autem sic: Domine, Domine, absque cuius nutu nec passer ad terram nec folium cadit arboris, precor clæmentiam tuam, ut tu, qui omnia nosti, ostendere digneris mihi peccatori, quis sit ille qui tanta bona erga me exhibere non desinit. Hæc uere, Domine, ideo peto, non ut temerario ausu pollutis[2]

[1] candelabrum] candelebrum (Mombritius).

[2] pollutis] polutis (Mombritius).

eum contingere quæram manibus, sed ut sciam famulum tuum qui inter homines degens, angelicam habet conuersationem, et magnificem nomen tuum benedictum in sæcula. Talibus dictis orabat, talibusque se hortabatur sermonibus: Auferam certe somnum ab oculis meis, excubabo sollicitus uigilansque pernoctabo; forsitan ostendet mihi Dominus seruum suum. Dixit, et dictum cœpit opere complere. Interea, paucis admodum euolutis diebus, ecce cultor æternitatis aduenit Nicolaus, et iteratæ uicis factum trino supplere cupiens numero æquale duorum iactauit talentum. Cuius sonitu excitatus homo, statim egressus, iam uadentem iamque fugientem tali subsequebatur uoce: Siste gradum, neque enim aspectui te subtrahæ nostro; olim te concupiui cernere. Sic fatus ocyor aduolat, spatioque correpto Nicolaum agnouit per umbras. Moxque humi prostratus osculari satagebat pedes eius. Quod sanctus pio ut erat pectore fieri prohibuit. Sed breuiter allocutus exegit ab eo ne cuiquam dum uitales carperet auras Nicolaum huius rei indicaret auctorem.

**Page 311, note 6.** Brit. Mus. Add. MS 22414, in the upper margin of fol. 1 r, has a heading beginning thus: *Lib̄ ep̄i* ⟨altered from *sc̄i*⟩ *Godehardi in hild̄.* Concerning Godehardus, bishop of Hildesheim (1022–38), and the possible relationship of this MS to him, see Coffman, *New Approach*, pp. 252–6, and Coffman, *Hildesheim*, pp. 269–75. The date of the MS, and of the text of the plays on fol. 3 v–4 r, has been discussed by Dümmler, in *Z.f.d.A.*, xxxv (1891), 401, and xxxvi (1892), 239; Coffman, *New Approach*, p. 245; Weydig, p. 47. The copying of the MS as a whole is assigned to the eleventh century in the official description, *Catalogue of Additions to the Manuscripts in the British Museum in the Years 1854–60: Additional MSS. 19720–24026* [London], 1875, p. 643, and this has been generally accepted as the date of the text of the plays. Aspects of their versification, however, point to the end of the eleventh century or the beginning of the twelfth as the date of the composition of the plays. For discussions of the plays themselves see Creizenach, i, 99; Dümmler, in *Z.f.d.A.*, xxxv (1891), 401–2, and xxxvi (1892), 238–9; E. Schröder, in *Z.f.d.A.*, xxxvi (1892), 239–40; Chambers, ii, 59–60; Coffman, *New Theory*, pp. 61–2; Weydig, pp. 46–7, 49–50, 53–60, 75–6. In regard to the cathedral school at Hildesheim see Detten, pp. 20–34.

**Page 329, note 1.** It is clear that the monasteries rather early conceived of St Nicholas as especially devoted to literary studies, for one of the most popular of his sequences, found in numerous MSS of the eleventh century, contains these verses (*A.H.*, liv, 95):

Adolescens amplexatur literarum studia,
Alienus et immunis ab omni lascivia.

In the form used in the plays under discussion the story probably arose as a modification of some established legend of St Nicholas, or as a misinterpretation of an iconographic representation. It may be an adaptation to the *clerici* of the legend of the saint's rescuing three officers condemned to death under Constantine, or under Eustathius, governor of Myra. See Mombritius, ii, 302–5; Cahier, i, 303–4, 354; S. Baring-Gould, *The Lives of the Saints*, xv, London, 1914, p. 67. In later versions of the story of the *clerici*, the murdered scholars are said to have been put into a pickling-tub, and representations of St Nicholas standing beside such a vessel containing three human figures are common in the later Middle Ages. Probably this iconographic design represented originally three converted pagans in a baptismal font, and the story of the three *clerici* may have arisen as a mistaken interpretation of it. See G. G. Coulton, *Art and the Reformation*, Oxford, 1928, pp. 281–3, 555–6; Meller, p. 16; Künstle, p. 461; Mâle, *XIII*e *Siècle*, pp. 338–9. For additional conjectures see Ermini, *Nicola*, pp. 117–9; P. Aebischer, in *Archivum Romanicum*, xv (1931), 383–99; Chambers, i, 369–70.

**Page 337, note 4.** The legend *Iconia Sancti Nicholai* is given as follows in Mombritius, ii, 306–7:

Cum de Affricæ partibus Vandalorum[1] exercitus applicuisset ad terram Calabrindem, atque eandem regionem igne succenderent, reperta est ibi a quodam barbaro in cuiusdam christicolæ domo sancti Nicolai imago in tabula honeste depicta. Quam protinus in sinu suo proiecit et abscondit, quamuis ab eo ignoraretur omnino quid esset. Cum autem peruenisset ad eos qui christicolas captiuos deducebant uinctos, interrogauit unum ex eis et ait: Rogo ut mihi indicetur cuius est figura in hac tabula tam pulchre depicta. Et hæc dicens demonstrauit eis achonam. Cum ergo eam contemplati essent Christiani, cum gemitu et lachrymis dixerunt: Imago hæc quam cernimus Sancti Nicolai dicitur, qui multis miraculis et uirtutibus apud Deum et homines existens clarus manifeste edocet se uiuere etiam post sepulchrum. Cumque uero hoc auditu percepisset ille barbarus, continuo abscondit eam propter suos socios, nemini ex hoc aliquid pandens. Cum autem reuersus esset exercitus Uandalorum in Aphricam cum plurimis captiuis et spoliis multis, rediit et ipse barbarus, qui Sancti Nicolai habebat tabulam in domum suam. Erat autem ipse thelonarius. Quadam autem die tulit ipsam achonam et posuit eam ante thelonarium suum, ubi erant omnia quæ habebat: aurum, et argentum, uestes. Et sic locutus est ei dicens: Nicolae, habeto custodiam super theloneum hoc, nam ego alibi necesse habeo proficisci. Hæc locutus imagini, discessit apertum omnino relinquens thelonæum, securus proficiscens quasi plurimos ibi custodes dimitteret. Cum autem secus eundem thelonæum latrones transirent et uidissent apertum et neminem custodem ibidem esse, dixerunt ad inuicem, ut uenientes nocte eadem diriperent omnia quæque intrinsecus erant posita. Quod ita factum est. Nam uenientes nocte omnia abstulerunt, aurum, argentum, uestes, et cætera, et sic profecti sunt. Sola achona deforis pendens superstes remansit. Hæc autem Dei dispensatione agebantur ut huiuscemodi occasione reperiretur quanti meriti Nicolaus esset, et apud Africanas regiones manifeste clares⟨c⟩eret. Veniente autem barbaro, cuius theloneum erat, reperit eum uacuum, nil omnino habentem nisi ipsum Sancti Nicholai achonam. Tunc plorans et gemens uæhementissimos stridores emittebat, et turbido aspectu conuersus in faciem imaginis beati Nicolai, quasi ad uiuentem hominem et ratione utentem, hæc uerba proferebat dicens: O Nicolae, bonum te custodem thelonæi mei posui. Quid fecisti? Redde mihi res meas; alioquin cædo te flagellis. Et cum hæc diceret, accepto flagello, tundebat Sancti Nicolai imaginem.

[1] Vandalorum] Vandolorum (Mombritius).

Cum uero fatigatus esset cædendo eam dixit ei: Certe in igne te proiiciam, si non reddideris causam meam. Piissimus autem confessor beatissimus Nicolaus nimia miseratione ductus super achonam suam, ac si ipse flagellis cæderetur, sub festinatione ad locum accessit propius, ubi latrones cuncta diuidebant quæ de illius Saraceni thelonæo abstulerant. Tunc dixit ad eos Sanctus Nicolaus: O infelices et miseri, quid facitis? Numquid ignoratis quoniam ego ipse ibidem eram quando hoc malum perpetrastis? Nam oculi mei conspexerunt quando has et illas res abstulistis. Quantitatem et numerum[1] etiam cunctarum rerum quas de thelonæo abstulerant singillatim eis exponens, addidit dicens: Scitote autem, quoniam furtum quod perpetrastis, si non mihi acquieueritis ut reuocetis cuncta quæ abstulistis, ego illud publice manifestare curabo. Nam sub mea cura uniuersa fuerunt posita, et ideo pro uestro scelere ego innocens quam grauiter flagellis cæsus sum. Credite mihi, quia nullomodo uobis parcam, si meis non acquiescitis consiliis, sed crastina die morti tradere uos faciam. Illi autem fures cum uiderent se depræhensos, existimantes quempiam fuisse de populis, qui eos explorauisset, nimium mente consternati, et ultra quam credi potest exterriti, uæhementer metu mortis coacti, per tetræ noctis silentia reportauerunt omnia, et in thelonæo reposuerunt. Mane autem facto, cum uenisset barbarus et uideret cunctam substantiam quam amiserat, flære cœpit præ gaudio, cui tale miraculum fuerat demonstratum per Sanctum Nicolaum. Tunc appræhensa imagine, deosculari eam cœpit dicens: O sancte Nicolae, fidelis et iuste, piissime et misericordissime serue Dei excelsi, quam sublimis, quam magnus, quam præpotens factus es, proximusque et familiaris Deo regi immortali, cui uiuens militare non cessasti, a quo potestatem accepisse comprobaris, ut talia facere possis qualia mihi gentili ex ære insensibili patrare dignatus es! Ab ista namque die credo in Christum, et in te. Credidit autem in Christum Dominum, et baptizatus est ipse et domus eius tota; et construxit ecclesiam in honorem Sancti Nicolai. In qua moratus est cum uxore sua et filiis pariterque glorificantes Dominum et Sanctum Nicolaum.

**Page 351, note 4.** The legend *Filius Getronis* is given as follows in Mombritius, ii, 307–9:

Sed si uestre caritati durius non est, uolo adhuc de mirabilibus beati Nicolai uobis enarrare miraculum. Beatus itaque et electus Domini nostri Iesu Christi, Nicolaus episcopus, dum uitam finiret, et de hac luce migraret ad Dominum, animam eius qui illi dedit eam, ad se de hac luce recepit. Clerici nanque et sacerdotes sui dum hoc conspicerent, gratias egerunt Deo, qui ita sui confessoris animam cum gloria eleuaret ad cælum. Tunc accepta aqua ut corpus lauarent beati Nicolai, appræhenderunt lintiamina sancti corporis et expoliare cœperunt. Erat autem ibidem quidam homo nomine Cethron, et cœpit rogare eosdem sacerdotes et clericos ut ostenderent in eum misericordiam, et ut aliquid de sancti uiri uestimentis sibi dari debuissent. Et dicebat eis cum lachrymis et desiderio magno: Ego ueni benedictionem a domino meo, Nicolao, accipere, et concessum mihi non fuit ut uel uitam eius conspicerem. Obsecro uos ut uel aliquid de uestimentis eius sancti corporis mihi præbeatis, ut id habeam tantum in honorem sanctissimi

[1] numerum] munerum (Mombritius).

domini mei. Presbyteri uero et clerici beatissimi Nicolai hæc audientes, et talem petitionem et desyderium cognoscentes, dederunt ei unum de lintiaminibus sanctissimi uiri. Cethron autem ut accepit uestimentum beati Nicolai, cum desyderio magno tulit lucellum nouum, ubi nullus usus hominum fuit, et cum gaudio reclusit illud, et ibat lætus dicens: Gratias tibi ago, Domine, quia de confessore tuo sanctissimo reliquias porto. Obsecro, Domine, ut per has beati Nicolai reliquias de lumbis meis des mihi filium. Reuersus denique Cethron in ciuitatem suam, quæ dicitur Excoranda, ad uxorem suam, quæ dicebatur Euphrosina, cœpit dicere: Ecce reliquias beati Nicolai Archiepiscopi quem tu desyderasti uidere. Deprecemur illum, ut per suas sacras reliquias aperiat Deus uuluam tuam et de tuis uisceribus det nobis filium. Tunc Euphrosina repleta gaudio dicebat: Domine, tibi gloria, qui nobis peccatoribus tantam gratiam concessisti, ut de beati Nicolai haberemus reliquiis. Et rogare cœpit uirum suum Cethron, ut ecclesiam in honore beati Nicolai construeret, ut per suas orationes adimpleret Deus desyderium suum. Cuius precibus Cethron benigne fauens, ecclesiam fabricare cœpit foras portas ciuitatis in parte orientis quasi stadiis duobus. Quæ dum completa fuisset, dedicauit eam Appolonius episcopus eiusdem ciuitatis in honorem beati Nicolai, in qua recundit linteamen illud. Tantum autem odorem cœperunt habere reliquie uestimenti sancti uiri, quod usque ad duo completa stadia locus ille splenderet miraculis, ut undecunque ibidem languentes[1] uenirent, statim Deus per beati Nicolai merita beneficia præstaret. Cæcos illuminabat, surdis auditum præbebat, et qui spiritus diuersis iniquitatibus habebant, sanabantur. Omnes denique gratias Deo et beatissimo Nicolao cœperunt agere, qui tanta miracula operari dignatus est in populo suo per seruum suum Nicolaum. Ornauit itaque Cethron latera muri coronis aureis, et decantabat Domino Deo laudem quottidie, et dicebat: Domine meus piissime et misericordissime, Nicolae, ego seruus tuus peto, ut adimpleas desyderium meum et depreceris pro me Dominum, ut de carne mea det mihi filium. Cumque quottidie hæc oraret, concepit Euphrosyna ex eo filium, et expleto tempore peperit eum in sexto die mensis Decembris, et uocauit eum Adeodatum, et ad omnes dicebat gratanter: Quia per beati Nicolai reliquias dedit mihi pius Dominus hunc quem conspicitis filium. Erat enim infans clarissimus et speciosus ualde. Post hæc omni anno cum lætitia magna cœperunt celebrare sollemnitatem beati Nicolai in anniuersario natiuitatis filii sui. Cum autem complesset puer annos septem, uenit Cethron et Euphrosyna cum filio suo et cum his qui inuitati erant ad festiuitatem beati Nicolai. Venerunt autem et Agareni et prædati sunt omnes uiros ac mulieres, inter quos etiam et puer est captus filius[2] Cethronis. Cethron uero cum uxore sua liberatus est. Oblito puero præ pauore et timore, uenerunt in ciuitatem suam Excorandum. Agareni uero duxerunt captiuos in Babyloniam, et diuidentibus inter se captos peruenit puer Adeodatus, filius Cethronis, in manum regis Marmorini. Euphrosina uero et Cethron cœperunt filium quærere. Et cum non inuenissent, sciderunt uestimenta sua et capillos cœperunt euellere, et facies suas percutientes atque lachrymantes, mater dicebat: Heu, heu, mihi, unice fili mi, quid miseræ matri, fili, de te accidit! Ego misera cum petitione magna a domino meo Nicolao cum uiro meo petii,

[1] languentes] langueutes (Mombritius).

[2] filius] filins (Mombritius).

et ille rogauit Dominum meum, et te nobis donauit. Non ideo petiuimus, ut oculis nostris uideremus de te talem perditionem, sed gaudium et exultationem in uita nostra de te expectauimus, et optabamus ut tu clauderes oculos nostros. Ecce nunc ego uacua sum de te, fili mi! O domine meus, beate Nicolae, confessor Christi, quia per te illum habui, tu illum mihi redde, ut uideam illum antequam moriar. Per tuam sanctam intercessionem uenter meus dolorem perpessus, et caput meum infirmatum est. Et postquam illum filium meum ante oculos meos uidi, præ gaudio non memini pressuræ sed gaudens permansi. O sancte Nicolae, miserearis miseriarum mearum, quia te sciente ego misera illum nutriui, ego laui, et nunc plenum est pectus meum doloribus, quia non uideo unicum filium meum. Sancte Nicolae, obsecro, redde filium meum, ut sicut me lætam fecisti quando illum mihi dedisti, ita et nunc quando in captiuitate est destitutus, obsecro, ut et certiorem me ex illo facias et reddas filium meum. Carnem non comedam, vinum non bibam quousque filium meum non uideam. Tunc cœpit Euphrosyna ieiunare et orare, et non comedebat nisi tribus in hebdomade diebus, et semper dicebat: Beate Nicolae, redde, obsecro, filium meum. Cum peruenisset autem propinquius sancte solemnitati beatissimi Nicolai, die quinto mense Decembrio, cœpit dicere uxori suæ, Euphrosyne, Cethron: Mulier, acquiesce consiliis meis, et pergamus ad beatissimi Nicolai sollemnitatem, et quidquid Dominus dederit nobis, pauperibus erogemus, et patrem nostrum sanctissimum rogemus. Forsitan sicut liberauit tres illos innocentes de laqueo mortis et de ira Constantini imperatoris et ad salutem adduxit, ita filium nostrum reuocabit. Credo equidem quia ab illo hæc mihi inspiratio euenit. Euphrosyna denique, ubi talia audiuit, commota sunt uiscera eius, et cœpit flære et facere sicut uir eius præceperat. Cumque in ecclesiam ingressa fuisset,[1] expandit ad cælum manus suas dicens: Domine Iesu Christe, Fili Dei uiui, respice in me peccatricem, exaudi me, et per merita huius beatissimi Nicolai sicut liberasti multos uiros de pelago mortis, et ad salutem adduxisti et tres innocentes de periculo mortis, sic libera, Domine, filium meum de manu regis Agarenorum, et duc eum ad me, ut cognoscamus et credamus quia tu es qui omnia potes, et uales eripere omnes qui in te confidunt a nexu, et uinculo mortis liberare, et es mirabilis in sanctis tuis in sempiternum, qui uiuis et regnas in sæcula sæculorum, Amen. Cumque orationem complesset, salutauit omnes, et refectionem cœpit parare clericis et pauperibus qui[2] ad solemnitatem uenerant sanctissimi Nicolai. Sacerdotes uero et leuitæ simul omnes canere cœperunt horas ad laudem Domini et beati confessoris et episcopi. Post actas horas omnes se ordinantes pariter cibum cœperunt inuicem sumere, et statim res mira et inaudita secuta est. Ipsa hora qua sacerdotes cibum sumere cœperunt in solemnitate beati Nicolai, eadem hora Rex qui erat in Babylonia, in cuius obsequio erat infans, cœpit dicere militibus suis atque magistratibus et ducibus: Dico uobis, beatissimi mei, quia ab hora qua natus sum usque modo non fuit mihi unquam comedendi uoluntas sicut modo est. Parate mihi cum festinatione cibum quo uesci debeam, et mensam ponite. Ministri uero cum talia audissent, posuerunt mensam, et omnes pariter cœperunt cibum sumere. Cœpit Rex post hæc clamare et dicere: Poculum mihi præbete, quia uelociter bibere cupio. Tunc infans qui erat in obsequio suo, cum talia audisset, parare

[1] fuisset] fnisset (Mombritius). [2] pauperibus qui] panperibus qni (Mombritius).

scyphum et aquam mundare cœpit, et subito commemorare inter se cœpit, et dicere: Heu me, quia expletus est annus quo captiuus ueni in obsequium regis. Et longa suspiria trahebat in sensu suo. Rex uero cum talia audisset suspiria, cœpit dicere ei: Dic mihi pro qua causa sic fortiter suspirasti? Infans uero tremefactus cum timore cœpit ei dicere: Domine Rex, recordatus sum subito in mea mente quia hodie expletus est annus, quo hic apud te captiuus existo, quia pater meus et mater mea in hac die faciebant magnam sollemnitatem in ecclesia Sancti Nicolai, domini nostri. Rex cum talia audisset, respondit et dixit ei: O miselli, quid uobis prodest ista cogitare cum ego uos apud me habeo? Et quis est qui de manu mea uos tollere possit, quandiu deus noster uult facere ut uos habere debeamus? Fer mihi bibere. Infans accepit scyphum ad potum parandum et aquam in manu sua ad lauandum scyphum. Subito uir Dei, Nicolaus, affuit et appræhendidit infantem per uerticem capilli capitis sui et reportauit et reddidit illum matri suæ. Cumque reficerentur omnes extra fores ecclesiæ, uiderunt illum ibidem stantem, et scyphum et aquam in manu tenentem, qui euntes interrogare cæperunt eum dicentes: Quis es tu? Et ille dicit: Ego sum Adeodatus, Cethronis filius. Cum audisset hæc Euphrosyna mater eius, commota sunt quippe uiscera eius; super eum cœpit flære præ gaudio, et currens amplexata est eum, et tenens collum filii sui, gaudere cœpit et dicere: Gratias tibi ago, Domine Iesu Christe, Fili Dei uiui, qui non me fraudasti a gratia tua, sed exaudisti filium meum, et uidi illum oculis meis antequam me uocares de hoc sæculo, qui cum Patre et Spiritu Sancto uiuis et regnas Deus per omnia sæcula sæculorum, Amen.

## CHAPTER XXVII

## PLAYS ON SUBJECTS FROM ESCHATOLOGY: THE WISE AND FOOLISH VIRGINS—ANTICHRIST

**Page 361, note 4.** Concerning descriptions of Paris MS lat. 1139 see above, p. 453. Photographic facsimiles of the pages occupied by the *Sponsus* are given by E. Monaci, *Facsimili di Documenti per la Storia delle Lingue e delle Letterature romanze*, Rome [1910], plates 37–42. These facsimiles are decidedly superior to those of Coussemaker, *Histoire*, plates xiii–xviii. A diplomatic print of the *Sponsus* is given by W. Foerster and E. Koschwitz, *Altfranzösisches Uebungsbuch*, 6th ed. by A. Hilka, Leipzig, 1921, cols. 91–8, 293–8, along with a virtually complete bibliography of earlier editions and textual commentaries. The same print and most of the collateral material are provided by E. Koschwitz, *Les plus anciens Monuments de la Langue française: Textes diplomatiques*, Leipzig, 1913, pp. 48–53. The text and the music are studied at length, with abundant bibliography, by L.-P. Thomas, *La Versification et les Leçons douteuses du Sponsus (Texte Roman)*, in *Romania*, liii (1927), 43–81; and by the same scholar, *Les Strophes et la Composition du Sponsus (Textes latin et roman)*, in *Romania*, lv (1929), 45–112. I am very grateful to Monsieur Thomas for allowing me to see the MS of this second study in advance of publication. The music is considered also by Liuzzi, *Vergini*, pp. 87–96. For literary comment see especially Chambers, ii, 61–2; Petit de Julleville, i, 27–34; Fischer, pp. 9–19; Sepet, *Drame*, pp. 24–9, 113–20. Byzantine influence upon the play is inferred by Liuzzi, *Vergini*, pp. 96–108.

**Page 368, note 6.** In the Sarum Breviary the eighth lesson of Matins on the feast of All Saints (Nov. 1) is followed by this rubric:[1]

Ista præcedens Lectio[2] legatur ab uno Puero, ut prædictum est; et interim procedant quinque Pueri de vestiario ordinatim in superpelliciis, capitibus velatis amictibus albis, et cereos ardentes in manibus tenentes, ad gradum chori accedant. Finita Lectione, simul incipiant ad altare conversi Responsorium. *R.* 8. *Audivi vocem de cælo venientem: Venite, omnes virgines sapientissimæ; oleum recondite in vasis vestris dum sponsus advenerit. V. Media nocte clamor factus est: Ecce sponsus venit. Oleum recondite.*

The five choir-boys, with their heads covered by amices, and with lights in their hands, obviously symbolize—and even impersonate—the five wise virgins. For reflections of the theme in the modern liturgy see Liuzzi, *Vergini*, p. 82.

**Page 370, note 2.** The letter of Adso concerning Antichrist is edited as follows by Sackur, pp. 104–13:

EPISTOLA ADSONIS AD GERBERGAM REGINAM DE ORTU ET TEMPORE ANTICHRISTI

Excellentissimæ reginæ ac regali dignitate pollenti Deo dilectæ omnibusque sanctis amabili, monachorum matri et sanctarum duci, dominæ reginæ Gerbergæ frater Adso suorum omnium servorum ultimus gloriam et pacem sempiternam.

Ex quo, domina mater, misericordiæ vestræ germen promerui, semper vobis in omnibus fidelis fui tanquam proprius servus. Unde quamvis indignæ sint apud Dominum preces orationis meæ, tamen pro vobis et pro seniore vestro domino rege, necnon et pro filiorum vestrorum incolumitate Dei nostri misericordiam exoro, ut vobis et culmen imperii in hac vita dignetur conservare, et vos faciat in cœlis post hanc vitam secum feliciter regnare. Quoniam si Dominus vobis prosperitatem dederit et filiis vitam longiorem, scimus indubitanter et credimus ecclesiam Dei exaltandam et nostræ religionis ordinem magis ac magis multiplicandum. Hoc ego fidelis vester opto et valde desidero; qui si potuissem vobis totum regnum acquirere, libentissime fecissem, sed quia illud facere non valeo, pro salute vestra filiorumque vestrorum Dominum exorabo, ut gratia eius in operibus vestris semper vos præveniat, et gloria illius pie et misericorditer subsequatur, ut divinis intenta mandatis possitis adimplere bona, quæ desideratis, unde corona vobis detur regni cœlestis. Igitur quia pium studium habetis scripturas audire et frequenter loqui de nostro redemptore, sive etiam scire de Antichristi impietate et persecutione, necnon et potestate eius et generatione, sicut mihi servo vestro

[1] *Sarum Breviary*, iii, 975. See Feasey, *Easter Sepulchre*, pp. 495–6.

[2] The eighth lesson is from a homily on the wise and foolish virgins.

dignata estis præcipere, volui aliqua vobis scribere et de Antichristo ex parte certam reddere, quamvis non indigeatis a me hoc audire, quæ apud vos habetis prudentissimum pastorem domnum Roriconem, clarissimum speculum totius sapientiæ atque eloquentiæ hac valde nostra ætate.

Ergo de Antichristo scire volentes primo notabitis, quare sic vocatus sit. Ideo scilicet, quia Christo in cunctis contrarius erit, id est Christo contraria faciet. Christus venit humilis, ille venturus est superbus. Christus venit humiles erigere, peccatores iustificare; ille e contra humiles deiciet, peccatores magnificabit, impios exaltabit semperque vitia quæ sunt contraria virtutibus docebit. Legem euangelicam dissipabit, demonum culturam in mundo revocabit, gloriam propriam quæret et omnipotentem Deum se nominabit. Hic itaque Antichristus multos habet suæ malignitatis ministros, ex quibus iam multi in mundo precesserunt, qualis fuit Antiochus, Nero, Domitianus. Nunc quoque nostro tempore multos Antichristos novimus esse. Quicumque enim sive laicus, sive canonicus sive monachus contra iustitiam vivit et ordinis sui regulam inpugnat et quod bonum est blasphemat, Antichristus est et minister sathanæ.

Sed iam de exordio Antichristi videamus. Non autem quod dico ex proprio sensu excogito vel fingo, in libris diligenter relegendo hæc omnia scripta invenio.

Sicut ergo auctores nostri dicunt, Antichristus ex populo Iudeorum nascetur de tribu scilicet Dan secundum prophetiam dicentem: *Fiat Dan coluber in via, cerastes in semita.* Sicut enim serpens in via sedebit et in semita erit, ut eos, qui per semitas iustitiæ ambulant, feriat et veneno suæ malitiæ occidat. Nascetur autem ex patris et matris copulatione, sicut et alii homines, non, ut quidam dicunt, de sola virgine. Sed tamen totus in peccato concipietur, in peccato generabitur et in peccato nascetur. In ipso vero conceptionis suæ initio diabolus simul introibit in uterum matris eius et ex virtute diaboli confovebitur et contutabitur in ventre matris et virtus diaboli semper cum illo erit. Et sicut in ventrem matris domini nostri Iesu Christi spiritus sanctus venit et eam sua virtute obumbravit et divinitate replevit, ut de spiritu sancto conciperet et quod nasceretur divinum esset et sanctum: ita quoque diabolus in matrem Antichristi descendet et totam eam replebit, totam circumdabit, totam tenebit, totam interius et exterius possidebit, ut diabolo per hominem co-operante concipiet, et quod natum fuerit, totum sit iniquum, totum malum, totum perditum. Unde et ille homo filius perditionis appellatur, quia in quantum poterit genus humanum perdet et ipse in novissimo perdetur.

Ecce audistis, qualiter nascatur, audite etiam locum, ubi nasci debeat. Nam sicut dominus et redemptor noster Bethleem sibi prævidit, ut ibi pro nobis humanitatem assumeret et nasci dignaretur, sic diabolus illi homini perdito, qui Antichristus dicitur, locum novit aptum, unde radix omnium malorum oriri debeat, scilicet civitatem Babiloniæ. In hac enim civitate, quæ quondam fuit inclita et gloriosa urbs gentilium et caput regni Persarum, Antichristus nascetur, in civitatibus Bethsaida et Corozaim nutriri et conversari dicitur, quibus civitatibus Dominus in euangelio improperat dicens: *Ve tibi Bethsaida, ve tibi Corozaim.* Habebit autem Antichristus magos, maleficos, diuinos et incantatores, qui eum diabolo inspirante nutrient et docebunt in omni iniquitate, falsitate et nefaria arte. Et maligni spiritus erunt duces eius et socii semper et comites indivisi. Deinde Hierosolimam veniens omnes christianos, quos ad se convertere non poterit, per varia tormenta iugulabit, et suam sedem in templo sancto parabit. Templum etiam destructum, quod Salomon Deo ædificavit, in statum suum restaurabit et circumcidet se et filium Dei omnipotentis se esse mentietur.

Reges autem et principes primum ad se convertet et deinde per illos ceteros populos. Loca vero, per quæ dominus Iesus Christus ambulavit, [calcabit] et prius destruet, quod Dominus illustravit, deinde per universum orbem nuntios mittet et prædicatores suos. Prædicatio autem eius et potestas tenebit a mari usque ad mare, ab oriente usque ad occidentem, ab aquilone usque ad septentrionem. Faciet quoque signa multa, miracula magna et inaudita. Faciet ignem de cœlo terribiliter venire, arbores subito florere et arescere, mare turbari et subito tranquillari; naturas in diversis figuris mutari, aquarum cursus et ordinem converti, aera ventis et commotionibus multis agitari et cetera innumerabilia et stupenda, mortuos etiam in conspectu hominum resuscitari, *ita ut in errorem inducantur, si fieri potest, etiam electi.* Nam quando tanta ac talia signa viderint etiam illi qui perfecti et electi Dei sunt, dubitabunt, utrum ipse sit Christus, qui in fine mundi secundum scripturas venturus est, an non.

Excitabit autem persecutionem sub omni cęlo super christianos et omnes electos. Eriget itaque se contra fideles tribus modis, id est terrore, muneribus et miraculis. Dabit in se credentibus auri atque argenti copias. Quos vero muneribus corrumpere non poterit, terrore superabit. Quos autem terrere non poterit, signis et miraculis seducere temptabit. Quos nec signis poterit, in conspectu omnium miserabili morte cruciatos crudeliter necabit. Tunc erit talis tribulatio, qualis non fuit super terram ex tempore, quo gentes esse cęperunt usque ad tempus illud. Tunc qui in agro sunt fugient ad montes dicentes: 'Cadite super nos', et collibus: 'Cooperite nos', et qui supra tectum, non descendet in domum suam, ut tollat aliquid de ea. Tunc omnis fidelis christianus, qui inventus fuerit, aut Deum negabit aut sive per ferrum sive per ignem fornacis sive per serpentes sive per bestias sive per aliquid aliud quodlibet genus tormentorum interibit, si in fide permanserit.

Hæc autem tam terribilis et timenda tribulatio tribus annis manebit in toto mundo et dimidio. Tunc breviabuntur dies propter electos. Nisi enim Dominus abbreviasset dies, non fuisset salva omnis caro. Tempus siquidem, quando idem Antichristus veniat vel quando dies incipiat apparere iudicii, Paulus apostolus in epistola ad Thessalonicenses: *Rogamus vos per adventum Domini nostri Iesu Christi*, manifestat eo loco, ubi ait: *quoniam, nisi venerit discessio primum et revelatus fuerit homo peccati et filius perditionis.* Scimus enim, quoniam post regnum Grecorum sive etiam post regnum Persarum, ex quibus unum quodque suo tempore magna gloria viguit et maxima potentia floruit ad ultimum quoque post cetera regna, regnum Romanorum cępit, quod fortissimum omnium superiorum regnorum fuit et omnia regna terrarum sub dominatione sua habuit, omnesque populorum nationes Romanis subiacebant et serviebant eis sub tributo. Inde ergo dicit Paulus apostolus, Antichristum non antea in mundum esse venturum, nisi venerit discessio primum, id est, nisi prius discesserint omnia regna a Romano imperio, quę pridem subdita erant. Hoc autem tempus nondum venit, quia, licet videamus Romanorum regnum ex maxima parte destructum, tamen, quamdiu reges Francorum duraverint, qui Romanum imperium tenere debent, Romani regni dignitas ex toto non peribit, quia in regibus suis stabit. Quidam vero doctores nostri dicunt, quod unus ex regibus Francorum Romanum imperium ex integro tenebit, qui in novissimo tempore erit. Et ipse erit maximus et omnium regum ultimus. Qui postquam regnum feliciter gubernaverit, ad ultimum Ierosolimam veniet et in monte Oliveti sceptrum et coronam suam deponet. Hic erit finis et consummatio Romanorum christianorumque imperii. Statimque secundum prędictam Pauli apostoli sententiam Antichristum dicunt mox affuturum, et tunc revelabitur quidem homo peccati, Antichristus videlicet, qui, licet homo sit, fons tamen erit omnium peccatorum; et filius perditionis, id est filius diaboli, non per naturam, sed per imitationem, quia per omnia adimplebit diaboli voluntatem; quia plenitudo diabolicę potestatis et totius mali ingenii corporaliter habitabit in illo, in quo erunt omnes thesauri maliciæ et iniquitatis absconditi.

Qui adversatur, id est contrarius est Christo Deo omnibusque membris eius, et extollitur, id est in superbiam erigitur super omne quod dicitur Deus, id est supra omnes deos gentium, Herculem videlicet, Apollinem, Iovem, Mercurium, quos pagani deos esse existimant. Super omnes istos deos extolletur Antichristus, quia maiorem et fortiorem se iis omnibus faciet: et non solum supra hos, sed etiam supra omne quod colitur, id est supra sanctam Trinitatem, quæ solummodo colenda et adoranda est ab omni creatura sua. Ita se extollet, ut in templo Dei sedeat, ostendens se, tanquam sit Deus. Nam sicut supra diximus, in civitate Babilonię natus Ierosolimam veniens circumcidet se dicens Iudeis: 'Ego sum Christus vobis repromissus, qui ad salutem vestram veni, ut vos, qui dispersi estis, congregem et defendam.' Tunc confluent ad eum omnes Iudei existimantes deum suscipere, sed suscipient diabolum, sive etiam in templo Dei sedebit Antichristus id est in sancta ecclesia, omnes christianos faciens martires et elevabitur et magnificabitur, quia in ipso erit caput omnium malorum diabolus, qui est rex super omnes filios superbiæ.

Sed ne subito et inprovise Antichristus veniat et totum simul omne genus humanum suo errore decipiat et perdat, ante eius exortum duo magni prophetæ mittentur in mundum, Enoch scilicet et Elias, qui contra impetum Antichristi fideles Dei divinis armis premunient et instruent eos et confortabunt et preparabunt electos ad bellum, docentes et predicantes tribus annis et dimidio; filios autem Israel quicunque eo tempore fuerint inventi, hi duo maximi prophetæ et doctores ad fidei gratiam convertent et a pressura tanti turbinis in parte electorum insuperabilem reddent. Tunc implebitur quod scriptura dicit: *Si fuerit numerus filiorum Israel sicut arena maris, reliquiæ salvæ fient.* Postquam vero per tres annos et dimidium prædicationem suam compleverint, mox incipiet excandescere Antichristi persecutio et contra eos primum Antichristus sua arma corripiet eosque interficiet, sicut in apocalipsi dicitur: *Et cum finierint*, inquit, *testimonium suum, bestia, quæ ascendet de abisso, faciet adversus eos bellum et vincet eos et occidet illos.* Postquam ergo isti duo interfecti fuerint, inde cęteros fideles persequens aut martires gloriosos faciet aut apostatas reddet. Et quicumque in eum crediderint, signum caracteris eius in fronte accipient.

Sed quia de principio eius diximus, quem finem habeat dicamus. Hic itaque Antichristus diaboli filius et totius maliciæ artifex pessimus, cum per tres annos et dimidium, sicut prædictum est, magna persecutione totum mundum vexabit et populum Dei variis pęnis cruciabit, postquam Helian et Enoch interfecerit et cęteros in fide permanentes martirio coronaverit, ad ultimum veniet iudicium Dei super eum, sicut beatus Paulus scribit dicens: *Quem dominus Iesus interficiet spiritu oris sui*; sive dominus Iesus interfecerit illum potentia virtutis suę sive archangelus Michael interfecerit illum, per virtutem domini nostri Iesu Christi occidetur, non per virtutem cuiuslibet angeli vel archangeli. Tradunt autem doctores, quod in monte Oliveti Antichristus occidetur in papilione et in solio suo, in illo loco, contra quem ascendit Dominus ad cęlos.

Debetis autem scire, quia, postquam fuerit Antichristus occisus, non statim veniet dies iudicii, nec statim veniet Dominus ad iudicium, sed sicut ex libro Danielis intelligimus, xl dies Dominus concedet electis, ut agant penitentiam, propterea, quia seducti sunt ab Antichristo. Postea vero quam hanc pœnitentiam expleverint, quantum temporis spatium fiat, quousque ad iudicium Dominus veniat, nullus est qui sciat, sed in dispositione Dei manet, qui ea hora seculum iudicabit, qua ante secula iudicandum esse prefixit.

Ecce, domna regina, ego fidelis vester quod pręcepistis fideliter implevi, paratus de cęteris obœdire quę fueritis dignata imperare.

**Page 371, note 1.** The earliest edition of the Tegernsee *Ludus de Antichristo* is that of B. Pez, *Thesaurus Anecdotorum Novissimus*, ii, Augsburg, 1721, part iii, pp. 187–96. This text is reprinted by T. Wright, *The Chester Plays*, ii, London, 1847, pp. 227 sqq., and by Migne, *P.L.*, ccxiii, 949 sqq. The text was re-edited by G. von Zezschwitz, *Vom römischen Kaisertum deutscher Nation: ein mittelalterliches Drama*, Leipzig, 1877, pp. 217–41, and from him revised by Froning, pp. 206–24. At the end of his edition Zezschwitz gives a facsimile of p. 12 of the MS. The content of the MS is described by W. Wattenbach, in *Neues Archiv der Gesellschaft für ältere deutsche Geschichtskunde*, xvii (1892), 33 sqq. The one brief passage in the play which has musical notation is indicated in the foot-notes. The text of the play has no heading, and what immediately precedes is irrelevant. For translations of the *Ludus* into German see especially Gundlach, iii, 814–37; Vetter, pp. 312–33. The play has been translated into English by Sarah F. Barrow and W. H. Hulme, *Antichrist and Adam* (*Western Reserve University Bulletin*, xxviii, no. 8), Cleveland, 1925, pp. 15–32. For references to German translations earlier than those of Gundlach and Vetter see Barrow and Hulme, p. 8. For discussions of the play see especially F. Kampers, *Die deutsche Kaiseridee in Prophetie und Sage*, Munich, 1896, pp. 59–63; Vetter, pp. 279–98; Wilken, pp. 145–52; Aschner, pp. 356–62; Meyer, *Abhandlungen*, i, 136–49, 334–8; Reuschel, pp. 2–4, 35–9; Golther, pp. 169–71; Scherer, pp. 450–5; Chambers, ii, 62–4; Creizenach, i, 72–8; Hase, pp. 14–15, 219; Froning, pp. 199–205; Michael, iv, 427–36; Duriez, pp. 585–93; Salzer, i, 157–62; Michaelis, pp. 61–87; Sepet, *Origines*, pp. 89–103; Wadstein, pp. 144–6; Rudwin, *Survey*, pp. 55–6; Manitius, iii, 1052–6.

## CONCLUSION

**Page 398, note 1.** The records concerning the persistence of the religious drama throughout the later Middle Ages and into modern times do not always discriminate between Latin plays or dramatic ceremonies performed in churches and vernacular plays performed outside. As bearing upon the former see, for example, Creizenach, i, 222–3; Chambers, ii, 96, 107, 389–90; Gasté, pp. 33, 52–3, 68, 76–9; Lefebvre, i, 4–5; Moléon, p. 305; Eberle, pp. 13, 145, 187, *et pass.*; Le Verdier, i, pp. xxxvi–xxxvii, xl–xliii, xlvii–xlviii. In regard to sixteenth-century vigilance and reform in the matter see the extracts from Kirchmayer and Gilpin in appendix C, and above, pp. 420 sq. The survival of the Easter sepulchre, and of one or another of the dramatic ceremonies associated with it, is surveyed by N. C. Brooks, *The* Sepulchrum Christi *and its Ceremonies in Late Medieval and Modern Times*, in *J.E.G.P.*, xxvii (1928), 147–61; and by O. Eberle, in *Geistliche Spiele*, pp. 52–3. Stapper (*Münster*, pp. 25, 39) records concerning Münster that, whereas the *Visitatio Sepulchri* was abolished about the beginning of the eighteenth century, the *Depositio* and *Elevatio* were continued into the nineteenth century.

**Page 410, note 2.** Chambers (ii, 105), following Petit de Julleville (i, 192, 417), finds the first use of *mystère* (*misterre*) in the sense of 'dramatic performance' in a charter granted by Charles VI to a Parisian *Confrérie de la Passion* in 1402. Creizenach (i, 161), using Roy (p. 11*), cites an earlier use of *mystère* in a document of 1374 relating to the *Confrérie de la Charité* at Rouen. Roy (p. 11*) regards this latter as 'le plus ancien exemple daté du mot *mystère*'. The derivation of *mystère* from Latin *misterium* (or *mysterium*), for which I have suggested fresh evidence above, is affirmed by G. Paris (*Journal des Savants*, 1892, p. 673). In the text above I have cited examples of *misterium* from the fourteenth century; for examples of its use to denote Church plays and dramatic ceremonies in the fifteenth century see Le Verdier, i, pp. xxxvi, xli, xlvii, xlviii. Petit de Julleville (i, 188) and Chambers (ii, 105) derive *mystère* (*mistère*) from Latin *ministerium*. F. Blatt (*Bulletin Du Cange: Archivum Latinitatis Medii Aevi*, fasc. 2 [1928], 80–1) cogently argues that from the fifth century onward *misterium* in the sense of 'service' was often used for *ministerium* in that sense, not through syncope, but through confusion and substitution. This substituted *misterium* may be the original of *misterium* meaning 'religious service, liturgical office or ceremony', as illustrated by Du Cange (v, 424) and by the text above. G. Körting (*Lateinisch-Romanisches Wörterbuch*, Paderborn, 1907, col. 655) derives *mystère* from Greek *μυστήριον*. W. Meyer-Lübke (*Romanisches etymologisches Wörterbuch*, Heidelberg, 1911) and E. Gamillscheg (*Etymologisches Wörterbuch der französischen Sprache*, Heidelberg, 1928) do not discuss the particular etymology before us. The evidence cited in the text above seems to support the following derivation: *misterium*, or *mysterium* ('liturgical office or ceremony') > *misterium* ('liturgical play') > *mystère*, or *mistère* ('religious play'). The use of English *mystery* in a dramatic sense is a modern invention, being found first, apparently, in [R. Dodsley,] *A Select Collection of Old Plays*, i, London, 1744, Preface, pp. xii, xiii. See *New English Dictionary* (*s.v.*); Pollard, p. xx; Chambers, ii, 105.

**Page 410, note 4.** The attitude of ecclesiastics and councils towards Church plays is reviewed by D'Ancona, i, 53–6; Creizenach, i, 94–5, 175–8; Chambers, ii, 98–103. The plays under consideration here do not come within the purview of J.-B. Eriau, *Pourquoi les Pères de l'Église ont condamné le Théâtre de leur Temps*, Paris and Angers, 1914; A. Reyval, *L'Église et le Théâtre: Essai historique*, Paris, 1924; P. Deslandres, *L'Église et le Théâtre*, in *Revue des Études historiques*, xci (1925), 131–6.

**Page 412, note 3.** A summary of information concerning the *Hortus Deliciarum* is given by A. Straub and G. Keller, ed., *Herrade de Landsberg: Hortus Deliciarum*, Strassburg, 1901, pp. v–vii. The single MS of the *Hortus* (about 324 leaves) was destroyed by fire in 1870, but provision had previously been made for reproducing about two-thirds of the miniatures, and much of the text had been transcribed. The miniatures are reproduced by Straub and Keller, in the work mentioned above. A. Bastard's transcript of the text is in the Bibliothèque Nationale, in Paris (see Straub and Keller, p. vi). The passage which I quote above is the text given by J. Walter, in A. Wilmart's *L'Ancien Cantatorium de l'Église de Strasbourg*, Colmar, 1928, pp. 95–7, as coming from 'fol. $315^r$ de l'original'. For references to the *Hortus Deliciarum* see also C. M. Engelhardt, *Herrad von Landsperg*, Stuttgart and Tübingen, 1818, pp. 104–5; Pearson, ii, 285–6; Creizenach, i, 94; Chambers, i, 318–9; ii, 98.

**Page 415, note 1.** The reformers in England seem to have had only slight relations with liturgical plays, and chiefly through the ceremonies of the *Depositio* and *Elevatio* at the Easter sepulchre. These relations are surveyed by Chambers, ii, 24–5. The generally tolerant attitude of the later years of Henry VIII is shown in the following passage from the *Articles about Religion set out by the Convocation, and published by the King's Authority*, of 1536:[1]

Creeping to the cross, and humbling ourselves to Christ on Good Friday, and offering there unto Christ before the same, and kissing of it in memory of our redemption by Christ made upon the cross; setting up the sepulchre of Christ, whose body after His death was buried . . . and all other like laudable customs, rites and ceremonies be not to be contemned and cast away, but to be used and continued as things good and laudable.

The *Rationale* or *Book of Ceremonies*, of 1538, speaks of the *Elevatio* thus:[2]

Upon Easter-day in the morning the ceremonies of the Resurrection be very laudable, to put us in remembraunce of Christ's Resurrection, which is the cause of our justification.

After the Edwardine *Injunctions* of 1547 began a general destruction of Easter sepulchres, which was interrupted somewhat during the reign of Mary. See Chambers, *loc. cit.* In 1557, Roger Edgeworth, Canon of Wells and Salisbury, could publish a sermon containing the following:[3]

The deuout ceremonies on Palme sondayes in processions and on good fridaies about the laying of the crosse and sacrament into the sepulchre,

[1] D. Wilkins, ed., *Concilia Magnæ Britanniæ et Hiberniæ*, iii, London, 1737, p. 822.

[2] J. Strype, *Ecclesiastical Memorials*, i, part 2, Oxford, 1822, p. 432.

[3] *Sermons very fruitfull, godly, and learned, preached and sette foorth by Maister Roger Edgeworth*, London, 1557, fol. $xciv^v$–$xcv^r$. See Feasey, *Ceremonial*, p. 53.

gloriouslye arayed, be so necessary to succour the labilitie of mans remembrance, that if they wer not vsed once euery yere, it is to be feared that Christes passion wold sone be forgotten.

The final disappearance of the *Depositio* and *Elevatio* was brought about, presumably, by the Elizabethan *Injunctions* of 1559, which forbade 'monuments of . . . idolatry and superstition'.[1]

**Page 417, note 3.** Isidore of Seville (*Etymologiæ*, xviii, 59) speaks of the Roman *spectacula* thus (Migne, *P.L.*, lxxxii, 660):

Hæc quippe spectacula crudelitatis, et inspectio vanitatum non solum hominum vitiis, sed de dæmonum jussis instituta sunt. Proinde nihil esse debet Christiano cum circensi insania, cum impudicitia theatri, cum amphiteatri crudelitate, cum atrocitate arenæ, cum luxuria ludi. Deum enim negat, qui talia præsumit, fidei Christianæ prævaricator effectus, qui id denuo appetit quod in lavacro jam pridem renuntiavit, id est, diabolo, pompis et operibus ejus.

**Page 418, note 1.** The use of the term *miracle* by William of Wadington and Robert of Brunne, as a designation for the forbidden *ludi*, *larvæ*, and *spectacula*, is confusing. A similar use may have been in the mind of Bishop Robert Grosseteste, of Lincoln, when he put the *ludos quos vocant miracula* on the same level with the May-games and carousings of the folk, as in the following address of about the year 1244 to his archdeacons (*Roberti Grosseteste Episcopi quondam Lincolniensis Epistolæ*, ed. H. R. Luard, London, 1861, pp. 317–8):

Faciunt etiam, ut audivimus, clerici ludos quos vocant miracula; et alios ludos quos vocant Inductionem Maii, sive Autumni; et laici scotales; quod nullo modo vos latere posset, si vestra prudentia super his diligenter inquireret . . . miracula etiam et ludos supra nominatos et scotales, quod est in vestra potestate facili, omnino exterminetis.

In records or popular utterances concerning the drama the word *miraculum* and its derivatives seem to be used in at least three different senses: (1) a forbidden show or entertainment, as in the references before us; (2) the wonderful events in the life of Christ which were dramatized (see the *Tretise of miraclis pleyinge* above, p. 414; Coffman, *Nomenclature*, pp. 460–1); and (3) the dramatization of a saint's legend (see the closing rubric *Finitur Miraculum* of the Fleury *Iconia Nicolai* above, pp. 348, 409). In regard to the possibility that *miraculum* 'came, especially in England, to stand for "religious play" in general,' see Chambers, ii, 104. The term is treated comprehensively by Coffman, *Nomenclature*, pp. 448–65. For uses of *miraculum* in medieval writings see also below, pp. 522, 541, 542.

**Page 420, note 2.** Disorder accompanying the dramatic performances of Easter is mentioned in the following ordinance adopted by the chapter at

[1] See H. Gee and W. J. Hardy, *Documents Illustrative of English Church History*, London, 1896, p. 428. See Chambers, ii, 25. Various ecclesiastical pronouncements concerning the Easter sepulchre between the years 1538 and 1565 are recorded by W. H. Frere, *Visitation Articles and Injunctions of the Period of the Reformation*, 3 vols., London, 1910, ii, 38, 48, 183–7, 194–5, 239, 244, 265, 277, 285–6; iii, 169.

Gerona in 1539, and published in [J. Villanueva,] *Viage literario a las Iglesias de España*, xii, Madrid, 1850, pp. 342–3:

Die sabbati X Maii MDXXXVIIII fuit comuni omnium tam præsentium in Capitulo quam infirmorum consultorum consensu facta sequens ordinacio sive statutum. Licet maiores nostri pia consideratione ad excitandam populi devotionem introduxerint, singulosque Canonicos in suo novo ingressu astrinxerint, ut eorum quilibet secundum ordinem antiquitatis in festo Paschæ Resurrectionis Redemptoris nostri Jhesu Christi in præsenti Ecclesia Gerundensi in Matutinis singulis annis faciant representationem, quæ vulgo *Les tres Maries* dicitur; tamen quia experimento compertum est, id quod ad Dei cultum laudem et honorem introductum fuerat, ad ipsius noxam et offensam tendere, multa scandala inde oriri, populi indevocionem excrescere, et infinita animarum ac corporum pericula insurgere, ac divinum officium plurimum perturbari, et denique Ecclesiæ decorem et honestatem inquinari: propterea Capitulum predictæ Ecclesiæ volens, ut tenetur, tot scandalis et periculis obviare, omnemque lasciviam, abusum et turpitudinem ab ipsa Ecclesia extirpare, post varios tractatus matura omnium deliberatione reformando statuit et ordinavit, quod de cœtero dicta representatio non possit fieri nisi in hunc qui sequitur modum. Videlicet: quod, finita verbetta,[1] tres Mariæ vestibus nigris, ut moris est, indutæ incipiant canere versus solitos in poste ubi invitatoria cantantur, et cantando eant ad altare maius, ubi sit paratum Cadafale cum multa luminaria, et ibi sint Apothecarius cum Uxore et Filiolo, necnon Mercator cum Uxore sua, qui non intrent nisi finita tercia lectione, et ibi fiat illa representatio[2] petitionis unguenti ad ungendum sacratissimum Corpus Christi, ut moris est. Quando ipsæ personæ representationem facturæ venient ad Ecclesiam, nulla sint tympana sive tabals, neque trompetæ, nec aliquod aliud genus musicorum, neque niger, neque nigra sive famula, nec crustula, sive flaons aliquo modo projiciantur. Hæc enim magis ad ludibrium quam ad Dei cultum populique rissum et indevotionem ac divini officii perturbationem tendere dinoscuntur. Representationes Centurionis, quæ fieri solebant[3] in Matutinis: Magdalenæ et Thomæ quæ fieri consueverant ante vel post Vesperas, vel in medio quibus erat consuetudo, immo corruptela piscandi omnino extirpari voluit atque decrevit dictum Capitulum, et nihil aliud quam quod supradictum est aliquatenus fieri prohibuit atque prohibet, nisi de expresso consensu ipsius Capituli nemine discrepante.

In regard to the abolishing of the *Visitatio Sepulchri* at Gerona in 1566 see *id.*, xiv, Madrid, 1850, p. 90.

[1] verbetta] Refers, presumably, to a trope of the last responsory.

[2] representatio] represantatio (Print).

[3] solebant] solebat (Print).

# APPENDICES

# APPENDIX A

## THE EASTER SEPULCHRE

THE most comprehensive and orderly study of the Easter sepulchre is by N. C. Brooks, *The Sepulchre of Christ in Art and Liturgy* (*University of Illinois Studies in Language and Literature*, vii, no. 2), Urbana, 1921. This study provides the basis for much of the present brief survey. Aspects of the subject are treated by A. Heales, *Easter Sepulchres: their Object, Nature and History*, in *Archaeologia*, xlii (1869), 263–308; H. P. Feasey, *The Easter Sepulchre*, in *The Ecclesiastical Review*, xxxii (1905), 337–55, 468–99; D. G. Dalman, *Das Grab Christi in Deutschland*, Leipzig, 1922; E. A. Stückelberg, *Die Verehrung des heiligen Grabes*, in *Schweizerisches Archiv für Volkskunde*, i (1897), 104–14; Young, *Dramatic Associations*, pp. 7–29; Bond, *Chancel*, pp. 220–41. The slightness of the treatment of the subject by A. Glock, *Zur Mysterienbühne*, in *Analecta Germanica, Hermann Paul zum 7. August 1906 dargebracht*, Amberg, 1906, pp. 3–18, is deprecated by Brooks, *Sepulchre*, p. 53. Briefer treatments, with bibliography, are provided by Chambers, ii, 21–5; Bergner, pp. 69–70, 261–2, 361–2; Otte, i, 365–7; Hirn, pp. 69, 84, 494. Sauer, pp. 155 sqq., 216, 430, 443; Rock, iii, 76–80; iv, 278–9. The subject is treated somewhat informally by C. J. Cox, *Some Somerset Easter Sepulchres and Sacristies*, in *Downside Review*, xlii (1924), 84 sqq. For modern uses of the *sepulchrum* see *Decreta*, iv, 419–41; Wetzer and Welte, v, 976–7; Dalman, p. 14; Brooks, *Sepulchrum Christi*, pp. 155 sqq.; *Geistliche Spiele*, pp. 52–3. Information concerning particular Easter sepulchres is referred to in foot-notes below. I do not, however, undertake to employ exhaustively the evidences found *passim* in the first volume of the present treatise.

### I

The natural model for representations of the *sepulchrum Christi* is the actual tomb on Golgotha, still preserved and venerated in Jerusalem as the Holy Sepulchre. The Gospels speak of this burial-place as having been hewn out of solid rock, and as having a door that was closed by rolling a large stone before it.[1] During the first three Christian centuries the site suffered neglect and desecration, from which Constantine rescued it during the early years of the fourth century. Over the tomb he probably built the structure called the Anastasis, and opposite this, a basilica called the Martyrium, these two buildings serving as two sides of an open court, or *atrium*, the remaining two sides being formed by walls.[2] Whether the Anastasis was built by Constantine, or slightly

[1] See Matt. xxvii, 60; Mark xv, 46; Luke xxiii, 53.

[2] The succession of buildings over and round the Holy Sepulchre is surveyed by A. Heisenberg in the first volume of his *Grabeskirche und Apostelkirche*, 2 vols., Leipzig,

later, it was in the form of a rotunda, on the west side of the *atrium*. Under the protection of the rotunda was the small eminence of natural rock constituting the *sepulchrum*, and immediately over this was a cone-shaped roof, or *ciborium*, resting on columns.[1] Under the cornice of this roof was a lattice, or grille; and over the exterior of the structure was much gold and silver ornamentation. The rock itself, probably quadrangular in shape, was hollowed out to form a cave, or grotto, the door being provided with a stone for closing it. Within the cave, on the right of a person entering, was a grave, in the form either of a sarcophagus above the level of the floor, or of a cavity sunk below this level.

The group of structures surrounding the *sepulchrum* was more or less completely destroyed by the Persians in the year 614, and was rebuilt during the decade 616–26, by Modestos, Patriarch of Jerusalem. The buildings of Modestos and his successors were completely destroyed by El Hakim, Caliph of Egypt, in 1010. Within the first half of the eleventh century Greek architects rebuilt them, following the general plan of Modestos. In the twelfth century the Crusaders contrived to unite all the sanctuaries near the Holy Sepulchre into a single architectural group, and this arrangement, modified by periodic alterations and restorations, survives in the complex structure of to-day.

Although, as has been shown above, the Holy Sepulchre was the scene of striking liturgical, and quasi-dramatic, ceremonials at a very early period, it was not the original setting of the Easter play, *Visitatio Sepulchri*.[2] The *Visitatio* originated in the West, and was enacted in the Anastasis in Jerusalem only after the Crusaders carried it there. Of its performance in Jerusalem we have no record earlier than a text of the play from the twelfth century.[3]

Indirectly, however, the Easter play was associated with the Holy Sepulchre through the attachment of the *Visitatio* to architectural imitations of that structure in the West. These imitations must have been inspired first by reports of early pilgrims and Crusaders,[4] but after the tenth and eleventh centuries the erection of them may have been encouraged by a desire to provide an appropriate *mise en scène* for the dramatic *Depositio*, *Elevatio*, and *Visitatio*. The Western sepulchres were circular or polygonal structures of varying dimensions, and for varying uses. In their cone-shaped roofs, and in other architectural details, they copied, more or less suggestively, the original in Jerusalem. They seem to have been especially esteemed in Germany, where they sometimes

1908. This monograph is used by Brooks, *Sepulchre*, pp. 9–12, and by C. Gurlitt, *Das Grab Christi in der Grabeskirche in Jerusalem*, in *Clemen Festschrift*, pp. 189–99.

[1] For additional evidence as to the shape of the Holy Sepulchre and its roof, or covering, see C. R. Morey, in *Clemen Festschrift*, pp. 153–66.

[2] Concerning early dramatic ceremonies at the Holy Sepulchre see above, i, 86 sqq.

[3] See above, i, 262.

[4] See Dalman, p. 11; Stückelberg, *Verehrung*, pp. 107–8.

served as chapels in cemeteries, or were erected in crypts, or in other parts of the church building.[1] Often the church itself took the circular form, with a pointed roof.[2] Similar structures, used as churches, chapels, or monuments, were by no means infrequent in France, Spain,[3] Italy,[4] and England.[5]

Although the Western imitations of the Holy Sepulchre must have served often as *mise en scène* for the dramatic ceremonies of Easter and Holy Week, the instances in which recorded or extant examples of these structures can be definitely associated with particular versions of the *Depositio*, *Elevatio*, and *Visitatio Sepulchri* are not numerous. These dramatic ceremonies in the cathedral of Aquileia, however, may be assumed to have been performed at the monument of the Holy Sepulchre in the north aisle near the west end of the church.[6] This round structure, erected in the eleventh century, is about 3.8 metres in diameter, and somewhat over two metres in height, and is surmounted by a conical roof, with a grille under the cornice. There is a door on the west side, and within are a niche and an altar.[7]

## II

In general, however, the sepulchres actually used for the *Depositio*, *Elevatio*, and *Visitatio Sepulchri* are not described in the dramatic texts, or elsewhere, in such a way as to identify them as reproductions of the Holy Sepulchre. Some of them clearly were not of this character; others may have been. I proceed, then, to a brief survey of some of the features of the dramatic sepulchres, without inquiring as to the possibility of Palestinian influence, beginning with those on the Continent.

As to the position of the *sepulchrum* in the church there was no fixed tradition. In many instances it is spoken of as being in the choir or presbytery.[8] This is its location, for example, in the *Visitatio* from Fleury,

[1] See Dalman, pp. 10–9.

[2] See Dalman, pp. 16, 19, 26–106; Brooks, *Sepulchre*, p. 88; Bergner, pp. 69–70, 361–2.

[3] Concerning French and Spanish churches reproducing the Holy Sepulchre see A. K. Porter, *Romanesque Sculpture of the Pilgrim Roads*, i, Boston, 1923, p. 185; C. Enlart, *Manuel d'Archéologie française*, i, Paris, 1902, p. 792; Stückelberg, *Verehrung*, pp. 110–1.

[4] Concerning the monument at Aquileia see Lanckoronski, pp. 4–5, 92, 105, 124–5.

[5] See Porter, *op. cit.*, p. 185.

[6] For the *Visitatio Sepulchri* of Aquileia see above, i, 320, and for the *sepulchrum* see plate ix. This sepulchre is described and illustrated by Lanckoronski, pp. 4–5, 92, 105, 124–5.

[7] For Easter plays from Constance, Eichstätt, Augsburg and Magdeburg see above, i, 283, 301, 311, 351, 631. In regard to reproductions of the Holy Sepulchre in these places information is given as follows: Constance = Dalman, pp. 15, 30 sqq., and his plates iii and iv; Brooks, *Sepulchre*, p. 89; Bergner, p. 361; Eichstätt = Dalman, pp. 56 sqq., and his plate vii; Augsburg = Dalman, pp. 16, 96 sqq.; Magdeburg = Bergner, pp. 361–2; Dalman, pp. 34–5, and his plate v. It is not to be assumed without further evidence, however, that the plays mentioned here were invariably associated with the particular sepulchres referred to. For the sepulchre at Constance see above, plate viii.

[8] See Brooks, *Sepulchre*, pp. 53–6.

as appears in the rubric *Cum autem venerint ⟨i.e. Mariæ⟩ in chorum, eant ad Monumentum.*[1] Sometimes it is specifically assigned to a place behind the altar, as at Parma: *Corpus Christi . . . reportetur, et in Paradiso post altare maius reverenter recondatur, ut in Sepulcro.*[2] Here the enclosure used as a sepulchre is called *Paradisus*. In England, as we shall see, the *sepulchrum* is virtually always in the choir, or chancel, on the north side. In most of the dramatic ceremonies from Germany, or from countries under German influence, it is in some other part of the church.[3] The usual positions were at or near the altar of the Holy Cross beside the door from the nave into the choir,[4] in the middle of the nave,[5] at the west end,[6] or at the altar of a saint somewhere in the nave or aisles.[7] Sometimes the sepulchre was in a chapel[8] or in the crypt.[9]

The forms of the sepulchre, in Continental churches, are various. As we should expect, from the fact that the altar was associated with the notion of burial,[10] the dramatic sepulchre was often merely the altar itself.[11] In such instances the angels usually stood behind or at the sides of the altar-table,[12] and at the words *Non est hic* the angels or the Marys quite commonly lifted the altar-cloth.[13] The Marys often peer within the grating under the altar-table, as if to verify the assertions of the angels.[14] Sometimes the sepulchre is more definitely localized as a small structure or receptacle upon the altar-table, or as a recess in some part of the altar.[15]

When the sepulchre was in a place apart from the main altar, it was often merely a space enclosed within curtains.[16] This arrangement is indicated in the following rubric from the usage of the diocese of Bamberg:[17]

Vbi notandum est quod in templo designari, atque tapete vel antipendio claudi, debet locus quidam ad repræsentandum Christi Sepulchrvm conueniens, in quo inter cætera stratum iaceat linteum, seu sudarium album et subtile, designans syndonem quo Christi corpus mortuum inuolutum fuit.

Within such an enclosure—and within other types of sepulchre—was often placed a receptacle, such as a coffer (*arca*), within which the buried object, or objects, could be securely kept.[18] Such a coffer—which

[1] See above, i, 394.

[2] See above, i, 125. See also the *Depositio* from Fécamp mentioned above, i, 555.

[3] See Brooks, pp. 55, 56–8.

[4] See the *Visitatio* from St Emmeram above, i, 295.

[5] See the *Visitatio* from Moosburg above, i, 361.

[6] See the *Visitatio* from Aquileia mentioned above in this appendix; Essen above, i, 333; Stapper, *Feier*, p. 88, note 1.

[7] See Zurich above, i, 314.

[8] See St Gall above, i, 621; see also Brooks, pp. 55, 65–6, 88–9; Wilmart, p. 105.

[9] See Würzburg above, i, 258.

[10] See above, i, 218 sqq.

[11] See Brooks, pp. 54–5, 59–61, 89.

[12] See Besançon above, i, 290.

[13] See Le Mans above, i, 289; Troyes, i, 292; Châlons, i, 279.

[14] See Tours above, i, 241. Concerning the altar-gratings, through which the grave or reliquary of a saint might be seen, see Bergner, p. 260.

[15] See the *Depositio* from the *Regularis Concordia*, devised under Continental influences, above, i, 133; Narbonne, i, 285. See also Brooks, pp. 61–2.

[16] See Brooks, pp. 63–4.

[17] See above, i, 323.

[18] See Brooks, pp. 62–3.

becomes the *sepulchrum* in the more intimate sense—is mentioned in the following rubric from Bamberg:[1]

Alius quoque deligatur locus pro Sepulchro Domini erigendo, qui inter cætera contineat unam arcam vel quid simile, quod claudi et obserari, atque in eo venerabile Sacramentum reponi, tutoque relinqui possit, usque ad tempus et horam Dominicæ Resurrectionis.

That the sepulchre was sometimes a temporary structure of wood, with a door, might be inferred as a probability, although we have no text describing such a contrivance unequivocally.[2] There is, however, a wood-cut of the year 1516 illustrating a prank of Till Eulenspiegel which shows that the sepulchre assumed to have been used in the *Visitatio* was a small house-shaped shelter, or kennel, with a saddle roof. In the front of the structure is an opening, and upon the threshold sits the actor impersonating the angel.[3]

At the close of the Middle Ages, and thereafter, a good many Continental churches were adorned with permanent sepulchres in the form of highly sculptured stone monuments.[4] Often the figures represent the Entombment, or a later scene. Probably such monuments were seldom, or never, used for the *Visitatio*; but they may often have been decorated and used for the *Depositio* and *Elevatio*. Sometimes the figure of Christ lying on the lid of a sarcophagus has a cavity in the breast, for receiving the Host in the *Depositio*. Sepulchres have been used ceremonially until relatively recent times, especially in Southern Germany, where the 'heilige Gräber', of a permanent or temporary sort, still serve at Eastertide for the exposition, rather than the burial, of the Host.[5]

## III

In England the Easter sepulchres usually took forms somewhat different from those prevailing on the Continent.[6] There were relatively few structures of any kind modelled upon the Holy Sepulchre in Jerusalem, and virtually no groups of elaborately sculptured figures of the sort that appeared in France and Germany at the end of the Middle

[1] *Agenda Bambergensia* . . ., Ingolstadt, 1587, p. 495, quoted by Young, *Dramatic Associations*, p. 115. See Brooks, p. 64. For the Bamberg *Depositio* and *Elevatio* from the *Agenda* see above, i, 172. As to the Essen curtained enclosure, or *tentorium*, containing an *archa*, see above, i, 333.

[2] In the dramatic texts the occasional mentions of *ostia* and *fenestræ* are indecisive. See Brooks, p. 65.

[3] See Brooks, p. 65, and for a reproduction of the wood-cut see his fig. 18. For a later note on the matter see Brooks, *Scogan's 'Quem quæritis' and Till Eulenspiegel*, in *M.L.N.*, xxxviii (1923), 57. Brooks speaks of the wood-cut as coming from a unique copy of *Ulenspiegel*, Strassburg, 1515, in the British Museum. I have seen the original only in *Ein kurtzweilig lesen von Dyl Ulenspiegel*, Strassburg, 1516, fol. xvi$^v$ (Brit. Mus. C. 57. c. 23. [1]).

[4] See Brooks, pp. 88–9; A. Philippe and P. Marot, in *Revue d'Histoire françiscaine*, i (1924), 144–66; Stückelberg, *Verehrung*, pp. 111–4; Otte, i, 365–7.

[5] See Brooks, *Sepulchre*, p. 66, 89; Brooks, *Sepulchrum Christi*, pp. 155–61.

[6] See Brooks, *Sepulchre*, pp. 71 sqq.

Ages. On the other hand we have abundant evidence of the earlier existence in England of temporary wooden sepulchres, and there are remains of scores of permanent structures in stone.

The essential part of the temporary sepulchre was inevitably some kind of wooden chest, or coffer, in which the cross, or cross and Host together, could be buried. Although church furniture of this nature could hardly be expected to survive the Reformation, one or two examples are still preserved. The one at Cowthorpe, Yorkshire, is 'a wooden chest, decorated with traceried panels, with posts at the angles, carrying a gabled roof with a fine cresting running along the ridge and eaves, and crocketed gables. Arched braces spring from the posts to the eaves of the roof'.[1] A less elaborate sepulchre chest is, or was, kept at Snitterfield Vicarage, Warwickshire.[2]

Probably many of the chests mentioned in English church records were not intended for independent use, but were relatively small coffers suitable for being placed within or upon or near permanent stone structures.[3] Of these permanent sepulchres some were built solely for use during the period from Good Friday to Easter; others served also as tombs of donors. Those in the former class may be divided into three groups:

(1) The simplest form is a mere recess in the north wall of the choir or chancel. Such recesses vary in shape and size, some being long and broad, and some being close to the level of the pavement. The earliest appear to be of the thirteenth century. Among the recorded examples are those at Twywell, Northamptonshire; Middleton, Lancashire; St Martin's, Canterbury; Bottesford, Lincolnshire; and Orpington, Kent.[4] Probably some of the cupboards or so-called aumbries, in the north walls of churches, were used as Easter sepulchres.[5]

(2) The more richly carved and vaulted sepulchres date from the fourteenth and fifteenth centuries. These differ from the ordinary recesses chiefly in being surmounted by highly decorated Gothic arches, and in having sculptured human figures on panels below the recess and elsewhere. Among the finest examples are those at Hawton,[6] Sibthorpe,[7]

[1] F. E. Howard and F. H. Crossley, *English Church Woodwork*, London [1917], p. 140. A photograph of this sepulchre is given there, on p. 143.

[2] It is described by Bloxam, ii, 116–9. See Brooks, *Sepulchre*, p. 75. A picture of the Snitterfield chest is given in *Birmingham and Midland Institute Archaeological Section: Transactions, Excursions, and Report for the Year 1894*, xx (1895), 80.

[3] Useful citations from records are made by Brooks, *Sepulchre*, pp. 72–9.

[4] For photographs of those at Twywell and Middleton see Bond, *Chancel*, pp. 226, 228. Concerning the others see Brooks, *Sepulchre*, p. 90; Feasey, *Easter Sepulchre* p. 346. The one in St Martin's, Canterbury, the so-called 'Bertha's Tomb', is commonly regarded as the burial place of the restorer of the church at the end of the twelfth century.

[5] See Feasey, *Easter Sepulchre*, p. 346.

[6] For illustrations of Hawton see Bond, *Chancel*, pp. 235, 237; Cox, *Church Fittings*, p. 272; Cox and Harvey, opposite p. 76; Rock, iv, opposite p. 279; above, plate iii.

[7] For Sibthorpe see Cox and Harvey, opposite p. 76.

and Arnold,[1] in Nottinghamshire; at Heckington,[2] Lincoln Cathedral,[3] and Navenby,[4] in Lincolnshire; at Northwold, Norfolk;[5] at Bampton, Oxfordshire;[6] at Patrington, Yorkshire;[7] at Harlington, Middlesex;[8] and in St Helen's, Bishopsgate, London.[9]

(3) The third type of sepulchre designed for the ceremonies of Easter may be called the chest-tomb. It takes the shape of a large stone chest, and has a flat top upon which a coffer could be set. This kind of sepulchre, of which there are relatively few, was placed in the northeast corner of the chancel, or against the north wall. Particularly well-known is the one at Porlock, Somerset.[10]

Aside from the structures erected exclusively for use as Easter sepulchres are those which served also as tombs of the donors, or of other prominent persons.[11] Such a monument would normally have a flat top, or at least a level space, upon which could be placed a coffer or the other objects necessary for the ceremonies of Easter. A considerable number of extant wills provide for tombs of this kind,[12] and examples may be seen at Woodleigh, Devonshire, and at Maxey, Northamptonshire.[13]

It hardly need be said that the review above does not account for all the exceptional forms of sepulchre that must have existed, nor does it describe the temporary features of decoration and illumination which were, often, no doubt, the most striking part of the setting for the dramatic ceremonies of Good Friday and Easter Day.[14]

[1] For Arnold see Cox and Harvey, p. 76.

[2] For Heckington see Bond, *Chancel*, p. 238; Cox, *Church Fittings*, p. 271; Rock, iii, 78. See also Bloxam, ii, 120–1.

[3] For Lincoln see Bond, *Chancel*, p. 232. See also Bloxam, ii, 121–2. This canopied and panelled sepulchre stands free of the wall, between two pillars of the north aisle.

[4] For Navenby see Bond, *Chancel*, p. 233.

[5] For Northwold see Bond, *Chancel*, p. 240; G. H. McGill, in *Norfolk Archaeology*, iv (1855), 120 sqq.

[6] For Bampton see Bond, *Chancel*, p. 229.

[7] For Patrington see Bond, *Chancel*, p. 239; Cox, *Church Fittings*, p. 271.

[8] For Harlington see Bond, *Chancel*, p. 231.

[9] For St Helen's see *London County Council: Survey of London*, ed. J. Bird and P. Norman, ix, part 1, London, 1924, plate 61, and p. 55.

[10] For an illustration see Bond, *Chancel*, p. 230. Bond (pp. 223, 236) regards as a chest-tomb Easter sepulchre the flat-topped monument against the north wall of the church of the Holy Trinity, at Stratford-on-Avon.

[11] See Brooks, *Sepulchre*, pp. 90–1.

[12] See Feasey, *Easter Sepulchre*, pp. 346–8.

[13] For illustrations see F. H. Crossley, *English Church Monuments*, London, 1921, p. 93; Bond, *Chancel*, p. 221.

[14] Records concerning the setting up, decorating and watching of the sepulchre are assembled and discussed by Brooks, *Sepulchre*, pp. 73–87. See the rubric concerning the *Visitatio* from Mont-Saint-Michel above, i, 575.

# APPENDIX B

## THE SHREWSBURY FRAGMENTS

THE fragments printed below are from religious plays composed partly in Latin and partly in English. The rubrics in the texts seem to indicate that the plays under consideration here may have been given in a church. Such plays represent a stage of dramatic development between the purely Latin plays of the Church, and the religious plays entirely in the vernacular performed under secular auspices outside. We still possess a fair number of such transitional compositions from Continental churches. See above, p. 423. From England the only known examples are those printed here.

The so-called Shrewsbury fragments, found in the Library of Shrewsbury School, MS VI (Mus. iii. 42), fol. $38^{r}$–$42^{v}$, were first made known by W. W. Skeat, in *The Academy*, Jan. 4, 1890, pp. 10–1, and were first edited by him in that periodical, Jan. 11, 1890, pp. 27–8. The text of Skeat has been re-issued, with editorial changes, but apparently without recourse to the MS, by the following: Manly, *Specimens*, i, pp. xxvii–xxxvii; O. Waterhouse, ed., *The Non-Cycle Mystery Plays* (*Early English Text Society*, Extra Series, civ), London, 1909, pp. 1–7; Adams, pp. 73–8. The most extended commentary is that of Waterhouse (*op. cit.*, pp. xv–xxvi), who draws largely from Skeat (*op. cit.*, pp. 10–1). As Skeat (p. 11) and Waterhouse (pp. xvi–xvii) have shown, the dialect of the English passages is essentially Northern. Forms more appropriate to the north-west Midlands, however, are present. The verbal resemblances to the *York Plays* were noted by Skeat (p. 11, and pp. 27–8 *passim*), and have been further studied by Frances H. Miller, in *M.L.N.*, xxxiii (1918), 91–5.

It will be observed that the texts which follow provide, in the main, only the part of a single actor in each of three plays: *Officium Pastorum*, *Visitatio Sepulchri*, and *Peregrinus*. In the texts themselves I have only sparingly inserted explanations or conjectures as to the parts not preserved. Abundant suggestions for further conjectures are found above in chapters ix to xv, and xvii.

The dramatic fragments are the following:[1]

### ⟨OFFICIUM PASTORUM⟩[2]

*Pastores erant in regione eadem uigilantes et custodientes gregem suum. Et ecce angelus Domini astitit iuxta illos, et timuerunt timore magno.*[3]

$iii^{us}$ Pastor.

⟨I. Pastor: . . . . . . . . . . . . . . . . . .

II. Pastor:⟩ *We! Tib!*

[1] The passages in English have no music. The footnotes indicate which of the Latin passages have.

[2] Shrewsbury MS VI (Mus. iii. 42), fol. $38^{r}$–$39^{r}$. For a facsimile of fol. $38^{r}$ see the frontispiece, plate xiii.

[3] See Luke ii, 8–9. This Latin passage is not provided with music, and appears not to be a choral liturgical piece.

⟨III. Pastor:⟩ *Telle on!*
⟨I. Pastor: . . . . . . . . . . . . . . . . . . .
II. Pastor:⟩ . . . . . . . . . . . . . . . . *þe nyght.*
⟨III. Pastor:⟩ *Brether, what may þis be,*
*þus bright to man and best?*
⟨I. Pastor: . . . . . . . . . . . . . . . .
II. Pastor:⟩ . . . . . . . . . . . . . . *at hand.*
⟨III. Pastor:⟩ *Whi say ȝe so?*
⟨I. Pastor: . . . . . . . . . . . . . . . .
II. Pastor:⟩ . . . . . . . . . . . . . . . . *warand.*
⟨III. Pastor:⟩ *Suche siȝt was neuer sene*
*Before in oure Iewery;*
*Sum merueles wil hit mene*
*That mun be here in hy.*
⟨I. Pastor: . . . . . . . . . . . . . . . . . . .
II. Pastor:⟩ . . . . . . . . . . . . . . . . *a sang.*
⟨III. Pastor:⟩ *Ȝe lye, bothe, by þis liȝt,*
*And raues as recheles royes!*
*Hit was an angel briȝt*
*þat made þis nobull*e *noyes.*
⟨I. Pastor: . . . . . . . . . . . . . . . . . . .
II. Pastor:⟩ . . . . . . . . . . . . . . *of prophecy.*
⟨III. Pastor:⟩ *He said a barn schuld be*
*In þe burgh of Bedlem born;*
*And of þis, mynnes me,*
*Oure fadres fond beforn.*
⟨I. Pastor: . . . . . . . . . . . . . . . . . . .
II. Pastor:⟩ . . . . . . . . . . . . . . . . *Iewus kyng*
⟨III. Pastor:⟩ *Now may we see þe same*
*Euen in oure pase puruayed;*
*þe angel nemed his name,—*
*'Crist, Saueour,' he saied.*
⟨I. Pastor: . . . . . . . . . . . . . . . . . . .
II. Pastor:⟩ . . . . . . . . . . . . . . . . *not raue.*
⟨III. Pastor:⟩ *Ȝone brightnes wil vs bring*
*Vnto þat blisful boure;*
*For solace schal we syng*
*To seke oure Saueour.* |

⟨Pastores:⟩

*Transeamus usque Bethelem, et uideamus hoc verbum quod factum est, quod fecit Dominus et ostendit nobis.*[1]

[1] For this processional of the *Pastores* see the *Officium Pastorum* of Rouen above, pp. 13, 17. The melody, however, differs from that found in the Rouen Gradual. See Loriquet, *Graduel*, ii, fol. $12^{r}$.

⟨I. Pastor: . . . . . . . . . . . . . . . . . .
II. Pastor:⟩ . . . . . . . . . . . . . . . . . *to knawe.*
⟨III. Pastor:⟩ *For no þing thar vs drede,*
*But thank God of alle gode;*
*þis light euer wil vs lede*
*To fynde þat frely fode.*[1]

⟨Pastores:⟩
*Saluatorem, Christum Dominum, infantem pannis involutum secundum sermonem angelicum.*

⟨I. Pastor: . . . . . . . . . . . . . . . . . .
II. Pastor:⟩ . . . . . . . . . . . . . . . . . *I mene.*[2]
⟨III. Pastor:⟩ *A! loke to me, my Lord dere.*
*Alle if I put me noght in prese!*
*To suche a prince without⟨en⟩ pere*
*Haue I no presand þat may plese.*
*But lo! a horn spone haue I here*
*þat may herbar an hundrith pese.*
*þis gift I gif þe with gode chere;*
*Suche dayntese wil do no disese.* |

*Fare wele now, swete swayn,*
*God graunt þe lifyng lang.*[3]

⟨Visitatio Sepulchri⟩[4]

Hic incipit Officium Resurreccionis in die Pasche.

⟨I. Maria: *Heu, misera! cur contigit*
*Videre mortem redemptoris?*
II. Maria: *Heu, consolatio nostra!*
*Ut quid taliter agere uoluit!*⟩
III[a] Maria: *Heu, redempcio Israel!*
*Ut quid mortem sustinuit!*[5]
⟨I. Maria: . . . . . . . . . . . . . . . . . .
II. Maria:⟩ . . . . . . . . . . . . . . . . . *payne.*
⟨III. Maria:⟩ *Allas! he þat men wend schuld by*
*Alle Israel, bothe knyght and knaue,*

[1] After this verse, a line is drawn across the page, and an asterisk refers to the Latin passage *Saluatorem . . . angelicum*, which I introduce here from fol. $42^{v}$, where it is entered, with music, by a later hand. For this Latin speech see the *Officium Pastorum* of Rouen above, pp. 13, 17. The melody of Shrewsbury, however, differs from that of Rouen. See Loriquet, *Graduel*, ii, fol. $12^{r}$–$12^{v}$.

[2] Guided by the *York Plays*, xv, 119, Skeat restores the full line: ⟨Now wat ȝe what⟩ I mene.

[3] Skeat adds here the closing lines from York Plays, xv, 130–1, with slightly altered spelling as follows:
And go we hame agayn
And mak mirth as we gang.

[4] Shrewsbury MS VI (Mus. iii. 42), fol. $39^{r}$–$40^{r}$.

[5] Latin speeches for the first two Marys are supplied, conjecturally, from the Easter play from Tours; see above, i, 441. See also a fragment from Fleury above, i, 666. In the Shrewsbury MS the speech of the third Mary (*Heu . . . sustinuit*) has no music.

*Why suffred he so forto dy,*
*Sithe he may alle sekenes saue?*

⟨I. Maria: . . . . . . . . . . . . . . . . .
II. Maria: . . . . . . . . . . . . . . . . .
III. Maria:⟩ *Heu! cur ligno fixus clauis*
*Fuit doctor tam suauis?*
*Heu! cur fuit ille natus*
*Qui perfodit eius latus?*[1]

⟨I. Maria: . . . . . . . . . . . . . . . . .
II. Maria:⟩ . . . . . . . . . . . . . . . . *is oght*
⟨III. Maria:⟩ *Allas! þat we suche bale schuld bide*
*þat sodayn sight so forto see,*
*þe best techer in world wide*
*With nayles be tacched to a tre!*
*Allas! þat euer so schuld betyde,*
*Or þat so bold mon born schuld be*
*For to assay oure Saueour side*
*And open hit withoute pite!*

⟨Omnes simul:⟩ *Iam, iam, ecce iam properemus ad tumulum,* |
*Vnguentes*[2] *dilecti corpus sanctissimum.*[3]

Et appropiantes Sepulcro can*tent*:
*O Deus! Quis reuoluet nobis lapidem ab hostio monumenti?*[4]

⟨I. Maria: . . . . . . . . . . . . . . . . .
II. Maria:⟩ . . . . . . . . . . . . . . *him leid.*
⟨III. Maria:⟩ *He þat þus kyndely vs has kend*
*Vnto þe hole where he was hid,*
*Sum socoure sone he wil vs send*
*At help to lift away þis lid.*

⟨Here must occur the dialogue between the Marys and the angel, beginning *Quem quæritis?*⟩

⟨I. Maria: . . . . . . . . . . . . . . . . . .
II. Maria: . . . . . . . . . . . . . . . . . .
III. Maria:⟩ *Alleluya schal be oure song,*
*Sithen Crist, oure Lord, by angellus steuen,*
*Schewus him as mon here vs among,*
*And is Goddis Son, heghest in heuen.* |[5]

⟨I. Maria: . . . . . . . . . . . . . . . . . .
II. Maria:⟩ . . . . . . . . . . . . . . . . *was gon.*

[1] Heu cur ligno . . . latus] Has no music.
[2] Vnguentes] The *u* is rubbed, but not erased.
[3] Iam, iam . . . sanctissimum] For this passage see, for example, the plays of Dublin and Tours above, i, 348, 441. The melody in the Shrewsbury MS, however, differs from the melodies in the two plays mentioned.
[4] This speech has music. Concerning this speech see above, i, 261–2.
[5] This is the last verse on the page, and under it a red line is drawn across the page.

⟨III. Maria:⟩ *Surrexit Christus, spes nostra;*
*Precedet vos in Galileam.*[1]
*Crist is rysen, wittenes we*
*By tokenes þat we haue sen þis morn!*
*Oure hope, oure help, oure hele, is he*
*And hase bene best, sithe we were born.*
*If we wil seke him for to se,*
*Lettes nought þis lesson be forlorn:*
*But gose euen vnto Galilee;*
*þere schal ȝe fynd him ȝow beforn.*[2]

## ⟨Peregrinus⟩[3]

Feria iiª in ebdomada Pasche Discipuli insimul cantent:
*Infidelis incursum populi*
*Fugiamus, Ihesu*[4] *discipuli!*
*Suspenderunt Ihesum patibulo;*
*Nul|li parcent eius discipulo.*[5]

⟨Luke:⟩ . . . . . . . . . . . . . . . *fast to fle.*

⟨Cleophas:⟩[6] *But if we fle, þai wil vs fang,*
*And ful felly þai wil vs flay.*
*Agayn to Emause wil we gang,*
*And fonde to get þe gaynest way.*
*And make in mynd euer vs amang*
*Of oure gode maister, as we may,*
*How he was put to paynes strang*
*On þat he tristed con him betray.*[7]

⟨Luke:⟩ . . . . . . . . . . . . . . . . . . *but agayn.*

⟨Cleophas:⟩ *By wymmen wordis wele wit may we*
*Crist is risen vp in gode aray;*
*For to oure self þe sothe say⟨d⟩ he,*
*Where we went in þis world away,*
*þat he schuld dye and doluen be*
*And rise fro þe dethe þe thrid day.*
*And þat we myȝt þat siȝt now se*
*He wisse vs, Lord, as he wele may.*

⟨Luke:⟩ . . . . . . . . . . . . . . . *.resoun*[8] *riȝt.*

[1] This Latin passage has no music. The possibilities as to the use of the sequence *Victimæ paschali*, from which these two lines derive, are fully shown in chapters x and xii.

[2] Under this verse a line is drawn across the page. Then follows the opening rubric (*Feria* iiª . . .) of the *Peregrinus*.

[3] Shrewsbury MS VI (Mus. iii, 42), fol. $40^{r}$–$42^{v}$.

[4] Ihesu] Ihesum (MS).

[5] These four Latin lines have music.

[6] That Cleophas is the speaker is mere conjecture. See below, p. 523, note.

[7] Beneath this verse, and the cue-words following it, a line is drawn across the page.

[8] resoun] rosoun (MS).

⟨Cleophas:⟩ *Et quomodo*[1] *tradiderunt eum summi sacerdotes et principes nostri in dampnacione⟨m⟩ mortis, et crucifixerunt eum.*[2]

*Right is þat we reherce by raw*
*þe materes þat we may on mene,* |
*How prestis and princes of oure lawe*
*Ful tenely toke him hom betwen,*
*And dampned him, withouten awe,*
*For to be dede with dole*[3] *bedene.*
*þai crucified him, wele we knaw,*
*At Caluary with caris kene.*

⟨Luke:⟩ . . . . . . . . . . . . . . . . . . *wraist.*

⟨Cleophas:⟩ *Dixerunt eciam se visionem angelorum vidisse, qui dicunt eum viuere.*[4]

*þe wymmen gret, for he was gon;*
*But ȝet þai told of meruales mo:*
*þai saw angellus stondyng on þe ston,*
*And sayn how he was farne hom fro.*
*Sithen of oures went ful gode wone*
*To se þat sight, and said right so.*
*Herfore we murne and makis þis mon;*
*Now wot þou wele of alle oure wo.*[5]

⟨Jesus:⟩ . . . . . . . . . . . . . . . *in þese.*

⟨Duo Discipuli insimul cantent:⟩

*Mane nobiscum, quoniam advesperascit, et inclinata est iam dies, alleluya.*[6]

⟨Jesus:⟩ . . . . . . . . . . . . . *wight*

⟨Cleophas:⟩ *Amend oure mournyng, maister dere,*
*And fonde oure freylnes for to felle*
*Herk, broþer, help to hold him here,*
*Ful nobel talis wil he vs telle.* |

⟨Luke:⟩ . . . . . . . . . . . . . *lent.*

⟨Cleophas:⟩ *And gode wyne schal vs wont non,*
*For þerto schal I take entent.*

⟨Luke:⟩ . . . . . . . . . . . . . . *he went.*

⟨Cleophas:⟩ *Went he is, and we ne wot how,*
*For here is noght left in his sted.*[7]
*Allas! where were oure wittis now?*
*With wo now walk we wil of red.*[8]

⟨Luke:⟩ . . . . . . . . . . . . . *oure bred.*

[1] quomodo] Skeat, and hence the other editors, read *quoniam*. The MS clearly and correctly has *quomodo*. See Luke xxiv, 20.

[2] For this Latin speech—which has no music here—see above, i, 459, 471, 477.

[3] dole] dele (MS), emended by Manly.

[4] For this Latin speech—which has no music—see Luke xxiv, 23.

[5] Beneath this verse, and the cue-words following it, a line is drawn across the page.

[6] This Latin speech has music. For parallels see the plays in chapter xv.

[7] sted] stid (MS).

[8] Beneath this verse, and the cue-words following it, a line is drawn across the page.

⟨Cleophas:⟩ *Oure bred he brak and blessed hit;*
*On mold were neuer so mased men,*
*When þat we saw him by vs sit,*
*þat we couthe noght consayue him þen.*

⟨Luke:⟩ . . . . . . . . . . . . . *ay.*

⟨Duo Discipuli insimul cantent:⟩
*Quid agamus, uel dicamus,*
*Ignorantes quo eamus,*
*Qui doctorem sciencie*
*Et patrem consolacionis*
*Amisimus?* | [1]

⟨Luke:⟩ . . . . . . . . . . . . . *gode state.*

⟨Cleophas:⟩ *We schal hom telle, withouten trayn,*
*Bothe word and werk, how* ⟨*that*⟩ *hit was.*
*I se hom sitt samyn in a playn;*
*Forthe in apert dar I not pas.*[2]

⟨Luke:⟩ . . . . . . . . . . . . *and wife.*

⟨Cleophas:⟩ *We saw him holle, hide and hewe;*
*þerfore be stille, and stint ȝoure strife.*
*þat hit was Crist ful wele we knewe;*
*He cutt oure bred withouten knyfe.*

⟨Omnes cantent:⟩
*Gloria tibi, Domine,*
*Qui surrexisti a mortuis,*
*Cum Patre et Sancto Spiritu*
*In sempiterna secula. Amen.*[3]

*Frater Thoma, causa* | *tristicie*
*Nobis tulit summa leticie.*[4]

In attempting to assign these fragments to a particular church one may seek guidance from the other liturgical pieces in the MS.[5] Since these pieces and the Latin passages in the plays are written by the same hand, one infers that the MS as a whole was used in a single community. The complete contents are as follows:

(1) Fol. $1^{r}$: The following occupies two-thirds of the page: *Montes exultastis sicut arietes, et colles sicut agni ovium, alleluya.*

(2) Fol. $1^{v}$: Blank.

[1] This Latin passage has music.

[2] Beneath this verse, and the cue-words following it, a line is drawn across the page.

[3] These four Latin lines—provided with music,—are the last stanza of the hymn *Ad cœnam agni*, printed in full above, i, 562.

[4] These two lines have music. The remainder of fol. $42^{v}$ is occupied by the passage *Saluatorem . . . angelicum,* inserted in the *Officium Pastorum* above. For scenes of the *Peregrinus* in which Thomas appears see above, i, 464, 479.

[5] In making the observations that follow, I have had the advantage of conferring with my friend, Mr. O. A. Silverman, of the University of Buffalo. I have found no significance in the names, Arthur Gill and William Bearsley, written in the margins of fol. $39^{v}$ and fol. $40^{r}$ respectively.

(3) Fol. $2^{r}$–$3^{v}$: The responsory *Centum quadraginta*, and the prose *Sedentem in superne maiestatis arce*. On fol. $2^{r}$–$2^{v}$ the text has been ineffectually erased, and a new text (*Simulacra gencium argentum et aurum* . . . ) has been written.

(4) Fol. $3^{v}$–$4^{v}$: The responsory *Centum quadraginta*, and the prose *Sedentem in superne*.

(5) Fol. $4^{v}$–$5^{v}$: A processional beginning: In die Purificacionis ad processionem: *Hodie*. Versus *Beata virgo Maria puerum*.

(6) Fol. $5^{v}$–$8^{r}$: A processional beginning: In die Palmarum: *En rex venit mansuetus tibi, Syon filie*.

(7) Fol. $8^{v}$–$14^{r}$: The part of the Jews from the Passions of Palm Sunday and of other days of Holy Week, beginning: In die Palmarum. Triplex: *Passio Domini nostri Ihesu Cristi secundum Matheum*.

(8) Fol. $14^{r}$–$15^{v}$: A processional beginning: In vigilia Pasche. Triplex: *Rex sanctorum angelorum*.

(9) Fol. $15^{v}$–$17^{v}$: A processional beginning: In die Pasche ad processionem. Triplex: *Salue festa dies*.

(10) Fol. $17^{v}$: A further passage from the processional of Easter beginning: In die Pasche. Triplex: *Crucifixum in carne*.

(11) Fol. $18^{r}$–$23^{v}$: A processional beginning: In die Pasche ad Vesperas: *Alleluya, alleluya, alleluya, alleluya. Laudate pueri*.

(12) Fol. $23^{v}$–$25^{v}$: A processional beginning: In translacione Sancti Cedde: *Salue festa dies*.

(13) Fol. $25^{v}$–$27^{r}$: A processional beginning: In die Ascencionis: *Salue festa dies*.

(14) Fol. $27^{r}$–$29^{r}$: A processional beginning: In die Pentecostes: *Salue festa dies*.

(15) Fol. $29^{r}$–$32^{v}$: A processional beginning: In ebdomada Pentecostes feria $ij^{a}$, $iij^{a}$ et $iiij^{a}$ cantabitur iste cantus ad processionem: *Sancti Spiritus assit*.

(16) Fol. $32^{v}$–$35^{r}$: A processional beginning: In festo Corporis Christi. Triplex: *Salue festa dies*.

(17) Fol. $35^{v}$–$37^{v}$: A processional beginning: In festo Dedicacionis Ecclesie: *Salue festa dies*.

(18) Fol. $38^{r}$–$42^{v}$: The dramatic fragments printed above.

(19) Fol. $43^{r}$: A passage from the processional of Palm Sunday beginning: *Unus autem ex ipsis, Cayphas nomine*.

Of these pieces the only one which points toward a particular church is the processional for the commemoration of St Chad (fol. $23^{v}$–$25^{v}$). Since this poem is not readily accessible elsewhere, I print it here:[1]

IN TRANSLACIONE SANCTI CEDDE

Salue, festa dies, toto venerabilis euo,
    Qua Ceddam Dominus sumpsit ad alta leuans.

[1] This text is not registered by Chevalier, *R.H.*

Salue, festa dies, toto venerabilis euo,
 Qua Ceddam Dominus sumpsit ad alta leuans.
Angelicus cetus veniens cum carmine letus
 Presciunt hunc celebrem mortis adire diem.
Puluere gustato tumbe, cum quoque liquore
 Languentum subito membra dolore carent.
Muti, leprosi, claudi, ceci, leprosi,
 Demonium pasci sunt per eum liberi.
Os iustum valde probat istum fixio thece,
 Qui fines liberos vendicat et tenet hos.
Hic reddit viuos plures in morte sopitos,
 Auxiliante Deo; laus cui sit iubilo.
Nobis collectis in laude tua, pater, assis,
 Succurrens precibus firmiter assiduis.

These verses clearly attach the MS to a church where St Chad was especially honoured.[1] The cult of this saint centred in Lichfield, where he resided as bishop of the immense diocese of Mercia in the seventh century, and where his relics were eventually translated from St Mary's Church to the cathedral. This translation was celebrated at the cathedral on August 2nd, St Chad's regular feast-day being March 2nd. One's natural temptation to assign the MS to Lichfield is increased by the following two entries in the Lichfield Statutes of the time of Hugh of Nonant (bishop 1188–98) as revised in the thirteenth or fourteenth century:[2]

Item in nocte Natalis representacio pastorum fieri consueuit et in diluculo Pasche representacio Resurreccionis dominice et representacio peregrinorum die lune in septimana Pasche sicut in libris super hijs ac alijs compositis continetur.

Et prouidere debet quod representacio pastorum in nocte Natalis domini et miraculorum in nocte Pasche et die lune in Pascha congrue et honorifice fiant.

These passages show that at Lichfield in the thirteenth or fourteenth century were performed the *Officium Pastorum*, *Visitatio Sepulchri*, and *Peregrinus*—precisely the types of play from which our fragments derive. It happens, however, that during the Middle Ages at least thirty churches were dedicated to St Chad, especially in the Midlands, one

[1] Concerning St Chad see Holweck, *Dictionary*, p. 204; *Acta Sanctorum*, *Martii*, i, 143–8; R. T. Hampson, *Medii Ævi Kalendarium*, ii, London, [1841] p. 44; S. Baring-Gould, *The Lives of the Saints*, iii, Edinburgh, 1914, pp. 23–7; Frances Arnold-Foster, *Studies in Church Dedications*, i, London, 1899, pp. 398–400; J. C. Wall, *Shrines of British Saints*, London, [1905] pp. 97–102. The Lichfield Cedda, or Ceadda, is to be distinguished from his brother Cedd, or Ceddus, who was bishop of the East Saxons. In the *Acta Sanctorum* the preferred spellings of the two names are *Ceadda* and *Ceddus*.

[2] Wordsworth, *Lincoln*, ii, 15, 23. See Chambers, ii, 108, 377.

being at Shrewsbury, and six others, in Shropshire.[1] Several of these, presumably, might have celebrated the translation of the saint, and have performed such liturgical plays as those under consideration here. In view of these possibilities we cannot at present assign the dramatic fragments with certainty to a particular church. The probabilities favour Lichfield, or its diocese.

[1] See Arnold-Foster, *op. cit.*, i, 400; iii, 345; F. Bond, *Dedications and Patron Saints of English Churches*, London, 1914, pp. 214–5. It appears that there was no such dedication at Beverley. S. Leighton (*Transactions of the Shropshire Archæological and Natural History Society*, 2d series, ix [1897], 295) thinks the verses to St Chad point to 'a possible connection with St Chad's in Shrewsbury, or at any rate, with the Diocese of Lichfield'. In a forthcoming publication Miss Mary H. Marshall will present a cogent reason for assigning the chief role in the fragmentary Shrewsbury *Peregrinus* to the companion of Cleophas rather than to Cleophas himself.

# APPENDIX C

## EXTRACTS FROM THE WRITINGS OF REFORMERS

### (i) *Gerhoh of Reichersberg* (1093–1169)

THE passage below is from *Libri Tres de Investigatione Antichristi*, written about 1161 by Gerhoh of Reichersberg. In regard to the author see *Catholic Encyclopedia*, vi, 472; Chambers, ii, 98–9; Meyer, p. 38. For references to Gerhoh see above, pp. 392, 411. The following is chapter 5, book 1, as edited by F. Scheibelberger, *Gerhohi Reichersbergensis Præpositi opera hactenus inedita*, i, Linz, 1875, pp. 25–8:

DE SPECTACULIS THEATRICIS IN ECCLESIA DEI EXHIBITIS

Et sacerdotes, qui dicuntur, jam non ecclesiæ vel altaris ministerio dediti sunt sed exercitiis avaritiæ, vanitatum et spectaculorum, adeo ut ecclesias ipsas, videlicet orationum domus, in theatra commutent ac mimicis ludorum spectaculis impleant. Inter quæ nimirum spectacula adstantibus ac spectantibus ipsorum feminis interdum et Antichristi, de quo nobis sermo est, non ut ipsi æstimant imaginariam similitudinem exhibent sed in veritate, ut credi potest iniquitatis ipsius mysterium pro parte sua implent. Quidni enim diabolus abutatur in serium rebus sibi exhibitis in vanitatis ludicrum, sicut Dominus quoque Jesus convertens in seria ludibria, quibus apud Judæos vel Pilatum in passione sua affectus est? Inde enim nunc regius honor, prophetalis vel sacerdotalis reverentia, insuper et divinus honor ei merito exhibetur, cum quia natus ex Deo, quin et secundum carnem ex regali ac sacerdotali prosapia omnia hæc jure paterno hæreditavit; tum etiam quia eadem per spineæ coronæ sceptrique simulati vel purpuræ gestationem per adorationis ei exhibitæ simulationem, per albæ vestis induitionem, per prophetandi a quo percussus fuisset exactionem dici et esse rex regum, Deus quoque sacerdos et propheta magnus commeruit. Per hæc enim, quæ dicta sunt, ut palam est, regia in eo sublimitas divinitatis majestas, sacerdotalis ac prophetalis dignitas irrisa sunt, sed ipse, qui est veritas, irrissionibus eorum in veritatis serium usus est. Quid ergo mirum si et isti nunc Antichristum vel Herodem in suis ludis simulantes eosdem non, ut eis intentioni est, ludicro mentiuntur sed in veritate exhibent, utpote quorum vita ab Antichristi laxa conversatione non longe abest? Horum enim locum quidem sanctum et vitam sanctitati contrariam si attendas quasi alienigenas in arce et abominationem desolationis videre te suspicaberis in loco sancto stantem. Contigit, ut comperimus, aliquando apud tales, ut eum quem inter ludicra sua quasi mortuum ab Elisæo propheta suscitandum exhiberent peracta simulatione mortuum invenirent. Alius item Antichristo suo quasi suscitandus oblatus intra septem dies vere mortuus, ut comperimus, et sepultus est. Et quis scire potest, an et cetera simulata Antichristi scilicet effigiem, dæmonum larvas, herodianam insaniam in veritate non exhibeant? Sicut enim in veritate a sapiente dicitur, quia maledicens impius diabolum maledicit se ipsum, ita consequenter dici ab eadem veritate potest, quod impius effigians diabolum vel ejus membrum effigiat vel exhibet se ipsum. Exhibent præterea imaginaliter et Salvatoris infantiæ cunabula, parvuli vagitum, puerperæ Virginis matronalem habitum, stellæ quasi sidus flammigerum, infantum necem, maternum Rachelis ploratum. Sed divinitas insuper et matura facies ecclesiæ abhorret spectacula theatralia, non respicit in vanitates et insanias falsas, immo non falsas sed jam veras insanias, in quibus viri totos se frangunt in feminas quasi pudeat eos, quod viri sunt, clerici in milites, homines se in dæmonum larvas transfigurant. Dumque hujusmodi vanitates et insaniæ sacramentorum dæmoniacorum celebrandorum locis et temporibus se ingerunt, quasi abominationem desolationis in loco sancto videre est. Paulo minus enim turpe est faciem ecclesiæ talibus vanitatum spectaculis christianos fœdare, quam olim in templo fuerit imagines Caji Cæsaris gentiles intulisse vel Pilatum. At si quis parietem hanc fodiat et lucernam evangelicæ animadversionis admoveat videbit certe abominationes majores his. Nam dum in semetipsis templum Dei violant, dum membra sua Deo dicata Beelfegor consecrant, dum mysterium sacerdotale et leviticum per contubernia feminarum polluunt, dum quæstum pietatem existimant, dum stipendiis Dei ministerio deputatis vanitatibus et non Deo militant, dum pauperum victualia in luxurias transferunt, quid nisi abominationem desolationis semetipsos in loco sancto constituunt? Et cum sint in cœtu talium nonnulli genere clari, litterarum scientia illustres, divitiis ampli, corporis et vestium cultu splendidi, ut tale quid de eis ab admirantibus etiam discipulis dici Domino vel cuilibet ejus vicario possit: Magister, aspice, quales lapides et quales structuræ. Magistro cœlesti non faciem rerum sed corda intuenti non est nec esse debet cura de talium structura lapidum, qui ab apostolicæ ædificationis dissident fundamento, dicetque de his: Amen dico vobis non relinquetur lapis super lapidem, qui non destruatur. Bonum quippe est male ædificata primo bene destrui, ut melior ædificatio de eisdem subsequi valeat lapidibus et impendiis.

### (ii) *Thomas Kirchmayer, or 'Naogeorgus'* (1511–63).

The following passage is from Thomas Naogeorgus ⟨Kirchmayer⟩, *Regnum Papisticum*, 1553, pp. 144–53. The author was a particularly fiery German reformer. In this long work in Latin hexameters he unreservedly exposes his hatred of the hierarchy, customs, and liturgy of the Roman Church. See C. H. Herford, *Studies in the Literary Relations of England and Germany in the Sixteenth Century*, Cambridge, 1886, pp. 119–24; Chambers, ii, 217–8; Wiener, *passim.*

Palmarum dies.

Hinc uenit alma dies, qua Christus creditur urbem
Ingressus Solymam, dorso gestatus aselli.
Tum ridenda iterum faciunt spectacla Papistæ,
Insigni ualde pompa, facieque seuera.
Ligneum habent asinum, et simulacrum equitantis in illo
Ingens: at uerò tabula consistit asellus,
Quatuor atque rotis trahitur, quem manè paratum
Ante fores templi statuunt. Populus uenit omnis
Arboreos portans ramos, salicesque uirentes,
Quos tempestates contra, cœlique fragorem
Adiurat pastor, multo grandique precatu.
Mox querno sese coram prosternit asello,
Sacrificus longa quem uirga percutit alter.
Postquam surrexit, grandes de corte scholarum
Se duo prosternunt itidem mirabili amictu,
Cantuque absurdo: qui ut surrexere, in acernum
Protendunt equitem digitos, monstrantque canentes
Hunc esse illum, qui quondam uenturus in orbem,
Credentem Israel à iure redemerit Horci,
Cuique uiam ramis turba exornarit oliuæ.
His decantatis, ramos dehinc protinus omnes
Conijciunt partim in simulacrum, partim in asellum,
Cuius et ante pedes magnus cumulatur aceruus.
Post hæc in templum trahitur, præeuntibus unctis
Consequitur populus, quamuis certamine magno
Quisque legat iactas asini ad uestigia frondes.
Falsò etenim summis præsertim uiribus illas
Contra hyemes pollere putant, et fulmina dira.
Impia nónne hæc sunt? ita nónne idola coluntur?
Vidi ego cordatos reges, sed ritibus istis
Imbutos, genibus flexis procumbere coram
Talibus idolis, summumque impendere cultum.
Est ubi nummati ciues, uulgoque uerendi,
Non paucis redimunt nummis sibi iura trahendi
Huc illuc asini, atque utuntur heriliter illis,
Non permittentes alium contingere quenquam.
Quippe putant magnum se Christo impendere honorem,
Mireque acceptos illi, et permulta mereri.
Si quis et hos asinos putet, haud errauerit hercle.
Talia quum faciant uncti, populusque tributim,
Illico sectantur pueri post prandia certum,
Dicitur æditu o precium, damnumque cauetur,
Assumuntque asinum, et per uicos atque plateas
Carmina cantantes quædam notissima raptant,

Quis nummo à populo, uel panes dantur, et oua.
Prædæ huius partem ludi præstare magistro
Coguntur mediam, ne exors sit solus aselli.
 Inde die Iouis usque ad solennia tempora Paschæ,
Impiaque et ridenda magis ceremonia gliscit,
Qua tamen eximij sibi Catholicique uidentur.
Campanis primum triduana silentia cunctis
Mandantur, tabulis pulsant de turribus altis.
Percurrunt etiam pueri plateasque forumque,
Et crepitus edunt magnos, ad templa uocantes.
Noctibus inde tribus nocturna ad cantica surgunt,
Malleolis sumptis, saxisue, aut fustibus, omnes.
Omnia ubi paulatim extinguit lumina custos,
Sacrificique altum rauco de gutture clamant.
Tum uerò exoritur sæuus crudusque tumultus:
Pulpita contundunt, et sedes, scamna, cathedras.
A furijs dicas agitari, et pneumate tristi
Bassaridum. Multi clauis figuntur ad ipsas
Sedes, nonnulli lapidum exanimantur ab ictu.
Ast alij plagas referunt, aut uulnera, cæsi
Fustibus. His factæ possunt seruire tenebræ,
Omnium et æqualis funesti insania ritus.
Impius hinc probris multis laceratur Iudas,
Et Maria è tenebris puerorum uoce citatur,
Vt sit propitia, et uitijs medeatur, et omni
Noxæ. Conueniunt hæc festo scilicet illi.
Luminibus post hæc accensis in cruce fixum
Idolum circumfertur, pendetque lucerna
Illius à collo, turbæ quo nempe sequenti
Monstret iter. Nonne hæc sunt ludicra mira Papatus?
Hac quoque luce triplex adiurat præsul oliuum,
Ampullasque genu flexo bis terque salutat.
Quem post Canonici facto sectantur eodem.
Dissilias risu cernens, mireris et unde
Sit multis uisum ampullis dixisse salutem.
Pransi consueto nudant altaria cultu,
Atque lauant, ramisque fricant, scopisque paratis,
Inde superfundunt laticem munusque Lyæi
In crucis effigiem, rogitantque uocantque patronum
Cuiusque altaris, dignetur ut esse clientum
Perpetuique memor cultus, placetque Tonantem.
Hinc celebrant monachi cœnam, et collegia quædam
Insigni pacis specie, rituque uenusto.
Mutuò namque sibi plantas terguntque lauantque,

Cœna Domini

Interea infestis animis et corde doloso.
Ceu quondam exemplo mandarit talia Christus,
Et non, ut fratrum se totum quisque saluti
Impendat, casuque lubens inseruiat omni,
Præbuit ut seipsum nobis et ad infima seruum.
Mox circum panes et pocula magna feruntur,
Vnde patres sancti fœmellis sæpe propinant
Non fictis animis, redeuntque frequenter in orbem.

Parasœue.

Luce sacerdotes duo circum altare sequenti
Idolum portant humeris Christi in cruce fixi,
Ruffa contectum casula, lugubre canentes.

Casula dicitur extima sacerdotum uestis, quando sacra faciunt.

Ante gradus tandem nudatum ueste reponunt
Strata super uillosa tapetia, suppositumque
Puluinar capiti. Hinc prostrati corpore toto,
Omnibus infigunt perfossis basia membris,
Ligneum et idolum summo uenerantur honore.
Hos dein certatim rasorum turba sequuntur,
Impietatis ut artifices ad talia semper
Præcedunt: post quos tractabile uulgus adorat,
Dona ferens pariter, nummos, Cereremque, uel oua,
Aucupium rasis gratum, cultusque scelesti
Speratum precium. Quo pacto idola coluntur,
Catholica hæc si sunt, Christique imitamina sponsæ?
Præterea ne quid simulacris ludere cessent,
Et pro derisu regnantem exponere Christum,
Assumunt aliam statuam pro more iacentem
Defuncti nuper, porrectis cruribus aptè,
Atque decussatim compostis pectore palmis,
Et pompa cantuque pio ad factum antè sepulchrum
Portant, sericeis tectam membra omnia peplis,
Sic tamen ut cerni possint multicia dicas
Serica, sic uisum transmittunt, cunctaque monstrant.
Præcedunt pueri tabulis in amœna crepantes,
Lumen et æditiuus præfert. Scit signa popellus,
In genua extemplò cadit, aut terræ oscula figit,
Extenditque manus, et multis pectora tundit,
Et statuam quernam diuinum ut numen adorat.
Ne iaceat uerò, inque sepulchro sola colatur,
Mysticus adfertur quoque et unà clauditur intus
Panis, ut impietas crescat, cultusque prophanus.
Sacrificus supplex statuam ueneratur inertem
Primus, et Assyrios pani succendit odores.
Multa statim populus comportat lumina circum,
Cancellisque hæret, noctemque diemque precatur

Curuatis genibus, uiolisque et flore sepulchrum
Omnigeno exornat, suaque affert munera largè.
Adsunt conducti quoque qui psalteria cantent
Alterius, defuncto homini uelut, atque nocenti,
Vt magis hinc plebes ad munera danda uocetur.

Sabbatum ante Pascha.

Ante diem Pas⟨c⟩hæ uetus aptè extinguitur ignis,
Et nouus è silicum uenis extunditur. Illum
Adiurat multis aduersum incommoda pastor.
Cuius quisque capit torrem molimine summo,
Fertque domum, ut quando tempestas ingruat atra,
Succenso, cœli plaga sit tutus ab omni.
Cereus hinc ingens, Pas⟨c⟩halis dictus, amœno
Sacratur cantu, cui ne mysteria desint
Thurea compingunt in facta foramina grana.
Hic ad honorem ardet uincentis tartara Christi
Nocte dieque quasi hoc uictu capiatur inani.
Post liquidas etiam baptismi consecrat undas
Vel præsul, uel Præpositus: nec enim amplius illæ
Baptismo prosunt, nec possunt tingere quenquam,
Præterito quarum ualuit toto usus in anno.
Magna procedunt pompa celebrique paratu
Candelis, crucibus, uexillis, chrismate, oliuo:
Circumeunt fontem nouies, diuosque precantur.
Fixi stant omnes tandem. Mox incipit ille,
Et ter tangit aquam, crucis effingitque figuras.
Grandia tum profert multa et plaustralia uerba,
Sanosque adiurat latices, et uexat ineptè,
Dum studet et credit meliores reddere multò
Omnipotentis quàm dextra ac benedictio fecit.
Pòst et candelam uexatas ponit in undas,
Terque suo flatu turbat pridiana obolenti
Prandia, et infuso tandem unctas chrismate reddit.
Attonitus spectat populus, creditque potentem
Vndis uim tribui tanto adiurantis hiatu,
Atque alijs, agitat quas gens doctissima, nugis.
Allatis igitur uasis de fontibus haurit,
Fertque domum contra morbos pecorisque suosque.
Inde silent tabulæ, et campanis pristina dantur
Iura, simulque suum capiunt ieiunia finem.

Pascha.

Nocte dein media consueta ad cantica surgunt.
Præuenit æditúus studio, rasusque sacerdos,
Et statuam è clauso tollunt, panemque, sepulchro:
Angelicasque indunt statuas, pepla rara tenentes
Aduersæ, uacua apparent reliqua omnia circum,

Immoti si non custodes usque manerent.
Sed puto nondum illos terræ sensisse tremorem,
Nec clarum ardentis uultum uidisse ministri.
Hinc aliam statuam uictricia signa ferentis
Imponunt aræ, cantantque animosius omnes:
Christum deuicto Satana, portisque refractis
Carceris inferni, uiuum redijsse sepulchro.
Quod tamen haud credunt: id quod testantur ubique
Cultibus ac studijs, dubio, factisque metuque.
Est ubi continuò ludi et spectacula dantur.
Vt tres conueniant Mariæ, uisantque sepulchrum,
Cumque Petro currat uelox Zebedeïa proles.
Hæc tam ridiculè fiunt gestuque iocisque,
Vt Crassum possint aut exhilarare Catonem.
Nocte statim, non expectata luce diei,
Carnes arripiunt quidam, comeduntque gulosè.
Cætera turba suas carnes, crassasque placentas,
Oua rubra, et raphanos, lactisque coagula dulcis,
Et quæcunque uolunt primo contingere gustu,
In templum confert, ut consecret antè sacerdos.
Discurrunt etiam monachi, uilesque domatim
Sacrifici, precium captantes atque lucellum,
Atque domi curant eadem cuicunque uolenti.
Degustant hodie raphanos ante omnia quidam,
Quartanam contra febrim, morbosque latentes.
Quid narrem hypocrisin magnam, cultumque coactum,
Quo cœnant plerique omnes de corpore Christi:
Non cœnaturi, si non horrenda timerent
Fulmina? Nullus enim nouit, creditque perennem
Se uitam nactum Christi morte atque triumpho.
Quis uerò ista doceret eos, quum cuncta Papatus
Dogmata, doctrinæ, cultus, ritusque repugnent?
Postridie lætos uulgò spaciantur in agros,
Et solitam repetunt uitam, linquuntque seuera.
I nunc, Iudæos ride, Turcasque cruentos,
Ob ritus cultusque suos, et dogmata praua.
Permultum sapiunt, si uis conferre Papistis.

Dies rogationum.

Hebdomas inde uenit, peregrè qua cum cruce uadunt
In uicinum aliquem uicum. Porrò inter eundum
Cantibus implorant diuos, Christique parentem
Præcipuè. Postquam uentum illuc, templa subintrant,
Regnantemque illic diuum diuamque precantur,
Vt seruet fruges, et grandinis atque pruinæ
Auertat mala, et annonæ leuet omne grauamen.

Pòst in cauponam properant, uel gramine strati
In uiridi prandent, largeque replentur Iaccho,
Absque cruce ut redeant interdum, gressibus atque
Incertis miserè titubent, reuomantque comesta.
Continuis omnes faciunt tribus ista diebus.
Cum crucibus multis persæpe uenitur in unum
Templum, cœtus ubi sua cantica clamat in auras
Quisque unde exoritur tristis confusio uocum,
Dum superare alios alij nituntur ineptè.
Sacrifici attendunt, placet hæc insania rasis,
Donaque uictrici tribuunt Baccheïa parti.
  Post uenit illa dies, superas qua Christus ad arces — Ascensio.
Scandit, quam celebrant itidem potuque ciboque
Prælargo: qua cuique aliqua est comedenda uolucris,
Haud scio quapropter. Post prandia templa petuntur.
Truncus ibi, qui tempus ad hoc est uisus in ara,
In summum trahitur demisso fune lacunar,
Cœtu sacrificum deducente atque canente.
Nam pietas horum consistit cantibus omnis.
Inde statim Satanæ præceps perturpis imago
Deijcitur, nonnunquam ardens, diruptaque prorsus.
Expectant pueri cupidè, uirgisque iacentem
Concidunt, lacerantque in paruas denique partes.
Post hæc deijcitur panis, quem barbara turba
Nuncupat oblatas, cui sæpe admixta papyrus
Imponit pueris. Fiunt magno omnia risu.
Ex laqueari etiam certa syphonibus arte
Eiaculantur aquas, si quem tinxisse laborant.
Atque ita finitur magno fabella cachinno.
  In Pentecoste mites albæque columbæ, — Pentecoste.
Funiculis leuiter uinctæ, mittuntur ab alto:
Lignea postremo cœlo dependet eodem.
Cernis ut idolis ludant, doceantque popellum,
Non secus ac pupis teneræ assueuere puellæ?

### (iii) *Barnabe Googe* (1540–94).

Kirchmayer's *Regnum Papisticum* was translated into English by Barnabe Googe under the title *The Popish Kingdome, or reigne of Antichrist, written in Latine verse by Thomas Naogeorgus, and englyshed by Barnabe Googe*, London, 1570. Concerning Googe see *D.N.B.*, xxii, 151–2; Wiener, pp. 105 sqq. The passage quoted under (ii) above from the *Regnum Papisticum* is rendered in *The Popish Kingdome* as follows (fol. $50^{r}$–$53^{v}$):[1]

[1] Googe actually translated from a later edition (1559) of Kirchmayer's book; but in the part with which we are concerned, the differences between the editions of 1553 and

Palme Sunday.

Here comes that worthie day wherein, our sauior Christ is thought,
To come vnto Jerusalem, on asses shoulders brought:
When as againe these Papistes fonde, their foolish pageantes haue,
With pompe and great solemnitie, and countnaunce wondrous graue.
A woodden Asse they haue, and Image great that on him rides,
But vnderneath the Asses feete, a table broade there slides,
Being borne on wheeles, which ready drest, and al things meete therfore
The Asse is brought abroade and set before the Churches doore:
The people all do come and bowes of trees and palmes they bere,
Which things against the tempest great, the Parson coniures there,
And straytwayes downe before the Asse, vpon his face he lies,
Whome there an other Priest doth strike with rodde of largest sise:
He rising vp, two lubbours great vpon their faces fall,
In straunge attire and lothsomely, with filthie tune they ball:
Who when againe they risen are, with stretching out their hande,
They poynt vnto the woodden knight, and singing as they stande
Declare that that is he that came, into the worlde to saue,
And to redeeme such as in him their hope assured haue:
And euen the same that long agone while in the streate he roade,
The people mette, and Oliue bowes so thicke before hym stroade.
This being soung, the people cast the braunches as they passe,
Some part vpon the Image, and some part vpon the Asse.
Before whose feete a wondrous heape, of bowes and braunches ly,
This done into the Church he strayght, is drawne full solemly:
The shauen Priestes before them marche, the people follow fast,
Still striuing who shall gather first the bowes that downe are cast:
For falsely they beleeue that these, haue force and vertue great,
Against the rage of winter stormes, and thunders flashing heate.
Are Idoles worshipt otherwise, are these not wicked things?
Euen I my selfe haue earst behelde, both wise and mightie Kings
Defilde with this religion vile, that on their knees haue kneelde,
Vnto these stockes, and honour due to God, to them did yeelde.
In some place wealthie Citizens, and men of sober chere
For no small summe doe hire this Asse, with them about to bere,
And manerly they vse the same, not suffering any by,
To touch this Asse, nor to presume vnto his presence ny:
For they suppose that in this thing, they Christ doe highly serue,
And well of him accepted are, and great rewardes deserue.
If any man shall happe to thinke, them Asses here in this,
I sure beleeue he is not much deceyude, nor thinkes amis.
When as the Priestes and people all haue ended this the sport,
The boyes doe after dinner come, and to the Church resort:

1559 are negligible. Googe's translation of 1570 is reprinted under the editorship of R. C. Hope, London, 1880.

The Sexten pleasde with price, and looking well no harme be done,
They take the Asse, and through the streetes, and crooked lanes they rone,
Whereas they common verses sing, according to the guise,
The people giuing money, breade, and egges of largest cise.
Of this their gaines they are compelde, the maister halfe to giue
Least he alone without his portion of the Asse shoulde liue.
From Thurseday then till Easter come, the fondest toyes haue place
Wherin these cathlikes think themselues, great men of wondrous grace

Maundy Thursday.

First three dayes space the belles are wilde, in silence for to lie,
When from the toppes of hawtie towres, with clappers lowd they crie.
The boyes in euery streat doe runne, and noyses great they make,
While as in calling men to Church their wooden clappers shake.
Thre nightes at midnight vp they rise, their Mattens for to heare,
Appoynted well with clubbes and staues, and stones in order theare:
The Sexten straightwayes putteth out the candles speedely,
And straight the Priest with rustie throte, alowde begins to cry.
Then furious rage begins to spring, and hurlyburly rise,
On pewes and deskes and seates they bounce, and beate in dredfull-wise:
Thou wouldst suppose they were possest, with sprightes and deuills all,
Or fury such as forceth them, that vpon Baccus call.
Some beaten downe with clubbes and staues, amongst the pewes do ly
And others almost brainde with stones, or wounded mortally.
Well serues the darckenesse for these deedes, and thereto doth agree,
The fashions like of euery one, that thus enraged bee.
Here wicked Iudas all to torne, with vile reproches lies,
And Marie in the darcke is calde vpon with childish cries.
That she be mercifull and helpe, and heale the faultes that bee,
And through hir powre deliuer them, from hurt and miseree.
These things vnto these feastes belonges, the candles being light,
An Image fastned to a crosse is caried all vpright:
A lanterne rounde about his necke, is hangde to shew the way,
Are not these popish foolish toyes, a pretie kinde of play?
This day the oyle and glasses of the Bishop hallowed bee,
And twise three times saluting them, he lowly bendes his knee.
The Cannons after doe the same, with laughter wouldst thou faint,
And woonder farre to see them make, their speechelesse glasse a saint.
Their dinner done, from th'aultar all their costly clothes they take,
And wash it, rubbing it with bowes, and bromes that they doe make:
Then water on they powre and wine crosswise there on they lay,
And to the patron of ech aultar, humbly doe they pray,
That they vouchsafe to looke vpon theyr seruaunts worshipping,
And to aswage the furie great, of Ioue the thundring King.

And here the Monkes their maundie make, with sundrie solemne rights
And signes of great humilitie, and wondrous pleasaunt sights.
Ech one the others feete doth wash, and wipe them cleane and drie,
With hatefull minde, and secret frawde, that in their heartes doth lye:
As if that Christ with his examples, did these thinges require,
And not to helpe our brethren here, with zeale and free desire,
Ech one supplying others want, in all things that they may,
As he himselfe a seruaunt made, to serue vs euery way.
Then strait the loaues doe walke, and pottes in euery place they skinke
Wherewith the holy fathers oft, to pleasaunt damsels drinke,
And sure with no dissembling heart, for true as steele they bee,
And often times they put in proofe their great fidelitee.

Good friday.

Two Priestes the next day following, vpon their shoulders beare,
The Image of the Crucifix, about the altar neare:
Being clad in coape of crimozen die, and dolefully they sing:
At length before the steps his coate pluckt of they straight him bring,
And vpon Turkey Carpettes lay him downe full tenderly,
With cushions vnderneath his heade, and pillowes heaped hie:
Then flat vpon the grounde they fall, and kisse both hande and feete,
And worship so this woodden God, with honour farre vnmeete.
Then all the shauen sort falles downe, and foloweth them herein,
As workemen chiefe of wickednesse, they first of all begin:
And after them the simple soules, the common people come,
And worship him with diuers giftes, as Golde, and siluer some:
And others corne or egges againe, to poulshorne persons sweete,
And eke a long desired price, for wicked worship meete.
How are the Idoles worshipped, if this religion here
Be Catholike, and like the spowes of Christ accounted dere?
Besides with Images the more, their pleasure here to take.
And Christ that euerywhere doth raigne, a laughing stocke to make,
An other Image doe they get, like one but newly deade,
With legges stretcht out at length and handes, vpon his body spreade:
And him with pompe and sacred song, they beare vnto his graue,
His bodie all being wrapt in lawne, and silkes and sarcenet braue,
The boyes before with clappers go, and filthie noyses make,
The Sexten beares the light, the people hereof knowledge take:
And downe they kneele, or kisse the grounde, their handes held vp abrod
And knocking on their breastes they make, this woodden blocke a God.
And least in graue he shoulde remaine, without some companie,
The singing bread is layde with him, for more idolatrie:
The Priest the Image worships first, as falleth to his turne,
And franckensence and sweete perfumes, before the breade doth burne:
With tapers all the people come, and at the barriars stay,

Where downe vpon their knees they fall, and night and day they pray:
And violets and euery kinde of flowres about the graue
They straw, and bring in all their giftes, and presents that they haue.
The singing men their Dirges chaunt, as if some guiltie soule,
Were buried there, that thus they may, the people better poule.
  On Easter eue the fire all, is quencht in euery place, **Easter eue.**
And fresh againe from out the flint, is fetcht with solemne grace:
The Priest doth halow this against great daungers many one,
A brande whereof doth euery man with greedie minde take home,
That when the fearefull storme appeares, or tempest blacke arise,
By lighting this he safe may be, from stroke of hurtfull skies:
A Taper great the paschall namde, with musicke then they blesse,
And franckensence herein they pricke, for greater holynesse:
This burneth night and day as signe, of Christ that conquerde hell,
As if so be this foolish toye, suffiseth this to tell.
Then doth the Bishop or the Priest, the water halow straight,
That for their baptisme is reserude: for now no more of waight
Is that they vsde the yeare before, nor can they any more,
Yong children christen with the same, as they haue done before.
With woondrous pompe and furniture, amid the Church they go,
With candles, crosses, banners, Chrisme, and oyle appoynted tho:
Nine times about the font they marche, and on the saintes doe call,
Then still at length they stande, and straight the Priest begins withall,
And thrise the water doth he touche, and crosses thereon make,
Here bigge and barbrous wordes he speakes, to make the deuill quake:
And holsome waters coniureth, and foolishly doth dresse,
Supposing holyar that to make, which God before did blesse:
And after this his candle than, he thrusteth in the floode,
And thrise he breathes thereon with breath, that stinkes of former foode:
And making here an ende, his Chrisme he poureth therevpon,
The people staring hereat stande, amazed euery one:
Beleeuing that great powre is giuen to this water here,
By gaping of these learned men, and such like trifling gere.
Therefore in vessels brought they draw, and home they carie some,
Against the grieues that to themselues, or to their beastes may come.
Then Clappers ceasse, and belles are set againe at libertee,
And herewithall the hungrie times of fasting ended bee.
  At midnight then with carefull minde, they vp to mattens ries, **Easter day.**
The Clarke doth come and after him, the Priest with staring eies:
The Image and the breade from out the graue (a worthie sight)
They take, and Angels two they place in vesture white,
And rounde about ech place appeeres, all voyde of standers by,
Saue onely that the watchmen there, amazed seeme to ly.
But yet I thinke the trembling of the earth they neuer see,

Nor of the heauenly messenger, the flaming maiestie.
An other Image of a Conquerour they forth doe bring,
And on the aultar place, and then, they lustily doe sing,
That Gates of hell a sunder burst, and Sathan ouerthrowne,
Christ from his graue is risen vp, and now aliue is knowne.
Which yet they thinke not so to be, as plainely doth appeere,
By their Religion, doubtes, and feare, and by their doings here.
In some place solemne sightes and showes, and Pageants fayre are playd,
With sundrie sortes of maskers braue, in straunge attire arayd,
As where the Maries three doe meete, the sepulchre to see,
And Iohn with Peter swiftly runnes, before him there to bee.
These things are done with iesture such, and with so pleasaunt game,
That euen the grauest men that liue, woulde laugh to see the same.
At midnight strait, not tarying till the daylight doe appeere,
Some gettes in flesh and glutton lyke, they feede vpon their cheere.
They rost their flesh, and custardes great, and egges and radish store,
And trifles, clouted creame, and cheese, and whatsoeuer more
At first they list to eate, they bring into the temple straight,
That so the Priest may halow them with wordes of wondrous waight.
The Friers besides, and pelting Priestes, from house to house doe roame,
Receyuing gaine of euery man that this will haue at home.
Some raddish rootes this day doe take before all other meate,
Against the quartan ague and such other sicknesse great.
What should I shew their forced fayth and great hypocrisie,
When as of Ch⟨r⟩ist they doe receyue the dredfull misterie?
Which they ne woulde if that they fearde not lightnings of the Pope,
For none of them beleeueth here, nor none of them doth hope
That they receyue eternall life, and euerlasting seate,
By death of Jesus Christ and by his crosse and triumph great.
For who should teache to them the same, since every Popes decree,
Their doctrine sayth, and all their rightes, to this contrarie bee?
Straight after this, into the fieldes they walke to take the viewe,
And to their woonted life they fall, and bid the reast adewe:
Go nowe and laugh the Jewes to scorne, and all the Turkes that bee,
For fayth, religion, lawes, and life, and their Idolatree.
Sure wondrous wise and good they be, if that thou wilt compare
Them with these doltish Papistes here, that blinde and beastly are.

Procession weeke.

Nowe comes the day wherein they gad abrode, with crosse in hande,
To boundes of euery field, and round about their neighbours land:
And as they go, they sing and pray to euery saint aboue,
But to our Ladie specially, whom most of all they loue.
When as they to the towne are come, the Church they enter in,
And looke what saint that Church doth guide, they humbly pray to him,
That he preserue both corne and fruite, from storme and tempest great,

And them defend from harme, and send them store of drinke and meat.
This done, they to the Tauerne go, or in the fieldes they dine,
Where downe they sit and feede a pace, and fill themselues with wine,
So much that oftentymes without the Crosse they come away,
And miserably they reele, till as their stomacke vp they lay.
These things three dayes continually are done, with solemne sport,
With many Crosses often they vnto some Church resort,
Whereas they all do chaunt alowde, wherby there streight doth spring,
A bawling noyse, while euery man seekes hyghest for to sing:
The Priestes giue eare, this madnesse them doth most of all content,
And wine to them that passe the reast, is from the Parson sent.
Then comes the day when Christ ascended to his fathers seate, Ascension day.
Which day they also celebrate, with store of drinke and meate.
Then euery man some birde must eate, I know not to what ende,
And after dinner all to church they come, and there attende.
The blocke that on the aultar still, till then was seene to stande,
Is drawne vp hie aboue the roofe, by ropes, and force of hande:
The Priestes about it rounde do stand, and chaunt it to the skie,
For all these mens religion great, in singing most doth lie.
Then out of hande the dreadfull shape of Sathan downe they throw,
Oft times with fire burning bright, and dasht a sunder tho,
The boyes with greedie eyes do watch, and on him straight they fall,
And beate him sore with rods, and breake him into peeces small.
This done, they wafers downe doe cast, and singing Cakes the while,
With Papers rounde amongst them put, the children to beguile.
With laughter great are all things done: and from the beames they let
Great streames of water downe to fall, on whom they meane to wet.
And thus this solemne holiday, and hye renowmed feast,
And all their whole deuotion here, is ended with a ieast.
On Whitsunday whyte Pigeons tame in strings from heauen flie, Whitsun-day.
And one that framed is of wood, still hangeth in the skie.
Thou seest how they with Idols play, and teach the people to,
None otherwise then little gyrles with Puppets vse to do.

### (iv) *George Gilpin, the Elder* (1514?–1602).

*The Bee hiue of the Romishe Churche. . . . Translated out of Dutch into Englishe by George Gilpin the Elder*, London, 1579, is a translation of a Calvinistic satire on Catholicism published in 1569 by Philipp van Marnix, Sainte-Aldegonde (1538–98), under the pseudonym Isaac Rabbotenu. See *D.N.B.*, xxi, 380. The following passage is from *The Bee hiue*, fol. 200v–201v:

In summe, Christ hath not done anie thing in his death and passion, but they do plaie and counterfeite the same after him, so trimlie and liuelie that no plaier nor iuggler is able to do it better.

Yea, do we not see likewise, that vppon good Friday they haue a Crucifixe, either of wood, or of stone, which they laie downe softlie vpon the ground, that euerie bodie may comme creeping to it, vpon handes and knees, and so kisse the feete of it, as men are accustomed to doe to the Pope of Rome: And then they put him in a graue, till Easter: at which time they take him vppe againe, and sing, Resurrexit, non est hic, Alleluia: He is risen, he is not here: God be thanked. Yea and in some places, they make the graue in a hie place in the church where men must goe vp manie steppes, which are decked with blacke cloth from aboue to beneath, and vpon euerie steppe standeth a siluer candlesticke with a waxe candle burning in it, and there doe walke souldiours in harnesse, as bright as Saint George, which keepe the graue, till the Priests come and take him vp: and then cometh sodenlie a flash of fire, wherwith they are all afraid and fall downe: and then up-startes the man, and they begin to sing Alleluia, on all handes, and then the clocke striketh eleuen.

Creeping to the Crucifixe and burying it.

Then againe upon Whitsunday they begin to play a new Enterlude, for then they send downe a Dove out of an Owles nest, deuised in the roofe of the church: but first they cast out rosin and gunpouder, with wilde fire, to make the children afraide, and that must needes be the holie ghost, which commeth with thunder and lightening.

The holy ghost on Whitsunday.

Likewise, upon Ascension day, they pull Christ vp on hie with ropes aboue the clouds, by a vice deuised in the roofe of the church, and they hale him vp, as if they would pull him vp to the gallowes: and there stande the poore Priests, and looke so pitifully after their God, as a dogge for his dinner.

The Crucifix ascendeth to heauen.

In summe, a man doeth often spende a pennie or two, to see a play of Robin hood, or a Morisse daunse, which were a great deale better bestowed vppon these apishe toies of these good Priests, which counterfeite all these matters so handsomlie, that it will do a man as much good to see them, as in frostie weather to goe naked.

I speake not of their perambulations, processions, and going about the towne, cariing their crucifixes alongst the streetes, and there play and counterfeite the whole passion, so trimlie with all the seuen sorrowes of our Lady, as though it had ben nothing else, but a simple and plaine Enterlude, to make boyes laugh at, and a litle to recreat heauie or sorrowfull hearts: for these matters fal out onlie vpon Church holy dayes or solemnities, when the Catholikes are determined to be merrie, and drink themselues so droncke, that they tumble from their seat: as you shall see our Maisters of Louen doo euery yere in their solemnitie, and especially at the seuenth yeres procession, which is, of the seuen sorrowes of our Ladie. All what soeuer Christ hath done, must bee set abroch to be counterfeite.

# APPENDIX D

## MISCELLANEOUS RECORDS AND REFERENCES

Here are brought together merely a few of the more striking records or mentions of plays or dramatic ceremonies associated with churches which have been omitted from the body of the present treatise, or have been merely referred to there. The list below makes no pretence to comprehensiveness or completeness. A large number of references to such records from England are given by Chambers, ii, Appendix W *passim*, and a more extensive collection of them is being made by another investigator.

### (i) *Beverley, Yorkshire.*

Contigit ut tempore quodam æstivo intra septa polyandri ecclesiæ Beati Johannis, ex parte aquilonari, larvatorum (ut assolet) et verbis et actu fieret repræsentatio Dominicæ resurrectionis. Confluebat eo copiosa utriusque sexus multitudo, variis inducta votis, delectationis videlicet, seu admirationis causa, vel sancto proposito excitandæ devotionis. Cum vero, præ densa vulgi astante corona, pluribus, et præcipue statura pusillis, desideratus minime pateret accessus, introierunt plurimi in ecclesiam; ut vel orarent, vel picturas inspicerent, vel per aliquod genus recreationis et solatii pro hoc die tædium evitarent. Ingressi igitur ecclesiæ limina adolescentuli quidam, casu fortuito ostium quoddam reperiunt semiapertum, quo per gradus ascenditur ad superiora murorum. Eo accurrentes levitate puerili, gradatim insuper murales ascendebant basilicæ testudines, ea ut reor intentione, ut per altas turriculorum fenestras, seu si qua vitrearum fenestrarum essent foramina, liberius personarum et habitus et gestus respicerent, et earundem dialogos auditu faciliori adverterent; Zaccheum in hoc imitantes, *qui cum esset statura pusillus, ut videret Jesum, arborem ascendit sycomorum.* Sed, ecce! intimatum est matriculariis quod agebatur ab adolescentulis; qui nimirum verentes ne puerorum indiscretio, desiderio videndi personas, quarum officio prætaxata transigebatur repræsentatio, fenestras vitreas perforaret, vel aliquo modo detereret, illos insequebantur cursu pernici; ipsosque temeritatis argutos, alapis gravioribus expalmatos coegerunt reverti.

Quidam vero puerorum, pœna sociorum conspecta, in insequentium manus formidans incidere, superiores secessit in partes, quoadusque deveniret cursu prærapido ultra crucem magnam, tunc temporis collocatam in altaris B. Martini confinio. Ibi vero stans et deorsum aspiciens, quadrato cuidam lapidi pedem imposuit incautius; qui a muro solutus et decisus, non sine fragore magno super lapideum decidit pavimentum; et, non obstante duritia, in infinitas partes est comminutus. Adolescentulus vero suo destitutus fulcimine, horrendo stupore percussus, solotenus corruit, et ibi per aliquantum temporis articulum exanimis jacuit, et mortuo simillimus. Circumstabant plurimi graviter suspirantes, de casu tali miserabiliter ingemiscentes, dolores suos lacrymarum exuberantia protestantes. Parentes ejus ejulabant, laniabant capillos, clamorem et ululatum crebris interrumpebant singultibus; ignorantes, quia in brevi Divina dispensatione tristitia in gaudium, ploratus in risum esset convertendus. Non passus namque Deus ecclesiam, in Sui et Confessoris honore dedicatam, quasi cæde humana pollui; sed volens eam majoris in posterum auctoritatis haberi, volens etiam testimonium perhibere veritatis, illi quæ interim fiebat suæ resurrectionis repræsentationi; in omnium qui aderant conspectu adolescentulum, qui mortuus credebatur, erexit incolumem, adeo ut nec aliquam in toto corpore suo esset perpendere læsionem. Factum est ergo, ut qui præ populi multitudine extra ecclesiam repræsentationi non poterant interesse, mirabilius viderent resurrectionis indicium intra corpus ecclesiæ; et non tantum resurrectionis, sed passionis Dominicæ. Per decisionem namque lapidis, sine manu decidentis a muro, plane indicabatur, sine admixtione virili, ex virgine Dominica Incarnatio: per utriusque casum, scilicet et lapidis et pueri, significabatur passio Ejusdem, hominis et Dei. Veruntamen lapis cadendo confractus typum gessit arietis occisi; adolescens vero typum Isaac permanentis illæsi. Unde Cujus passionis secundum humanitatem signum fuit ruina; Ejus etiam resurrectionis secundum Divinitatem signum exstitit erectio miraculosa.[1]

(ii) *Cividale.*

De Repræsentatione ludi Christi. Anno Domini mcclxxxxviii. die vii. exeunte Majo, videlicet in die Pentecostes, et in aliis sequentibus duobus diebus, facta fuit repræsentatio Ludi Christi; videlicet Passionis, Resurrectionis, Ascensionis, adventus Spiritus Sancti, et adventus Christi ad Judicium in Curia Domini Patriarchæ (Raimundi a Turre) Austriæ Civitatis, Forijulii, honorifice, et laudabiliter per Clerum Civitatensem.[2]

Anno Domini mccciiii. facta fuit per Clerum, sive per Capitulum Civitatense Repræsentatio: sive factæ sunt Repræsentationes infrascriptæ. Imprimis de Creatione primorum parentum, deinde de Annunciatione Beatæ Virginis, de Partu, et aliis multis: et de Passione et Resurrectione, Ascensione et adventu Spiritus Sancti, et de Anti-

[1] James Raine, ed., *The Historians of the Church of York and its Archbishops*, i, London, 1879, pp. 328–30, from a thirteenth-century *continuator* of the *Vita* of St John of Beverley. See also *Acta Sanctorum*, Maii, ii, 187–8; Chambers, ii, 338–9; A. F. Leach, in *Furnivall Miscellany*, pp. 206–8.

[2] Rubeis, p. 354, from 'Julianus Canonicus in Chronico Forojuliensi'. See L. A. Muratori, *Antiquitates Italicæ Medii Ævi*, ii, Milan, 1739, Diss. 29, *De Spectaculis et Ludis publicis*, col. 849; D'Ancona, i, 91; Chambers, ii, 77–8.

christo, et aliis: et demum de adventu Christi ad Judicium. Et prædicta facta fuerunt solemniter in Curia Domini Patriarchæ in Festo Pentecostes cum aliis duobus sequentibus; præsente Rev. D. Ottobono Patriarcha Aquilegiensi, D. Jacobo q. D. Ottonelli de Civitate Episcopo Concordiensi, et aliis multis Nobilibus de Civitatibus, et Castris Forijulii, die xv. exeunte Majo.[1]

(iii) *Dunstable, Bedfordshire.*

Gaufridus Abbas. Hic, ex illustri Cenomanensium et Normannorum progenie exortus, non solum morum honestate præditus, sed divina scientia satis extitit adornatus. Qui, defuncto Abbate Ricardo, cunctorum hujus ecclesiæ fratrum electione, assensu etiam Anglorum Regis, Henrici Primi, hanc Abbathiam, etsi invitus, suscepit gubernandam.

Iste de Cenomannia, unde oriundus erat, venit, vocatus ab Abbate Ricardo, dum adhuc sæcularis esset, ut scholam apud Sanctum Albanum regeret. Et cum venisset, concessa fuit schola alii magistro, quia non venit tempestive. Legit igitur apud Dunestapliam, expectans scholam Sancti Albani, sibi repromissam; ubi quemdam ludum de Sancta Katerina,—quem 'Miracula' vulgariter appellamus,—fecit. Ad quæ decoranda, petiit a Sacrista Sancti Albani, ut sibi capæ chorales accommodarentur, et obtinuit. Et fuit ludus ille de Sancta Katerina.

Casu igitur, nocte sequenti, accensa est domus Magistri Gaufridi; et combusta est domus, cum libris suis et capis memoratis. Nesciens igitur quomodo hoc damnum Deo et Sancto Albano restauraret, seipsum reddidit in holocaustum Deo, assumens habitum religionis in Domo Sancti Albani. Et hæc fuit causa, quare tantum habuit diligentiæ, ut capas chorales in eadem, postea in Abbatem promotus, faceret pretiosas.[2]

(iv) *Leconfield, Yorkshire.*

Item My Lord useth and accustomyth to gyfe yerely if his Lordship kepe a Chapell and be at home them of his Lordschipes Chapell if they doo play the Play of the Nativite uppon Cristynmes-Day in the mornnynge in my Lords Chapell befor his Lordship—xxs.[3]

Item My Lorde useth and accustomyth to gyf yerely when his Lordshipe is home and hath an Abbot of Miserewll ⟨*i.e.* Misrule⟩ in Cristynmas in his Lordschippis Hous uppon New-Yers-day in rewarde—xxs.[4]

Item My Lord usith and accustomedith to gyfe yerely if his Lordship kepe a Chapell and is at home in rewarde to them of his Lordshipe

[1] Rubeis, p. 354, from same source.

[2] H. T. Riley, ed., *Chronica Monasterii S. Albani*, i, London, 1867, pp. 72–3, from *Gesta Abbatum Monasterii Sancti Albani, Sectio Prima, a Matthæo Parisiensi, pro majori parte, conscripta*. See Chambers, ii, 366.

[3] [Thomas Percy, ed.,] *The Regulations and Establishment of the Household of Henry Algernon Percy*, London, 1827, p. 343. This entry and the two following ones are from a list of customary rewards drawn up during the first quarter of the sixteenth century.

[4] *Id.*, p. 344.

Chapell and other his Lordshipis Servauntes that playth the Play of Resurrection upon Estur-Day in the Mornnynge in my Lordis 'Chapell' befor his Lordshipe—xxs.[1]

(v) *London.*

Londonia pro spectaculis theatralibus, pro ludis scenicis, ludos habet sanctiores, repræsentationes miraculorum quæ sancti confessores operati sunt, seu repræsentationes passionum quibus claruit constantia martyrum.[2]

(vi) *Regensburg.*

Anno Domini 1194 celebratus est in Ratispona ordo creacionis angelorum et ruina Luciferi et suorum, et creacionis hominis et casus et prophetarum sub Celestino III papa, regnante Hainrico imperatore et semper augusto et Chounrado regente inibi episcopatum, septima Idus Februarii.[3]

(vii) *Riga.*

Eadem hyeme factus est *ludus prophetarum* ordinatissimus, quem *Latini Comœdiam* vocant, in media *Riga*, vt fidei Christianæ rudimenta gentilitas fide etiam disceret oculata. Cuius ludi et comœdiæ materia tam neophytis, quam paganis, qui aderant, per interpretem diligentissime exponebatur. Vbi autem armati *Gedeonis* cum *Philistæis* pugnabant; pagani, timentes occidi, fugere cœperunt, sed caute sunt reuocati. Sic ergo admodum breue tempus siluit Ecclesia, in pace quiescendo. Iste autem ludus quasi præambulum, præludium et præsagium erat futurorum malorum. Nam in eodem ludo erant bella, vtpote *Dauid*, *Gedeonis*, *Herodis*. Erat et doctrina *Veteris et Noui Testamenti*, quia nimirum per bella plurima, quæ sequuntur, conuertenda erat gentilitas, et per doctrinam Veteris et Noui Testamenti erat instruenda, qualiter ad verum pacificum et ad vitam perueniat sempiternam.[4]

(viii) *Witney*, *Oxfordshire.*

In the Dayes of ceremonial Religion they used at *Wytney* to set foorthe yearly in maner of a Shew, or Enterlude, the Resurrection of our Lord and Saviour *Chryste*, partly of Purpose to draw thyther some Concourse of People that might spend their Money in the Towne, but cheiflie to allure by pleasant Spectacle the comon Sort to the Likinge of Popishe Maumetrie; for the which Purpose, and the more lyvely thearby to exhibite to the Eye the hole Action of the Resurrection, the Preistes

[1] *Id.*, p. 345. See Chambers, ii, 375.

[2] J. C. Robertson, ed., *Materials for the History of Thomas Becket*, iii, London, 1877, p. 9, from the section *De ludis*, in the description of London introducing the *Vita S. Thomæ* by William Fitzstephen (†1170–82). See Chambers, ii, 379–80.

[3] *Monumenta Germaniæ Historica, Scriptores*, ed. G. H. Pertz, xvii, Hannover, 1861, p. 590, from *Annales Ratisponenses*, ed. W. Wattenbach. See Creizenach, i, 64.

[4] J. D. Gruber, ed., *Origines Livoniæ Sacræ et Civilis*, Frankfort and Leipzig, 1740, p. 34, from *Gesta Alberti Livoniensis Episcopi*, under the year 1204. See Creizenach, i, 64–5.

garnished out certein smalle Puppets, representinge the Parsons of *Christe*, the Watchmen, *Marie*, and others, amongest the which one bare the Parte of a wakinge Watcheman, who (espiinge *Christ* to arise) made a continual Noyce, like to the Sound that is caused by the Metinge of two Styckes, and was therof comonly called, *Jack Snacker* of *Wytney*.[1]

### (ix) *York*.

Item inueniet ⟨thesaurarius⟩ stellas cum omnibus ad illas pertinentibus, preter cirpos, quos inueniet Episcopus Puerorum futurorum ⟨fatuorum?⟩, vnam in nocte Natalis Domini pro pastoribus, et ij[as] in nocte Epiphanie, si debeat fieri presentacio iij[um] regum.[2]

[1] W. Lambarde, *Dictionarium Angliæ Topographicum et Historicum: An Alphabetical Description of the Chief Places in England and Wales*, London, 1730, p. 459. This work was written in the sixteenth century.

[2] Wordsworth, *Lincoln*, ii, 98, from York Statutes of the thirteenth century. See Chambers, ii, 399.

# LIST OF BOOKS

The following list is offered not as a complete bibliography of the subjects included in the present treatise, but primarily as an elucidation of the abbreviated references in the foot-notes and appendices. Abbreviated references to periodicals (see, for example, BROOKS) are explained in alphabetical entries in the list itself.


*A.H.* G. M. Dreves and C. Blume, ed., *Analecta Hymnica Medii Ævi*, Leipzig, 1886 sqq.

ADAMS. J. Q. Adams, ed., *Chief Pre-Shakespearean Dramas*, Boston, New York, &c., [1924].

ALBERS, *Consuetudines*. B. Albers, ed., *Consuetudines Monasticæ*, 5 vols., Monte Cassino, 1900–12.

ALLEN, *Institutions*. A. V. G. Allen, *Christian Institutions*, New York, 1897.

ALLEN, *Lyric*. P. S. Allen, *The Romanesque Lyric*, Chapel Hill, 1928.

ALT. H. Alt, *Theater und Kirche in ihrem gegenseitigen Verhältniss historisch dargestellt*, Berlin, 1846.

ANZ. H. Anz, *Die lateinischen Magierspiele*, Leipzig, 1905.

ARENS. F. Arens, ed., *Der Liber Ordinarius der Essener Stiftskirche*, Paderborn, 1908.

ASCHNER. S. Aschner, *Zum Ludus de Antichristo*, in *Münchener Museum für Philologie des Mittelalters und der Renaissance*, i [1911–12], 355–62.

ATCHLEY. E. G. C. F. Atchley, *A History of the Use of Incense in Divine Worship* (*Alcuin Club Collections*, xiii), London, 1909.

AUBER. C. A. Auber, *Histoire et Théorie du Symbolisme religieux*, 4 vols., Paris, 1870–84.

BÄUMER. S. Bäumer, *Histoire du Bréviaire*, trans. R. Biron, 2 vols., Paris, 1905.

BARBIERI. L. Barbieri, ed., *Ordinarium Ecclesiæ Parmensis e vetustioribus excerptum reformatum A. 1417*, Parma, 1866.

BARROW AND HULME. *Antichrist and Adam: Two Mediaeval Religious Dramas*, trans. Sarah F. Barrow and W. H. Hulme (*Western Reserve University: Bulletin*, xxviii, no. 8), Cleveland, 1925.

BARTHÉLEMY. *Rational ou Manuel des divins Offices de Guillaume Durand*, trans. C. Barthélemy, 5 vols., Paris, 1854.

BARTHOLOMAEIS. V. De Bartholomaeis, *Le Origini della Poesia drammatica italiana*, Bologna, [1924].

BARTHOLOMAEIS, *Teatro*. V. De Bartholomaeis, *Il Teatro abruzzese del Medio Evo*, Bologna, [1924].

BASKERVILL, *Folk Festivals*. C. R. Baskervill, *Dramatic Aspects of Medieval Folk Festivals in England*, in *Studies in Philology* (University of North Carolina), xvii (1920), 19–87.

BASKERVILL, *Wooing Plays*. C. R. Baskervill, *Mummers' Wooing Plays in England*, in *M.P.*, xxi (1924), 225–72.

BATIFFOL. P. Batiffol, *History of the Roman Breviary*, trans. A. M. Y. Baylay, London, 1912.

BAUDRILLART. A. Baudrillart, A. Vogt, and U. Rouziès, *Dictionnaire d'Histoire et de Géographie ecclésiastiques*, Paris, 1912 sqq.

BEATTY. A. Beatty, *The St George, or Mummers', Play: A Study in the Protology of the Drama*, in *Transactions of the Wisconsin Academy of Sciences, Arts and Letters*, xv, part 2 (1906), 273–324.

BECKERS. O. Beckers, *Untersuchungen über das Spiel von den Zehn Jungfrauen*, Breslau, 1904.

BEESON. C. H. Beeson, *A Primer of Medieval Latin*, Chicago, [1925].

BEISSEL. S. Beissel, *Geschichte der Verehrung Marias in Deutschland während des Mittelalters*, Freiburg, 1909.

BELLOTTE. A. Bellotte, *Ritus Ecclesiæ Laudunensis redivivi . . . ex vetustissimis MSS codicibus vindicati*, Paris, 1652.

BERGNER. H. Bergner, *Handbuch der kirchlichen Kunstaltertümer in Deutschland*, Leipzig, 1905.

BERLINER. R. Berliner, *Denkmäler der Krippenkunst*, Augsburg, 1926 sqq.

*BIBLIA SACRA*. See HETZENAUER.

BINTERIM. A. J. Binterim, *Die vorzüglichsten Denkwürdigkeiten der christkatholischen Kirche*, 7 vols., Mainz, 1825–41.

BISHOP. E. Bishop, *Liturgica Historica*, Oxford, 1918.

BLOXAM. M. H. Bloxam, *The Principles of Gothic Ecclesiastical Architecture*, 3 vols., London, 1882.

BLUME, *Repertorium*. C. Blume, *Repertorium Repertorii: Kritischer Wegweiser durch U. Chevalier's Repertorium Hymnologicum* (*Hymnologische Beiträge*, ii), Leipzig, 1901.

BÖHME. M. Böhme, *Das lateinische Weihnachtspiel* (*Beiträge zur Kultur- und Universalgeschichte*, xl), Leipzig, 1917.

BOEHMER. E. Boehmer, *Sponsus: Mystère des Vierges sages et des Vierges folles*, in *Romanische Studien*, ed. E. Boehmer, iv (1879–80), 99–111.

BOHATTA. H. Bohatta, *Liturgische Bibliographie des xv. Jahrhunderts mit Ausnahme der Missale und Livres d'Heures*, Vienna, 1911.

BOHNSTEDT. K. K. R. Bohnstedt, *Vie Saint Nicholas, altfranzösisches Gedicht, Erlangen*, 1897.

BOND, *Chancel*. F. Bond, *The Chancel of English Churches*, Oxford, 1916.

BOUTILLIER. F. Boutillier, *Drames liturgiques et Rites figurés ou Cérémonies symboliques dans l'Église de Nevers*, in *Bulletin de la Société Nivernaise des Sciences, Lettres et Arts*, 2e série, viii (1880), 441–521.

BRAUN, *Altar*. J. Braun, *Der christliche Altar in seiner geschichtlichen Entwicklung*, 2 vols., Munich, 1924.

BRAUN, *Gewandung*. J. Braun, *Die liturgische Gewandung im Occident und Orient nach Ursprung und Entwicklung, Verwendung und Symbolik*, Freiburg, etc., 1907.

BRAUN, *Handlexikon*. J. Braun, *Liturgisches Handlexikon*, Regensburg, 1924.

BRINKMANN. H. Brinkmann, *Zum Ursprung des liturgischen Spieles*, in *Xenia Bonnensia: Festschrift zum fünfundsiebzigjährigen Bestehen des Philologischen Vereins und Bonner Kreises*, Bonn, 1929, pp. 106–43.

BROOKS, *Easter Plays*. N. C. Brooks, *Liturgical Easter Plays from Rheinau Manuscripts*, in *J.E.G.P.*, x (1911), 191–6.

BROOKS, *Himmelfahrtsfeier*. N. C. Brooks, *Eine liturgisch-dramatische Himmelfahrtsfeier*, in *Z.f.d.A.*, lxii (1925), 91–6.

BROOKS, *Lamentations*. N. C. Brooks, *The Lamentations of Mary in the Frankfurt Group of Passion Plays*, in *J.E.G.P.*, iii (1900–1), 415–30.

BROOKS, *Neue Osterfeiern*. N. C. Brooks, *Neue lateinische Osterfeiern*, in *Z.f.d.A.*, l (1908) 297–312.

BROOKS, *New Texts*. N. C. Brooks, *Some New Texts of Liturgical Easter Plays*, in *J.E.G.P.*, viii (1909), 463–88.

BROOKS, *Osterfeiern*. N. C. Brooks, *Osterfeiern aus Bamberger und Wolfenbüttler Handschriften*, in *Z.f.d.A.*, lv (1914), 52–61.

BROOKS, *Rheinau*. N. C. Brooks, *A Rheinau Easter Play of the Late Sixteenth Century*, in *J.E.G.P.*, xxvi (1927), 226–36.

BROOKS, *Sepulchre*. N. C. Brooks, *The Sepulchre of Christ in Art and Liturgy* (*University of Illinois Studies in Language and Literature*, vii, no. 2), Urbana, 1921.

BROOKS, *Sepulchrum Christi*. N. C. Brooks, *The* Sepulchrum Christi *and its Ceremonies in Late Mediaeval and Modern Times*, in *J.E.G.P.*, xxvii (1928), 147–61.

BROUSSOLLE. J. C. Broussolle, *Théorie de la Messe*, Paris, 1913.

CABROL, *Églises*. F. Cabrol, *Les Églises de Jérusalem: la Discipline et la Liturgie au quatrième Siècle*, Paris, 1895.

CABROL, *Origines*. F. Cabrol, *Les Origines liturgiques*, Paris, 1906.

CABROL, *Prayer*. F. Cabrol, *Liturgical Prayer: Its History and Spirit*, London, 1925.

CABROL AND LECLERCQ. F. Cabrol and H. Leclercq, *Dictionnaire d'Archéologie chrétienne et de Liturgie*, Paris, 1907 sqq.

CAHIER. C. Cahier, *Caractéristiques des Saints dans l'Art populaire*, 2 vols., Paris, 1867.

CAHOUR. A. Cahour, *Du Drame liturgique*, in *Études de Théologie, de Philosophie et d'Histoire*, nouv. sér., i (1859), 362–83; ii (1860), 37–63, 234–42.

CARGILL. O. Cargill, *Drama and Liturgy*, New York, 1930.

*CARMINA BURANA*. See SCHMELLER.

CASTELLANI. A. Castellani, ed., *Liber Sacerdotalis nuperrime ex libris Sancte Romane Ecclesie et quarumdem aliarum ecclesiarum et ex antiquis codicibus . . . collectus*, Venice, 1523.

*CATHOLIC ENCYCLOPEDIA*. *The Catholic Encyclopedia*, 16 vols., New York, [1907–14].

CHAMBERS. E. K. Chambers, *The Mediaeval Stage*, 2 vols., Oxford, 1903.

CHAMBERS, *Divine Worship*. J. D. Chambers, *Divine Worship in England in the Thirteenth and Fourteenth Centuries*, London, 1877.

CHAMPOLLION-FIGEAC. J. J. Champollion-Figeac, ed., *Hilarii Versus et Ludi*, Paris, 1838.

CHARVET. E. Charvet, *Recherches sur les anciens Théâtres de Beauvais*, Beauvais, 1881.

CHASLES. Madeleine Chasles, *Le Drame liturgique*, in *La Vie et les Arts liturgiques*, iii (1916–17), 65–70, 121–34, 169–81, 258–66, 297–307, 403–12.

CHEVALIER, *Bayeux*. U. Chevalier, ed., *Ordinaire et Coutumier de l'Église cathédrale de Bayeux* (*Bibliothèque liturgique*, viii), Paris, 1902.

CHEVALIER, *Laon*. U. Chevalier, ed., *Ordinaires de l'Église cathédrale de Laon* (*Bibliothèque liturgique*, vi) Paris, 1897.

CHEVALIER, *R.H.* U. Chevalier, *Repertorium Hymnologicum: Catalogue des Chants, Hymnes, Proses, Séquences, Tropes en usage dans l'Église latine depuis les Origines jusqu'à nos Jours*, 6 vols., Louvain and Brussels, 1892–1920.

CLARK. J. M. Clark, *The Abbey of St Gall*, Cambridge, 1926.

*CLEMEN FESTSCHRIFT.* W. Worringer *et al.*, ed., *Festschrift zum sechzigsten Geburtstag von Paul Clemen*, Bonn, 1926.

CLÉMENT. F. Clément, *Histoire générale de la Musique religieuse*, Paris, 1861.

CLICHTOVEUS. J. Clichtoveus, *Elucidatorium Ecclesiasticum*, Paris, 1516.

CLOETTA, *Beiträge.* W. Cloetta, *Beiträge zur Litteraturgeschichte des Mittelalters und der Renaissance*, 2 vols., Halle, 1890–2.

CLOETTA, *Époux.* W. Cloetta, *Le Mystère de l'Époux*, in *Romania*, xxii (1893), 177–229.

COFFMAN, *Hildesheim.* G. R. Coffman, *A Note concerning the Cult of St Nicholas at Hildesheim*, in *The Manly Anniversary Studies in Language and Literature*, Chicago, 1923, pp. 269–75.

COFFMAN, *Miracle Play.* G. R. Coffman, *The Miracle Play in England*, in *Studies in Philology* (University of North Carolina), xvi (1919), 56–66.

COFFMAN, *New Approach.* G. R. Coffman, *A New Approach to Medieval Latin Drama*, in *M.P.*, xxii (1924–5), 239–71.

COFFMAN, *New Theory.* G. R. Coffman, *A New Theory concerning the Origin of the Miracle Play*, Menasha, 1914.

COFFMAN, *Nomenclature.* G. R. Coffman, *The Miracle Play in England—Nomenclature*, in *P.M.L.A.*, xxxi (1916), 448–65.

COHEN, *Mise en Scène.* G. Cohen, *Histoire de la Mise en Scène dans le Théâtre religieux français du Moyen Âge*, Paris, 1926.

COHEN, *Pèlerins.* G. Cohen, *La Scène des Pèlerins d'Emmaüs*, in *Mélanges de Philologie romane et d'Histoire littéraire offerts à M. Maurice Wilmotte*, i, Paris, 1910, pp. 105–29.

COHEN, *Théâtre.* G. Cohen, *Le Théâtre en France au Moyen Âge.* i. *Le Théâtre religieux*, Paris, [1928].

COHEN AND YOUNG. G. Cohen and K. Young, *The Officium Stellæ from Bilsen*, in *Romania*, xliv (1916–7), 357–72.

CORBLET. J. Corblet, *Histoire dogmatique, liturgique et archéologique du Sacrement de l'Eucharistie*, 2 vols., Paris, 1885–6.

COUSSEMAKER. E. de Coussemaker, *Drames liturgiques du Moyen Âge*, Rennes, 1860.

COUSSEMAKER, *Histoire.* E. de Coussemaker, *Histoire de l'Harmonie au Moyen Âge*, Paris, 1852.

COX, *Church Fittings.* J. C. Cox, *English Church Fittings, Furniture and Accessories*, London, [1923].

COX, *Churchwardens' Accounts.* J. C. Cox, *Churchwardens' Accounts from the Fourteenth Century to the Close of the Seventeenth Century*, London, [1913].

COX AND HARVEY. J. C. Cox and A. Harvey, *English Church Furniture*, New York, 1907.

CRAIG. H. Craig, *The Origin of the Old Testament Plays*, in *M.P.*, x (1912–3), 473–87.

CRAWFORD. J. P. W. Crawford, *Spanish Drama before Lope de Vega* (*Publications of the University of Pennsylvania, Extra Series in Romanic Languages and Literatures*, vii), Philadelphia, 1922.

CRAWFORD, *Nicholas*. Mary S. Crawford, *Life of St Nicholas*, Philadelphia, 1924.

CREIZENACH. W. Creizenach, *Geschichte des neueren Dramas*, 2d ed., 3 vols., Halle, 1911–23.

CROMBACH. H. Crombach, *Primitiæ Gentium seu Historia SS. Trium Regum Magorum Evangelicorum*, Cologne, 1654.

CROSSE. G. Crosse, *The Religious Drama*, London, [1913].

CUISSARD. C. Cuissard, *Mystères joués à Fleury et à Orléans*, in *Lectures et Mémoires de l'Académie de Sainte-Croix d'Orléans*, iv (1880), 284–313.

*D.N.B.* *Dictionary of National Biography*, ed. Leslie Stephen *et al.*, New York, 1885 sqq.

DALMAN. G. Dalman, *Das Grab Christi in Deutschland*, Leipzig, 1922.

D'ANCONA. A. D'Ancona, *Origini del Teatro italiano*, 2 vols., Turin, 1891.

DANIEL, *Codex*. H. A. Daniel, *Codex Liturgicus Ecclesiæ Universæ in epitomen redactus*, 4 vols., Leipzig, 1847–53.

DANIEL, *Thesaurus*. H. A. Daniel, *Thesaurus Hymnologicus*, 5 vols., Halle and Leipzig, 1841–56.

DANJOU. F. Danjou, *Le Théâtre religieux et populaire au xiii*e *Siècle: Le Mystère de Daniel*, in *Revue de la Musique religieuse, populaire et classique*, iv (1848), 65–78. After page 96 of this volume, the play of Daniel from British Museum MS Egerton 2615 is printed on pages separately numbered 1 to 32.

DANKÓ, *Feier*. J. Dankó, *Die Feier des Osterfestes nach der alten römisch-ungarischen Liturgie*, in *Oesterreichische Vierteljahresschrift für katholische Theologie*, xi (1872), 103–38, 175–208.

DANKÓ, *Hymnarium*. J. Dankó, *Vetus Hymnarium Ecclesiasticum Hungariæ*, Budapest, 1893.

DAVIDSON. C. Davidson, *Studies in the English Mystery Plays*, in *Transactions of the Connecticut Academy of Arts and Sciences*, ix (1892–95), 125–297. Published separately ('Printed by authority of Yale University', 1892), with page-numbers 1–173. References throughout are to the separate reprint.

*DECRETA*. *Decreta Authentica Congregationis Sacrorum Rituum*, 7 vols., Rome, 1898–1927.

DELAMARE. R. Delamare, *Le De Officiis ecclesiasticis de Jean d'Avranches, Archevêque de Rouen (1067–1079)*, Paris, 1923.

DESCHAMPS DE PAS. L. Deschamps de Pas, *Les Cérémonies religieuses dans la Collégiale de Saint-Omer au xiii*e *Siècle: Examen d'un Rituel manuscrit de cette Église*, in *Mémoires de la Société des Antiquaires de la Morinie*, xx (1886–7), 97–211.

DESJARDINS. G. Desjardins, *Histoire de la Cathédrale de Beauvais*, Beauvais, 1865.

DETTEN. G. von Detten, *Ueber die Dom- und Klosterschulen des Mittelalters*, Paderborn, 1893.

DIONYSIUS. [P. L. Dionysius,] *Antiquissimi Vesperarum Paschalium Ritus Expositio*, Rome, 1780.

*DIRECTORIUM CHORI*. *Directorium Chori ad usum omnium Ecclesiarum in quibus Officium Divinum juxta Ritum S. Romanæ Ecclesiæ cantari solet*, Rome, 1889.

DONDI OROLOGIO. F. S. Dondi Orologio, *Dissertazione sopra li Riti, Disciplina, Costumanze della Chiesa di Padova sino al xiv Secolo*, Padua, 1816.

DOUHET. J. Douhet, *Dictionnaire des Mystères* (J. P. Migne, ed., *Nouvelle Encyclopédie théologique*, vol. xliii), Paris, 1854.

DU CANGE. C. D. Du Cange, *Glossarium Mediæ et Infimæ Latinitatis*, 10 vols., Niort, 1883–7.

DUCHESNE. L. Duchesne, *Christian Worship, its Origin and Evolution*, trans. M. L. McClure, London, 1927.

DÜRRE. K. Dürre, *Die Mercatorszene im lateinisch-liturgischen, altdeutschen und altfranzösischen religiösen Drama*, Göttingen, 1915.

DU MÉRIL. E. Du Méril, *Origines latines du Théâtre moderne, Paris*, 1849. Reproduced in facsimile, Leipzig and Paris, 1897.

DU MÉRIL, *Poésies*. E. Du Méril, *Poésies inédites du Moyen Âge*, Paris, 1854.

DURANDUS. *Rationale Diuinorum Officiorum Guilhelmi Mimatensis Ecclesie Episcopi*, Strassburg, 1486.

DURIEZ. G. Duriez, *La Théologie dans le Drame religieux en Allemagne au Moyen Âge*, Paris and Lille, [1914].

DURIEZ, *Apocryphes*. G. Duriez, *Les Apocryphes dans le Drame religieux en Allemagne au Moyen Âge* (*Mémoires et Travaux publiés par des Professeurs des Facultés catholiques de Lille*, x), Lille, 1914.

EBERLE. O. Eberle, *Theatergeschichte der innern Schweiz* (*Königsberger deutsche Forschungen*, v), Königsberg, 1929.

ERMINI. F. Ermini, *Lo Stabat Mater e I Pianti della Vergine nella Lirica del Medio Evo*, Città di Castello, 1916.

ERMINI, *Nicola*. F. Ermini, *Il Miracolo drammatico di San Nicola di Mira e la Leggenda dei tre Chierici risuscitati*, in *Studi medievali*, iii (1930), 110–20.

EVEILLON. [J. Eveillon,] *De Processionibus Ecclesiasticis Liber*, Paris, 1655.

FALCONIUS. N. C. Falconius, ed., *Sancti Confessoris Pontificis et celeberrimi Thaumaturgi Nicolai Acta Primigenia*, Naples, 1751.

FARAL, *Jongleurs*. E. Faral, *Les Jongleurs en France au Moyen Âge*, Paris, 1910.

FARAL, *Mimes*. E. Faral, *Mimes français du xiii$^{e}$ Siècle*, Paris, 1910.

FEASEY, *Ceremonial*. H. J. Feasey, *Ancient English Holy Week Ceremonial*, London, 1897.

FEASEY, *Easter Sepulchre*. H. P. Feasey, *The Easter Sepulchre*, in *The Ecclesiastical Review*, xxxii (1905), 337–55, 468–99.

FISCHER. O. Fischer, *Die mittelalterlichen Zehnjungfrauenspiele*, in *Archiv für das Studium der neueren Sprachen und Literaturen*, cxxv (1910), 9–26.

FLETCHER. J. M. J. Fletcher, *The Boy-Bishop at Salisbury and Elsewhere*, Salisbury, [1921].

FLOOD. W. H. Grattan Flood, *Irish Origin of the* 'Officium Pastorum', in *The Month*, cxxxviii (1921), 545–9.

*FLORIACENSIS VETUS BIBLIOTHECA*. *Floriacensis Vetus Bibliotheca . . . Joannis a Bosco*, Lyons, 1605.

FOERSTER AND KOSCHWITZ. W. Foerster and E. Koschwitz, *Altfranzösisches Uebungsbuch*, 6th ed. by A. Hilka, Leipzig, 1921.

FORTESCUE, *Ceremonies*. A. Fortescue, *The Ceremonies of the Roman Rite Described*, London, 1920.

FORTESCUE, *Mass*. A. Fortescue, *The Mass*, London, 1917.

FRANZ, *Benediktionen.* A. Franz, *Die kirchlichen Benediktionen im Mittelalter,* 2 vols., Freiburg, 1909.

FRANZ, *Messe.* A. Franz, *Die Messe im deutschen Mittelalter*, Freiburg, 1902.

FRANZ, *St Florian.* A. Franz, *Das Rituale von St Florian aus dem zwölften Jahrhundert*, Freiburg, 1904.

FRERE, *Ceremonial.* W. H. Frere, *The Principles of Religious Ceremonial*, London, 1906.

FRERE, *Sarum.* W. H. Frere, *The Use of Sarum*, 2 vols., Cambridge, 1898–1901.

FRERE, *Winchester Troper.* W. H. Frere, ed., *The Winchester Troper* (*Henry Bradshaw Society*, viii), London, 1894.

FRONING. R. Froning, *Das Drama des Mittelalters* (*Deutsche National-Litteratur*, ed. J. Kürschner, xiv), Stuttgart, [1891].

FULLER. J. B. Fuller, ed., *Hilarii Versus et Ludi*, New York, [1929].

*FURNIVALL MISCELLANY. An English Miscellany presented to Dr. Furnivall in honour of his seventy-fifth birthday*, Oxford, 1901.

GASELEE. S. Gaselee, ed., *The Oxford Book of Medieval Latin Verse*, Oxford, 1928.

GASTÉ. A. Gasté, *Les Drames liturgiques de la Cathédrale de Rouen*, Évreux, 1893. Reprinted from *Revue catholique de Normandie*, ii (1893), 349–72, 477–500, 573–605. A briefer form of this study appeared in *Annales de la Faculté de Lettres de Caen*, iv, 1–18, 95–131.

GAUTIER, *Origines.* L. Gautier, *Origines du Théâtre moderne*, in *Le Monde* (1872), Aug. 17, pp. 1–2; Aug. 28, p. 1; Aug. 30, pp. 1–2; Sept. 4, pp. 1–2.

GAUTIER, *Poésie.* L. Gautier, *La Poésie religieuse dans les Cloîtres des ix$^e$–xi$^e$ Siècles*, Paris, 1887.

GAUTIER, *Tropes.* L. Gautier, *Histoire de la Poésie liturgique au Moyen Âge: Les Tropes*, Paris, 1886.

GAYLEY, *Comedies.* C. M. Gayley, ed., *Representative English Comedies: From the Beginnings to Shakespeare*, New York, 1907.

GAYLEY, *Forefathers.* C. M. Gayley, *Plays of Our Forefathers*, New York, 1907.

*GEISTLICHE SPIELE. Jahrbuch der Gesellschaft für schweizerische Theaterkultur*, ed. O. Eberle, iii (1930–1). This volume is composed of articles under the general title *Geistliche Spiele.*

GERBERT, *De Cantu.* M. Gerbert, *De Cantu et Musica Sacra*, 2 vols., St Blaise, 1774.

GERBERT, *Monumenta.* M. Gerbert, *Monumenta Veteris Liturgiæ Alemannicæ*, 2 vols., St Blaise, 1777–9.

GERBERT, *Vetus Liturgia.* M. Gerbert, *Vetus Liturgia Alemannica*, 3 Parts (paged continuously), St Blaise, 1776.

GESER. W. Geser, *Ein Weihnachtsspiel im hohen Mittelalter*, in *Stimmen aus Maria-Laach*, lxiii (1902), 533–48.

GESSLER. J. Gessler, *Le Drame liturgique de Munsterbilsen*, Antwerp, 1928.

GIESEBRECHT. W. von Giesebrecht, *Geschichte der deutschen Kaiserzeit*, 6 vols., Leipzig, 1881–95.

GLOCK. A. Glock, *Zur Mysterienbühne*, in *Analecta Germanica, Hermann Paul zum 7. August, 1906, dargebracht*, Amberg, 1906, pp. 1–18.

GOLTHER. W. Golther, *Die deutsche Dichtung im Mittelalter*, Stuttgart, 1912.

GOUGAUD. L. Gougaud, *La Crèche de Noël avant Saint François d'Assise,* in *Revue des Sciences religieuses*, ii (1922), 26–34.

GRADUALE. *Graduale Sacrosanctæ Romanæ Ecclesiæ de Tempore et de Sanctis*, Rome, 1908.

GRENIER. P. N. Grenier, *Introduction à l'Histoire générale de la Province de Picardie* (*Mémoires de la Société des Antiquaires de Picardie. Documents inédits concernant la Province*, iii), Amiens, 1856.

GRIESHABER. F. K. Grieshaber, *Ueber die Ostersequenz Victimæ Paschali und deren Beziehung zu den religiösen Schauspielen des Mittelalters*, Carlsruhe, 1844.

GRÖBER. G. Gröber, *Grundriss der romanischen Philologie*, 2 vols., Strassburg, 1897–1906.

GRÜNEWALD. A. Grünewald, *Die lateinischen Einschiebsel in den deutschen Gedichten von der Mitte des 11. bis gegen Ende des 12. Jahrhunderts*, Göttingen, 1908.

GUNDLACH. W. Gundlach, *Heldenlieder der deutschen Kaiserzeit*, 3 vols., Innsbruck, 1894–9.

HAGER. G. Hager, *Die Weihnachtskrippe*, Munich, 1902.

HARTKER. *Antiphonale du B. Hartker*, published in facsimile in *Paléographie musicale*, ii[e] série, i, Solesmes, 1900. (See *Paléographie musicale* below. The MS of Hartker is in two volumes [St Gall MSS 390–391], but in my references I usually follow the continuous paging of the facsimile).

HARTMANN, *Dreikönigsspiel*. K. A. M. Hartmann, *Ueber das altspanische Dreikönigsspiel*, Bautzen, 1879.

HARTMANN, *Repertorium*. P. Hartmann, *Repertorium Rituum*, Paderborn, 1913.

HASE. K. Hase, *Miracle Plays and Sacred Dramas*, London, 1880. Trans. by A. W. Jackson from K. Hase, *Das geistliche Schauspiel*, Leipzig, 1858.

HASKINS. C. H. Haskins, *The Renaissance of the Twelfth Century*, Cambridge, 1927.

HASTINGS, *Bible*. J. Hastings, ed., *A Dictionary of the Bible*, 5 vols., New York, 1898–1904.

HASTINGS, *Dictionary*. J. Hastings, ed., *A Dictionary of Christ and the Gospels*, 2 vols., New York, 1906–8.

HASTINGS, *Encyclopædia*. J. Hastings, ed., *Encyclopædia of Religion and Ethics*, 12 vols., New York, 1908–22.

HASTINGS, *Theatre*. C. Hastings, *The Theatre: its Development in France and England, and a History of its Greek and Latin Origins*, London, 1902.

HAUTCŒUR, *Documents*. E. Hautcœur, *Documents liturgiques et nécrologiques de l'Église collégiale de Saint-Pierre de Lille*, Lille and Paris, 1895.

HAUTCŒUR, *Histoire*. E. Hautcœur, *Histoire de l'Église collégiale et du Chapitre de Saint-Pierre de Lille*, 3 vols., Lille and Paris, 1896–9.

HEALES. A. Heales, *Easter Sepulchres: their Object, Nature and History*, in *Archaeologia*, xlii (1869), 263–308.

HEDLEY. J. C. Hedley, *The Holy Eucharist*, London, 1923.

HENDERSON. W. G. Henderson, ed., *Processionale ad usum insignis et præclaræ Ecclesiæ Sarum*, Leeds, 1882.

HERRMANN. M. Herrmann, *Forschungen zur deutschen Theatergeschichte des Mittelalters und der Renaissance*, Berlin, 1914.

HETZENAUER. M. Hetzenauer, ed., *Biblia Sacra*, Regensburg, 1929.

HEYNE. Hildegard Heyne, *Das Gleichnis von den klugen und törichten Jungfrauen*, Leipzig, 1922.

HILKA AND SCHUMANN. A. Hilka and O. Schumann, ed., *Carmina Burana*, i–ii, Heidelberg, 1930.

HIRN. Y. Hirn, *The Sacred Shrine*, London, 1912.

*HISTOIRE LITTÉRAIRE. Histoire littéraire de la France*, 35 vols., Paris, 1733–1921.

HOEYNCK. F. A. Hoeynck, *Geschichte der kirchlichen Liturgie des Bisthums Augsburg*, Augsburg, 1889.

HOLWECK, *Calendarium*. F. G. Holweck, *Calendarium Liturgicum Festorum Dei et Dei Matris Mariæ*, Philadelphia, 1925.

HOLWECK, *Dictionary*. F. G. Holweck, *A Biographical Dictionary of the Saints*, St Louis and London, 1924.

HOLWECK, *Fasti*. F. G. Holweck, *Fasti Mariani*, Freiburg, 1892.

ILVONEN. E. Ilvonen, *Parodies de Thèmes pieux dans la Poésie française du Moyen Âge*, Helsingfors, 1914.

*J.E.G.P. The Journal of English and Germanic Philology* [before 1902 *The Journal of Germanic Philology*], Urbana, 1897 sqq.

JACOBSEN. J.-P. Jacobsen, *Essai sur les Origines de la Comédie en France au Moyen Âge*, Paris, 1910.

JEANROY. A. Jeanroy, *Le Théâtre religieux en France du xi^e^ au xiii^e^ Siècles*, Paris, 1924.

JENNEY. A. M. Jenney, *A Further Word as to the Origin of the Old Testament Plays*, in *M.P.*, xiii (1915–6), 59–64.

JULIAN. J. Julian, *A Dictionary of Hymnology*, London, 1907.

KEHREIN. J. Kehrein, *Lateinische Sequenzen des Mittelalters*, Mainz, 1873.

KEHRER, *Legende*. H. Kehrer, *Die 'Heiligen Drei Könige' in der Legende und in der deutschen bildenden Kunst bis Albrecht Dürer*, Strassburg, 1904.

KEHRER, *Literatur*. H. Kehrer, *Die heiligen drei Könige in Literatur und Kunst*, 2 vols., Leipzig, 1908–9.

KELLNER. K. A. H. Kellner, *Heortology*, London, 1908.

KLAPPER. J. Klapper, *Der Ursprung der lateinischen Osterfeiern*, in *Zeitschrift für deutsche Philologie*, l (1923), 46–58.

KLEIN. J. L. Klein, *Geschichte des Dramas*, 13 vols., Leipzig, 1865–76.

KÖPPEN. W. Köppen, *Beiträge zur Geschichte der deutschen Weihnachtsspiele*, Marburg, 1892.

KRESSNER. A. Kressner, *St Nicolaus in der Tradition und in der mittelalterlichen Dichtung*, in *Archiv für das Studium der neueren Sprachen und Literaturen*, lix (1878), 33–60.

KRETZMANN. P. E. Kretzmann, *The Liturgical Element in the Earliest Forms of the Medieval Drama* (*University of Minnesota Studies in Language and Literature*, iv), Minneapolis, 1916.

KRETZMANN, *Harrowing of Hell*. P. E. Kretzmann, *A Few Notes on 'The Harrowing of Hell'*, in *M.P.*, xiii (1915–6), 49–51.

KÜNSTLE. K. Künstle, *Ikonographie der Heiligen*, Freiburg, 1926.

LANCKORONSKI. K. Lanckoronski, G. Niemann, and H. Swoboda, *Der Dom von Aquileia*, Vienna, 1906.

LA PIANA, *Rappresentazioni*. G. La Piana, *La Rappresentazioni sacre nella Letteratura bizantina dalle Origini al Sec. ix, con Rapporti al Teatro sacro d'Occidente*, Grottaferrata, 1912.

LA PIANA, *Review*. G. La Piana, review in *Bollettino di Letteratura critico-religiosa*, i (1914–5), 217–24.

LANGE. C. Lange, *Die lateinischen Osterfeiern*, Munich, 1887.

LANGE, *Auferstehungsfeiern*. C. Lange, *Liturgisch-dramatische Auferstehungsfeiern aus Venedig, Gran, Meissen und Worms*, in *Z.f.d.A.*, xli (1897), 77–83.

LANGE, *Programm*. C. Lange, *Die lateinischen Osterfeiern*, in *Jahresbericht über die Realschule erster Ordnung in Halberstadt*, Programm no. 223, Halberstadt, 1881, pp. 1–35.

LANGE, *Ungedruckte Osterfeiern* (*1*). C. Lange, *Ungedruckte lateinische Osterfeiern*, in *Z.f.d.A.*, xxviii (1884), 119–29.

LANGE, *Ungedruckte Osterfeiern* (*2*). C. Lange, *Ungedruckte lateinische Osterfeiern*, in *Z.f.d.A.*, xxix (1885), 246–59.

LE VERDIER. P. Le Verdier, ed., *Mystère de l'Incarnation et Nativité de Notre Sauveur et Rédempteur Jésus-Christ représenté à Rouen en 1474*, 2 vols., Rouen, 1885–6.

LEFEBVRE. L. Lefebvre, *Histoire du Théâtre de Lille de ses Origines à nos Jours*, 5 vols., Paris, 1901–7.

LEGG. J. W. Legg, ed., *The Sarum Missal*, Oxford, 1916.

LEGRIS. A. Legris, *La Liturgie rouennaise en Italie*, in *Revue des Questions historiques*, nouvelle série, xlix (1913), 450–60.

LIETZMANN. H. Lietzmann, *Einführung in das römische Brevier*, Bonn, 1917.

LINDNER. A. Lindner, *Plainte de la Vierge*, Upsala, 1898.

LINTILHAC. E. Lintilhac, *Histoire générale du Théâtre en France. i. Le Théâtre sérieux du Moyen Âge*, Paris, [1904].

LIUZZI, *Espressione*. F. Liuzzi, *L'Espressione musicale nel Dramma liturgico*, in *Studi medievali*, nuova serie, ii (1929), 74–109.

LIUZZI, *Vergini*. F. Liuzzi, *Drammi musicali dei Secoli xi–xiv. i. Le Vergini savie e le Vergini folli*, in *Studi medievali*, nuova serie, iii (1930), 82–109.

LORIQUET, *Graduel*. H. Loriquet, J. Pothier, and A. Collette, ed., *Le Graduel de l'Église cathédrale de Rouen au xiii^e Siècle*, 2 vols., Rouen, 1907.

LÜERS. F. Lüers, *Die deutschen Lieder der Carmina Burana*, Bonn, 1922.

LUZARCHE. V. Luzarche, *Office de Pâques ou de la Résurrection*, Tours, 1856.

*M.L.N. Modern Language Notes*, Baltimore, 1886 sqq.

*M.P. Modern Philology*, Chicago, 1903 sqq.

MACRI. D. Macri, *Hierolexicon*, 2 vols., Bologna, 1765–7.

MAGNIN, *Lectures*. Lectures by C. Magnin reported in *Journal général de l'Instruction publique*, iv (1835), 245–6, 370–2, 395–6, 418–9, 455–6, 478–80, 514–6. I refer only to the lectures relevant to the present treatise.

MAGNIN, *Review*. C. Magnin, review of L. J. N. Monmerqué and F. Michel, *Théâtre français au Moyen Âge*, Paris, 1839, in *Journal des Savants* (1846), pp. 5–16, 76–93, 449–65.

MAÎTRE. L. Maître, *Les Écoles épiscopales et monastiques en Occident avant les Universités* (*768–1180*), Paris, 1924.

MÂLE, *Moyen Âge*. E. Mâle, *L'Art religieux de la Fin du Moyen Âge en France*, Paris, 1922.

MÂLE, *xii^e Siècle*. E. Mâle, *L'Art religieux du xii^e Siècle en France*, Paris, 1922.

MÂLE, *xiii^e Siècle*. E. Mâle, *L'Art religieux du xiii^e Siècle en France*, Paris, 1919.

MANITIUS. M. Manitius, *Geschichte der lateinischen Literatur des Mittelalters* (*Handbuch der klassischen Altertums-Wissenschaft*, ed. I. von Müller, ix, Abteilung ii, Th. i–iii), 3 vols., Munich, 1911–31.

MANLY, *Literary Forms*. J. M. Manly, *Literary Forms and the New Theory of the Origin of Species*, in *M.P.*, iv (1906–7), 577–95.

MANLY, *Miracle Play*. J. M. Manly, *The Miracle Play in Mediaeval England*, in *Essays by Divers Hands, being the Transactions of the Royal Society of Literature of the United Kingdom*, new series, vii, ed. Margaret L. Woods, London, 1927, pp. 133–53.

MANLY, *Specimens*. J. W. Manly, *Specimens of the Pre-Shakespearean Drama*, 2 vols., Boston, 1900.

MANTZIUS. K. Mantzius, *A History of Theatrical Art in Ancient and Modern Times*, 6 vols., London, 1903–21.

MARBACH. C. Marbach, *Carmina Scripturarum*, Strassburg, 1907.

MARIN. E. Marin, *Saint Nicolas, Évêque de Myre* (*vers 270–341*), Paris, 1917.

MARTENE. E. Martene, *De Antiquis Ecclesiæ Ritibus*, 4 vols., Venice, 1788.

MARTINUCCI. P. Martinucci, *Manuale Sacrarum Cæremoniarum*, 2 parts, 4 vols., Regensburg and Rome, 1911–5.

*MÉLANGES*. [*Mélanges des Bibliophiles français*, vol. vii, Paris, 1831–2.] This rare volume has no title-page or date. I use the title on the cover of the copy in the British Museum (Shelf-mark, G. 297). The second article in the volume, to which all my references apply, has continuous page-numbers from 1 to 272. The reputed editor of the texts to which I refer is L. J. N. Monmerqué.

MELLER. W. C. Meller, *The Boy Bishop and Other Essays on Forgotten Customs and Beliefs of the Past*, London, 1923.

MÉRIMÉE. H. Mérimée, *L'Art dramatique à Valencia depuis les Origines jusqu'au Commencement du xvii*[e] *Siècle* (*Bibliothèque méridionale*, 2[e] série, vol. xvi), Toulouse, 1913.

MEYER. W. Meyer, *Fragmenta Burana* (*Festschrift zur Feier des Hundertfünfzigjährigen Bestehens der Königlichen Gesellschaft der Wissenschaften zu Göttingen: Abhandlungen der philologisch-historischen Klasse*), Berlin, 1901.

MEYER, *Abhandlungen*. W. Meyer, *Gesammelte Abhandlungen zur mittellateinischen Rythmik*, 2 vols., Berlin, 1905.

MICHAEL. E. Michael, *Geschichte des deutschen Volkes vom dreizehnten Jahrhundert bis zum Ausgang des Mittelalters*, 6 vols., Freiburg, 1897–1915.

MICHAELIS. E. A. F. Michaelis, *Zum Ludus de Antichristo*, in *Zeitschrift für deutsches Altertum*, liv (1913), 61–87.

MIGNE, *P.G.* J. P. Migne, ed., *Patrologiæ Cursus Completus: Series Græca*, 161 vols., Paris, 1857–66.

MIGNE, *P.L.* J. P. Migne, ed., *Patrologiæ Cursus Completus: Patrologia Latina*, 221 vols., Paris, 1844–64.

MILCHSACK. G. Milchsack, *Die Oster- und Passionsspiele. i. Die lateinischen Osterfeiern*, Wolfenbüttel, 1880.

MOLÉON. Le Sieur de Moléon [Jean Baptiste Le Brun des Marettes], *Voyages liturgiques de France*, Paris, 1718.

MOLITOR. R. Molitor, *Passionsspiel und Passionsliturgie*, in *Benediktinische Monatsschrift*, v (1923), 105–16.

Mombritius. B. Mombritius, *Sanctuarium seu Vitæ Sanctorum*, 2 vols., Paris, 1910.

Monaci. E. Monaci, *Facsimili di Documenti per la Storia delle Lingue e delle Letterature romanze*, Rome, [1910].

Mone, *Hymni*. F. J. Mone, ed., *Hymni Latini Medii Ævi*, 3 vols., Freiburg, 1853–55.

Mone, *Schauspiele*. F. J. Mone, *Schauspiele des Mittelalters*, 2 vols., Karlsruhe, 1846.

Monmerqué. See *Mélanges*.

Monmerqué and Michel. L. J. N. Monmerqué and F. Michel, *Théâtre français au Moyen Âge*, Paris, 1865.

Moreau, *Explication réaliste*. E. de Moreau, *L'Explication réaliste des Cérémonies de la Sainte Messe*, in *Nouvelle Revue théologique*, xlviii (1921), 400–19.

Moreau, *Explications allégoriques*. E. de Moreau, *Les Explications allégoriques des Cérémonies de la Sainte Messe au Moyen Âge*, in *Nouvelle Revue théologique*, xlviii (1921), 123–43.

Morf. H. Morf, *Das liturgische Drama von den fünf klugen und den fünf thörichten Jungfrauen*, in *Zeitschrift für romanische Philologie*, xxii (1898) 385–91.

Morley. H. Morley, *English Writers*, 11 vols., London, etc., 1887–95.

Moroni. G. Moroni, *Dizionario di Erudizione storico-ecclesiastica*, 103 vols., Venice, 1840–61.

Moser. H. J. Moser, *Geschichte der deutschen Musik*, 3 vols., Stuttgart and Berlin, 1926–8.

Motter. T. H. V. Motter, *The School Drama in England*, London, 1929.

Mühlbacher. E. Mühlbacher, *Die literarischen Leistungen des Stiftes St Florian bis zur Mitte des 19. Jahrhunderts*, Innsbruck, 1905.

Müller, *Geschichte*. N. Müller, *Zur Geschichte des Gottesdienstes der Domkirche zu Berlin in den Jahren 1540–1598*, in *Jahrbuch für Brandenburgische Kirchengeschichte*, 2. und 3. Jahrgang [2. Abteilung], Berlin, 1906, pp. 337–551.

Müller, *Statuten*. N. Müller, *Die Statuten des neuen Stifts zu Halle a. S. und des Doms zu Köln-Berlin und Bruchstücke des Breviarius dieser Kirchen*, in *Jahrbuch für Brandenburgische Kirchengeschichte*, 2. und 3. Jahrgang [2. Abteilung], Berlin, 1906, pp. 233–336.

Muller. H. F. Muller, *Pre-history of the Mediaeval Drama: The Antecedents of the Tropes and the Conditions of their Appearance*, in *Zeitschrift für romanische Philologie*, xliv (1924–5), 544–75.

Nagl. J. W. Nagl, *Deutsch-oesterreichische Literaturgeschichte*, 2 vols., Vienna, 1899–1914.

Nunn. H. P. V. Nunn, *An Introduction to Ecclesiastical Latin*, Cambridge, 1922.

Otte. H. Otte, *Handbuch der kirchlichen Kunst-archäologie des deutschen Mittelalters*, 2 vols., Leipzig, 1883–5.

Owst. G. R. Owst, *Preaching in Mediaeval England*, Cambridge, 1926.

*P.M.L.A.* *Publications of the Modern Language Association of America*, Baltimore, etc., 1884 sqq.

Paetow. L. J. Paetow, *A Guide to the Study of Medieval History*, New York, 1931.

*Paléographie Musicale*. *Paléographie musicale: les principaux Manuscrits de Chant grégorien, ambrosien, mozarabe, gallican publiés en Fac-similés phototypiques par les Bénédictins de Solesmes*, Solesmes, or Tournai, 1889 sqq. Deuxième Série, i (*Antiphonale du B. Hartker*), Solesmes, 1900.

PAS. J. de Pas, *Mystères et Jeux scéniques à Saint-Omer aux xv^e et xvi^e Siècles*, in *Mémoires de la Société des Antiquaires de la Morinie*, xxxi (1913), 343–77.

PEARSON. K. Pearson, *The Chances of Death and other Studies in Evolution*, 2 vols., London and New York, 1897.

PERDRIZET. P. Perdrizet, *Étude sur le Speculum Humanæ Salvationis*, Paris, 1908.

PETIT DE JULLEVILLE. L. Petit de Julleville, *Les Mystères*, 2 vols., Paris, 1880.

PFEIFFER. H. Pfeiffer, *Klosterneuburger Osterfeier und Osterspiel*, in *Jahrbuch des Stiftes Klosterneuburg*, i (1908), 3–56.

PFEIFFER, *Klosterneuburger Osterspiel*. H. Pfeiffer, *Das Klosterneuburger Osterspiel*, in *Musica Divina: Sonderheft Klosterneuburg*, i (1913), 158–76.

PIOLIN, *Recherches*. P. Piolin, *Recherches sur les Mystères qui ont été représentés dans le Maine*, Angers, 1858. Reprinted from *Revue de l'Anjou et du Maine*, iii (1858), 161–82, 228–46, 321–35; iv (1858), 1–18.

PIOLIN, *Théâtre*. P. Piolin, *Le Théâtre chrétien dans le Maine au cours du Moyen Âge*, Mamers, 1892. Reprinted from *Revue historique et archéologique du Maine*, xxix (1891), 24–36, 209–40, 249–78; xxx (1891), 45–71; xxxi (1892), 167–85, 314–45; xxxii (1892), 24–55.

PLATER AND WHITE. W. E. Plater and H. J. White, *A Grammar of the Vulgate*, Oxford, 1926.

POLLARD. A. W. Pollard, *English Miracle Plays, Moralities and Interludes*, Oxford, 1904.

PROCTOR AND WORDSWORTH. F. Proctor and C. Wordsworth, ed., *Breviarium ad usum insignis Ecclesiæ Sarum*, 3 vols., Cambridge, 1879–86.

RABY. F. J. E. Raby, *A History of Christian-Latin Poetry from the Beginnings to the Close of the Middle Ages*, Oxford, 1927.

REICH. H. Reich, *Der Mimus*, i, 2 parts (paged continuously), Berlin, 1903.

REINERS, *Tropen*. A. Reiners, *Die Tropen-, Prosen- und Präfations-Gesänge des feierlichen Hochamtes im Mittelalter*, Luxemburg, 1884.

REINERS, *Unbekannte Tropen-Gesänge*. A. Reiners, *Unbekannte Tropen-Gesänge des feierlichen Messamtes im Mittelalter*, Luxemburg, 1887.

REUSCHEL. K. Reuschel, *Die deutschen Weltgerichtsspiele* (*Teutonia*, iv), Leipzig, 1906.

RIETSCHEL, *Lehrbuch*. G. Rietschel, *Lehrbuch der Liturgik*, 2 vols., 1900–9.

RIETSCHEL, *Weihnachten*. G. Rietschel, *Weihnachten in Kirche, Kunst und Volksleben*, Bielefeld and Leipzig, 1902.

ROCK. D. Rock, *The Church of Our Fathers*, ed. G. W. Hart and W. H. Frere, 4 vols., London, 1905.

ROHAULT DE FLEURY, *Messe*. C. Rohault de Fleury, *La Messe: Études archéologiques sur ses Monuments*, 8 vols., 1883–9.

ROHAULT DE FLEURY, *Vierge*. C. Rohault de Fleury, *La Sainte Vierge: Études archéologiques et iconographiques*, 2 vols., Paris, 1878.

ROY. E. Roy, *Le Mystère de la Passion en France du xiv^e au xvi^e Siècle*, Dijon and Paris, [1903–4].

RUBEIS. J. F. B. M. de Rubeis, *Dissertationes Duæ*, Venice, 1754.

RUDWIN, *Prophetensprüche*. M. J. Rudwin, *Die Prophetensprüche und -Zitate im religiösen Drama des deutschen Mittelalters*, Leipzig, 1913.

RUDWIN, *Survey.* M. J. Rudwin, *A Historical and Bibliographical Survey of the German Religious Drama* (*University of Pittsburgh Studies in Language and Literature*), Pittsburgh, 1924.

RUDWIN, *Teufel.* M. J. Rudwin, *Der Teufel in den deutschen geistlichen Spielen des Mittelalters und der Reformationszeit* (*Hesperia*, vi), Göttingen, 1915.

RUEFF. H. Rueff, *Das rheinische Osterspiel der Berliner Handschrift MS. Germ. Fol. 1219* (*Abhandlungen der Gesellschaft der Wissenschaften zu Göttingen*, Philol.-Hist. Klasse, Neue Folge, xviii, i), Berlin, 1925.

SACKUR. E. Sackur, *Sibyllinische Texte und Forschungen*, Halle, 1898.

SALZER. A. Salzer, *Illustrierte Geschichte der deutschen Literatur von den ältesten Zeiten bis zur Gegenwart*, 3 vols., Munich, [1903–12].

SALZER, *Osterfeiern.* A. Salzer, *Die Anfänge des modernen Dramas: Die Osterfeiern*, in *Studien und Mitteilungen zur Geschichte des Benediktinerordens*, xxxii (1911), 330–3.

SANTI, *Essen.* [A. De Santi,] *Vita liturgica nell'antica Collegiata di Essen*, in *La Civiltà cattolica* (1909), iv, 451–62, 703–11; (1910), i, 705–14.

SANTI, *Palme.* [A. De Santi,] *La Domenica delle Palme nella Storia liturgica*, in *La Civiltà cattolica* (1906), ii, 3–18, 159–77.

SANTI, *Pasqua.* A. De Santi, *Il Mattino di Pasqua nella Storia liturgica*, Rome, 1917. This is a revision of the author's article in *La Civiltà cattolica* (1907), ii, 3–22.

*SARUM BREVIARY.* See PROCTOR AND WORDSWORTH.

*SARUM MISSAL.* See LEGG.

*SARUM PROCESSIONAL.* See HENDERSON.

SAUER. J. Sauer, *Symbolik des Kirchengebäudes und seiner Ausstattung in der Auffassung des Mittelalters*, Freiburg, 1924.

SCHEIBELBERGER. F. Scheibelberger, ed., *Gerhohi Reichersbergensis Præpositi opera hactenus inedita*, i, Linz, 1875. (No more vols. published.)

SCHERER. W. Scherer, *Zum Tegernseer Antichristspiel*, in *Z.f.d.A.*, xxiv (1880), 450–5.

SCHIFFMANN, *Drama.* K. Schiffmann, *Drama und Theater in Oesterreich ob der Enns bis zum Jahre 1803* (*Jahresbericht des Museum Francisco-Carolinum*, lxiii), Linz, 1905.

SCHIFFMANN, *Review.* K. Schiffmann, review of H. Anz, *Die lateinischen Magierspiele*, Leipzig, 1905, in *Anzeiger für deutsches Altertum und deutsche Literatur*, xxxi (1907), 12–7.

SCHMELLER. J. A. Schmeller, ed., *Carmina Burana*, Breslau, 1894.

SCHMIDT. K. W. C. Schmidt, *Die Darstellung von Christi Höllenfahrt in den deutschen und den ihnen verwandten Spielen des Mittelalters*, Marburg, 1915.

SCHNEIDERHAN. J. Schneiderhan, *Roswitha von Gandersheim, die erste deutsche Dichterin*, Paderborn, 1912.

SCHÖNBACH, *Marienklagen.* A. Schönbach, *Ueber die Marienklagen*, Graz, 1874.

SCHÖNBACH, *Review.* A. Schönbach, review of E. Wilken, *Geschichte der geistlichen Spiele in Deutschland*, Göttingen, 1872, in *Zeitschrift für deutsche Philologie*, iv (1873), 364–70.

SCHÖNBACH, *Sanct Lambrecht.* A. Schönbach, *Ueber einige Breviarien von Sanct Lambrecht*, in *Z.f.d.A.*, xx (1876), 129–97.

SCHÖNEMANN. O. Schönemann, *Der Sündenfall und Marienklage*, Hanover, 1855.

SCHUBIGER, *Sängerschule*. A. Schubiger, *Die Sängerschule St Gallens vom achten bis zwölften Jahrhundert*, Einsiedeln and New York, 1858.

SCHUBIGER, *Spicilegien*. A. Schubiger, *Musikalische Spicilegien* (v. Band der *Publikation älterer praktischer und theoretischer Musikwerke*, herausgegeben von der Gesellschaft für Musikforschung, Jahrgang iv, Lieferung ii), Berlin, 1876.

SCHÜTTPELZ. O. Schüttpelz, *Der Wettlauf der Apostel und die Erscheinungen des Peregrinispiels im geistlichen Spiel des Mittelalters.* (*Germanistische Abhandlungen*, no. 63), Breslau, 1930.

SCHWAN. E. Schwan, *Zu den ältesten französischen Denkmälern*, in *Zeitschrift für romanische Philologie*, xi (1887), 469–73.

SCHWIETERING. J. Schwietering, *Ueber den liturgischen Ursprung des mittelalterlichen geistlichen Spiels*, in *Z.f.d.A.*, lxii (1925), 1–20.

SEITZ. J. Seitz, *Die Verehrung des heiligen Joseph in ihrer geschichtlichen Entwicklung bis zum Konzil von Trient dargestellt*, Freiburg, 1908.

SEPET, *Drame*. M. Sepet, *Le Drame chrétien au Moyen Âge*, Paris, 1878.

SEPET, *Origines*. M. Sepet, *Origines catholiques du Théâtre moderne*, Paris, [1901].

SEPET, *Prophètes*. M. Sepet, *Les Prophètes du Christ*, Paris, 1878. Reprinted from *Bibliothèque de l'École des Chartes*, xxviii (1867), 1–27, 211–64; xxix (1868), 105–39, 261–93; xxxviii (1877), 397–443.

SLEUMER. A. Sleumer, *Kirchenlateinisches Wörterbuch*, Limburg, 1926.

*SOISSONS RITUAL*. *Rituale seu Mandatum insignis Ecclesiæ Suessionensis, tempore Episcopi Nivelonis exaratum, sumptibus et curis Historicæ, Archeologicæ ac Scientificæ Suessionensis Societatis editum*, Soissons and Paris, 1856.

SONDHEIMER. I. Sondheimer, *Die Herodes-partien im lateinischen liturgischen Drama und in den französischen Mysterien*, Halle, 1912.

STAMMLER. W. Stammler, *Das religiöse Drama im deutschen Mittelalter*, Leipzig, 1925.

STAPPER, *Agende*. R. Stapper, *Die älteste Agende des Bistums Münster*, Münster, 1906.

STAPPER, *Feier*. R. Stapper, *Die Feier des Kirchenjahres an der Kathedrale von Münster im hohen Mittelalter*, Munster, 1916. Reprinted from *Zeitschrift für vaterländische Geschichte und Altertumskunde*, lxxv (1917), 1–181.

STAPPER, *Kleve*. R. Stapper, *Mittelalterliche Ostergebräuche der Stiftsherren zu Kleve*, in *Römische Quartalschrift für christliche Altertumskunde und für Kirchengeschichte*, xxxv (1927), 171–82.

STAPPER, *Münster*. R. Stapper, *Liturgische Ostergebräuche im Dom zu Münster*, in *Zeitschrift für vaterländische Geschichte und Altertumskunde*, lxxxii (1924), 19–51.

STENGEL. E. Stengel, *Zum Mystère von den klugen und thörichten Jungfrauen*, in *Zeitschrift für romanische Philologie*, iii (1879), 233–7.

STÖTZNER. P. Stötzner, *Osterfeiern herausgegeben nach einer Zwickauer Handschrift aus dem Anfange des 16. Jahrhunderts*, Programm no. 594, Zwickau, 1901.

STONE, *Eucharist*. D. Stone, *A History of the Doctrine of the Holy Eucharist*, 2 vols., London, 1909.

STONE, *Pseudo-Augustinian Sermon*. E. N. Stone, *A Translation of Chapters xi–xvi of the Pseudo-Augustinian Sermon against Jews, Pagans and Arians*, *concerning the Creed* (*University of Washington Publications in Language and Literature*, iv, no. 3, pp. 195–214), Seattle, 1928.

STROPPEL. R. T. Stroppel, *Liturgie und geistliche Dichtung, 1050–1300* (*Deutsche Forschungen*, xvii), Frankfort, 1927.

STRECKER. K. Strecker, ed., *Hrotsvithæ Opera*, Leipzig, 1906.

STÜCKELBERG, *Himmelfahrt*. E. A. Stückelberg, *Gebräuche bei der Feier von Christi Himmelfahrt*, in *Schweizerisches Archiv für Volkskunde*, xiii (1909), 150–1.

STÜCKELBERG, *Verehrung*. E. A. Stückelberg, *Die Verehrung des heiligen Grabes*, in *Schweizerisches Archiv für Volkskunde*, i (1897), 104–14.

STUDER. P. Studer, ed., *Le Mystère d'Adam*, Manchester, 1918.

STURDEVANT. Winifred Sturdevant, *The Misterio de los Reyes Magos: Its Position in the Development of the Mediaeval Legend of the Three Kings* (*Johns Hopkins Studies in Romance Literatures and Languages*, x), Baltimore and Paris, 1927.

SWETE. H. B. Swete, *Church Services and Service-Books before the Reformation*, London, 1896.

TANQUEREY. F. J. Tanquerey, *Plaintes de la Vierge en Anglo-français*, Paris, 1921.

TAYLOR. H. O. Taylor, *The Mediaeval Mind*, 2 vols., New York, 1919.

THALHOFER. V. Thalhofer, *Handbuch der katholischen Liturgik*, 2 vols., Freiburg, 1912.

THIEN. H. Thien, *Ueber die englischen Marienklagen*, Kiel, 1906.

THIERS. J.-B. Thiers, *Traité de l'Exposition du Saint Sacrement de l'Autel*, 2 vols., Avignon, 1777.

THOMAS, *Strophes*. L.-P. Thomas, *Les Strophes et la Composition du Sponsus* (*Textes latin et roman*), in *Romania*, lv (1929), 45–112.

THOMAS, *Versification*. L.-P. Thomas, *La Versification et les Leçons douteuses du Sponsus* (*Texte roman*), in *Romania*, liii (1927), 43–81.

THURSTON. H. Thurston, *Lent and Holy Week*, London, 1904.

TIDDY. R. J. E. Tiddy, *The Mummers' Play*, Oxford, 1923.

TISCHENDORF, *Apocalypses*. C. von Tischendorf, *Apocalypses Apocryphæ*, Leipzig, 1866.

TISCHENDORF, *Evangelia*. C. von Tischendorf, *Evangelia Apocrypha*, Leipzig, 1876.

TOLHURST. J. B. L. Tolhurst, ed., *The Ordinale and Customary of the Benedictine Nuns of Barking Abbey* (*Henry Bradshaw Society*, lxv, lxvi), 2 vols., London, 1927–8.

TRAUBE. L. Traube, *Zur Entwicklung der Mysterienbühne*, in L. Traube, *Vorlesungen und Abhandlungen*, iii, Munich, 1920, pp. 293–330. Reprinted from *Schauspiel und Bühne*, ed. J. Lepsius and L. Traube, Munich, 1880, i, 49–73; ii, 15–33.

TUNISON. J. S. Tunison, *Dramatic Traditions of the Dark Ages*, Chicago, 1907.

USENER. H. Usener, *Das Weihnachtsfest* (*Religionsgeschichtliche Untersuchungen*, i), Bonn, 1889.

VALE. G. Vale, *Il Dramma liturgico pasquale nella Diocesi Aquileiese*, in *Rassegna Gregoriana*, iv (1905), 193–202.

VALENTIN. V. Valentin, *Tempel und Theater*, in *Die Grenzboten* (Leipzig), xlix (1890, 4th Quarter), 66–78, 114–25.

VALLE DE PAZ. Ida del Valle de Paz, *Sulle Origini e lo Svolgimento del Teatro religioso in Italia*, Udine, 1924.

VAN DOREN. R. Van Doren, *Étude sur l'Influence musicale de l'Abbaye de Saint-Gall* (*viii*^e^ *au xi*^e^ *Siècle*), Louvain, 1925.

VAN MIERLO. J. Van Mierlo, *Een Utrechtsch Antiphonarium—Bijdrage tot de Geschiedenis van het liturgisch Drama in de Nederlanden*, in *Leuvensche Bijdragen op het Gebied van de Germaansche Philologie*, viii (1908–9), 1–75.

VENZMER. B. Venzmer, *Die Chöre im geistlichen Drama des deutschen Mittelalters*, Ludwigslust, 1897.

VERMEYLEN. A. Vermeylen, *Le Théâtre dans l'Église*, Brussels, 1901.

VETTER. F. Vetter, *Das Tegernseer Spiel vom deutschen Kaisertum und vom Antichrist*, in *Münchener Museum für Philologie des Mittelalters und der Renaissance*, ii [1913–4], 279–333.

VIGOUROUX. F. Vigouroux, ed., *Dictionnaire de la Bible*, 5 vols., 1895–1912.

VILLANUEVA. J. Villanueva, *Viage literario á las Iglesias de España*, 22 vols., Madrid, 1803–52.

VILLETARD, *Corbeil*. H. Villetard, ed., *Office de Pierre de Corbeil* (*Bibliothèque musicologique*, iv), Paris, 1907.

VILLETARD, *Giudei*. H. Villetard, *I Giudei nella Liturgia*, in *Rassegna Gregoriana*, ix (1910), 429–44.

VULGATE. See HETZENAUER.

WACKERNAGEL. P. Wackernagel, *Das deutsche Kirchenlied*, 5 vols., Leipzig, 1864–77.

WACKERNELL. J. E. Wackernell, *Altdeutsche Passionsspiele aus Tirol*, Graz, 1897.

WADDELL. Helen Waddell, *The Wandering Scholars*, London, 1927.

WADSTEIN. E. Wadstein, *Die eschatologische Ideengruppe*, Leipzig, 1896.

WAGNER. P. Wagner, *Origine et Développement du Chant liturgique*, Tournai, 1904.

WALTHER. H. Walther, *Das Streitgedicht in der lateinischen Literatur des Mittelalters*, Munich, 1920.

WAPELHORST. I. Wapelhorst, *Compendium Sacræ Liturgiæ juxta Ritum Romanum*, 10th ed., New York, 1925.

WARD. A. W. Ward, *A History of English Dramatic Literature to the Death of Queen Anne*, 3 vols., London, 1899.

WEBER, *Kunst*. P. Weber, *Geistliches Schauspiel und kirchliche Kunst in ihrem Verhältnis erläutert an einer Ikonographie der Kirche und Synagoge*, Stuttgart, 1894.

WEBER, *Praefigurationen*. T. Weber, *Die Praefigurationen im geistlichen Drama Deutschlands*, Marburg, 1919.

WECHSSLER. E. Wechssler, *Die romanischen Marienklagen*, Halle, 1893.

WEINHOLD. K. Weinhold, *Weihnacht-Spiele und -Lieder aus Süddeutschland und Schlesien*, Vienna, 1875.

WERNER. J. Werner, *Notkers Sequenzen*, Aarau, 1901.

WETZER AND WELTE. H. J. Wetzer and B. Welte, *Kirchenlexikon*, 12 vols., Freiburg, 1886–1901.

WEYDIG. O. Weydig, *Beiträge zur Geschichte des Mirakelspiels in Frankreich*, Erfurt, 1910.

WIENER. F. Wiener, *Naogeorgus im England der Reformationszeit*, Berlin, 1907.

WIEPEN. E. Wiepen, *Palmsonntagsprozession und Palmesel*, Bonn, 1903.

WILHELM. F. Wilhelm, *Der Ludus de Antichristo* (*Münchener Texte*, ed. F. Wilhelm, i), Munich, 1912.

WILKEN. E. Wilken, *Geschichte der geistlichen Spiele in Deutschland*, Göttingen, 1872.

WILMART. A. Wilmart, ed., *L'ancien Cantatorium de l'Église de Strasbourg: Manuscrit additionnel 23922 du Musée Britannique . . . avec un Mémoire de M. l'Abbé J. Walter*, Colmar, 1928.

WILMOTTE. M. Wilmotte, *Études critiques sur la Tradition littéraire en France*, Paris, 1909.

WINDAKIEWICZA. S. Windakiewicza, *Dramat liturgiczny w Polsce średniowiecznej*, in *Rozpraw Wydzialu filologicznego Akademii Umiejetności w Krakowie*, xxxiv (1903), 340–55.

WINTERFELD. P. von Winterfeld, *Deutsche Dichter des lateinischen Mittelalters*, Munich, 1913.

WIRTH. L. Wirth, *Die Oster- und Passionsspiele bis zum xvi Jahrhundert*, Halle, 1889.

WONISCH. O. Wonisch, *Osterfeiern und dramatische Zeremonien der Palmweihe* (*St Lambrechter Quellen und Abhandlungen*), Graz, [1927].

WORDSWORTH, *Ceremonies*. C. Wordsworth, *Ceremonies and Processions of the Cathedral Church of Salisbury*, Cambridge, 1901.

WORDSWORTH, *Lincoln*. C. Wordsworth, ed., *Statutes of Lincoln Cathedral*, 2 vols., Cambridge, 1892–7.

WORDSWORTH, *Notes*. C. Wordsworth, *Notes on Mediaeval Services in England*, London, 1898.

WORDSWORTH AND LITTLEHALES. C. Wordsworth and H. Littlehales, *The Old Service-Books of the English Church*, London, n.d.

WRIGHT. T. Wright, *Early Mysteries and Other Latin Poems of the Twelfth and Thirteenth Centuries*, London, 1838.

WÜLCKER. R. P. Wülcker, *Das Evangelium Nicodemi in der abendländischen Literatur*, Paderborn, 1872.

WÜRDTWEIN. S. A. Würdtwein, *Commentatio Historico-Liturgica de Stationibus Ecclesiæ Moguntinæ*, Mainz, 1782.

YOUNG, *Dramatic Associations*. K. Young, *The Dramatic Associations of the Easter Sepulchre* (*University of Wisconsin Studies in Language and Literature*, x), Madison, 1920.

YOUNG, *Easter Play*. K. Young, *The Origin of the Easter Play*, in *P.M.L.A.*, xxix (1914), 1–58.

YOUNG, *Harrowing of Hell*. K. Young, *The Harrowing of Hell in Liturgical Drama*, in *Transactions of the Wisconsin Academy of Sciences, Arts, and Letters*, xvi, part ii, (1909), 889–947.

YOUNG, *Home of the Easter Play*. K. Young, *The Home of the Easter Play*, in *Speculum*, i (1926), 71–86.

YOUNG, *Joseph*. K. Young, *A Liturgical Play of Joseph and His Brethren*, in *M.L.N.*, xxvi (1911), 33–7.

YOUNG, *Miracle Play*. K. Young, *Concerning the Origin of the Miracle Play*, in *The Manly Anniversary Studies in Language and Literature*, Chicago, 1923, pp. 254–68.

YOUNG, *Officium Pastorum*. K. Young, *Officium Pastorum: A Study of the Dramatic Developments within the Liturgy of Christmas*, in *Transactions of the Wisconsin Academy of Sciences, Arts, and Letters*, xvii, part i (1912), 299–396.

YOUNG, *Officium Stellae*. K. Young, *A New Text of the Officium Stellae*, in *M.L.N.*, xxvii (1912), 68–71.

YOUNG, *Ordo Prophetarum*. K. Young, *Ordo Prophetarum*, in *Transactions of the Wisconsin Academy of Sciences, Arts, and Letters*, xx (1922), 1–82.

YOUNG, *Ordo Rachelis*. K. Young, *Ordo Rachelis* (*University of Wisconsin Studies in Language and Literature*, iv), Madison, 1919.

YOUNG, *Passion-Play*. K. Young, *Observations on the Origin of the Mediæval Passion-Play*, in *P.M.L.A.*, xxv (1910), 309–54.

YOUNG, *Peregrinus*. K. Young, *A New Version of the* Peregrinus, in *P.M.L.A.*, xxxiv (1919), 114–29.

YOUNG, *Poema Biblicum*. K. Young, *The* Poema Biblicum *of Onulphus*, in *P.M.L.A.*, xxx (1915), 25–41.

YOUNG, *Presentation*. K. Young, *Philippe de Mézières' Dramatic Office for the Presentation of the Virgin*, in *P.M.L.A.*, xxvi (1911), 181–234.

YOUNG, *Purification*. K. Young, *Dramatic Ceremonies of the Feast of the Purification*, in *Speculum*, v (1930), 97–102.

YOUNG, *Rouen*. K. Young, *A Contribution to the History of Liturgical Drama at Rouen*, in *M.P.*, vi (1908–9), 201–27.

YOUNG, *Some Texts*. K. Young, *Some Texts of Liturgical Plays*, in *P.M.L.A.*, xxiv (1909), 294–331.

YOUNG, *Trois Rois*. K. Young, *La Procession des Trois Rois at Besançon*, in *The Romanic Review*, iv (1913), 76–83.

*Z.F.D.A.* *Zeitschrift für deutsches Alterthum* [*und deutsche Literatur* added later], Leipzig, etc., 1841 sqq.

ZEZSCHWITZ. G. von Zezschwitz, *Vom römischen Kaisertum deutscher Nation: ein mittelalterliches Drama*, Leipzig, 1877.

# INDEX

Abbreviations: Annun., Annunciation; Ant., Antichrist; Ascens., Ascension; assoc., associated; Benediktb., Benediktbeuern; C. of St P., Conversion of St Paul; Dan., Daniel; Dep., Depositio; El., Elevatio; F. As., Festum Asinorum; Fil. Get., Filius Getronis; Ic. St Nic., Iconia Sancti Nicolai; L. de Reg. Æg., Ludus de Rege Ægypti; L. Pasch., Ludus Paschalis; m (after a reference), mentioned; Off. Past., Officium Pastorum; Off. St., Officium Stellæ; Or. de I. et R., Ordo de Isaac et Rebecca; Or. Jos., Ordo Joseph; Or. Proph., Ordo Prophetarum; Or. Rach., Ordo Rachelis; Per., Peregrinus; Present., Presentation; Purif., Purification; R. of L., Raising of Lazarus; Tr. Cler., Tres Clerici; Tr. Fil., Tres Filiæ; V. S., Visitatio Sepulchri. Parenthetical numbers and letters (see *Angel*) apply to classifications under other major entries mentioned. Thus under *Angel*, the parenthetical numbers and letters apply to classifications under *Visitatio Sepulchri*, *Officium Stellæ*, and *Ordo Rachelis*.

PRINTED IN GREAT BRITAIN
AT THE UNIVERSITY PRESS, OXFORD
BY VIVIAN RIDLER
PRINTER TO THE UNIVERSITY